Do This in Remembrance of Me

Also in the SCM Studies in Worship and Liturgy series

The Collect in the Churches of the Reformation
Edited by Bridget Nichols

Rethinking the Origins of the Eucharist
Martin Stringer

Liturgy and Interpretation
Kenneth Stevenson

Comfortable Words: Polity, Piety and the Book of Common Prayer
Edited by Stephen Platten and Christopher Woods

SCM STUDIES IN WORSHIP
AND LITURGY

Do This in Remembrance of Me

The Eucharist from the Early Church to the Present Day

Bryan D. Spinks

scm press

Published in 2013 by SCM Press
Editorial office
3rd Floor
Invicta House
108–114 Golden Lane
London
EC1Y 0TG

SCM Press is an imprint of Hymns Ancient & Modern Ltd (a registered charity)
13A Hellesdon Park Road
Norwich NR6 5DR, UK

www.scmpress.co.uk

British Library Cataloguing in Publication data

A catalogue record for this book is available from the British Library

978-0-334-05307-1

Typeset by Manila Typesetting Company

Contents

Foreword by Teresa Berger vii
Preface xi
Abbreviations xv

Introduction: In Search of the Meals behind the Last Supper: Cultural Background and Eucharistic Origins 1

1 Some Early Eucharistic Practices and Beliefs from Ignatius to Origen 30
2 The Shaping of Early Eucharistic Prayers: 'Paleoanaphoras' 52
3 Eucharistic Theologies in the Fourth- and Fifth-Century Homilies and the Emergence of the Classical Anaphora 68
4 The Egyptian Anaphoral Traditions and the Divine Liturgy of the Coptic Orthodox Church 94
5 The Eucharist and Anaphoras of the Byzantine Synthesis 121
6 The Syriac Liturgical Traditions 141
7 The Ethio-Eritrean ('Ge'ez') and Armenian Traditions 171
8 The Classical Western Rites 190
9 From the Romano-Western Synthesis to the Tridentine Reforms: Liturgy, Commentaries and Eucharistic Theologies 211
10 Luther and Lutheran Eucharistic Liturgies 246
11 The Reformed Tradition: From Ulrich Zwingli to Eugène Bersier 272
12 The Anglican Tradition: From Thomas Cranmer to the Tractarian Disputes 313
13 The Radical Reformation and Some New Churches of the Eighteenth and Nineteenth Centuries 347
14 The Twentieth-Century Liturgical and Ecumenical Movements: From Vatican II to 'Lima' 1982 377
15 Some Trends in a Postmodern Era 407
Afterword: Some Crumbs from Beneath the Table 436
Appendix 1: The Classical Anaphoral Families 446
Bibliography 447
Index 502

Contents

Preface
Abbreviations

Foreword

TERESA BERGER

With this book on the Eucharist from the early Church to the present day, Bryan Spinks offers us the fruits of his 40 years of indefatigable, passionate commitment to scholarly inquiry into the history of Christian liturgy. Having displayed his skills in this field in numerous prior publications, he here focuses his attention on what surely constitutes the key challenge for any historian of Christian liturgy, namely how to map the development of eucharistic celebrations from the threshold of the Upper Room all the way to cyberspace. To my knowledge, Bryan Spinks is the first scholar who maps the terrain in precisely this sweeping arch – even the most recent books to date on eucharistic development have stopped short of the digital world, although eucharistic practices have by now migrated online (whether scholars of liturgy approve or not).

The diachronic breadth of the present book is matched by a splendid synchronic or, more appropriately, ecclesial breadth. From the Eastern Churches in all their diversity – both Orthodox and Oriental – through Roman Catholic and Protestant communities to modern and contemporary ecclesial formations, Spinks surveys the history of the Eucharist with an amazingly wide lens. I doubt that there is another book on eucharistic history available that displays not only the standard Eastern and Western narratives but also describes, for example, the eucharistic practices of the ancient Church of the East as well as those of the small yet intriguing nineteenth-century English Catholic Apostolic Church or the much larger (Mormon) Church of Jesus Christ of Latter-Day Saints. Bryan Spinks attends to all of these traditions and more, and he does so with many years of scholarly research into a richly diverse array of liturgical traditions at his fingertips. Here too, Spinks's book is unmatched in its breadth. This history of the Eucharist is marked by a deep passion for the subject matter as a whole, not only for customary high points.

That said, *Do This in Remembrance of Me* appears at a complicated time in liturgical historiography as a scholarly discipline. Vital challenges have been raised for the traditional ways of writing liturgy's past. These challenges are related to major shifts in historiography broadly conceived (e.g., the turns to social history, history 'from below', gender history and micro-history, to name but a few). The probing questions about the way historians construct the object of their inquiry put pressure also on the work of historians of liturgy as they struggle with how to study and narrate liturgy's past. Bryan Spinks is aware of these pressures, yet refuses to be either immobilized by them or lured into an endless theorizing of all the pressures that disables one from ever daring to write anything approaching an actual historiographic narrative again. Instead, Spinks presents a clear choice of what he considers essential for a history of the Eucharist (within the harsh constraints of a one-volume, single-authored book). Essential for him are the textual witnesses to the rite, and their renowned interpreters. It is no secret that I have argued for privileging other sites for the writing of liturgical history. It is equally clear that what Bryan Spinks has chosen to focus on will always remain one key building block for any history of the Eucharist, no matter how many other angles one explores. There is, after all, no unmediated access ever to the past; and for the more distant past, written texts especially remain of primary importance. Moreover, a fresh look at these sources is particularly important in liturgical history-writing at this point in time, since some of our key sources have come to be read and interpreted very differently today from how they were read even 50 years ago. Last but not least, privileging a eucharistic history rooted in key textual witnesses clearly does not mean that other ways of narrating this history – for example with a focus on the gathered assembly, or on the importance of gender differences in shaping eucharistic celebrations – are not also important. The beautiful cover of the present book says as much: it shows a detail from a communion service of a group of Moravians at Fetters Lane in London in 1753. Not only is the gathered congregation the central focus of this image, but men and women are separated by gender in this eucharistic assembly – as, indeed, they were for most of liturgical history.

There remains of course the basic question of what – in the face of greatly diversified scholarly methods in historiography – a book on eucharistic history must include. The answers will vary depending on each scholar's historiographic lenses. That diversity in and of itself can be seen as a good: it witnesses to the fact that no narrative of eucharistic development can tell the whole story (not least because there is an 'inner side' to this history that cannot be mapped with historical tools). Such a witness is important especially at a point in time when the grand, linear, evolutionary narratives of earlier scholarship have lost credibility. This scholarship downplayed, among other things, the fragmentariness of the extant sources and the diversity of the evidence, which defies harmonization.

With this background of changes in liturgical historiography, *Do This in Remembrance of Me* opts for and displays, as no other book I know, a diachronic and synchronic breadth of eucharistic texts and interpretations. This breadth, moreover, is presented by a pre-eminent historian of liturgy who reads ferociously in the field. As Bryan Spinks's colleague at Yale – our offices are across the hall from each other – I stand as an eyewitness to the phenomenal workload that lies behind this book. I have seen and can testify to the never-ending boxes of new books that piled up outside Bryan's office; while inside the piles grew higher and higher on his desk, until the man himself was hard to see behind the piles. And then there were the periodic email updates about individual book chapters he was working on, such as one message that announced, with obvious relief: 'I am finally out of Egypt!'

As Bryan Spinks's colleague at Yale, I have also had the privilege of worshipping with him. Given Bryan's vast knowledge of different eucharistic practices and his openness to contemporary pastoral necessities and cultural sensibilities, no eucharistic service at which Bryan presides is ever simply a repetition. I remember one 'blended' Eucharist at Yale Divinity School a couple of years ago, which Bryan concelebrated with a UCC pastor and a Maronite priest (only Bryan could bring these two together!). The service included Christian New Age music, a twentieth-century setting of the Kyrie, a contemporary Maronite setting for the Fraction, and a medieval trope setting for the Gospel. The words of institution – as they now appear in the Maronite *Sharar* – were chanted in Syriac. As a whole, the eucharistic service that day both served the worshipping community of Yale Divinity School well and also expressed – in the vibrant language of liturgical celebration – the breadth of Bryan's appreciation of eucharistic practice through time.

With the mention of eucharistic practice I come to a last, yet ultimately primary point. The biblical book of Numbers will help me arrive at this point. In this book, we read a story of spies sent to explore the Promised Land, a land reportedly of milk and honey (Num. 13.1—14.9). While two spies returned with grapes, pomegranates and figs, the others brought back only tales of ambiguity. Christians who read this story in the context of the story of Jesus and his table practices have long perceived eucharistic overtones in what the two spies brought back from the Promised Land. These eucharistic overtones are beautifully displayed, for example, in the early thirteenth-century Redemption Window in the Corona Chapel of Canterbury Cathedral, where the image of the two spies appears directly underneath the image of Jesus' crucifixion. The Redemption Window might be said to display, in glass, a history of eucharistic allusions running through the biblical witness as a whole. The faithful who looked up at this window during the celebration of the Eucharist entered into the biblical stories, which stretched forth into their own eucharistic celebration. In other words, past presence and real presence fused in this liturgical moment. I hope that in some small way readers of Bryan Spinks's book may similarly glimpse something of the power of eucharistic practice, past and present. Because if indeed the subject matter of this book is not merely an arcane Christian food ritual, but rather the very way in which God seeks to be present in the world and nourish it with divine life, then the manifold ways in which Christians have celebrated this reality through the centuries are of utmost importance for us today, too.

Preface

The nineteenth-century Mercersberg theologian John Williamson Nevin wrote:

> The Question of the Eucharist is one of the most important belonging to the history of religion. It may be regarded as in some sense central to the whole Christian system. For Christianity is grounded in the living union of the believer with the person of Christ; and this great fact is emphatically concentrated in the mystery of the Lord's Supper.[1]

Ever since my first liturgical studies as an undergraduate at the University of Durham with Arthur Couratin, I have wanted to write a book on both eucharistic liturgies and theologies, but hitherto the right time never seemed to present itself. I was delighted therefore when Dr Natalie Watson invited me to do just that. Only when I began the work did I realize just how difficult such a task is.

First, for someone from an English-speaking and/or Anglican perspective, any book on eucharistic liturgy is already totally overshadowed by Dom Gregory Dix's now classic *The Shape of the Liturgy*. A classic it is, similar to Darwin's *On the Origin of Species*. Both contain brilliant ideas, and both contain much information which is now so hopelessly out of date as to be quite dangerous, but each is a classic and thus in many ways can never be replaced.

A second problem is how much to write, and what to include and not to include. Books on eucharistic liturgy frequently totally ignore the corresponding developments in eucharistic theology, and vice versa. Liturgy scholars often privilege a particular era or area, and, for example, expend much detail on the first seven centuries and then leap for a quick visit to two or three Reformation rites before leaping into the modern era, with both of the latter seeming to be mere footnotes to the former. Alternatively, the early period is briefly summarized in generalities and the Eastern rites are lumped together as one, all as a prelude to the main business of either the Reformation or contemporary Western eucharistic liturgical rites. In attempting to avoid all these, I quickly became aware that I knew too much in certain areas and in other areas practically nothing at all. The challenge has been to write not only more broadly but also at the same depth across the different epochs and traditions. Not all can be included. Southern Baptists, Disciples of Christ and American Presbyterians may all feel that they have been passed over, and equally the Old Catholics, many of

1 John Williamson Nevin, *The Mystical Presence and the Doctrine of the Reformed Church on the Lord's Supper*, ed. Linden J. DeBie, Eugene: Wipf and Stock, 2012, p. 47.

the Swiss Reformed cities and many Anglican provinces will experience a real absence in this work.[2] However generous a word length, it is always necessary to select and exclude, and some of the latter comes as much by ignorance of the material as by deliberate choice. Since I have previously written two volumes on the English Congregationalist eucharistic tradition, I judged it unnecessary to give more than a brief reference in this work. I hope those who feel they have been overlooked or ignored will understand and forgive the omission.

After investigating current scholarship regarding the New Testament evidence pertaining to the Last Supper and Lord's Supper, I have chosen from the various theological themes of the Eucharist that emerge to investigate the concepts of sacrifice, presence and eschatology in a wide variety of eucharistic liturgies, with particular focus on the verbal heart of the rites, namely the Eucharistic Prayer, anaphora or Great Thanksgiving. It is not that other theological themes are unimportant, as evidenced in the wider themes in Horton Davies's masterful book, *Bread of Life and Cup of Joy*.[3] It is simply that the themes I have selected are ones that surface most prominently in subsequent eucharistic theological debate.

I am aware that in some circles historical development is thought unimportant and old-fashioned, but such circles are not ones that I move in or feel at home with, and so I have attempted as far as possible to discuss current scholarly opinion on the history of the rites and the anaphoras. Although the popular little adage *Lex orandi, lex credendi* (the rule of prayer established the rule of belief) is important, the idea that doctrine only flowed from liturgy and that doctrine never impacted and changed liturgical practice is pious humbug and wishful thinking. Therefore this study also engages with some of the eucharistic theologies that often accompanied and meshed with the liturgical practices. It is hoped that the resulting study will be a useful guide to the primary texts contained in *Prex Eucharistica*, *Coena Domini* and *Prayers of the Eucharist, Early and Reformed*, as well as older collections such as Brightman's *Liturgies Eastern and Western*. I deal mainly with texts, but I am well aware that the text is always for performance, and always presupposes a body of people and a suitable space at a particular time and a particular culture. These are important, but are not the primary focus of this particular study.

Needless to say, this book could not have been possible without the generous help and advice of many others. I am grateful to the Episcopal Church Foundation for a grant from the Conant Fund to cover the cost of travel and study for this book. Material has been generously sent by Rachel Melvin of Pristine Press; Emmanuel Fritsch provided me with copies of his important papers on the Ethio-Eritrean rite; Howard Gardner sent material on the Essex Peculiar People; and Dr Anthony Gelston furnished me with his most recent papers on the East Syrian tradition; Gabriel Aydin kindly allowed me to use his translation of the Syriac commentary of Jacob of Edessa.

I am greatly indebted to Professor Harold Attridge of Yale Divinity School for his guidance on the New Testament material; to Professors Vasilios Marinis, Yale Divinity School, and Fr Professor Stefanos Alexopoulos now of Catholic

2 For recent developments in Eucharistic liturgy among the Old Catholics, see the essays in *Internationale Kirchliche Zeitschrift* 103: Heft 1–2 (January–June 2013).

3 Grand Rapids: Eerdmans, 1993.

University, Washington, for help with the Byzantine rite; to Mary Farag of Yale Graduate School for assistance with the Coptic material; Fr Emmanuel Fritsch CSSp for corrections and advice on the Ethio-Eritrean rite, and Fr Professor Daniel Findikyan of St Nersess Armenian Seminary, New Rochelle, New York, for reading the section on the Armenian rite; Professor Harald Buchinger of the University of Regensburg for assistance on the medieval West; Professor Markus Rathey, Yale University, on Lutheran rites, and Professor Robin Leaver, Visiting Professor, Yale University, on the Radical Reformation and eighteenth- and nineteenth-century developments; and my colleague Professor Melanie Ross, Yale Divinity School, for help with and comments on the sections on contemporary theology. A special thanks to my colleague Professor Teresa Berger for comments on many of the chapters, including the medieval West, the Reformed tradition, twentieth-century reforms and theology, and the postmodern material, as well as helping to make my Essex English a little more grammatically correct. She has also kindly written the Foreword to this work.

I am grateful to my colleagues and the support staff at the Yale Institute of Sacred Music, and especially to my Director, Professor Martin Jean, for his unfailing support and encouragement. I am most grateful to Natalie Watson and the staff of SCM Press for giving me the opportunity to write this book.

I owe a great debt of gratitude to my wife Care who has been extremely patient, having had a spouse missing completely in mind, and sometimes body too, for the best part of 18 months while this work was being completed.

Lastly, my previous works were always read in draft and commented upon by my close friend, Kenneth Stevenson. His untimely death from leukaemia in 2011 has meant that this work has not had the benefit of his sharp eye, wide learning and humour. Fond memories of him have spurred me on while writing *Do This in Remembrance of Me.*

Bryan D. Spinks
Bishop F. Percy Goddard Professor of Liturgical Studies and Pastoral Theology,
Yale Institute of Sacred Music and Yale Divinity School
Feast of St George, Patron Saint of England, 2013

Abbreviations

Brightman	F. E. Brightman, *Liturgies Eastern and Western*, Oxford: Oxford University Press, 1896.
CD	Irmgard Pahl (ed.), *Coena Domini I. Die Abendmahlsliturgie der Reformationskirchen im 16./17. Jahrhundert*, Freiburg: Universitätsverlag Freiburg Schweiz, 1983.
ET	English Translation.
nd	no date of publication.
np	no publisher.
PE	Anton Hänggi and Irmgard Pahl (eds), *Prex Eucharistica*, Freiburg: Éditions Universitaires Fribourg Suisse, 1968; 2nd edn 1998.
PEER	R. C. D. Jasper and G. J. Cunming (eds), *Prayers of the Eucharist: Early and Reformed*, New York: Pueblo Publishing, 1980, and subsequent reprints, Collegeville: Liturgical Press.

Abbreviations

Introduction

In Search of the Meals behind the Last Supper: Cultural Background and Eucharistic Origins

> At the heart of it all is the eucharistic action, a thing of an absolute simplicity – the taking, blessing, breaking and giving of bread and the taking, blessing and giving of a cup of wine and water, as these were first done with their new meaning by a young Jew before and after supper with His friends on the night before He died. Soon it was simplified still further, by leaving out the supper and combining the double grouping before and after it into a single rite. So the four-action Shape of the Liturgy was found by the end of the first century. He had told His friends to do this henceforward with the new meaning 'for the *anamnesis*' of Him, and they have done it always since.
>
> Was ever another command so obeyed? For century after century, spreading slowly to every continent and country and among every race on earth, this action has been done, in every conceivable human circumstance, for every conceivable human need from infancy and before it to extreme old age and after it, from the pinnacles of earthly greatness to the refuge of fugitives in the caves and dens of the earth.[1]

This quotation from Gregory Dix has become one of those 'purple passages' that is often quoted in relation to the Eucharist, both in general essays on eucharistic liturgy and especially in Anglican homilies. Its rhetoric is superb, but its assumptions are ones that today have to be considerably nuanced. Quite apart from whether or not the Eucharist did ever become a four-action shape as argued by Dix,[2] the very notion that all eucharistic meals celebrated by those who claimed in some way to be 'Christian' in the first three centuries always consisted of an Anamnesis ('remembrance') of Jesus' death, were always related to the Last Supper Jesus had with his disciples, and always used bread and wine mixed with water, are ones that more recent scholarship has called into question. Such questioning is not a return to the older extreme liberal Protestant claim that 'sacraments' were invented by Paul and borrowed from Hellenistic mystery religion, a view that was recirculated in English-speaking countries in the 1950s translations of the works of Rudolf

1 Gregory Dix, *The Shape of the Liturgy*, London: Dacre Press, 1945, pp. 743–4.

2 Bryan D. Spinks, 'Mis-shapen: Gregory Dix and the Four Action Shape of the Liturgy', *Lutheran Quarterly* 4 (1990), pp. 161–77.

Bultmann.[3] Recent scholarship questions a simplistic notion that every Christian community celebrated its sacred meal with the foundational narrative found in 1 Corinthians 15 and the Synoptic Gospels always in mind. Dix favoured a *chaburah* setting (a religious fellowship meal) for the Last Supper over against a specific Passover meal, but since in both rites (and we know precious little about a *chaburah*) the post-meal prayer is the *birkat ha-mazon*, he suggested that this prayer is the locus for what became the anaphora, *qurbana* or Eucharistic Prayer. Focus on the *berakot* forms of Jewish prayers, and the *birkat ha-mazon* in particular, became popular in the 1970s and 1980s. More sober scholarship of Jewish prayers questions whether these 'statutory' prayers were the only or the predominant form in the first century, and also underscores the fact that the forms that have come down to us post-date our earliest Christian forms. Stefan Reif observed:

> In pursuit of this reconstruction, liturgists have sometimes turned for guidance to the authoritative Jewish prayer-books of almost a thousand years later, or even of the more modern period, and sought to extrapolate backwards, making assumptions that defy the vast chasm of history, geography and ideology that separate one millennium from another. Those who have adopted such a position have transplanted some or all of the rabbinic rites and customs of tenth-century Babylon or early medieval Europe to first-century Judaea and the surrounding Jewish diaspora and have declined to distinguish the continuity of some liturgical traditions from the patent novelty of others.[4]

We have scant information as regards the actual forms of Jewish meal prayer in the first century CE and therefore precious little on which to speculate about some evolution of Christian Eucharistic Prayers. What does seem safe to say is that by the fourth century there emerged from the different geographical areas of Christianity, rites which, both by osmosis and because of the emergence of a canon of Scripture, used bread and wine mixed with water, and related these in prayer in some way or other to a sacrifice fulfilled by Jesus in his death, and linking the bread and wine to his body and blood. Some of the possible forms and influences on the way to the emergence of what is usually understood today as 'the Eucharist' need to be considered further.

The wider cultural setting: the Greco-Roman Symposium

Although the Synoptic Gospels all record a version of the Last Supper, they do so within the longer narratives of the ministry of Jesus which include a variety of meals he attended. Common in these meals is that Jesus is shown as breaking

3 German scholars such as Otto Pfleiderer, Albert Eichhorn and Wilhelm Heitmüller had espoused such a view, and it was assumed by the English Congregationalist Harry Bulcock in his *A Modern Churchman's Manual*, London: Union of Modern Free Churchmen, 1941. Rudolf Bultmann's *The Theology of the New Testament*, ET in various editions in the 1950s and 1960s, continued to suggest this link.

4 Stefan C. Reif, *Judaism and Hebrew Prayer: New Perspectives on Jewish Liturgical History*, Cambridge: Cambridge University Press, 1993, p. 53.

Jewish purity rules by eating with 'sinners'.[5] Many New Testament scholars therefore view the 'Last Supper' alongside the other meals either attended by Jesus or provided by him (e.g. the feedings of the 5,000 and the 4,000). Viewing the meals together, Dennis Smith and Hal Taussig have argued that there is nothing particularly special about these meals – many of which, including the 'Last Supper', they regard as the creations of either the early Church or the evangelist – but rather, they reflect the influence of the Greco-Roman Symposium.[6] They argue that Christians were not significantly different from those in their culture, and meals had been influenced by the common customs and etiquette of the Greco-Roman Symposium or banquet.

The Greco-Roman banquet took place in the evening and consisted of two parts. First was the *deipnon,* which was the meal proper and consisted of a number of courses. The second was the Symposium, or Roman *convivium,* which was a time of serious wine drinking and included entertainment with music, perhaps jugglers, and frequently prostitutes. Generally it was regarded as a male event, though more recent scholarship has shown that beginning in the Late Republican era, the meals became gender-inclusive with wives attending, and children too sometimes, and in this context the 'entertainment' would be appropriate for mixed company.[7] An appetizer course was added to precede the *deipnon.* Guests were greeted by slaves, had their feet washed, and reclined for the meal. The Symposium proper usually included a libation of wine to the gods. In more educated or philosophically minded gatherings, a post-prandial discussion or talk was an expected part of the Symposium.

It is evident that some characteristics of this elite banquet were copied, adapted and developed throughout the Mediterranean world. It was, for example, copied by clubs or societies (*collegia*) formed by less wealthy groups, who would meet perhaps once a year for a feast. It also seems to have influenced the later Jewish Passover ritual, which incorporated hors d' oeuvre as well as reclining.[8] Joseph Tabory, commenting on the changes in the Passover ritual after the destruction of the Jerusalem Temple in 70 CE, notes:

> the paschal meal has changed from a sacrificial meal, in which the food was the main event of the evening, into a type of sympotic meal which itself went through changes. The seder as we know it is similar to the second-stage

5 Craig L. Blomberg, *Contagious Holiness: Jesus' Meals with Sinners*, Downer's Grove: InterVarsity Press, 2005.

6 Dennis E. Smith and Hal E. Taussig, *Many Tables: The Eucharist in the New Testament and Liturgy Today*, London: SCM Press, 1990; Dennis E. Smith, *From Symposium to Eucharist: The Banquet in the Early Christian World*, Minneapolis: Fortress Press, 2003; Hal Taussig, *In the Beginning was the Meal: Social Experimentation and Early Christian Identity*, Minneapolis: Fortress Press, 2009.

7 For women and children being present, see Blake Leyerle, 'Meal Customs in the Greco-Roman World', in Paul F. Bradshaw and Lawrence A. Hoffman (eds), *Passover and Easter: Origin and History in Modern Times*, Notre Dame: University of Notre Dame Press, 1999, pp. 29–61, esp. 43–5.

8 Baruch M. Bokser, *The Origins of the Seder: The Passover Rite and early Rabbinic Judaism*, Berkeley: University of California Press, 1984; Joseph Tabory, 'Towards a History of the Paschal Meal', in Bradshaw and Hoffman (eds), *Passover and Easter*, pp. 62–80.

symposium, in which discussions and conversations became the main elements of the evening, and many of these discussions are related to the foods consumed during the evening.[9]

It is not too difficult to suggest a Symposium influence on the 'Last Supper' traditions, where the Johannine Jesus washes the feet of the disciples, where the guests recline, they dip (hors d' oeuvre), have a blessing rather than a libation to a pagan deity, and sing (psalms). Likewise, there are a number of elements in Paul's description of the Lord's Supper at Corinth that reflect the Symposium. Hal Taussig in particular wishes to see practically every meal in the New Testament as simply a version of the Greco-Roman banquet in which *deipnon* and *kline* always carry a technical meaning.[10] He also suggests that all of the hymns that can be found in the New Testament, from the 'Logos' hymn of John 1, reconstructions in Philippians and Colossians, and the heavenly songs of the Book of Revelation, were sung during the passing of the cup at the Christian Symposium.[11] However, as Blomberg points out, precisely because such Greek customs did permeate Second Temple Judaism, we may not infer any particular kind of meal just from a reference to diners reclining.[12] *Deipnon* simply became a word to indicate an evening meal, and 'reclining' became synonymous with dining or eating, and the terms *anaklino, katakeimai* and *anapipto* were used to refer to being at table, regardless of what position one was able to take.[13] When Mark 6.30–44 uses the words *symposia* and *anaklinai* for the feeding of the 5,000, it can hardly imply a Greco-Roman banquet with couches and wine. Furthermore, though the similarities or parallels between the Greco-Roman banquet and Jewish and New Testament meals are interesting, the dissimilarities are also important. Fergus King notes that the sharing of food, wine and culture (discourse, music, etc.) are common in Greco-Roman social life. However, sharing a meal was an indicator of some kind of social link, family (real or fictive), political, economic or religious.[14] The religious differences between the Jewish milieu and the Greco-Roman world are important considerations. S. R. Shimoff has observed:

> The affluent Jews in Hellenistic Eretz Israel had aspirations of forming an elite aristocracy, and adopted many of the more innocent Greco-Roman practices (e.g. names, clothing style, etc.). But the Greco-Roman banquet was rooted in idolatry, and was marked by flagrant hedonism. Whatever else might be said about these banquets, it is clear that they were not appropriate expressions

9 Tabory, 'Towards a History of the Paschal Meal', pp. 73–4.

10 Taussig, *In the Beginning was the Meal*, p. 23. Tausig's work takes as proven the views of Matthias Klinghardt, Burton Mack and Dennis Smith, and seems to be merely an elaborate justification for the fellowship meals he sometimes arranges at Union Theological Seminary, New York.

11 Taussig, *In the Beginning was the Meal*, pp. 104–9.

12 Blomberg, *Contagious Holiness*, p. 95.

13 Reta Halteman Finger, *Of Widows and Meals: Communal Meals in the Book of Acts*, Grand Rapids: Eerdmans, 2007.

14 Fergus J. King, *More than a Passover: Inculturation in the Supper Narratives of the New Testament*, Frankfurt am Main: Peter Lang, 2007, p. 72.

> of traditional Jewish religious values. The Greco-Roman banquet thus represented an important boundary condition, the limiting case of how far a Jew might go in accepting, adopting, or adapting Hellenistic cultural practices.
>
> In a sense, then, if we want to appreciate the true extent of hellenization among Jews in Eretz Israel, and how the rabbis reacted to hellenization, Greco-Roman banquets are of special significance; no other Hellenistic practice was at once so culturally-attractive and so religiously-reprehensible.[15]

It seems not unreasonable to conclude that it is not what the New Testament meals might have in common with Greco-Roman Symposia that are of particular importance, but rather, their *differences* and their *theological significance*.

Jewish antecedents

Whatever degree of cultural assimilation, Jesus lived, moved and had his being in Jewish culture and religion. The Hebrew Scriptures and the literature of the Second Temple period are needed to unlock terms such as the Kingdom of God, Messiah and Son of Man that feature in the Gospels. He is recorded as teaching in synagogues, and in and around the Temple. The Gospel traditions do not hide the discontinuity, but for all Jesus' transformation of Judaism,[16] he does not cease to be a first-century Jewish Galilean teacher. It is therefore logical to look for Jewish antecedents and cultural settings for the Eucharist.

The Synoptic Gospels place the Last Supper within a Passover context/setting which was strongly defended by Joachim Jeremias.[17] However, others have seen considerable objections to this simple identification, such as the fact that the Fourth Gospel places the crucifixion at the time of the slaughter of the Passover lambs. Various solutions have been offered to reconcile the Synoptic and Fourth Gospel dating. In 1957 Annie Jaubert argued strongly that the difference is to be accounted for by the use of different calendars. The Synoptic writers used the calendar as preserved in the Qumran Community whereas St John used the official Jewish calendar.[18] This view, which has apparently been espoused by Pope Benedict XVI, has been re-examined and defended recently by Stéphane Saulnier.[19] Colin J. Humphreys has refined the astronomical calculations of J. K. Fotheringham.[20] Working with new computing techniques and with astronomer

15 S. R. Shimoff, 'Banquets: The Limits of Hellenization', *Journal for the Study of Judaism* 27:4 (1996), pp. 443–4.

16 I borrow here the title of John Riches' book, *Jesus and the Transformation of Judaism*, London: Darton, Longman and Todd, 1980.

17 Joachim Jeremias, *The Eucharistic Words of Jesus*, London: SCM Press, 1966.

18 A. Jaubert, *La date de la Cène*, Paris: Gabalda, 1957; *The Date of the Last Supper*, New York: Alba House, 1965.

19 Pope Benedict XVI, 'Jesus is the New and True Lamb', Maundy Thursday Homily, 6 April 2007, http://www.zenit.org/article-19348?l=english; Stéphane Saulnier, *Calendrical Variations in Second Temple Judaism: New Perspectives on the 'Date of the Last Supper' Debate*, Leiden: Brill, 2012.

20 J. K. Fotheringham, 'The Evidence of Astronomy and Technical Chronology for the Date of the Crucifixion', *Journal of Theological Studies* 34 (1934), pp. 146–62.

Graeme Waddington as well as noted biblical scholars, Humphreys provides evidence for use of the pre-exilic calendar by Samaritans, Zealots and some Essenes alongside the official Jewish calendar. It was a lunar calendar but counted the day from sunrise to sunrise. Humphreys plausibly suggests that since Jesus saw himself as the new Moses, he deliberately used the same calendar.

> By choosing to hold his last supper as a Passover meal using the pre-exilic calendar, Jesus was holding his last Passover meal on the *exact* anniversary of the first Passover meal described in the book of Exodus. Jesus was therefore symbolically identifying himself as the new Moses, which is consistent with his words at the last supper.[21]

Humphreys shows that the only possible date could be 3 April 33 CE, and that the Qumran calendar in that year kept Passover after the official Jewish date. However, some New Testament scholars, while accepting the reliability of Humphreys' calculations, will question the reliability of the Gospel statements upon which he based those calculations. Perhaps the meal is given a Passover setting by the Synoptics for theological reasons rather than historic reasons, or perhaps the Fourth Gospel and 1 Corinthians 5.7 have deliberately theologized the event to make the crucified Christ the ultimate paschal lamb. What can be said is that the *cumulative witness* of the New Testament associates the last meal with the time of Passover, even if it was not actually celebrated on the Passover. Another problem is that although Jeremias could confidently recreate the Passover ritual at the time of Jesus, current scholarship is less confident of being able to do that. The accounts of the Seder in the Mishnah and Tosefta post-date the destruction of the Temple and are already adjusting the ritual to a rabbinic setting, and Shmuel Safrai views the Last Supper accounts as giving valuable information about Passover in the Second Temple period prior to the Talmudic developments.[22] Philo's account is contemporary with the New Testament, and he records the following:

> In this festival [=Passover] many myriads of victims from noon till eventide are offered by the whole people, old and young alike, raised for that particular day to the dignity of the priesthood. For at other times the priests according to the ordinance of the law carry out both the public sacrifices and those offered by private individuals. But on this occasion the whole nation performs the sacred rites and acts as priests with pure hands and complete immunity. The reason for this is as follows . . . So exceedingly joyful were they [for their exodus] that in their enthusiasm and impatient eagerness, they naturally enough sacrificed without waiting for priests. This practice was . . . sanctioned by the law once in every year to remind them of their duty of

21 Colin J. Humphreys, *The Mystery of the Last Supper: Reconstructing the Final Days of Jesus*, Cambridge: Cambridge University Press, 2011, p. 194.

22 Shmuel Safrai, 'Early Testimonies in the New Testament of Laws and Practices Relating to Pilgrimage and Passover', in R. Steven Notley, Marc Turnage and Brian Becker (eds), *Jesus' Last Week: Jerusalem Studies in the Synoptic Gospels*, vol. 1, Leiden: Brill, 2006, pp. 41–51, esp. 47–50.

> thanksgiving . . . On this day every dwelling-house is invested with the outward semblance and dignity of a temple. The victim is then slaughtered and dressed for the festal meal which befits the occasion.[23]

This of course tells us something of the Temple, but nothing of the 'domestic' meals that followed, though it is clear that it included unleavened bread, bitter herbs, the paschal lamb and wine. Joseph Tabory suggests that if the material that does not belong to the earliest stratum of the Mishnah is extracted, then the pre-70 CE Passover ritual consisted of the following:

1 They poured the first cup . . . he recites the blessing for the day.
2 They brought unleavened bread, lettuce and fruit puree . . . they bring the paschal lamb.
3 They pour him the second cup . . . he expounds the biblical passage, 'My father was a wandering Aramean' until the end of the section.
4 They poured the cup; he recites the grace after meals.
5 The fourth [cup], he recites the *Hallel*, and says over it the blessing of the song.[24]

Though this may well be something like the Passover meal ritual at the time of Jesus, and, at least according to the Synoptics, it included bread and a cup of wine, we cannot be certain that Jesus observed the usual rituals. Following Jeremias, liturgical scholars such as Louis Ligier, Louis Bouyer and Thomas Talley have all urged that the *berakot* used at the Passover meal are the origins of the prayers over the bread and wine of the Eucharist.[25] The problem here is the assumption that there were standard invariable *berakot* recited at the Passover Seder in the early first century, and that Jesus and the Christian community faithfully used them. Both assumptions are questionable, though this will be considered only later in this study.

Other scholars have suggested other Jewish antecedents, though with hardly convincing arguments. Bernhard Lang, for example, has attempted to find a Temple ritual for the origin of the Last Supper.[26] He used Old Testament references to reconstruct a hypothetical Temple sacrifice which included the slaughter of an animal, and the presentation of bread and wine. This sacrifice was a substitute for and represented the one offering, and Lang suggested that the priests said 'This is N's Blood', N being the name of the sacrifice, and later, 'This is N's Body'. He suggests that Jesus jettisoned the Temple sacrifice, but kept the rite of bread and wine and the formula and applied it to himself. While it does seem that the Temple and its priesthood played a greater part in the early

23 Philo, 'Special Laws', 2:145–146, in Bokser, *Origins of the Seder*, p. 9.

24 Tabory, 'Towards a History of the Paschal Meal', p. 64.

25 Jeremias, *The Eucharistic Words of Jesus*; Louis Bouyer, *Eucharist: Theology and Spirituality of the Eucharistic Prayer*, Notre Dame: University of Notre Dame Press, 1968; Louis Ligier, 'The Origins of the Eucharistic Prayer: From the Last Supper to the Eucharist', *Studia Liturgica* 9 (1973), pp. 176–85; T. J. Talley, 'The Eucharistic Prayer of the Ancient Church according to Recent Research: Results and Reflections', *Studia Liturgica* 11 (1975), pp. 138–58.

26 Bernhard Lang, *Sacred Games: A History of Christian Worship*, New Haven: Yale University Press, 1997, pp. 215–19.

development of Christianity than the New Testament explicitly says (especially if Acts 6.7 has historical worth), this ritual seems to reside in the mind of Lang rather than Temple history, and his statement that his explanation 'must remain conjectural' is something of an understatement.

Cesare Giraudo put forward the argument that the Eucharist was derived from the literary form of the *todah* as found in the Old Testament, and he has been followed by Xavier Léon-Dufour.[27] The *zebah todah* (sacrifice of praise) is listed among the communion sacrifices in Leviticus, and was accompanied by prayer with a particular structure, such as Joshua 24.2–15, Deuteronomy 26.5–10 and Ezra 9.6–15. However, as Paul Bradshaw has noted, the Old Testament texts that Giraudo cited do not accompany a cultic act, and there is no reason to resort to the literary forms to explain the later Eucharistic Prayer.[28] Since, as Léon-Dufour admits, the *todah* is impossible to reconstruct in any detail, like Lang's proposal, we are interpreting something that we have (the accounts of the Eucharist and the later prayers) by something we do not have (a hypothetical *todah*).[29]

John O'Neill accepted that the Last Supper was not a Passover meal, and instead he sought the origin of the meal among small Jewish groups who used a ritual with bread and wine. He cited the mention of bread and wine, and particularly the meal mentioned in the Jewish romance known as *Joseph and Aseneth*, together with Proverbs 9.5 and Ecclesiastes 9.7. He linked these with the priestly blessing of bread and wine in the Qumran Community (1 QS 6.4–5), and concluded that Jesus knew and shared the theology of Qumran.[30]

Joseph and Aseneth was not written by the Qumran Community, nor found in its library. It is dated by most scholars somewhere between 100 BCE and the rule of Trajan (98–117 CE), and reflects a Greek-speaking environment.[31] The book itself is concerned with the marriage of a Jew to an Egyptian woman and with the problem of dietary laws. Six passages from this work speak of a meal, and specifically of bread and a cup. The bread is variously described in these passages as 'blessed bread of life' or 'bread of life', and a 'cup of blessing' or 'blessed cup of immortality'. Clearly there are echoes here of the Bread of Life in the Fourth Gospel, and the cup of blessing in 1 Corinthians 10. However, there is no evidence that it influenced or was influenced by the New Testament material. Christopher Burchard's careful analysis argued that what was crucial in this narrative was that Jews set apart food by blessings or *berakot*:

> The idea seems to be that the benedictions will somehow imbue food, drink, and ointment with the spirit of life, making them the earthly substitute for

27 Cesare Giraudo, *La struttura letteraria della preghiera euaristica*, Analecta Biblica 92, Roma: Pontificium Institutum Biblicum, 1981; Xavier Léon-Dufour, *Sharing the Eucharistic Bread: The Witness of the New Testament*, New York: Paulist Press, 1987.

28 Paul Bradshaw, 'Zebah Todah and the Origins of the Eucharist', *Ecclesia Orans* 8 (1991), pp. 245–60.

29 Léon-Dufour, *Sharing the Eucharistic Bread*, p. 42.

30 John O'Neill, 'Bread and Wine', *Scottish Journal of Theology* 48 (1995), pp. 169–84. See p. 183 for the statement that Jesus shared the theology of the Qumran community.

31 For the work being a later Christian story, Ross S. Kraemer, *When Aseneth Met Joseph: A Late Antique Tale of the Biblical Patriarch and his Egyptian Wife, Reconsidered*, Oxford: Oxford University Press, 1998.

> celestial manna which is spirit of life by essence. The spirit will in turn permeate a person as he or she consumes blessed food and drink and applies blessed ointment to the skin.[32]

Although noting a similar interest in theology with manna in John 6 and 1 Corinthians 10, Burchard nevertheless concluded:

> The result of this research seems to be that [*Joseph and Aseneth*] is irrelevant to the origin of the Lord's Supper . . . What [it] can do perhaps is to help explain why the central rite of that new religious movement, Christianity, was a solemn form of consuming ἄρτος and ποτήριον, why gestures concerning just these two things were remembered from, or attributed to, Jesus' last supper (such gestures are what Mark 14.22–24 par. is about, after all, not a meal), and why a narrative concerning them was formed at all.[33]

Quite apart from the fact that the antecedents that O'Neill adduced are quite disparate, there is not the slightest evidence in the New Testament to suggest that, with reference to the Qumran Community, Jesus 'shared their theology'.[34] However, a number of scholars have attempted to show parallels within the Essene and Qumran communities, and given the prominence of the Essene quarter of Jerusalem it is surmised that Jesus may have had some knowledge of this sect. Josephus recounts the meals of the Essenes as follows:

> And as for their piety towards God, it is very extraordinary; for before sun-rising they speak not a word about profane matters, but put up certain prayers which they have received from their forefathers, as if they made a supplication for its rising. After this every one of them are sent away by their curators, to exercise some of those arts wherein they are skilled, in which they labor with great diligence till the fifth hour. After which they assemble themselves together again into one place; and when they have clothed themselves in white veils, they then bathe their bodies in cold water. And after this purification is over, then every one meet [*sic*] together in an apartment of their own, into which it is not permitted to any of another sect to enter; while they go, after a pure manner, into the dining-room, as into a certain holy temple, and quietly set themselves down; upon which the baker lays them loaves in order; the cook also brings a single plate of one sort of food, and sets it before every one of them; but a priest says grace before meat; and it is unlawful for anyone to taste of the food before grace be said. The same priest, when he hath dined, says grace again after meat; and when they begin, and when they end, they praise God, as he that bestows their food upon them; after which they lay aside their [white] garments, and betake themselves to their labors again till the evening; then they return

32 Christopher Burchard, 'The Importance of Joseph and Aseneth for the Study of the New Testament: A General Survey and a Fresh Look at the Lord's Supper', *New Testament Studies* 33 (1987), p. 117.

33 Burchard, 'The Importance of Joseph and Aseneth', pp. 118–19.

34 O'Neill, 'Bread and Wine', p. 183.

> home to supper, after the same manner; and if there be any strangers there, they sit down with them. Nor is there ever any clamor or disturbance to pollute their house, but they give everyone leave to speak in their turn; which silence thus kept in their house appears to foreigners like some tremendous mystery; the cause of which is that perpetual sobriety they exercise, and the same settled measure of meat and drink that is allotted them, and that such as is abundantly sufficient for them.[35]

Josephus' observation on the concern for purity is borne out by the evidence of the Qumran documents, which if not actually Essene, were very similar. In the *Manual of Discipline* we find the following:

> Whenever there are ten men of the Council of the Community there shall not lack a Priest among them. And they shall all sit before him according to their rank and shall be asked their counsel in all things in that order. And when the table has been prepared for eating, and the new wine for drinking, the Priest shall be the first to stretch out his hand and bless the first-fruits of the bread and new wine. (1 QS 6.4–6)[36]

Not only is there a blessing of food and drink, but someone had to be present to interpret the Torah (1 QS 6.15–23). There is also a need for purity (1 QS 5.13). In the *Rule of the Congregation* a procedure is set out for a/the Messianic feast for when the Priest Messiah comes:

> the chiefs of the [clans of Israel] shall sit before him, [each] in the order of his dignity, according to [his place] in their camps and marches. And before them shall sit all the heads of [family of the congreg]ation, and the wise men of [the holy congregation,] each in the order of his dignity.
>
> And [when] they shall gather for the common [tab]le, to eat and [to drink] new wine, when the common table shall be set for eating and the new wine [poured] for drinking, let no man extend his hand over the first-fruits of bread and wine before the Priest; for [it is he] who shall bless the first-fruits of bread and wine, and shall be the first [to extend] his hand over the bread. Thereafter, the Messiah of Israel shall extend his hand over the bread, [and] all the congregation of the Community [shall utter a] blessing, [each man in the order] of his dignity. (1QSa2.20–21)[37]

The text is fragmentary, and in his fourth edition Vermes's translation implies that there is only one Messiah, not two. What is interesting here is that unlike the Symposium and the Last Supper, the participants sit, as in the feeding of the four and five thousand. Lawrence Schiffman comments, 'The messianic banquet, in keeping with the approach of the sect, would embody the traditions of

35 Josephus, 'The Wars of The Jews or The History of The Destruction of Jerusalem: Book II', http://www.ccel.org/j/josephus/works/war-2.htm.

36 Geza Vermes, *The Dead Sea Scrolls in English*, London: Penguin, 1975, p. 81.

37 Vermes, *The Dead Sea Scrolls in English*, p. 121.

Israel, not those of the Hellenistic pagans.'[38] Furthermore, 4Q434a contains the fragments of a grace after meals, though the exact occasion is not known:

> Your []. Your [. . .] to be comforted concerning the mourning, afflicted (city) which. [to d[est]roy nations, and He will cu[t o]ff peoples, and the wicked. [. . .] He renews works of heaven and earth, and they shall rejoice. And His glory fills [the whole earth . . . For] their [gu]ilt He will atone and (the One) abounding in goodness will comfort them . . . [. . .] . . . to eat its fruit and its goodness. BLANK [. . .] BLANK
>
> Like a man whose mother comforts him, so will He comfort them in Jerusal[em . . . like a bridegroom] over a bride, over her [fore]ver He will dwe[ll . . . fo]r His throne is forever and ever and His glory.[. . .] and all nations [. . .] to it and there shall be in it a hos[t . . .] . . . and their pleasant [la]nd [. . .] . . . ornamentat[ion]. [. . .]. I will bless [. . .] Blessed be the name of the Most Hi[gh . . .] BLANK [. . .] . . . [. . .] Your kindness upon me [. . .] you have established for the Torah [. . .]. the book of Your laws.[39]

Certainly we have here a community with strict purity rules that practised regular, apparently daily, meals which served as boundary markers, and these meals may prefigure the Messianic meal of 1QSa. Exactly how normative the fragment of the grace actually was is impossible to know. However, in the context of the Eucharist, Fergus King rightly notes that there are intriguing similarities: a meal involving bread and wine with Messianic significance.[40]

The Jewish material gives a broad context in which the meals in the Gospels and the distinct Last Supper narratives of Jesus can be evaluated.

The meals of Jesus and his Last Supper

It has already been noted that a number of New Testament studies have been concerned to view the Last Supper of the Synoptic Gospels in a wider context of a succession of meals Jesus attended or hosted rather than in isolation, and therefore it is useful to look at this wider context before specific discussion of the Last Supper narratives and the Johannine Supper.

To those whose field is other than New Testament scholarship, it is at times difficult to gain any overview or a sense of a consensus. This is partly because on the one hand scholars such as Willi Marxsen, J. D. Crossan and Burton Mack (followed by Smith and Taussig), building on the older form-critical methods of Bultmann, tend to regard many of the meals, and particularly the Last Supper, as being creations of the early communities and their storytellers, and not a living historical memory of what Jesus

38 Lawrence H. Schiffman, *The Eschatological Community of the Dead Sea Scrolls*, Atlanta: Scholars Press, 1989, p. 56.

39 James R. Davila, *Liturgical Works: Eerdmans Commentaries on the Dead Sea Scrolls*, Grand Rapids: Eerdmans, 2000, pp. 174–5.

40 King, *More than a Passover*, p. 85.

actually did.[41] Valeriy Alikin argued that originally Christians celebrated a ritual with bread and wine, believing that they were the body of Christ, and later this was projected onto an imagined Last Supper instituted by Jesus.[42] Kathleen E. Corley, noting the important role women played in funerary rituals, concluded that the Last Supper narratives were an etiological legend that 'ground the cult of the eucharist in the life and deeds of Jesus. Thus, a memorial meal originally founded by women and the poor is here attributed to a man (Jesus).'[43] On the other hand, following the approach of Birger Gerhardsson that tight rules governed transmission of religious material in Jewish circles, scholars such as Richard Bauckham and Craig Blomberg accord a much higher degree of historical worth to the meal narratives.[44] In spite of this divide, which certainly has implications for the origins of the Eucharist, there are some broad agreements on the focus or motifs of the meals in the Gospels.

In Mark, generally regarded as the earliest written Gospel (*c.* 65 CE), Jesus is engaged in controversy over table company, as well as fasting in 2.15ff. The first crucial meal is the feeding of the 5,000 (6.30–44), and, after teaching on clean and unclean (7.14–23), there is the feeding of the 4,000. La Verdiere sees those two meals of 'Breaking the Bread' as bringing to a conclusion the first part of Mark, which asks the question, 'Who is Jesus?'[45] La Verdiere writes:

> In setting out the universal mission of the Church, Mark relies on Eucharistic imagery, in particular on two stories of Jesus' breaking bread for large crowds. The section shows how the breaking of the bread, which at first was for Jewish men (*andres*) only (6:34–44) came to include Gentiles as well. Along with Gentiles, the breaking of the bread would include women as well as men (8:1–9). The section also shows what was needed, on the Jewish side and on the Gentile side, for those developments to be possible.[46]

Important here is that both feedings recall not only the manna in the wilderness of Exodus 16, but also the feeding of 100 men by Elisha in 2 Kings 4.42–44. Blomberg draws attention to the use of the verb *chortazein*, 'to completely

41 Willi Marxsen, *The Beginnings of Christology together with the Lord's Supper as a Christological Problem*, Philadelphia: Fortress Press, 1979; John D. Crossan, *The Historical Jesus: The Life of a Mediterranean Jewish Peasant*, San Francisco: Harper, 1991; Burton L. Mack, *A Myth of Innocence: Mark and Christian Origins*, Philadelphia: Fortress Press, 1991.

42 Valeriy A. Alikin, *The Earliest History of the Christian Gathering: Origin, Development and Content of the Christian Gathering in the First to the Third Centuries*, Leiden: Brill, 2010.

43 Kathleen E. Corley, *Maranatha: Women's Funerary Rituals and Christian Origins*, Minnapolis: Fortress Press, 2010, p. 108. This study has too many assertions that lack a convincing argument.

44 Birger Gerhardsson, *Memory and Manuscript: With Tradition and Transmission in Early Christianity*, Grand Rapids: Eerdmans, 1998, originally published separately 1961 and 1964; Richard Bauckham, *Jesus and the Eyewitnesses: The Gospels as Eyewitness Testimony*, Grand Rapids: Eerdmans, 2006; Blomberg, *Contagious Holiness*.

45 Eugene La Verdiere, *The Eucharist in the New Testament and the Early Church*, Collegeville: Liturgical Press, 1996, pp. 50–1.

46 La Verdiere, *Eucharist in the New Testament*, p. 52.

satisfy', which suggests that these meals are a foreshadowing of the Messianic banquet, and so also echo Isaiah 25.6–9 and 55.1–2.[47] They also point to the Last Supper narrative with the words and actions of taking, giving thanks and blessing. According to La Verdiere, the second part of Mark's Gospel poses the question of what it means to be a follower of Christ, or a disciple. This line of inquiry is the focus of the literary-critical approach of George Ossom-Batsa who suggests the following structure of the Last Supper in Mark's passion narrative:

Mark 14.17–21 Prediction – Judas' treason
Mark 14.22–25 The Meal
Mark 14.16–31 Prediction – the fall of the disciples.

He suggests that in Mark the narrative explains the passion, and teaches about discipleship:

> Mark clearly demonstrates that even though the disciples did not merit the establishment of the communion because of the repeated failures, Jesus offered himself in the Eucharist as a foretaste of the new mode of existence in the διαθήκη established by the outpouring of his blood.[48]

Matthew is generally regarded as being written *c.* 85 CE and coming from a Jewish-Christian community, where the Torah still has some importance. The community had been expelled from the Synagogue, and became committed to the Gentile mission. The community lived in the wake of the destruction of the Jerusalem Temple, and the consolidation of rabbinic Judaism. Matthew redacted the Marcan Gospel material, and so reproduced the question of eating with sinners and fasting (Matt. 9.10–17), and the two feeding narratives. According to La Verdiere, Matthew has modified the accounts to reflect the way the Eucharist was celebrated in his communities.[49] Matthew includes the Q saying that the Son of Man comes eating and drinking ('the consummate party animal')[50] in contrast to John the Baptist. The Messianic banquet theme is found in the parable of the wedding feast (Matt. 22.1–14) and the bridesmaids (Matt. 25.1–13). In addition there is an eschatological meal saying in Matthew 8.11 about many coming from east and west to sit at table with Abraham, Isaac and Jacob in the Kingdom of Heaven, which recalls Isaiah 25.6–7. The Last Supper narrative is redacted to stress a concern of the Matthean communities found throughout this Gospel, the forgiveness of sins.[51] Daniel Stökl Ben Ezra has argued that the Barabbas narrative in Matthew 27.15–23 has been shaped by the Jewish ritual of Yom Kippur. Certainly the ritual of Yom Kippur inspired the writer of the Letter to the Hebrews, and so a connection

47 Blomberg, *Contagious Holiness*, pp. 106 and 58–9.

48 George Ossom-Batsa, *The Institution of the Eucharist in the Gospel of Mark: A Study of the Function of Mark 14.22–25 within the Gospel Narrative*, Frankfurt am Main: Peter Lang, 2001, p. 75.

49 La Verdiere, *Eucharist in the New Testament*, p. 73.

50 So the title of Blomberg, *Contagious Holiness*, Chapter 4.

51 Blomberg, *Contagious Holiness*, pp. 75–6. Matthew 1.21 announces that the child is to be named Jesus, because he will save his people from their sins.

was current in first-century Christian communities. It may be that Yom Kippur theology of forgiveness has impacted the Matthean cup saying.[52]

It is in Luke–Acts that a concentration of meals and references to eating is found, which inspired Robert Karris's title, *Eating Your Way through Luke's Gospel.*[53] La Verdiere devoted a separate study to the meals in the Lucan tradition.[54] He identifies ten meals that lead up to and then follow the Last Supper narrative. Three are told in the origins of the Church in Jesus' ministry:

1 The banquet at the home of Levi (5.27–39).
2 The dinner at the home of a Pharisee (7.36–50).
3 The breaking of the bread in Bethsaida (9.10–17).

Four meals take place in the journey to Jerusalem:

1 The hospitality offered at the home of Martha (10.38–42).
2 A second dinner at the home of a Pharisee (11.37–54).
3 A third such dinner, on the Sabbath (14.1–35).
4 The hospitality extended by Zacchaeus (19.1–10).

After the Last Supper narrative (which in the manuscript tradition of Luke has two versions) there are two post-resurrection meals:

1 The meal at Emmaus (24.13–35).
2 The meal of fish with the entire community in Jerusalem (24.36–49).[55]

Luke is regarded as writing for a Gentile audience, and La Verdiere believes that in these meals there is influence of the Greco-Roman Symposium.[56] Blomberg, however, comes to a different conclusion, arguing that the kinds of table fellowship involved in each of these passages vary greatly. There are banquets thrown by Pharisees in chapters 7, 11 and 14, in which Jesus is the 'rude' guest, and the one occasion that a clear Symposium pattern emerges (14.1–24) Jesus tries to turn it into an anti-symposium.[57] Some writers lay stress on the Lucan idea of hospitality and inclusivity in these meals, suggesting an 'open' table.[58] It is certainly noticeable that the (Q) saying of Matthew 8.11 is expanded in Luke to include north and south as well as east and west (Luke 13.28–29). However, the Last Supper narrative seems to have been a 'closed' table for the 12 apostles who will judge the 12 tribes of Israel. As regards Luke's Last Supper narrative, La

52 Daniel Stökl Ben Ezra, *The Impact of Yom Kippur on Early Christianity*, Tübingen: Mohr Siebeck, 2003, pp. 165–71.

53 Robert J. Karris, *Eating Your Way through Luke's Gospel*, Collegeville: Liturgical Press, 2006.

54 Eugene La Verdiere, *Dining in the Kingdom of God: The Origin of the Eucharist according to Luke*, Chicago: Liturgy Training Publications, 1994.

55 La Verdiere, *Dining in the Kingdom of God*, p. 13.

56 La Verdiere, *Dining in the Kingdom of God*, p. 21.

57 Blomberg, *Contagious Holiness*, p. 161.

58 So Karris, *Eating Your Way through Luke's Gospel*, p. 98; La Verdiere, *Dining in the Kingdom of God*, p. 192.

Verdiere believes that there are two traditions that have been joined (regardless of the longer or shorter text). The Last Supper tradition (22.14–18) has been joined to the Lucan communities' Lord's Supper (22.19–20). The Lord's Supper in these communities is suggested by the breaking of bread (Acts 2.42, 46, the difficulties of the community at table 6.1–7), and the meals involving Paul in Acts 16.34, 20.7–12 and 27.33–38. What is important is that in the Synoptic Gospels the Last Supper narratives are all in the immediate context of the passion narrative, and are an integral part of it. N. T. Wright aptly observes that the Last Supper is 'the central symbolic action which provides the key to Jesus' implicit story about his own death'.[59] But by the same token, the purpose of the narratives is to interpret the greater narrative, and they do not purport to be explicit liturgical instructions, even though later that is how they have come to be read.

Given that in 1 Corinthians food is a prominent subject and that in 10.16–17 Paul speaks of cup and bread, and in 11.17–22 the Lord's Supper has the sequence of bread and then cup, this has been taken by many to suggest more than one meal pattern among the Corinthians. The Fourth Gospel is silent on any Institution Narrative at the final meal with the disciples, and instead gives prominence to service and foot-washing. However, given the 'eucharistic' teaching related to the feeding of the 5,000 in John 6, when added to this plethora of meals, it is not altogether surprising that some scholars have felt that there were once several or many meal traditions associated with the Jesus movement, not all of which were related to the Last Supper tradition. Xavier Léon-Dufour posited a threefold development of the meal tradition.[60] Building on the (questionable) idea of a *todah* meal, he suggested that the first Christians reacted as good Jews by joyously celebrating the God who delivered his Son Jesus from death and was bringing them into the eschatological kingdom. The *todah* was permeated with the idea of covenant, and so recalling the covenant promised in Jeremiah 31.31–34, the concept of a new covenant was added. A third stage was the adding of an idea of atoning covenant in Isaiah 53. The Supper accounts reveal two complementary traditions, the cultic (Mark and Matthew) and the testamentary (Luke and Paul). Bruce Chilton identified six 'types' of Eucharist.[61] The first type of Eucharist was Jesus' practice of fellowship meals – eating with sinners. The second type was after Jesus had cleansed the Temple, when he made the bold claim that the bread and wine of his fellowship meals were his 'flesh' and 'blood', adding a sacrificial dimension. A third type was found among Petrine circles, which emphasized the concept of covenant. From the group around James in Jerusalem came the 'Last Supper', or *seder* tradition, which privileged Jews and established the group's authority. Resistance to this came from the Pauline communities, which insisted that the meal came from the night he was betrayed, and not the Passover, and that the terms 'This is my body' and 'This is my blood' were taken as autobiographical, and it is this tradition that has influenced the Synoptic Gospels. A sixth type he finds in John, where the feeding of the 5,000 occurs at Passover; Jesus is identified as the heavenly manna, and gives his own flesh. Paul Bradshaw seems to weave

59 N. T. Wright, *Jesus and the Victory of God*, Minneapolis: Fortress Press, 1996, p. 554.

60 Léon-Dufour, *Sharing the Eucharistic Bread*, pp. 176–9.

61 Bruce Chilton, *A Feast of Meanings: Eucharistic Theologies from Jesus through Johannine Circles*, Leiden: Brill, 1994.

some of these 'types' together in his projected development of the Eucharist.[62] Most recently Martin Stringer has suggested that in Pauline and Johannine communities the 'Last Supper' was an annual celebration at Passover, and thus had a quite different emphasis from a more regular weekly community meal called the 'breaking of the bread', whereas Valeriy Alikin concludes that the Supper was shared/celebrated every Sunday evening by the early communities.[63] As will be seen, certainly alongside the Last Supper narratives in the Synoptic Gospels and 1 Corinthians, the *Didache* testifies to a community, or communities, that celebrated a meal with bread and wine, and associated with Jesus, but not with his words associating the bread and wine with his body and blood. Similar evidence from the second century attests 'Eucharists' with bread only or bread and water. This certainly suggests that the Eucharist was not always thought of in the manner of Dix's purple prose quoted at the beginning of this Introduction. However, such precise reconstructions of possible developments or 'types' *behind* the New Testament texts remain speculative exercises. What is perhaps more useful to consider are the theological meanings and functions *in* the narratives, since it is upon these that later orthopraxy and orthodoxy have come to rest.

The Lord's Last Supper narratives

The four Narratives of Institution of the Last Supper in the New Testament are: 1 Corinthians 11.23–27; Mark 14.22–25; Matthew 26.26–29; Luke 22.14–19a (shorter text) or 14–20 (longer text). Paul in 1 Corinthians 11 recites what the Lord did on the night he was betrayed (he doesn't say it was Passover) as a pattern for the churches at Corinth to follow in terms of behaviour rather than a liturgical text. The Synoptics, by contrast, give the narrative accounts in a sequence of events of the passion. Some scholars think that the latter are coloured by liturgical practice, and although that may be the case, since we have no liturgical practice with which to compare them, this is simply speculation. There is an affinity between Mark and Matthew, with an emphasis on covenant offering of Sinai, and also between Luke and the Pauline account where there are allusions to the new covenant of Jeremiah. In addition, the usual dating of the four documents means that Paul (*c.* 54 CE) and Mark (*c.* 65 CE) pre-date the destruction of the Temple, whereas Matthew and Luke (*c.* 80–85 CE) write for communities that no longer know the Jerusalem Temple as a living cult.

Paul introduces the narrative with the words παρέλαβον and παρέδωκα – I received and handed on – and these terms are also found in chapter 15 of his letter where he gives an account of eye witnesses of the resurrection. Some commentators believe that these words reflect rabbinical technical terms, *qibbêl* and *mâsar,* for handing on sacred teaching as accurately as possible.[64] It is surmised

62 Paul F. Bradshaw, *Reconstructing Early Christian Worship*, London: SPCK, 2009, pp. 18–19.

63 Martin Stringer, *Rethinking the Origins of the Eucharist*, London: SCM Press, 2011; Alikin, *Earliest History of the Christian Gathering*.

64 W. D. Davies, *Paul and Rabbinic Judaism*, 3rd edn, London: SPCK, 1970, p. 246; Gerhardsson, *Memory and Manuscript*, p. 290; King, *More than a Passover*, p. 194.

that Paul is handing on what he had learnt (catechesis) during his stay in Antioch in the early 40s CE.[65] The context seems to be that a division along social lines had developed in Corinth with wealthier members gathering for the Lord's Supper dining in the *triclinium* (dining room), and less wealthy members having a lesser fare in the *atrium* (courtyard). In his recent study of the Pauline Supper, Panayotis Coutsoumpos argues that the meal envisaged here was not based on the Symposium, or the *convivium*, but the Greco-Roman *Eranos*, which was like a 'pot-luck' dinner.[66] However, the sequence suggests that the meal was separated from a ritual of bread and wine. Whereas Stringer puts forward the suggestion that the Lord's Supper at Corinth was an annual event at Passover, Coutsoumpos thinks that Paul's comments suggest that the Supper was held continually at possibly weekly intervals, and not merely as an annual recollection of the Lord's death. No time is specified by Paul but the context suggests that the abuse was not a memory of an annual event, but something that was happening with some regularity. This does not necessarily mean that the Lord's Supper at Corinth verbally recalled the Last Supper, but the Last Supper tradition known to Paul is the exemplar for the Corinthians' Lord's Supper.

Paul's narrative states that Jesus gave thanks (εὐχαριστήσας) over the bread and likewise the cup, implying two Eucharistic Prayers. Of the bread saying, Coutsoumpos suggests that it derives from a Greek-speaking community's tradition, indicated by the possessive pronoun at the beginning (μοὑ) and the fact that the words 'which is for you' cannot be retranslated back into Aramaic.[67] As noted, the cup saying is anchored in the new covenant of Jeremiah. After both the bread and cup sayings, Paul records Jesus as saying, 'Do this in remembrance of me'. The word 'Anamnesis' has occasioned much discussion throughout the Church's history, not only as to whether the Semitic background implies a dynamic making present rather than the Enlightenment's mental reflection, but also whether it includes an Anamnesis by God as well as humans. Some scholars cite parallels in Greco-Roman memorial or funerary meals, but the Hebrew *zikkaron* seems to underlie the term, and recalls Jewish cultic celebrations such as the Passover, which is often linked with a sacrifice, and serves as a proclamation. This latter is made explicit in the Pauline narrative, for the Lord's Supper is to be celebrated to proclaim the Lord's death until he comes. There is a distinct eschatological dimension, for when the Lord comes, the Kingdom will be established and the Messianic banquet will be celebrated.

The Marcan narrative, as we have noted, is placed after the prediction of betrayal and followed by a warning of Peter's denial, the setting is the time of Passover, and Jesus is with the Twelve. After taking bread, Jesus blessed (εὐλογήσας) and broke and said, 'Take: this is my body'. For the cup, Jesus 'gave thanks', as in Paul. Many New Testament scholars regard these as synonyms, but in Jewish prayer forms they appear to be distinct prayer genres, suggesting a *berakah* over

65 So Jerome Kodell, *The Eucharist in the New Testament*, Wilmington: Michael Glazier, 1988, p. 71.

66 Panayotis Coutsoumpos, *Paul and the Lord's Supper: A Socio-Historical Investigation*, Frankfurt am Main: Peter Lang, 2005, pp. 46–51.

67 Coutsoumpos, *Paul and the Lord's Supper*, p. 120.

the bread and an *eucharistia* over the cup.[68] After they had drunk from the cup he said, 'This is my blood of the covenant, which is poured out for many.' This echoes the Sinai covenant, when Moses splashed the blood of offerings on the altar and on the people (Ex. 24.5–8). 'For many' means, potentially, all. Jesus then vows not to drink of the fruit of the vine until he drinks it new in the Kingdom of God, which is also an eschatological reference to the Messianic banquet.

The Matthean community added little to Mark's narrative, which was its source, other than adding 'for the forgiveness of sins' after the 'many' of the cup saying. This community, which regarded Jesus as a new Moses, was happy to leave the Sinai covenant emphasis of the Marcan narrative. The eschatological saying replaces Kingdom of God with Kingdom of my Father.

The difficult question regarding Luke is the two readings, and that regardless of which is earlier, a cup is passed around prior to the bread. We have either the sequence cup–bread (shorter) or cup–bread–cup (longer). In favour of the shorter reading is the fact that it is difficult to see why a later scribe should have omitted the fuller saying over the bread and the cup with its saying. Verse 17 reads:

> Then, taking a cup, he gave thanks and said, 'Take this and share it among you, because from now on, I tell you, I shall not drink wine until the kingdom of God comes.'

Jesus then takes bread, gives thanks, breaks and gives it with the words 'This is my body'. Given the eschatological emphasis and a vow of abstention in verse 17, it might explain why in the Acts of the Apostles Luke talks of 'Breaking of the Bread' – it might have been a bread-only ritual. However, Fergus King noted that although from the time of Westcott and Hort in the nineteenth century through the 1950s most scholars favoured the shorter text, an increasing number have preferred the longer text, but there is certainly no unanimity.[69] The majority of manuscripts support the longer text, and it can be defended on the grounds that Luke the historian is linking the Last Supper with specific cups of the Passover *Seder*. If the longer text is given priority, then we have a sequence of a cup with an eschatological emphasis that is shared, bread identified in some way with 'my body which will be given for you', and a command to do this in remembrance. Then likewise with the cup which is 'the new covenant in my blood which will be poured out for you'. Though this sequence has much in common with the Pauline narrative, it is far from identical.

From the four accounts, several points may be noted.

Liturgical prayers

Even though the narrative is not a liturgical text, it narrates the performance of a liturgical rite. There were separate prayers over bread and cup(s), either a

68 Joseph Heinmann, *Prayer in the Talmud: Forms and Patterns*, New York and Berlin: De Gruyter, 1977, pp. 90–3.

69 King, *More than a Passover*, p. 223.

berakah and a *eucharistia* (Mark and Matthew) or two (Paul) or three (Luke) *eucharistia* prayers.

Liturgical formulae and actions

Bread and a cup were distributed with formulae, associating the bread with the body of Jesus and the cup as his blood of the covenant. The word for bread, *artos*, does not allow us to decide whether it was leavened or unleavened, though King suggests that it designates wheat bread, which was more up-market than barley bread: 'The choice of bread as the food element might well give an indication of how God, or Jesus, perceived those who partook of it. They shared in a rich foodstuff, and, by implication, were accorded a high status.'[70] The content of the cup is not specified, but the most natural inference is that it was wine, to which water was normally added in Mediterranean cultures. As regards the interpretative words, if they were spoken in Aramaic or Hebrew, there was no 'is', and so subsequent debates over whether or not 'is' means 'real identity' are somewhat alien to the Semitic mind and grammar. It has been debated whether a Jewish mindset could envisage eating someone's body (or in Aramaic, *bisra*/flesh) and drinking blood, which was condemned in the Old Testament. It is this theme that John 6 discusses at length. However, the words spoken concerning the bread and cup are perhaps best understood in terms of the symbolic acts of the Old Testament prophet, which not only declared but helped bring about that which God wills. The Hebrew *dabar* means both word and deed, and the prophetic symbolism was a mode of divine speech. Proto-Isaiah walked naked, Ezekiel took a brick to portray a siege and he refused to mourn when his wife died. Nicholas Perrin has argued that Jesus deliberately 'fulfils' some of the Old Testament prophecies to do with the Messiah and the Temple.[71] The triumphal entry into Jerusalem on a donkey was deliberately arranged and fulfils Zechariah 9.9. The cleansing of the Temple in which Jesus quotes from Isaiah and Zechariah was deliberately orchestrated. The Last Supper was also prearranged – the man with a water jar, and an 'upper room' (and according to Humphreys, a deliberately calculated date). In the deliberate celebration of the supper with the interpretative words (either by Jesus or the subtle creations by later Christians makes no difference), the commemoration of the Exodus is consciously transformed as prophetic symbolism of the impending death of Jesus. Scott McKnight has argued that since the Passover sacrifice was not an atoning one, but a protecting one, then 'Jesus' death protects from God's judgement, and that judgement surely finds its clearest expression in Jesus' warnings about Jerusalem's destruction', though he argues this in association with the

70 King, *More than a Passover*, p. 215.

71 Nicholas Perrin, *Jesus the Temple*, London and Grand Rapids: SPCK and Baker, 2010. See also G. K. Beale, *The Temple and the Church's Mission*, Downers Grove: InterVarsity Press, 2004, pp. 176–80, and S. Kim, 'Jesus – The Son of God, the Stone, the Son of Man and the Servant: The Role of Zechariah in the Self-Identification of Jesus', in G. F. Hawthorne and O. Betz (eds), *Tradition and Interpretation in the New Testament: Essays in Honor of E. E. Ellis*, Tübingen: Mohr Siebeck, 1987, pp. 134–48.

bread saying.[72] If Yom Kippur has influenced the Matthean saying, the food also symbolizes the forgiveness of sins that the death of Jesus seals. Bread and wine become the cultic meal of the (new) covenant, and the words thus have sacrificial overtones. Nicholas Perrin writes:

> if we grant the Last Supper as a historical reality (as almost all scholars do), then it may be – and repeatedly has been – argued that whatever Jesus intended at that mysterious meal, at least part of what he wished to accomplish was a kind of sacrifice. Moreover, it was a sacrifice in which he invited his disciples to partake. Their having done so equally implies their own conscious participation in a priestly meal. It was, after all, only priests who were allowed to feed themselves on the sacrificial meal.[73]

Perrin may here be overstating the implications, but certainly the concept of sacrifice hovers over the context of the meal and what it foreshadowed.

The command to repeat the ritual

The command to do this in remembrance is not found in Mark or Matthew. It is found after the bread and cup sayings in Paul, and after the bread saying in Luke, though the Greek ὡσαύτως, 'likewise' or 'the same manner', may well imply the command with the cup. Whatever the implications for the New Testament texts, the rituals that evolved to become the Eucharist presuppose the intention to repeat them.

As already noted, there has been much discussion over the Greek term *anamnesis* and the Hebrew *zikkaron*, particularly as to whether it is humanity or God who does the 'remembrance', or both.[74] Furthermore, most commentators suggest that the Semitic 'remembrance' carries with it a sense of making the past present. Margaret Barker has made the intriguing proposal that the word is in fact linked with the Bread of the Presence (Lev. 24), which, like other cereal offerings, is described as an '*azkanah*, which may be translated as a "memorial offering" or even possibly an "invocation offering"'.[75] She notes that Psalms 38 and 70 are entitled *l'hazkiyr*, 'for memorial offering' though both contain an invocation (Ps. 38.22 and Ps. 70.5), and the LXX renders the title of Psalm 38 *eis anamnesin peri sabbatou*. She surmises that the Bread of the Presence set before the Lord each Sabbath was a memorial of the eternal covenant, and Jesus (or some early Christian

72 Scot McKnight, *Jesus and His Death: Historiography, the Historical Jesus, and Atonement Theory*, Waco: Baylor University Press, 2005, p. 281.

73 Perrin, *Jesus the Temple*, p. 177.

74 For some of the literature, see Max Thurian, *The Eucharistic Memorial*, 2 vols, London: Lutterworth, 1960 and 1961; David Gregg, *Anamnesis in the Eucharist*, Bramcote: Grove Books, 1976; Brian J. Vickers, 'The Lord's Supper: Celebrating the Past and Future in the Present', in Thomas R. Schreiner and Matthew R. Crawford (eds), *The Lord's Supper: Remembering and Proclaiming Christ until He Comes*, Nashville: B&H Academic, 2010, pp. 313–40

75 Margaret Barker, *The Great High Priest: The Temple Roots of Christian Liturgy*, London: T & T Clark, 2003, p. 88.

communities) regarded the Last Supper as the new Bread of the Presence.[76] In the light of the incident on eating grain on the Sabbath and the appeal to David (Mark 2.23–28 and parallels) there may be overtones of the Bread of the Presence, but as intriguing as Barker's argument is, there are too many hypotheses involved. However, the Last Supper accounts do seem to have been magnets that have attracted a variety of First and Second Temple cultic resonances and overtones.[77]

The eschatological dimension

All four narratives suppose that the Last Supper and, for Paul the Lord's Supper somehow point to the apocalyptic *eschaton*. In the Gospels Jesus will abstain from wine until it is drunk anew in the Kingdom, and therefore the Messianic meal. For Paul, the Supper proclaims (prophetic symbolism reiterated) the death of the Lord until he comes. When he comes, he brings the new age. R. Steven Notley, Nicholas Perrin and Margaret Barker all suggest that the Second Temple speculation on Melchizedek as the heavenly figure who would inaugurate the eternal Jubilee has either been deliberately taken up by Jesus or has been projected upon him. Melchizedek brought forth bread and wine; the new priest-messiah also brought forth bread and wine, pointing to the Kingdom.[78]

It has been observed that although John's Gospel has a Last Supper, which was held near Passover, there is no Last Supper Institution Narrative. However, the theme of 'ingesting Jesus' is prevalent in this Gospel.[79] Of particular significance is the discourse on eating the flesh (*sarx*) of Jesus as heavenly manna in chapter 6, which follows the feeding of the 5,000. Some commentators such as Bultmann have regarded the Fourth Gospel as anti-sacramental (or regarded 'sacramental' material as a later redaction), but others such as C. H. Dodd and Raymond Brown thought otherwise, and regard chapter 6 as eucharistic teaching.[80] Jesus is depicted as the new Moses, who gives heavenly manna, which is himself: 'I am the Bread of Life.' In the discourse at the Johannine Supper, Jesus announces he is also the True Vine. Both are used to stress that Christ dwells within his followers. If the True Vine points towards wine, then according to Freedman, 'the ingesting motif is an effective vehicle for conveying the soteriology of the Gospel and ties this expression of soteriology to the Eucharist tradition'.[81]

---

76 Barker, *The Great High Priest*, pp. 88–9.

77 For a general survey of some of these, see Brant Pitre, *Jesus and the Jewish Roots of the Eucharist: Unlocking the Secrets of the Last Supper*, New York: Doubleday, 2011.

78 R. Steven Notley, 'The Eschatological Thinking of the Dead Sea Sect and the Order of Blessings in the Christian Eucharist', in R. Steven Notley, Marc Turnage and Brian Becker (eds), *Jesus' Last Week: Jerusalem Studies in the Synoptic Gospels*, vol. 1, Leiden: Brill, 2006, pp. 121–38; Perrin, *Jesus the Temple*; Barker, *The Great High Priest*.

79 Jane S. Webster, *Ingesting Jesus: Eating and Drinking in the Gospel of John*, Leiden: Brill, 2003.

80 Rudolph Bultmann, *The Gospel of John*, Philadelphia: Westminster Press, 1964; C. H. Dodd, *The Interpretation of the Fourth Gospel*, Cambridge: Cambridge University Press, 1953; Raymond Brown, *The Gospel according to John*, 2 vols, Anchor Bible 29 and 29a, New York: Doubleday, 1966.

81 Webster, *Ingesting Jesus*, p. 153, referencing William Freedman, 'Literary Motif: A Definition and Evaluation', *Novel* 4 (1971), pp. 123–31.

A first-century 'eucharistic' rite: *Didache* 9–10

The *Didache* or *Teaching of the Twelve Apostles* was discovered by Archbishop Philotheos Bryennios in 1873. It is known from two Greek manuscripts and also a Coptic version. Although few scholars have accepted Joan Hazelden Walker's arguments for a pre-Marcan or even pre-Pauline dating for this document, the date of *c.* 80 CE is preferred by most, and Palestine or Syria are still regarded as probable origins.[82] Much recent debate has revolved around the relationship of the *Didache* to the Gospel of Matthew, and whether one used the other, or whether both drew on an independent tradition.[83] What is important is that here we have a document of comparable dating to the New Testament (in places it was regarded as canonical Scripture).

Jonathan Draper observes that it reflects the perspective of a Jewish–Christian community concerned with the preparation and socialization of Gentile converts.[84] Though there seems to be agreement that the present document is composite, and that chapters 1–6 are the oldest, and perhaps were or came to be used as instruction or catechesis, it is the theology of this composite document that has been most under scrutiny, and this in turn affects the context of what it says on baptism. Jonathan Reed observed that although chapters 7–10 are tied to chapters 1–6 by means of the connecting phrase ταῦτα πάντα προειπόντες (having first recited all these things), this section contains far fewer verbal parallels to the Hebrew Scriptures. Whereas the Hebrew Scriptures are the authority for much of these first chapters, from 7 onwards it is Jesus who becomes the authority, though as the lawgiver. However, the new lawgiver simply reinforces the Jewish nature of the older Torah. Reed notes how the identity of the Church is tied to the vine, which in the Old Testament is the identity of Israel, and that the community is the inheritor of the Davidic kingdom. Malachi 1.11 is used without any anti-Jewish polemic, and the role of the High Priest is reinterpreted and applied to the offices of prophets and teachers. The community also appropriates apocalyptic passages for itself. Reed concluded:

> The community of the *Didache* found an important source for its epic imagination within the stories, themes, and passages of the Hebrew Scriptures, and in fact has transferred important items within the tradition to its own epic: past temple sacrifices are now communal meals; officiating priests are now prophets, teachers, and apostles; and the temple is now the church. The

---

82 Joan Hazelden Walker, 'A Pre-Marcan Dating for the Didache: Further Thoughts of a Liturgist', *Studia Biblica* 3 (1978), pp. 403–11.

83 Jonathan Draper (ed.), *The Didache in Modern Research*, Leiden: Brill, 1996; Clayton N. Jefford (ed.), *The Didache in Context*, Leiden: Brill, 1995; Huub Van De Sandt, *Matthew and the Didache: Two Documents from the same Jewish–Christian Milieu*, Minneapolis: Royal Van Gorcum, Assen and Fortress Press, 2005; Kurt Niedwimmer, *The Didache*, Minneapolis: Fortress Press, 1998; Huub Van De Sandt and David Flusser, *The Didache: Its Jewish Sources and Its Place in Early Judaism and Christianity*, Assen and Minneapolis: Royal Van Gorcum and Fortress Press, 2002; Aaron Milavec, *The Didache: Faith, Hope and Life of the Earliest Christian Communities, 50–70 CE*, New York: Newman Press, 2003; Thomas O'Loughlin, *The Didache: A Window on the Earliest Christians*, London: SPCK, 2010.

84 Jonathan Draper, 'Ritual Process and Ritual Symbol in Didache 7–10', *Vigiliae Christianae* 54 (2000), p. 122.

> community views itself as the true Israel, has grafted itself into the Davidic lineage, and has gathered itself from within the diaspora. The community also has a complete set of ethical guidelines or laws. It has, in short, brought the past into the present in order to give meaning and justification to its shape and very existence.[85]

Nathan Mitchell presupposed a similar construct in his examination of baptism in the *Didache*. He noted that chapters 1–5 are concerned with the yoke of the law, meaning the Torah, and suggests that one can attain salvation only by becoming a fully observant Jew. This becomes mitigated in the later chapters, but, notes Mitchell, the Christology of the *Didache* may be characterized as one whereby believers continue to preach the preaching of Jesus, but they do not yet preach Jesus. Furthermore, there is a distinct absence of important Pauline themes. The meal prayers occur in chapters 9–10, and give an order of cup/bread. Each is accompanied by a short prayer beginning 'We give thanks'. A longer prayer of thanks is provided after the meal. Although 9.1 clearly says 'Concerning the eucharist, give thanks thus', some scholars have preferred to classify this as an agape, especially since chapter 14 also speaks of a loaf and thanksgiving on the Lord's day or the day appointed by the Lord. However, if it is accepted that the term 'Eucharist' had a much wider meaning in the first three centuries, and was not always associated with the Institution Narratives of the New Testament, then there is no need to conclude that this was not a Eucharist. Equally, though, it is the Eucharist of *this particular community*, and not necessarily representative of all other Christian communities at this time.

The origin and nature of the prayers, and particularly the post-prandial prayer have occasioned much debate. Louis Finkelstein argued that *Didache* 10 was a rearrangement of the three strophes of the *birkat ha-mazon* meal prayer, and many have accepted this argument.[86] His view was compounded by the claim of Louis Bouyer that a Hebrew version of *Didache* 10 had been found at Dura Europos.[87] Though Bouyer provided no footnote, this appears to have been a reference to J. L. Teicher's misleading translation of a fragment of a meal prayer, which in fact has no correlation with the *Didache*'s text.[88] Appeal has also been made to *Jubilees* 22.1–9, which witnesses to a tripartite meal prayer on the lips of Abraham. Recent Jewish scholarship shows that there was no common agreed original text of this meal prayer in Jewish households in the mid-first century, and therefore there is no fixed text with which the *Didache* can be compared.[89] Although published in 1964 in Hebrew, it was not until the publication of the English edition in 1977 that the work of Joseph Heinemann began to make an impact on Christian liturgical scholars, particularly the rather

---

85 Jonathan Reed, 'The Hebrew Epic and the *Didache*', in Jefford (ed.), *The Didache in Context*, pp. 224–5.

86 Louis Finkelstein, 'The Birkat Ha-mazon', *Jewish Quarterly Review* 19 (1928–9), pp. 211–62.

87 Bouyer, *Eucharist*, pp. 27 and 116.

88 J. L. Teicher, 'Ancient Jewish Eucharistic Prayers in Hebrew', *Jewish Quarterly Review* 54 (1963), pp. 99–109.

89 See Milavec, *Didache*, pp. 416–21.

uncritical assumption that standard Jewish prayer forms were all extremely ancient and pre-dated Christian forms. Heinemann noted:

> The Jewish prayers were originally the creations of the common people. The characteristic idioms and forms of prayer, and indeed the statutory prayers of the synagogue themselves, were not in the first place products of the deliberations of the Rabbis in their academies, but were rather the spontaneous, on-the-spot improvisations of the people gathered on various occasions to pray in the synagogue. Since the occasions and places of worship were numerous, it was only natural that they should give rise to an abundance of prayers, displaying a wide variety of forms, styles, and patterns. Thus, the first stage in the development of the liturgy was characterized by diversity and variety – and the task of the Rabbis was to systematize and to impose order on this multiplicity of forms, patterns, structures. This task they undertook after the fact; only after the numerous prayers had come into being and were familiar to the masses did the Sages decide that the time had come to establish some measure of uniformity and standardization.[90]

Turning his attention to the work particularly of Finkelstein and the quest for an original text, Heinemann stated:

> [T]he widely accepted goal of the philological method – viz., to discover or to reconstruct the one 'original' text of a particular composition by examining and comparing the extant textual variants one with the other – is out of place in the field of [early] liturgical studies. We must not try to determine by philological methods the 'original' text of any prayer without first determining whether or not such an 'original' text ever existed.[91]

Avi Shmidman's work on the development of the *birkat ha-mazon* draws attention to the many different supplications and variations, and, not least, the poetic forms of this prayer tradition, which also warns against the idea of any original form.[92] Furthermore, the Dura Europos Meal Prayer Fragment and the meal prayer of 4Q434a from Qumran witness to a plurality of forms.[93] It is precisely Finkelstein's positing of an original text of the *birkat ha-mazon* and his comparison with *Didache* 10 that has been addressed by Araon Milavec and Jonathan Schwiebert in their work on this Church Order. Schwiebert noted:

> A major difficulty with using Finkelstein's *Birkat ha-mazon* at all, despite careful provisos, is that we cannot assume a fixed entity of 'Judaism' even in the early second century, especially a monolithic *diaspora* Judaism, to which

90 Heinmann, *Prayer in the Talmud*, p. 37.

91 Heinmann, *Prayer in the Talmud*, p. 43.

92 Avi Shmidman, 'Developments within the Statutory Text of the Birkat ha-Mazon in Light of Its Poetic Counterparts', in Albert Gerhards and Clemens Leonhard (eds), *Jewish and Christian Liturgy and Worship: New Insights into Its History and Intersection*, Leiden: Brill, 2007, pp. 109–26.

93 Jacob Neusner, *A History of the Jews in Babylonia: 1. The Parthian Period*, 2nd edn, Leiden: Brill, 1969, p. 161; Davila, *Liturgical Works*, pp. 174–5.

> a Jewish follower of Jesus (or at least one who certainly *sounds* Jewish) can react by manipulating certain phrases of a fixed prayer tradition.[94]

Milavec points out that the text that Finkelstein gave was his own reconstruction of an urtext, based on much more recent texts of the meal prayer, but with the conviction that the 'briefest form' is nearest the original. Milavec observes that the briefest form is in fact in the Mishnah, and that if Finkelstein had followed what the Mishnah says, he could not have possibly constructed the text that he did; instead, 'his expectation of finding the source for the Eucharistic Prayers of the Didache would have entirely evaporated'.[95] In fact, in order to make his comparison more convincing, Finkelstein used *Didache* 10 to assist his reconstruction of an urtext of the *birkat ha-mazon*, and then of course was able to find parallels in *Didache* 10.

Milavec also notes the very different style of the prayers of the *Didache* to that of the *birkat ha-mazon*. This is discussed further by Schwiebert, who draws attention to the great overlap, if not repetition, found between the prayers of *Didache* 9.2, 9.3 and 10.1. They have a strong internal relationship, and not really an external relationship to any single source, but as noted by Van de Sandt and Flusser, they have parallels with a variety of Jewish sources.[96] Since they pre-date the later statutory Jewish meal prayers, they can perhaps tell us more about the development of Jewish prayer than supposed Jewish forms can tell us about the *Didache*. And of course, why a post-prandial prayer should become the source of a pre-prandial prayer has no good explanation, and that is probably because there is not one. If *Didache* prayers are of value at all in paleoanaphoral speculation, logic suggests it is the prayers of *Didache* 9 rather than 10 that should be the object of attention. Even the texts of the *Didache* are fluid, since 10.7 says that prophets may give thanks in whatever manner they wish. That is not to say that the *Didache* prayers do not reflect Jewish patterns (which, given the concerns of this community, we would expect) but they are prayers that are peculiar to this community. One may agree with Schwiebert's observation as regards *Didache* 10:

> One can probably surmise, then, that a threefold after-dinner prayer was traditional (compare *Jub.* 22:1–9), and that our group simply took it for granted. But it would be too much to claim that the prayers of *Didache* 10 derive their meaning from a polemical, conscious reorientation of a *fixed* Jewish prayer form.[97]

The three prayers give a structure of 9.2, a single strophe, two strophes in 9.3–4, two strophes, and then the post-meal prayer of three stropes, and an eschatological invocation, 10.2–6. Schwiebert discusses the verbal parallels between the three prayers, particularly the opening and closing of each prayer, which give

94 Jonathan Schwiebert, *Knowledge and the Coming Kingdom: The Didache's Meal Ritual and Its Place in Early Christianity*, London: T & T Clark, 2008, pp. 118–19.

95 Milavec, *Didache*, p. 420.

96 Van de Sandt and Flusser, *Didache*, p. 313.

97 Schwiebert, *Knowledge and the Coming Kingdom*, p. 119.

them a highly formal structure. The first two doxologies in 9 match those in 10, and much of 9.4 is found in 10.5:

> First for the cup:
> *We thank you* our *Father, for* the holy vine of David your servant, *which you made known to us through Jesus your servant. To you be the glory to the ages.*
> Then for the fragment (*klasmatos*, broken bread):
> *We thank you*, our *Father, for* the life and knowledge, *which you made known to us through Jesus your servant. To you be the glory to the ages.*
> Then, after you are full, give thanks like this:
> *We thank you*, holy *Father, for* your holy name, which you made to dwell in our hearts, and for the knowledge and faith and immortality, *which you made known to us through Jesus your servant. To you be the glory to the ages.*

Alan Garrow has argued that the prayers of 9 and 10 are a redaction of what originally were two separate, alternative accounts of a prayer that creates a transition between a full and a symbolic meal – in effect two 'eucharistic' rituals that have been redacted as one.[98] His argument is based on the parallels in language between the prayer of 9 and that of 10, together with the fact that 10 concludes with what appears to be an invitation to receive holy things. As logical as this may be, rather like Chilton's arguments of the meals behind the meal, it is speculative, and in the document as redacted, the prayers seem to be intended to be sequential.

The first prayer over the cup gives thanks for 'the holy vine of David, your servant (child)'. Jonathan Draper notes that the expression has no exact verbal source, but echoes a number of Old Testament references to the Davidic house, concluding that it is 'an imprecise and ambiguous ritual expression in the Eucharistic Prayer of the *Didache,* which draws on a rich symbolic tradition in the culture of Israel'.[99]

The prayer that accompanied the loaf speaks of life and knowledge which were made known through Jesus, your servant (child), and then develops into a petition for the ingathering of the scattered Church just as the loaf was once scattered over the mountains. The post-prandial prayer gives thanks to God for the (his) holy name dwelling in our hearts, that as creator he has given food and drink for enjoyment, and gives the community spiritual food and drink. A further request for the ingathering of the Church follows, and it concludes with an eschatological invocation:

> May grace come and may this world pass away. Hosanna to the God of David. If anyone is holy, let him advance; if anyone is not, let him be converted. Maranatha. Amen.

98 Alan J. P. Garrow, *The Gospel of Matthew's Dependence on the Didache*, London: T & T Clark, 2003, p. 28.

99 Draper, 'Ritual Process', p. 150.

Given that this community preached what Jesus preached, but did not preach Jesus, we should not be surprised that the meal, like the whole document, has no reference to the death of Jesus, and thus no association of the bread and wine with his body and blood. Schwiebert concludes:

> Thus, the *Didache*'s meal ritual has three distinct phases, each marked by a formal *eucharisteō*-prayer, and each phase represents increased emphasis and therefore communal importance. Bread is emphasized more than the cup; the eschatological gathering of the community, however, is the topic of greatest concern.[100]

Van de Sandt has recently suggested that the use of 'what is holy' in *Didache* 9.5 suggests a channeling of Temple sanctity to the community meal, which he links also with *Didache* 14.1–3.[101]

Didache 14.1–3 also mentions 'Eucharist' and a loaf, and confession of failings so that the offering (*thusia*) may be a pure offering as in Malachi 1.11. Here, then, the ritual that is celebrated on the Lord's Day, and called a Eucharist, is given a sacrificial dimension. There is no mention of the sacrifice of Christ, and so the document seems to have in mind that the ritual action and prayers of a holy community constitutes a sacrifice. Schwiebert is probably correct when he says,

> In calling their common meal a 'sacrifice', then, the author of *Didache* 14.1–3 is simply highlighting its *sacred* quality, in much the same way that the remark in 9.5 does. The terms 'pure' (καθαρὰ) and 'made common' or 'profaned' (κοινωθῇ) in 14.1–2 properly belong to a temple context – purity associated with a shrine and sacrificial rites.[102]

It perhaps reflects the post-70 CE situation, where what now constituted sacrifice was a heightened issue. Though different from the Gospel and Pauline Institution Narratives, this community did regard its meal with cup and bread as, in some sense, a sacrifice.

Some observations

Whatever the precise origin or origins of what later emerged as the Eucharist, the meal traditions of the Gospels are best understood within their Semitic environment, and by what apparently distinguished them from other Jewish meal traditions. From the brief overview of these first-century CE witnesses to 'eucharistic meals', it is possible to identify several theological motifs.

100 Schwiebert, *Knowledge and the Coming Kingdom*, p. 72.

101 Huub van de Sandt, 'Why does the Didache Conceive of the Eucharist as a Holy Meal?', *Vigiliae Christianae* 65 (2011), pp. 1–20.

102 Schwiebert, *Knowledge and the Coming Kingdom*, p. 167.

Euchology/eucharistias/doxology

Meals in the ancient world did not make a clear distinction between 'secular' and 'religious' meals. Meals frequently included invocations and prayers to a deity or deities. In the Jewish setting of Christianity, meals such as the feeding of the 5,000 and the Emmaus meal included 'blessing', which seems to refer to the *berakah*-style of Jewish prayer. The Last Supper narratives have 'blessed' and 'gave thanks', this latter being another liturgical genre. No meal prayer texts are given in the Gospels or by Paul, but we do find some in the *Didache*. The purpose of these prayers seems to bless God for his mighty acts, recited over the bread and cup. We have no idea of how similar or how different the meal prayers of other communities were.

Sacrifice, covenant and soteriology

The narratives of the Last Supper carry echoes of the Sinai covenant sacrifice, or the new covenant foretold by Jeremiah. Sacrificial protecting and atoning dimensions are also expressed in the 'given for you' and 'given for many for the forgiveness of sins' in the interpretative words. The ritual in the narratives points to the impending death of Jesus. Andrew McGowan has recently commented that to consider 'Eucharist' and 'sacrifice' together historically is to engage with two changing realities. Christian meals are immediately connected to a broader language of logic of offerings and sacrifices, of which meals were typically a part, but their place in the system was dynamic, and the meals change the meaning of 'sacrifice' even as they employ it.[103]

Christology and presence/association of identity

The interpretative words of Jesus regarding the bread suggest some prophetic identity of the bread with himself. In the narratives that have a command to repeat the rite, for the Christian communities the saying quite naturally associates the identity with some sort of presence of the Risen Lord. The Emmaus meal suggests that the elements are a means of divine disclosure of the Risen One.

Ecclesiology

Many scholars stress that Jesus ate with sinners, prostitutes and tax collectors, and see those meals as illustrating the hospitality of God who reaches out to all. Strangely, in the accounts of the Last Supper in the Synoptics, the meal seems to have been reserved for the Twelve, and though others may well have been understood to be present in the 'Upper Room', this was not an 'open table'. In

103 Andrew McGowan, 'Eucharist and Sacrifice: Cultic Tradition and Transformation in Early Christian Meals', in Matthias Klinghardt and Hal Taussig (eds), *Meals and Religious Identity in Early Christianity*, Tübingen: A. Francke, 2012, pp. 191–206.

1 Corinthians Paul addressed a whole number of issues to do with behaviour of members of the community, and for at least one grave offence required exclusion from the community. There is no suggestion that the Lord's Supper in Corinth was an open meal; on the contrary, participation required not only adherence to a certain way of life, but also participation in a worthy manner rather than in an unworthy manner (ἀναξίως). The *Didache* represents a community that invites Gentiles in, but only in so far as they become, as far as possible, Jews. The meal requires instruction and baptism, and is a boundary marker.

Eschatology

In the Last Supper narratives Jesus speaks of not drinking from the fruit of the vine again until he drinks it new in the Kingdom. Paul speaks of the Lord's Supper as proclaiming the death of the Lord until he comes. The prayers of the *Didache* ask for the ingathering of the Church, and invoke the Lord to come. The meals, therefore, had some proleptic dimension that pointed to the Messianic banquet.

These are by no means exhaustive of the theological motifs suggested by these meal narratives, but these may serve as a basic grid in discussing the development of the eucharistic liturgy and eucharistic theology, though in the subsequent history it has been sacrifice and presence that have dominated discussion and argument, and inevitably in the chapters that follow these will figure more prominently than other motifs.

1

Some Early Eucharistic Practices and Beliefs from Ignatius to Origen

The liturgical evidence for celebration of the Eucharist in the pre-Nicene period is sparse. Since it seems that the prayers uttered were extemporary,[1] there was no need for manuscript copies, and there was no one central theological school of thought. What may be gleaned about the rites tells us only what some communities did, and where we have theological expositions, they tell us only what that particular writer thought and taught.

Justin Martyr (*c.* 100–*c.* 165): a community in Rome

Among the most important sources are the writings of Justin Martyr. Originally from Samaria, and a philosopher by training, Justin ended his days as a Christian teacher in Rome in the mid-second century. Paul's letters indicate that Christianity was already found in Rome in the 50s CE, and he refers to various groups meeting in private houses. It may be that some of the Roman Tituli churches in the city were built over foundations of what were once private homes of Christian patrons and patronesses.[2] However, other groups appear to have centred on a teacher and modelled themselves on the philosophical schools.[3] Justin seems to have been head of one such school model which was located at the house of Martin over the Tiburtine baths. His famous pupil, Tatian, was to write a harmony of the Gospels, the *Diatessaron*. Justin's Palestinian origin and Tatian's Syriac abilities may point to a particular ethnic make-up for his Church.[4] Rome was the political centre of the Empire, and had large numbers of ethnic immigrants, including many from Syria and Palestine.

Justin's *First Apology* addressed to the emperor Antoninus Pius, *c.* 150, and the *Dialogue with Trypho* provide information about the eucharistic practice of his assembly and something of Justin's understanding of the Eucharist. Perhaps

1 Allan Bouley, *From Freedom to Formula: The Evolution of the Eucharistic Prayer from Oral Improvisation to Written Texts*, Washington: Catholic University of America Press, 1981.

2 See the Introduction to Hugo Brandenburg, *Ancient Churches of Rome: From the Fourth to the Seventh Centuries*, Turnhout: Brepols, 2005; Allan Doig, *Liturgy and Architecture: From the Early Church to the Middle Ages*, Aldershot: Ashgate, 2008, pp. 6–10.

3 J. S. Jeffers, *Conflict at Rome: Social Order and Hierarchy in Early Christianity*, Minneapolis: Fortress Press, 1991.

4 It is thought by most scholars that the *Diatessaron* was first written in Syriac, but very quickly translated (probably by Tatian himself) into Greek.

it is because the *First Apology* was addressed to a hostile outsider that it is limited in its language and in what it reveals, since he was concerned to portray Christianity as a harmless movement. On the other hand, when we consider who was likely to read this and how it circulated, it may be that it was addressed to pagan philosophical schools, or even to other Christian churches of the house model, since it was Christian groups who circulated and copied the work. The *Dialogue with Trypho*, an imaginary Jewish opponent (though it may have some factual basis), is more theological.

In chapter 65 of the *First Apology* Justin describes a baptism, after which the candidates join the eucharistic assembly, which is making common prayers. At the end of these common prayers, or intercessions, came the Kiss of Peace. Bread and a cup of water mixed with wine are brought to the presiding one, who takes them and offers a prayer at great length. At the conclusion the people respond with Amen. The deacons distribute communion and take it to those who are absent – no doubt for a variety of reasons, and not just sickness. It may be that more of the membership were absent than were present. In *1 Apol.* 66 a little more information regarding the origin of this rite is given to the Emperor, and an analogy is drawn between the Eucharist and the mysteries of Mithras; or rather, these are contrasted. The Sunday Eucharist is described in *1 Apol.* 67 – a similar pattern to a baptismal Eucharist, though of course without the details of a baptism. There are readings from the memoirs of the apostles (Gospels?) or from the writings of the prophets. Justin's understanding of the term 'prophets' included the books of Hystaspes and the Sibyl, and it may be that the memoirs included Epistles or even what later would be regarded as non-canonical Christian writings. After the readings, the president gives a discourse – a homily. Then they all stand and offer prayers. Then bread and wine and water are brought, and the president offers prayers and thanksgivings. At the end the people say Amen, and the distribution is as in chapter 65.

Such is the pattern of the eucharistic liturgy. There is no substantial meal mentioned, just bread and a mixed cup. Justin does not go into great detail, presumably because he is addressing a non-Christian audience. He gives a description that can be easily understood, and that leaves no room for suspicion of lewd or outrageous practices. We have a service that is bipartite. The first part seems to be reading of Scripture, homily and intercession; and the Kiss of Peace. The second, the bringing of bread, and wine and water, is followed with thanksgivings and distribution of communion.

Two points need further comment. First, Andrew McGowan has questioned the authenticity of the mention of wine. Justin compared the Christian meal with the rites of Mithras, and the latter used water in its ritual, not wine. McGowan notes that in 1891 Adolf von Harnack had suggested that in *1 Apol.* 65 the president offers ὕδατος καὶ κράματος, which literally means 'of water and of wine mixed with water'.[5] No such ambiguity or suspicion of emendation arises in the second reference in *1 Apol.* 65 and in 67, where it is simply wine with water, but McGowan has suggested that in accordance with other evidence of other ecclesial groups using water rather than wine, Justin's assembly also used only water.

5 Andrew McGowan, *Ascetic Eucharists: Food and Drink in Early Christian Ritual Meals*, Oxford: Clarendon Press, 1999.

However, although Harnack may be correct about the oddity of water added to wine mixed with water, there is no reason to doubt the other two references, and it would seem that Justin's community knew a 'mixed cup', which was simply the common custom of diluting neat wine.

Second, there is the nature of the prayers associated with the bread and the cup. In *1 Apol.* 65 we have the following:

1 The president offers praise and glory to the Father of all in the name of the Son and of the Holy Spirit. That is, there was something trinitarian about it.
2 He gives thanks at some length for being counted worthy. It was therefore long, and had something to do with salvation.
3 It concluded with an Amen said by all; the president prays on behalf of the congregation.

In *1 Apol.* 66 we have:

Jesus' Words of Institution are quoted, but as an explanation of why the rite is performed at all. There is no evidence here that the words formed part of the prayers, except perhaps there is a connection between the Prayer of the Word, or whatever this phrase means, and the certain formulae of the Mithras rites.

There has been, and continues to be, disagreement over the precise meaning of the words *di' euches logou tou par' autou* (δι' εὐχῆς λόγου τοῦ παρ' αὐτοῦ).

In a paper published posthumously, Edward Ratcliff argued that it referred to the Institution Narrative, which was recited first in baptismal Eucharists so that candidates knew why they were doing this. It later became a regular feature of all Eucharistic Prayers.[6] G. J. Cuming argued that the Greek is best rendered 'a form of words which is from Jesus' and means the Institution Narrative.[7] In a rejoinder, A. Gelston argued that it is 'through a word of prayer that is from him', and simply means that a Thanksgiving Prayer is recited because Jesus gave thanks. It does not, in his view, mean the Words of Institution.[8] More recently Michael Heintz has argued for the rendering 'through the prayer of the Word [Logos]', and had in mind the later isolated references for asking for consecration of the elements through the Logos.[9] Given that 'Logos epikleses' seem to be an exception rather than the rule, the leap to a theology of consecration that Heintz suggests at the end of his discussion seems improbable. The meaning of the phrase must remain ambiguous, but since not until the fourth century do we find clear evidence of a recitation of the Institution

6 E. C. Ratcliff, 'The Eucharistic Institution Narrative of Justin Martyr's *First Apology*', *Journal of Ecclesiastical History* 22 (1971), pp. 97–102, reprinted in A. H. Couratin and D. H. Tripp (eds), *E. C. Ratcliff: Liturgical Studies*, London: SPCK, 1976, pp. 41–8.

7 G. J. Cuming, ΔΙ' ΕΥΧΗΣ ΛΟΓΟΥ, *Journal of Theological Studies* 31 (1980), pp. 80–2.

8 A. Gelston, ΔΙ' ΕΥΧΗΣ ΛΟΓΟΥ, *Journal of Theological Studies* 33 (1982), pp. 172–5.

9 Michael Heintz, 'δι' εὐχῆς λόγου τοῦ παρ' αὐτοῦ (Justin Apology 1.66.2): Cuming and Gelston Revisited', *Studia Liturgica* 33 (2003), pp. 35–6.

Narrative forming part of the prayer(s) over the elements, Ratcliff's and Cuming's suggestions seem the least likely.[10]

In *1 Apol.* 67 we have:

1 Prayers and thanksgivings are offered (note the plural).
2 The president offers according to his ability – extempore.
3 At the end the people say Amen.

This information may be supplemented by the *Dialogue with Trypho* (*Dial.*). There the argument is about the correct exegesis of certain Old Testament passages.

In *Dial.* 41.1 Justin takes up the subject of the offering of Leviticus 14, which was for the cleansing of leprosy. Justin sees this as a type of the Eucharist. The leper is the sinner; the cleansing, baptism; the offering, which is a thank offering, is the Eucharist. He also states that the Eucharist was handed down to us to do in remembrance (*eis anamnesin tou pathous . . . poiein*) of the suffering of Christ, and it is an opportunity for giving thanks for the creation of the world and for the redemption of humankind. He sees it as the fulfilment of Malachi 1.11. Trypho, his imaginary opponent, argued that God rejected Temple sacrifices, but accepts the sacrifice of praise and thanksgiving offered in the synagogue. Justin sees the pure sacrifice of Malachi as being the Eucharist offered by Christians. We see here the concept of sacrifice being applied to the Eucharist with the same proof text as in the *Didache*.

Dial. 116/117 may be usefully summarized:

1 Prayers and thanksgivings can only be accepted by God when offered by worthy men.
2 God accepts sacrifices from no one but his priests.
3 Christians are made worthy through baptism, and are the true priestly race and can offer acceptable sacrifices.
4 These sacrifices are effected by thanksgiving over the bread and wine.
5 These effect the remembrance of the passion.

In summary, Justin tells us that the Sunday worship of his assembly, which included receiving bread and wine mixed with water, was celebrated because of the words of Institution of Jesus (*1 Apol.* 66), though we do not know that these words were recited during the ritual celebration. The 'presidential' prayer, or prayers, he was accustomed to hearing in the circles in which he mixed at Rome were extempore, of considerable length and could be described as praise or glory made to the Father in the name of the Son and the Holy Spirit, and included thanksgiving for creation and redemption. Whether his theology of sacrifice in memory of the passion was articulated in the prayer we do not know – his texts are silent on this matter. However, this meal would appear to be a different pattern from the Jewish–Christian group which produced the *Didache* some 70 or more years before, though for both communities Malachi 1.11 was linked to the Eucharist as in some sense an offering.

10 Paul F. Bradshaw, *Eucharistic Origins*, London: SPCK, 2004, pp. 1–23.

How representative the teaching was and how widely disseminated and accepted, we simply do not know. All we know is that this is what his ecclesial group did, but it tells us nothing of what other groups may or may not have done. It is because of these limitations that the little evidence we do have is best examined by geographical location, though the provenance of some of the material is uncertain. Some of the writers, like Justin, had lived in different parts of the Mediterranean world and may be recording information that they regarded was common to the communities they knew and had known. On the other hand, some may well have been attempting to promote their understanding and preferred ritual as a norm among a variety of understandings and practices. It may be coincidence, but the deep structures of Justin's meeting – Scripture, exposition, prayers, Kiss of Peace, bread and water mixed with wine over which prayers and thanksgiving were recited, and sharing the 'eucharistized' bread and wine – were in fact to become the foundational elements of the Eucharist that emerged in later centuries.

Further Roman and Western evidence

Justin Martyr wrote from Rome, but, as noted, may well represent a Syrian/Palestinian assembly, and he cannot be taken as representing all groups in Rome. Prior to Justin, the first letter of Clement of Rome has been interpreted as making reference to the Eucharist (chapters 40–41) and perhaps witnessing to the type of prayer/prayers that might have been recited at the meal (chapters 59–61). George Blond admitted that the word *eucharistia* does not occur, and *eucharistein* occurs twice, but in a different context he suggested that the following was a reference to the Eucharist understood as a sacrifice replacing the Temple sacrifice:

> He has bidden us celebrate the offerings (*prosphoras*) and the services (*leitourgias*) not randomly or without order but at determined times and hours. He himself has determined by his supreme will where and by whom he wants them celebrated, so that everything may be done in a holy manner, according to his good pleasure, and in a way acceptable to his will. Those, therefore, who present their offerings (*prosphoras*) at the appointed time are acceptable and blessed, for in obeying the prescriptions of the Master they do not go astray.[11]

In chapters 59–61 a long prayer is given, which gives thanks for God's saving work, includes petitions and then returns to praise of God. It may well be similar to prayers that were offered in association with a eucharistic meal, but it is not set forth as such. Likewise, although the Eucharist is referred to as a sacrifice in the *Didache* and seems to have been an early, though undefined description of the ritual meal, and may therefore be alluded to in chapters 40–41, Martin Stringer is correct to conclude that in *1 Clement* there is no evidence for the

11 George Blond, 'Clement of Rome', in Willy Rordorf et al. (eds), *The Eucharist of the Early Christians*, New York: Pueblo Publishing, 1978, p. 28.

practice of a meal or for any rite containing the sharing of bread and cup in Rome until the witness of Justin Martyr.[12]

Irenaeus, Bishop of Lyons, wrote a treatise against heretics towards the end of the second century. His native town was in fact Smyrna, though he claimed to have spent so much time mastering the 'Gaulish' language that he had forgotten his own.[13] According to Damien Casey, 'Irenaeus is a genuinely catholic thinker for whom nothing is left out of the economy of salvation and for whom truth is always to be found in the whole.'[14] This of course begs questions of what was 'catholic' at the end of the second century, because those later judged as heretical groups did not conceive of themselves as such. What Irenaeus stressed were the principles of continuity and harmony against innovation and strife and the positive nature of created matter over against those groups that disdained the body. He was thus critical of a group who followed a certain Markus who feigned to give thanks over 'the cup mixed with wine' and invoked 'Grace' to drip her own blood into the cups. Markus had women co-celebrants, and, according to Irenaeus, he would utter the following prayer over a cup: 'May that Grace who is before all things, unthinkable and unspeakable, fill your inner self and increase in you her knowledge, planting the mustard seed in good ground.'[15] Against such distortions of the gospel he has received, Irenaeus unfolds what he believes to be the true teaching about the eucharistic meal as part of creation and the redemption of the body. He first of all asserts that the ritual meal was given to the Church by Jesus and is a sacrifice of some sort:

> The Lord gave directions to his disciples to offer first-fruits to God from God's own creatures, not as though God stood in need of them, but that they themselves may be neither unfruitful nor ungrateful. Thus, he took the bread, which comes from creation, and he gave thanks, saying: 'This is my Body'. He did likewise with the cup, which is part of the creation to which we ourselves belong, declaring it to be his blood, and [so] he taught the new offering of the new covenant. This is the offering which the church received from the apostles and which it offers throughout the whole world, to God who provides us with nourishment, the first-fruits of divine gifts in this new covenant.[16]

Irenaeus appeals to Malachi 1.11 – the same proof text as in the *Didache* and Justin – and can describe the ritual meal as 'the oblation of the Church', which the Lord taught should be offered as a pure sacrifice, 'offering from God's own creation, with thanksgiving'. It might be expected that Irenaeus would link the concept of sacrifice to the death of Christ and atonement, but since his argument

---

12 Martin Stringer, *Rethinking the Origins of the Eucharist*, London: SCM Press, 2010, p. 156.

13 'Adver. Haer. 1. Preface. 3', in David N. Power, *Irenaeus of Lyons on Baptism and Eucharist: Selected Texts with Introduction, Translation and Annotation*, Alcuin/Grow Liturgical Study 18, Bramcote: Grove Books, 1991, p. 14.

14 Damien Casey, 'Irenaeus: Touchstone of Catholicity', in B. Neil, G. D. Dunn and Lawrence Cross (eds), *Prayer and Spirituality in the Early Church, Vol. 3: Liturgy and Life*, Strathfield, Australia: St Paul's Publications, 2003, pp. 147–55, 149.

15 'Adver. Haer 1.13.2', in Power, *Irenaeus*, p. 14.

16 'Adver. Haer. IV.17.5', in Power, *Irenaeus*, pp. 15–16.

is against those who write off the material creation, his interest is in seeing this as offering fruits of creation, namely bread and wine. He further adds:

> Then again, how can they say that the flesh goes to corruption and does not partake of life, when it is nourished by the Lord's body and blood? Therefore, either let them change their opinion or refrain from offering the things just mentioned. But our opinion agrees with the eucharist, and the eucharist in turn confirms our opinion. For we offer to God those things which belong to God, proclaiming fittingly the communion and unity of the flesh and the spirit. For as the bread, which is produced from the earth, when it receives the invocation of God is no longer common bread, but the eucharist, consisting of two realities, the earthly and the heavenly, so also our bodies, when they receive the eucharist, are no longer corruptible, but have the hope of resurrection.[17]

Two things are of interest in this passage. First, we encounter an idea of 'presence'. In the eucharistic food Christians are nourished by the Lord's body and blood, and Irenaeus can describe the eucharistic food (though he mentions only bread) as combining earthly (material) and heavenly (spiritual) realities. Second, because of this there is an eschatological dimension. Being nourished by the Lord's body and blood means that our bodies become 'the hope of the resurrection'. The eschatological and 'heavenly' dimension is further emphasized:

> Thus the Word wills that we too should offer a gift at the altar, frequently and without interruption. There is, therefore, an altar in heaven, for towards that place are our prayers and offerings directed. There is also a temple, as John says in the Apocalypse: 'And the temple of God was opened [Rev. 11.9]', as there is a tabernacle, 'For behold', he says, 'the tabernacle in which God will dwell with human beings [Rev. 21.3].'[18]

Irenaeus later links the concepts of incarnation, Eucharist and resurrection. He asks:

> When, therefore, both the cup that has been mixed and the bread that has been made, receive the word of God and become the eucharist of Christ's body and blood, from which the substance of our flesh is increased and made consistent, how can they deny that flesh is capable of receiving the gift of God which is eternal life, [since] it is nourished by Christ's body and blood and is his member?[19]

As with the reference to 'word' in Justin, there is speculation as to whether 'receive the word of God' is a reference to recital of the Words of Institution or some consecratory invocation as might be hinted at in the reference to 'invocation of God'. As with Justin, there is no definitive answer. Irenaeus certainly

17 'Adver. Haer. IV.18.5', in Power, *Irenaeus*, p. 21.
18 'Adver. Haer. IV.18.5', in Power, *Irenaeus*, p. 22.
19 'Adver. Haer. V.2.3', in Power, *Irenaeus*, p. 23.

attests to concepts of offering, presence and eschatology. His concern with correct practice and his condemnation of those groups whom he believed to have held heretical views also suggests an ecclesiological dimension. One does not eat and drink holy food with the heretics.

Syria and Asia Minor

Ignatius of Antioch (c. 35–c. 107)

Ignatius of Antioch was martyred in the reign of Trajan (98—117). In the seven letters that are usually counted as authentic, there are some statements that may be pertinent to the Eucharist as this bishop understood it at the beginning of the second century.[20] In some of the letters there is mention of the 'altar', and some have regarded this as suggesting that Ignatius saw the Eucharist as a sacrifice, which may be so, but the word is also patient of other more general interpretations.[21] Likewise there is a reference to the Eucharist that seems simply to mean thanksgiving in prayer.[22] In *Philadelphians* 4 Ignatius writes:

> Be careful then to participate in only the one eucharist, for there is only one flesh of our Lord Jesus Christ and one cup to unite us in his blood, one altar just as there is one bishop with the presbytery and deacons, my fellow servants, so that whatever you do you do according to God.

The emphasis here is on ecclesial unity. Ignatius was a bishop of Antioch, but it is unclear that at this early date he was the sole bishop in Antioch, and he seems to be attempting some sort of unity gathered around himself and his celebrations of a eucharistic ritual. In Ephesians 20.1–2 he says that the breaking of the bread is the medicine of immortality and the antidote to dying, suggesting that the Eucharist imparts eternal life. In Romans 7.2–3 he speaks of his desire for the bread of God, which is the flesh of Jesus Christ, and for drink, his blood, which appear to have eucharistic overtones. He also seems to make reference to some group or groups who held a docetic Christology, suggesting that they abstain from the Eucharist because they do not believe the Eucharist to be the flesh of Christ. However, it is difficult to say exactly what Ignatius intended by his reference to the Eucharist as the flesh of Christ. In a recent article, Frederick C. Klawiter has argued that all Ignatius' statements must be interpreted in the context of his refutation of a heterodox Christology, his understanding of martyrdom and the unity of the Church:

20 For a useful summary of the recessions and present views, see the very good summary in Stringer, *Rethinking the Origins of the Eucharist*, p. 129.

21 Stringer, *Rethinking the Origins of the Eucharist*, p. 133.

22 See Raymond Johanny, 'Ignatius of Antioch', in Johanny and Rordorf (eds), *Eucharist of the Early Christians*, pp. 48–70, e.g. Ephesians 13.1.

> Ignatius' statement that 'the eucharist is the flesh of Jesus Christ' affirms that the risen, crucified humanity of Jesus is, indeed, present in Eucharistic fellowship – in the unity of love of members sharing bread/wine in an Episcopal assembly. But it is incorrect to infer from this belief that Ignatius held to a realistic identity between Christ and the Eucharistic food.[23]

Andrew McGowan draws attention to the fact that Ignatius describes his own impending death as a bread-offering and as a libation poured out for God (Rom. 2.2), thus preferring to see his own martyrdom in terms of the cultic images of bread and wine and not animal sacrifice.[24] There does seem to be a link between the martyrdom of Christ as proleptically shown forth in the Eucharist and the Eucharist and martyrdom of the Christian. Although the Lord's Day is important for Ignatius, there is no indication that a Eucharist meal was celebrated every Lord's Day. Stringer remarks of the Eucharist, 'Very little more can be said with certainty about Ignatius' letters.'[25]

Didascalia

The *Didascalia* is a Church Order that is usually dated to early third-century North Syria (though the province of Syria then was not the same as the present country Syria). Recent studies have drawn attention to the importance of gender differentiation in this document, and part of the rationale for the Church Order is to impose some hierarchical structure and rules and limit the role of women.[26] *Didascalia* 12 sets out from east to west of the church building a seating arrangement, with the bishop and presbyters, lay men and then young girls, married women, elderly women and widows.[27] Teresa Berger has noted that this may reflect the wider Greco-Roman separation of sexes at respectable Symposia meals.[28] Mention of the Eucharist is incidental to broader concerns that seem to underlie the document's origin. In 2.58 the document discusses protocol when there are visiting presbyters and bishops from other churches. The visiting bishop should 'offer the oblation', but if he is unwilling he should

23 Frederick C. Klawiter, 'The Eucharist and Sacramental Realism in the Thought of St. Ignatius of Antioch', *Studia Liturgica* 37 (2007), p. 129.

24 Andrew McGowan, 'Eucharist and Sacrifice: Cultic Tradition and Transformation in Early Christian Meals', in Matthias Klinghardt and Hal Taussig (eds), *Meals and Religious Identity in Early Christianity*, Tübingen: A. Francke, 2012, p. 199.

25 Stringer, *Rethinking the Origins of the Eucharist*, p. 139.

26 Charlotte Methuen, 'Widows, Bishops and the Struggle for Authority in the *Didascalia Apostolorum*', *Journal of Ecclesiastical History* 46 (1995), pp. 197–213 and '"For Pagans Laugh to Hear Women Teach": Gender Stereotypes in the *Didascalia Apostolorum*', *Studies in Church History* 34 (1998), pp. 23–35; Teresa Berger, *Gender Differences and the Making of Liturgical History: Lifting a Veil on Liturgy's Past*, Aldershot: Ashgate, 2011.

27 Alistair Stewart-Sykes, *The Didascalia Apostolorum: An English Version with Introduction and Annotation*, Turnhout: Brepols, 2009, p. 174. Stewart-Sykes wishes to date the document to the fourth century, but his arguments are not compelling.

28 Teresa Berger, *Women's Ways of Worship: Gender Analysis and Liturgical History*, Collegeville: Pueblo, 1999, pp. 34–6 and 54–6.

at least 'speak over the cup'.[29] R. H. Connolly wished to see the latter as a reference to reciting the Words of Institution relating to the cup, but he assumed that the narrative was part of the prayer.[30] A more likely interpretation is that there was a series of prayers or separate prayers over the bread and cup, and the visiting bishop was expected to recite at least one of the prayers.[31] More intriguing is the reference in 6.22:

> but you, in accordance with the Gospel and in accordance with the power of the Holy Spirit gather in the cemeteries to read the Holy Scriptures and to offer your prayers to God without hesitation and offer an acceptable eucharist, the likeness of the royal body of Christ, both in your congregations and in your cemeteries and on the departure of those who sleep. You set pure bread before him, which is formed by fire and sanctified by the invocation, offering without demur and praying for those who sleep.[32]

The passage once again witnesses to the Eucharist as being regarded in some way as a sacrifice or oblation that is offered. The reference to the cemeteries is a reminder that many early Christians saw these as legitimate and logical places for gathering for worship.[33]

Acts of Thomas *and other apocryphal* Acts

These apocryphal *Acts* are thought to have originated in East Syria, probably Edessa, somewhere between 220 and 230.[34] Although existing in translation in a number of languages, the primary texts are in Syriac and Greek. It is generally thought that Syriac was the original language, but that some parts of the Greek preserve an earlier version than the present Syriac redaction.[35] There are six references to eucharistic rituals, and with the exception of that in chapter 29 all follow or complete the initiation ritual. Three of the accounts include prayer texts.

---

29 Stewart-Sykes, *Didascalia Apostolorum*, p. 176.

30 R. H. Connolly, *Didascalia Apostolorum: The Syriac Version Translated and Accompanied by the Verona Latin Fragments, with an Introduction and Notes*, Oxford: Clarendon Press, 1929, pp. 122–3.

31 Marcel Metzger, 'The Didascalia and the Constitutiones Apostolorum', in Johanny and Rordorf (eds), *Eucharist of the Early Christians*, pp. 194–219.

32 Stewart-Sykes, *Didascalia Apostolorum*, pp. 255–6.

33 See further, Ramsay MacMullen, *The Second Church: Popular Christianity* A.D. *200–400*, Atlanta: Society for Biblical Literature, 2009.

34 See the discussion in Jan N. Bremmer, 'The *Acts of Thomas*: Place, Date and Women', in Jan N. Bremmer (ed.), *The Apocryphal Acts of Thomas*, Louvain: Peeters, 2001, pp. 74–90. For the text, see Harold W. Attridge, *The Acts of Thomas*, Salem: Polebridge Press, 2010.

35 See Harold W. Attridge, 'The Original Language of the *Acts of Thomas*', in Harold W. Attridge, John J. Collins and Thomas H. Tobin (eds), *Of Scribes and Scrolls: Studies on the Hebrew Bible, Intertestamental Judaism, and Christian Origins presented to John Strugnell on the Occasion of his Sixtieth Birthday*, Lanham: University of America Press, 1990, pp. 241–50.

Chapters 49–50

The apostle then ordered his deacon to prepare a table, and they put up a bench which they found there. He spread out a linen cloth on it and set out the bread of blessing. The apostle stood by and said,

'Jesus, who deemed us worthy to partake of the eucharist of your sacred body and blood, now we make bold to approach your eucharist and to call upon your holy name. Come and partake with us.'

And he began to speak:

'Come, perfect compassion; Come, fellowship of the male; Come, Lady, you who understand the mysteries of the chosen one, Come, Lady, you who share in all the contests of the noble athlete, Come, Respite, you who reveal the magnitudes of every greatness, Come, Lady, you who make manifest what is secret and render visible what is hidden; the sacred dove which gives birth to twin nestlings. Come, hidden Mother; Come, Lady, you who are manifest in your own activities, and who furnish joy and repose to those who cleave to you; Come and share with us in this eucharist that we make in your name, and in the love by which we are united at your summons.'

And when he had spoken, he marked the sign of the cross on the bread, broke it, and began to distribute it. He gave it first to the woman, saying, 'May this be for the remission of sins and eternal transgressions'. And after her he distributed also to the others who had received the seal.[36]

Chapter 133

After they had been baptized and clothed, he set bread on the table, blessed it, and said,

'Bread of life, those who eat of which remain incorruptible, bread that fills hungry souls with your blessing: You are the one who has been deemed worthy to receive a gift, that you might become for us forgiveness of sins, that those who eat of you might be immortal. We pronounce over you the name of the Mother, of an ineffable mystery, and of the hidden authorities and powers: we pronounce over you your name, Jesus.'

36 Attridge, *Acts of Thomas*, p. 53.

And he said, 'May the power of the blessing come and let the bread be consecrated, so that all the souls who partake of it might be released from their sins.'

Then he broke it and gave it to Sifor, and his wife and daughter.'[37]

Chapter 158

When they emerged [from the water] he took bread and a cup, blessed them, and said:

> 'We eat your holy body that was crucified for us, and we drink for our salvation your blood that was shed for us. Therefore, let your body become our salvation and your blood produce remission of sins. In return for the gall that you drank on our account, let the gall of the devil be removed from us. In return for the vinegar that you drank for us, let our weakness be empowered. In return for the spittle that you received on our account, may we receive the dew of your beneficence. By the reed with which they beat you on our account, may we receive the perfect dwelling. Because you received a crown of thorns on our account, may we who love you put on an unfading crown. In return for the shroud in which you were wrapped, let us gird ourselves with your unconquerable power. In return for the new tomb and the burial, may we receive renewal of soul and body. Because you arose and came back to life, may we arise to life and stand before you in just judgment.'

He broke the eucharistic bread and gave it to Vizan, Tertia, Manashar, and Sifor's wife and daughter, and said,

> 'May this eucharist bring you salvation, joy, and health of soul.' And they said, 'Amen.' Then a voice was heard saying, 'Amen. Fear not, but only believe.'[38]

In the first account, in which the Syriac has toned down the wilder eroticism of the Greek,[39] we have mention of a deacon, who sets the table and a linen cloth and places the bread upon the table – here the deacon has a liturgical

37 Attridge, *Acts of Thomas*, p. 101.
38 Attridge, *Acts of Thomas*, pp. 117–18.
39 So the first few lines of the Syriac of chapter 50 read: 'Come, gift of the Exalted; Come, perfect mercy; Come, Spirit of holiness; Come, revealer of the mysteries of the Chosen among the Prophets.'

role in terms of laying the table. Next there is an interesting brief exhortation or explication to the congregation of what is about to happen and why. Jesus has made them worthy to partake of the Eucharist, so now the apostle will call upon his name to come and have fellowship with them. The prayer is in fact not a thanksgiving but an invocation – an Epiklesis – calling on the divinity under various names to 'come' and participate in the Eucharist.[40] Here a divine presence is invoked, not apparently on the elements but in the action or fellowship. There is a remarkable pile up of divine names and epithets. Then, reflecting its Syrian provenance and Syriac grammar, 'Come fellowship of the male', and later, sacred dove, bearer of the twins and hidden Mother. In Syriac 'Spirit' is grammatically feminine, and as early as the *Odes of Solomon* we find female sexual and bodily imagery applied to the Spirit. The term 'come' seems linked to the Maranatha of Paul and Revelation, though here Jesus and the Spirit seem interchangeable. There are a number of references to things that are hidden being made manifest. The term Eucharist seems interchangeable with agape/lovefeast, and possibly the communities of Thomas saw no marked difference between one or the other. Of interest also in the Syriac version is the clause 'by which we are united at your summons/we are gathered together at thy call'. The later Syrian writers, Ephrem and Aphrahat, quote versions of the Words of Institution in which 'Do this whenever you are gathered in my name' are on the lips of Jesus. This would appear to be a Syriac peculiarity, perhaps deriving from Tatian's *Diatessaron*.

There is a ceremonial action – the apostle marked the bread with the cross, he broke it and distributed it with the words 'May this be for the remission of sins and eternal life' – here picking up the words of the Gospels 'for the remission/forgiveness of sins'.

In the second account, which is a baptismal Eucharist, bread is placed on the table and blessed. Both Jesus and the bread apparently are both simultaneously addressed through the language of the Fourth Gospel.[41] The thought seems to be that the element over which Jesus is named will be for forgiveness of sins and those who eat it will be immortal. But there is also invocation – the naming of the Name – the Mother of the ineffable mystery and of hidden authorities and powers, identified as the name of Jesus. The power is invoked to come and settle on the bread so that those who receive will be released from their sins. In chapter 158 it is Christ who is addressed, with an emphasis on the passion and its fruits. There is a reference to the gall and vinegar, the spitting, the reed with which he was smitten and the crown of thorns, the linen cloth, the grace and burial. But the invocation ends with being anchored in the resurrection. The words of administration request salvation, joy and health for the soul.

Of the six accounts, four mention only bread. Of the two accounts that include a cup, that in chapter 121 in the Greek contains water, while the cup's contents in chapter 158 is not specified, and this account notes that only the bread is

40 For a thorough discussion of these invocations, see Susan E. Myers, *Spirit Epicleses in the Acts of Thomas*, Tübingen: Mohr Siebeck, 2010.

41 Myers, *Spirit Epicleses*, reads this as being addressed to the bread, and analogous to ch. 157, where the oil is addressed (p. 135). It seems to me to be ambiguous and addressed to both Christ as the bread of life, and the bread as being the bread of life.

received by the participants. The Syriac recension hints that a 'mingled cup' (Mygdonia objects to the copious amount of wine that nurse brings in chapter 120) featured in chapter 121, and specifies wine in chapter 133 and a mixed cup in chapter 158. This may reflect a variety of co-existing practices, with some communities using only bread for their meal ritual, others using bread and water and others using wine mixed with water. Equally, it may be that the Syriac redactor made alterations to bring former practice into what was emerging as the more normative practice.

In summary, these accounts witness to communities that apparently knew different rituals – sometimes with bread only, sometimes bread and cup of water and sometimes bread and wine. There were extemporary prayers over the elements, which varied between an Epiklesis and an embryonic proclamation of salvation history in very general terms. This is also found in the *Acts of John*, which are dated second or third century, with Egypt, East Syria and Asia Minor all being suggested as place of origin.[42] There are two particular accounts of the Eucharist:

(A)

And when he had said this John prayed; and he took bread, and brought it into the sepulchre to break it, and he said,

'We glorify thy name that converteth us from error and pitiless deceit; we glorify thee who hast shown before our eyes what we have seen; we testify to thy goodness, in various ways appearing; we praise thy gracious name, O Lord; <we thank thee> who hast convicted those that are convicted by thee; we thank thee, Lord Jesus Christ, that we confide <in thy grace>, which is unchanging; we thank thee who hadst need of (our) nature that is being saved; we thank thee that hast given us this unwaving <faith> that thou alone art <God> both now and for ever; we thy servants, that are assembled and gathered (?) With <good> cause, give thanks to thee, O holy one.'

And when he had made this prayer and glorified (God) he gave to all the brethren the Lord's Eucharist, and went out of the sepulchre.[43]

(B)

And he asked for bread, and gave thanks with these words:

'What praise or what offering or what thanksgiving shall we name as we break this bread, but thee alone, Lord Jesu? We glorify thy name that was

42 Recent opinions about the date and provenance of the *Acts of John* differ widely, from the second half of the second century in Egypt; the first half of the third century in East Syria; and the second quarter of the second century in Asia Minor.

43 Wilhelm Schneemelcher (ed.), *New Testament Apocrypha*, vol. 2, London: Lutterworth Press, 1965, pp. 253–4.

spoken by the Father; we glorify thy name that was spoken through the Son. We glorify thine entering of the Door; we glorify thy Resurrection that is shown us through thee; we glorify thy Way; we glorify thy Seed, thy Word, thy Grace, thy Faith, thy Salt, thine inexpressible Pearl, thy Treasure, thy Plough, thy Net, thy Greatness, thy Diadem, him that for us was called the Son of Man, that granted us the truth, repose, knowledge, power, commandment, confidence, hope, love, liberty and refuge in thee. For thou alone, O Lord, art the root of immortality and the fount of incorruption and the seat of the ages, who now art called all these things on our account, that calling on thee through them we may know thy greatness, which at the present is invisible to us, but visible only to the pure as it is portrayed in thy manhood only.'

And he broke the bread and gave to all of us, praying over each of the brethren that he would be worthy of the Lord's grace and of the most holy Eucharist. And he partook of it himself and said, 'May there be for me also a part with you', and, 'Peace be with you, my beloved'.[44]

In both accounts we have bread only, and both give an order of thanksgiving or prayer, breaking the bread, giving, and the second adds the Peace after the distribution. The first appears to be addressed to Christ, though to the Name as perhaps in Philippians 2.9. The name is 'glorified' – though 'Praise' and 'Thanksgiving' are also used. It is a vague prayer mainly concerned with salvation in abstract terms. The words assembled and gathered occur here as in the *Acts of Thomas*. The prayer is a thanksgiving and there is no petition for anything at all. It is one prayer. And although it is concerned with salvation, it is ahistorical; there is no anchoring of the prayer either in Old Testament salvation history or in the Gospel narratives. 'We thank thee who hadst need of our nature that is being saved' may be an oblique reference to the incarnation.

In the second account, the prayer is quite explicitly addressed to the Son. Once more there is concern with the Name – described here as spoken through the Father and through the Son. There is a cryptic reference to entering by the door – is this an allusion to St John's Gospel and the door of the sheepfold, or is this the door of heaven as in the book of Revelation? We have a number of key gospel concepts and imagery from John and Matthew – resurrection, the Way, seed, Logos, grace, faith, salt, pearl, treasure, plough, net, greatness, diadem. There is reference to the Son of Man and a list of benefits, and then what appears to be a reference to salvation in terms of immortality and the incarnation. There is a single prayer, with little direct historical reference. Again, although calling on the name is mentioned, it is an invocation of glorification to the Son, with a list of spiritual benefits which the Son has bequeathed. Other apocryphal *Acts*, such as those of Paul and Peter, also have brief references to Eucharists with bread and water.[45]

---

44 Schneemelcher (ed.), *New Testament Apocrypha*, vol. 2, pp. 255–6.

45 M. R. James, trans., 'The Acts of Peter', *The Apocryphal New Testament*, Oxford: Clarendon Press, 1924, http://www.earlychristianwritings.com/text/actspeter.html; 'Acts of Paul', http://www.earlychristianwritings.com/actspaul.html.

The Gospel of Philip

The *Gospel of Philip* is one of the documents from the Nag Hammadi library, which is thought by many to be a collection of Valentinian documents. Modern scholarship regards the library as representing Gnostic Christianity, but the works date from a time when the authors thought of themselves as devout and learned Christians.[46] Valentinus spent some time in Rome, but he was an Egyptian and the library was uncovered in the desert outside Nag Hammadi in Egypt. However, the *Gospel of Philip* is regarded by many as originating in Antioch or Edessa and dated to the end of the second century or early third century. The recent study by Hugo Lundhaug argues a core theme of Philip is deification to become the perfect man just like Jesus was.[47] Part of the deificatory process involves partaking of five 'mysteries', including baptism, chrismation and the Eucharist: 'when Christ came, the perfect man, he brought bread from heaven so that man would be nourished with the food of man' (55.10).[48] Chapter 75.1 refers to the bread, the cup and the oil, and Segelberg argued that the oil was blessed in addition to the bread and wine, but was not itself part of this eucharistic meal.[49] David Tripp suggested that it meant that the bread was baked with oil.[50] The chapter continues:

> The cup of prayer contains wine and it contains water, for it is laid down as the type of the blood over which thanks is given. And it fills with the Holy Spirit and it is that of the completely perfect man. Whenever we drink this we will receive the perfect man. (75.14–20)[51]

This might suggest some invocation of the Spirit in addition to thanksgiving, but the information is too sparse to allow any firm conclusions as to what might have been recited at such Eucharists. However, this community seems to have used wine and water in the cup. Valeriy Alikin suggests that the rite envisages that those who partake become a perfect person in which all division is removed, and that, so he implies, is different from participating in the death, resurrection and glorification of Jesus.[52] However, that seems to ignore the Christology in this Gospel which underlies the concept of the perfect person. It would seem the end results – forgiveness of sins and eternal life by being in Christ – are very similar.

46 Alistair Logan, *Gnostic Truth and Christian Heresy*, Edinburgh: T & T Clark, 1996; Alistair Logan, 'The Mystery of the Five Seals: Gnostic Initiation Reconsidered', *Vigiliae Christianae* 51 (1997), pp. 188–206.

47 Hugo Lundhaug, *Images of Rebirth: Cognitive Poetics and Transformational Soteriology in the Gospel of Philip and the Exegesis on the Soul*, Leiden: Brill, 2010.

48 Text Lundhaug, *Images of Rebirth*, pp. 468–539.

49 Eric Segelberg, 'The Coptic-Gnostic Gospel according to Philip and its Sacramental System', *Numen* 7 (1960), p. 195.

50 D. H. Tripp, 'The "Sacramental System" of the Gospel of Philip', *Studia Patristica* 17.1 (1982), p. 258.

51 Lundhaug, *Images of Rebirth*, op. cit.

52 Valeriy A. Alikin, *The Earliest History of the Christian Gathering: Origin, Development and Content of the Christian Gathering in the First to Third Centuries*, Leiden: Brill, 2010, p. 138.

North Africa: Tertullian and Cyprian

Two important witnesses from Latin-speaking North Africa are Tertullian and Cyprian. Tertullian (*c.* 160–*c.* 220) records that his community was used to celebrating 'the sacrament of the Eucharist, commanded by the Lord at the time of the supper, and to all, we receive even at our meetings before daybreak, and from the hands of no others than the heads of the Church'.[53] Elsewhere he referred to the feast of Christians called agape, love, and this seems to be a separate religious meal from what he calls the Eucharist.[54] Alikin suggests that the Eucharist was celebrated in the morning in this community and the agape in the evening.[55] However, Andrew McGowan has argued that the terms Eucharist and agape are still at this time interchangeable, and that the agape is the evening Eucharist, and at the daybreak meetings the elements were received that had been consecrated at the evening Eucharist.[56] Although Tertullian speaks of offering oblations, which could refer to the Eucharist, the context is such that it could equally refer to the offering of prayer generally. What is most interesting in Tertullian, though, is his emphasis on the bread and wine being the body and blood of Christ. In attacking Marcion (who according to Tertullian regarded the physical as evil and taught that Christ's body was a phantom), he asserted the importance of the human senses and in passing asked whether the taste of wine was different from 'that which He consecrated in memory of His blood',[57] and also referred to 'the bread by which he represents his own proper body, thus requiring in his very sacraments the "beggarly elements" of the Creator'.[58] Tertullian made considerable use of the terms *figura* and *figurare* in contradistinction to Marcion's docetism. Concerning Christ's cross he wrote:

> This tree it is which Jeremiah likewise gives you intimation of, when he prophesies to the Jews, who should say, 'Come, let us destroy the tree with the fruit, (the bread) thereof,' that is, His body. For so did God in your own Gospel [Marcion only used St. Luke's Gospel] even reveal the sense, when he called His body *bread*; so that, for the time to come, you may understand that He has given to His body the figure of bread, whose body the prophet of old figuratively turned into bread, the Lord Himself designing to give by and by an interpretation of the mystery.[59]

---

53 Tertullian, 'De Corona 3.3', *The Chaplet, or De Coronoa*, http://www.tertullian.org/anf/anf03/anf03-10.htm#P1019_415012.

54 'Apol. 39', *The Apology*, S. Thelwall, trans. http://www.tertullian.org/anf/anf03/anf03-05.htm#P253_53158.

55 Alikin, *Earliest History of the Christian Gathering*, p. 143.

56 Andrew McGowan, 'Rethinking Agape and Eucharist in Early North African Christianity', *Studia Liturgica* 34 (2004), pp. 165–76.

57 'De Anima 17.13', *A Treatise on the Soul*, trans. Peter Holmes, http://www.tertullian.org/anf/anf03/anf03-22.htm#P2560_840932.

58 'Ad. Marcion 1.14', Christian Classics Electronic Library, 1998, http://www.tertullian.org/anf/anf03/anf03-28.htm#P3804_1266834.

59 'Ad. Marcion, 3.19', Christian Classics Electronic Library, 1998, http://www.tertullian.org/anf/anf03/anf03-30.htm#P4763_1515567.

In a much longer passage Tertullian asserted that Jesus

> declared plainly enough what He meant by the *bread*, when He called the bread His own body. He likewise, when mentioning the cup and making the *new* testament to be sealed 'in His blood,' affirms the reality of His body.[60]

He also wrote that 'the flesh feeds on the body and blood of Christ, that the soul likewise may fatten on *its* God'.[61]

It is difficult to know precisely how Tertullian understood the term *figura*. He also used the term *repraesentatio*, which Paul Bradshaw suggests might be better understood as 'manifest'.[62] Bradshaw notes that Tertullian seems to teach that just as bread and wine in the Old Testament prefigure the body and blood of Christ, so also at the Last Supper they are a *figura* of his body and blood; but that does not necessarily mean that Tertullian thought the same about the Lord's Supper.[63] This is strictly correct of course, though perhaps Bradshaw is being over-cautious here, since the inference is that in the Lord's Supper the bread and wine are also *figura/repraesentatio* of the body and blood of Christ. Tertullian also used the Latin term *sacramentum* for the Greek *mysterion*. In Latin secular usage the word carried the meaning of a solemn oath and thus could (and later, would) give a rather different emphasis from *mysterion*.

The other great African theologian was Cyprian, Bishop of Carthage (d. 258). From Cyprian we learn that at his time the Eucharistic Prayer began with 'Lift up your hearts' with the response 'We lift them to the Lord'. It is his *Epistle* 63 that is of most significance for the Eucharist. Addressed to Bishop Caecilius, in this letter Cyprian attacks the practice (as witnessed in the Syrian *Acts of Thomas*) of using only water in the cup at the Eucharist, although he also objects to using only wine. He insists on the practice found in Justin Martyr, of wine and water mingled together. Thus he wrote:

> Know then that I have been admonished that, in offering the cup, the tradition of the Lord must be observed, and that nothing must be done by us but what the Lord first did on our behalf, as that the cup which is offered in remembrance of Him should be offered mingled with wine.[64]

He appealed to the example of Jesus at the Last Supper:

> For, taking the cup on the eve of His passion, He blessed it, and gave it to His disciples, saying, 'Drink ye all of this; for this is my blood of the New Testament, which shall be shed for many, for the remission of sins. I say unto you,

60 'Ad. Marcion 4.40', Christian Classics Electronic Library, 1998, http://www.tertullian.org/anf/anf03/anf03-31.htm#P5230_1636728.

61 'De Res. Carn. 8', Christian Classics Electronic Library, 1998, http://www.tertullian.org/anf/anf03/anf03-41.htm#P9676_2650295.

62 Bradshaw, *Eucharistic Origins*, p. 96.

63 Bradshaw, *Eucharistic Origins*, p. 95.

64 Cyprian, *Epistle* 63.2, in Alexander Roberts and James Donaldson (eds), *The Ante-Nicene Fathers: The Writings of the Fathers down to A.D. 325*, vol. 5, Buffalo: Christian Literature Company, 1886.

> I will not drink henceforth of this fruit of the vine, until that day in which I shall drink new wine with you in the kingdom of my Father.' In which portion we find that the cup which the Lord offered was mixed, and that that was wine which He called His blood. Whence it appears that the blood of Christ is not offered if there be no wine in the cup, nor the Lord's sacrifice celebrated with a legitimate consecration unless our oblation and sacrifice respond to His passion.[65]

Just as water is mixed with flour to produce bread, so only water mingled with wine will be the blood of Christ:

> For because Christ bore us all, in that He also bore our sins, we see that in the water is understood the people, but in the wine is showed the blood of Christ. But when the water is mingled in the cup with wine, the people is [*sic*] made one with Christ, and the assembly of believers is associated and conjoined with Him on whom it believes; which association and conjunction of water and wine is so mingled in the Lord's cup, that that mixture cannot any more be separated. Whence, moreover, nothing can separate the Church – that is, the people established in the Church, faithfully and firmly persevering in that which they have believed – from Christ, in such a way as to prevent their undivided love from always abiding and adhering. Thus, therefore, in consecrating the cup of the Lord, water alone cannot be offered, even as wine alone cannot be offered. For if any one offer wine only, the blood of Christ is dissociated from us; but if the water be alone, the people are dissociated from Christ; but when both are mingled, and are joined with one another by a close union, there is completed a spiritual and heavenly sacrament. Thus the cup of the Lord is not indeed water alone, nor wine alone, unless each be mingled with the other; just as, on the other hand, the body of the Lord cannot be flour alone or water alone, unless both should be united and joined together and compacted in the mass of one bread; in which very sacrament our people are shown to be made one, so that in like manner as many grains, collected, and ground, and mixed together into one mass, make one bread; so in Christ, who is the heavenly bread, we may know that there is one body, with which our number is joined and united.[66]

Cyprian is insistent that the priest (bishop) must do as Christ did, and then the bread and wine will be what Christ said they would be. It might be inferred that Cyprian's churches recited the Words of Institution at the Eucharist as a warrant or declaration of intention to imitate Christ, but he does not actually say that. His concern in this letter is the mixed chalice, and even in the passage just cited, he sees the mingling as an expression of the unity of the Church. However, he does imply that the priest (bishop) in imitating Christ offers an oblation:

65 Cyprian, '*Epistle* 63.9', in Alexander Roberts and James Donaldson (eds), *The Ante-Nicene Fathers: Hippolytus, Cyprian, Caius, Novatian*, New York: Charles Scribner's Sons, 1903.

66 Cyprian, '*Epistle* 63.13', in Roberts and Donaldson (eds), *The Ante-Nicene Fathers*, 1903.

> And again the Lord in the Gospel repeats this same saying and says, 'Ye reject the commandment of God that ye may keep your own tradition'. Moreover, in another place He establishes it, saying, 'Whosoever shall break one of these least commandments, and shall teach men so, he shall be called the least in the kingdom of heaven'. But if we may not break even the least of the Lord's commandments, how much rather is it forbidden to infringe such important ones, so great, so pertaining to the very sacrament of our Lord's passion and our own redemption, or to change it by human tradition into anything else than what was divinely appointed! For if Jesus Christ, our Lord and God, is Himself the chief priest of God the Father, and has first offered Himself a sacrifice to the Father, and has commanded this to be done in commemoration of Himself, certainly that priest truly discharged the office of Christ, who imitates that which Christ did; and he then offers a true and full sacrifice in the Church to God the Father, when he proceeds to offer it according to what he sees Christ Himself to have offered.[67]

Although it is disputed as to exactly how this should be interpreted, it once more underscores the early concern to understand the Eucharist in sacrificial terms. In Epistle 57.3 he wrote:

> Yea, it is the great honour and glory of our episcopate to have granted peace to martyrs, so that we, as priests, who daily celebrate the sacrifices of God, may prepare offerings and victims for God.

This seems to suggest a daily Eucharist in the mid-third century.

Egypt

The two great early witnesses to Egyptian Christianity are Clement of Alexandria and Origen. Clement's method of allegory, typology and allusion makes it difficult to know with any clarity what he believed about the Eucharist. In a very thorough essay, André Méhat, following a study by T. Camelot, noted that there are four passages in Clement that are certain references to the Eucharist, and another 40 that might be allusions.[68] In *Stromata* 1.19 Clement considers Proverbs 9.17, with its references to stolen bread and sweet water of theft and applies it to those who use bread and water in the Eucharist rather than water and wine. This latter – the mixed cup – he interprets as reflecting the spiritual and physical make-up of humans and their sanctification. In *Paedagogus* II.2 he refers the flesh and blood of John 6.34 to faith and hope by which the Church grows. In *Strom.* 1.10 he refers to Jesus taking the bread, blessing it, breaking it, 'that we might eat it, according to logikos', which may mean reason, but which

67 Cyprian, 'Epistle 63.14', in Roberts and Donaldson (eds), *The Ante-Nicene Fathers.*

68 André Méhat, 'Clement of Alexandria', in Johanny and Rordorf (eds), *Eucharist of the Early Christians*, pp. 99–131; T. Camelot, 'L' Eucharistie dans l'Ecole d'Alexandrie', *Divinitas* 1 (1957), pp. 71–92.

Méhat argues means 'with the intervention of the divine Logos'.[69] In a passage in *Strom.* 7.7 it has been conjectured that he is referring to the posture during the Eucharistic Prayer:

> Prayer is, then, to speak more boldly, converse with God. Though whispering, consequently, and not opening the lips, we speak in silence, yet we cry inwardly. For God hears continually all the inward converse. So also we raise the head and lift the hands to heaven, and set the feet in motion at the closing utterance of the prayer, following the eagerness of the spirit directed towards the intellectual essence; and endeavouring to abstract the body from the earth, along with the discourse, raising the soul aloft, winged with longing for better things, we compel it to advance to the region of holiness, magnanimously despising the chain of the flesh.[70]

Although this would certainly be appropriate with a Eucharistic Prayer in mind, Clement's words are too open for such a precise identification. Robin Darling Young has suggested that the Eucharist underlies Clement's views on Christ's saving work and Christian life and martyrdom.[71] She draws attention to a passage in the sermon on the rich man:

> For this also He came down. For this He clothed Himself with man. For this He voluntarily subjected Himself to the experiences of men, that by bringing Himself to the measure of our weakness whom He loved, He might correspondingly bring us to the measure of His own strength. And about to be offered up and giving Himself a ransom, He left for us a new Covenant–testament: My love I give unto you. And what and how great is it? For each of us He gave His life, – the equivalent for all. This He demands from us in return for one another.[72]

Young observes that in the *Paedagogus* milk, word and blood are all related to the symbol of the Lord's passion and teaching and that Scripture has named wine the symbol of the sacred blood. In her view, the ritual of the Eucharist is the entry of salvation in the *Protrepticuss* and the pattern of Christian life in the *Paedagogus* and communicates knowledge in the breaking of the bread.[73] However, as suggestive as all this might be, Clement's language is too imprecise to make such a conclusion.

Harald Buchinger points out similar problems with interpreting Origen: 'The spiritualizing principal trait of his hermeneutic makes it frequently difficult

69 Méhat, 'Clement of Alexandria', p. 117.

70 Clement of Alexandria, 'The Stromata, or Miscellanies', in Peter Kirby (ed.), *Early Christian Writings* (2013), http://www.earlychristianwritings.com/text/clement-stromata-book7.html.

71 Robin Darling Young, 'The Eucharist as Sacrifice According to Clement', in Roch A. Kereszty (ed.), *Rediscovering the Eucharist: Ecumenical Conversations*, New York: Paulist Press, 2003, pp. 63–91.

72 *Sermon Index.net*, http://www.sermonindex.net/modules/articles/index.php?view=article&aid=18010.

73 *Sermon Index.net*, http://www.sermonindex.net/modules/articles/index.php?view=article&aid=18010. Art. cit., pp. 82, 84 and 89.

to distinguish Eucharistic-theological statements from more general theological reflections.'[74] Furthermore, although Origen taught in Alexandria, he later moved to Caesarea, and so any liturgical information may reflect the latter rather than the former domicile. Patrick Jacquemont draws attention to two passages, one in *Contra Celsum* and another in a homily on Jeremiah where Origen says, 'We have a symbol of our thanksgiving to God in the bread which is called "eucharist"', and 'If you go up with him (the Lord) to celebrate the Passover, he gives you the cup of the new covenant; he also gives you the bread of blessing. In short, he gives you the gift of his own body and his own blood.'[75] Both suggest an acceptance of a presence. In another passage in *Contra Celsum* he seems to refer to a Eucharistic Prayer:

> But we give thanks to the Creator of all, and, along with thanksgiving and prayer for the blessings we have received, we also eat the bread presented to us; and this bread becomes by prayer a sacred body, which sanctifies those who sincerely partake of it. (*Contra Celsum* 8.33)[76]

Whether 'thanksgiving' and 'prayer' imply separate prayers is difficult to know, and whether the prayer(s) included a 'Logos' Epiklesis or a Spirit Epiklesis is likewise open to speculation, though since in his Homily on Leviticus (13,6) Origen gives the Holy Spirit a specific place in making the mysteries holy, Buchinger is inclined to think he knew an Epiklesis of the Spirit.[77] Gregory Dix argued that Origen's references in *De Principiis* to Isaiah 6.3 and its exegesis showed that the Sanctus was part of the Egyptian Eucharistic Prayer.[78] However, whatever the influence of his exegesis on some later Egyptian anaphoras, there is nothing that Origen says that allows us to conclude that this was a feature in the Egyptian Eucharistic Prayers known to him.

Concluding remarks

The evidence for eucharistic practices and beliefs in the two centuries following the crystallization of the early Christian communities is sparse and is both geographically and community specific. Certain themes and general ritual (thanksgiving) seem to have been common, but it is impossible to extrapolate some common liturgical shape or some universal doctrinal understanding of the eucharistic rite. It was a time of pluriformity.

---

74 Harald Buchinger, 'Early Eucharist in Transition? A Fresh Look at Origen', in Albert Gerhards and Clemens Leonhard (eds), *Jewish and Christian Liturgy and Worship: New Insights into Its History and Intersection*, Leiden: Brill, 2007, p. 207.

75 Patrick Jacquemont, 'Origen', in Johanny and Rordorf (eds), *Eucharist of the Early Christians*, pp. 183–93. 'Contra Celsum 8.57'; Homiliae in Jeremiam 19.13; H. Chadwick, trans. *Origen: Contra Celsum*, Cambridge, 1953, p. 495.

76 Origen, 'Origen. Contra Celsum', in *Early Christian Writings*, Peter Kirby (2013), http://www.earlychristianwritings.com/text/origen168.html.

77 Buchinger, 'Early Eucharist in Transition?', p. 218.

78 Gregory Dix, 'Primitive Consecration Prayers', *Theology* 37 (1938), pp. 261–83.

2

The Shaping of Early Eucharistic Prayers: 'Paleoanaphoras'

Pre-Nicene paleoanaphoras

In the very varied and diverse pre-Nicene documentation there is very little about the form and content of the prayers prayed in association with the bread, water or mixed wine. There are the meal prayers of the *Didache*, though the meal was not associated with the body and blood of Christ. Justin Martyr speaks of prayers and thanksgivings, and the plural, if not simply rhetoric, might imply a series of prayers, or even possibly separate prayers over the bread and cup (as perhaps indicated in the *Didascalia*). In the *Acts of Thomas* and *Acts of John* we have considerable variety of content and form. Some are short prayers of praise or glorifying of the Name, and some are in the form of invocation to the Spirit to come upon the ritual action and/or the elements. However, scholars also identify a number of other Eucharistic Prayers as pre-Nicene, though it is extremely difficult to give any precise dating to them.

The Anaphora of Addai and Mari

The Anaphora of Addai and Mari is one of three anaphoras used by the Church of the East or Assyrian Church. It is also used with slight adaptation by the Chaldean and the Syro-Malabar Churches. It has a 'twin' in the Maronite Church, called *Sharar*, or the Anaphora of St Peter III. Although this latter may conserve some earlier readings of the underlying common text, in comparison with the East Syrian anaphora it has undergone considerable expansion. Most scholars believe that Addai and Mari is the oldest anaphora still in use today and probably dates from the late third century.

And the priest says: Peace be with you. *And they reply*: And with you and your spirit. *And the deacon says*: Give peace to one another in the love of Christ. *And they say*: For all the Catholikoi. *And the deacon proclaims*: Let us give thanks and intercede. *And the priest says*: The grace of Our Lord, etc. *And they reply*: Amen. *And the priest says*: Life up your minds. *And they reply*: Towards you, O God. *And the priest says*: The oblation is offered to God the Lord of all. *And they reply*: It is fit and right. *And the deacon says*: Peace be with us.

And the priest recites quietly:

Worthy of praise from every mouth, and thanksgiving from every tongue is the adorable and glorious name of the Father and the Son and the Holy Spirit, who created the world by his grace and its inhabitants in his compassion, and redeemed mankind in his mercy, and has effected great grace towards mortals.

Your majesty, O Lord, a thousand thousand heavenly beings worship and myriad myriads of angels, hosts of spiritual beings, ministers (of) fire and of spirit, with cherubim and holy seraphim, glorify your Name, *Qanona* (= raising the voice). Crying out and glorifying. *And they reply*: Holy, Holy.

And the priest recites quietly: And with these heavenly powers we give thanks to you, O Lord, even we, your lowly, weak and miserable servants, because you have effected in us a great grace which cannot be repaid, in that you put on our humanity so as to quicken us by your divinity. And you lifted up our poor estate, and righted our fall. And you raised up our mortality. And you forgave our debts. You justified our sinfulness and you enlightened our understanding. And you, our Lord and our God, vanquished our enemies and made triumphant the lowliness of our weak nature through the abounding compassion of your grace.

Qanona. And for all. *And they reply*: Amen. *And the deacon says*: In your minds.

And the priest recites quietly:

You, O Lord, in your unspeakable mercies make a gracious remembrance for all the upright and just fathers who have been pleasing before you in the commemoration of the body and blood of your Christ which we offer to you upon the pure and holy altar as you have taught us. And grant us your tranquility and your peace all the days of the world. *Repeat. And they reply*: Amen.

That all the inhabitants of the earth may know that you alone are God, the true Father, and you have sent our lord Jesus Christ, your Son and your beloved, and he, our Lord and God, taught us in his life-giving gospel all the purity and holiness of the prophets, apostles, martyrs and confessors and bishops and priests and deacons, and of all the children of the holy catholic church, who have been marked with the mark of holy baptism.

And we also, O Lord, – *Thrice* – your lowly, weak and miserable servants who are gathered together and stand before you at this time have received by tradition of the example which is from you rejoicing, and glorifying, and magnifying, and commemorating and praising, and performing this great and dread mystery of the passion and death and resurrection of our Lord Jesus Christ.

May (s)he come, O Lord, your Holy Spirit and rest upon this oblation (*of*)
And the deacon says: Be in silence:

of your servants, and bless and hallow it, that it may be to us, O Lord, for the pardon of debts and the forgiveness of sins, and a great hope of resurrection

from the dead and a new life in the kingdom of heaven with all who have been pleasing before you.
And for all your marvelous economy towards us we give you thanks and praise you without ceasing in your Church redeemed by the precious blood of your Christ, with open minds and with uncovered faces.

Qanona. As we offer up. *And they reply*: Amen.

This prayer has the following structure:

- Opening dialogue.
- Praise and thanksgiving to the Name.
- Sanctus.
- Thanksgiving for redemption.
- *Doxology.*
- Commemoration of the righteous fathers and offering, and request for peace.
- Commemoration of the Church (clergy and all the baptized).
- Praise offered because of the example received from Christ.
- Epiklesis.
- *Doxology.*

One of the most obvious features of this anaphora is that it lacks an Institution Narrative. A narrative has been added to the Chaldean text and the Syro-Malabar, both in communion with Rome, but these are interpolations into the manuscript tradition and examples of 'Latinization'. Instead, the anaphora alludes to the Last Supper in the words 'received by tradition the example which is from you'. Some have argued that it once had a narrative that for some reason has fallen out of the text, though those so arguing usually do so from dogmatic presuppositions.[1] The majority of scholars believe that the prayer never had an Institution Narrative and dates from a time before the narrative was regarded as a *sine qua non* of an anaphora. The community did what the Lord said, namely, gave thanks over bread and wine, without having to remind God as to why it was celebrating this ritual. Ever since a seminal article by the English liturgical scholar Edward Ratcliff, scholars have speculated about an earlier form underlying the present anaphora.[2] Ligier, Bouyer, Talley, Sanchez Caro and Wegman all saw the tripartite *birkat ha-mazon*, as morphed in *Didache* 10, as providing the building block of Addai and Mari.[3] A paleoanaphora could be reconstructed by

1 Bryan D. Spinks, *Worship: Prayers from the East*, Washington, DC: Pastoral Press, 1994, pp. 1–45; Uwe Michael Lang, 'Eucharist without Institution Narrative? The Anaphora of Addai and Mari Revisited', in Uwe Michael Lang (ed.), *Die Anaphora von Addai und Mari: Studien zu Eucharistie und Einsetzungsworten*, Bonn: Nova and Vetera, 2007, pp. 31–65.

2 Spinks, *Worship: Prayers from the East*, pp. 1–19; Anthony Gelston, *The Eucharistic Prayer of Addai and Mari*, Oxford: Clarendon Press, 1992. For essays on the theology of this anaphora, see Bosco Puthur (ed.), *Studies on the Anaphora of Addai and Mari*, LRC Publications 9, India: Kochi, 2004.

3 Louis Ligier, 'Anaphores orientales et prières juives', *Proche-Orient Chrétien* 13 (1963), pp. 3–20; T. J. Talley, 'The Eucharistic Prayer of the Ancient Church According to Recent Research: Results and Reflections', *Studia Liturgica* 11 (1976), pp. 138–58; H. Wegman, 'Généalogie hypothétique de la prière eucharistique', *Questiones Liturgique* 61 (1980), pp. 263–78; J.-M.

removing those elements that did not seem in accordance with the Jewish *birkat ha-mazon*, though, as one might predict, the scholars differed on precisely what that core consisted of. In an article published in 2002, Sarhad Jammo reiterated the *birkat ha-mazon* theory, arguing that the Sanctus, Epiklesis and the paragraph that refers to the 'example from you' are later additions to the original core.[4] However, as noted in the Introduction, more recent scholarship has questioned the methodology of any reconstructions that assume that the *birkat ha-mazon* is even the basis of *Didache* 10, quite apart from underlying any other anaphora. More recent studies suggest that two core elements in Addai and Mari are probably the doxological-Sanctus section and also the Epiklesis.

In my study of the Sanctus in the Eucharistic Prayer I argued that Addai and Mari is our earliest example of an anaphoral Sanctus, and I posited several possible origins, including the so-called Jewish 'mystical' tradition, evolving from speculation on the vision of Ezekiel and the *merkavah*, and found in the Second Temple apocalypses, some of the Qumran texts, and eventually blossoming in the later Hekhalot literature.[5] The leading scholars in this field at that time were Scholem and Gruenwald. Their work has been critiqued and taken much further in more recent works by David Halperin, Martha Himmelfarb, Rachel Elior and Peter Schäfer.[6] Schäfer, for instance, dislikes the term 'mystical' and is dubious about the Qumran material being part of this general development, though Daniel Falk and Philip Alexander make a good case that at least the Songs of the Sabbath Sacrifice stand within this diffuse tradition.[7] Despite such differences, there is broad agreement on the various themes found in this literature. One common theme in the apocalypses is that the seer sees, hears and joins in the angelic praises of heaven, and beholds the Glory of the Throne. This is true of Enoch, as well as the apocalypses of Isaiah and Zechariah. As this tradition or traditions developed in the apocalypses and later Hekhalot literature, the *qedussah* (Sanctus) becomes more and more central. Schäfer notes:

> The heavenly liturgy culminates in a description of God himself as he approaches on the highest heaven – or rather, not a description of God but of the horror experienced by those present and kept at bay by the fire emanating from the mouth of the keruvim (= cherubim), ofannim, and holy

---

Sanchez Caro, 'La anaphora de Addai y Mari y la anaphora maronita Sarrar: intent de reconstrucción de la Fuente primitive común, *Orientalia Christiana Periodica* 43 (1977), pp. 107–20.

4 Sarhad Jammo, 'The Anaphora of the Apostles Addai and Mari: A Study of Structure and Historical Background', *Orientalia Christiana Periodica* 68 (2002), p. 14.

5 Bryan D. Spinks, *The Sanctus in the Eucharistic Prayer*, Cambridge: Cambridge University Press, 1991.

6 D. J. Halperin, *The Faces of the Chariot*, Tübingen: J. C. B. Mohr, 1988; Martha Himmelfarb, *Ascent to Heaven in Jewish and Christian Apocalypses*, New York: Oxford University Press, 1993; Rachel Elior, 'From Earthly Temple to Heavenly Shrines. Prayer and Sacred Song in the Hekhalot Literature and Its Relation to Temple Traditions', *Jewish Studies Quarterly* 4 (1997), pp. 217–67; Rachel Elior, *The Three Temples: On the Emergence of Jewish Mysticism*, Oxford: The Littman Library of Jewish Civilization, 2004; Peter Schäfer, *The Origins of Jewish Mysticism*, Princeton: Princeton University Press, 2011.

7 Daniel Falk, *Daily, Sabbath, and Festival Prayers in the Dead Sea Scrolls*, Leiden: Brill, 1998; Philip Alexander, *The Mystical Texts*, London: T & T Clark, 2006.

> creatures when they utter the Qedushah (strikingly, the [Hekhalot] text finds it necessary to emphasize that this is precisely the time when Israel pronounces the Qedushah in its synagogues on earth).[8]

In Schäfer's view the majority of this disparate literature witnesses to a *unio liturgica*, where those who ascend (or descend) to the Chariot enter into a common liturgy with the angels, though this would seem to assume either a common language or that language is transcended.[9]

The influence of this whole tradition on theology and liturgy in early Christianity is being more and more acknowledged. Its influence on the Sanctus unit in the anaphora has been explored in much more detail by Gabriele Winkler in her important study, *Das Sanctus* (2002),[10] and in numerous supporting articles. Winkler noted the link between Enoch and the Ethiopian Anaphora of the Apostles, suggesting that the *qedussah* of the former explains the Sanctus and Benedictus of the latter.[11] As regards Addai and Mari, after a thorough comparison with *Ma'aseh Merkavah* and noting the sequence of cherubim and seraphim and the word glorify, she concluded:

> Thus the root of the leitmotive of 'praise' in the ante Sanctus of the East-Syrian Anaphora of the Apostles (of Addai and Mari) very likely has nothing to do with the Jewish threefold *Berakah* after the meal, as has often been assumed, but seemingly has its origin in the shape of the Jewish Qeduššа, where the Cherubim sing the 'Praise' (going back to Ezek. 3:12) and the Seraphim the 'Holy' (Isa. 6:3).[12]

Winkler's comparisons of course seem mainly based on philology, but Meßner and Lang have argued that the Ethiopian Anaphora of the Apostles is an artificial product of a rather late date, redacted certainly not earlier than the fourteenth century.[13] The influence of Enoch, even if valid, tells us nothing of the origin of the Sanctus in the first centuries. Similarly, it is difficult, if not impossible, to date *Ma'aseh Merkavah*. The point at issue, however, is not textual origin, but rather whether we can detect the same influences at work.

8 Schäfer, *Origins of Jewish Mysticism*, p. 255. See also Elliot K. Ginsburg, '"The *neshamah* is always praying": Towards a Typology of Prayer in Jewish Mystical Tradition (a first offering)', in Bronwen Neil, Geoffrey D. Dunn, and Lawrence Cross (eds), *Prayer and Spirituality in the Early Church*, vol. 3, Liturgy and Life, Strathfield NSW, Australia: St Paul's Publications, 2003, pp. 353–92.

9 See John C. Poirier, *The Tongues of Angels*, Tübingen: Mohr Siebeck, 2010.

10 Gabriele Winkler, *Das Sanctus: Über den Ursprung und die Anfänge des Sanctus und sein Fortwirken*, Rome: Pontificio Istituto Orientale, 2002.

11 Gabriele Winkler, 'A New Witness to the Missing Institution Narrative', in Maxwell E. Johnson and L. Edward Phillips (eds), *Studia Liturgica Diversa: Essays in Honor of Paul F. Bradshaw*, Portland: Pastoral Press, 2004, pp. 117–28, 127.

12 Gabriele Winkler, 'The Sanctus: Some Observations with Regard to Its Origins and Theological Significance', in Neil, Dunn and Cross (eds), *Prayer and Spirituality in the Early Church*, vol. 3, pp. 129–33.

13 R. Meßner and M. Lang, 'Ethiopian Anaphoras: Status and Tasks in Current Research via an Edition of the Ethiopian Anaphora of the Apostles', *Jewish and Christian Liturgy and Worship*, Leiden: Brill, 2007, pp. 185–205.

The opening lines of Qumran's 4QBerakhot286 1ii are remarkably similar to the opening of Addai and Mari in tone and style.[14] The continued influence of the *merkavah* mysticism in Syriac circles can be seen in Aphrahat and has been discussed recently in the study by Stephanie K. Skoyles Jarkins, where she draws attention to two particular passages in the *Demonstrations*.[15] Winkler's evidence leads to the conclusion that in Addai and Mari, the central part of the opening section of the anaphora (*Oratio ante Sanctus*) presupposes the presence of the Sanctus which 'stands so to speak in the epicenter' of the whole prayer'.[16]

A good number of scholars have noted the distinction in eucharistic epikleses between the form which asks the Father for the Spirit to be sent and forms that ask that the Holy Spirit come. On the basis of the term *maranatha,* the conviction of the antiquity of the Anaphora of St Basil and Addai and Mari, scholars such as Sebastian Brock, Gabriele Winkler and I have suggested that the term 'come' is an older tradition and also distinctive as regards geography.[17] At least in the Syriac tradition, this is the preferred term in the *Acts of Thomas*, a work that, as Sebastian Brock has noted, is used by or alluded to in two places in Addai and Mari: 'you put on our humanity' and 'you raised up our mortality'.[18] Indeed, there is also considerable overlap of theme and vocabulary between sections of Addai and Mari and the Hymn of Thomas: there it is the Name that is glorified (cf. *Sharar*); there are ministers of flaming fire; the Holy ones are in tranquility and rest; a pure and holy offering is offered; and God assembles the worlds (cf. *Sharar*) for his glory.

The epikleses in Thomas have been discussed by Gabriele Winkler and more recently in an extended study by Susan Myers.[19] Comparing these prayer invocations to prayer forms in Judaism, pagan religions and magical texts of a similar period, Myers concluded:

---

14 James R. Davila, *Liturgical Works: Eerdmans Commentaries on the Dead Sea Scrolls*, Grand Rapids: Eerdmans, 2000, p. 49.

15 Stephanie K. Skoyles Jarkins, *Aphrahat the Persian Sage and the Temple of God*, Piscataway: Gorgias Press, 2008.

16 Gabriele Winkler, 'Unsolved Problems Concerning the Background and Significance of the Vocabulary of Praise in some of the Oldest Eucharistic Prayers', in Bert Groen, Steven Hawkes-Teeples and Stefanos Alexopoulos (eds), *Inquiries into Eastern Christian Worship*, Leuven: Peeters, 2012, p. 159.

17 Gabriele Winkler, 'Further Observations in Connection with the Early Form of the Epiklesis', in G. Winkler (ed.), *Studies in Early Christian Liturgy and Its Context*, Aldershot: Ashgate, 1997, pp. 66–80; Sebastian Brock, 'Invocations to/for the Holy Spirit in Syriac Liturgical Texts: Some Comparative Approaches', in R. F. Taft and Gabriele Winkler (eds), *Comparative Liturgy Fifty Years after Anton Baumstark (1872–1948)*, Rome: Pontificio Istituto Orientale, 2001, pp. 377–406; Bryan D. Spinks, 'The Consecratory Epiklesis in the Anaphora of St James', *Studia Liturgica* 11 (1976), pp. 19–38.

18 Sebastian Brock, 'Some Early Witnesses to the East Syriac Liturgical Tradition', *Journal of Assyrian Academic Studies* 18 (2004), p. 9; 'The Acts of Thomas', ET in W. Wright (ed.), *The Apocryphal Acts*, vol. II, London: Williams and Norgate, 1871, pp. 248 and 249. See also Harold W. Attridge, *The Acts of Thomas*, Salem: Polebridge Press, 2010.

19 Winkler, 'Further Observations'; Susan E. Myers, *Spirit Epicleses in the Acts of Thomas*, Tübingen: Mohr Siebeck, 2010.

> The epicleses are notable in their repetition of the anaphoral 'come', their use of short epithets for the divine figure, and their request that the Spirit join with them in the ritual action. Although there are ancient prayers that evidence some similarities, no ancient prayer appears to be closely related in form to the epiclesis.[20]

In other words, the Epiklesis appears to be a quite distinct Christian form of invocation. The *Acts of Thomas* attest to communities where the Eucharist – which sometimes seems to have been bread only and other times bread and cup (though the content of the cup is unspecified) – could apparently be celebrated with these brief invocations rather than a thanksgiving or doxological proclamation as in, for example, the prayers of the *Didache*. Chapter 50 of the *Acts of Thomas* uses the term 'come' successively throughout the invocation in the imperative. As with its counterpart in chapter 27 over oil, it is addressed to Christ, but as a feminine figure reminiscent of the *Odes of Solomon*. In chapter 27 Jesus is described as fellowship of the male and lady, but also Holy Spirit, and it seems that the names of the Son and the Spirit were interchangeable, or at least not clearly distinguished. In chapter 50 the words of distribution ask that the bread be for the remission of sins and eternal transgressions. In chapter 133 again bread is blessed, and here it is the Bread of Life, presumably Jesus, who is addressed. It includes the proclamation, 'You are the one who has been deemed worthy to receive a gift, that you might become for us forgiveness of sins, that those who eat of you might be immortal.' The petition in this asks, 'May the power of the blessing and thanksgiving come and abide upon this bread, that all the souls, which take of it, may be renewed, and their sins may be forgiven'. In chapter 158 Jesus is addressed:

> We eat your holy body that was crucified for us, and we drink for our salvation your blood that was shed for us. Therefore, let your body become our salvation and your blood produce remission of sins.

When these are compared with the short and succinct Epiklesis of Addai and Mari, we find the jussive, 'and may there come', as in the *Acts of Thomas* chapter 133; the request for remission of sins and eternal life all echo the prayers in the *Acts of Thomas*; and if bless is original to the earliest reading, that too is found in Thomas. Given the centrality of the Epiklesis in the *Acts of Thomas*, there is every reason to regard the Epiklesis of Addai and Mari as belonging to its most ancient core. In the light of the most recent scholarship, any attempt to 'reconstruct' an earlier stratum of Addai and Mari which does not incorporate the Sanctus and Epiklesis would seem misplaced. However, it may be the case that any attempt at all to reconstruct some earlier form is misplaced, since it assumes that the few ancient texts we have – *Didache* and the *Acts of Thomas* and *Acts of John* – were normative for everywhere. It may be safer to conclude that Addai and Mari is simply an early pre-Nicene Eucharistic Prayer and certainly the oldest one in continuous use.

20 Myers, *Spirit Epicleses*, p. 177.

Strasbourg Gr.254

The Strasbourg Papyrus, which consists of six fragments, was first published by Andrieu and Collomp in 1928.[21] These editors drew attention to the parallels with the Alexandrian Anaphora of St Mark and its Coptic version, St Cyril, and regarded the fragments as a fragmentary part of St Mark. However, with the emergence of articles and books focusing on the *birkat ha-mazon* as the parent of all subsequent Christian Eucharistic Prayers, a number of scholars including Edward Kilmartin, Herman Wegman, Geoffrey Cuming, W. H. Bates and Enrico Mazza, argued that far from being a fragment of a longer anaphora, the text was a complete prayer.[22] It begins with thanksgiving (though this part has lacunae), moves to offering and then supplication with intercessions (also lacunae) and concludes with a doxology. It has a bipartite movement from praise to intercession, like the *birkat ha-mazon* and Didache 10, and can be termed a Christian *berakah* or a Christian *eucharistia*.[23] Jasper and Cuming conclude:

> Scholars have drawn attention to the similarity of the prayer's structure to Jewish prayers such as the Blessing for food. Originally the prayer may have consisted of three 'panels': thanksgiving, offering, intercession, rounded off by a *chatimah*. This suggests a very early date, perhaps *c.* 200, which is supported by the length of the prayer (very much the same as that in the *Apostolic Tradition*) and the quotation from Malachi 1:11, found also in the *Didache*, Justin, Irenaeus, and Tertullian, but not often used by later writers.[24]

In the light of more recent studies it seems unhelpful to see any analogy between the two prayers. As Walter Ray once observed, it is not possible to discover a precise genetic link with any particular Jewish prayer.[25]

The text of this anaphora reads:

> to bless [you] . . . . [night] and day . . .
>
> [you who made] heaven [and] all that is in [it, the earth and what is on earth,] seas and rivers and [all that is] in [them]; [you] who made man [according to your] own image and likeness. You made everything through your wisdom,

21 M. Andrieu and P. Collomp, 'Fragments sur papyrus de l'anaphore de saint Marc', *Revue des sciences religieuses* 8 (1928), pp. 489–515.

22 Edward Kilmartin, 'Sacrificium Laudis: Content and Function of Early Eucharistic Prayers', *Theological Studies* 35 (1974), pp. 268–87; H. A. J. Wegman, 'Une anaphore incomplète? Les Fragments sur Papyrus Strasbourg Gr. 254', in R. van den Broek and M. J. Vermeseren (eds), *Studies in Gnosticism and Hellenistic Religions*, Leiden: Brill, 1981, pp. 432–50; G. J. Cuming, 'The Anaphora of St Mark: A Study in Development', *Le Muséon* 95 (1982), pp. 115–29; W. H. Bates, 'Thanksgiving in the Liturgy of St Mark', in Bryan D. Spinks (ed.), *The Sacrifice of Praise*, Rome: CLV Edizioni Liturgiche, 1981, pp. 107–19; Enrico Mazza, 'Una Anafora incomplete? Il Papiro Strasbourg Gr. 254', *Ephemerides Liturgicae* 99 (1985), pp. 425–36.

23 Cuming, 'Anaphora of St Mark: A Study in Development', pp. 115–29; Bates, 'Thanksgiving', p. 113.

24 *PEER*, p. 53.

25 Walter Ray, 'The Strasbourg Papyrus', in Paul F. Bradshaw (ed.), *Essays on Early Eastern Eucharistic Prayers*, Collegeville: Liturgical Press, 1997, p. 44.

the light [of?] your true Son, our Lord and Savior Jesus Christ; giving thanks through him to you with him and the Holy Spirit, we offer the reasonable sacrifice and this bloodless service, which all the nations offer you, 'from sunrise to sunset,' from south to north, [for] your 'name is great among all the nations, and in every place incense is offered to your holy name and a pure sacrifice'.

Over this sacrifice and offering we pray and beseech you, remember your holy and only Catholic Church, all your peoples and all your flocks. Provide the peace which is from heaven in all our hearts, and grant us also the peace of this life. The . . . . of the land peaceful things towards us, and towards your [holy] name, the prefect of the province, the army, the princes, councils . . . (*About one-third of a page is lacking here, and what survives is in places too fragmentary to be restored.*)

[for seedtime and] harvest . . . preserve, for the poor of [your] people, for all of us who call upon [your] name, for all who hope in you. Give rest to the souls of those who have fallen asleep; remember those of whom we make mention today, both those whose names we say [and] whose we do not say . . . [Remember] our orthodox fathers and bishops everywhere; and grant us to have a part and lot with the fair . . . of your holy prophets, apostles, and martyrs. Receive(?) [through] their entreaties [these prayers]; grant them through our Lord; through whom be glory to you to the ages of ages.[26]

The present writer has questioned whether in fact this is the only interpretation of the fragments and argued that on analogy with Addai and Mari which is divided by a doxology, it might be the first of a number of units making up a once longer anaphora.[27] More recently Michael Zheltov, in the light of another Egyptian Eucharistic Prayer, the Barcelona Anaphora, the manuscript of which is earlier than the Strasbourg fragments, has suggested that Strasbourg is a fragment of a more developed anaphora.[28] Save an important discovery of a complete version of the fragments, it is unlikely to be proven one way or the other. If it is a complete prayer, then, like Addai and Mari, there is no Narrative of Institution, though also no Sanctus and Epiklesis. Because of the lacunae, only one 'praise word' survives – bless. As already noted, it may be that other words included thanksgiving and glory. God is blessed night and day, as creator of heaven earth, rivers and man in God's image and likeness. A wisdom Christology is utilized. Giving thanks through the Son and Spirit, the Church offers a reasonable sacrifice and bloodless service, in fulfilment of Scripture – Malachi 1.11. If there is an early Institution Narrative or mandate for observing the Eucharist, it seems to have been Malachi 1.11. This has been linked with

26 *PEER*, pp. 53–4.

27 Bryan D. Spinks, 'A Complete Anaphora? A Note on Strasbourg Gr. 254', *Heythrop Journal* 35 (1984), pp. 51–9.

28 Michael Zheltov, 'The Anaphora and the Thanksgiving Prayer from the Barcelona Papyrus: An Underestimated Testimony to the Anaphoral History of the Fourth Century', *Vigiliae Christianae* 62 (2008), pp. 467–504. For the Barcelona Anaphora, see ch. 4.

Romans 12.1, and bloodless service is found in the Jewish *Testament of Levi*. It is usually thought to refer to the purity of verbal prayer rather than the animal sacrifice of the Temple. For Christianity the sacrifice on the cross had rendered the Temple superfluous, and to utter thanksgiving in remembrance was a bloodless service. There then follow prayers for the Church, for peace–shalom, for those in authority including the army; then for the departed. The prayers are made through Jesus Christ.

Apostolic Constitutions VII.25 and 26

The *Apostolic Constitutions* (*AC*) is a Church Order,[29] and dates from *c.* 380 in the region of Antioch. The compiler seems to have had semi-Arian or Eunomian christological concerns and subordinates Jesus the Son to God the Father. He has collected and edited a number of more ancient texts in order to substantiate his own Christology. He has used the *Didascalia*, the *Didache*, the so-called *Apostolic Tradition* (see below), as well as some Hellenistic synagogue prayers. In Book VIII he reproduces an anaphora which accords with fourth-century patterns. However, in Book VII he uses and edits the prayers of *Didache* 9 and 10. In his version, *Didache* 9 is extended and makes reference to the blood and body (in that order) of Jesus:

> Be always thankful, as faithful and honest servants, and concerning the eucharist, say thus: We thank you, our Father, for the life which you have made known to us through Jesus your Child, through whom you made all things and take care of the whole [world]; whom you sent to become man for our salvation; whom you permitted to suffer and to die; whom you raised up, and have been pleased to glorify, and have set down on your right hand; by whom also you have promised us the resurrection of the dead. Do you, O Lord almighty, eternal God, so gather together your Church from the ends of the earth into your kingdom, as this [corn] was once scattered, and is now gathered together and become one loaf. We also give you thanks, our Father, for the precious blood of Jesus Christ, [which was] shed for us, and for his precious body, of which we celebrate this figure [*antitupa*], as he himself has ordered us, to show forth his death: for through him glory [is to be given] to you for ever. Amen.[30]

Didache 10 is used as a post-prandial prayer, but here too a reference to the blood and body of Christ has been added to *Apostolic Constitutions*' version.

Marcel Metzger suggested that this reworking of the *Didache* represents a eucharistic rite which may still have been in use when the compilation was

29 See Paul F. Bradshaw, *The Search for the Origins of Christian Worship*, London: SPCK, 1992, ch. 4.

30 Marcel Metzger, *Les Constitutions Apostoliques*, vol. III, Sources Chrétiennes 336, Paris: Les Éditions du Cerf, 1987, pp. 52–4; ET in W. Jardine Grisbrooke, *The Liturgical Portions of the Apostolic Constitutions: A Text for Students*, Alcuin/GROW Liturgical Study 13–14, Nottingham: Grove Books, 1990, p. 18.

redacted and was for ordinary occasions.[31] Enrico Mazza has suggested that in what the manuscripts entitle the 'Mystical Eucharist', 'this anaphora presupposes some intermediate phases between it and its source'.[32] Yet, as Bradshaw observes, given the longer 'classical' anaphora that the compiler gives in *AC* VIII, it is hard to believe that both types could have been current alongside one another in the same liturgical community.[33] It may, as Mazza suggested, represent a phase of development, when 'Eucharist' meant not any thanksgiving meal of Christians, but a meal linked specifically to the death of Jesus; but the prayer may also have been the creation of the compiler and never used. If it is the former, it certainly shows a concern for salvation history as well as linking the celebration with the cup and bread with the blood and body of Jesus. There is still no full narrative but a reference to antitypes, comparable to the reference to the 'example' in Addai and Mari, but, unlike the East Syrian prayer, *AC* VII.25 has no Sanctus and Epiklesis.

The so-called *Apostolic Tradition*

The Eucharistic Prayer in this document has come down to us in Latin and Ethiopic and exists in expanded forms in the Syriac *Testamentum Domini* and the Greek fourth-century collection, *Apostolic Constitutions*, Book VIII. Apart from the Latin version, it is found in Church Orders and works associated with Egypt and Syria, and although the original language was Greek, no Greek version has survived. The conventional reconstruction of events, which is presupposed by most textbooks until very recently and still found in popular books on the history of worship, is as follows.

In 1551, a statue was discovered which bore no name, but included a list of titles of works, many of which are accepted as being titles of the theologian Hippolytus. Among this list of titles are two – *Peri Chrismaton* and *Apostolike Paradosis* – of Spiritual gifts and Apostolic Tradition. Copies of these works were unknown. E. Schwarz in 1910 and R. H. Connolly in 1916 independently noted that in a number of Church Orders having an Egyptian and Syrian provenance, there was a common body of material, a 'liturgical Q' on analogy with the 'Q' material common to the Gospels of Matthew and Luke. They extracted the common material and for internal reasons identified it as the missing *Apostolic Tradition* (*AT*) of Hippolytus listed on the plinth of the statue. In the popular story, Hippolytus was an anti-pope, who was martyred with Pope Pontianus and who on account of his conservative views was at emnity with the discipline and trinitarian theology of Popes Zephyrinus and Callistus. The *Apostolic Tradition* would therefore represent a conservative approach to liturgical tradition. Thus it is concluded that the *Apostolic Tradition* represents a conservative and

31 Marcel Metzger, 'The Didascalia and the Constituiones Apostolorum', in Raymond Johanny and Willy Rordorf (eds), *The Eucharist of the Early Christians*, trans. Matthew J. O'Connell, Collegeville: Liturgical Press, 2001, pp. 194–219.

32 Enrico Mazza, *The Origins of the Eucharistic Prayer*, Collegeville: Liturgical Press, 1995, p. 60.

33 Bradshaw, *Eucharistic Origins*, p. 117.

thus reliable type of liturgy that was found at Rome *c.* 215 and probably having its roots in the late second century.

The liturgical text was made prominent among liturgists through the editions by the Anglican scholar Dom Gregory Dix and the Roman Catholic scholar Dom Bernard Botte.[34] As a result of their work and on the assumption that these texts date from *c.* 215, the Ordination Prayers and the Eucharistic Prayer have been very influential in modern revisions. For example, in the Roman Missal, the second Eucharistic Prayer was inspired by the *Apostolic Tradition* text, and in the Church of England, the third Eucharistic Prayer of the *Alternative Service Book 1980* was based upon it. For some inexplicable reason there seemed to be an almost uncontested assumption that if these prayers were dated 215, they were authoritative and could be transplanted into late twentieth-century churches.

To the discerning inquirer there were already some question marks over this liturgical Q. Not everyone thought that the Hippolytus of this work was the anti-pope of Rome. Second, in important articles in 1924 George La Piana had drawn attention to the complicated relationships of different ethnic groups in Rome, divided by their different languages.[35] We cannot conclude that this liturgy and Eucharistic Prayer, originally written in Greek, would be representative of all the Christian communities in Rome at this time. J. M. Hanssens had argued at length that Hippolytus was from Egypt and that the *Apostolic Tradition* represents Egyptian usage.[36] Last, the Eucharistic Prayer, which is only found in Latin and Ethiopic, is offered as the type of prayer that a bishop might pray at his ordination Eucharist. There is no suggestion that this was the type of prayer offered *every* Sunday.

In recent years, the status of the whole document and its Eucharistic Prayer has been called into question. Jean Magne questioned whether the liturgical Q was indeed the missing work of Hippolytus.[37] He has been followed by Marcel Metzger, and subsequently many others have seriously questioned the authenticity of the liturgical Q.[38] Perhaps the most damaging critique was the large tome by Allen Brent, in which he drew attention to the fact that, first, the headless statue which has been restored as Hippolytus had in fact been of a woman.[39] Second, he noted that none of the documents identified by Schwarz and company carried the title 'Apostolic Tradition' and that names associated with Church Orders are ciphers. Brent went on to examine the rest of the Hippolytus corpus, concluding

34 Gregory Dix, *The Treatise on The Apostolic Tradition*, London: SPCK, 1937; Bernard Botte, *La Tradition Apostolique de Saint Hippolyte*, Münster: Aschendorff, 1963.

35 George La Piana, 'The Roman Church at the End of the Second Century', *Harvard Theological Review* 18 (1925), pp. 201–77; 'Foreign Groups in Rome during the First Centuries of the Empire', *Harvard Theological Review* 20 (1927), pp. 183–403.

36 Jean Michel Hanssens, *La Liturgie d'Hippolyte*, Rome: Pontificio Istituto Orientale, 1965.

37 Jean Magne, *Tradition Apostolique sur les Charismes et Diataxeis des Saints Apôtres*, Paris: np, 1975.

38 Marcel Metzger, 'Nouvelles perspectives pour le prétendue Tradition apostolique', *Ecclesia Orans* 5 (1988), pp. 241–59; 'Enquêtes autour de la prétendue Tradition apostolique', *Ecclesia Orans* 9 (1992), pp. 7–36.

39 Allen Brent, *Hippolytus and Roman Church in Third Century: Communities in Tension before the Emergence of a Monarch-Bishop*, Leiden: Brill, 1995.

that it derives from a time when a monarchical bishop emerged in Rome replacing the older polity of churches each having presbyter-bishops. The statue of a woman, so he argued, was a corporate icon of the distinctive community that had achieved a continuing influence under the pseudonym of Hippolytus and that contained at least two authors. As for the liturgical Q, Brent opined that the assumption of an autograph named 'Apostolic Tradition', which once existed as the work of a single, 'real' author is chimerical. Paul Bradshaw has suggested that while some elements in this document may be of the early third century, as a living document it reached its present state probably in the early fourth century and has a variety of layers of material reflecting different times and community practice.[40] This has been reiterated and examined in more detail in the commentary by Paul Bradshaw, Ed. Phillips and Maxwell Johnson.[41] Alistair Stewart-Sykes, even though arguing for a mid-third-century redaction, also concedes that there is more than one layer of material in the rite.[42] Although the prayer has archaic features – Jesus is described as child and the angel of God's will – it also has features that suggest a fourth-century date, particularly the inclusion of the Words of Institution within the prayer. Paul Bradshaw has noted that references to the Words of Institution in Justin and many other documents seem to be a catechetical rather than a euchological context. It would seem, therefore, that the Eucharistic Prayer may be a fourth-century creation looking back in time to an imagined third-century ideal. However, the material, and the prayer, continued to have a life as living texts as it was redacted and adapted in subsequent Church Orders. Whatever else may be said of the anaphora, it is not the universal Eucharistic Prayer of Rome in 215. Matthieu Smyth has shown quite convincingly that far from this prayer being Roman, it can be situated in the first half of the fourth century, somewhere west of Antioch and Palestine, and is structurally related to the Anaphora of St John Chrysostom.[43]

The document gives two eucharistic accounts – one after the ordination of a bishop, in which a Eucharistic Prayer is given, and one after a baptism, which is only a brief outline. Neither rite describes a Word service as Justin Martyr does. We have a sequence:

- Intercessions.
- Kiss of Peace.
- Giving thanks over bread and wine which are antitypes or the likeness of the body and blood.

40 Paul F. Bradshaw, 'Redating the Apostolic Tradition: Some Preliminary Steps', in Nathan Mitchell and John F. Baldovin (eds), *Rule of Prayer, Rule of Faith: Essays in Honor of Aidan Kavanagh*, OSB, Collegeville: Liturgical Press, 1996, pp. 3–17.

41 Paul F. Bradshaw, Maxwell E. Johnson and L. Edward Phillips, *The Apostolic Tradition: A Commentary*, Minneapolis: Fortress Press, 2002.

42 Alistair Stewart-Sykes, *Hippolytus: On the Apostolic Tradition*, New York: St Vladimir's Seminary Press, 2001. For the problem in a wider context, J. A. Cerrato, 'The Association of the Name Hippolytus with a Church Order now known as *The Apostolic Tradition*', *St Vladimir's Theological Quarterly* 48:2 (2004), pp. 179–94.

43 Matthieu Smyth, 'The Anaphora of the So-Called "Apostolic Tradition" and the Roman Eucharistic Prayer', in Maxwell E. Johnson (ed.), *Issues in Eucharistic Praying*, Collegeville: Liturgical Press, 2010, pp. 71–98.

- In the case of a baptism, also thanks over milk and honey.
- The breaking of the bread.
- The words of administration at a baptismal Eucharist are, 'The bread of heaven in Christ Jesus', and, in turn with a cup of water, milk and wine, 'In God the Father almighty. And in the Lord Jesus Christ. And in the Holy Spirit and the holy Church.'

The Eucharistic Prayer of the *Apostolic Tradition* has the following structure:

- Dialogue – *Dominus vobiscum.*
- Thanksgiving for redemption, concluding with the Institution Narrative.
- Anamnesis (remembering) and oblation (offering of bread and cup).
- Petition for the Spirit – an Epiklesis.
- Closing doxology.

The dialogue serves to present the assembly before God in prayer. It is almost identical to that of the later Roman canon of the Mass – the only real link between this prayer and later Roman tradition. The *Dominus vobiscum* – the Lord be with you – is from Ruth 2.4 and Luke 1.28 and is thus Semitic in origin. Robert Taft has used a computer on Greek literature to show that the expression was known in Greek, and therefore a Greek origin is probable. 'Let us give thanks to the Lord' may well derive from the opening salutation on Jewish table prayers, the *birkat ha-zimmun*, the precise form of which varied to the number of males present. However, Taft has again shown that the version in the Christian prayer has Greek parallels – almost as a chant at a football game to get a crowd in the mood.[44]

The prayer begins with thanksgiving and not with the word 'blessing'. As we have seen, there seems to be a preference in Christian prayer for thanksgiving rather than blessing. The thanksgiving is to God, through Jesus Christ – reflecting the belief that Jesus the High Priest is our true intercessor, and we approach God through him. The substance of the thanksgiving is christological – it is about salvation history in Christ and is almost creed-like. It contains archaisms – Beloved Child, or servant Jesus Christ, as in the *Didache*, and he is the messenger or angel of your counsel. The Institution Narrative is the first example of its inclusion as part of the prayer, though it forms the climax of the thanksgiving. There is a transition – a remembering of the death and resurrection and the offering of the bread and cup to God. The petition for the Spirit is textually difficult. The Latin does not make grammatical sense and has given rise to a vast number of articles suggesting a reconstruction of the original Greek, either to make it a full explicit Epiklesis asking for a change in the bread and wine, or removing any reference to the Spirit at all. The Latin consists of three sections: Invocation of the Spirit; gathering into one; and prayer for the fruits of communion. The overall sense of this prayer therefore seems to be this: the rite of bread

44 Robert F. Taft, 'The Dialogue before the Anaphora in the Byzantine Eucharistic Liturgy. III: Let us Give Thanks to the Lord – It is Fitting and Right', *Orientalia Christiana Periodica* 55 (1989), pp. 63–74.

and wine – the remembrance – is the means by which the Church is enabled, in the Holy Spirit, to praise and glorify God.

The Eucharistic Prayer is found only in the Latin recension of this Church Order. In expanded form it is found also in the *Testamentum Domini*, found in Syriac and Ethiopian.[45] The Syriac was made from a Greek text no longer extant, though very recently Simon Corcoran and Benet Salway have identified a Greek fragment preserved on a parchment scrap that had been used as binding.[46] It may be that the Ethiopian is derived from a Coptic or even directly from a Greek version. However, like all prayers in these later Church Orders, there is no evidence of actual liturgical use, though as will be noted later, both the version of the so-called *Apostolic Tradition* and the expansion in *Testamentum Domini* were influential in the Ethiopian Orthodox Church.

Concluding remarks: a Jewish urtext or progenitor?

If we take what little evidence we have – the prayers from the *Acts of Thomas* and *Acts of John, Didache* 9—10, Addai and Mari, Strasbourg 254, *Apostolic Constitutions* 7.25 and even the prayer of the *Apostolic Tradition*, we have extremely varied prayers, with little in common. The earlier attempts made by scholars to trace these all back to the Jewish *birkat ha-mazon*, or to any particular Jewish prayer, is problematic.[47] It is one thing to find Semitisms in the texts, but quite another to attempt to trace them to a single prayer source. Allan Bouley, in his study published in 1981, questioned the assumption that Jesus, who challenged so many elements of what later emerged as rabbinic Judaism, used the 'standard' Jewish prayers at the Last Supper since that 'would have confusedly linked Jesus' covenant cup with the food, land, city and probably the Passover of the former covenant, whereas the meaning of all of these was being changed in the very celebration of the supper'.[48] As noted already, Stefan Reif had called in question any reconstruction of standard forms of Jewish prayer in

45 For details, see Grant Sperry-White, *The Testamentum Domini: A Text for Students, with Introduction, Translation, and Notes*, Alcuin/GROW Liturgical Study 19, Bramcote: Grove Books, 1991.

46 Simon Corcoran and Benet Salway, 'A Newly Identified Greek Fragment of the *Testamentum Domini*', *Journal of Theological Studies* 62 (2011), pp. 118–35.

47 Here the names Louis Ligier, Thomas Talley, Herman Wegman and Enrico Mazza are legendary. Louis Bouyer argued strongly for equal consideration of the synagogue *berakoth*, though Professor Giraudo would argue for the importance of the *todah* form as described in the Old Testament writings. Louis Ligier, 'Anaphores orientales et priers juives', *Proche-Orient Chrétien* 13 (1963), pp. 3–20; T. J. Talley, 'The Eucharistic Prayer of the Ancient Church According to Recent Research: Results and Reflections', *Studia Liturgica* 11 (1976), pp. 138–58; H. Wegman, 'Généalogie hypothétique de la prière eucharistique', *Questions Liturgiques* 61 (1980), pp. 263–78; Mazza, *Celebration of the Eucharist*; Louis Bouyer, *Eucharist: Theology and Spirituality of the Eucharistic Prayer*, Notre Dame: Notre Dame University Press, 1968; Cesare Giraudo, *La struttura letteraria della preghiera eucaristica: Saggio sulla genesi letteraria di una forma: toda veterotestamentaria, beraka giudaica, anafora Cristiana*, Rome: Pontifico Istituto Biblico, 1989.

48 Allan Bouley, *From Freedom to Formula: The Evolution of the Eucharistic Prayer from Oral Improvisation to Written Texts*, Washington: Catholic University of America, 1981, p. 79.

the early common era.[49] In his study of the prayers of the Dead Sea Scrolls, Daniel Falk concluded that the liturgical prayers of the sectarians were collected and collated from forms used in the Second Temple. Nevertheless, with reference to the quest for original Jewish prayer texts, Falk observed:

> This enterprise is fraught with problems since it proceeds on the dubious assumption that the prayers were from the beginning literary creations fixed by an authority, and that they developed in a linear fashion. Furthermore, the rabbinic discussions presuppose alternative texts and for the most part refer to prayers without reproducing them, so that one cannot safely assume that the content known from the medieval prayer-books is in mind.[50]

The implications of these more recent studies for evaluating the development of the anaphora are stated quite clearly by Gabriele Winkler:

> Neither the long favored *birkat ha-mazon* ancestry nor other theories like those revolving around the Synagogue or the Old Testament *todah*, can satisfactorily explain all the structural and textual shapes of the varied early evidence.[51]

Even if there are Jewish echoes in some of the early Christian material, there was less reason for Gentile communities to be wedded to Jewish prayer forms. The evidence that we do have (and it is rather like having only a few pieces of a 1,000-piece jigsaw) may best be interpreted as pointing to a great diversity of Eucharistic Prayers and diverse content, which gradually, through 'euchological osmosis', came to emerge in the fourth century as what is termed the classical anaphora. The early material also witnesses to a variety of themes in the prayers, but three particular themes emerge. First, there is recognition that the Eucharist is somehow an offering or sacrifice, and Malachi 1.11 features prominently. Second, we can begin to see a concern to articulate presence – either of Christ or his salvific work – in association with the elements. Third, eschatology is expressed through remembrance of the departed and the wider Church, as well as in association with the elements that are received for remission of sins, or other spiritual fruits and benefits. In Addai and Mari the community expresses a realized eschatology in that the worshippers 'give you thanks and praise you without ceasing in your Church redeemed by the precious blood of your Christ, with open mouths and with uncovered faces'.

49 Stefan Reif, *Judaism and Hebrew Prayer: New Perspectives on Jewish Liturgical History*, Cambridge: Cambridge University Press, 1993.

50 Daniel K. Falk, *Daily, Sabbath, and Festival Prayers in the Dead Sea Scrolls*, Leiden: Brill, 1998, p. 2.

51 Winkler, 'A New Witness', p. 118.

3

Eucharistic Theologies in the Fourth- and Fifth-Century Homilies and the Emergence of the Classical Anaphora

The Eucharistic Prayers of the 'classical' period are difficult to date in terms of their first appearance as written texts. Some information, though, of their shape and content and something of the understanding of certain influential presbyters and bishops are contained in some fourth- and fifth-century commentaries and catechetical homilies that have survived. We have the mystagogical catechetical homilies (*MC*) attributed to Cyril of Jerusalem, *c.* 384; the liturgical homilies of Theodore of Mopsuestia, *c.* 390, and perhaps reflecting Antioch as well as Mopsuestia; Ephrem the Syrian for Edessa and Nisibis; John Chrysostom's writings for Antioch and Constantinople; Ambrose for Milan and Augustine for Hippo, North Africa.

The *Mystagogic Catecheses* (*MC*) attributed to Cyril of Jerusalem

Cyril was Bishop of Jerusalem, 350–386/7, with periods of exile in between.[1] His episcopate began during the resurgence of Arianism, and his own orthodoxy has been questioned.[2] There are two sets of catechetical lectures or homilies attributed to him. The first, 18 baptismal lectures (BC), are accepted as authentic. The date and authorship of the five *MC*, given after baptism and that include an outline of the eucharistic liturgy and anaphora, are, however, disputed, particularly since there are notable differences between them concerning the baptismal ritual. Three manuscripts attribute them to Cyril and his successor John and one manuscript of the *MC* is attributed to John. The quest to prove or disprove Cyrilline authorship of *MC* has become something of a popular pastime. Two of the most recent studies are those by Alexis Doval and Juliette Day. Doval studied with Edward Yarnold and followed the latter's conviction that *MC* was by Cyril, but the older Cyril, and that changes had taken place in the liturgy since his earlier BC.[3] Juliette

1 Jan Willem Drijvers, *Cyril of Jerusalem: Bishop and City*, Leiden: Brill, 2004.

2 See Robert C. Gregg, 'Cyril of Jerusalem and the Arians', in Robert C. Gregg (ed.), *Arianism: Historical and Theological Reassessment*, Cambridge, MA: Philadelphia Patristic Foundation Ltd, 1985, pp. 85–119; Drijvers, *Cyril of Jerusalem*, Appendix 1.

3 Alexis Doval, *Cyril of Jerusalem Mystagogue*, Washington: Catholic University of America, 2001, pp. 135–49; E. J. Yarnold, 'The Authorship of the *Mystagogic Catecheses* Attributed to Cyril of Jerusalem', *Heythrop Journal* 19 (1978), pp. 143–61.

Day, by contrast, argued that the baptismal liturgy presupposed by *MC* does not accurately reflect the baptismal rite known to Cyril in BC and that *MC* reflects a period after 397 and more likely fifth-century usages and understanding. The hagiopolite rite of *MC*, she suggested, might be an interpretation of a version of the 'Hippolytus' documents that lie behind the Egyptian *Canons of Hippolytus* and the Antiochene *Apostolic Constitutions*.[4]

The views of Doval and Day may now need to be refigured in light of Abraham Terian's edition of Macarius of Jerusalem's Letter to the Armenians. In the early decades of the twentieth century N. Akinian had argued that this letter was mistakenly attributed to Macarius I of Jerusalem, but that in fact the Macarius was Macarius II of the sixth century. Akinian's view did not go unchallenged, but his view seems to have prevailed and explains why scholars have ignored it until now. Abraham Terian has made a compelling case for the authenticity of the letter and dates it 335. The letter discusses baptismal procedures and only mentions the Eucharist briefly.[5]

Juliette Day has questioned whether or not Terian has proved his case, since she notes that at a number of places he admits that the document – found in three late redactions – has been interpolated, and she has reiterated her view that the BC cannot be harmonized with the quite different ritual sequence given in *MC*.[6] In a recent article, Maxwell Johnson has noted that by limiting the investigation to baptism only, Day has left unanswered the view shared by many liturgical scholars that the anaphora outlined in *MC* 4–5 reflects an earlier form of euchology than might be expected if the document is from the end of the fourth century.[7] Regardless of whether the author was Cyril or John (and here they will be called 'Cyril'), *MC* witnesses to an anaphora that has much in common with the classical Anaphora of St James, which came to be associated with Jerusalem.

Literary antecedents of the Greek Anaphora of St James are found in a paragraph preceding the final bidding in a sermon of Eusebius of Caesarea delivered sometime between the years 314 and 319 at the opening of the new cathedral at Tyre and in *MC*. In his sermon, Eusebius writes:

> Such is the great temple which the Word, the great *Creator* of the universe, has built throughout the world beneath the *sun*, having fashioned on *earth* that intelligible image of those things that lie beyond the vaults of *heaven*; so that by the *whole creation* and by the rational, living beings upon earth, his Father is honoured and reverenced. But the region above the heavens and the

4 Juliette Day, *The Baptismal Liturgy of Jerusalem: Fourth- and Fifth-Century Evidence from Palestine, Syria and Egypt*, Aldershot: Ashgate, 2007, pp. 134–8.

5 Abraham Terian, *Macarius of Jerusalem: Letter to the Armenians*, Crestwood: St Vladimir's Seminary Press, 2008, p. 79.

6 Juliette Day, 'The Catchetical Lectures of Cyril of Jerusalem: A Source for the Baptismal Liturgy of Mid-Fourth Century Jerusalem', in David Hellholm et al. (eds), *Ablution, Initiation, and Baptism: Late Antiquity, Early Judaism, and Early Christianity*, Beihefte zur Zeitschrift für die Neutestamentliche Wissenschaft und die Kunde der Älteren Kirche, Berlin: De Gruyter, 2011, pp. 1175–200.

7 Maxwell E. Johnson, 'Christian Initiation in Fourth-Century Jerusalem and Recent Developments in the Study of the Sources', *Ecclesia Orans* 26 (2009), p. 153.

> models there of the things on earth, and the *Jerusalem* above, as it is called, and *the heavenly* mount Sion, and the supramundane city of the living God, in which the myriad *choirs* of *angels* and *assembly of the first-born written in heaven*, honour their Maker and sovereign Ruler of the universe with *praises* [*theologiais*] unutterable and inconceivable to us – such as no mortal can worthily *hymn*.[8]

The allusions are certainly there, though without the anaphoral text of St James (see Chapter 6) this would not be an obvious allusion. On the other hand, *MC* clearly outlined an anaphora in *MC* 5, which has affinities with St James.

In *MC* 4 Cyril began with a reference to the Institution Narrative and quotes a form that some have thought may be a liturgical formula and similar to one quoted by Eusebius of Caesarea.[9] Cyril argued that since Jesus turned water into wine at Cana in Galilee, it is certainly not incredible to believe that he turns wine into his blood. Because of this,

> Therefore with fullest assurance let us partake as of the Body and Blood of Christ: for in the figure [ἐν τύπῳ] of Bread is given to thee His Body, and in the figure of Wine His Blood; that thou by partaking of the Body and Blood of Christ, mightest be made the same body and the same blood with Him.[10]

Cyril argued that the bread and wine should not be contemplated as bare elements, because Jesus had declared them his body and blood. What seems bread and wine, and tastes like them, are not bread and wine, but the body and blood of Christ, though partaking of them is spiritual.[11]

In *MC* 5 Cyril outlines the eucharistic celebration. It is an instruction for the newly baptized and acquaints them with what they will see and hear whenever they attend the Divine Liturgy at Jerusalem. Bradshaw and Johnson warn that 'we must be careful not to assume that it quotes the prayer precisely and completely in every respect'.[12] However, each section is introduced with *eita,* next, as though he is giving the actual sequence. The deacon gives water to the priest (bishop) and the presbyters to wash their hands as a symbol of purity. Then after the exchange of the Kiss of Peace came the *Sursum corda* – 'Lift up your hearts', with the reply 'We lift up our hearts to the Lord'. The Priest says, 'Let us give thanks to the Lord', with the response, 'It is meet and right'. The main body of the anaphora follows:

> After this, we call to mind heaven and earth and sea; sun and moon and stars; all Creation, rational and irrational, visible and invisible; angels, archangels,

8 Eusebius, *Church History* X. 4.69–72. M. H. Shepherd, 'Eusebius and the Liturgy of St James', *Yearbook of Liturgical Studies* 4 (1963), pp. 109–25.

9 D. S. Wallace-Hadrill, 'Eusebius and the Institution Narrative in the Eastern Liturgies', *Journal of Theological Studies* 4 (1953), pp. 41–2.

10 Cyril, *MC* 4:3, in F. L. Cross (ed.), *St Cyril of Jerusalem's Lectures on the Christian Sacraments*, London: SPCK, 1966, pp. 27, 68.

11 Cyril, *MC* 4:6 and 9, in Cross (ed.), *St Cyril of Jerusalem's Lectures*, pp. 69, 71.

12 Paul F. Bradshaw and Maxwell E. Johnson, *The Eucharistic Liturgies: Their Evolution and Interpretation*, Collegeville: Liturgical Press, 2012, p. 80.

virtues, dominions, principalities, powers, thrones; the cherubim with many faces; saying with full effect the (words) of David, 'Magnify the Lord with me.' We call to mind also the seraphim, whom Isaiah saw in the Holy Spirit standing in a circle round the throne of God, with two wings veiling the face, and with two the feet, and with two flying, and saying, 'Holy, holy, holy (is the) Lord of Sabaoth.' The reason why we say this hymn of praise which has been handed down to us from the seraphim is that we may share with the supernatural armies in their hymnody.

Then, having sanctified ourselves with these spiritual hymns, we beseech God, the lover of man, to send forth the Holy Spirit upon the (gifts) set before him, that he may make the bread the body of Christ, and the wine the blood of Christ; for everything that the Holy Spirit has touched, has been sanctified and changed.

Then, after the spiritual sacrifice, the bloodless service, has been perfected, we beseech God over that sacrifice of propitiation, for the common peace of the churches, for the stability of the world, for emperors, for armies and auxiliaries, for the sick, for the oppressed; and, praying in general for all who need help, we all offer this sacrifice.

Then we call to mind also those who have fallen asleep; first patriarchs, prophets, apostles, martyrs; that God, through their prayers and advocacy, may receive our supplication. Then also for the holy fathers and bishops who have fallen asleep before us; for we believe that it will be the greatest profit to the souls for whom supplication is offered in the presence of the holy and most dread sacrifice.

In the same way, offering our prayers for those who have fallen asleep, even though they were sinners . . . we offer Christ slain for our sins, propitiating God, the lover of man, for them and for ourselves.[13]

If this is a full account, then the Jerusalem Anaphora known to Cyril had the following:

Mention of creation and angelic beings
Sanctus
Epiklesis
Intercession for the Living
Intercession of the Dead
(Lord's Prayer).

Compared with *AC* VIII, there is no thanksgiving for the work of Christ, no Institution Narrative and no Anamnesis (remembering and offering), and this raises a number of questions. Emmanuel Cutrone subjected the lectures to a theological examination, and he noted Cyril's concern with 'ikon-mimesis' – that is, the identification of the believer with Christ, especially the events in his life. Cutrone argued that had the anaphora known to Cyril contained these elements, they would have been ideal for his purpose and method. For Cutrone, Cyril was unable to use them because they were simply not in the Jerusalem

13 *PEER*, pp. 85–6.

Anaphora at that time.[14] It could be that Jerusalem had a conservative Eucharistic Prayer, and these elements had not been introduced in the time of Cyril. This would make more sense if the *MC* were early in Cyril's career, but are less credible if they date *c.* 384 or even later, since these elements would be more likely to have found their way in the Eucharistic Prayer by this time. It has also been suggested that since Cyril had discussed the Institution Narrative in *MC* 4, he saw no need to mention it again when he discussed the anaphora and so passed over it. This was argued by Edward Yarnold and more recently by Anthony Gelston.[15] Another possible explanation is that since cantillation was used in public prayer (the ancient world did not differentiate between 'said' and 'sung' when they used 'said'), Cyril only mentioned those parts that were cantillated and would be heard, whereas some parts were recited in a low, inaudible voice.[16] It may be, therefore, that the thanksgiving for redemption and the Institution Narrative were said in a low voice.[17] Geoffrey Cuming suggested at one time that the words 'after the spiritual sacrifice, the bloodless service has been perfected' is a reference to the Institution Narrative and Anamnesis, and that the anaphora known to Cyril was similar to that found in Egypt, with a sequence of Sanctus, Epiklesis, Institution Narrative, Anamnesis.[18] It remains a fact, though, that Cyril does not actually mention the Narrative in his discussion of the elements of the anaphora and by analogy with the Strasbourg Papyrus and Addai and Mari, he may not have known one as part of the anaphora.

The anaphora he outlines did not apparently give thanks for creation, but commenced as a hymn of the creation to the creator, wending its way to the Sanctus. The thought seems to be that the worshippers make a spiritual ascent and are sanctified by singing the Sanctus, and, standing before God like the seraphim, they ask for a true communion and descent of the Spirit and make requests for the living and departed. C. L. Beukers argued that the reference

14 E. C. Cutrone, 'Cyril's Mystagogical Catechesis and the Evolution of the Jerusalem Anaphora', *Orientalia Christiana Periodica* 44 (1978), pp. 52–64.

15 Edward Yarnold, 'Anaphoras without Institution Narratives?', *Studia Patristica* 30 (1997), pp. 395–410; Anthony Gelston, 'Cyril of Jerusalem's Eucharistic Prayer: The Argument from Silence', *Studia Patristica* 46 (2010), pp. 301–5.

16 Robert F. Taft, 'Was the Eucharistic Anaphora Recited Secretly or Aloud? The Ancient Tradition and What Became of It', in Roberta R. Ervine (ed.), *Worship Traditions in Armenia and the Neighboring Christian East*, Crestwood: St Vladimir's Seminary Press and St Nersess Armenian Seminary, 2006, pp. 15–57; Gregory Woolfenden, 'Praying the Anaphora: Aloud or in Silence', *St Vladimir's Theological Quarterly* 51 (2007), pp. 179–202. See also Stig Simeon R. Frøyshov, 'The Early Development of the Liturgical Eight-Mode System in Jerusalem', *St Vladimir's Theological Quarterly* 51 (2007), pp. 139–78; John Arthur Smith, *Music in Ancient Judaism and Early Christianity*, Farnham: Ashgate, 2011; Alan Cabaniss, *Pattern in Early Christian Worship*, Macon: Mercer University Press, 1989, p. 16.

17 It may be noted that the post-Sanctus of the Syriac Anaphora of St James is said silently, though the Institution Narrative is chanted; in Greek James, only the interpretative words of Jesus are intoned aloud.

18 Geoffrey Cuming, 'Egyptian Elements in the Jerusalem Liturgy', *Journal of Theological Studies* 25 (1974), pp. 117–24. See Bryan D. Spinks, 'The Jerusalem Liturgy of the Catecheses Mystagogae: Syrian or Egyptian', *Studia Patristica* 17.2 (1989), pp. 391–5. This paper was given at the Oxford Patristic Conference 1983, after which Cuming announced to the audience that he had changed his mind on this matter, but he never recorded this change of mind in print.

for emperors in the plural pointed to the time when the Empire was led by two emperors and hence is to be dated 382, though others have seen the plural as simply reflecting the general prayer as commended in 1 Timothy 2.2.[19] For Cyril, the Epiklesis seems to be of paramount importance, and it asks for the Spirit to be sent (ἐξαποστεῖλαι) and that the elements be made (ποιήσῃ) the body and blood of Christ, 'for whatsoever the Holy Spirit has touched is sanctified and changed'. If Macarius' letter to the Armenians is to be dated 335, then even at that time the Epiklesis was regarded as the important part of the Eucharist, for the letter remarks, 'the tale of expiation is behind the veil, where the Holy Spirit descends'.[20] In *MC* the Eucharist is a spiritual sacrifice and a sacrifice of propitiation, and thus requests for living and departed can be made. The main emphases seem to be praise as creation's hymn, eschatology (realized for the congregation joining with angels to sing Sanctus, and future for the departed), presence in the elements, and the rite is regarded as a sacrifice.

Theodore of Mopsuestia (*c.* 350–428)

Theodore was a presbyter at Antioch for ten years and a close friend of St John Chrysostom. He became Bishop of Mopsuestia in 392. It is possible that his catechetical homilies were delivered when he was a presbyter at Antioch, but equally possible that they were delivered at Mopsuestia. In his lifetime Theodore was a respected teacher of the Church, and he died in 428. In the later christological controversy between Cyril of Alexandria and Nestorius of Constantinople, Theodore's memory came under a cloud since he had been Nestorius' teacher. In 553, in a failed attempt to heal the divisions that stemmed from the Council of Chalcedon in 451, Theodore was posthumously condemned and his works destroyed. The catechetical homilies survive in Syriac translation, conserved in the Church of the East tradition. However, it is clear that his teaching on matters liturgical was influential throughout the East, before and after his condemnation.

The homilies are each preceded by what might be termed a short synopsis, entitled in Syriac *sūrat ktāb*. A. Mingana, in his edition, called these a synopsis.[21] The French edition of Tonneau and Devreesse translated it as 'texte du livre' and understood it to be an 'ordo', or service summary, of which the homily was an expansion – the very opposite of a synopsis of the homilies.[22] This latter view was accepted by Enrico Mazza, who has argued that the 'ordo' preserves an outline of the liturgy of the early part of the fourth century which Theodore has had to expand in the homilies, since the liturgy of his day or area

19 C. L. Beukers, 'For Our Emperors, Soldiers and Allies': An Attempt at Dating the Twenty-third Catechesis by Cyrillus of Jerusalem', *Vigiliae Christianae* 15 (1961), pp. 177–84.

20 Terian, *Macarius of Jerusalem*, p. 91.

21 A. Mingana, *Commentary of Theodore of Mopsuestia on the Lord's Prayer and on the Sacraments of Baptism and the Eucharist*, Woodbrooke Studies 6, Cambridge: Heffers, 1933.

22 R. Tonneau and Robert Devreesse, *Les Homélies Catéchétiques de Théodore de Mopsueste*, Rome: Vatican City, 1949.

was more fully developed.[23] More recently Clemens Leonhard has convincingly shown this to be erroneous. Theodore wrote in Greek. The *sūrat ktāb* quotes the Peshitta and is an eighth-century summary or synopsis by the Church of the East redactor of each of the homilies. The summaries might tell us something of the Church of the East liturgy, but they most certainly do not represent an 'ordo' that was earlier than Theodore's homilies.[24]

According to Theodore, Christ truly acts in the Eucharist, but he does so through the mediation of the visible priest. The priest mediates and renders present the action of Christ, who is imaged in the liturgical actions.[25] Using Neoplatonist thought, the liturgical action mirrors the divine reality. The actions of the liturgy represent various stages of the life and work of Christ. Thus he wrote:

> This, then, is the reason why he gave us the bread and the chalice: these are the food and the drink which keep us alive in this world. But he called the bread his body and the chalice his blood because the passion affected his body and wounded it and made his blood flow. He used food and drink as symbols of the two means of his passion, his body and blood, in order to make known to us our enduring, immortal life, in expectation of which we receive this sacrament which gives us, so we believe, a firm hope of the blessings to come.[26]

Like Cyril, he attached great importance to the work of the Spirit in the Eucharist. He argued that just as the Spirit gave immortality to the dead Christ in the resurrection, so the bread and wine become life-giving because of the descent of the grace of the Holy Spirit that transforms them.[27] The bread and wine are memorials of the passion, and therefore what 'we perform in the liturgy is a kind of sacrifice'.[28] The bishop (high priest) 'performs a kind of representation of the liturgy of this sacrifice that is too great for words. By this means he performs for you a visible representation of these indescribable heavenly realities and of the spiritual, immaterial powers.'[29]

Deacons, wearing a stole on their left shoulder, represent angels and ministering spirits. When they bring out the bread and wine Theodore exhorts his listeners to 'imagine that Christ our Lord is being led out to his passion'.[30] They bring up the bread and place it on the altar to complete the representation of the passion, 'so from now on we should consider that Christ has already undergone

23 Enrico Mazza, *The Origins of the Eucharistic Prayer*, Collegeville: Liturgical Press, 1995, pp. 287–331.

24 Clemens Leonhard, 'Did Theodore of Mopsuestia Quote an Ancient "Ordo"?', *Studia Liturgica* 34 (2004), pp. 191–204.

25 See Frederick G. McLeod, 'The Christological Ramifications of Theodore of Mopsuestia's Understanding of Baptism and the Eucharist', *Journal of Early Christian Studies* 10 (2002), pp. 37–75.

26 'Homily 4:9', in Edward Yarnold, *The Awe-Inspiring Rites of Initiation: The Origins of the RCIA*, Collegeville: Liturgical Press, 1994, p. 215.

27 'Homily 4:11', in Yarnold, *Awe-Inspiring Rites of Initiation*, p. 217.

28 'Homily 4:11', in Yarnold, *Awe-Inspiring Rites of Initiation*, p. 219.

29 'Homily 4:15' and '21', in Yarnold, *Awe-Inspiring Rites of Initiation*, pp. 219 and 224.

30 'Homily 4:23' and '25', in Yarnold, *Awe-Inspiring Rites of Initiation*, pp. 225 and 227.

the passion and is now placed on the altar as if in a tomb'.[31] It is interesting that in Theodore's theology, the bread and wine already are in some sense the body and blood of Christ – the dead, lifeless body. The deacons spread the cloth on the altar, and this represents the dead body of Christ being laid out in the tomb. Theodore continued:

> So now we re-enact this angelic service in commemoration of those who during the Lord's passion and death at every moment came and stood by. This is why the deacons stand round waving their fans, offering a kind of honour and veneration to the body that is laid out on the altar; in keeping it free from the filth of bird-droppings, they remind all present to regard the body as awesome and truly holy, for by virtue of its union with the divine nature it is truly the Lord. So it is right that they should lay it out, and stand watch by it with great reverence.[32]

In Theodore's tradition at this time, this ceremonial laying of the table took place in silence.[33] The silence is broken when the bishop says the prayer over the offerings, which included asking for grace to be made worthy of this ministry. Next come the Peace and the exchange of the Kiss of Peace, followed by the Washing of Hands and the Diptychs (the commemoration of the living and the dead).[34] The bishop then comes forward 'to perform the liturgy', which seems to refer to the Anaphora and Communion, and these are outlined in Homily 5.

Theodore outlines the opening dialogue of the anaphora, beginning with the Grace (2 Cor. 13.14), 'Lift up your hearts' and 'Let us give thanks to the Lord'.[35] The bishop, 'filled with awe', is the tongue of the Church and speaks words of praise, giving adoration and worship to the majesty of the Father, Son and Spirit, a trinitarian focus.[36] All creation and especially the invisible powers praise God, and this leads to the Sanctus. After the Sanctus, Theodore explained:

> Then he proclaims the transcendent mercy that God bestowed on us when he revealed his plan for us in Christ. For Christ, 'though he was in the form of God,' determined to 'take the form of a servant'; he assumed a perfect and complete man for the salvation of the human race, thus cancelling the ancient and cruel burdens of the law and death's long-established hold over us, and conferring upon us favours beyond our description or comprehension. For Christ our Lord accepted the passion in order to exterminate death utterly by his resurrection; and he has promised that we too can share with him in the enjoyment of this future.
>
> So it was necessary for Christ to give us this mystery with its power to lead on to our future. Through it we are born again in the sign of baptism, commemorate our Lord's death by this dread liturgy, and receive his body and

31 'Homily 4:26', in Yarnold, *Awe-Inspiring Rites of Initiation*, p. 228.
32 'Homily 4:27', in Yarnold, *Awe-Inspiring Rites of Initiation*, p. 229.
33 'Homily 4:28', in Yarnold, *Awe-Inspiring Rites of Initiation*, p. 229.
34 Robert Taft, *The Diptychs*, Rome: Pontificium Institutum Studiorum Orientalium, 1991.
35 'Homily 5:2–4', in Yarnold, *Awe-Inspiring Rites of Initiation*, pp. 239–41.
36 'Homily 5:5', in Yarnold, *Awe-Inspiring Rites of Initiation*, p. 241.

> blood as our immortal and spiritual food. When he was about to go to meet his passion, he bequeathed this food to his disciples, so that we might receive his body and blood by means of this bread and wine – we who all believe in Christ and continue to commemorate his death.[37]

Since Theodore immediately moves to discuss the Epiklesis of the Spirit, there has been speculation as to whether or not his anaphora included a recitation of the Institution Narrative and how this might relate to Cyril and to Addai and Mari. Though implied above, it is certainly not quoted. However, it may be that this is because in the anaphora known to Theodore, as in many anaphoras of the West Syrian shape, the narrative is simply the climax of the salvific work of Christ, and not regarded as a 'consecratory formula'. It is clear from Homily 4 and other writings of Theodore, that the narrative was important for his Christology, in that it was part of the obedience of his humanity in keeping the law to observe the Passover. He wrote:

> It was necessary that He also should perform this service according to the Divine law, which was something that harmonised with the (Mosaic) law; and if He did not perform a priestly service according to the law, He would not have been a high priest, as He would then be performing a priestly service not according to the law of God.[38]

As with *MC*, it is impossible to give a definitive opinion on whether Theodore's anaphora contained the Words of Institution or not, but it is clear that, as with *MC*, it was the Epiklesis that held great importance for him. For Theodore, since the bread and wine typify the slain body and blood of Christ, the Epiklesis is needed for the 'resurrection' of the elements, or rather, to make them life-giving for the communicants. So Theodore wrote:

> Just as our Lord's body was clearly revealed as immortal when it had received the Spirit and his anointing, so too in the liturgy the bread and wine that have been offered receive at the coming of the Holy Spirit a kind of anointing by the grace that comes upon them. From this moment we believe that they are the body and blood of Christ, free from death, corruption, suffering and change, like our Lord's body after the resurrection.[39]

The Epiklesis was for the *grace* of the Holy Spirit, and it was for the elements *and* the congregation. There followed commemorations of the living and the dead. Theodore also gave an extended explanation of the signing of the cross over the elements and the Fraction and the Commixture – the dropping of a piece of the bread into the chalice. He also explained that the bishop concluded

37 'Homily 5:10', in Yarnold, *Awe-Inspiring Rites of Initiation*, pp. 244–5.

38 Theodore of Mopsuestia, 'VI.80', in A. Mingana (ed.), *Woodbrooke Studies, Vol. 5: Commentary of Theodore of Mopsuestia on the Nicene Creed*, Cambridge: Heffers, 1932. See Bryan D. Spinks, 'Theodore of Mopsuestia and the Institution Narrative in the East Syrian Anaphora', *Studia Patristica* 40 (2006), pp. 109–14.

39 Cyril, 'Homily 5:12', in Yarnold, *Awe-Inspiring Rites of Initiation*, p. 246.

with a prayer asking God to 'approve of the sacrifice, and that the grace of the Holy Spirit may come upon the world'. He also announced, 'What is holy for the holy' as an invitation to communion. The people replied, 'One holy Father, one holy Son, one Holy Spirit' and 'Glory be to the Father and to the Son and to the Holy Spirit to the ages of ages. Amen.' And thus, 'We receive from the dread, ineffable altar an immortal and holy food.' The bread is received in the right hand.

Reviewing Theodore's outline, the Fraction has attracted some symbolic actions though no formulae are mentioned, and likewise the deacons brought the bread and wine in silence. The Communion, however, does have a brief preparation with dialogue between celebrant and people. Theodore's theology of the Eucharist, in summary, is that the actions as a whole somehow re-present the suffering, death and resurrection of Jesus, and the calling of the Holy Spirit on the elements makes them 'alive', or the life-giving body and blood of Jesus for those who receive. His anaphora praised God and included the Sanctus, and a rehearsal of the salvific work of Christ, perhaps with quotations from Philippians 2.9–11, though it is not positively asserted that the Institution Narrative was rehearsed. It certainly had an Epiklesis asking for the grace of the Holy Spirit on the elements and people, and commemorations of the living and the dead. Theodore refers to the Eucharist as a sacrifice and offering, but his emphasis is very much on the Holy Spirit 'raising from the dead' the bread and wine to be the body and blood of Christ. Thus the Eucharist is a representation of the resurrection, and is itself an eschatological sign.

The Syrian tradition and Ephrem (*c.* 306–73)

In 1920 Ignatius Rahmani published a short Syriac commentary on baptism and the Eucharist.[40] Its attribution to St John Chrysostom is incorrect for many reasons, but Sebastian Brock has republished the text along with a Sogdian translation, and he dates it to the early fifth century.[41] It was later used and expanded in different ways by East and West Syrian commentators. It mentions the reading of the Scriptures, the exchange of peace, and like Theodore, describes the altar as the place of Christ's sepulchre, and that '[t]he bread and wine on it are a symbol of the body of Jesus Christ, (the body) in which blood was also present'.[42] The priest represents the soul of Christ, the tongue of the ecclesial assembly, and a 'painter who depicts spiritual things in the Mysteries'.[43] It mentions the Sanctus, the deacons 'bending down', the Lord's Prayer, the 'Holy to the Holy', communion, and a thanksgiving prayer after communion.

As noted, the commentary was common to both the East and West Syrian traditions; but so also were and are the works of St Ephrem the Syrian.

40 I. E. Rahmani, *I Fasti della Chiesa Patriarchale Antiochena*, Rome: Pontificio Istitulo Orientale, 1920, reprint, Piscataway: Gorgias Press, 2010.

41 Sebastian P. Brock, 'An Early Syriac Commentary on the Liturgy', *Journal of Theological Studies* 37 (1986), pp. 387–403.

42 Brock, 'Early Syriac Commentary', p. 391.

43 Brock, 'Early Syriac Commentary', p. 391.

His theology is preserved mainly in his hymns and metrical homilies, and his teaching on the Eucharist has been the subject of an exhaustive study by Pierre Yousif, who notes that Ephrem considered the Eucharist as essentially the paschal mystery in the Church, and that is the centre of his eucharistic thinking.[44] Joseph Amar has observed:

> To express the fullness of the mystery that is Christ, Ephrem juxtaposes images of the actual body of the historical Jesus with allusions to the eucharistic body of Christ, until, like particles in a kaleidoscope, the images merge and resolve into a single, integrated whole.[45]

Ephrem's method and love of typology means that references and allusions to the Eucharist abound throughout his writings. The summary presented here will concentrate on the more obvious references.

In *Hymns on the Nativity* 4, Ephrem contrasts the temporal and limited nature of Old Testament eucharistic types and other New Testament meals with the eternal and eschatological nature of Christ's institution of the Eucharist. Thus with reference to feeding the four and five thousand:

> They consumed the seven loaves of bread that He broke, and they finished also the five loaves of bread that He multiplied.
> The one loaf of bread that He broke conquered the creation; for however much it is divided it multiplies all the more.
> Again, a great deal of Wine filled the water jugs; it was poured out and consumed although there had been a great deal.
> Although small was the drink of the cup that He gave, very great was its power – infinite.
> In the cup that accepts all wines, the mystery remains the same.
> The one loaf of bread He broke cannot be confined, and the one cup that He mingled cannot be limited. (vv. 91–5)[46]

The sacrificial nature of the Eucharist is emphasized by juxtaposition of the Paschal and other lambs with Christ the Lamb of God. At his birth the shepherds

> carried and offered to Him: suckling lamb to the Paschal Lamb, the first-born to the First-born, a sacrifice to the Sacrifice, a temporal lamb to the True Lamb. A fitting sight that a lamb to the Lamb should be offered. (*Hymns of the Nativity* 7.5)[47]

It is Christ who legitimizes the Passover of Moses:

44 Pierre Yousif, *L'Euchariste chez Saint Éphrem de Nisibe*, Rome: Pontificio Istituto Orientale, 1984, p. 400: 'Ephrem . . . considère l'Eucharistie essentiellement comme *mystère pascal dans l'Eglise*. C'est là le centre de sa pensée eucharistique'.

45 Joseph P. Amar, 'Perspectives on the Eucharist in Ephrem the Syrian', *Worship* 61 (1987), p. 446.

46 ET in Kathleen E. McVey, *Ephrem the Syrian: Hymns*, Mahwah: Paulist Press, 1989, pp. 96–7.

47 McVey, *Ephrem the Syrian*, p. 116.

> The Lamb gave Moses instructions that it (the lamb) be not cooked in water, for the spit is a sign of His Cross . . .
>
> The Lamb gave orders concerning His symbol that they should eat it with unleavened bread – new bread and new flesh to depict a symbol of His newness, for gone was the old leaven of Eve which made all stale with age. Everything had grown old and everything had wasted away, but through the unleavened bread that renovates all the leaven that ages all is made useless. Blessed is that Bread who has made everything new! (*On the Crucifixion* 2.4 and 5)[48]

This is treated at greater length in *Hymns of the Unleavened Bread*:

> The true lamb stood up and broke his body for the upright ones who had eaten the paschal lamb. *Response: Praise to the messiah who, through his body, rejected the unleavened bread of the people along with the people!*
>
> He slaughtered and ate the paschal [lamb], and he broke his body; he removed the shadow, and he gave the truth.
>
> He ate the unleavened bread, [and] in the unleavened bread, his body became for us the true unleavened bread.
>
> There the symbol was completed, [symbol] that had pursued [him] from the days of Moses until then. (19.1–4)[49]

Ephrem combines the soteriological theme of the Institution Narrative with that of the Epistle to the Hebrews:

> He broke the bread with his hands as a symbol for the sacrifice of his body. He mixed the cup with his hands as a symbol for the sacrifice of his blood. He sacrificed and offered himself, the priest of our atonement.
>
> He clothed himself in the priesthood of Melchizedek, his type, who did not offer sacrifices. He have the bread and the wine, but he dismissed the priesthood [which was] weary from libations. (*Hymns of the Unleavened Bread* 2.7–8)[50]

Two other prominent themes in Ephrem are that of presence, and the eschatological significance of the Eucharist. In *Hymns of the Nativity* 16 Ephrem says:

> Let bread and the mind portray You. Dwell in bread and in those who eat it. In hidden and revealed [form] let your church see You as [does] the one who bore You.
>
> Whoever hates your bread is like that one who hates your body. A distant one who loves Your bread [is like] a near one who cherishes Your image.

---

48 ET in Sebastian Brock and George Kiraz (eds), *Ephrem the Syrian: Selected Poems*, Provo: Brigham Young University Press, 2006, pp. 127, 129.

49 J. Edward Walters (ed.), *Hymns on the Unleavened Bread*, Piscataway: Gorgias Press, 2011, p. 84.

50 Walters, *Hymns on the Unleavened Bread*, p. 20.

> Your bread is far more honorable than Your body . . . Behold, Your image is portrayed with the blood of the grapes upon the bread and portrayed upon the heart by the finger of love with the pigments of faith. (vv. 4–5, 6, 7)[51]

Ephrem follows others of the Eastern tradition in associating the presence with the Holy Spirit, which is also 'fire':

> In Your bread there is hidden the Spirit who is not consumed, in Your Wine there dwells the fire that is not drunk: the Spirit is in Your Bread, the Fire in Your Wine – a manifest wonder, that our lips have received.
>
> To the angels who are spiritual Abraham brought food for the body, and they ate. The new miracle is that our mighty Lord has given to bodily man fire and Spirit to eat and to drink.[52]

> See, Fire and Spirit are in the womb of her who bore you, see, Fire and Spirit are in the river in which You were baptized. Fire and Spirit are in our baptismal font, in the Bread and Cup are Fire and Holy Spirit. (*Hymns of Faith* 10.8, 11, 17)[53]

In this last stanza, Ephrem draws a careful parallel between the incarnation, the proclamation of sonship at the baptism of Jesus, and the indwelling of the bread and wine – the Holy Spirit being the agent in all three. Yet the Eucharist has an eschatological purpose. As found in Irenaeus, Ephrem frequently uses the term 'medicine of life' for the Eucharist, alluding to the gift of immortality/eternal life. It is the reversal of the curse of death of the garden of paradise (*Hymns on Virginity* 31.5), and Christ's body to satisfy the hunger of death (*Hymns on Virginity* 37.5). It is a wedding feast (*Hymns of Faith* 10.18).

Does Ephrem tell us anything about the anaphora he was familiar with? In Sermon 4 he alluded to the Institution Narrative, and this has raised speculation as to whether he is referring to an anaphoral Institution Narrative, particularly since he has Jesus saying 'and when you are gathered together in my name . . . do in my memory that which I have done'.[54] A similar 'gathered in my name' is found in Aphrahat, and (as discussed later) in the East Syrian Anaphora of Theodore the Interpreter; it has been surmised by Bernard Botte that a similar form of narrative was originally in Addai and Mari and subsequently fell out.[55] However, quite apart from the unlikelihood of Addai and Mari having had a narrative, Ephrem's allusions are spread through several lines of his sermon, and not as a single block, and may simply be poetic allusion to the biblical narrative that he is discussing. In a recent essay, Andrew Palmer has suggested that the liturgy of Edessa is reflected in Ephrem's *Hymns of Faith*

---

51 McVey, *Ephrem the Syrian*, p. 149–50.

52 Brock and Kiraz, *Ephrem the Syrian*, p. 207.

53 Brock and Kiraz, *Ephrem the Syrian*, p. 211.

54 Edmund Beck, *Ephraem Syrus: Sermones in Hebdomadam Sanctam*, Louvain: CSCO, 1979, t.181, p. 32.

55 Bernard Botte, 'L'Anaphore Chaldéenne des Apôtres', *Orientalia Christiana Peridoica* 15 (1949), pp. 273–4. The narrative in Aphraat is in *De Pasch.*

4 and 5, which are dated to 372.[56] He draws attention to possible parallels regarding Daniel 7.10 and the Sanctus of Addai and Mari, but it may be simply that both Addai and Mari and Ephrem are using Daniel 7.10. Little else in the *Hymns* convincingly parallels the anaphora. Ephrem may make many allusions to the liturgy, but they are too buried in his poetic images to be of significant help. However, his reverend treatment of the mystery of the Eucharist with metaphor and image rather than philosophical discussion is key to this more Semitic theological approach. *Raza* (*rozo*), mystery, is the means by which God reveals himself to humanity, and although potentially anything could be a *raza*, for Ephrem the Eucharist is certainly a most crucial mystery by which God manifests himself to the Church.[57]

John Chrysostom

John Chrysostom was born in Antioch *c.* 347, and in 374/5 became a monk. He was ordained presbyter in 381, and gained a reputation as an eloquent and effectual preacher. His appointment as Bishop of Constantinople was not a success, and he made many enemies. He was finally deposed and lived in exile until his death in 407. He preached a good number of catechetical homilies on baptism, but his eucharistic teaching has to be gleaned from passing references and commentaries. In a homily on Matthew 26.26–28, Chrysostom contrasts the type (the Passover) with the truth (the Last Supper). Jesus '[gave] thanks, to teach how we ought to celebrate this sacrament, and to show that not unwillingly doth He come to the passion, and to teach us whatever we may suffer to bear it thankfully, thence also suggesting good hopes'.[58] In a homily on 1 Corinthians he called the Eucharist 'awful mysteries', though his main concern here was to stress the one body of the Church and the need for liberality and love, particularly of the poor.[59] In his *Treatise on Priesthood*, Chrysostom wrote:

> For the priestly office is indeed discharged on earth, but it ranks among heavenly ordinances; and very naturally so: for neither man, nor angel, nor archangel, nor any other created power, but the Paraclete Himself, instituted this vocation, and persuaded men while still abiding in the flesh to represent the ministry of angels. Wherefore the consecrated priest ought to be as pure as if he were standing in the heavens themselves in the midst of those powers. Fearful, indeed, and of most awful import, were the things which were used

56 Andrew Palmer, 'The Fourth-Century Liturgy of Edessa Reflected in Epraim's *Madroshe* 4 and 5 on Faith', in István Perczel, Réka Forrai and György Geréby (eds), *The Eucharist in Theology and Philosophy: Issues of Doctrinal History in East and West from the Patristic Age to the Reformation*, Leuven: Leuven University Press, 2005, pp. 320–62.

57 Bryan D. Spinks, 'Sacramental Theology in the East Syrian Tradition', *Moscow Theological Conference* (in Russian), Moscow, 2009, vol. III, pp. 537–51, English: http://petru440.livejournal.com/258975.html.

58 John Chrysostom, 'Homilies on Matthew, Homily 28', Christian Classics Ethereal Library, http://www.ccel.org/ccel/schaff/npnf110.toc.html.

59 John Chrysostom, 'Homilies on 1 Corinthians, Homily 24', New Advent, http://www.newadvent.org/fathers/220124.htm.

before the dispensation of grace, as the bells, the pomegranates, the stones on the breastplate and on the ephod, the girdle, the mitre, the long robe, the plate of gold, the holy of holies, the deep silence within. But if any one should examine the things which belong to the dispensation of grace, he will find that, small as they are, yet are they fearful and full of awe, and that what was spoken concerning the law is true in this case also, that 'what has been made glorious has no glory in this respect by reason of the glory which excels'. For when you see the Lord sacrificed, and laid upon the altar, and the priest standing and praying over the victim, and all the worshippers empurpled with that precious blood, can you then think that you are still among men, and standing upon the earth? Are you not, on the contrary, straightway translated to Heaven, and casting out every carnal thought from the soul, do you not with disembodied spirit and pure reason contemplate the things which are in Heaven? Oh! What a marvel! What love of God to man! He who sits on high with the Father is at that hour held in the hands of all, and gives Himself to those who are willing to embrace and grasp Him. And this all do through the eyes of faith! Do these things seem to you fit to be despised, or such as to make it possible for any one to be uplifted against them?

Would you also learn from another miracle the exceeding sanctity of this office? Picture Elijah and the vast multitude standing around him, and the sacrifice laid upon the altar of stones, and all the rest of the people hushed into a deep silence while the prophet alone offers up prayer: then the sudden rush of fire from Heaven upon the sacrifice – these are marvellous things, charged with terror. Now then pass from this scene to the rites which are celebrated in the present day; they are not only marvellous to behold, but transcendent in terror. There stands the priest, not bringing down fire from Heaven, but the Holy Spirit: and he makes prolonged supplication, not that some flame sent down from on high may consume the offerings, but that grace descending on the sacrifice may thereby enlighten the souls of all, and render them more refulgent than silver purified by fire. Who can despise this most awful mystery, unless he is stark mad and senseless? Or do you not know that no human soul could have endured that fire in the sacrifice, but all would have been utterly consumed, had not the assistance of God's grace been great.[60]

The Eucharist is given a sacrificial dimension, no doubt helped by the title of his treatise and reflecting a duty of priesthood, namely 'to offer'. He also seems to allude to the Epiklesis in the anaphora. It may be that in a homily on Ephesians Chrysostom alludes to the anaphoral Sanctus.[61] However, much discussion has centred on the meaning of his statement in his *Homily on the Betrayal of Judas* 1.6.

For it is not man that makes the oblations become (*proskeimena genesthai*) the body and blood of Christ, but this one, the Christ crucified for us. Sup-

60 John Chrysostom, 'On the Priesthood, Book III', New Advent, http://www.newadvent.org/fathers/19223.htm.

61 John Chrysostom, 'Homilies on Ephesians, Homily 14', http://www.sacred-texts.com/chr/ecf/113/1130027.htm.

> plying the outward appearance, the priest stands upright, proclaiming those words. But the power and the grace are of God. 'This is my body,' he says. This word refashions (*metarruthmizei*) the oblations. And just as that utterance which said, 'Be fertile, and multiply, and fill the earth', indeed was spoken once, became deed empowering our nature for procreation for all time; so, too, this utterance, once spoken, at each table in the churches from until today and until his second coming produces the completed sacrifice.[62]

Some have argued that Chrysostom taught that the recitation of the Words of Institution were consecratory, rather than the Epiklesis of the Spirit. It is unlikely that Chrysostom saw the need for an either/or, but accepted a both/and on this question. It does appear that he assumed that the words were recited in the anaphoras known to him. Whether that anaphora is the Greek anaphora that bears his name will be discussed later in this study.

Ambrose of Milan (339–397)

Ambrose was born in Trier in 339, and was elected Bishop of Milan in 373, following the death of the Arian bishop Auxentius. His thoughts on the Eucharist are mainly to be found in *De Mysteriis* and *De Sacramentis*. In the former, Ambrose seems to imply that the Words of Institution play a crucial role in the elements becoming the body and blood of Christ. Noting the Old Testament 'miraculous' changes of various elements, he argued:

> Marah was a most bitter stream, so that the thirsting people could not drink. Moses cast wood into the water, and the water lost its bitterness, which grace of a sudden tempered. (Exodus 15:25). In the time of Elisha the prophet one of the sons of the prophets lost the head from his axe, which sank. He who had lost the iron asked Elisha, who cast in a piece of wood and the iron swam. This, too, we clearly recognize as having happened contrary to nature, for iron is of heavier nature than water.
>
> We observe, then, that grace has more power than nature, and yet so far we have only spoken of the grace of a prophet's blessing. But if the blessing of man had such power as to change nature, what are we to say of that divine consecration where the very words of the Lord and Saviour operate? For that sacrament which you receive is made what it is by the word of Christ. But if the word of Elijah had such power as to bring down fire from heaven, shall not the word of Christ have power to change the nature of the elements? You read concerning the making of the whole world: '*He spoke and they were made, He commanded and they were created.*' Shall not the word of Christ, which was able to make out of nothing that which was not, be able to change things which already are into what they were not? For it is not less to give a new nature to things than to change them.

62 John Chrysostom, 'Homily on the Betrayal of Judas 1.6', ET in Edward J. Kilmartin, 'John Chrysostom's Influence on Gabriel Qatraya's Theology of Eucharistic Consecration', in *Theological Studies* 42 (1981), pp. 444–57, p. 452.

But why make use of arguments? Let us use the examples He gives, and by the example of the Incarnation prove the truth of the mystery. Did the course of nature proceed as usual when the Lord Jesus was born of Mary? If we look to the usual course, a woman ordinarily conceives after connection with a man. And this body which we make is that which was born of the Virgin. Why do you seek the order of nature in the Body of Christ, seeing that the Lord Jesus Himself was born of a Virgin, not according to nature? It is the true Flesh of Christ which was crucified and buried, this is then truly the Sacrament of His Body.

The Lord Jesus Himself proclaims: 'This is My Body.' (Matthew 26:26.) Before the blessing of the heavenly words another nature is spoken of, after the consecration the Body is signified. He Himself speaks of His Blood. Before the consecration it has another name, after it is called Blood. And you say, Amen, that is, It is true. Let the heart within confess what the mouth utters, let the soul feel what the voice speaks.

Christ, then, feeds His Church with these sacraments, by means of which the substance of the soul is strengthened.[63]

The logic seems to be that if prophetic words caused changes in the Old Testament, and if Christ was born of a virgin, then the creative word of God needs no justification when bread and wine are received as the body and blood of Christ. Edward Kilmartin saw a parallel here with John Chrysostom and suggested that when Ambrose became a bishop he immersed himself in the Greek Fathers, and Chrysostom was his inspiration here. However, Kilmartin added that since Ambrose did not have the 'Platonic horizon of thought' of the Greek theologians, his interpretation took a rather different trajectory in the Latin-speaking world.[64]

In *De Sacramentis*, Ambrose not only discusses the meaning of the Eucharist, but also quotes portions of an anaphora that has many similarities with that of Rome, but also sufficient differences which have parallels in a *Post Secreta* in the *Missale Gothicum* and a *Post Pridie* in the *Liber Ordinam* for some to suggest it is more akin to 'Gallican' or 'Hispano-Mozarabic' anaphoras.[65] It is perhaps best regarded as distinctly Milanese.

Ambrose appealed to the Epistle of the Hebrews to show that Christian mysteries or sacraments were older than Jewish mysteries, since it was Melchizedek and not Abraham who brought forth bread and wine.[66] However, Melchizedek is none other than Christ.[67] A little later Ambrose argues as he did in *De Mysteriis*, namely that at the consecration the bread becomes the body of Christ on account of Christ's word that brings sacraments into existence:

63 Ambrose of Milan, 'On the Mysteries', 9: 51–55, http://www.newadvent.org/fathers/3405.htm.

64 Edward J. Kilmartin, *The Eucharist in the West: History and Theology*, Collegeville: Liturgical Press, 1998, pp. 15 and 21.

65 Matthieu Smyth, *La Liturgie Oubliée: La Priére Eucharistique en Gaule antique et dans l'Occident non Roman*, Paris: Les Éditions du Cerf, 2003, pp. 38–47.

66 Ambrose, '*De Sacramentis* 4.10', in Yarnold, *Awe-Inspiring Rites of Initiation*, p. 131.

67 Ambrose, '*De Sacramentis* 4.13', in Yarnold, *Awe-Inspiring Rites of Initiation*, p. 132.

> before consecration it was not the body of Christ, but after the consecration I tell you that it is now the body of Christ. He spoke and it was made, he commanded and it was created . . . and that, though wine and water are poured into the chalice, through the consecration effected by the heavenly word it becomes his blood.[68]

Ambrose then asks if his readers wish to know how the consecration takes place by the power of the heavenly words, and quotes from an anaphora:

> The bishop says: *Make for us this offering approved, reasonable, acceptable, because it is the figure of the body and blood of our Lord Jesus Christ; who, the day before he suffered, took bread in his holy hands, looked up to heaven to you, holy Father, almighty, eternal God, and gave thanks, blessed, and broke it, and handed it when broken to his apostles and disciples, saying, 'Take and eat from this, all of you; for this is my body, which will be broken for many.'*
>
> Notice this. *Likewise after supper, the day before he suffered, he took the cup, looked up to heaven to you, holy Father, almighty, eternal God, gave thanks, blessed, and handed it to his apostles and disciples, saying: 'Take and drink from this, all of you, for this is my blood.'* See, all those words up to 'Take,' whether the body or the blood, are the evangelist's; then they are Christ's words, 'Take and drink from this, all of you; for this is my blood'.
>
> Notice these points. He says, 'Who, the day before he suffered, took bread in his holy hands.' Before it is consecrated, it is bread; but when the words of Christ are added, it is the body of Christ. Then hear his words: 'Take and eat from this, all of you; for this is my body'. And before the words of Christ, the cup is full of wine and water; when the words of Christ have been employed, the blood is created which redeems his people. So you see in what ways the word of Christ has power to change everything. Our Lord Jesus himself therefore bore witness that we should receive his body and blood. Ought we to doubt his faith and witness? . . .
>
> So you do not say 'Amen' to no purpose: you confess in spirit that you are receiving the body of Christ. When you seek it, the bishop says to you, 'The body of Christ,' and you say 'Amen,' which means 'It is true'. What your tongue confesses, let your feelings retain, so that you may know that this is a sacrament whose likeness has come first.
>
> Now you must learn how great a sacrament it is. See what he says: 'As often as you do this, so often you will make remembrance of me until I come again.'
>
> And the bishop, says: *Therefore, remembering his most glorious Passion and resurrection from the dead, and ascension into heaven, we offer to you this spotless victim, reasonable victim, bloodless victim, this holy bread and this cup of eternal life; and we pray and beseech you to receive this offering on your altar on high by the hands of your angels, as you vouchsafed to receive*

68 Ambrose, '*De Sacramentis* 4.16', and '19', in Yarnold, *Awe-Inspiring Rites of Initiation*, pp. 134–5.

the gifts of your righteous servant Abel, and the sacrifice of our patriarch Abraham, and that which the high priest Melchizedek offered to you.[69]

Ambrose suggests that repetition of the Words of Institution is an important factor in the bread and wine becoming the figure (*figura*) of the body and blood of Christ, and he carefully distinguished the prayers and petitions of the priest from the 'Word of God' that brings about the sacrament. In *De fide*, Ambrose wrote: 'However as often as we receive the sacraments, which are transfigured [*transfigurantur*] by the mystery of the holy prayer into the flesh and blood, we proclaim the death of the Lord.'[70] Edward Kilmartin has argued that divorced from the Greek platonic background, Ambrose's teaching would lead to a somatic presence that was seen as directly opposed to a 'spiritual' presence. He also suggests that the teaching of Ambrose in *De officiis ministrorum*, as well as in *De Sacramentis*, was that the Eucharist is a sacrifice offered by Christ the High Priest and the congregation, which was significantly different from the Greek concept of Anamnesis or commemoration of the sacrifice of the cross.[71] It is significant that the anaphora to which Ambrose alludes apparently had no explicit petition for the Spirit to come upon the bread and wine, but simply a request (of course one could argue that the request is made 'in the Spirit') for the Father to approve what is the figure of the body and blood of Christ, and that becomes the body and blood of Christ when Christ's eternal Logos in the Words of Institution are uttered. What is offered is the *immaculatam hostiam*, the spotless sacrifice or victim, though it seems to be also a reference to the Church itself as the body of Christ.[72]

Augustine of Hippo (354–430)

If Ambrose gives a window into the West as represented by Milan, his famous convert Augustine gives us a perspective as a North African Latin theologian. Augustine tells us very little about the eucharistic rite of his day, though Van Der Meer confidently reconstructed a 'Sunday in Hippo'.[73] Augustine is important for the particular framework for understanding knowledge, including sacraments, with the distinction of *res* (things, reality) and *signum* (signs that point to a reality). As R. A. Markus points out, for Augustine *signum* played an important part in the meanings of Scripture, but also the theory of language, his discussion of miracles, of the relation of God to the world, and human knowledge of the world and self-knowledge.[74] In his work of 389, *De Magistro*, Augustine discussed the meaning of signs and of spoken words, suggesting that the purpose of both is either to teach or to remind. Speech is a recalling to mind

69 ET from *PEER*, pp. 145–6. The italics here are confined to allusions to the Roman *canon missae*.

70 Ambrose, '*De fide* 4.10.124', in Kilmartin, *Eucharist in the West*, p. 17.

71 Kilmartin, *Eucharist in the West*, pp. 18–19.

72 Kilmartin, *Eucharist in the West*, pp. 20–1.

73 F. Van Der Meer, *Augustine the Bishop*, London and New York: Sheed and Ward, 1961, pp. 388–402.

74 R. A. Markus, 'St Augustine on Signs', *Phronesis* 2 (1957), p. 60.

since the memory is where words are stored, and in considering them there is brought to mind the realities of which the words are signs. Signs direct us to things. He returned to this in more detail in his *De Doctrine Christiana*. There, as Rowan Williams has noted, God is supremely *res*, thing, and he has provided a *signum* in the Word made flesh.[75] Most signs relate to thought, but some relate to sight, some to hearing and some to taste, 'and in the sacrament of His body and blood He signified His will through the sense of taste'.[76] Sacraments are thus signs that point to a reality. Kilmartin recalls Augustine's words in *Enarrationes in Psalmos* 98.9, where he said:

> Understand spiritually what I have spoken. It is not the body, which you see, that you will eat, nor drink that blood which is shed . . . I have commended to you a sacrament; understand spiritually, it will make you live.[77]

According to Kilmartin, Augustine's stress on faith or belief results in the corporal visible sign in the sacrament losing something of its importance, since it is only a necessary step to attain the invisible, the eternal, or the *res*.[78]

In a sermon on Easter, Augustine wrote:

> we come now to what is done in the holy prayers which you are going to hear, that with the application of the word we may have the body and blood of Christ. Take away the word, I mean, it is just bread and wine; add the word, and it is now something else. And what is that something else? The body of Christ, and the blood of Christ. So take away the word, it is bread and wine; add the word and it will become a sacrament.[79]

This would appear to refer to the Words of Institution as being necessary to interpret the signs so they point to the proper *res*. Yet in his work on the Trinity, between 399 and 412, he wrote that by means of signs the apostle Paul

> was able to proclaim the Lord Jesus Christ, either through his speech, through a letter, or through the sacraments of the Lord's Body and Blood; when we speak of Christ's Body and Blood we certainly do not refer to Paul's speech, or to the parchment and ink, or to the expressive sounds made by his tongue, or to the sign of the letters imprinted on skins. Only what is taken from the fruits of the earth and consecrated by a mystical prayer do we rightly receive to benefit our spiritual health, doing so in memory of what the Lord endured for us. Although human hands make this visible, it is only through

75 Rowan Williams, 'Language, Reality and Desire in Augustine's *De Doctrina*', *Journal of Literature and Theology* 3 (1989), pp. 138–50.

76 Augustine, 'De Doctrina Christiana II.3.4', http://www.georgetown.edu/faculty/jod/augustine/ddc.html.

77 Kilmartin, *Eucharist in the West*, p. 27.

78 Kilmartin, *Eucharist in the West*, p. 26.

79 Sermon 229.3 in *Sermons*, vol. 6, trans. Edmund Hill, ed. John Rotelle, New Rochelle: New City Press, 1993, p. 266.

> the invisible action of God's Spirit that it is sanctified to become so great a sacrament.[80]

Here 'mystical prayer' and the invisible action of the Spirit seem to be foremost for it to be a sacrament. It may be, however, that 'presence' in the elements is not Augustine's main focus for the Eucharist. In another Easter sermon he asserted:

> The bread that you see upon the altar, the bread when consecrated by the word of God, is the Body of Christ. The cup, or rather what the cup contains, when sanctified through the word of God, is the Blood of Christ. Through these Christ the Lord desired to entrust us with his Body and with his Blood, which he shed for the forgiveness of sins. If you receive them in a fitting manner, then you are what you received, for the apostle says, 'We though many are one bread, one body.'[81]

Augustine was much more concerned about Christians being worthy and being the body of Christ, and elsewhere he asserted that 'we are what we receive'.[82] This also seems to be his focus as regards the concept of sacrifice:

> Then after the sanctification of God's sacrifice, because God desired that we ourselves be his sacrifice – something made clear when the sacrifice was first instituted – and because the sacrifice is to be a sign of what we are, then when the sanctification is completed, we say the Lord's Prayer . . .[83]

The same teaching is found in *The City of God*:

> Christ is both the priest who offers as well as the victim that is offered. He desired that the sacramental sign of this should be the daily sacrifice of the Church. Since the Church is Christ's body and he is its head, the Church learns to offer itself through him.[84]

Thus Augustine emphasized the ecclesiological implications of the Eucharist; the sacramental action is a sign of the Church being the body of Christ, and itself is offered in the Eucharist. However, it is important to bear in mind that, like many theologians, Augustine did not write a systematic treatment of the Eucharist and his references to it are scattered in a variety of writings; he is not as consistent or as crystal clear as modern writers would wish.

---

80 Augustine, 'On the Trinity III. IV. 10', in Laurence J. Johnson (ed.), *Worship in the Early Church: An Anthology of Historical Sources*, vol. 3, Collegeville: Liturgical Press, 2009, p. 24.

81 Augustine, 'Sermon 227', in Johnson, *Worship in the Early Church*, p. 68.

82 Augustine, 'Sermon 57', in Johnson, *Worship in the Early Church*, p. 59.

83 Augustine, 'Sermon 227', in Johnson, *Worship in the Early Church*, p. 69.

84 Augustine, *The City of God*, 'X. 20', in Johnson, *Worship in the Early Church*, p. 33.

The classical anaphora of *Apostolic Constitutions* VIII and the anaphoral families

In contrast to the varied Eucharistic Prayer forms of the purported pre-Nicene period, those that are dated from the later fourth century onwards have a much more homogeneous form and content. They vary from geographical region, but even this is variable as will be seen. This euchological osmosis is illustrated by the anaphora found in *Apostolic Constitutions* (*AC*) VIII. In contrast with the rite outlined in *AC* VII, in *AC* VIII we have a much fuller text and rite. There is mention of lections, sermon, Litanies and prayers of dismissal, prayers for catechumens, energumens, illuminands and penitents, intercessions of the faithful which take the form of litany, the giving of the Peace, the preparation of the gifts, the anaphora, communion rites, thanksgiving for communion and dismissal. The structure accords quite well with Justin Martyr's outline, though in comparison it has been fleshed out. Justin's ritual sequence may not have been the only eucharistic sequence, but it was the one that seems to have emerged as universal by the fourth century. Justin, it will be recalled, outlined readings, homily, intercessions, the Kiss of Peace, the bringing of a cup and bread, prayers and thanksgivings and communion. Subsequent development elaborated this sequence particularly at places that Gregory Dix called second and tertiary stratum, but Robert Taft calls soft points.[85] These were at the beginning of the service, at the bringing and placing of bread and wine on the table, before receiving communion, and after communion. Assemblies at worship do not like prolonged silences, and so prayers and chants gradually filled the silence of bringing the bread and wine to the table. Preparation and worthy reception attracted devotional prayers prior to receiving communion. Additionally, a ritual act psychologically needs a gentle introduction and a gentle conclusion, thus attracting 'gathering' and 'dismissal' rites. These will be noted in passing in subsequent chapters, though only discussed in any detail where the prayer formulae shed light on developing theologies of the Eucharist.

It is interesting that we have a rubric that notes that at this point in the rite the bishop puts on a splendid robe – our first real reference to some specialized vesture. Whether it was to reflect a cultic role or had more to do with an imperial governmental role is uncertain. The identity of the compiler remains a secret until the parousia. There have been guesses. Jasper and Cuming suggest the Eunomian bishop, Julian in Cilicia *c.* 364.[86] Eunomias himself has been suggested, with parallels drawn from his writings and the *AC*.[87] On the other hand, with modern revisionist ideas on Arianism, it could be that the

85 Robert Taft, 'How Liturgies Grow: The Evolution of the Byzantine Divine Liturgy', *Orientalia Chrisiana Periodica* 43 (1977), pp. 355–78; expanded version in Robert Taft, *Beyond East and West: Problems in Liturgical Understanding*, Washington: The Pastoral Press, 1984, pp. 167–92.

86 *PEER*, p. 100.

87 Georg Wagner, 'Zur Herkunft der Apostolischen Konstitutionen', *Mélanges Liturgiques offert au R. P. Bernard Botte osb*, Louvain: Abbaye du Mont César, 1972, pp. 525–37; Thomas A. Kopecek, 'Neo-Arian Religion: The Evidence of the Apostolic Constitutions', in Robert C. Gregg (ed.), *Arianism: Historical and Theological Reassessments*, Cambridge, MA: The Philadelphia Patristic Foundation, 1985.

compiler was just an old-fashioned Eusebian.[88] The compiler has incorporated the Eucharistic Prayer found in the Latin and Ethiopic versions of the *Apostolic Tradition* (*AT*), and it may be that he knew a Greek version of this Church Order. Raphael Graves also demonstrates that the compiler used material from the Jewish–Hellenistic prayers that he had incorporated in *AC* VII, particularly in the names of Old Testament personages, and the angelic hierarchy.[89] However, he has considerably extended and enlarged the prayer to take into account contemporary (*c.* 380) usage in his region of Antioch, and Graves suggests material that has parallels in the Greek Anaphoras of St John Chrysostom and Byzantine St Basil. The compiler has also used the composition to reinforce his non-Nicene Christology for which he found support in earlier pre-Nicene sources. It is simply not known whether the anaphora was ever used, or is simply the ideal and tendentious composition of the compiler.[90] However, it does reflect some of the content of other fourth-century anaphoras that originated in this region. Bouley comments that '[t]he author has to a great extent reworked traditional material in order to produce a cohesive, carefully structured, ideal text'.[91]

The anaphora that the compiler presents begins with the Grace from 2 Corinthians, which is the common introduction in most of the Eastern rites. In contrast to the prayer of *AT* we no longer lift up our hearts, but our minds, the *nous*, which Bouyer notes is the most spiritual part of the soul in Hellenistic anthropology.[92]

There is a long thanksgiving for creation, and much of the material here is borrowed from his Jewish synagogal prayers in *AC* VII. The Father is described as knowledge, without beginning, eternal vision . . . who created all things through the only begotten Son. But the Son was begotten before the ages. That subordination is intended is shown by the later description of the Son as 'notable worshipper'. The prayer mentions cherubim, seraphim and angelic orders arranged in descending rank, followed by the visible creation. The thanksgiving is for the whole of creation of the Father, which includes the Son before the ages, the heavenly beings in descending order after the Son, and man. The fall is recounted, and Old Testament personages such as Abraham, the Exodus and finally Joshua. Then the Sanctus is introduced. Here the text says that the paraclete and Jesus worship the Father.

The Sanctus is followed by Romans 1.25, 'Blessed is he for ever. Amen.'

---

88 Joseph T. Lienhard, 'The "Arian" Controversy: Some Categories Reconsidered', *Theological Studies* 48 (1987), pp. 415–37; Rowan Williams, *Arius: Heresy and Tradition*, London: Darton, Longman and Todd, 1987; Lewis Ayres, *Nicea and Its Legacy: An Approach to Fourth-Century Trinitarian Theology*, New York: Oxford University Press, 2006.

89 Raphael Graves, 'The Anaphora of the Eighth Book of the Apostolic Constitutions', in Paul F. Bradshaw (ed.), *Essays on Early Eastern Eucharistic Prayers*, Collegeville: Liturgical Press, 2002, pp. 173–94.

90 My former teacher, Canon Arthur Couratin, used to refer to the compiler as a 'sacristy creeper' and an 'armchair liturgist'.

91 Allan Bouley, *From Freedom to Formula: The Evolution of the Eucharistic Prayer from Oral Improvisation to Written Texts*, Washington: Catholic University of America, 1981, p. 231.

92 Louis Bouyer, *Eucharist: Theology and Spirituality of the Eucharistic Prayer*, Notre Dame: University of Notre Dame Press, 1968, p. 253.

In most anaphoral traditions, the Sanctus is followed by the Benedictus, 'Hosanna in the highest. Blessed is he who comes in the name of the Lord.' The recital of Isaiah 6.3 in the synagogue is followed by Ezekiel 3.11, 'Blessed be the glory of the Lord from this place', and in the synagogal prayers of *AC* VII, the compiler reproduces the Jewish response. It has been suggested that here we have the transition from using the Jewish form, to Romans 1.25, before morphing to 'Blessed is he who comes in the Name of the Lord'. In other words, this is an early or primitive feature. That is one possible explanation. Another is that since the compiler is semi-Arian, 'Blessed is he who comes in the Name of the Lord' was too high a Christology for him, and inappropriate, and Romans 1.25 may be a deliberate substitution for the more common use of the Benedictus. Interestingly, the Benedictus occurs in *AC* VIII, but after the anaphora at the invitation to communion.

The post-Sanctus picks up on the word 'Holy' and there follows a rehearsal of redemptive history – the law, the prophets and finally Christ (the new Joshua), with a précis of the Gospel, and one or two words from *AT*.

A mini-Anamnesis introduces the Institution Narrative, but it makes it clear that the remembering is part of the thanksgiving. In other words, the narrative is a rehearsal of salvation history and not a formula for consecration.

The Anamnesis after the narrative is an expanded form of *AT*:

> Remembering then his Passion and death and resurrection from the dead, his return to heaven and his future second coming, in which he comes with glory and power to judge the living and the dead, and to reward each according to his works, we offer you, King and God, according to his commandment, this bread and this cup, giving you thanks through him that you have deemed us worthy to stand before you and to serve you as priests.[93]

Thus the bread and cup are offered, and so in some sense are regarded as a sacrifice. This Anamnesis is followed by the Epiklesis, asking God to send the Holy Spirit 'upon this sacrifice' and *apophenei* the bread the body of Christ, and the cup the blood of Christ. The Greek word for send is *katapempo*, which is also found in the Anaphora of St John Chrysostom and also associated with Antioch. The verb *apophenei* means declare or manifest. There is a sense of revelation asked for by the action of the Spirit on the elements rather than conversion. The purpose of the 'manifestation' of the elements as the body and blood of Christ is for spiritual benefits:

> that those who partake of it may be strengthened to piety, obtain forgiveness of sins, be delivered from the devil and his deceit, be filled with Holy Spirit, become worthy of your Christ, and obtain eternal life, after reconciliation with you, almighty Master.[94]

A list of intercessions follows: for the celebrant, the clergy, the temporal rulers, for departed clergy, for the congregation, the city, the sick, those in trouble,

93 *PEER*, p. 110.
94 *PEER*, p. 111.

catechumens, penitents and weather, terminating in a doxology which again subordinates the Son.

The structure and component parts of this anaphora, though in different sequence and with different arrangements, became standard in most subsequent anaphoras, and these may be divided into broad, though not exclusive, geographical families. It is unlikely that those compiling or expanding anaphoras thought of the structures and components in quite the manner outlined in the chart (see Appendix 1 on p. 446), which is mainly a convenient scholarly device. The geographical groupings are not rigid, and Egypt used, and uses, anaphoras of 'West Syrian' shape in addition to the peculiar 'Egyptian' pattern of St Mark (Greek)/St Cyril (Coptic), and these were not necessarily imported to Egypt from elsewhere.

Concluding remarks

These writings, some intended for a lay audience and some for a clerical audience (commentaries), yield some information of the shape of Eucharistic Prayers in certain places (Jerusalem, the area of Antioch, and Milan) as well as some theological reflection on the meaning of the ritual and prayers. The evidence seems to show that in the East there was interest in or excitement about the work of the Spirit in the transformation of the bread and wine, whereas in Milan at least there is no indication that there was any petition for the Spirit to come upon the elements or ritual, but rather an emphasis on the recitation of the Words of Institution as consecratory. However, this dichotomy may not have been recognized by the writers themselves at the time.

The fourth century witnessed the so-called Constantinian Peace, and the public role enjoyed by the churches resulted in changes and rapid growth. It was easier to have some sense of unity among the churches, and monarchical episcopacy emerged with bishops having jurisdiction over large geographical areas, and certain sees were accorded special importance and authority. With the cessation of persecution, larger and more lavish buildings for worship were built, and liturgy developed accordingly. It is this period that gave rise to the 'classical' anaphoras, which, though having their distinct family and local differences, also seem to have emerged in a period of osmosis or synthesis. Anaphoras tended to have common elements, even if not in the same sequence. It is noticeable that apart from *AT*, no pre-Nicene Eucharistic Prayer text includes the Institution Narrative, though this in the post-Nicene period became a *sine qua non*. Paul Bradshaw has suggested that the narrative was added to the anaphora for catechetical reasons as the liturgy itself became increasingly catechetical and didactic, perhaps in response to the increase of numbers of Christians after the Constantinian peace.[95] With the establishment of a canon of Scripture, it was perhaps also used to root out any survivals of bread and water Eucharists that were fellowship meals unconnected with the Last Supper. Maxwell Johnson has made a very plausible argument that the narrative came to be part of the anaphora as martyrdom declined. He notes that Ramsay MacMullen has argued

95 Bradshaw, *Eucharistic Origins*, pp. 140–1.

convincingly that, based on archaeological evidence of the size of church buildings, only 5 per cent of the Christian population – the elite – regularly attended the Sunday liturgy. Ninety-five per cent, the second church, flocked to cemeteries to celebrate a meal (some form of Eucharist?) at the graves of the martyrs, as well as their departed families. That fact is already noted in the *Didascalia*. The Church hierarchy responded with sermons of disapproval, and more effectively by building churches over the graves of the martyrs, and then by removing the martyrs' bodies to the inside of churches in order to lure in some of the 95 per cent.[96] Martydom as evidenced in the *Acts of the Martyrs* was seen as Christ-like living out the passion of Christ. Johnson argues that, with the decline, living out the passion was transferred to sharing the Eucharist:

> The sacrificial connotations and implications of adding the narrative of institution to the Eucharistic Prayer may well be directly related also to the cessation of martyrdom, by emphasizing the very cost of discipleship implied by sharing the cup of Christ in the Eucharist, that is, both the public liturgy and reception in holy communion of the body and blood of Christ *sacrificed*![97]

The fourth century also witnessed the Arian struggle, doctrinally settled in 325 at Nicaea but not finally settled until the late 370s; and with the Council of Constantinople, 381, a mature trinitarian theology was formulated. The fifth century, however, witnessed the christological disputes ignited by the dispute between Nestorius of Constantinople and Cyril of Alexandria, and in the wake of the Councils of Ephesus (431) and of Chalcedon (451), the division of the Eastern Churches into Chalcedonians, miaphysites and dyophysites gave rise to rival bishops and distinct rites associated with Alexandria, Jerusalem, Antioch, Constantinople and Seleucia–Ctesiphon, and then, later, Byzantine, Egyptian, Church of the East, Syrian Orthodox, Maronite, Ethiopian and Armenian rites. The West, avoiding large splits, would have liturgical families – Roman, Milanese, Gallican, Hispano-Mozarabic (Visigothic) and Celtic, giving rise to a hybrid Western rite with local uses.

---

96 Ramsay MacMullen, *The Second Church: Popular Christianity* AD *200–400*, Atlanta: Society for Biblical Literature, 2009. See also Ann Marie Yasin, *Saints and Church Spaces in the Late Antique Mediterranean*, Cambridge: Cambridge University Press, 2009.

97 Maxwell E. Johnson, 'Sharing "The Cup of Christ!": The Cessation of Martyrdom and Anaphoral Development', in Steven Hawkes-Teeples, Bert Groen and Stefanos Alexopoulos (eds), *Studies on the Liturgies of the Christian East: Selected Papers of the Third International Congress of the Society of Oriental Liturgy Volos, May 26–30, 2010*, Leuven: Peeters, 2013, pp. 109–26. Another version of this paper is entitled 'Martyrs and the Mass: The Interpolation of the Narrative of Institution into the Anaphora', *Worship* 87 (2013), pp. 2–22.

4

The Egyptian Anaphoral Traditions and the Divine Liturgy of the Coptic Orthodox Church

The Coptic Church of Egypt today is the main successor to the historic Egyptian tradition. It uses three eucharistic rites, which are preserved in both Greek and Coptic (Sahidic and Bohairic): St Basil, which is used the most frequently; St Gregory, used for seven major feasts; and St Cyril (the Greek version is named St Mark) in the month of Kiahk and in Lent.[1] Christianity in Egypt seems to have been a diffuse and decentralized movement in the first two or three centuries, and in spite of the efforts on the part of bishops, there were groups of monks and others who operated outside any central authority. At one time it seems that the bishop of Alexandria was more like a chief presbyter, elected and ordained by other presbyters. However, Alexandria became the perceived centre of the Egyptian Church, its bishop ranking second to Rome and, after 381 CE, third after Rome and Constantinople, and its liturgical use would become the standard for Egypt. It has already been noted that, in addition to the testimony of Clement of Alexandria and Origen, a number of liturgical scholars have regarded the lacunae fragment Strasbourg Papyrus Gr.254 as being a complete Egyptian 'paleoanaphora', from which the Anaphora of St Mark (Greek) and St Cyril (Coptic) may have developed. This may be the case. However, there are other anaphoras and fragments that suggest a once wider selection and pattern of anaphoras than the three that are used today in the Coptic Church, and these need to be considered.

Sarapion, Barcelona and St Thomas

There are two Egyptian anaphoras that can be dated at least to the mid or late fourth century, and they provide us with two distinct patterns of anaphora. A third, which is fragmentary, is probably late fourth or early fifth century.

The 'euchology' of Sarapion, Bishop of Thmuis in the Nile delta, *c.* 339–60, is a collection of prayers contained in an eleventh-century manuscript (MS Lavra 149) and was published first by A. Dimitrievskij in 1894 and then by

1 Ioannes Malak, 'The Eucharistic Divine Liturgy According to the Rite of the Coptic Church of Alexandria', in J. Madey (ed.), *The Eucharistic Liturgy in the Christian East*, Kottayam: Prakasam Publications and Paderborn, 1982: Ostkirchendienst, p. 11.

Georg Wobbermin in 1898.[2] Questions concerning the ordering of these prayers need not concern us unduly, other than to note that the sequence in the manuscript begins with the anaphora and is followed by a prayer for the Fraction, a laying on of hands after the Fraction, and a prayer after the distribution of communion.[3] Recent studies include those by R. Barrett-Leonard and Maxwell E. Johnson.[4]

Bernard Botte had questioned whether Sarapion was the author of this collection, since in his view there were words and phrases that pointed to the compiler being an Arian or a Pneumatomachian, and since Sarapion was a friend of Athanasius, he could not have written these. Botte preferred to speak of 'Pseudo-Sarapion'.[5] Geoffrey Cuming regarded Botte's arguments as unconvincing, and demonstrated that on Botte's evidence even Athanasius could be convicted of similar errors![6] The thorough study by Maxwell Johnson indicates that there is nothing in this collection that prevents us from accepting the attribution to Sarapion. Whether Sarapion wrote all the prayers himself, or whether some are from another hand (as a 'collection' often implies), and are thus even earlier, does not alter the mid-fourth-century *terminus ad quem* for the anaphora.

The euchology contains a number of prayers for a eucharistic service: for a prayer for Sunday, a prayer after the sermon, prayers for various groups of people and for the harvest, an anaphora, a prayer during the Fraction and a blessing and prayer after the Communion. The anaphora begins, not with thanksgiving or blessing, but with praise, hymning and glorifying the uncreated (*ageneton*, but according to Cuming probably should be read as *agenneton*, unbegotten) Father of the only-begotten Jesus Christ, and God is then described in negative epithets or alpha-privatives (*theologia negativa*), an Egyptian concern already found in Clement of Alexandria.[7] Thereafter *ainoumen*, we praise you, becomes the key praise word. God is praised for being known through the Son, one who spoke through him, and who reveals the Son to his saints. God is also praised for gifts and attributes such as the giver of immortality. This is praise to the Father for the revelation of and through the Son. Louis Bouyer described it as 'a curious mixture of Johannine imagery, tending towards a kind of harmless Gnosticism and a vaguely mystagogical philosophical jargon which was already

---

2 A. Dimitrievskij, *Ein Euchologium aus dem 4 Jahrhundert, verfasst von Sarapion Bischoff von Thmuis*, Kiev, 1894; G. Wobbermin, *Altchristliche liturgische Stücke aus der Kirche Ägyptens nebst einem dogmatischen Brief des Bischofs Serapion von Thmuis*, Leipzig and Berlin, 1898.

3 G. J. Cuming, 'Thmuis Revisited: Another Look at the Prayers of Bishop Sarapion', *Theological Studies* 41 (1980), pp. 568–75.

4 R. Barrett-Leonard, *The Sacramentary of Sarapion of Thmuis: A Text for Students*, Alcuin/GROW Liturgical Study 25, Bramcote: Grove Books, 1993; Maxwell E. Johnson, *The Prayers of Sarapion of Thmuis: A Literary, Liturgical and Theological Analysis*, Rome: Pontificio Istituto Orientale, 1995.

5 B. Botte, 'L'Eucologue de Sérapion est-il authentique?', *Oriens Christianus* 48 (1964), pp. 50–6.

6 Cuming, 'Thmuis Revisited'.

7 Clement of Alexandria, 'Stromata Book 5.12', http://www.earlychristianwritings.com/text/clement-stromata-book5.html.

present in Clement of Alexandria in the preceding century', and the Johannine backdrop at least should be borne in mind.[8]

The opening hymn of praise suddenly shifts gear, and the remainder of the prayer is contextually an extended series of intercessions, introduced by the petition, 'We pray, make us living men.'[9] It asks:

> Give us a spirit of light, that we may know you, the true God and him whom you have sent, Jesus Christ. Give us holy Spirit, that we may be able to speak and expound your unspoken mysteries. May the Lord Jesus Christ and the Holy Spirit speak in us and hymn you through us.

This leads into Ephesians 1.21, and an angelic hierarchy and the Sanctus (but no Benedictus) and what is a peculiarly Egyptian element, a Sanctus–Epiklesis. After the recitation of the Sanctus, the prayer asks:

> Full is heaven, full also is earth of your excellent glory, Lord of powers. Fill also this sacrifice with your power and your partaking.

It continues, 'To you we offered this bread, the likeness of the body', in the past tense. The Words of Institution follow, and include words from *Didache* 9.2–4. A further Epiklesis follows, asking that the Logos be sent on the bread and wine so that the bread will become the body of the Logos and the cup will become the blood of Truth. The eschatological benefits of the 'medicine of life' include healing of every disease, empowering of all advancement and virtue, and not for condemnation. Brief intercession is made for mercy for the people, and for angelic support for the Church. Prayers for the departed and prayer for those who offered (offerings and eucharistic gifts) lead into a doxology, 'through your only-begotten Jesus Christ in Holy Spirit'.

Of note, therefore, is that the Sanctus and the Institution Narrative (with a part of the *Didache*) come within the intercessory part of the prayer, and it is the Logos who is the agent of descent upon the elements.

The integrity of the prayer as it now stands has been questioned both by Enrico Mazza and by Maxwell Johnson. Mazza seized upon the use of *Didache* 9.2–4, noting its use in another Egyptian anaphoral fragment, *Deir Balyzeh*. He suggests that both have drawn on an older liturgical rite of the *Didache* and *Apostolic Constitutions* VII.25. Mazza also wants to speak with Botte of pseudo-Sarapion (he ignored Cuming's article), and argued that the Logos Epiklesis is the work of a Pneumatomachian.[10] Maxwell Johnson argued that Sarapion had expanded an earlier anaphora, particularly in the pre-Sanctus and Sanctus section, which present a pattern AB–BA–BA. By removing some elements, a chiastic pattern A–B–A emerges, which he thinks was the earlier

8 Louis Bouyer, *Eucharist: Theology and Spirituality of the Eucharistic Prayer*, Notre Dame: University of Notre Dame Press, 1968, p. 203.

9 *PE*, pp. 128–32; *PEER*, pp. 76–8.

10 E. Mazza, *The Origins of the Eucharistic Prayer*, Collegeville: Liturgical Press, 1995, ch. 6. The chapter originally appeared as 'L'anafora di Serapione: una ipostesi de interpretazzione', *Ephemerides Liturgicae* 95 (1981), pp. 510–28.

text. He follows Mazza in regarding the *Didache* quotation as coming from an earlier surviving living liturgical rite but against Mazza, he defends the integrity of the Logos Epiklesis.[11] Johnson has also continued to favour Egypt as the place of origin of the Sanctus, and draws attention to Georg Kretschmar and Robert Taft's arguments that the exegesis of Isaiah 6.3 that Origen learned from his Hebrew teacher has influenced the introduction and context of the Egyptian anaphoral Sanctus.[12] Johnson drew attention to the petition, 'May the Lord Jesus Christ and Holy Spirit speak in us and hymn you through us', together with a singular 'Face' from Isaiah 6.3 as indicating that here the two seraphim are identified as the Son and the Spirit. More recently he and Paul Bradshaw, while acknowledging Winkler's arguments concerning the importance of *merkavah* mysticism, rejected her view that Syria (with Addai and Mari) is the likely place of origin, maintaining that 'we continue to find it highly suggestive that the earliest fourth-century anaphoras we possess having the *Sanctus* are Egyptian'.[13]

We have already noted that most scholars attribute Addai and Mari to the third century, and the most recent scholarship considers the Sanctus and Epiklesis as being core parts of this anaphora from its origin. The key to this and the Egyptian Sanctus may indeed be the common influence of *merkavah*, and we will return to this theme when considering the next anaphora, the Barcelona Papyrus. It is of course possible that Origen's exegesis lies behind this anaphora. But equally important is Bouyer's observation of Johannine imagery. 'May the Lord Jesus Christ and the Holy Spirit speak in us and hymn you through us' may be simply reflecting the indwelling of the Son and the Spirit found in passages such as John 14.14, 23; 15.4; 17.23, as well as Romans 8.11, Galatians 7.10, Ephesians 5.19, Colossians 3.16 and Revelation 8.10–11. We cannot join the heavenly worship unless Christ and the Holy Spirit first dwell in us, and they offer the hymn in, with and through us. Maxine West, in one of the Gregory Dix Award essays, compared the concerns of several of the prayers in the Sarapion collection with the theological and pastoral concerns of the Desert Fathers. She wrote:

> The understanding is that the angels worship God, as portrayed by the Trishagion, and that this becomes possible for Christians, made spiritual in baptism. This is salvation for it places Christians in God's presence and may explain the frequent requests to be made 'living' and the use of 'life' and 'living' in the collection; eternal life is worshipping God in his presence as do the angels.
>
> This 'angelic' worship is understood by these monks as particularly important. A story is told of a revelation to Anthony that he is equalled in virtue by

11 Johnson, *Prayers of Sarapion of Thmuis*, *passim*.

12 G. Kretschmar, *Studien zur frühchristlichen Trinitätstheologie*, Tübingen: Mohr, 1956; R. F. Taft, 'The Interpolation of the Sanctus into the Anaphora: When and Where? A Review of the Dossier', Part I, *Orientalia Christiana Periodica* 57 (1991), pp. 281–308; Part II, 58 (1992), pp. 83–121.

13 Paul F. Bradshaw and Maxwell E. Johnson, *The Eucharistic Liturgies: Their Evolution and Interpretation*, Collegeville: Liturgical Press, 2012, p. 121.

> a doctor who 'every day sings the Trishagion with the angels', illustrating also that this state is accessible to lay people. Is it perhaps too fanciful to suggest that it was this understanding of Isa. 6.3 which caused the sanctus to be used in Egypt?[14]

This explanation at least has the merit of anchoring the Sanctus into the rest of the Johannine flavour of Sarapion, over against an intrusive and subordinationist Christology and Pneumatology of Origen's teacher. The Sanctus–Epiklesis unit is an Egyptian peculiarity, and found in fragments of other anaphoras, and in Mark/Cyril. In Sarapion, God is asked to fill the sacrifice with power, which, as Mary Farag has demonstrated, is equated in the Egyptian tradition with the Son and is a christological term.[15]

The reference to the *Didache* within the Institution Narrative may have a non-liturgical explanation. It is often overlooked that for a long time in Egypt the *Didache* was regarded as canonical literature.[16] A quotation from *Didache* 9 is probably less a witness to a survival of some primitive Eucharist than it is a conscious use of a sacred book thought to be apostolic, and perhaps no more remarkable in an Egyptian context than is the quotation from Ephesians 1.21. It is simply an imaginative use of Egyptian scriptural sources.

There has been much discussion concerning the Logos Epiklesis, and it is often postulated that there was a transition from invocation of the Logos to the Spirit.[17] Sarapion may therefore preserve an earlier and specifically Egyptian form of Epiklesis. However, it is not necessarily more primitive than a Spirit Epiklesis. Athanasius frequently used Logos and Spirit as interchangeable, and Sarapion pre-dates 381, when many still did not see a sharp distinction between Logos and Spirit. It may simply be a peculiarity of Sarapion, and quite consistent with his Sanctus–Epiklesis request for 'power' as understood as the Son. The anaphora thus opens with praise for the revelation of and through the Son, and then turns to petition, making a series of requests. It asks for enlightenment and indwelling to join in the Sanctus with angels, and requests that this sacrifice be filled with *dunamis*, Christ. It is a sacrifice that has been offered (preparation of the elements and placing them on the altar?) and is a 'bloodless service', a term found in the *Testament of Levi*. The bread and wine are a likeness of the body and blood of Christ, and God is requested that the Logos come so that the bread and wine become (*hina genetai*) the body of the Logos and the blood of

14 E. Maxine West, 'The Sacramentary of Serapion: Worthless Heresy or Precious Resource?', Gregory Dix Essay 1995, typescript p. 25.

15 Mary Farag, 'Δύναμις Epicleses: An Athanasian Perspective', *Studia Liturgica* 39 (2009), pp. 63–79.

16 Bart D. Ehrman, 'The New Testament Canon of Didymus the Blind', *Vigiliae Christianae* 37 (1983), pp. 1–12; Lee Martin McDonald and James A. Sanders, *The Canon Debate*, Peabody: Henrickson, 2002, p. 493.

17 R. F. Taft, 'From Logos to Spirit: On the Early History of the Epiclesis', in Andreas Heinz and Heinrich Rennings (eds), *Gratias Agamus. Studien zum eucharistischen Hochgebet: Für Balthasar Fischer*, Freiburg: Herder, 1992, pp. 489–502; Maxwell E. Johnson, 'The Archaic Nature of the Sanctus, Institution Narrative, and Epiclesis of the Logos in the Anaphora Ascribed to Sarapion of Thmuis', in *The Christian East: Its Institutions and Its Thought: A Critical Reflection*, OCA 251, Rome: Pontificio Istituto Orientale, 1996, pp. 671–702.

Truth, all being Johannine concerns and adding to the Johannine flavour of the prayer that Bouyer had noted. Eschatological fruits are requested for the communicants, the Church and the departed.

Equally important now in assessing the Egyptian anaphoral tradition is that contained in the Barcelona Papyrus published by R. Roca-Puig.[18] For some years scholars were tantalized by the publication in short extracts over prolonged periods of this text. Roca-Puig finally published a full edition of this Greek anaphora in 1984.[19] As his edition indicates, a fourth-century provenance is given to this anaphora, which suggests that it is equally as important as Sarapion and Strasbourg Gr.254 in assessing the Egyptian tradition. Michael Zheltov has recently noted:

> This papyrus is in fact the oldest manuscript known to contain Christian liturgical prayers conserved in their integrity – while, for example, the famous Strasbourg papyrus, P. Straßb. inv. 254, dates from the 4th–5th centuries and has many lacunae in its text, – giving our codex seminal importance for liturgical scholarship.[20]

Zheltov argues that since Strasbourg Gr.254 is but a fragment, the Barcelona Anaphora should be given priority in assessing the Egyptian tradition. He noted:

> Nevertheless, despite the plain fact that this papyrus, probably connected in some way with the Pachomian monastic community, is the oldest liturgical manuscript containing a full anaphora, its important testimony is almost completely neglected by modern liturgical scholars.[21]

Walter Ray has rightly pointed out that the dating of a manuscript or papyrus should not be confused with the date of its content, and thus has defended the 'priority' of Strasbourg Gr.254 over Barcelona.[22] However, giving priority of one over the other would seem to rest on prior assumptions and convictions about the shape or content of an anaphora at a given epoch (in Ray's case the wish to interpret Strasbourg Gr.254 in the light of *Didache* 10 and the *birkat ha-mazon*), and it may be wiser simply to take both as fourth-century witnesses

18 The material on Barcelona and Thomas is adapted from Bryan D. Spinks, 'Revisiting Egyptian Anaphoral Development', in David A. Pitt, Stefanos Alexopoulos and Christian McConnell (eds), *A Living Tradition: On the Intersection of Liturgical History and Pastoral Practice. Essays in Honor of Maxwell E. Johnson*, Collegeville: Liturgical Press, 2012, pp. 195–210.

19 R. Roca-Puig, *Anàfora De Barcelona: I Altres Pregàries 9 Missa del segle IV*, Barcelona: Grafos, 1984.

20 Michael Zheltov, 'The Anaphora and the Thanksgiving Prayer from the Barcelona Papyrus: An Underestimated Testimony to the Anaphoral History in the Fourth Century', *Vigiliae Christianae* 62 (2008), p. 468.

21 Zheltov, 'Anaphora and the Thanksgiving Prayer', p. 469.

22 Walter Ray, 'The Strasbourg Papyrus', in Paul F. Bradshaw (ed.), *Essays on Early Eastern Eucharistic Prayers*, Collegeville: Liturgical Press, 1997, pp. 39–56, p. 46.

to more than a simplistic single Egyptian anaphoral tradition rather than to attempt a Solomon's judgement.

The Barcelona Anaphora was already known in part in the Coptic parchment Louvain 27, so this anaphora existed in both Greek and Coptic. A further Greek fragment is preserved in PVindob. G 41043.[23]

Up our hearts. We have to the Lord.

Let us also give thanks. Fitting and Right.

It is fitting and right to praise You, to bless You, to hymn You, to give You thanks, o Master, God Pantocrator of our Lord Jesus Christ, Who created all things from non-existence into being, all: heaven and the earth, the sea, and all that is in them, through Your beloved child Jesus Christ, our Lord, through whom You have called us from darkness into light, from ignorance to knowledge of the glory of His name, from decay of death into incorruption, into life eternal; Who sits on the chariot, Cherubim and Seraphim before it, who is attended by thousands of thousands and myriads of angels, archangels, thrones and dominions, hymning and glorifying, with whom we are also hymning, saying: 'Holy, Holy, Holy Lord of Sabaoth! Heaven and earth are full of Your glory, in which you have glorified us through Your Only-Begotten, the firstborn of every creature, Jesus Christ, our Lord, Who sits on the right hand of Your greatness in heaven, Who is coming to judge the living and the dead, <the remembrance of whose death we do>. Through Him we offer You these Your creations, the bread and the cup: we ask and beseech You to send onto them Your holy and Comforter Spirit from Heaven, to represent them materially and to make the bread the Body of Christ and the cup the Blood of Christ, of the New Covenant – as He Himself, when He was about to hand <Himself>, having taken bread and given thanks, broke it and gave it to His disciples, saying 'Take, eat, this is my body;' likewise after supper, having taken a cup and given thanks, He gave it to them, saying: 'Take, drink the blood, which is shed for many for remission of sins.' And we also do the same in Your remembrance, like those – whenever we meet together, we make the remembrance of You, of the holy mystery of our Teacher and King and Savior Jesus Christ. Even so, we pray to You, Master, that in blessing you will bless and in sanctifying sanctify . . . for all communicating from them for undivided faith, for communication of incorruption, for communion of the Holy Spirit, for perfection of belief and truth, for fulfillment of all Your will, so that in this and again we will glorify Your all-revered and all-holy name, through Your sanctified Child, our Lord Jesus Christ, through Whom glory [be] to You, power unto the unblended ages of ages.[24]

23 For the Louvain, see *PEER*, pp. 81–2; for the Greek fragment, Jürgen Hammerstaedt, *Griechische Anaphorenfragmente aus Ägypten und Nubien*, Opladen/Wiesbaden: Westdeutscher Verlag, 1999, p. 156.

24 Zheltov, 'Anaphora and the Thanksgiving Prayer', pp. 487–92.

Zheltov usefully summarizes the structure thus:[25]

- Introductory dialogue.
- Preface with four initial praise verbs, creation narrative and a christological section.
- Pre-Sanctus.
- Oblation and Epiklesis I.
- Institution Narrative.
- Anamnesis.
- Epiklesis II.
- Concluding doxology.

He notes that the Sanctus–Epiclesis I–Institution is an Egyptian characteristic, and it also has the short form of the Sanctus with no Benedictus. Like Strasbourg Gr.254, it has the quotation from Psalm 146.6/Nehemiah 9.6, and 'O Master, God Pantocrator of our Lord Jesus Christ', which has a parallel in another lesser-known Egyptian anaphora, that of Athanasius. Its close parallels to other Egyptian anaphoras and works even led Zheltov to wonder if Athanasius may have been its author.[26] There are certain elements that are peculiar, such as the interruption of the post-Sanctus and Epiklesis by a christological reference, a lack of intercessions and the fact that Epiklesis II is a sanctification of the communicants, not the gifts. One particularly interesting element is the quotation in the Barcelona Anaphora from *1 Clement* 59.2. While for twenty-first-century Western scholars this is a quotation from the Fathers, in a fourth-century Egyptian context it is in fact a quotation from canonical Scripture. It is frequently overlooked in liturgical discussions that both Clement of Alexandria and Didymus the Blind regarded *1 Clement* as well as the *Didache* as sacred texts alongside the Gospels and Pauline Epistles, and Codex Alexandrinus included *1* and *2 Clement*.[27] Furthermore, although Barcelona lacks the careful Sanctus–Epiklesis unit with a pick-up on 'Fill' found in Sarapion, that pick-up is present in the Louvain Coptic fragment, and hinted at in the PVindob. G 41043. Sebastià Janeras has suggested the copyist of Barcelona has accidently omitted to repeat the phrase 'for full is heaven of your holy glory', which is certainly possible.[28] Equally, the other two fragments might suggest that the link phrase was added. Whichever of these might be the case, the cumulative literary evidence shows that some recensions of this anaphora did have the characteristic Egyptian link.

25 Zheltov, 'Anaphora and the Thanksgiving Prayer', p. 493.

26 Zheltov, 'Anaphora and the Thanksgiving Prayer', p. 497.

27 Bart D. Ehrman, 'The New Testament Canon of Didymus the Blind', *Vigiliae Christianae* 37 (1983), pp. 1–21, esp. 16–18; Bruce M. Metzger, *The Canon of the New Testament*, Oxford: Clarendon Press, 1987, pp. 134, 214, 225. Rufinus was taught by Didymus and he also accords these books a special place. Metzger, *Canon*, p. 234. Lee Martin McDonald and James A. Sanders, *The Canon Debate*, Peabody, MA: Henrickson, 2002, p. 493.

28 Sebastià Janeras, 'Sanctus et Post-Sanctus dans l'anaphore du *P.Monts.Roca inv.no.154b–155a*', *Studi sull Oriente Christiano* 11 (2007), pp. 9–13.

In a recent essay Paul Bradshaw considered the Barcelona text and Zheltov's arguments.[29] Although he concluded that it probably dates no later than the middle of the fourth century, and 'thus represents one of the oldest anaphoras known to us, probably as old as the *Sacramentary of Sarapion* and as the anaphora in the *Apostolic Tradition* in its fully developed form', his assessment was made with the claim that there is 'a growing consensus among liturgical scholars that in other extant early Eucharistic Prayers both the Sanctus with its surrounding material and also the Institution Narrative were usually fourth-century additions to an older core', though this 'growing consensus' was footnoted only by reference to a section of Maxwell Johnson's work of 1995 on Sarapion.[30] Johnson in turn had referred to the older studies of Talley, Giraudo, Wegman, Cuming and Mazza on the relationship of the Jewish *berakah* and Strasbourg Gr.254. As we have noted in earlier chapters, more recent scholarship has moved away from this paradigm, and the philological tour de force of Gabriele Winkler on the *merkavah* background to the Sanctus makes it extremely difficult to continue to maintain that the Sanctus is always a later intrusion.[31] What is intriguing in this respect is the fact that Barcelona has an explicit *merkavah* reference, apparently with reference to Christ, 'who sits on the chariot, Cherubim and Seraphim before it'. It is precisely these references and the hitherto neglected fragment of the Anaphora of Thomas that Mary Farag draws attention to as requiring a reassessment of the origins of the Sanctus in the anaphora and, in turn, what constitutes an 'Egyptian' pattern.

The anaphoral fragment named Thomas is found in the Great Euchology of the White Monastery. This manuscript was copied in the tenth century, and is a compilation of earlier anaphoras.[32] It certainly includes in Coptic the anaphoras of the Syrian Orthodox Church such as Severus of Antioch and John

---

29 Paul F. Bradshaw, 'The Barcelona Papyrus and the Development of Early Eucharistic Prayers', in Maxwell E. Johnson (ed.), *Issues in Eucharistic Praying in East and West: Essays in Liturgical and Theological Analysis*, Collegeville: Liturgical Press, 2010, pp. 129–38.

30 Paul F. Bradshaw, 'The Barcelona Papyrus and the Development of Early Eucharistic Prayers', paper circulated to the North American Academy of Liturgy Problems in Early Liturgy Seminar 2010, p. 7; revised published version (see note above), pp. 138, 132–3, footnote 16, p. 138. The same concern with the *birkat ha-mazon* surfaces in Walter Ray's recent article, 'The Barcelona Papyrus and the Early Egyptian Eucharistic Prayer', *Studia Liturgica* 41 (2011), pp. 211–29. Ray has yet to address the studies of Gabriele Winkler that undermine his a priori assumptions.

31 Gabriele Winkler, *Das Sanctus: Über den Ursprung und die Anfänge des Sanctus und sein Fortwirken*, OCA, Rome: Pontificio Istituto Orientale, 2002; 'The Sanctus: Some Observations with Regard to its Origins and Theological Significance', in Bronwen Neil, Geoffrey D. Dunn and Lawrence Cross (eds), *Prayer and Spirituality in the Early Church, Vol. 3: Liturgy and Life*, Strathfield, NSW: St Paul's Publications, 2003, pp. 111–31; 'A New Witness to the Missing Institution Narrative', in Maxwell E. Johnson and L. Edward Phillips (eds), *Liturgica Diversa Studia: Essays in Honor of Paul F. Bradshaw*, Portland: Pastoral Press, 2004, pp. 117–28. With reference to the Ethiopic anaphora of the Apostles and East Syrian Addai and Mari, Winkler concludes on p. 128, 'The interesting fact remains, however, that both the Syriac and the Ethiopic "Anaphora of the Apostles" had (= the Ethiopic anaphora) or have (= the Syriac "Anaphora of the Apostles") no Institution Narrative, but contained the Sanctus from the beginning'.

32 Alin Suciu, 'À propos de la datation du manuscript contenant le Grand Euchologe du Monastère Blanc', *Vigiliae Christianae* 65 (2011), pp. 189–98.

Bostra.[33] However, it also contains anaphoras of the Coptic Orthodox Church, and includes two otherwise unknown anaphoras – the evangelist Matthew, which is an entire anaphora, and the fragment of St Thomas.[34] I give here the English translation of Thomas given by Mary Farag:

> Who can make his mind heavenly and place his thoughts in Paradise and place his heart in the heavenly Jerusalem and see God the invisible, the incomprehensible, the unattainable, the uncreated, the immeasurable? As for He who accurately measured the entire creation, His workmanship no one comprehends, except He Himself and [His] good Father and the Holy Spirit. [These] three are one, a single divinity, a single lordship, three hypostases, a perfect Trinity in a single divinity. These three are one: he who collected all the waters that were upon the earth into a single gathering and called it the sea and established the four river-branches flowing into it, (a sea that) can neither become overfilled nor lack (for water), He who bounded the waters in three parts and placed one part in heaven, one part upon the earth, and one part under the earth, He who created the sun and the moon and the stars and appointed the sun to shine upon His creations by day and the moon by night, the evening [star] and Arcturus and the morning star to shine upon the earth. And You also created the angels and the archangels, the principalities and the authorities, the powers and all the powers that are in the heavens. And by Your hands, along with Your good Father and the Holy Spirit, You also created man according to Your image and according to Your likeness. And you also created Paradise and placed the man whom You created in it to cultivate it and to praise You,
>
> *Pre-Sanctus*
>
> You whom the angels praise, You whom the archangels worship,
>
> [in Greek] *Those who are seated stand*
>
> You whom the powers hymn, You whose holy glory the authorities sing, You to whom the thrones sing the doxology of victory,
>
> [in Greek] *Look towards the east.*
>
> You before whom stand Your two honored creatures, the Cherubim and the Seraphim, each of them with six wings, with two wings they cover their faces on account of the great glory of Your divinity, and with two they cover their

33 Though for some 'Egyptian' elements in Severus see Bryan D. Spinks, 'The Anaphora of Severus of Antioch: A Note on its Character and Theology', in J. Getcha and A. Lossky (eds), Θυσία αἰνέσεω: *Mélanges liturgiques offerts à la mémoire de l'archevêque Georges Wagner (1930–1993)*, Paris: Presses Saint Serge, 2005, pp. 345–51.

34 Emmanuel Lanne, *Le Grand Euchologe du Monastère Blanc*, Patrologia Orientalis 28.2, Paris: Firmin-Didot, 1958. Matthew and Thomas are given in French translations. For the German of Matthew, Angelicus M. Kropp, 'Die Koptische Anaphora des Heiligen Evangelisten Matthäus', *Oriens Christianus* 29 (1932), pp. 111–25. And Italian, G. Maestri, 'Un contributo alla conoscenza dell'antica liturgia egiziana: Studio dell'anafora del santo evangelista Matteo', *Memoriam Sanctorum Venerantes Miscellanea in onore di Monsignor Victor Saxer, Studi Di Antichita Cristiana* 48 (1992), pp. 525–37.

feet on account of the great fire emanating from around Your throne, O God, the Creator,

[in Greek] *Let us attend.*

and with two they fly, while hymning and praising You, glorifying You with unwearying mouth and unceasing tongue and never-silent lips, hymning You, glorifying You, saying,

[in Greek] *Holy, holy, holy, Lord Sabaoth. Heaven and earth are full of Your holy glory.*

Holy are you, holy are you, holy are you, Lord Sabaoth. Truly heaven and earth are full of Your holy glory. Fill now this sacrifice also with the joy of Your Holy Spirit.

You placed the man whom You had created in the paradise of delight and commanded him that from every tree in . . .[35]

The fragment begins with a trinitarian proclamation of creation, though centred upon the Second Person, and fills out the briefer reference to heaven, earth, the sea and all that is in them found in Strasbourg Gr.254 and Barcelona. It has the 'Egyptian' Sanctus–Epiclesis unit, with the request, 'Fill now this sacrifice also with the joy of Your Holy Spirit', though it also has the repetition of the trice holy, which is usually classed as a 'West Syrian' trait. Mary Farag has argued that the prayer fragment reflects the Eunomian christological controversies of the late fourth century and was composed about that time, pointing to the emphasis on God's incomprehensible nature, and the unique knowledge of the Son, as well as a reference to the throne of God. She asserts:

> These four reflections of anti-Eunomian polemic in Thomas (use of Ezekiel's vision, the properties of divinity and lordship in the Trinity, Jn 1:18, and the (in)visibility and (in) comprehensibility of God) both reveal the coherence of Thomas' initial lines and provide a benchmark for dating. The Anaphora of Thomas is most likely a composition of the end of the fourth century or of the fifth: that is, no earlier than the Eunomian controversy in the second half of the fourth century, yet no later than the controversy's immediate relevancy, which quickly declined in the first half of the fifth century.[36]

However, what is of the utmost importance is the commentary she provides on the background to the apparent expansion of the Egyptian concern with Psalm 146.6. Noting the echoes of *merkavah/hekhalot* interests in Barcelona, Farag compares the preoccupation with the details of the creation in the *hekhalot* literature with the account of creation in the Thomas fragment. The opening

35 Mary Farag, 'The Anaphora of St Thomas the Apostle. Translation and Commentary', *Le Muséon* 123 (2010), pp. 321–3. My italics, and Farag provides the rest of the text of the presupposed Sanctus.

36 Farag, 'Anaphora of St Thomas the Apostle', pp. 327–8. See also T. Kopecek, *A History of Neo-Arianism*, Patristic Monograph series, 8, vol. 2, Cambridge: The Philadelphia Patristic Foundation, 1979, pp. 542–3.

of the anaphora with a question has a parallel in the Anaphora of Matthew, and also in the Anaphora of Severus, which has Egyptian elements. Farag calls attention to the questions that are posed in *Ma'aseh Merkavah*, both in narrative frames and prayer texts, and observes that there is a confluence of a number of themes in both texts:

> Vision of God (and the tension between immanence and transcendence).
> The state of one's heart/mind/thoughts.
> Knowledge and its endurability.
> God as specifically creator.
> Creation of heaven and earth.
> Angelic retinue including thrones.
> Fiery throne.
> The glory of God.
> Abundant verbs of praise.
> Standing facing eastward at sunrise.
> Human and angelic participation in the Sanctus/*qedushah*.[37]

Farag suggests that the anaphora was influenced by the prayer corpus of *Ma'aseh Merkavah*, which is regarded as having a Palestinian provenance, and concludes that '[b]y its clear reflection of characteristic *merkavah* speculation, this cosmopolitan anaphora pinpoints Jewish mysticism as the likely influential source not only of the Sanctus, but of the entire unit of Sursum Corda, creation-centered Preface, and Sanctus'.[38]

The importance of the Anaphora of Thomas is that if Farag's dating is correct, then together with Barcelona, our understanding of early Egyptian anaphoral patterns is widened. Like the Barcelona Anaphora, Thomas has no pre-Sanctus intercessory unit which has been regarded by some as the hallmark of the Egyptian anaphora. Yet both Thomas and Barcelona *are* genuinely Egyptian anaphoras. Taken with Sarapion, they witness to a range of fourth- and fifth-century Egyptian anaphoral patterns.

The Grand Euchology of the White Monastery also contains an anaphora that is attributed to Matthew.[39] It is possible that it represented some local tradition in Southern Egypt. The prayer begins by contrasting the inability of 'fleshly language or the human intelligence' to speak of God's marvels, but tells of the 'rational spirits and incorporeal powers' who bless God without ceasing. The cherubim carry the chariot, and the seraphim stand in fear and tremble with awe. The opening of the anaphora once more shows the continuing influence of *merkavah* mysticism. The Post-Sanctus leads quickly into the Institution Narrative. The Epiklesis prays:

> We ask and beseech you . . . that . . . you will send us your Holy Spirit, the Paraclete, The spirit of Truth, upon this bread and this cup and that you will change them to the body and blood of our Lord Jesus Christ . . .

37 Farag, 'Anaphora of St Thomas the Apostle', p. 353.
38 Farag, 'Anaphora of St Thomas the Apostle', p. 357.
39 Text with French translation, Lanne, *Grand Euchologe du Monastère Blanc*, pp. 345–67.

There are also echoes of the Syrian Anaphora of *Testamentum Domini*.

The *Deir Balyzeh* Papyrus, written in Upper Egypt between the sixth and eighth centuries, represents another 'local' Egyptian tradition.[40] The fragment begins with intercessions, and leads into the Sanctus with Ephesians 1.21. The Sanctus–Epiklesis unit follows, but here God is asked to fill us with glory and to send down the Holy Spirit upon the creatures to make the bread the body of our Lord, and the cup his blood. This is followed by a petition based on *Didache* 9, similar to Sarapion. The Narrative of Institution follows, after which is a fragmentary Anamnesis proclaiming the death, confessing the resurrection, and a petition for the Spirit for the congregation for strengthening and increasing faith and hope of the eternal life to come. Alistair C. Stewart has recently reviewed this fragment, and suggests that what we have in the papyrus leaves are scattered prayers, and in his view the final intercessory lines for the Holy Spirit in fact represent a fragment of a post-communion, or at least a post-anaphoral, prayer.[41] In the light of this he proposes a theory that anaphoral development in Egypt was by various independent prayer units being built up and included into a single prayer.[42] If this holds true for Mark/Cyril, then Strasbourg Gr.254 might, after all, have been one of a series of units from which this anaphora developed. Other fragments collected by Hammerstaedt witness again to local variations, as do two Coptic ostraka in the British Museum.[43] Canon 26 of Pope Gabriele II Ibn Turaik (1131–45) apparently brought to an end the use of other anaphoras:

> It has reached my feebleness that certain people in the provinces of the Sa'id celebrate the Liturgies not in conformity with, and otherwise than the three known ones which are the Liturgy of Saint Basil, and that of Saint Gregory, and the Liturgy of St Cyril. I have forbidden anyone to act deliberately thus, until he has come to the cell, and his Liturgies have been verified.[44]

The Coptic Divine Liturgy

The main liturgy now in use in the Coptic Church is ascribed to St Basil. The outline of the liturgy is as follows:[45]

---

40 C. H. Roberts and B. Capelle, *An Early Euchologium: The Dêr-Balizeh Papyrus Enlarged and Reedited*, Louvain: Université de Louvain Institut Orientaliste, 1949; *PE*, pp. 124–7; *PEER*, pp. 79–81.

41 Alistair C. Stewart, *Two Early Egyptian Liturgical Papyri: The Deir Balyzeh Papyrus and the Barcelona Papyrus with Appendices Containing Comparative Material*, Alcuin/GROW Joint Liturgical Study 70, Norwich: Canterbury Press, 2010, p. 7.

42 Stewart, *Two Early Egyptian Liturgical Papyri*, p. 21.

43 Jürgen Hammerstaedt, *Griechische Anaphorenfragmente Aus Ägypten und Nubien*, Wiesbaden: Westdeutsches Verlag GmbH, 1999. Stewart, *Two Early Egyptian Liturgical Papyri*, pp. 52–3.

44 O. H. E. Burmester, 'The Canons of Gabriel Ibn Turaik, LXX Patriarch of Alexandria', *Orientalia Christiana Periodica* 1 (1935), pp. 5–45, p. 41.

45 The text is from Fr Abraam D. Sleman, available at CopticChurch.net. For a broad sweep of recent history, see Hany N. Takla, 'Coptic Liturgy: Past, Present, Future', www.stshenouda.com/coptman/colgsurv.pdf. See also Heinzgerd Brakmann, 'Le Déroulement de la Messe Copte.

A The Offertory

1 The Prothesis (Preparation)
Vesting. Prayer of preparation of the altar. Agpia (canonical hours). Hand washing. The Creed.

2 Choosing the Lamb
The Rite of choosing the Lamb (selecting the communion loaf). The Procession of the Lamb. The Blessing of the Lamb.

3 The Thanksgiving
Opening Greeting. Prayer of Thanksgiving.

4 The Prayer of Offertory. (The bread and wine are covered.)

B The Liturgy of the Catechumens

1 The Absolutions
The Absolution to the Son.
The Absolution of the Ministers.

2 The Lections
Introductory prayers with incense.
The Pauline Epistle with prayer.
The Catholic Epistle with prayer.
The Acts of the Apostles with prayer with incense.
The Synaxarium (saints' biographies).
The Trisagion.
The Litany of the Gospel.
The Psalm.
The Gospel and prayer.
Sermon.

3 The Prayer of the Veil

4 The Long Litanies
The Litany of Peace.
The Litany of the Fathers.
The Litany of the Congregation.

5 The Creed

6 The Pre-anaphora
Washing of hands.
Prayer of Reconciliation.
Holy Kiss.

C The Liturgy of the Faithful

1 The Anaphora

2 The Fraction
Prayer before the Fraction.
Prayer of the Fraction (seasonal Propers).
Lord's Prayer.
Priest's inaudible prayers.
Holy things for holy people.

Structure et Histoire', in A. M. Triacca and A. Pistoia (eds), *L'Eucharistie: Célébrations, Rites, Piétés*, Rome: CLV Edizione Liturgiche, 1995, pp. 107–32.

3 **Prayer of Confession**
4 **Communion** (Hymns/chants during the communion.)
5 **Post-Communion**
Prayer of Thanksgiving.
Prayer of Laying on of Hands (Dismissal).
Dismissal.

When this outline is compared with the information given by Justin Martyr, and later by the compiler of *Apostolic Constitutions* VIII, it amply illustrates the growth of soft points in the liturgy.

Although in current usage, when the Mark/Cyril or Gregory Anaphoras are used, much of Parts A and B of St Basil are used.[46] However, Greek manuscripts of St Mark were edited by G. J. Cuming, and, as one might expect, the shape of the Greek rite is more akin to the Byzantine rite as found in the eighth-century manuscript Barbarini 336 and less developed than the older texts of Coptic Cyril.[47]

Greek Mark

The Prothesis.
Incense prayers.
Prayer of the prothesis.
First Prayer of the Morning.
Prayer for the Emperor.
Prayer for the Patriarch.
Little Entrance.
Prayer of the Trisagion.
Scripture readings: Epistle and Gospel.
The Synapte.
Three Prayers.
The Great Entrance.
The Kiss of Peace.
Offertory and Creed.
Anaphora.
Prayer of the Lord's Prayer.
Prayer of Inclination.
Elevation.
Fraction.
Communion.

46 ET *The Three Coptic Liturgies (Arabic, Coptic and English)*, Copts in Chicago, 2008; *The Coptic Liturgy of Saint Mark the Apostle, Commonly known as the Liturgy of St Cyril*, http://www.saintmark.com. This latter seems to have all the litanies and diptyches transposed to the end of the anaphora to conform to the shape of St Basil.

47 G. J. Cuming, *The Liturgy of St Mark Edited from the Manuscripts with a Commentary*, Rome: Ponificium Institutum Studiorum Orientalium, 1990; Stefano Parenti and Elena Velkovska (eds), *L'Eucologio Barberini gr.336*, Bibliotheca Ephemerides Liturgicae Susidia 80, Rome: CLV Edizioni Liturgiche, 2000.

Thanksgiving after Communion.
The Prayer behind the Ambo and the Dismissal.

Coptic Cyril

Prothesis (as Basil).
First Prayer of the Morning.
Prayer of the Prothesis.
Absolution of the Son.
Absolution of the ministers.
Incense Prayer.
The Three Prayers.
Pauline Epistle.
(Prayer for the Patriarch.)
Catholic Epistle.
Acts of the Apostles.
Trisagion.
Gospel.
(Prayers with some overlap with the Synapte.)
Prayer of the Veil.
Prayers.
Creed.
Kiss of Peace.
Anaphora.
Consignation, Fraction and Lord's Prayer.
Prayer of Inclination.
Elevation and Commixture.
Communion.
Thanksgiving.
Dismissal.

Again, this comparison gives some indication of how rites grow, borrow, but also have quite independent texts.

With regard to the present Divine Liturgy of St Basil, as in all the Eastern rites, an elaborate ritual preparation of vesting and preparation of the elements prefaces the public liturgy. These are the concern of the clergy, and were likely once simple and informal. If vesture is worn it has to be put on, and preparation may well invoke a prayer for worthiness. In the East it seems that the custom of selection of bread and wine for the celebration was carried out by deacons at the beginning of the service, and transferred prior to the anaphora. This seems later to have become the function of the priest. What was a utilitarian necessity, done in a devout manner, became a rite in its own right. Thus, although no part of the liturgy of the whole assembly, the priest's preparation of himself, the elements and, in the Egyptian rite, placing them on the altar before the liturgy of the faithful, now form an introductory rite, combined with the recitation of one of the Offices. One of the characteristics of soft-point growth is a tendency to anticipate later core parts of the rite. The leavened loaf, the Lamb, which is stamped in the centre with a large cross surrounded by 12 smaller crosses representing the 12 apostles and has the words of the Trisagion, is marked by a cross from the wine which is mixed with water. The priest also signs the Lamb. The prayer of Offertory includes the placing of the elements under a cloth (Prospherine) and the priest prays to the Son that he will 'show your face upon this bread and upon this cup', and is asked to bless, sanctify, purify and change them so that they become 'your holy body' and 'your precious blood', and requests spiritual/eschatological benefits. This would seem to be a consecration before the consecration.

The present beginning of the liturgy of the catechumens, with 'absolutions', is a preparation for the Word, but the earlier beginning may be marked by the greeting before the prayer of thanksgiving. The lections in this tradition have also been multiplied in comparison to earlier testimonies. These are interspersed with prayers, since every reading must now have its prayerful introduction and conclusion. The Trisagion in the non-Chalcedonian tradition is christological:

> Holy God, Holy Mighty, Holy Immortal, who was born of the Virgin, have mercy upon us. Holy God, Holy Mighty, Holy Immortal, who was crucified for us, have mercy upon us. Holy God, Holy Mighty, Holy Immortal, who rose from the dead and ascended into heaven, have mercy upon us.

The older text, preserved in the Byzantine rite, is 'Holy God, Holy Mighty, Holy Immortal, have mercy upon us'. This chant was already in existence at the time of the Council of Chalcedon (451), where it was attributed to a group of 'Oriental bishops', though according to an interpolated passage in the Bazaar of Heracleides (*c.* 451–470), it was introduced by Proclus of Constantinople (434–436) to make an earthquake stop.[48] It appears that in Syria the addressee was understood as being the Son, which was probably the original intention, but in Constantinople, the acclamation was taken to refer to the Trinity.[49] According to Severus of Antioch, it was a fellow non-Chalcedonian Patriarch of Antioch, Peter the Fuller, who introduced the addition 'who was crucified for us', giving it a pointed christological meaning in accordance with his understanding of the Christology of Cyril of Alexandria. Interestingly, in another homily, Severus noted that 'the Alexandrians, the Libyans, and the Egyptians do not sing at all in church this praise of Christ', which Cuming took to mean that they were singing the Trisagion in its original form.[50] For those who gave the chant a trinitarian meaning, the addition was seen as teaching Theopaschitism, that the Godhead was capable of suffering, and ultimately the Byzantine tradition gave it a solely

48 Sebastian Brock, 'The Origins of the Qanona "Holy God, Holy Mighty, Holy Immortal" according to Gabriel of Qatar (Early 7th Century)', *The Harp* 21 (2006), pp. 173–85. See Hans-Joachim Schultz, *The Byzantine Liturgy*, New York: Pueblo Publishing, 1986, pp. 22–4; Volker L. Menze, *Justinian and the Making of the Syrian Orthodox Church*, Oxford: Oxford University Press, 2008, pp. 165–75.

49 Sebastià Janeras, 'Le Trisagion: Une Formule Brève en Liturgie Comparée', in Robert F. Taft and Gabriele Winkler (eds), *Comparative Liturgy Fifty Years after Anton Baumstark (1872–1948)*, Rome: Pontificio Istituto Orientale, 2001, pp. 495–562.

50 Severus of Antioch, *Homélies Cathedrals*, PO 29, Paris: Firmin-Didot, 1960, homilies 125 and 124 respectively; Cuming, *Liturgy of St Mark*, p. 95.

trinitarian interpretation, and saw the non-Chalcedonian version as heretical. Matti Moosa, accepting the testimony of Ephrem of Amida and Zachariah of Mitylene, argues that the 'non-Chalcedonian' phrase was in fact used in Antioch from the time of Eustatius of Antioch in the fourth century.[51] Whatever the precise origin, at some stage the Egyptians did adopt the non-Chalcedonian version, which continued to be expanded in a christological sense. What is of interest is the position of the Trisagion in the Coptic rite. Whereas in the Byzantine rite it entered the liturgy as an entrance chant, in the Coptic rite its position is firmly as part of the readings of Scripture and as a prelude to the Gospel.

The Creed was introduced by Timothy of Constantinople, a non-Chalcedonian, at the beginning of the sixth century, to show he accepted the Councils of Nicaea (325) and Constantinople (381). His Chalcedonian successor could hardly remove it because it would suggest he did not accept those councils. However, the Creed was usually regarded as belonging to the faithful, not to catechumens. The Prayer of the Veil, which is placed after the readings, refers to offering 'this awesome and bloodless sacrifice' and prays that this 'mystery' will be for the forgiveness of sins. Cyril of Jerusalem's rite knew the Lord's Prayer prior to communion, and the invitation 'Holy things for the Holy', which Robert Taft has described as the ancient communion call with a congregational response.[52] Theodore of Mopsuestia had given an explanation for the Fraction, and Sarapion witnesses to post-communion thanksgiving prayers in Egypt in the fourth century. These communion and post-communion components continued to attract more material. Much of this was devotional material that fulfilled a need. The Fraction in the Coptic rite, though less complex than in the Syrian Orthodox rite, is certainly a complicated action.[53] Each of the three liturgies has its own Fraction Prayer, and there are a further 17 from which the celebrant can choose for certain festivals.[54] That in St Gregory differs in the older Greek and Sahidic manuscripts from that found in the later Greek and Bohairic manuscripts.[55] However, it is the elaborate preparation of the elements prior to the older beginning of the liturgy, with prayer that is almost an 'anaphora before the anaphora', together with prayer for worthiness, that has heightened theologies of eucharistic offering and presence.

The Egptian Anaphoras of St Basil, St Mark/Cyril and St Gregory

The Anaphora of St Basil is known in a number of recensions and languages. It is of the 'West Syrian' or 'Syro-Byzantine' family, but as we have argued above, this should be taken to refer to a structure rather than a precise geographical

51 Matti Moosa, *The Maronites in History*, Piscataway: Gorgias Press, 2005, p. 72.

52 Robert Taft, '"Holy Things for the Saints": The Ancient Call to Communion and Its Response', in Gerard Austin (ed.), *Fountain of Life*, Washington, DC: Pastoral Press, 1991, pp. 87–102.

53 Gregory Tillett, 'The Fraction in the Coptic Orthodox Liturgy', *The Glastonbury Review* (1999), http://www.coptic.org/language/tilett.htm.

54 Ugo Zanetti, 'Fraction Prayers in the Coptic Liturgy', *The Harp* 27 (2011), pp. 291–302.

55 Ugo Zanetti, 'Deux prières de la fraction de la liturgie de Grégoire, en grec et en copte', *Orientalia Christiana Periodica* 78 (2012), pp. 291–333.

origin. The name of St Basil of Caesarea has been associated with an anaphora since the time of Leontius of Byzantium in the sixth century. Following the important study by H. Engberding in 1931, scholars have worked with the understanding that there are two main families of the Anaphora of St Basil:[56]

1 Byzantine Basil and its derivations such as the Armenian and Syriac.
2 Egyptian Basil, in Greek, Sahidic and Bohairic.

Though having some things in common, they represent two quite distinct recensions, with the Egyptian seemingly earlier.[57] What has puzzled scholars is how the name Basil should have become attached to an Egyptian anaphora. Basil did visit Egypt *c.* 356–357, when a layman, but there is no evidence to illuminate why he should have been thought to be connected with this anaphora. In contrast, it has been argued that Basil himself expanded the Byzantine version, both in its christological and trinitarian content.[58]

More recently however, Gabriele Winkler has taken much further the insights of A. Renoux concerning the Armenian Anaphora of Gregory the Illuminator (the great missionary of the Armenian Church at the beginning of the fourth century), which is in fact a form of St Basil that is less developed than the Byzantine and Egyptian versions.[59] Winkler has also argued that the name of Basil is not a helpful starting point for discussing the relationship of these anaphoras, and she doubts that Basil of Caesarea was personally involved with any of them. Winkler's painstaking philological approach, which certainly does not suggest that in every respect Gregory the Illuminator (arm.Bas.1) has the earlier readings, inclines her to argue for an even earlier Syriac urtext. This could be the case, but there are few Syriac versions of St Basil preserved in Syrian Orthodox manuscripts, and those known to me are later Syriac versions of the Byzantine anaphora, with embellishments. Whatever may be the ultimate origins of the Basilian anaphoras, nothing has altered the fact that the Egyptian recension is quite distinct, and there are also distinctions between the Greek, Sahidic and

56 Hieronymus Engberding, *Das Eucharistische Hochgebet der Basileiosliturgie: Textgeschichtliche Untersuchungen und kritische Ausgabe*, Münster: Aschendorff, 1931.

57 For an excellent overview of the present state of the question and studies, see Anne Vorhes McGowan, 'The Basilian Anaphoras: Rethinking the Question', in Maxwell E. Johnson (ed.), *Issues in Eucharistic Praying in East and West: Essays in Liturgical and Theological Analysis*, Collegeville: Liturgical Press, 2010, pp. 219–61. See also D. Richard Stuckwisch, 'The Basilian Anaphoras', in Paul F. Bradshaw (ed.), *Essays on Early Eucharistic Prayers*, Collegeville: Liturgical Press, 1997, pp. 109–30.

58 B. Capelle, 'Les liturgies "basiliennes" et S. Basile', in *Un témoin archaïque de la liturgie copte de S. Basile*, J. Doresse and E. Lanne, Louvain: Publications Universitaires Louvain, 1960; Boris Bobrinskoy, 'Liturgie et Ecclésiologie Trinitaire de Saint Basile', in B. Botte (ed.), *Eucharisties d'Orient et d'Occident*, Paris: Les Éditions du Cerf, Paris 1970, pp. 197–240; Albert Houssiau, 'The Alexandrine Anaphora of St Basil', in L. C. Sheppard (ed.), *The New Liturgy*, London: Darton, Longman and Todd, 1970, pp. 228–43.

59 A. Renoux, 'L'anaphore arménienne de Saint Grégoire l'Illuminateur', in Botte (ed.), *Eucharisties d'Orient et d'Occident*, pp. 83–108; Gabriele Winkler, *Die Basilius-Anaphora: Edition der beiden armenischen Redaktionen und der relevanten Fragmente, Übersetzung und Zusammenschau aller Versionen im Lichte der orientalischen Überlieferungen*, Anaphorae Orientales 2, Rome: Pontificio Istituto Orientale, 2005.

Bohairic Egyptian versions which have been the concern of the study by Achim Budde.[60] The oldest manuscript is a seventh-century Sahidic manuscript, and the first part of the anaphora up to the post-Sanctus is missing. Its editors dated the anaphora to the fourth century. In comparison with the Sahidic and Greek, the Bohairic versions show signs of expansion. Budde has not attempted to reconstruct an urtext, but arranges the texts in parallel with the conviction that the variants speak for themselves as to how an anaphoral tradition was localized, or as local examples of 'improvization'.[61] He does not suggest that it is an Egyptian composition, but that it has been 'Egyptianized'. Hieronymous Engberding, Alphonse Raes and, more recently, Todd Johnson have drawn attention to parts of Egyptian Basil that make it distinctly Egyptian, and in terms of paleoanaphoras, it raises the question of whether some earlier Egyptian Eucharistic Prayer had been fused or thoroughly incorporated into what has become Eg.Bas.[62] Even with the priority of arm.Bas.1, Winkler admits that the Egyptian version is not unimportant, and has its own particular distinctive readings.[63] Among these are the opening *oratio theologica*, with the reference to Psalm 146.6 or Nehemiah 9.6ff, which has parallels in the other Egyptian anaphoras, and the lack of a Benedictus following the Sanctus. The Institution Narrative is introduced with 'for' or 'because', which is an Egyptian characteristic, and the narrative itself is close to that found in Mark/Cyril. The narrative also has *katallangelo* of 1 Corinthians 11 on the lips of Jesus. Eg.Bas has the distinct 'Egyptian' aorist form for the offering (we have offered), and the doxology also is a distinct form, having parallels in three Coptic sources. The cumulative inference would seem to be that, even if the final pattern of Eg.Bas was not a home-grown Egyptian creation, the anaphora represents a prayer tradition that was honed on Egyptian soil and at an early date and perhaps might have influenced the shaping of the Anaphora of Sarapion.

The anaphora opens with praise of God who is 'I am, truly Lord God, existing before the ages, reigning until the ages', and as creator, 'you made heaven and earth and the sea and all that is in them'. The latter, echoing Psalm 146.6 or Nehemiah 9.6ff, have parallels in Strasbourg Gr.254, Mark/Cyril and Barcelona. God sits 'on the throne of [your] glory', leading into the angelic hierarchy and Sanctus, which is a central concern of the *hekhalot* literature, and, with Thomas, indicates the influence on Egyptian anaphoral development. The post-Sanctus rehearses the saving work of Christ and leads to the Institution Narrative, 'this great mystery', which serves as part of the narrative of salvation. Stephen Davis has drawn attention to two particular expansions in the

60 Achim Budde, *Die ägyptische Basilios-Anaphora: Text–Kommentar–Geschichte*, Münster, Aschendorff, 2004.

61 Budde, *Basilios-Anaphora*, p. 551.

62 H. Engberding, *Das eucharistiche Hochgebet der Basileiosliturgie: Textgeschichtliche Untersuchungen und kritische Ausgabe*, Theologie des christlichen Ostens 1, Münster: Verlag Aschendorff, 1931; A. Raes, 'Un nouveau document de la liturgie de S. Basile', *Orientalia Christiana Periodica* 26 (1960), pp. 401–11; Todd E. Johnson, 'Recovering Ägyptisches Heimatgut: An Exercise in Liturgical Methodology', *Questiones Liturgique* 76 (1995), pp. 182–98.

63 Winkler, *Basilius-Anaphora*.

Bohairic.[64] In the Words of Institution, Christ is said to take the bread in his 'holy hands which are spotless and without blemish, blessed and life-giving'. The life-giving dimension of the eucharistic elements was a particular emphasis of Cyril of Alexandria:

> But He is also within us in another way by means of our partaking in the oblation of bloodless offerings, which we celebrate in the churches, having received from Him the saving pattern of the rite, as the blessed Evangelist plainly shows us in the passage which has just been read. For He tells us that 'He took a cup, and gave thanks, and said, Take this, and divide it with one another'. Now by His giving thanks, by which is meant His speaking to God the Father in the manner of prayer, He signified to us that He, so to speak, shares and takes part in His good pleasure in granting us the life-giving blessing which was then bestowed upon us: for every grace, and every perfect gift comes to us from the Father by the Son in the Holy Spirit. And this act then was a pattern for our use of the prayer which ought to be offered, whenever the grace of the mystical and life-giving oblation is about to be spread before Him by us: and so accordingly we are wont to do. For first offering up our thanksgivings, and joining in our praises to God the Father both the Son and the Holy Spirit, we so draw near to the holy tables, believing that we receive life and blessing both spiritually and corporeally: for we receive in us the Word of the Father, Who for our sakes became man, and Who is Life, and the Giver of life.[65]

Life-giving became a particular term that later Copts and Syrian Orthodox added to their anaphoral texts to emphasize not only adherence to Cyril's teaching, but also that their Eucharist alone was the true Eucharist.[66] The transformation of the elements is also further emphasized in the Bohairic expansion of the Epiklesis. The Sahidic and Greek versions call upon the Spirit to come and 'descend upon us and these gifts that have been set before you, and may sanctify them and make them holy of holies'. The Bohairic asks that the Spirit may descend to 'purify them, change them, and manifest them as a sanctification of Your saints'.[67] All the Egyptian versions pray for the living first and then the

64 Stephen J. Davis, *Coptic Christology in Practice: Incarnation and Divine Participation in Late Antique and Medieval Egypt*, Oxford: Oxford University Press, 2008, pp. 92–4.

65 Cyril of Alexandria, http://www.ccel.org/ccel/pearse/morefathers/files/cyril_on_luke_13_sermons_135_145.htm.

66 Patrick T. R. Gray, 'From Eucharist to Christology: The Life-giving Body of Christ in Cyril of Alexandria, Eutyches and Julian of Halicarnassus', in István Perczel, Réka Forrai and György Geréby (eds), *The Eucharist in Theology and Philosophy: Issues of Doctrinal History in East and West from the Patristic Age to the Reformation*, Leuven: Leuven University Press, 2005, pp. 23–35; Bryan D. Spinks, 'Carefully Chosen Words? The Christological Intentionality in the Institution Narrative and the Epiclesis of the Syriac Anaphora of St James', in Steven Hawkes-Teeples, Bert Groen and Stefanos Alexopoulos (eds), *Studies on the Liturgies of the Christian East: Selected Papers of the Third International Congress of the Society of Oriental Liturgy Volos, May 26–30, 2010*, Leuven: Peeters, 2013, pp. 239–57.

67 See Budde, *Basilios-Anaphora*, p. 161; ET Fr Abraam D. Sleman (ed.), *St Basil Liturgy*, www.copticchurch.net. In present usage this is whispered by the priest and is not audible to the congregation.

dead. Davis draws attention to the emphasis on the role of the saints, with the words 'Since, Master, it is a command of your only-begotten Son that we should share in the commemoration of your saints', and, earlier in the anaphora, 'that we may have a share and an inheritance together with all your saints who have pleased you since the beginning'. Davis cites the comment of E. Renaudot, that the saints are those who have become 'sanctified completely in soul, body, and spirit, having become co-corporeal (*σύσσωμοι*), co-participating (*συμμέτοχοι*) and co-formed (*σύμμορφοι*) with Christ', and therefore the priest, on behalf of the people, asks God to grant that same sanctification through pure participation 'in the most pure sacrament'.[68] Davis sees further development of this theology in the prayers following the Pauline Epistle and Catholic Epistle readings. What the three linguistic versions of Egyptian Basil reveal, then, is a heightened concern for the eschatological fruits of the bread and wine, and their transformation. This, however, is also closely connected with the process of sanctification of the communicants and the communion of the living with the saints who have gone before. This is further reinforced in the prayer before the Fraction and the Fraction Prayer (the latter resembles a mini-anaphora) where the holy body and honoured blood are worshipped, and the elements are purified by the Spirit so that we can be purified.

The Anaphora of Mark/Cyril

In addition to Strasbourg Gr.254 (whether a complete early paleoanaphora from which the anaphora developed, or a fragment of an already developed anaphora), Mark/Cyril is also known in two early fragments, a British Museum wooden tablet in Coptic dating from the eighth century, and a sixth-century parchment with the same text in Greek.[69] These latter contain the (post-) Sanctus–Epiklesis unit, Institution Narrative, Anamnesis ('Proclaiming'), Epiklesis of the Holy Spirit, and intercession for spiritual gifts. Strasbourg parallels the opening section. Whatever the development, present Mark/Cyril results in a shape which, although having some things in common with the Roman *canon missae*, is regarded as uniquely Egyptian (see the chart, Appendix I, p. 446).

In comparison with Strasbourg Gr.254, the opening praise verbs have been multiplied, and the list of 'water features' of the earth have been expanded. The praise transitions to 'offering this reasonable and bloodless service' and a paraphrase of Malachi 1.11.[70] At this point the anaphora moves from offering into intercession, obscured in the Greek, but made clear in the Coptic:

> And over this sacrifice and this offering we pray and beseech you, for you are good and love humanity: remember, Lord, the holy and only catholic and apostolic Church . . .

68 Davis, *Coptic Christology in Practice*, p. 95; E. Renaudot, *Liturgiarum Orientalium Collectioi*, Farnborough: Gregg International, [1847] 1970, p. 75.

69 *PEER*, pp. 54–6; Anton Hänggi and Irmgard Pahl, *Prex Eucharistica*, Fribourg: Éditions universitaires Fribourg Suisse, 1968, 2nd edn 1998, pp. 120–3.

70 *PE*, pp. 102–15 (Mark) and 135–9 (Cyril); *PEER*, pp. 59–66.

Earlier scholarship regarded all intercession as a 'late' development, and in Mark/Cyril was judged to be an interpolation.[71] However, Strasbourg Gr.254 is evidence that from the beginning this anaphoral family moved swiftly from praise–offering–intercession. The present intercessions have been expanded with material being added from the Three Prayers, the Synapte, the Anaphora of St James, and *1 Clement* 59 (the latter being regarded as 'Scripture' in the older Egyptian tradition).[72] As with Sarapion, the majority of the anaphora is therefore in an intercessory context. The lengthy intercession ends with the introduction to the Sanctus – Ephesians 1.21. The Sanctus–Epiklesis unit asks God to fill the sacrifice with his blessing 'through the descent of your [all-] Holy Spirit', and the Narrative of Institution follows, 'For our Lord and God and King of all, Jesus the Christ, in the night when he was handed over . . .'. The Anamnesis is a 'proclaiming', and the gifts are mentioned as having been set (aorist), pointing back to the beginning of the anaphora. A second Epiklesis asks for the sending of the Spirit to sanctify and perfect (the Coptic adds 'change') and make the bread and wine the body and blood of Christ. The Holy Spirit is given many attributes, similar to those found in the Anaphora of St James. The Epiklesis is followed by further petition for the fruits of worthy communion:

> that they may become to all of us who partake of them for faith, for sobriety, for healing, [for temperance, for sanctification,] for renewal of soul, body, and spirit, for fellowship in eternal life and immortality, for the glorifying of your [all-]holy name, for forgiveness of sins; that in this as in everything your all-holy and honorable and glorified name may be glorified and praised and sanctified, with Jesus Christ and the Holy Spirit.[73]

Cyril of Alexandria summed up his eucharistic teaching with what appear to be allusions to the text of a comparable anaphora known to him in the fifth century:

> Proclaiming the death in the flesh of the Only-begotten Son of God, that is, of Jesus Christ, and confessing His return to life from the dead and His ascension into heaven, we celebrate the bloodless service in the Churches, and we thus approach the sacramental gifts and are sanctified, being partakers both of the holy flesh and of the precious blood of Christ the Saviour of us all; not receiving it as common flesh – surely not! – nor as the flesh of a man sanctified and associated with the Word in a unity of dignity, or at least as having Divine indwelling, but as truly life-giving [*zoopoion*], and as the Word's very own. For being naturally Life as God, when he became One with his own flesh He rendered it life-giving.[74]

71 R.-G. Coquin, 'L'anaphore alexandrine de saint Marc', *Le Muséon* 82 (1969), pp. 307–56.

72 See Cuming, *Liturgy of St Mark*, p. 109, for detailed parallels and sources.

73 *PEER*, p. 66.

74 Text in T. Herbert Bindley and F. W. Green, *The Oecumenical Documents of the Faith*, London: Methuen and Co., 1950, pp. 215–16.

The Anaphora of St Gregory

The third Egyptian anaphora in use today is named after Gregory Nazianzus. Although there are Armenian and Syriac anaphoras of the same name, that is the only thing that they have in common with the Egyptian anaphora. This anaphora is addressed throughout to God the Son. Josef Jungmann, in his classic work *The Place of Christ in Liturgical Prayer*, argued that the anaphora was no earlier than the sixth century, since because it was addressed to the Son, it was a product of the non-Chalcedonian miaphysite Christology.[75] More recent scholarship demonstrates that prayer to Christ pre-dates the non-Chalcedonian splits.[76] Anton Baumstark suggested that this anaphora had been expanded by Gregory himself and brought to Egypt by Syrian monks.[77] Ernst Hammerschmidt, in his edition of the Coptic (Bohairic) text, suggested that it was to be dated between the last years of the fourth century and the early part of the fifth century.[78] José Manuel Sánchez Caro compared the I–Thou style of the post-Sanctus with the writings of Gregory, and concluded that the Nazianzen bishop could have compiled it himself. Thus, for example, 'You delivered to me the precepts of the law' is, in the thought of Gregory, an allusion to the law given to Adam, represented in the Tree of Knowledge.[79] He concluded that this section was consistent with the anti-Arian stance of Gregory. Albert Gerhards, in his critical edition of the Greek text, took this further, arguing that the anaphora may have been composed by Proclus of Constantinople (d. 446) who knew Gregory's writings, adding an anti-Nestorian element, and subsequently the anaphora was 'Egyptianized'.[80] This would account for its 'West Syrian' pattern but with some 'Egyptian' characteristics.

The opening praise section to the Sanctus consists of praise verbs, a *theologica negativa* (not inconsistent with Gregory's theology) and the praise of the angels. Though not full of intercessions in the manner of Mark/Cyril, it does, in the manner of Sarapion, switch to intercession. Whereas Sarapion asked for Jesus and the Holy Spirit to hymn in us, Gregory requests:

> Accept from us also our voices together with the unseen. Count us among the powers in the heavens. Let us also sing together with them – having cast away from us all remembrance of unbefitting thoughts – and cry out with what is sent up by them, with unsilenced voices and mouths . . .[81]

75 Josef Jungmann, *The Place of Christ in Liturgical Prayer*, 2nd edn, London: Geoffery Chapman, 1965.

76 See Bryan D. Spinks (ed.), *The Place of Christ in Liturgical Prayer: Trinity, Christology, and Liturgical Theology*, Collegeville: Liturgical Press, 2008.

77 Anton Baumstark, *Die Chrysostomosliturgie und die syrische Liturgie des Nestorios*, Chrysostomika, Rome: Tipografia Poliglotta, 1908, pp. 846–8.

78 Ernst Hammerschmidt, *Die Koptische Gregoriosanaphora. Syrische und Griechische Einflüsse Auf Eine Ägyptische Liturgie*, Berlin: Akademie Verlag, 1957.

79 José Manuel Sánchez Caro, *Eucharistia e Historia de la Salvacion*, Madrid: Biblioteca de Autores Cristianos, 1984, p. 323.

80 Albert Gerhards, *Die griechische Gregoriosanaphora: Ein Beitrag zur Geschichte des Eucharistischen Hochgebets*, Münster: Aschendorff, 1984.

81 ET, Pope Shenouda III, 'Saint Gregory the Theologian: According to the Rites of the Coptic Orthodox Church', http://www.copticchurch.net/topics/liturgy/stgregory.pdf, p. 33.

The very lengthy rehearsal of Christ's saving work is expressed in a You–me, or I–Thou style:

> You fulfilled your law for me. You showed me the way to rise from my fall,

The priest prays just before the Words of Institution:

> I offer to you, o my Master the symbols of my freedom. I write my deeds in keeping with your words. You are he who has given me this service which is full of mystery. You granted me to offer up your flesh in bread and wine.

The Epiklesis prays:

> You our Master, through your voice yourself, change these gifts that are here. You, being with us, prepare for us this service which is full of mystery. Implant in us the remembrance of your holy service. Send down upon us the grace of your Holy Spirit that he may purify and change these holy offerings present here into the body and blood of our salvation.[82]

Lengthy intercessions for living and departed follow, as in Eg.Bas.

Concluding remarks

It would seem that Egypt used anaphoras of a variety of patterns, and those that show similarities to the 'West Syrian' pattern were not necessarily foreign imports. They appear to be home grown, or certainly 'Egyptianized' immediately they had cleared Customs! The elements, as already found in Theodore of Mopsuestia, were treated as sacred types from their selection for the service. The Egyptian anaphora speaks of them having been offered at some point before the anaphora. This may account also for the intercessions being placed immediately after the opening praise, and the idea that the Eucharist is the fulfilment of the sacrifice of Malachi 1.11. Presence is invoked twice – immediately after the Sanctus and again just before the end of the anaphora. In later versions in Bohairic, the request for change is stated more clearly. The Institution Narrative seems to serve less as the culmination of thanksgiving for Christ's saving earthly life than in its intercessory context, serving as a solemn warrant for the rite. The eschatological gifts of communion are emphasized in the light of the Egyptian concern found in Cyril of Alexandria, that the elements become life-giving to those who receive them. The focus of belief – offering and presence – is heightened by the elaborate ritualized preparation of the elements and the altar prior to the older commencement of the liturgy. These particular aspects find emphasis in the late Pope Shenouda III's book entitled *Priesthood*. On the concept of eucharistic sacrifice he wrote:

82 My translation of Hammerschmidt and the present text. Both the Greek and the Coptic have variants.

> We remember and preach his atonement and His sacrificial death on the cross, until His Second Coming. We remember His limitless Love. But all this memory does not warrant forgetting that; 'This Is My Body . . . This Is My Blood'. Also the expression 'Each time you eat' and 'Each time you drink' denotes perpetuity of the original offering made on Maundy Thursday.[83]

On presence he wrote:

> **We proclaim in the Liturgy that this is the TRUE BODY and TRUE BLOOD of our Lord Jesus Christ.** This proclamation is not based on a contrived, preconceived idea of ours. It is also NOT a theological novelty. We have taken what the Lord said as gospel truth in simplicity, as spiritual people and not as argumentative theorists. We accept it as is because the Lord uttered it. We dare not add to His utterance, nor can we mix it with our earthly wisdom in contradiction with the Word. We urge those who claim to be 'Evangelical' to follow the gospel truth.[84]

The English translation unfortunately used the term transubstantiation, though the Coptic tradition has never signed up to Western medieval Aristotelian terminology. The Arabic words used are forms of the root حول (ḥwl), with the basic meaning of 'to change'. Coptic–Arabic glossaries offer حول (ḥwl) as a possible Arabic translation for the Coptic term used in the Bohairic Basilian epiclesis, change.[85] Pope Shenouda was contrasting the Coptic belief with a perceived Protestant belief:

> He did not say 'This is symbolic of My Body & this is symbolic of My Blood'. Saint Paul did not speak of 'discerning the Lords Symbolic Body' but rather, He said: *(1 Cor 11:29) For he who eats and drinks in an unworthy manner eats and drinks judgment to himself, not discerning the Lord's body.* **Hence if one says that he is only partaking of a symbol, such person is not discerning of the Lord's body.** Those who are sincere about the biblical truth should carefully consider the above verses, which were uttered by Christ and Saint Paul His disciple.[86]

Although Tadros Malaty has emphasized that consecration is by uttering the words of Christ himself and by 'asking the Father to send His Holy Spirit upon the oblations to be transformed into the Immortal Body and Blood of Christ in order that their effect may be accomplished in us', Athanasius Iskander probably better represents the Eastern concern to be less circumscript when

83 H. H. Pope Shenouda III, 'Priesthood', trans. Amir Hanna, revised Maher Malek, COEPA 1997, http://tasbeha.org/content/hh_books/Priesthd/index.html.

84 Shenouda III, 'Priesthood'.

85 In the Arabic translation of St Basil's Liturgy commonly used today, however, a different Arabic word is used (root نقل, nql). I am grateful to Mary Farag and Fr Athanasius Farag for this information.

86 Shenouda III, 'Priesthood'.

he says that 'the change of the gifts is a "hidden mystery" that is exalted far above the limits of human thoughts or the power of speech . . . it is revealed to us, the "babes" who in faith, believe in the mystery without any probing into the nature of the mystery, the "babes" who cry out aloud, "I believe, *so be it*".'[87]

87 Tadros Y. Malaty, *Christ in the Eucharist*, Orange, CA: Coptic Orthodox Christian Center, 2001, p. 158; Athanasius Iskander, *Understanding the Liturgy*, reprints of articles first published in *Parousia* September 1993–March 1997, Kitchener, Ontario: St Mary's Coptic Orthodox Church, nd, p. 51, Article of March 1996, p. 7.

5

The Eucharist and Anaphoras of the Byzantine Synthesis

The Byzantine rite is the name given to the liturgies used by the Eastern Orthodox (those Churches in communion with the Ecumenical Patriarch of Constantinople, such as Greek, Russian and Serbian Orthodox), together with some dissident breakaways, and, with some modifications, the Eastern Catholics (those uniate groups that are in communion with Rome). The Eucharist, or Divine Liturgy, has a complex history, and its primary core is derived from the liturgy as celebrated in Hagia Sophia or the 'Great Church' in Constantinople until the fall of that city to the Ottomans in 1453. Robert Taft divides its development into five phases:

1. The paleo-Byzantine or pre-Constantine era, about which we know little.
2. The imperial phase during the late patristic period, especially from the reign of Justinian I (527–565) and his immediate successors, creating a system of cathedral liturgy that lasted until sometime after the Latin Conquest (1204–61), thus overlapping with phases 3–4.
3. The 'Dark Ages', 610–*c.* 850, including the Iconoclasm disputes, culminating in the Studite reform.
4. The Studite era (800–1204).
5. The final neo-Sabaitic synthesis after the Latin Conquest.[1]

Certain features are derived from the stational or processional liturgies in Constantinople, adapted for the very different settings of small parish churches. It is also an amalgamation or synthesis of the traditions of Antioch and Caesarea marked particularly by the use of the Anaphoras of St John Chrysostom and St Basil. By the eleventh century the Liturgy of St John Chrysostom (prayers and the anaphora) came to be the dominant and usual rite used.[2] The Byzantine

1 Robert F. Taft, *The Byzantine Rite: A Short History*, Collegeville: Liturgical Press, 1992, pp. 18–19; 'The Liturgy of the Great Church: An Initial Synthesis of Structure and Interpretation on the Eve of Iconoclasm', *Dumbarton Oaks Papers* 34–5 (1980–1), pp. 45–75; expanded and reprinted in *Liturgy in Byzantium and Beyond*, Variorum, Aldershot: Ashgate, Ch. 1.

2 St Basil is used on the Sundays of the Great Lent, Thursday and Saturday of Holy Week, the vigils of the Nativity and Theophany, as well as the feast of St Basil. Stefanos Alexopoulas has argued that Chrysostom became the preferred anaphora after the iconoclastic disputes because Basil lent itself to the arguments of the iconoclasts. Stefanos Alexopoulas, 'The Influence of Iconoclasm on Liturgy: A Case Study', in Roberta R. Ervine (ed.), *Worship Traditions in Armenia and the Neighboring Christian East*, Crestwood: St Vladimir's Press with St Nersess

rite also borrowed and used the Jerusalem Anaphora of St James; although this was probably once more widely used, it is usually limited now to the feast of St James. This synthesis, as celebrated in splendour in Hagia Sophia, provoked the comment of the envoys of Prince Vladimir of Kiev:

> the Greeks led us to the edifices where they worship their God, and we knew not whether we were in heaven or on earth. For on earth there is no such splendor or such beauty, and we were at a loss how to describe it. We only know that God dwells there among men, and their service is fairer than the ceremonies of other nations. For we cannot forget that beauty.[3]

The contemporary Byzantine Divine Liturgy, St John Chrysostom and St Basil, has the following outline:[4]

- [Vesting prayers.]
- [PROTHESIS–elaborate preparation of the bread (the Lamb) and chalice.]
- Preparation and opening dialogue.
- ENARXIS.
- Initial Blessing Litany (Great Synapte) and Prayer 1.
- Antiphon 1.
- Litany (Little Synapte) and Prayer 2.
- Antiphon 2 Litany (Little Synapte) and Prayer 3.
- Antiphon 3 with added refrains (*Ho Monogenes*), or Beatitudes.
- LITTLE ENTRANCE [This was the more ancient beginning of the Liturgy.]
- Trisagion prayer and chant.
- Procession to the throne.
- Epistle or Acts.
- Gospel.
- Ektene.
- Litany of the Catechumens Prayer (John Chrysostom or Basil).
- Dismissal of Catechumens.
- Litany of the Faithful with prayers (John Chrysostom or Basil).
- Cherubic Hymn Prayer of the Cherubic Hymn.
- Incensation.

Seminary, 2006, pp. 127–37; see also Stefano Parenti, 'La "vittoria" nella chiesa de Constantinopoli della Liturgia di Crisostomo sulla Liturgia de Basilio', in Robert F. Taft and Gabriele Winkler (eds), *Comparative Liturgy Fifty Years after Anton Baumstark (1872–1948)*, Rome: Pontifico Istituto Orientale, 2001, pp. 907–28. There is also a liturgy of the pre-sanctified. For this latter, see Stefanos Alexopoulas, *Presanctified Liturgy in the Byzantine Rite: A Comparative Analysis of Its Origins, Evolution, and Structural Components*, Liturgia Condenda 21, Leuven: Peeters, 2009.

3 S. H. Cross and O. P. Sherbowitz-Weltzor, *The Russian Primary Chronicle: Laurention Text*, Cambridge, MA: The Medieval Academy of America, 1953, pp. 110–11.

4 I have used Antiochene Orthodox Christian Archdiocese of North America, *The Liturgikon: The Book of Divine Services for the Priest and Deacon*, Grand Rapids: Dickinson Press, 1989. The Deacon's parts have been omitted in this outline.

- GREAT ENTRANCE (transfer of bread and chalice from the prothesis room through the *naos* to the altar through the Royal (central) doors).
- *Orate fratres* dialogue.
- Litany and Prayer of the *Proskomide.*
- Kiss of Peace.
- Nicene Creed.
- ANAPHORA (John Chrysostom or Basil).
- Litany and prayer.
- Lord's Prayer.
- Prayer of Inclination (John Chrysostom or Basil).
- Prayer of Elevation: 'Holy things for the holy'.
- Chant.
- Fraction and adding of the Zeon (warm water) to the chalice.
- Communion gifts returned to the altar and censed.
- Litany and Prayer of Thanksgiving (John Chrysostom or Basil).
- Dismissal Prayer behind the ambo.
- Prayer of consumption of the gifts.
- Final blessing and distribution of the *antidoron* (the bread not used for the communion).

The development of this complex rite has been carefully documented in studies by Robert Taft, in which he has given an almost exhaustive examination of the manuscripts and printed editions of this rite, as well as some of the classic commentaries.[5] These commentaries follow the tradition of the allegorical methods already encountered in Cyril of Jerusalem and Theodore of Mopsuesta, and even though the latter was condemned in 553 his method has none the less been extremely influential in the Byzantine synthesis. Equally influential was *The Ecclesiastical Hierarchy* of Pseudo-Dionysius the Areopagite. This seems to have been the work of a non-Chalcedonian Syrian, first attested to in the writings of Severus of Antioch, and brought to the attention of the Chalcedonians in conversations in 532. Pseudo-Dionysius combined an Alexandrian approach to theology with Neoplatonism, seeking the true spiritual reality behind the earthly image: 'we must penetrate what is most holy. When we have uncovered the intelligible character of the first of the images, we must gaze upon its godlike beauty.'[6] His method was to describe the rite and then turn to the spiritual interpretation. The rite he describes may well have been similar to that of Antioch, or even of the Liturgy of St James.[7]

5 Robert Taft, *The Great Entrance: A History of the Transfer of Gifts and other Pre-anaphoral Rites of the Liturgy of St. John Chrysostom*, Rome: Pontificum Institutum Studiorum Orientalium, 1975; *The Diptychs*, Rome: Pontificium Institutum Studiorum Orientalium, 1991; *The Precommunion Rites*, Rome: Pontificio Istituto Orientale, 2000; *The Communion, Thanksgiving, and Concluding Rites*, Rome: Pontificio Istituto Orientale, 2008. The studies are in succession to Juan Mateos, *La Célération de la Parole dans la Liturgie Byzantine: Étude historique*, Rome: Pontificorum Institutorum Studiorum Orientalium, 1971.

6 ET in Thomas L. Campbell, *Dionysius the Pseudo-Areopagite: The Ecclesiastical Hierarchy*, Lanham: University Press of America, 1981, p. 36.

7 Campbell, *Dionysius the Pseudo-Areopagite*, p. 139.

> When the bishop has finished a holy prayer near the divine altar, he commences by incensing it and goes around the whole enclosure of the holy place. He goes back again to the divine altar and starts the sacred chanting of the Psalms with the whole ecclesiastical order accompanying him in the holy language of the Psalter. Next comes the reading of the Sacred Scriptures by the deacons. After these readings the catechumens leave the sacred precincts, along with the possessed and the penitents. Those worthy of beholding and sharing divine things remain. Some of the deacons stand near the closed doors of the holy place, while others perform some other duty proper to their rank. After the whole body of the church has sung as a confession the hymn of the Catholic faith, with the priests, the members of the diaconal ministry chosen for it place the holy bread and the chalice of benediction on the divine altar. Then the divine bishop pronounces a sacred prayer and proclaims 'the holy peace be to everyone.' When all have given the kiss of peace to one another, the mystical recitation of the holy diptychs takes place.
>
> After the bishop and the priests have washed their hands in water, the bishop takes up his position at the center of the divine altar, and the chosen deacons alone stand nearby with the priests. When the bishop has praised the sacred works of God, he consecrates the most divine mysteries, and holds up to view the things celebrated, reverently brought forth under the symbols. Having shown the gifts of God, the bishop proceeds to holy communion in them and invites the others to do likewise. After he has received and distributed the supremely divine Communion, he ends with a holy thanksgiving. Although the multitude has seen only the divine symbols, he himself is always hierarchically raised by the supremely divine Spirit to the holy archetypes of the mysteries by means of blessed and spiritual visions on account of the purity of his godlike condition.[8]

Theodore's ideas and those of Dionysius inspired further commentaries, such as those of Maximus the Confessor (seventh century), St Germanus (eighth century), Nicholas Cabasilas (fourteenth century) and two by Symeon of Thessalonike (fifteenth century).[9] Although hitherto most scholars, accepting the Greek Vita, have regarded Maximus as a well-connected and well-to-do person of Constantinople, who describes the rite of Constantinople, some scholars have followed Brock in preferring the biographical details preserved in a hostile Syriac source, which attributes a Palestinian origin for Maximus with only a brief stay in Constantinople. It may be, therefore, that Maximus is a witness

8 Campbell, *Dionysius the Pseudo-Areopagite*, pp. 34–5.

9 English translations cited here: George C. Berthold, *Maximus Confessor: Selected Writings*, New York: Paulist Press, 1985; Paul Meyendorff, *St. Germanus of Constantinople: On the Divine Liturgy*, Crestwood: St Vladimir's Seminary Press, 1984; J. M. Hussey, P. A. McNulty and Nicholas Cabasilas, *A Commentary on the Divine Liturgy*, London: SPCK, 1960; Steven Hawkes-Teeples, *St. Symeon of Thessalonika: The Liturgical Commentaries*, Toronto: Pontifical Institute of Medieval Studies, 2011. There are other commentaries, such as the eleventh-century Protheoria, and by Nicholas and Theodore of Andida. See René Bornert, *Les Commentaires Byzantins de la Divine Liturgie du VIIe au XVe Siècle*, Paris: Institut Français d'Etudes Byzantines, 1966.

to Palestinian rather than Constantinopolitan usage, though the commentary is so vague that it could be any rite.[10] The commentaries tend to presuppose a celebration by a bishop, and it is also the case, as with all ancient commentaries, that they do not necessarily comment on everything that is useful for modern scholarly reconstructions.

As with the Coptic rite, the present vesting prayers and the prothesis are a later, post-ninth-century development.[11] In the earliest Byzantine manuscript, Barberini 336, there is one prayer for the prothesis, and no prayers for vesting. The preparation of vesting and the careful cutting of the bread are examples of ever-intensifying clerical piety. Germanus describes the vesture and its meaning, and this finds extended treatment in Cabasilas and Symeon.[12] Although the prothesis is described by Germanus, Paul Meyendorff notes that this section of the commentary originally came just before the transfer of the gifts, but was moved to a new position before the liturgy, reflecting the later development.[13] Of the prothesis, Cabasilas explained that the elements are not brought to the altar immediately and 'sacrificed', but are first dedicated since Christ was dedicated to God from the beginning.[14] However, whereas for Theodore the elements represented the slain body of Christ, for Cabasilas the ceremonies known to him for the prothesis also reflect the incarnation:

> As long as it remains in the *prothesis* the bread thus separated from the rest is still only bread. But it has acquired a new characteristic – it is dedicated to God; it has become an offering, since it represents our Lord during the first phase of his life on earth, when he became an oblation. Now this happened at the moment of his birth, as has been said, for, as the first-born, he was offered up from birth, in accordance with the Law. But the pains which Christ endured afterwards for our salvation, his Cross and Death, had been symbolized beforehand in the Old Testament. That is why the

10 Taft, *Great Entrance*; Hans-Joachim Schulze, *The Byzantine Liturgy*, New York: Pueblo Publishing, 1986; Hugh Wybrew, *The Orthodox Liturgy: The Development of the Eucharistic Liturgy in the Byzantine Rite*, London: SPCK, 1989; Paul F. Bradshaw, Paul F. and Maxwell E. Johnson, *The Eucharistic Liturgies: Their Evolution and Interpretation*, Collegeville: Liturgical Press, 2012, do not address this question, though oddly they attribute his work to the sixth century. For the Palestinian argument, see Sebastian Brock, 'An Early Syriac Life of Maximus the Confessor', *Analecta Bollandiana* 91 (1973), pp. 299–346. For other scholars, see footnote 35 in Joseph Patrich, 'Archaeological and Literary Evidence for the Evolution of the "Great Entrance"', in Béatrice Caseau, Jean-Claude Cheynet, and Vincent Déroche (eds), *Pèlerinages et Lieux Saints dans l'Antiquité et le Moyen Âge: Mélangues offerts à Pierre Maraval*, Paris: Association des Amis du Centre d'Histoire et Civilisation de Byzance, 2006, p. 347. For a recent strong argument for Constantinople, see Robert F. Taft, 'Is the Liturgy Described in the Mystagogia of Maximus Confessor Byzantine, Palestinian, or Neither?', *in Bollettino della Badia Greca di Grottaferrata* 8 (2011), pp. 223–270.

11 For a good discussion on the development of the prothesis, see Thomas Pott, *Byzantine Liturgical Reform*, Crestwood: St Vladimir's Seminary Press, 2010, pp. 197–228.

12 For a recent discussion on origin and development, see Warren T. Woodfin, *Embodied Icon: Liturgical Vestments and Sacramental Power in Byzantium*, New York: Oxford University Press, 2012.

13 Meyendorff, *St. Germanus*, p. 13.

14 Cabasilas, *Commentary on the Divine Liturgy*, p. 31.

> priest marks the loaf with these symbols before carrying it to the altar and sacrificing it.[15]

The loaf is leavened bread, the top flattened and stamped with a round wooden stamp bearing the inscription IC XC NIKA (Jesus Christ Conquers).[16] Symeon explained the ritual cutting with the 'lance' (liturgical knife) thus:

> Then, by means of the lance, typifying the one which pierced the Lord, he cuts out the four-part seal of the prosphora, adding the words of Isaiah, 'Like a lamb he was led to slaughter', and the rest, showing the mystery proclaimed beforehand. When he says, 'That His life is being taken up from the earth', inserting the lance from the side, he takes out the four-sided bread with the seal, and sets it on the diskos.
>
> The diskos, then, typifies the heavens, and for that reason, it is round, and holds the Master of heaven. What is called the 'asterisk' represents the stars, especially the one at the birth of Christ, just as the veils represent the firmament, the swaddling clothes, the shroud, and the burial cloths. For He was incarnate for this reason: in order that he might be slain for us. But the prothesis also offers the figure of the cave and the manger. The chalice typifies that one in which the Savior offered His blood in the sacred-service.[17]

There is here a developing eucharistic theology, but in a ritual that is solely clerical and not part of the public liturgy.

Both Cabasilas and Symeon know of the opening blessing and the antiphons, though Pseudo-Dionysius and Maximus presuppose that the Liturgy of the Word begins soon after the entrance of the bishop. As Taft has shown, the initial blessing in the contemporary rite does not appear until the eleventh century. All the initial litanies (*Synapte*), antiphons and the Trisagion (which was a refrain) reflect the stational liturgy of Constantinople, where the people and clergy assembled in a certain place and processed singing psalms with antiphons to the church in which the Divine Liturgy was to be celebrated.[18] The public liturgy began when the bishop entered the Church, followed by the people,[19] signified by the 'Little Entrance' when the Gospel book is processed; after a greeting, the lections were read and a homily, or homilies, was given.[20] It would seem that the stational antiphons were popular, and the 'Office of the Three Antiphons' was adopted for use on those days when there was no station. In the sixth century the Trisagion became the antiphon for the Introit psalm, and then subsequently the psalm dis-

15 Cabasilas, *Commentary on the Divine Liturgy*, p. 36.

16 See E. S. Drower, *Water into Wine: A Study of Ritual Idiom in the Middle East*, London: John Murray, 1956.

17 Symeon, 'On the Sacred Liturgy', Hawkes-Teeples, *St. Symeon of Thessalonika*, p. 185.

18 See John F. Baldovin, *The Urban Character of Christian Worship: The Origins, Development, and Meaning of Stational Liturgy*, Rome: Pontificorum Institutum Studiorum Orientalium, 1987.

19 Berthold, *Maximus*, pp. 198–9.

20 Robert Taft, 'How Liturgies Grow: The Evolution of the Byzantine Divine Liturgy', in Robert Taft (ed.), *Beyond East and West: Problems in Liturgical Understanding*, Washington, DC: The Pastoral Press, 1984, pp. 167–92.

appeared.[21] The *ektene* or litany after the Gospel also derives from stational liturgies.[22] The dismissal of the catechumens and others, and the closing of the doors (the latter commented upon by Maximus), are ancient elements of the rite.

The Great Entrance was, as in Theodore, the moment when the deacons transferred the selected bread and wine from the *skeuophylakion* – at Hagia Sophia a circular structure, detached from the church to its north, where the faithful deposited their offerings – bread, wine, oil, food, donations and tithes, but elsewhere a prothesis room.[23] Later, with the introduction of the tripartite sanctuary, the prothesis would take place in the north room. In Theodore, the Great Entrance was carried out in silence, and liturgy often abhors a silence. Taft suggests that the older core in the Byzantine rite was the transfer of the gifts by the deacons, an oration said by the priest (Prayer of the *Proskomide*) and the cherubic hymn, added under Justin II in 573–574, sung by the people. The celebrant also washed his hands. Cabasilas explained the meaning of the Great Entrance thus:

> The priest, having said the doxology aloud, comes to the altar of preparation, takes the offerings, and reverently holding them head-high departs. Carrying them thus, he goes to the altar, after walking in slow and solemn procession through the nave of the church. The faithful chant during this procession, kneeling down reverently and devoutly, and praying that they may be remembered when the offering is made. The priest goes on, surrounded by candles and incense, until he comes to the altar. This is done, no doubt, for practical reasons; it was necessary to bring the offerings which are to be sacrificed to the altar and set them down there, and to do this with all reverence and devotion. This is the way in which kings of old brought their gifts to God; they did not allow others to do it for them, but brought their offerings themselves, wearing their crowns. Also, this ceremony signifies the last manifestation of Christ, which aroused the hatred of the Jews, when he embarked on the journey from his native country to Jerusalem, where he was to be sacrificed; then he rode into the Holy City on the back of an ass, escorted by a cheering crowd.[24]

Symeon defended the custom of the faithful prostrating before the elements:

> For we do not commit idolatry in prostrating ourselves to the divine gifts – far from it! – but we give honor to the gifts offered to God through prayers, though they are not yet consecrated; <we do so> since they are sanctified by the presentation, are hallowed by most divine prayers and are antitypes of the body of Christ and His blood.[25]

Symeon was able to find 'divine meaning' in much of the minutiae of the placing of the gifts:

21 Taft, 'How Liturgies Grow', p. 176.

22 Taft, 'How Liturgies Grow', p. 177.

23 Taft, *Great Entrance*; Joseph Patrich, art. cit.

24 Cabasilas, *Commentary on the Divine Liturgy*, p. 65.

25 Symeon, 'Explanation of the Divine Temple', Hawkes-Teeples, *Liturgical Commentaries*, p. 129.

> When the divine gifts have been set on the sacred altar, they are covered 1) because Jesus was not recognized by all from the beginning, and 2) because, though incarnate, He did not thereby give up the hidden quality of His divinity or His foreknowledge, but is always incomprehensible and infinite, and is know only insofar as he reveals Himself.[26]

The Creed, as noted in a previous chapter, was added by a non-Chalcedonian and was retained by the Chalcedonians. The Kiss of Peace found in St Paul and Justin Martyr is an ancient core ritual. Other than the Sanctus, the anaphora is not commented upon by Maximus, because the anaphora by this time was recited silently.[27] The anaphora is summarized in some detail by Germanus, and in his day the normal anaphora was that of St Basil. He highlighted the work of the Holy Spirit in the anaphora:

> And again the priest asks God to accomplish and bring about the mystery of His Son – that is, that the bread and wine be changed into the body and blood of Christ God – so that it might be fulfilled that 'Today I have begotten you' (Ps 2:7). Then the Holy Spirit, invisibly present by the good will and volition of the Father, demonstrates the divine operation and, by the hand of the priest, testifies, completes, and changes the holy gifts which are set forth into the body and blood of Jesus Christ our Lord . . .[28]

The research of Taft on the post-anaphoral communion rites suggests that the litany and prayer have been influenced from the Divine Office, though a litany and collect were part of the rite by *c.* 375.[29] The Lord's Prayer, though attested to by St John Chrysostom, was a recent introduction to the rite of Constantinople, *c.* 385.[30] The Prayer of Inclination, according to Taft, was a fourth-century addition serving as a final blessing over non-communicants who left at this point.[31] The chants, he suggests, are the remnant of a pre-communion psalm.[32] The elevation with 'holy things for holy people' is already found in *AC* VIII and in Theodore.

The Fraction in the Byzantine rite, as in most Eastern rites, is highly stylized and elaborate. The 'Lamb' is marked by the bread stamp IC/XC/NI/KA. This guides the celebrant into separating it into four and arranging it in the form of a cross on the diskos. The portion stamped IC is then placed in the chalice, the commingling. Unique to this rite is the addition of the *zeon*, or warm water. According to Taft, it was customary in domestic usage to drink wine cut with

26 Symeon, 'Explanation of the Divine Temple', p. 131.

27 Berthold, *Maximus*, p. 22. Pace Berthold, this is the Sanctus and not the Trisagion. Robert Taft, 'Was the Eucharistic Anaphora Recited Secretly or Aloud? The Ancient Tradition and What Became of It', in Roberta R. Ervine (ed.), *Worship Traditions in Armenia and the Neighboring Christian East*, Crestwood: St Vladimir's Seminary Press and St Nersess Armenian Seminary, 2006, pp. 15–57, p. 41.

28 Meyendorff, *St. Germanus*, pp. 97–9.

29 Taft, *Precommunion Rites*, p. 65.

30 Taft, *Precommunion Rites*, p. 66.

31 Taft, *Precommunion Rites*, p. 193.

32 Taft, 'How Liturgies Grow', pp. 184–6; Taft, *Precommunion Rites*, pp. 261–318.

hot water, and a desire to keep the chalice warm right up until communion to signify the living body and blood led to delaying the infusion of hot water until just before the Great Entrance, and then more hot water was added just before communion. The final practice was adding plain unheated water at the prothesis and hot water just prior to communion.[33] Whatever its origins in drinking customs, Symeon articulated its theological meaning:

> Then he also pours hot water into the chalice. He does this to witness that even when the Lord's body was dead and separated from His divine soul, it remained vivifying, since the divinity had not been taken from Him nor all the energies of the Spirit separated from Him. Since, then, the warm water represents the image of life on account of the heat, it is added at the moment of communion, so that, touching the lips to the chalice and receiving the blood in communion, we are confident that we are drinking from that vivifying breast, with the introduction and the feel of the heat typifying that the divinity has not been taken away, for it is written that our God is fire.[34]

Communion was once by bread in the hand and by drinking from the chalice, and this is still the case with the clergy, and in the rubrics of the Liturgy of St James. For the laity, communion is in the bread soaked in the chalice of wine, administered on a spoon. Communion was followed by a litany and prayer of thanksgiving, and concluding rites. The giving of the unblessed bread, the antidoron, may have been a vestige of a meal or distribution of charity, but with the decline in communicating (already complained of by St John Chrysostom), this rite has become a communion substitute. The Prayer 'Behind the Ambo' was once a prayer recited by the clergy on their way back to the *skeuophylakion*, but by the tenth century was moved to after the dismissal.[35]

The Byzantine anaphoras

The Byzantine rite has three anaphoras – St John Chrysostom (CHR), St Basil (Byz.Bas) and St James. All belong to the 'Syro-Byzantine' family, and there is evidence of mutual influence between them. However, each also has its own distinct history and theological ethos.

The Greek Anaphora of St John Chrysostom

Apostolic Constitutions (*AC*) VIII is believed to reflect the environs of Antioch *c.* 380, and it may also be the case that the anaphora of the so-called *Apostolic Tradition* had its origins in the same vicinity. This was suggested in 1961 by Massey Shepherd, and its affinities with West Syrian anaphoras rather than

33 Taft, *Precommunion Rites*, pp. 441–502.

34 Taft, *Precommunion Rites*, p. 488; Symeon, 'Explanation of the Divine Temple', p. 151.

35 For details of all these, see Robert F. Taft, *The Communion, Thanksgiving, and Concluding Rites*, Rome: Pontificio Istituto Orientale, 2008.

Rome has been more recently demonstrated by Matthieu Smyth.[36] The Greek anaphora named after St John Chrysostom is thought to be of a comparable date to *AC* and may well have been an anaphora used in Antioch when Chrysostom was a presbyter there, and brought by him to Constantinople when he became bishop. Our earliest manuscript, Barberini 336, dates from the eighth century.[37] The modern text has only slight variations. Georg Wagner subjected the anaphora to a careful comparison with the writings of Chrysostom, and suggested that he might have compiled the anaphora that bears his name.[38] Few have accepted these conclusions. Franz Van de Pavard did the reverse, reconstructing the liturgy of Antioch from the allusions in Chrysostom's writings, though this presumes that one knows the liturgy for which one is finding allusions to.[39] The matter is further complicated by the fact that the anaphora has a Syriac 'twin' (not that named St John Chrysostom, which, apart from the name, has nothing in common with CHR) called Twelve Apostles. Compared with the Greek text, the Syriac text is either less expanded or has been abbreviated. Some scholars have thought that the Syriac preserves the earlier text, but in the opinion of Sebastian Brock, and also of Georg Wagner, the Syriac style reflects the seventh century.[40] It may be the case, therefore, that an earlier common text lies behind both CHR and Syriac Twelve Apostles. Robert Taft, using the *Thesaurus Linguae Graecae* (*TLG*) database, ran a computer search for similarities between Chrysostom's writings and CHR, and concluded that at two particular places there is a strong possibility that Chrysostom had expanded an earlier version of the prayer.[41] Thus in the opening praise, the Greek text has:

> For you are God, ineffable, inconceivable, invisible, incomprehensible, existing always in the same way.[42]

36 M. H. Shepherd, 'The Formation and Influence of the Antiochene Liturgy', *Dumbarton Oaks Papers* 15 (1961), pp. 25–44; Matthieu Smyth, 'The Anaphora of the So-called "Apostolic Tradition" and the Roman Eucharistic Prayer', in Maxwell E. Johnson (ed.), *Issues in Eucharistic Praying in East and West*, Collegeville: Liturgical Press, 2011, pp. 71–97.

37 Stefano Parenti and Elena Velkovska (eds), *L'Eucologio Barberini gr.336*, Rome: CLV Edizioni Liturgiche, 1995, pp. 32–40. For the manuscript tradition of the whole liturgy, see A. Jacob, 'La Tradition Manuscrite de la Liturgie de Saint Jean Chrysostome', in B. Botte et al. (eds), *Eucharisties d'Orient et d'Occident*, 2 vols, Paris: Les Éditions du Cerf, 1970, pp. 109–38.

38 G. Wagner, *Der Ursprung der Chrysostomusliturgie*, Münster: Aschendorff, 1973.

39 Franz Van de Pavard, *Zur Geschichte der Messliturgie in Antiocheia und Konstantinopel gegen Ende des vierten Jahrhunderts*, OCA 187, Rome: Pontificio Istituto Orientale, 1970.

40 H. Engberding, 'Die syrische Anaphora der zwölf Apostel und ihre Paralleltexte', *Oriens Christianus* 12 (1937), pp. 213–47; A. Raes, 'L'authenticité de la Liturgie Byzantine de S. Jean Chrysostome', *Orientalia Christiana Periodica* 24 (1958), pp. 5–16; G. Khouri-Sarkis, 'L'Origine syrienne de l'anaphore byzantine de saint Jean Chrysostome', *L'Orient Syrien* 7 (1962), pp. 3–68; Sebastian Brock, private communication; Wagner, *Ursprung*.

41 Robert F. Taft, 'The Authenticity of the Chrysostom Anaphora Revisited: Determining the Authorship of Liturgical Texts by Computer', *Orientalia Christiana Periodica* 56 (1990), pp. 5–51. Cf. G. J. Cuming, 'Pseudonymity and Authenticity, with Special Reference to the Liturgy of St. John Chrysostom', *Studia Patristica* 15 (1984), pp. 532–8.

42 *PE*, pp. 224ff; *PEER*, pp. 132ff.

Not only are these absent from the Syriac text, but among all the Greek writers in the *TLG*, no one but Chrysostom uses all four epithets together, and no one but Chrysostom uses them in the exact order as found in the anaphora. The same holds for 'existing always in the same way', and also later in the anaphora, 'seen and unseen benefits'. Taft argues that it is plausible to conclude that Chrysostom took an already existing anaphora of Antioch and reworked it into what we know as CHR. Given Brock's and Wagner's opinions on the date of the Syriac syntax of Twelve Apostles, how far that text represents that earlier anaphora is another question, but it may be a later translation of an earlier version of an anaphora of Antioch. However, in an important linguistc analysis of the Greek text, Daniel Sheerin has shown that CHR exhibits many of the features of artistic prose, especially those associated with the so-called Second Sophistic, and employs these with considerable economy.[43] In other words, this is not an off-the-cuff prayer, but a polished piece of Greek rhetoric, compiled for public recitation, yet with linguistic restraint, or, in the words of Kucharek, 'a masterpiece of conciseness and clarity'.[44]

CHR (Barberini text) hymns, gives thanks and worships God and the only begotten Son and the Holy Spirit, and very succinctly covers creation, the fall, restoration and granting of the Kingdom to humanity. 'We give you thanks also for this ministry (λειτουργίας)' which God is asked to receive even though he receives the praise of the celestial beings in the Sanctus.[45] The saving work of Christ is again succinct – 'When he had come and fulfilled all the dispensation for us' – and the anaphora moves into the Institution Narrative. The Anamnesis has the words, 'offering you your own from your own, in all and for all', and 'we offer also this reasonable and bloodless service', the latter found in the Egyptian anaphoral tradition, though before the Words of Institution. What is being offered – praise, liturgical action, the bread and wine? Kenneth Stevenson regarded CHR as a 'logical extension of that early imprecision' seen also in the Strasbourg Papyrus.[46] What of presence/consecration? Although the Barberini text has the words 'Take, eat etc.' and 'Drink this etc.' said in a loud voice (*ekphonesis*), it is not known how old such a convention was. The petition for consecration is in the Epiklesis, though the Barberini omits the words in brackets:

> we pray and beseech and entreat you, send down your Holy Spirit on us and on these gifts set forth; and make this bread the precious body of your Christ, [changing it by your Holy Spirit,] Amen; and that which is in this cup the precious blood of your Christ, changing it by your Holy Spirit, Amen; so that they may become to those who partake for vigilance of soul, for fellowship of the Holy Spirit, for the fullness of the Kingdom, for boldness toward you, not for judgment or condemnation.

43 Daniel J. Sheerin, 'The Anaphora of the Liturgy of St. John Chrysostom: Stylistic Notes', in David Jasper and R. C. D. Jasper (eds), *Language and the Worship of the Church*, Basingstoke: Macmillan Press, 1990, pp. 44–81.

44 Casimir Kucharek, *The Byzantine–Slav Liturgy of St. John Chrysostom: Its Origin and Evolution*, Allendale: Alleluia Press, 1971, p. 575.

45 See further, Bryan D. Spinks, *The Sanctus in the Eucharistic Prayer*, Cambridge: Cambridge University Press, 1991, pp. 74–6.

46 Kenneth Stevenson, *Eucharist and Offering*, New York: Pueblo Press, 1986, p. 42.

The request is for the Spirit to be sent down (*κατάπεμψον*) on the communicants and the gifts set forth (*προκείμενα*) and to change (*μεταβαλών*) them. But the change is for fruits of communion-vigilance of soul, for koinonia of the Spirit, the fullness of the Kingdom and confidence in salvation. The intercessory nature of the Epiklesis leads into further offering of the reasonable service for intercessions for those already gone before (the righteous perfected in faith), and then the living, ending in a request for unity in worship – 'one mouth and one heart'. The sequence of departed–living is already reflected in the *Acts of Thomas*, 'for he is the judge of the dead and the living'.

Byzantine Basil (Byz.Bas)

In the previous chapter it has been noted that the pioneering work of H. Engberding on the various linguistic versions of the Anaphora of St Basil shows that there are two main versions, namely the Egyptian and the Byzantine.[47] This was still the presupposition of the important study by John Fenwick.[48] The work of Gabriele Winkler on the old Armenian version, known as St Gregory the Illuminator, means that this too is an important text for understanding the relationship of the various versions, and also suggests that the attribution to Basil has 'more to do with the clamour for authority in the context of a divided Christianity than with historical fact'.[49] In an essay in 1960, Bernard Capelle compared portions of Byz.Bas with the writings of St Basil and argued that the Cappadocian saint had expanded the anaphora that bears his name.[50] This was taken further by Boris Bobrinskoy who compared Basil's understanding of the economy of the Trinity, of the Holy Spirit and ecclesiology with the anaphora, concluding that the latter reflects Basil's theology and pastoral concerns.[51] Winkler is less convinced that Basil was involved in expanding Byz.Bas and instead argues that the Christology in the anaphora is that of the Antiochene Synod of 341, summoned in the aftermath of and opposition to the Council of Nicaea in 325, and not the Cappadocian trinitarian theology. She cites the pre-existence of the Son, 'before eternity', and his characterization as the living word, wisdom, power and true light of the Father, as well as his depiction of

47 See Chapter 4. Hieronymus Engberding, *Das Eucharistische Hochgebet der Basileiosliturgie: Textgeschichtliche Untersuchungen und kritische Ausgabe*, Münster: Aschendorff, 1931.

48 John R. K. Fenwick, *The Anaphoras of St. Basil and St. James: An Investigation into Their Common Origin*, Rome: Pontificium Institutum Orientale, 1992.

49 Gabriele Winkler, *Die Basilius-Anaphora: Edition der beiden armenischen Redaktionen und der relevanten Fragmente: Übersetzung und Zusammenschau aller Versionen im Lichte der orientalischen Überlieferungen*, Anaphorae Orientales 2, Rome: Pontificio Istituto Orientale, 2005; 'Preliminary Observations about the Relationship between the Liturgies of St. Basil and St. James', *Orientalia Christiana Periodica* 78 (2010), p. 7.

50 B. Capelle, 'Les liturgies "basiliennes" et S. Basile', in J. Doresse and E. Lanne (eds), *Un témoin archaïque de la liturgie copte de S. Basile*, Louvain: Publications Universitaires Louvain, 1960.

51 Boris Bobrinskoy, 'Liturgie et Ecclésiologie Trinitaire de Saint Basile', in Botte (ed.), *Eucharisties d'Orient et d'Occident*, vol. 2, pp. 197–240.

the Son as εἰκών of the Father.[52] The influence of this synod is to be found in various ways in all the versions of the anaphora, and thus Winkler prefers to speak of the anaphora as being '*Antiochene* not only in its liturgical shape but, surprisingly enough, in its Christology as well'.[53] This would not necessarily rule out a Cappadocian origin of the core, and since Gregory the Illuminator came to Armenia from Caesarea, the core might be a Cappadocian anaphora.

The Barberini text unfortunately is incomplete, and Jasper and Cuming use Grottaferrata MS G b vii of the ninth or tenth century to provide a complete text.[54] They note that in comparison with the Egyptian Anaphora of Basil, the Byzantine version is twice as long, and in places the wording is very similar to St John Chrysostom, suggesting some mutual influencing. There are more praise words than in the Egyptian version, and the majesty and wonder of God, including alpha-privatives, leads to the angelic praise and Sanctus. The post-Sanctus is an incredibly comprehensive survey of salvation history, from the expulsion from paradise and the sending of the prophets to a detailed summary of the saving work of Christ, with biblical allusions and quotes, such as Galatians 4.4, Philippians 2.9–11 and Hebrews 1.2.[55] The transition to the Words of Institution reads: 'And he left us memorials of his saving passion, these things which we have set forth according to his commandments', which is reminiscent of the Institution-Anamnesis of Addai and Mari. In fact there are a number of features in Basil that echo Addai and Mari.[56] Yet, even if this might signal a time when there was no narrative in some earlier core of the Basil Anaphoras, the narrative flows as just a specific detailed event in salvation history. The opening of the narrative is formulated on the basis of borrowings from John 6.15 and 1 Corinthians 11.23, and for both the bread and the cup the narrative has the verbs gave thanks, blessed and sanctified.[57] The Anamnesis, according to Winkler, in all versions of Basil is based on the Antiochene Creed of 341.[58] Like Chrysostom, it offers to God 'your own from your own'. The Epiklesis is prefaced by a statement that the antitypes of the body and blood were 'set forth', and, like Addai and Mari and the early Syriac tradition, it asks for the Spirit to come (ἐλθεῖν), and like Chrysostom, upon the congregation as well as the gifts. God is asked to bless and sanctify the gifts 'set forth' and show or manifest (ἀναδεῖξαι) them to be the 'precious' body and blood of Christ. The fruits of communion

52 Gabriele Winkler, 'The Christology of the Anaphora of St. Basil in Its Various Redactions, with Some Remarks Concerning the Authorship of Basil', in Bryan D. Spinks (ed.), *The Place of Christ in Liturgical Prayer: Trinity, Christology, and Liturgical Theology*, Collegeville: Liturgical Press, 2008, pp. 118–19.

53 Gabriele Winkler, 'Preliminary Observations about the Relationship between the Liturgies of St. Basil and St. James', *Orientalia Christiana Periodica* 78 (2010), pp. 5–55, p. 7.

54 *PEER*, pp. 114–23; *PE*, pp. 230–42.

55 See Fenwick, *Anaphoras of St. Basil and St. James*, pp. 98–122.

56 Gabriele Winkler, 'Unsolved Problems Concerning the Background and Significance of the Vocabulary of Praise in Some of the Oldest Eucharistic Prayers', in Bert Groen, Steven Hawkes-Teeples and Stefanos Alexopoulas (eds), *Inquiries into Eastern Christian Worship*, Leuven: Peeters, 2012, pp. 135–72.

57 See further, Winkler, 'Preliminary Observations', p. 37; Fenwick, *Anaphoras of St. Basil and St. James*, p. 124.

58 Winkler, 'Christology of the Anaphora of Basil', p. 119; Winkler, *Basilius-Anaphora*, pp. 866–70.

requested are fellowship with one another, not partaking for judgement, and for mercy and grace with the saints, which then leads into the intercessions for the departed and then the living. Stevenson noted that this anaphora opens with a reference to a sacrifice of praise and then shifts to a gift offering. The 'set forth' of the antitypes recalls perhaps Theodore of Mopsuestia, that the bread and wine typify the dead body and blood of Christ, and the coming of the spirit sanctifies them to be the precious body and blood of Christ.[59] The final doxology is addressed equally to Father, Son and Holy Spirit – reflecting at least the concern of St Basil himself about the need to change the final doxologies of prayers to exclude the Arian and Eunomean appeal to the liturgy to support subordination of the Son.[60]

The Greek Liturgy and Anaphora of St James

St James has a slightly different outline. That given below is from Brightman's text, and Mercier's critical edition, though a modern English version with adaptations is used by the monks of New Skete, New York.[61]

- [Prothesis. Private prayer for worthiness].
- [Vesting Prayer.]
- Prayer of Entrance.
- Prayer of Incense.
- Prayer of the Enarxis.
- Prayer.
- *Ho monogenes* and prayer.
- Prayer, Litany and Trisagion.
- Epistle.
- Gospel.
- Prayer after the Gospel.
- Litany and dismissal of the Catechumens.
- Cherubic Hymn.
- Prayer of the Great Entrance.
- Prayer of Incense.
- Prayer of Holy Basil.
- Prayer of Offering.
- Prayer of Incense.
- Creed.
- Peace.
- Litany.

59 See Stevenson, *Eucharist and Offering*, p. 40.

60 See Geoffrey Wainwright, *Doxology: The Praise of God in Worship, Doctrine and Life: A Systematic Theology*, New York: Oxford University Press, 1980; James B. Torrance, *Worship, Community, and the Triune God of Grace*, Carlisle: Paternoster Press, 1996.

61 F. E. Brightman, *Liturgies Eastern and Western*, Oxford: Oxford University Press, [1896] 1967, pp. 31–68; B.-Ch. Mercier, *La Liturgie de Saint Jacques*, Paris: Firmin-Didot, 1946; Orthodox Eastern Church, Monks of New Skete, *The Divine Liturgy of Our Father Among the Saints, James of Jerusalem*, New York: Monks of New Skete, 1996.

- Prayer of the Priest.
- Prayer of the Faithful.
- Prayer of the Oblation.
- Prayer of the Veil.
- Anaphora.
- Prayer and Lord's Prayer.
- Prayer of Inclination.
- Elevation and 'Holy Things for the holy'.
- Fraction.
- Prayer before Communion.
- Communion.
- Prayers of the Incense.
- Prayer of Inclination.
- Post-Communion Thanksgiving.
- Dismissal.
- Final Prayer.

The Anaphora of St James is associated with the Brother of the Lord and Jerusalem. It exists in Greek, Syriac, Georgian, Armenian, Old Slavonic and Ethiopian, but the main two versions are the Greek and Syriac, and the Syriac is clearly dependent upon the Greek.[62] In Chapter 3 we have already noted the possible allusion to the anaphora by Eusebius, and also by the *MC* attributed to Cyril of Jerusalem. If the outline given by Cyril was an accurate piece-by-piece summary, then in his day there was no rehearsal of the saving work of Christ after the Sanctus and no recitation of the Words of Institution. The Anaphora of James does have these elements, and it also has material in common with Eg.Bas. John Fenwick made the plausible argument that the present anaphora can be explained by the anaphora known to Cyril being expanded by slotting in the additional elements or blocks from Eg.Bas.[63] That may have been one way that anaphoral osmosis occurred and certainly explains why these two anaphoras have material in common.

Whatever the truth of its prehistory, the present anaphora is quite masterful in the way that its construction unfolds the economic Trinity in prayer. The opening praise, which could be read as an expansion of Romans 1.20, acknowledges that it is fitting to worship God, and then lists how creation itself (the sun, moon, choirs of stars, the sea and the earth), as well as the heavenly Jerusalem and the Church that is above, and all the angelic hierarchy, sing together the

62 Mercier, *Liturgie de Saint Jacques*; Ἀλκιβιάδης Καζαμίας, *Ἡ Θεία Λειτουργία τοῦ Ἁγίου Ἰακώβου τοῦ Ἀδελφοθέου καὶ τὰ νέα σιναϊτικὰ χειρόγραφα* (Θεσσαλονίκη 2006); Stig Symeon Frøyshov, 'The Georgian Witness to the Jerusalem liturgy: New Sources and Studies', in Bert Groen et al. (eds), *Inquiries into Eastern Christian Worship*, Leuven: Peeters, 2012, pp. 227–67; Lili Khevsuriani, Mzekala Shanidze, Micahel Kavtaria, Tinatin Tseradzee and Stéphane Verhelst, *Liturgia Ibero-Graeca Sancti Iacobi. Editio–translatio–retroversio–commentarii*, Münster: Aschendorff, 2011. See also John D. Witvliet, 'The Anaphora of St James', in Paul F. Bradshaw (ed.), *Essays on Early Eastern Eucharistic Prayers*, Collegeville: Liturgical Press, 2002, pp. 153–72.

63 Fenwick, *Anaphoras of St. Basil and St. James*.

Sanctus, which is described as the 'victory hymn of your magnificent glory'.[64] The post-Sanctus, as noted, echoes Byz.Bas, though it is not as full in its rehearsal of salvation history. After the Words of Institution, the Anamnesis prays, 'we offer this awesome and bloodless sacrifice', echoing Cyril's 'bloodless service', and Winkler believes that it too has been influenced by the Synod of Antioch (341).[65] The Epiklesis of the Greek text is in fact a double Epiklesis and one in which the salvific work of the Spirit is rehearsed as a parallel with the work of Christ:

> Have mercy on us, Lord, God the Father, almighty; have mercy on us, God, our Saviour. Have mercy on us, O God, according to your great mercy, and send out (*ἐξαπόστειλον*) upon us and upon these holy gifts set before your all-Holy Spirit, the Lord and giver of life, who shares the throne and the kingdom with you, God the Father and your only-begotten Son, consubstantial and coeternal, who spoke in the law and the prophets and in your new covenant, who descended in the likeness of a dove upon our Lord Jesus Christ in the river Jordan and remained upon him, who descended upon your holy apostles in the likeness of fiery tongues in the Upper Room of the holy and glorious Zion on the day of the holy Pentecost; send down (*κατάπεμψον*) Master, your all-Holy Spirit himself upon us and upon these holy gifts set before you, that he may descend (*ἐπιφοιτήσαν*) upon them, and by his holy and good and glorious coming may sanctify them, and make this bread the holy body of Christ, and this cup the precious blood of Christ.

In Cyril's *MC*, the verb used for the Epiklesis is *ἐξαποστεῖλαι*, which we may conclude is the original Jerusalem epikletic verb. The second verb, *κατάπεμψον*, is found in CHR, and also Egyptian Gregory, and may be an Antiochene word. It appears that Greek James has a doublet, in which the Antiochene Epiklesis formula has been inserted after the Jerusalem formula. This is confirmed by the fact that the doublet is absent in the Syriac version, and, though present in some Georgian texts, is also absent from the older Georgian manuscripts.[66] The term *ἐπιφοιτήσαν*, which Jasper and Cuming translate as 'descend upon', is a non-biblical term, but more accurately means visiting or residing, and is found in association with the Spirit in the writings of John Chrysostom, which may have a Syriac origin.[67] The fruits of communion requested are for the forgiveness of sins, eternal life, sanctification of souls and bodies, for bringing forth good works and for strengthening the Church. The intercessions, though, pray first for the Holy Places (of Jerusalem) and the living, and then the departed.

---

64 *PE*, pp. 244–60; *PEER*, pp. 90–9.

65 Winkler, 'Preliminary Observations', p. 41.

66 See Bryan D. Spinks, 'The Consecratory Epiklesis in the Anaphora of St. James', *Studia Liturgica* 11 (1976), pp. 19–38. For the Georgian, see *Liturgia Ibero-Graeca Sancti Iacobi*, pp. 84–5, Greek retroversion pp. 212–13 and commentary pp. 343–4. Winkler noted the double Epiklesis in the Georgian texts published by Michael Tarchnišvili, for example, 'Eine neue Georgische Jakobusliturgie', *Ephemerides Liturgicae* 62 (1948), pp. 49–82.

67 Spinks, 'Consecratory Epiklesis'; Sebastian Brock, 'Invocations to/for the Holy Spirit in Syriac Liturgical Texts: Some Comparative Approaches', in Robert Taft and Gabriele Winkler (eds), *Comparative Liturgy Fifty Years after Anton Baumstark*, Rome: Pontificium Institutum Orientalium Studiorum, 1998, pp. 377–406 and 391–95, and note 71.

Concluding observations and remarks

Although Bradshaw and Johnson are correct that the Eastern rites do not really compartmentalize moments such as 'presence' and 'sacrifice', and that they are more holistic, none the less there are particular highlights or moments of emphasis.[68] A theology of offering and presence is articulated in many of the later developments in the Byzantine rite – the whole prothesis is concerned with preparing the 'Lamb', already an antitype of the body and blood of Christ. This is also true in the elaborate Fraction, as well as the theology associated with the *zeon*. However, though not unimportant, they are both moments of solely clerical activity, and the prothesis is not technically part of the public liturgy. The older theology of the Eucharist is articulated in the anaphora, with secondary developments such as the Cherubic hymn, the Prayer of the *Proskomide* and the 'Holy things for holy people'. Here we find some ideas of offering, or presence and eschatological emphases.

The Cherubic Hymn of the sixth century exhorts:

> Let all mortal flesh keep silent and stand with fear and trembling and ponder nothing worldly within itself, for the King of kings and Lord of Lords cometh forth to be slain and given as food to the faithful.

The hymn regards the bread and wine as being brought forth to be offered as a sacrifice as food for the faithful. The *Proskomide* prayer of St John Chrysostom is a prayer requesting that the ministers be brought forth to the altar, that they may be enabled to offer and that they will be made worthy so that the sacrifice will be accepted and the Spirit will come upon them, upon the gifts and upon the people; 'gifts and spiritual sacrifices' will be offered.[69] That of Byz.Bas is also a prayer of approach for the ministers, that they may be worthy to offer 'this rational and bloodless sacrifice', asking that it be accepted as the gifts of Abel, Abraham, Moses and Aaron, and the peace-offerings of Samuel. These had entered the liturgy by the ninth century but, as Taft notes, they do not offer now, but pray that the offering in the anaphora will not be vitiated by unworthiness.[70] It is within the anaphoras themselves that any offering takes place. In CHR, a ministry of praise is offered, or asked to be accepted, even though the Sanctus is sung in heaven. Later what is offered is 'your own from your own, in all and for all', and it is a 'reasonable and bloodless service'. Byz.Bas offers a 'reasonable service', and the likeness of the holy body and blood of Christ has been set forth. St James offers the 'awesome and bloodless sacrifice' and the holy gifts are 'set before you'. Stevenson concluded that there was a theological richness here stemming from continued reflection of the Eucharist.[71]

All three anaphoras are concerned with the action of the Holy Spirit to effect some transformation of the elements. Byz.Bas has the imprecise 'show' or manifest, in the sense that the elements will be an epiphany of God in Christ. CHR

68 Bradshaw and Johnson, *Eucharistic Liturgies*, p. 192.

69 Taft, *Great Entrance*, p. 357; Stevenson, *Eucharist and Offering*, pp. 106–7.

70 Taft, *Great Entrance*.

71 Stevenson, *Eucharist and Offering*, p. 45.

and James have 'make', and CHR also has 'change'. Germanus stresses that it is the Holy Spirit who is the agent. Indeed, in the Syro-Byzantine Anaphoras the Institution Narrative, from a literary point of view, is the climax of salvation history, and it is in the Epiklesis that petition for the elements to be manifested as or made the body and blood of Christ is made. Cabasilas suggests that the change/transformation from bread to the body of Christ for us to eat is the immolation or sacrifice.[72] Yet already in Cabasilas the difference with the Latin Church is discussed. He argued that it is not a recitation of a narrative that consecrated, but a petition, and this is echoed by Symeon. Michel Zheltov has recently argued that there is ample evidence for many Byzantine writers regarding the Words of Institution as 'consecratory' as well as those who emphasized the Epiklesis, though he concludes that rather than a preference for one set of words over another, it is the reverence towards the manual acts throughout the celebration that is more telling.[73] Certainly given that liturgy is a text to be performed, his observations are important, but this does not alter the fact that, linguistically, the thrust of asking for change of the gifts is in the Epiklesis.[74]

Yet the goal is for a worthy and fruitful communion, and the requests that follow in the Epikleses cannot be separated from the petition for the Spirit. Byz.Bas stresses the communion with the saints and so remembers the saints who have gone before as well as the needs of the saints temporal; in James the fruits are forgiveness, sanctification, good works, and strengthening the Church; in Chrysostom they are for vigilance of soul, fellowship with the Holy Spirit and the fullness of the Kingdom. These are the final goal of the offering of praise, the bloodless service and the request for change in the elements by the Spirit.

Contact and controversy with the Latin Church in the thirteenth century, exposure to Western medieval education and then contact with the Western Reformation disputes all have led to Eastern Orthodoxy embracing and using later Western sacramental terminology, though without the complex scholastic underpinning of the terminology. Patriarch Jeremiah II (1536–95) responded to Lutheran teaching insisting that sacraments have a definite matter and form, and an instrumental cause.[75] Perhaps most famous was the Confession of Faith of Dosethius, or Synod of Jerusalem (1672):

> In the celebration of this we believe the Lord Jesus Christ to be present. He is not present typically, nor figuratively, nor by superabundant grace, as in the other Mysteries, nor by a bare presence, as some of the Fathers have said concerning Baptism, or by impanation, so that the Divinity of the Word is united to the set forth bread of the Eucharist hypostatically, as the followers

72 Cabasilas, *Commentary on the Divine Liturgy*, p. 81.

73 Michel Zheltov, 'The Moment of Eucharistic Consecration in Byzantine Thought', in Maxwell E. Johnson (ed.), *Issues in Eucharistic Praying in East and West*, Collegeville: Liturgical Press, 2011, pp. 263–306.

74 See Aftimos Skaf, 'Analyse Textuelle de L'Anamnèse et de l'épiclèse dans la Liturgie de Saint Jean Chrysostome', in Ayoub Chawan (ed.), *Mélanges offerts à Jean Tabet*, Lebanon: Publications de l'Institut de Liturgie à l'Université Saint-Esprit de Kaslik, 2005, pp. 93–105.

75 Nicolas Kazarian, 'The Sacramental Theology of Patriarch Jeremias II', 5th International Theological Conference of the Russian Orthodox Church, Moscow 2007, http://theolcom.ru/ru/full_text.php?TEXT_ID=343.

> of Luther most ignorantly and wretchedly suppose. But [he is present] truly and really, so that after the consecration of the bread and of the wine, the bread is transmuted, transubstantiated, converted and transformed into the true Body Itself of the Lord, Which was born in Bethlehem of the ever-Virgin, was baptized in the Jordan, suffered, was buried, rose again, was received up, sits at the right hand of the God and Father, and is to come again in the clouds of Heaven; and the wine is converted and transubstantiated into the true Blood Itself of the Lord, Which as He hung upon the Cross, was poured out for the life of the world. (John 6:51) Further [we believe] that after the consecration of the bread and of the wine, there no longer remains the substance of the bread and of the wine, but the Body Itself and the Blood of the Lord, under the species and form of bread and wine; that is to say, under the accidents of the bread. Further, that the all-pure Body Itself, and Blood of the Lord is imparted, and enters into the mouths and stomachs of the communicants, whether pious or impious. Nevertheless, they convey to the pious and worthy remission of sins and life eternal; but to the impious and unworthy involve condemnation and eternal punishment.[76]

Latin teaching would also be promulgated in Russia by Peter Moghila in the seventeenth century, and brought to a halt by the council under Patriarch Ioakim II in 1690. On the whole, Orthodoxy has spoken of change, *metabole*, or transmutation of the gifts in the Epiklesis, though often the term transubstantiation is selected in translation. Undoubtedly with a Russian flavour, the Eastern Orthodox understanding of the Eucharist in terms of presence was articulated by Sergius Bulgakov.[77] Bulgakov suggests that transubstantiation and Protestant reactions to it simply attempt to interpret the Eucharist within the limits of the world and materialism. In contrast, the Orthodox view sees the Eucharist as analogous to the incarnation but the 'body' of Christ is the risen and ascended body. The spiritual body is truly separated from the material corporeality of this world.[78] No transformation is required for the Orthodox transmutation, because, by God's will, the body and blood of Christ are – in this place, in this sanctuary – this bread and wine, and they do not need to be transformed into anything for this purpose.[79] Bulgakov wrote:

> Thus, the transmutation of the bread and wine into the body and blood of Christ signifies not the tabernacling of the heavenly Christ *substantialiter* into these accidents [bread and wine], which are then viewed as a kind of unchanging shell, but their direct conversion without any limitation and remainder into the body and blood of Christ – a true transmutation. The fact that the body and blood in their earthly nature remain what they were has no significance here. As such, they have become other than themselves; they no longer have independent existence as things of this world but belong to the

76 Dosethius, 'The Confessions of Dositheus (Eastern Orthodox, 1672)', Dennis Bratcher (ed.), http://www.crivoice.org/creeddositheus.html.

77 Sergius Bulgakov, *The Holy Grail and the Eucharist*, Hudson: Lindisfarne Books, 1997.

78 Bulgakov, *The Holy Grail and the Eucharist*, p. 99.

79 Bulgakov, *The Holy Grail and the Eucharist*, p. 111.

> body of Jesus, in the same way that the bread and fish that He ate in the presence of His disciples belonged to His body. The Lord, who in His spiritual and glorious body abides at the right hand of God the Father, creates, in the transmutation, a body for Himself from the bread, matter of this world, and animates it with His blood. This transmutation does not require the 'transubstantiation' of the thing itself, the bread and wine; it even excludes such a 'transubstantiation', for no *thing* exists in the world into which they could be transformed: the glorified body of the Lord abides *outside* of this world. The Lord instituted the sacrament of the Eucharist in His earthly abiding when He had an earthly body. But this body was transfigured into the body of the Resurrection, and then in the Ascension it became supramundane. The transmutation of the eucharistic elements must therefore be understood not as the 'transubstantiation' of one material into another but as the connection of the Lord's spiritual body with the eucharistic matter of this world. And the institution of this connection is the transmutation, which is not a physical but a metaphysical act. This act is directly analogous to the Incarnation and signifies the appearance of Christ on earth after the Ascension; and the eucharistic matter is the mediating mode of this appearance.[80]

The bread and wine become the 'metacosmic being' of the Lord's body.[81] The 'heaven on earth' splendour of the ceremonial tries to express this in ritual, but perhaps the word 'mysterion' – beyond our explanation – typifies best the Orthodox belief.

80 Bulgakov, *The Holy Grail and the Eucharist*, pp. 115–16.
81 Bulgakov, *The Holy Grail and the Eucharist*, p. 124.

6

The Syriac Liturgical Traditions

The Syriac language and the theology of the early Syrian Fathers such as Ephrem and Aphrahat are shared by three Churches that historically are divided by Christology: the Church of the East, or Assyrian Church but often referred to as East Syrian; the Syrian Orthodox Church or West Syrian; and the Maronite Church. The Church of the East, historically centred on Edessa, and then Nisibis and Seleucia-Ctesiphon, did not accept the decrees of the Councils of Ephesus (431) and Chalcedon (451); though not especially espousing the Christology of Nestorius, it refused to condemn him. Its historic homeland was mainly within the Persian Empire and so it enjoyed some isolation from the Byzantine and Roman worlds. It was a great missionary church, reaching China and possibly Japan, as well as founding the Thomas Christians of Kerala, India.[1] The Syrian Orthodox Church derives from those who accepted the Council of Ephesus, but who regarded the Council of Chalcedon as a departure from the Christology of Cyril of Alexandria as codified at Ephesus. Under the leadership of John of Tella, Severus of Antioch and, later, Jacob of Burdana, a separate clerical hierarchy was established, and the Church flourished in the Syriac-speaking hinterland of Antioch.[2] The Church is thus a non-Chalcedonian Church. In the sixteenth century it received the Syriac legacy of the splintering Thomas Church in India. The Maronite Church is a Chalcedonian Church which gathered around the monastic community of St Maron and gradually moved south to find protection in the mountains of Lebanon. It was rediscovered by the Latin Crusades, and it found it politically useful to recognize the Roman supremacy.[3] Most scholars tend to agree with W. F. Macomber that beneath the subsequent liturgical developments of these three Churches there was an earlier shared common core.[4] Division over Christology did not prevent subsequent mutual liturgical borrowing. As noted in an earlier chapter, Sebastian Brock has drawn attention to an early liturgical commentary, which dates from about 400 and was used in

1 Wilhelm Baum and Dietmar Winkler, *The Church of the East: A Concise History*, London: Routledge, 2010; Christopher Baumer, *The Church of the East: An Illustrated History of Assyrian Christianity*, New York: I. B. Tauris, 2006.

2 Volker L. Menze, *Justinian and the Making of the Syrian Orthodox Church*, Oxford: Oxford University Press, 2008.

3 Matti Moosa, *The Maronites in History*, Piscataway: Gorgias Press, 2006; Paul Naaman, *The Maronites: The Origins of an Antiochene Church*, Collegeville: Liturgical Press, Cistercian Publications, 2011.

4 W. F. Macomber, 'A Theory on the Origins of the Syrian, Maronite and Chaldean Rites', *Orientalia Christiana Periodica* 39 (1973), pp. 235–42.

the Syrian Orthodox tradition, but was also known to East Syrian commentators and translated into Sogdian (middle Iranian) by the Church of the East.[5]

The Church of the East or East Syrian Holy Qurbana

Today the eucharistic rite is contained in two liturgical books, the *Hūdrā* and the *Taksa*, and the rite has been almost uniform since the tenth or eleventh centuries.[6] Whatever may have been the diversity perhaps known at the time of Ephrem and Aphrahat, a move towards standardization for those Churches in the orbit of Seleucia-Ctesiphon is already found in Canon 13 of the Synod of Seleucia-Ctesiphon, held in 410, prior to the christological splits. That Synod decreed that the eucharistic liturgy should in future be uniformly celebrated according to 'the western rite that the Bishops Isaac (Seleucia-Ctesiphon) and Marutha (Martyropolis) have taught us'.[7] A further standardization and reform of the East Syrian rites is attributed to Catholicos Iso'yahb III (649–659), who is traditionally regarded as the originator of the *Hūdrā*. The Liturgical Homilies of Narsai (d. 503) and of Gabriel Qatraya (*c.* 615) pre-date the reform of Iso'yahb III and so allow us to see something of the development of the rite.[8] There are three particular homilies by Narsai that are pertinent, though Homily XVII is thought by many scholars to be either a much later work, or it has been interpolated to bring it into line with the liturgy as it had developed at a later date, and so must be used with some caution. Other commentaries show great dependence on that of Gabriel Qatraya, and include those of Abraham Qatraya Bar Lipah, An Anonymous Exposition, Yohannan Bar Zobi (*c.* 1250) and Patriarch Timothy II (fourteenth century), as well as an Arabic commentary by 'Ammar al-Basri, dated *c.* 838.[9]

5 Sebastian Brock, 'An Early Syriac Commentary on the Liturgy', *Journal of Theological Studies* 37 (1986), pp. 387–403.

6 For the development of the *Hūdrā,* see Awa Royel, 'From Mosul to Turfan: The *Hūdrā* in the Liturgy of the Assyrian Church of the East. A Survey of its Historical Development and its Liturgical Anomolies at Turfan', forthcoming in proceedings of the VIII Christianity in Iraq Conference, May 2011.

7 Cited by Macomber, 'A Theory on the Origins of the Syrian, Maronite and Chaldean Rites', p. 239.

8 R. H. Connolly, *The Liturgical Homilies of Narsai*, Cambridge: Cambridge University Press, 1909; Sebastian Brock, 'Gabriel of Qatar's Commentary on the Liturgy', *Hugoye: Journal of Syriac Studies* 6:2 (2003), pp. 197–248.

9 For Abraham and the Anonymous Author, see R. H. Connolly, *Anonymi Autoris Expositio Officiorum Ecclesiae Georgio Arbelensi vulgo adscripta*, Rome: Gabalda and Paris: Corpus Scriptorum Christianorum Orientalium, 1923; Robert Matheus (ed.), *A Commentary on the Mass (which has been attributed to, but is not really) by the Nestorian, George, Bishop of Mosul and Arbel, translated from the Syriac by R. H. Connolly*, Kottayam: OIRSI 243, 2000; Albert Khoraiche, '<<L'Explication de tous les Mysteres Divins>> de Yohannan Bar Zo'bi selon le manuscript Borgianus Syriacus 90', *Euntes Docete* 19 (1966), pp. 386–426; Thomas Mannooramparampil, *John Bar Zo'bi: Explanation of the Divine Mysteries*, Kottayam: OIRSI 157, 1992; Khalil Chalfoun, 'Baptême et Eucharistie chez 'Ammār al-Başri'', *Parole de L'Orient* 27 (2002), pp. 321–34. The section on the Eucharist in the work on the sacraments by Timothy II has been translated by Jose Kochuparampil in a dissertation, Rome 2000.

The present Holy Qurbana has the following order:[10]

- Making of the loaves and adding the *Malka.*
- Preparation of the chalice.
- Washing of hands.
- Vesting.
- *Gloria in excelsis* (Luke 1.14, said three times).
- Lord's Prayer introduced and ended with a version of Sanctus as a refrain.
- Prayer before the *Marmitha.*
- *Marmitha* (meaning 'elevation', is two or three psalms appointed). Or, *Aqqapta.*
- Prayer of the Anthem of the Sanctuary.
- *'Onita d-qanke* (Anthem of the Sanctuary – sung in procession to the bema).
- *Lakhu mara* (a hymn, during which the cross is venerated).
- *Lakhu mara* prayer.
- Trisagion.
- Old Testament Readings – Law and Prophets (Easter – Prophets and Acts of Apostles).
- *Surraya* (Psalm).
- Prayer before the Apostles.
- *Turgama* (explication).
- Pauline reading.
- *Zummara* (Alleluia chant).
- Veneration of the Gospel.
- Gospel and Homily.
- Litanies – *Ba'uta, karosuta* and 'Angel of Peace'.
- Blessing and imposition of hands.
- Dismissals.
- Washing of hands (in the Urmiah edition, this comes after the Creed).
- Onita of the mysteries.
- Transfer of elements from the Gazza (niche in the wall) to the altar.
- Creed.
- Prayer of Access.
- First *Gighla-kussapa* (whispered private prayer), *ghanta* (prayer said bowed) and *qanona* (aloud).
- Peace.
- Diptychs.
- Unveiling of the Mysteries and Incensation.
- Anaphora (divided into *Gighla*).

10 I have followed mainly the Urmiah edition: Assyrian Church of the East, *The Liturgy of the Holy Apostles Adai and Mari*, Piscataway: Gorgias Press, [1890] 2002, and the outline given in Pierre Yousif, 'Le Déroulement de la Messe Chaldéenne', in F. Casingena-Trévedy and I. Jurasz (eds), *Les liturgies syriaques*, Paris: Geuthner, 2006, pp. 59–99. See also his earlier essay, 'The Divine Liturgy according to the Rite of the Assyro-Chaldean Church', in J. Madey (ed.), *The Eucharistic Liturgy in the Christian East*, Kottayam: Prakasam Publications and Paderborn: Ostkirchendienst, 1982, pp. 174–237.

- Prayer for Peace of Christ.
- Prayer of Approach and psalm verses.
- Consignation, Fraction and Comminution.
- Prayer of Absolution.
- Lord's Prayer.
- Holy Things for the Holy.
- Communion of the clergy.
- (Rite of Penance.)
- Communion of the laity.
- *Tesbohta* (Hymn of Praise).
- Prayer of Thanksgiving.
- Second Prayer of Thanksgiving.
- Priests' Kiss of Peace in the sanctuary.
- *Huttama* (Blessing).
- People kiss the cross in the priest's hands and receive blessed bread.

There are some differences between the Church of the East's usage and the two offshoot Churches that are in communion with Rome, the Chaldean and the Syro-Malabar Churches. The rite of penance, for example, has been inserted as a pre-communion rite in the Church of the East, but in the two Uniate Churches, a Latinized rite of confession has replaced the indigenous rite and is not included in the Eucharist.[11] Although not part of the public liturgy, the elements are prepared beforehand with some elaborate baking rituals, and are placed in a niche ready for transfer to the altar prior to the anaphora. Vesture takes place with prayers and a washing of the hands.[12]

Sarhad Jammo made a detailed study of the Liturgy of the Word, and his conclusions, which are reflected here, shed light on some of the development of the rite.[13] The rite described by Gabriel Qatraya commenced with the *Marmitha*. The Lord's Prayer seems to have been a standard addition made in the time of Timothy the Great (780–823), though it probably had been used in some places prior to then. The opening Gloria is found first in manuscripts of the fifteenth century, but again it may have been used long before that in some places. The *Aqqapta* seems to have been the older entrance of the bishop into the sanctuary and beginning of the rite. After the prayers and chants in the sanctuary the clergy processed to the bema, or raised platform, that stood in the middle of the nave in Syrian churches; this is mentioned by Qatraya, who interpreted it as a symbol of Jesus going into the wilderness to fight Satan.[14] According to Jammo, the *Laku mara* is one of the oldest elements of the East Syrian rite, and served once as the Introit hymn.[15] On the other hand, the Trisagion, as well as parts

---

11 Jacques Isaac, *Taksa D- Hussaya: Le rite du Pardon dans l'Église syriaque orientale*, Rome: Pontificium Institutum Orientale, 1989, pp. 170–5.

12 For a description of the preparation and baking, and a description of a celebration of the liturgy, see E. S. Drower, *Water into Wine: A Study of Ritual Idiom in the Middle East*, London: John Murray, 1956, pp. 69–75, 159–73.

13 Sarhad Y. Hermiz Jammo, *La Structue de la Messe Chaldéenne du Début jusq'à l'Anaphore: Etude Historique*, Rome: Pontificium Institutum Orientalium Studiorum, 1979.

14 Brock, 'Gabriel of Qatar's Commentary', p. 10.

15 Jammo, *La Structure de la Messe Chaldéenne du Début jusqu'à l'Anaphore*, p. 86.

of the Litanies after the homily, are almost certainly Byzantine imports. Awa Royel writes:

> The first part of the diaconal litany, or the *Bā'ūthā*, is most likely an import from Byzantium borrowed by the East Syrian rite, most probably during the sojourn of the patriarch Mar Ābā I (540–52) in the West . . . The second part of the litany, or the *kārōzūthā*, was already mentioned by name in the first synod of the Church of the East (410), and is in all likelihood authentically East Syrian. The last part, or the *Angelus Pacis*, seems to be of Byzantine origin with modifications to suit the faithful gathered for prayer, rather than for the catechumens.[16]

The first reference to the Trisagion in the East Syrian rite is contained in the tractate of Patriarch Iso'yahb of Arzōn (582/3–595/6), and may well derive also from Mar Ābā's visit to Constantinople; and like the Byzantine rite, it is given a trinitarian interpretation.[17] The blessing and imposition of hands appears to be what Aidan Kavanagh called a *missa*,[18] or dismissal, but here the prayer is concerned with the clergy. The second blessing is for the people, but there is no blessing of the catechumens before their dismissal.

The ceremonies and prayers that immediately precede the anaphora are quite variable in the manuscripts and printed texts, as, for example, the position of the washing of the hands. It was the tradition in this rite for the archdeacon to choose the celebrant at this point, and that priest would carry the elements to the altar and unveil them. Since Theodore of Mopsuestia was an important theologian for this tradition, it is no surprise that Narsai gives similar teaching on the transfer of gifts:

> As an eagle the priest hovers before them, and prepares the food of perfect age for them to be nourished withal. The living sacrifice he prepares, he sets before their eyes; and he summons them to examine it with affection of soul. A dread mystery he begins to depict spiritually; and he mixes his words as paints before the beholders. With the pen of his word he draws an image of the Crucified King; and as with the finger he points out His passion, also His exaltation. Death and life his voice proclaims in the ears of the people; and forgiveness of iniquity he distributes, he gives, in the Bread and the Wine. A mystery of death he shews first to mortal man; and then he reveals the power of life that is hidden in his words.
>
> As for one dead he strews a bed with the sacred vessels; and he brings up, he sets thereon the bread and wine as a corpse. The burial day of the King he transacts mystically; and he sets soldiers on guard by a representation. Two deacons he places like a rank (of soldiers), on this side and on that, that they may be guarding the dread Mystery of the King of kings. Awe and love lie upon the faculties of their minds while they look intently upon the bread and

16 Awa Royel, 'East Meets East: Byzantine Liturgical Influences on the Rite of the Church of the East', *Journal of the Canadian Society for Syriac Studies* 8 (2008), pp. 44–55, 49–50.

17 Royel, 'East Meets East', p. 51.

18 Aidan Kavanagh, *Confirmation: Origins and Reform*, New York: Pueblo, 1988.

> wine, as upon the King. With bright apparel they are clothed exteriorly upon their bodies; and by their garments they shew the beauty of their minds. By their stoles (*oraria*) they depict a sign of the heavenly beings that were clothed in beauteous garments at the temple of the tomb. Two angels the disciples saw in the tomb of our Lord, who were attending the place of His body as though it were His body (itself). And if spiritual beings in fear honoured the place of His body, how much more should corporeal beings honour the Mystery that has honoured them? After the manner of the two watchers the two deacons are standing now to hover over the Mysteries.[19]

Qatraya emphasizes the theological shift that takes place as the anaphora is recited:

> *Up to here the Church depicts, through her types, the Mystery/symbol of the death and burial of Christ. From now on the priest approaches to depict the type of the Resurrection* through the recital of the holy words from his mouth, and by the sign (rushma) of the cross which is in his hand.[20]

In Homily XXXII, which is on the Priesthood, Narsai briefly describes the Fraction:

> And he stretches out his hands and breaks the spiritual Bread; and he signs the type of the Body and Blood that died and was raised up.[21]

Homily XVII gives a more detailed description but, as noted above, this homily may not be by Narsai for reasons that will be discussed shortly.[22] Concerning communion, Qatraya explained that it is a symbol of our participation that we shall have with Christ in the Kingdom of Heaven.[23] The eucharistic bread is leavened and made from wheat, but it has olive oil added in the making, as well as *Malka*, a special mix that is renewed every year and must be added to the communion bread dough. The origin of the *Malka* is found in the thirteenth-century work *Book of the Bee* by Shlemon of Basra. Shlemon wrote:

> Some men have a tradition that when our Lord broke his body for his disciples in the upper room, John the son of Zebedee hid a part of his portion until our Lord rose from the dead. And when our Lord appeared to his disciples and to Thomas with them, he said to Thomas, 'Hither with your finger and lay it on my side and be not unbelieving, but believing'. Thomas put his finger near to the Lord's side and it rested upon the mark of the spear, and the disciples saw the blood from the marks of the spear and nails. And John took that piece of consecrated bread, and wiped up that blood with it; and the Easterns, Mâr

19 Narsai, 'Homily XXI', in Connolly, *Liturgical Homilies of Narsai*, pp. 55–6.
20 Qatraya, in Brock, 'Gabriel of Qatar's Commentary on the Liturgy', p. 214.
21 Narsai, 'Homily XXXII', in Connolly, *Liturgical Homilies of Narsai*, p. 67.
22 Narsai, 'Homily XVII', in Connolly, *Liturgical Homilies of Narsai*, p. 23.
23 Qatraya, in Brock, 'Gabriel of Qatar's Commentary on the Liturgy', p. 220.

> Addai and Mâr Marî, took that piece, and with it they sanctified this unleavened bread which has been handed down among us.[24]

A rather different origin is given by Bar Zo'bi, and the ultimate origin may have been to do with ecclesiastical jurisdiction and unity.[25]

The East Syrian anaphoras

The East Syrian rite has three anaphoras – Addai and Mari, Nestorius and Theodore the Interpreter. It once knew other anaphoras, but only a sixth-century fragment has survived, and it was edited and published by R. H. Connolly.[26] When it is recalled that Addai and Mari has no Institution Narrative, this fragment contains what seems to be a halfway stage towards a full narrative:

> And because he was about to be taken up from our place and exalted to the place of the spiritual beings from which he had come down, he left in our hands a pledge of his holy body, that through his body he might be near to us and at all times be united to us through his power. For before the time of his crucifixion and the hour in which he was about to be glorified he took bread and wine which his will had made, (and) made it holy with a spiritual blessing. And he left this awesome mystery to us, and allowed us a good likeness, that we should continually do as he did, and live through his mysteries.[27]

Addai and Mari is the main anaphora used throughout the year. Nestorius is used on five occasions – Epiphany, the Friday of St John the Baptist, the memorial of the Greek Doctors, the Wednesday of the Rogation of the Ninevites and Maundy Thursday. Theodore is used from the first Sunday of the Annunciation–Nativity period until the Sunday of the Hosanna. Under Latin pressure, the Syro-Malabar and Chaldean Churches suppressed Nestorius and Theodore since they were named after heresiarchs. However, they were restored in the Chaldean Church in 1901 under the titles Second (Theodore) and Third (Nestorius) hallowing, and were restored in the Syro-Malabar Church in 1996. Since Addai

---

24 Shlemon of Basra, *Book of the Bee*, ed. and trans. E. A. Wallis Budge, Oxford, 1886, p. 102, accessed at http://www.sacred-texts.com/chr/bb/bb47.htm.

25 See Bryan D. Spinks, 'The Mystery of the Holy Leaven (Malka) in the East Syrian Tradition', in Maxwell E. Johnson (ed.), *Issues in Eucharistic Praying in East and West*, Collegeville: Liturgical Press, 2010, pp. 63–70; Awa Royel, 'The Sacrament of the Holy Leaven (*Malkā*) in the Assyrian Church of the East', *International Congress on the Anaphora of Mar Addai & Mari*, Rome, October 2011, forthcoming.

26 R. H. Connolly, 'Sixth-Century Fragments of an East-Syrian Anaphora', *Oriens Christianus* NS 12–14 (1925), pp. 99–128.

27 A. Gelston, *The Eucharistic Prayer of Addai and Mari*, Oxford: Clarendon Press, 1992, p. 75; A. Gelston, 'A Fragmentary Sixth-Century East Syrian Anaphora', in *Studia Patristica* 64 (2013), pp. 106–9.

and Mari has been fully discussed in an earlier chapter, it is the anaphoras Nestorius and Theodore that will be considered here.[28]

The term *Gighla* (see summary on p. 143) refers to a cycle or liturgical set of units – a *kussapa*, a *ghanta* and a *qanona*. The East Syrian anaphoras are divided in this manner. The *kussape* prayers tend to be private prayers of the priest. Although this genre of prayer may well have originated in the fourth or fifth centuries, the prayers were not inserted into the manuscripts until the eleventh century – and are not in every manuscript. The earliest *Hūdrā* we have, the tenth-century *Mar Esa'ya* text from Mosul, does not contain the *kussape* prayers. They do have their own interesting spirituality and theology, but they do not form part of the most ancient core of the anaphoras.[29]

The Anaphoras of Nestorius and Theodore have a structure that makes them distinctly East Syrian, namely that the intercessions come *before* the Epiklesis and not after. Some of the manuscripts of Nestorius and Theodore have colophons or headings about their origin:

> By the grace of God we begin to write the Quddasa (Hallowing) of my Lord Nestorius, Patriarch of Byzantium, the martyr, but not of blood, and persecuted for the truth of orthodox confession. Mar Ābā the Great, the Catholicos of blessed memory, when he went up to Roman territory, translated (*'phq*) the Quddasa of Mar Nestorius from Greek into Syriac and all his compositions, as Mar John the Catholicos indicates in the memre which he composed on the Fathers.
>
> In the power of the Lord Jesus Christ we begin to write the Quddasa of Mar Theodore, the Interpreter of godly books, which Mar Aba the Catholicos translated (*'phq*) and interpreted (*phsqh*) from Greek in to Syriac when he went up to new Rome and he translated it with the help of Mar Thomas the doctor of Edessa.

The clear implication is that Mar Ābā, who was Catholicos between 540 and 552, was responsible for introducing these anaphoras into the Church of the East, and since Mar Thomas died in 533, Theodore at least must have been in use prior to that date. Before becoming Catholicos, Mar Ābā travelled widely in the eastern Roman Empire. He was responsible for collecting works of Nestorius, including the *Bazaar of Heraclides*, and having them translated into Syriac.[30] The implication of the colophons is that Mar Ābā also collected

28 The music for the Divine Liturgy is available: compiled by L. Yakubova, music scores by A. Sahakyan, *Chants from the East: The Liturgical Music of the Assyrian Church of the East*, Chicago: Sponsored by the Assyrian Universal Alliance Foundation, 2009; Vahan Artsruni, CD, *Chants from the East, Sacred Episodes and Sacred Rituals*, music and documentary, Chicago: Assyrian Universal Alliance Foundation, 2007.

29 Bryan D. Spinks, 'Priesthood and Offering in the *kuššāpē* of the East Syrian Anaphoras', *Studia Liturgica* 15 (1984), pp. 104–17.

30 Sebastian Brock has pointed out that in Mar Ābā's letter to the clergy of Susa (c. 544), his language is quite traditional and shows no signs of Nestorius' technical terms. This was in part due the fact that the Church of the East was much more concerned with espousing and championing the theology of Nestorius' teacher, Theodore of Mopsuestia, than the Christology of Nestorius himself. Sebastian P. Brock, 'The Christology of the Church of the East in the

anaphoras named Nestorius and Theodore the Interpreter and had them translated into Syriac. There are, however, problems with taking the colophons simply at face value. The first is that Homily XVII attributed to Narsai quotes parts of each of these anaphoras. Thus they either pre-date Mar Ābā, or they have been interpolated into the Homily, or the Homily is indeed 'Pseudo-Narsai'. The cumulative evidence would suggest that the two anaphoras were indeed introduced by Mar Ābā. However, it is highly unlikely that there were two Greek anaphoras named Nestorius and Theodore that were simply translated into Syriac. Nestorius was only Patriarch for three years and would hardly have had time to introduce his own anaphora, and even more unlikely to have changed the structure. Mar Ābā would have found in use in Constantinople the Anaphoras of Byz.Bas, CHR (Twelve Apostles) and St James. Although Georg Wagner believed that Theodore's catechetical lectures presuppose the Anaphora of Theodore, Anthony Gelston came to the opposite conclusion, and Gelston is on more solid ground.[31] Important here are the Syriac terms used in the colophons, where *'phq* can mean translate but also publish, promulgate, set forth, and *phsqh*, which can mean translate, interpret or explicate.[32] The internal evidence suggests that Nestorius is based upon CHR, with occasional parallels with St Basil and St James. However, it is no wooden translation from the Greek, but has been rendered into the Syriac idiom, and has also borrowed from Addai and Mari. Perhaps 'incultured redaction' is the appropriate description. Theodore draws on Addai and Mari and Nestorius, and in places shows an awareness of Theodore's catechetical homilies, but again it is a Syriac composition and not a mere translation.[33]

The East Syrian anaphoras have a rather different opening dialogue from other anaphoral families, which in its simplest form in Addai and Mari is expanded in

Synods of the Fifth to Early Seventh Centuries: Preliminary Considerations and Materials', in G. D. Dragas (ed.), *Askum-Thyateira: A Festschrift for Archbishop Methodios of Thyateira and Great Britain*, London: Thyateira House, 1985, p. 127. For a modern defence, see Andrew Younan, *The Mesopotamian School and Theodore of Mopsuetsia*, 2009, available at http://www.lulu.com/content/5537694.

31 Georg Wagner, *Der Ursprung der Chrysostomusliturgie*, Münster: Aschendorff, 1973; Anthony Gelston, 'Theodore of Mopsuestia: the Anaphora and Mystagogical Catechesis 16', *Studia Patristica* 26 (1993), pp. 21–34.

32 Louis Costaz, *Syriac–English Dictionary*, Beirut: Éditions de l'Imprimerie Catholique, 1963, pp. 208, 294.

33 Douglas Webb, 'Le Sens de L'Anaphore de Nestorius', in Alexander Schmemann (ed.), *La Liturgie: sons sens, son esprit, sa méthode*, Rome: CLV, 1982, pp. 349–72; 'The Anaphora of Theodore the Interpreter', *Ephemerides Liturgicae* 104 (1990), pp. 3–22; P. Youssif, 'The Anaphora of Mar Theodore: East Syrian; Further Evidence', *Studia Anselmiana* 110, *Analecta Liturgica* 17 (1993), pp. 571–91; Anthony Gelston, 'The Relationship of the Anaphoras of Theodore and Nestorius to that of Addai and Mari', in George Karukaparampil (ed.), *Tuvaik: Studies in Honour of Rev. Jacob Vellian*, Syrian Church Series XVI, Kottayam: Manganam, 1995, pp. 20–6; 'The Origin of the Anaphora of Nestorius: Greek or Syriac?', *Bulletin of John Rylands University Library of Manchester* 78 (1996), pp. 73–86; Bryan D. Spinks, *Mar Nestorius and Mar Theodore the Interpreter: The Forgotten Eucharistic Prayers of East Syria*, Joint Liturgical Study 45, Alcuin Club/GROW, Cambridge: Grove Books, 1999.

Theodore and even more so in Nestorius.[34] They open with the 'Grace', but the second exhortation in Nestorius and Theodore is:

> Above in the heavenly heights, in the dread places of glory, where the waving of the wings of the Cherubim does not cease, and the alleluias and sweet chanting of the Holies by the Seraphim, there let your minds be.
>
> *To you God of Abraham, Isaac and Israel, glorious King.*

The third has undergone expansion, and the formula in the *Mar Esa'ya* manuscript of the tenth century is much shorter than the modern *textus receptus* of Nestorius (*Mar Esa'ya* underlined; common material in Theodore in bold):

> **The living and reasonable oblation of our first fruits and the unslain and acceptable sacrifice of the Son of our race**, [our kinsman] which the prophets figured in mystery, and the apostles proclaimed openly, and the martyrs bought with the blood of their necks, and the teachers expounded in the churches, and the priests sacrificed on the altar, and the Levites bore upon their arms, and the peoples received for the pardon of all their debts, and **for all the entire creation, is offered to God the Lord of all.**
>
> *It is fitting and right.*

In Nestorius the initial praise has parallels with CHR and Byz.Bas, but to the alpha-privatives of CHR have been added 'uncompounded', 'impassible and immortal', and 'not circumscribed'. These are words that became important in the Antiochene anxiety with the implications of the Christology of Cyril of Alexandria, and can be interpreted as safeguards against some of the more extreme and unqualified statements of Cyril.[35] In the post-Sanctus Byz.Bas seems to have been the inspiration where use is made of Hebrews 1.3, 2 Corinthians 4.4, Colossians 1.15, Philippians 2.6–7 and Galatians 4.4. Nestorius has:

> who being in your likeness and effulgence from you and the image of your Being, it was not robbery that he regarded that he is your equal, but emptied himself and took the form of a servant, perfect man, who from a reasonable, intelligent and immortal soul and from a mortal human body and conjoined it to him and united it with him in glory, power and honour, to the Son of a passible nature, which was fashioned by the power of the Holy Spirit for the salvation of all and was from a woman and was under the law, that he might redeem those under the law and enliven all those who were dead in Adam.

---

34 For critical texts, see Sébastien Naduthadam, 'L'Anaphore de Mar Nestorius. Edition Critique et Etude', thesis presented to the Institut Catholique de Paris, 1992; Jacob Vadakkel, *The East Syrian Anaphora of Mar Theodore of Mopsuestia: Critical Edition, English Translation and Study*, Vadavathoor, Kottayam: Oriental Institute of Religious Studies India, 1989. ET in Spinks, *Mar Nestorius*.

35 Bryan D. Spinks, 'The Anaphora of Nestorius: Antiochene Lex Credendi through Constantinopolitan Lex Orandi?', *Orientalia Christiana Periodica* 62 (1996), pp. 273–94.

Nestorius had claimed to be only following his deceased teacher, Theodore of Mopsuestia, and in this passage we see a number of both their concerns. 'Perfect man' is a phrase from Theodore's homilies on the Creed. It found its way into the Formula of Reunion that Cyril ratified, and later into the Chalcedonian Definition. The form of the union for Theodore and Nestorius was by conjunction, a term that Cyril repudiated. Obedience to the law is also a crucial theme in Theodore's writings that have survived. And whereas Byz.Bas expands the Galatians phraseology 'born of a woman' by adding the title *theotokos*, as one would expect, no such title is found in this anaphora.[36] The Words of Institution include the words 'after he had performed Passover with his disciples, according to the Law of Moses, he introduced his own Passover before he died'. This again was important in Theodore's Christology that Christ obeyed all the Jewish law, and it finds emphasis here. The Words of Institution spell out the obedient suffering.[37] The intercessions follow the Anamnesis and accord with the theology of Theodore's catechetical homilies. The bread and wine typify the dead body and blood of Christ – the sacrifice – and so the sacrifice is pleaded, and intercession is made over the 'slain' sacrifice. Only at the end is the Holy Spirit invoked to make the dead body life-giving for the communicants.[38] The form of the Epiklesis is as follows:

> And may there come, my Lord, the grace of the Holy Spirit and may it [she] dwell and rest upon this oblation which we offer before you and may it [she] bless and sanctify it and make this bread and this cup the Body and Blood of our Lord Jesus Christ, changing and sanctifying them for us by the activity of the Holy Spirit, so that the partaking of these glorious and holy mysteries may be to all who receive them, eternal life and resurrection from the dead and the pardon of the body and soul.

The verb 'come' is in Addai and Mari and Byz.Bas, though it is the grace of the Spirit that is requested.[39]

The verbs 'bless', 'sanctify', 'make' and 'change' are all found in the redactor's sources. The eschatological fruits requested in Addai and Mari are amplified in Nestorius, drawing on his other sources.

The Anaphora of Theodore's initial praise may be seen as an expansion of that found in Addai and Mari, which is concerned with the Name. The work of creation is regarded as a work of the Trinity, and it is the Spirit that makes mortals worthy of offering praise in the Sanctus. It uses the technical term *qnome* for 'persons' of the Trinity. Though named after Theodore, unlike Nestorius, there are no obvious 'Theodorian' terms or phrases in the post-Sanctus of this anaphora. The Institution Narrative has a form that echoes Aphrahat

36 Spinks, 'Anaphora of Nestorius', pp. 283–7. See also Jose Kochuparampil, 'Redemptive Economy in the Third East Syrian Anaphora attributed to Mar Nestorius', forthcoming in the papers of the Fourth Congress of the Society of Oriental Liturgy, Notre Dame University, Lebanon: Louaize, 2012. Nestorius declined to use *theotokos*, preferring *christotokos*.

37 Bryan D. Spinks, 'Theodore of Mopsuetia and the Institution Narrative in the East Syrian Anaphora', *Studia Patristica* 40 (2006), pp. 109–14.

38 Bryan D. Spinks, 'Anaphora of Nestorius', pp. 287–92.

39 See Bryan D. Spinks, 'The Epiclesis in the East Syrian Anaphoras', ch. 6 in *Worship: Prayer from the East*, Washington: Pastoral Press, 1993.

and Ephrem, where Jesus says, 'And perform this whenever you gather for my memorial', with the post-narrative pick-up, 'And as we have been commanded, we are gathered together . . .'. This anaphora offers 'this living and holy and acceptable sacrifice, the mystery of the Lamb of God who takes away the sins of the world'. In the intercessions there is one point where the Theodorian christological concerns find expression, 'God the Logos put on complete humanity, our Lord Jesus Christ, and was perfected and was declared righteous in the power of God and the Holy Spirit, . . .'. The Epiklesis follows Nestorius in asking for the grace of the Spirit to come; unlike Nestorius, but as in Theodore's catechetical homily, the grace of the Spirit is asked for us as well as for the elements. As with the structure of Nestorius, this perfectly fits the eucharistic theology of Theodore of Mopsuestia, in that the intercessions are recited pleading 'the mystery of the Lamb of God', and only finally is the grace of the Holy Spirit requested to make the elements the risen and life-giving body and blood of Christ.

A very similar theological concern is found in Narsai and Gabriel Qatraya. Narsai, in Homily XXI, says:

> By the power of His will the priest distributes life in the Bread, and drives out iniquity and makes the Spirit dwell in the midst of the members (of the body). The power of the Spirit comes down unto a mortal man, and dwells in the bread and consecrates it by the might of His power.[40]

Qatraya is certainly writing after the introduction of these two anaphoras; he thus knows two anaphoras with the Institution Narrative and one (Addai and Mari) without. He argues that the narrative is like the original creation blessing of the earth – 'it travels through all generations up till eternity, without being held back'.[41] But that is not quite the same as regarding them as consecratory. Qatraya says:

> *The fact that when the priest invokes the Spirit and she hovers he joins the Body to the Blood, and the Blood to the Body: a symbol of the returning of the soul of* our Lord *within his body, and his resurrection from the dead.* For the priest resurrects the Body symbolically through the agency of the Spirit.
>
> *The fact that, after the tabernacling of Grace, the priest does not make the sign of the cross again over the Mysteries (is) because the Mysteries have been completed by* the dissolution *of death.*[42]

It is also implied in his explanation of John 6:63, 'The Spirit gives life, but the body profits nothing':

> For the body of our Lord Christ does not possess of its own (human) nature New Life, and was going to give (this) to others too; rather, through the grace of the Holy Spirit which was given to him (sc. the Man) as a result of his resurrection from the dead, and by the perfect conjunction with the divine Nature,

40 Narsai, 'Homily XXI', in Connolly, *Liturgical Homilies of Narsai*, p. 58.

41 Qatraya, in Brock, 'Gabriel of Qatar's Commentary on the Liturgy', p. 217.

42 Brock, 'Gabriel of Qatar's Commentary on the Liturgy', p. 216.

> he was raised up, and became the gatherer of immortality to others, just as he said, 'Just as I am alive because of my Father, so whoever eats me will also live because of me'. (John 6:54) Accordingly, with awe and great attention we ought to approach this Mystery, and not in an ordinary fashion.[43]

Bar Zo'bi draws on Narsai and Qatraya, and in similar words to Qatraya says:

> For when the priest summons the Spirit he comes down in power, he joins the body to the blood and the blood to the body. This signifies the awesome return of the soul of Jesus, which returned to the Body which became living and immortal. The priest raises the Body to life figuratively by the operation of the Holy Spirit who comes down (on it) and abides (in it).
>
> After the descent of the Holy Spirit on the sacrifice, the priest no longer signs the Mysteries by the sign of the cross. This shows that the Mysteries are completed with all their rites and that Christ is raised and death has been vanquished and life reigns.[44]

George of Arbela drew a parallel between the divine and human natures of Christ and the sacramental presence:

> But certain godly men have said that these Mysteries (raze) are strictly the body and blood of Christ and not a mystery (raza) of His body and blood. But we say to them, that some things are by nature, and some are (only) adjuncts, which are (united) with the nature. Those that are by nature cannot be received into a union, but the nature itself makes them its own appropriation . . . And if these things are so, the bread and wine also have become the body and blood, not by nature, but by union. And when we call them body and blood after a manner, we also style them 'Mysteries,' that they may be recognized to be mysteries of the body and blood – since by nature they are distinct. But if they are strictly body and blood, they are not mysteries: and if they are mysteries they are not body and blood – since by a mystery is represented some attribute that it [the thing which represents] has not by nature. No natural things are mysteries, and no mysteries are natural things . . . so the bread and wine are the body and blood of Christ by a union and by a mystery: by nature (they are) bread and wine . . . But it behooves us to preserve the natures, and to perform mysteries by means of a union.[45]

It would seem that the dyophysite Christology is here being applied to the Eucharist.

The concept of offering in these two anaphoras is rendered by two verbs: *'aseq* (Aph'el of *slq*), raise up or send up, is generally used for offering praise, and *qareb* (Pa'el of *qrb*) for offering in connection with the eucharistic action. The noun used is *qurbana*, though after the recital of the Narrative of Institution they

43 Brock, 'Gabriel of Qatar's Commentary on the Liturgy', pp. 216–17.

44 Khoraiche, 'L'Explication des Mysteres divins', p. 409.

45 R. H. Connolly, *A Commentary on the Mass by the Nestorian George: Bishop of Mosul and Arbel (10th century)*, Kottayam: OIRSI Publications 243, 2000, pp. 106–8.

both also used the term *debhā* (feminine *debhtā* in Theodore). Under the influence of the catechetical and other writings of Theodore of Mopsuestia, there seems to be a sequence of offering of praise, offering the mystery of the passion which is associated with the recital of the Institution Narrative, then the pleading of the sacrifice in the intercessions, and then the Spirit is invoked to make the oblation life-giving for those who receive it.[46] It is the eschatological fruits of communion that are crucial in the thought of these anaphoras – eternal life and resurrection from the dead, pardon of body and soul, the light of knowledge and for uncovered faces towards God, and united one to another (Nestorius), as well as the forgiveness of sins, salvation of body and soul, new life in the Kingdom of Heaven, and to inherit the good things that have been prepared and will not pass away (Theodore). This is the focus of the short statement of belief on the Eucharist in the thirteenth/fourteenth-century writer Adisho in *The Pearl*. Adisho seems to have been influenced by Western terminology when he speaks of the matter of the sacrament as being wheat and wine, and the form being Christ's life-giving word and the descent of the Holy Spirit. The crux, though, is:

> Whenever we approach these sacraments we meet with Christ himself and him we bear upon our hands and kiss and in partaking thereof, we are being united with him, his holy body mixing with our bodies, and his innocent blood mingling with our blood, and by faith we know him that is in heaven and him that is in the Church, to be but one body.[47]

The classical commentators of the Church of the East are still foundational for sacramental thought in this tradition, as is evidenced in Awa Royel's *Mysteries of the Kingdom*.[48] Royel notes that the Church of the East accepts that the one non-repeatable sacrifice of Christ is perpetuated as a *raza*, mystery, in the Eucharist. Furthermore,

> the Assyrian Church of the East strictly, continuously and in keeping with the Apostolic Tradition of the blessed apostles of Christ and the words of Sacred Scripture itself, believes that the bread and wine consecrated at the Eucharistic celebration of the Church *are indeed the very Body and Blood of Jesus Christ*, according to his own word.[49]

However, he appeals to George of Arbela in rejecting the nature/accident terminology of Aristotelian categories and speaks instead of the elements being truly the Body and Blood of Christ, not in nature but in terms of sacramentality.[50]

46 Bryan D. Spinks, 'Eucharistic Offering in the East Syrian Anaphoras', *Orientalia Christiana Periodica* 50 (1984), pp. 347–71.

47 Adisho, *The Book of Marganitha (The Pearl)*, trans. Mar Eshai Shimun XXIII, Ernakulam, Kerala: Mar Themotheus Memorial Printing, 1965, p. 57.

48 Bishop Mar Awa Royel, *Mysteries of the Kingdom: The Sacraments of the Assyrian Church of the East*, CIRED, San Jose: Medius Corp, 2011.

49 Royel, *Mysteries of the Kingdom*, p. 257.

50 Royel, *Mysteries of the Kingdom*, p. 272.

The West Syrian (Syrian Orthodox) Holy Qurbono (Qurobo)

The West Syrian rite is that which was developed from the rites of Antioch and Jerusalem by the clerics and monastics who could not accept Chalcedon since they regarded it as a betrayal of Cyril of Alexandria's teaching. Though leaders among this group such as Severus of Antioch were Greek-speaking, the churches flourished in the more rural hinterland, which was Syriac-speaking, and the 'West Syrian' dialect became their liturgical language. Baby Varghese explains:

> The Monastic movement played a vital role in shaping the liturgical and the spiritual traditions of the Syrian Orthodox Church. The monasteries often enjoyed considerable freedom in the case of liturgical matters. The socio-political conditions of the Syrians as a minority made it rather difficult to bring the dioceses and the monasteries under a centralized authority, as in the Byzantine or Latin traditions . . . People lived in close relationship with ascetics who always maintained simple faith and traditions of folk wisdom. This has left traces in the liturgical texts and in the commentaries. Liturgical diversity seems to have been rooted in the monastic background.[51]

The surviving manuscripts witness to many local differences that co-existed, and thus it is very difficult to argue for some simple developmental evolution of the rite. This is further complicated by two distinct usages, the 'East' which was under the Maphrian of Tikrit/Mosul and influenced by the use of Seleucia-Ctesiphon, and the 'West', which was directly under the Patriarch of Antioch and reflected the usage of Antioch and Edessa. Sharing a Mesopotamian background with the Church of the East has meant that, in spite of their mutual hostility over Christology, they have shared the legacy of the hymns of Ephrem, and there are some common elements between their otherwise distinctive rites.[52] Not until the fifteenth century did the rite become more uniform, but even today there are differences between the Syrian Orthodox rite and its offshoots in India, the Syrian Orthodox Church of India and the Malankar Orthodox Syrian Church, and the Uniate Syro-Malankara Church. In addition, in the nineteenth century a breakaway group influenced by Anglicans of the Church Missionary Society led to the formation of the Mar Thoma Church, which adopted some Protestant principles such as refusing to pray for the departed, and nuanced the request for consecration of the bread and wine. Influenced by the work of Pseudo-Dionysius who seems to have been a non-Chalcedonian, liturgical commentaries include two by Jacob of Edessa (*c.* 633–708), George of the Arabs (d. 724), John of Dara (d. *c.* 825), Moses Bar Kepha (d. 903) and Dionysius Bar Salibi (d. 1171).[53]

---

51 Baby Varghese, *West Syrian Liturgical Theology*, Aldershot: Ashgate, 2004, p. 3.

52 Baby Varghese, 'Some Common Elements in the East and West Syrian Liturgies', *The Harp* 13 (2000), pp. 65–76.

53 Gabriel Aydin, *Jacob of Edessa: Commentary on the Holy Qurobo made to George the Stylite of Sarug from Ms. Berlin Sachau 218* (private translation); BL ms. Add.14496, ET in C. E. Hammond and F. E. Brightman, *Liturgies Eastern and Western*, Oxford: Clarendon Press, 1896, pp. 490–4; George of the Arabs and Moses Bar Kepha, in R. H. Connolly and H. W. Codrington,

The present ordo of the Syrian Orthodox Church has the following outline:[54]

- *The First Service*:
  - Opening Prayer.
  - Psalm 51.
  - Entry into the sanctuary (Psalm 43.4).
  - Kissing and going around the altar (Psalm 18.27–28).
  - Preparation of the bread and wine.
  - Service of Penitence: *Promion-Sedro*; *Qolo, Etro, Eqbo, Hutomo* and Lord's Prayer.

- *The Second Service*
  - Opening Prayer.
  - Washing of the Hands.
  - Vesting.
  - Kneeling before the altar.
  - General commemoration, and commemoration of names, holding the paten and chalice.
  - General *Promion-Sedro.*
  - Censing of the paten and chalice.
  - *Hutomo.*
  - *Qaumo* (Trisagion, Lord's Prayer and Creed).
  - *The public celebration.*
  - *M'anito* of Mar Severus.
  - Trisagion.
  - Lections (now Epistle and Gospel).
  - *Promion-Sedro.*
  - Blessing of the censer and censing.
  - Creed.
  - Kneeling before the altar.
  - Silent commemoration of names.
  - Prayer of Peace.
  - Prayer of Imposition of the Hands.
  - Prayer of the Veil.
  - Anaphora with sixfold canon (intercessions).
  - Rites before the Fraction.
  - Fraction and Consignation.

Two Commentaries on the Jacobite Liturgy, London: Williams and Norgate, 1913; Baby Varghese, *John of Dara: Commentary on the Eucharist*, Kottayam: SEERI, 1999; Jean Sader, *Le Lieu de Culte et la Messe Syro-Occidentale selon le 'De Oblatione' de Jean de Dara. Étude d'archéologie et de liturgie*, Rome: Pontificio Istituto Orientale, 1983; Baby Varghese, *Dionysius Bar Salibi: Commentary on the Eucharist*, Kottayam: SEERI, 1999.

54 For a description, see H. W. Codrington, *Studies of the Syrian Liturgies*, reprinted from the *Eastern Churches Quarterly*, London: Coldwell Ltd, 1952; K. P. Paul, *The Eucharist Service of the Syrian Jacobite Church of Malabar*, reprint, Piscataway: Gorgias Press, 2003; Archdiocese of the Western United States, DVD, *Understanding the Syriac Orthodox Divine Liturgy*, 2009.

- Lord's Prayer.
- Rites before the *Sancta Sanctis*.
- Holy Things for the Holy.
- Communion.
- Post-anaphoral hymns.
- Post-Communion Prayer for the Ineffable Love of God.
- Post-communion imposition of hands asking for divine blessing on the faithful.
- Prayer of Dismissal.
- Farewell prayer to the altar.

In common with the Coptic and Byzantine rites, the West Syrian rite has become prefixed by two preliminary preparations of the celebrant, known as the service of Melchizadek and the service of Aaron. They are carried out in the sanctuary behind the closed curtain that at times is drawn to hide clerical rites from the congregation. As with the Byzantine rite, these preliminary rites were once much simpler and shorter, and in the West Syrian rite did not take their present form until perhaps the fifteenth century. The rites have been studied by Baby Varghese, and the manuscript tradition from the tenth century shows not only simpler forms, but also considerable variations and differences between manuscripts.[55] This 'local variation' of what were private priestly prayers probably accounts for the fact that the early commentaries are almost silent about any preparation.

The bread and wine are prepared at this preliminary rite and are set on the altar and covered with a veil. For the anaphora, the veil is simply removed. That this was not always and everywhere the case is evidenced by older references to deacons preparing and placing the elements on the altar, and also to a procession with the chalice and paten from the altar, around the nave and back to the altar.[56] George of the Arabs speaks of the service of the psalm as the commencement of the liturgy, followed by the Trisagion (miaphysite version) and the hearing of the holy Scriptures.[57] John of Dara speaks of a *Sedro* and then the *M'anito* of entrance, and a second *Sedro*.[58] As to the lections, Dionysius Bar Salibi speaks of a reading from the Old Testament prophets, the Acts of the Apostles, an Epistle and the Gospel.[59] George of the Arabs, John of Dara and Moses Bar Kepha mention the dismissal of various groups, but Dionysius passes over this in silence, perhaps indicating that it had fallen into disuse.

Three prayers precede the anaphora, but Moses Bar Kepha implies that the commemorations (the reading from the Book of Life) came after the Prayer

---

55 Baby Varghese, 'Early History of the Preparation Rites in the Syrian Orthodox Anaphora', in René Lavenant (ed.), *Symposium Syriacum VII*, Rome: Pontificio Istituto Orientale, 1998, pp. 127–38.

56 See Varghese, 'Early History of the Preparation Rites', pp. 129–31. The references are in The Order of the Reception of a Bishop, *c.* sixth century, a canon in John of Tella, and in the commentaries of Moses Bar Kepha and Dionysius Bar Salibi.

57 Connolly and Codrington, *Two Commentaries*, p. 16.

58 Varghese, *John of Dara*, p. 59.

59 Varghese, *Dionysius Bar Salibi*, p. 22.

of Peace.[60] The ceremonies of the Fraction, which take place with the curtain closed, are perhaps the most complex of all traditions. The bread, the stamp of which allows for a division into 12, is partially broken in half and a tip dipped in the wine. There are then complex details for further breaking and arranging, and different patterns each with a name are used at different times of the liturgical year. There are different rules if more than one bread is used. Patterns include 'the Lamb', 'the Son of Man' and 'the Cross'.[61] Communion of the laity is by particles of the bread which have been smeared with the wine. A rather nice end to the rite is the priest's private prayer of farewell to the altar:

> Farewell, O Holy and divine altar of the Lord. Henceforth I know not whether I shall return to Thee or not. May the Lord make me worthy to see Thee in the Church of the Firstborn which is in heaven, and in this covenant do I trust. Farewell, O holy and atoning altar. May the Holy Body and the atoning Blood that I have received from Thee be to me for remission of debts and for the forgiveness of sins and for confidence before the awful judgement-seat of our Lord and our God, forever. Farewell, O Holy Altar-Table of Life and entreat our Lord Jesus Christ that my remembrance may not cease from Thee henceforth and forever, world without end, Amen.[62]

'Bread of blessing' is distributed after the liturgy, as in the Coptic and Byzantine traditions.

The West Syrian anaphoras

The West Syrian (Syriac) tradition has the largest number of anaphoras of any Church, though only a few have been edited.[63] The anaphoras (there may still be some to come to light) at present according to H.-J. Feulner number 83.[64] Not all of these anaphoras are contained in any one book, and most are no longer in use. For example, only 12 anaphoras are contained in *The Book of the Divine Liturgies* used in the Syrian Orthodox Church of the United States of America and Canada (1991). However, this large number of anaphoras witness to local variations and differences co-existing, and a continued tradition of compiling new eucharistic prayers. They range from the sixth century (though Twelve Apostles and St James may have an earlier origin) to the fifteenth century. The attributions given to some are obviously pseudepigraphal, but others at least

60 Connolly and Codrington, *Two Commentaries*, p. 41.

61 For illustrations, see the appendix in P. T. Givergis Paniker, 'The Holy Qurbono in the Syro-Malankara Church', in J. Madey (ed.), *The Eucharistic Liturgy in the Christian East*, Kottayam: Prakasam Publications and Paderborn: Ostkirchendienst, pp. 135–71.

62 K. Mani Rajan, *Queen of the Sacraments*, Kottayam: The Travancore Syriac Othodox Publishers, 2008, pp. 164–5.

63 In the series edited by Alphonse Raes, *Anaphorae Syriacae*, Rome: Pontificio Istituto Orientale, 1939.

64 Hans-Jürgen Feulner, 'Zu den Editionen orientalischer Anaphoren', in H-J. Feulner, E. Velkovska and R. F. Taft (eds), *Crossroads of Cultures: Studies in Liturgy and Patristics in Honor of Gabriele Winkler*, Rome: Pontificio Istituto Orientale, 2000, pp. 251–82.

indicate a *terminus post quem* date. In a study in 1926 Hermann Fuchs presented what is still a useful classification, dividing them into six groups, within two broad divisions:[65]

1 *Texts with non-Syrian ascriptions*

This group includes pseudepigraphal anaphoras that are definitely translations from Greek, *c.* sixth to *c.* seventh centuries (such as Timothy of Alexandria, Severus of Antioch and John of Bostra); probably translations from the Greek but without external distinguishing marks from the text, dating perhaps from the seventh century (such as Caelestine of Rome, Eustathius of Antioch and Julius of Rome); and late original Syriac texts with pseudepigraphal names but belonging to the second millennium (such as St John Chrysostom, John the Evangelist and Dioscorus of Alexandria).[66]

2 *Texts with Syrian names*

These include texts belonging to the second millennium, mainly twelfth to fifteenth centuries (including John Bar Susa (d. 1072), Dionysius Bar Salibi (d. 1171), Michael the Patriarch (1199) and Ignatius Behnan (1454); pseudepigraphal texts whose alleged names belong to the first millennium (Moses Bar Kepha (903), Marutha of Tikrit (649) and Philoxenus of Mabbug (523)) and the rest of the anaphoras of the first millennium (such as Cyriacus of Tikrit (d. 817) and Jacob of Serug (517)).[67]

Some of the later anaphoras may well have been compiled by the person whose name they carry, but many are probably just honorific titles. The Anaphora of Severus of Antioch is a case in point. Severus was Greek-speaking and did not write in Syriac. It is true that there are some parallels in the anaphora with Greek anaphoras – (Egyptian), and Severus was in exile in Egypt. Theoretically he could have compiled an anaphora, and he certainly knew the Egyptian anaphoras. However, no Greek original of Severus is known, and there is no direct evidence therefore to believe that he compiled the Syriac anaphora. On the other hand, the narrative of salvation history does reflect his theology of *theoria*, and it may have been compiled by someone who was steeped in his theology.[68] However, the foundational anaphoras of this tradition were versions of the Anaphoras of CHR and St James. These were in turn developed, improvised, abbreviated and changed, and the resulting new anaphoras in turn inspired or served as models for further improvisation and entirely new texts.

---

65 Hermann Fuchs, *Die Anaphora des Monophysitischen Patriarch Jöhannan I*, Münster: Aschendorff, 1926.

66 Fuchs, '*Die Anaphora*', pp. xxxii–lii.

67 Fuchs, '*Die Anaphora*', pp. lxi–lxxi. Sebastian Brock has recently suggested that the anaphora attributed to Marutha may well have been compiled by him. Lecture at Yale University, 11 April 2013.

68 Bryan D. Spinks, 'The Anaphora attributed to Severus of Antioch: A Note on its Character and Theology', in J. Getcha and A. Lossky (eds), *Θυσία αἰνέσεως: Mélanges liturgiques offerts à la mémoire de l'archevêque Georges Wagner (1930–1993)*, Paris: Presses Saint Serge, 2005, pp. 345–51.

It is not possible to consider all the anaphoras of this tradition here. Discussion will centre on the Syriac versions of the two foundational anaphoras and reference will be made to other anaphoras to illustrate something of the range of style and significant theological expressions.[69]

One of the characteristics of these anaphoras identified by Kenneth Stevenson is a tendency to play down the concept of offering in the Anamnesis.[70] This is particularly so in the case of the Anaphora of the Twelve Apostles, which is the Syriac twin of CHR. The 'missing oblation' in the Syriac version has been investigated by John Fenwick in exploring how fourth-century anaphoras might have been formed.[71] The opening praise is paralleled in the Greek, though it lacks the alpha-privatives (according to Taft, possibly Chrysostom's own additions), and the lead into the Sanctus is rather different from the Greek anaphora.[72] Parallels become fewer from the Institution Narrative onwards. The Narrative of Institution in the Syriac seems to have been expanded, but the Epiklesis is shorter, though it reproduces the request to 'send' the Holy Spirit. It is not that the concept of offering is absent – in the intercessions 'this rational sacrifice' is offered on behalf of all humanity – but there is no offering verb in the Anamnesis. Brock has expressed the view that the style of the Syriac points to the sixth or seventh century, and concludes with Taft that Twelve Apostles and CHR have a lost common ancestor.

Syriac James is in most places a word-for-word translation from the Greek version, apparently undertaken at a time of consolidation of the non-Chalcedonians in the first half of the sixth century, either in the time of John of Tella or under Jacob of Burdana.[73] There was a growing concern among the non-Chalcedonians for accurate and authoritative translations of the biblical books into Syriac, which resulted in a literalism, and this seems to have also played a significant part in the Syriac version of St James.[74] There are, however,

69 See Mar Athanasius Yeshue Samuel (ed.), *Anaphoras: The Book of the Divine Liturgies according to the Rites of the Syrian Orthodox Church of Antioch*, Lodi: Mar Athanasius Samuel, 1991. The Mar Thoma Church has tended to nuance the concept of sacrifice and the Eucharist, and also the petitions for consecration. In the missal of 1925 the Epiklesis of James read: 'May the Holy Spirit overshadowing the bread, make it unto those who receive the same the Body of Christ our Lord. Amen. And this wine in the cup unto those who receive the same the precious Blood of Christ our Lord. Amen.' The present English version of the *Qurbana Thaksa* has seven anaphoras, but with standard petitions for consecration, 'May the Holy Spirit sanctify this bread that it may be the body of our Lord Jesus Christ,' etc. Malankara Mar Thoma Syrian Church, *Qurbana Thaksa in English*, np, 2006.

70 Kenneth Stevenson, *Eucharist and Offering*, New York: Pueblo Press, 1986, p. 64.

71 John R. K. Fenwick, '*The Missing Oblation: The Contents of the Early Antiochene Anaphora*, Alcuin/GROW Liturgical Study 11, Bramcote: Grove Books, 1989.

72 Sebastian Brock, 'The Syriac Anaphora of the Twelve Apostles: An English translation', in Getcha and Lossky (eds), *Θυσία αἰνέσεως*, pp. 65–75. Brock's translation includes common material underlined. In the same volume, see Gohar Haroutiounian Thomas, 'L'anamnèse et l'histoire du salut dans les anaphors de la famille syrienne occidentale', pp. 113–26.

73 Menze, *Justinian and the Making of the Syrian Orthodox Church*.

74 For details, see Bryan D. Spinks, 'Carefully Chosen Words? The Christological Intentionality in the Institution Narrative and the Epiclesis of the Syriac Anaphora of St. James', in Steven Hawkes-Teeples, Bert Groen and Stefanos Alexopoulos (eds), *Studies on the Liturgies of the Christian East*, Leuven: Peeters, 2013, pp. 239–57.

some significant differences in Syriac James that point to particular eucharistic theological emphases in this tradition. First, and shared with Twelve Apostles, whereas the Greek Institution Narrative has Jesus say that his body and the cup are for remission of sins, the Syriac anaphoras add 'and for eternal life'. This, I have argued, is directly related to Cyril of Alexandria's teaching that the Eucharist is life-giving (*zôopoion*). Chalcedonians shared this belief, but for non-Chalcedonians their claim was worthless, since, unless one held Cyril's Christology, the elements could not be an icon of the hypostatic union, and hence the Chalcedonian Eucharist was akin to poison rather than life-giving.[75] Severus was firmly wedded to Cyril's Christology, as evidenced in his letters to Sergius the Grammarian, with large quotations from Cyril, and regarded himself as the heir to Cyril's thought.[76] In his letter to the monks of the East he warned against those who do not confess that

> the true flesh of God and the Logos which is from the holy God-bearer and ever-virgin Mary and from the Holy Spirit, which was hypostically united to him, so that from the fact that he came to be with us as God who became man he was named Emmanuel.[77]

In a letter to Pope Victor he states:

> For the bread that is consecrated on the holy tables and mystically transmuted is itself truly the body, the body of him in whose name it was in fact transmuted, that is of him who voluntarily died and rose for our sakes.[78]

Elsewhere Severus writes:

> The priest who stands before the altar, since he fulfills a mere ministerial function, pronouncing his words as in the person of Christ, and carrying back the rite that is being performed to the time at which He began the sacrifice for His apostles, says over the bread, 'This is my body which is given for you: this do in remembrance of me': while over the cup again he pronounces the words, 'This cup is the new testament in my blood, which is shed for you.' Accordingly it is Christ who still even now offers, and the power of His divine words perfects the things that are provided so that they may become His body and blood. But the priest who stands, since he fulfils a mere subsidiary function only, makes no addition whatever to the rites that are performed.[79]

The Words of Institution thus become christologically important. This is connected with the West Syrian understanding of Luke 1.35. Whereas the East

75 Spinks, 'Carefully Chosen Words?'

76 Iain Torrance, *Christology after Chalcedon: Severus of Antioch and Sergius the Monophysite*, Norwich: Canterbury Press, 1988.

77 E. W. Brooks, *A Collection of Letters of Severus of Antioch*, Patrologia Orientalis 12, Paris: Firmin-Dodot, 1919.

78 Brooks, *Collection of Letters*, pp. 262–3.

79 Severus, in E. W. Brooks, *The Sixth Book of the Select Letters of Severus*, Part II, London: Williams and Norgate, 1904, pp. 238–9.

Syrian commentators (as with most modern commentators) regarded the power of the most high and the Holy Spirit as synonyms, the West Syrians regarded power of the most high as referring to the Logos. In the Epiklesis of Greek James the doublet was noted, and the request was for the Spirit to come upon, *epiphoitesan*. In Syriac James there is no doublet, but this non-biblical Greek word has been rendered by *maggen*, overshadowing, which is the verb (*gn*) used in the Peshitta in Luke 1.35 and John 1.14. In other words, in line with Cyril of Alexandria, what happens in consecration at the Eucharist is regarded as a parallel with the incarnation. Moses Bar Kepha explicitly explained:

> Again, we say thus: just as in the case of the holy Virgin Mary the Father willed that the Son should be incarnate, but the Son came down into the womb of the Virgin and became incarnate, and the Spirit also came down to the Virgin and caused the Son to be incarnate of her: so here also in the case of the altar: the Father wills that the Son be united hypostatically to the bread and wine, and that they become His body and His blood; but the Son comes down that He may be hypostatically united to them; and the Spirit also comes down that He may unite them to Him, even as He caused Him to be incarnate of the Virgin.[80]

Similarly Dionysius Bar Salibi:

> The body and blood are called mysteries, because they are not what is seen. In appearance, they are bread and wine; but they are recognized (to be) and are the body and blood of God. As Jesus who was seen as a man, was God, so too those which are seen as bread and wine are the body and blood. Even though the (Holy) Spirit makes the mysteries the body and blood, they are those of the Son, as was effected in (the womb of) the Virgin. Even though the Spirit formed the body for the Son, it was the Son who took the body. As the angel said: *He who is to be born from you is Holy, and he is from the Holy Spirit* (Luke 1:35). Even though the Holy Spirit was the cause in that He fashioned the body, He who was conceived and born, is the Son. Similarly (on) the altar, which is the figure of the womb and the tomb, the Holy Spirit overshadows and transforms the bread and wine and makes them the body and blood of the Word, who became flesh only once in the womb. Although it is the body of the Son, it is given to us by the Father, through the Holy Spirit.[81]

Thus, whereas the emphasis in the East Syrian rite is on rendering the elements that typify the dead body of Christ life-giving by the coming of the Spirit on analogy with the *resurrection*, in the West Syrian rite the analogy is the Logos and Spirit at the *incarnation*.

In comparison with the two foundational anaphoras, those in this tradition vary widely in length and sophistication.[82] Some are short and the temptation

80 Moses Bar Kepha, in Connolly and Codrington, *Two Commentaries*, p. 60.

81 Varghese, *Dionysius Bar Salibi*, p. 70.

82 Baby Varghese, 'West Syrian Anaphoras Other than St. James and their Theological Importance', in John Berchmans and James Puthuparampil (eds), *Liturgy of St. James: Its Impact on Theologizing in India*, Pune: BVP Publications, 2009, pp. 32–46.

is to view them as 'early' when in fact they are the product of a later time when what was needed was precis and brevity. In Jacob of Serug, Severus of Antioch and Timothy of Alexandria, the opening praise of God is very lengthy, and there is considerable embellishment of the angelic hosts and their attributes and activities leading to the Sanctus. In contrast is that of the Anaphora of Dionysius Bar Salibi:

> It is meet and right to glorify and praise the Father, the Son and the Holy Spirit, one true God. With the thousands of thousands and the myriads of myriads of fiery hosts who stand before you and unceasingly glorify you, may we also be worthy to praise you thrice, crying out and saying . . .

In this same anaphora the post-Sanctus is a brief transition to the Institution Narrative. In some of the anaphoras the Institution Narrative is considerably expanded in detail, but in others it is minimal, and in at least two anaphoras the words of Jesus are conflated in similar manner to the fragment of the East Syrian Anaphora.[83] Thus the Anaphora of Thomas of Harkel has:

> When he befittingly took the form of a servant, as the one who has to fulfill the preparations for our salvation, he took bread and wine and sanctified and broke and gave to his apostles saying: 'Take, receive from it, believe and be assured that you eat my body and drink my blood for the remembrance of my death until I come.'

The Anamnesis in most of the West Syrian anaphoras is addressed to the Son. The epikleses have developed to reflect the incarnational eucharistic theology and also to reflect varied activities of the Spirit. Sebastian Brock has made an analysis of the Epiklesis in some 40 anaphoras, and found that most were addressed to the Father and fall into three main segments:[84]

1 An introduction either by the verb 'send', or 'may there come' with the Spirit as subject.
2 The consecratory action, with a variety of verbs.
3 The effects of consecration on the communicants.

In the Anaphoras of Eustathius I and John Bar Shusan the verb 'pour out' is employed, and in Ignatius the Maphrian, 'cause to reside'. Accompanying verbs include rest, reside and one instance of hover. While most epikleses direct the Spirit to the offerings/mysteries/gifts/sacrifice, a few direct it to the altar. Though

83 A. Raes, 'Les Paroles de la consecration dans les Anaphoraes Syriennes', *Orientalia Christiana Periodica* 3 (1937), pp. 486–504, though Raes's title betrays a Western Catholic bias as to the narratives function.

84 Sebastian Brock, 'Towards a Typology of the Epicleses in the West Syrian Anaphoras', in H.-J. Feulner, E. Velkovska and R. F. Taft (eds), *Crossroads of Cultures: Studies in Liturgy and Patristics in Honor of Gabriele Winkler*, Rome: Pontificio Istituto Orientale, 2000, pp. 173–92. See also Aho Shemunkasho, *Konsekration und Konsekrationsgeschehen in der Syrischen eucharistischen Anaphora und in der Liturgie der anderen Mysterien*, Piscataway: Gorgias Press, 2008.

this tradition has emphasized an incarnational eucharistic theology, with the Institution Narrative representing the Logos, it is the Spirit that is regarded as the 'seal'. In one of his commentaries Jacob of Edessa mentions the words of Jesus, but adds 'After the invocation of the Holy Spirit, he (the priest) fulfilled/completed the holy sacraments'.[85] Dionysius Bar Salibi commented:

> After having invoked the Holy Spirit, the priest stands erect from inclination and says: *May He overshadow* . . . and then he signs three crosses over the bread and three over the chalice, to indicate that by the will of the Father, God the Word descends and overshadows the mysteries and perfects them by the Holy Spirit.[86]

Eschatological fruits asked for include absolution of offences, forgiveness of sins, confidence and shamelessness, glory and edification of the Church (Mark the Evangelist); cleansing of souls and bodies from all blemishes, remission of sins and life eternal (St Peter); purification of heart, cleansing of thoughts and sanctification of souls (St John the Evangelist); partakers of joy and the ability to offer praises and thanksgiving (Xystus).

One other feature of these many anaphoras is the grouping of the intercessions into six, though those of the 'East' (Tikrit) usage are longer than the 'West' usage. The Six Canons are 'The Living Fathers', 'The Living Brethren', 'The Kings', 'The Saints', The Doctors of the Church' and 'The Departed'.[87]

A modern commentary on the liturgy by Ishaq Saka sheds some light on current thinking. Concerning the Institution Narrative, he writes:

> The priest relates the story as written by the evangelists concerning how the Lord Christ ordained this mystery in the upper room. This account is informational and historical and nothing else. For this reason the claim of some churches that transubstantiation occurs at the recital of these words is completely without foundation.[88]

Later he asserts:

> The transubstantiation, discussed earlier, occurs as the Holy Spirit transforms the bread and the wine into the Body and Blood of Christ.[89]

As in the case of the Coptic Church, transubstantiation is the translator's chosen word; 'transmutation' is probably more representative of Syrian Orthodox thought. Ishaq Saka, though, clearly sees the Narrative of Institution as narrative history and the Epiklesis as the centre of consecration. The link between our

85 Aydin, *Berlin Sachau* 218, p. 5 (private translation).

86 Varghese, *Dionysius Bar Salibi*, p. 78.

87 For details, see Phillip Tovey, 'Observations on the Six Intercessions in the Holy Qurbana', *Essays in West Syrian Liturgy*, Kottayam: OIRSI 199, 1998.

88 Ishaq Saka, *Commentary on the Liturgy of the Syrian Orthodox Church of Antioch*, Piscataway: Gorgias Press, 2008, p. 76.

89 Saka, *Commentary*, p. 80.

spiritual growth, the sacrifice of the cross and the Eucharist finds theological expression in an Encyclical of Patriarch Ignatius Zakka in 1991:

> This bloodless sacrifice is a remembrance of the Sacrifice on the Cross and an extension of it and the continuation of its benefits. Furthermore, its true offerer is the Lord Christ, who gave Himself as a redemptive offering on the cross.
>
> The Lord Jesus offers Himself on the Holy Altar as a bloodless sacrifice in the form of bread and wine. The Holy Bible said about Him, 'You are a priest forever, according to the order of Melchizedek' (Hebrews 5.6). Melchizedek was a king of the Holy City and its priest during the time of Abraham, the father of the Patriarchs, and his sacrifice was bread and wine; symbolizing the sacrifice of the new covenant just as he was a symbol of Jesus, the great priest.
>
> The priest who offers the sacrifice of the new covenant, represents the Lord Jesus. Therefore, the believers who participate in the Holy Eucharist, should be of one accord with the priest, who offers the sacrament, in order to receive Christ's blessings. They should also receive the Holy Communion. For, if the physical food nourishes the body, the Holy Eucharist is the food of the soul which makes its partaker worthy to be united with Christ. Concerning this matter, the Lord says: 'Those who eat My flesh and drink My blood abide in Me and I in them' (John 6:56). St. Paul explains this relationship between Christ and the true believer by saying: 'I have been crucified with Christ; it is no longer I who live, but Christ lives in me . . .' (Galatians 2:20).
>
> Therefore, the Holy Eucharist, grants us the Spiritual life in Christ and makes us abide in Him; so we grow and become strengthened spiritually.[90]

The Maronite rite

Writing in 1948, Archdale King asserted:

> The Maronite rite is a variant of the West Syrian liturgy, which in the course of centuries has been considerably Romanised. It has the distinction of being the only Oriental rite which is not used by any body of dissidents.[91]

It is true that since the thirteenth century this Syriac Church has been in communion with Rome, and historically claims never to have officially broken communion with any ecclesial body since its fifth-century origins, and has no 'Orthodox' counterpart. However, King's liturgical observations need considerable qualification, since the Maronite rite has considerable layers. Many scholars believe that the earliest distinctive Maronite rite is preserved in manuscript

90 Syriac Orthodox Church of Antioch: Archdiocese for the Eastern United States, 'The Holy Eucharist', http://syrianorthodoxchurch.org/library/patriarchal-encyclical-letters/the-holy-eucharist.

91 Archdale King, *The Rites of Eastern Christendom*, vol. 1, Pisacataway: Gorgias Press reprint, 2007, p. 211.

Paris 71 (dated 1454) and is clearly related to the East Syrian rite of Addai and Mari. The anaphora, the Third Anaphora of Peter, but commonly known by the first Syriac word of the pre-anaphoral prayer, *Sharar* (confirm/fortify), is a 'non-identical twin' of Addai and Mari, containing most of the East Syrian anaphoral text but having considerable additional material. The shared liturgical heritage between the Maronites and the East Syrian tradition is also demonstrated in a variety of recently edited liturgical fragments.[92] Other manuscripts show increasing adoption of or influence by Syrian Orthodox usage. Rome printed a missal for the Maronite Church in 1592/94, which was officially adopted in 1596. It was compiled/edited by Thomas Terracina and contained 14 anaphoras.[93] *Sharar*, which in older manuscripts always appeared first, was now placed last. However, as we have noted, the West Syrian anaphoras all have their own particular Institution Narratives. The 'Romanization tendency' in this missal replaced the narratives with a single common narrative translated from the Roman anaphora, the *canon missae*.[94] It was printed in large type, and in some of the anaphoras the Epiklesis was altered so as to refer to the communicants only and not the elements. A further missal was printed in 1716, under the guidance of Michel Metoscita and Andrew Scandar, and in this edition three anaphoras, including *Sharar*, were omitted, and the Roman *canon missae* and the Anaphora of St John Maron were added, as well as a liturgy of the pre-sanctified which had been constructed by butchering *Sharar*.[95] A third edition of 1763 reduced the anaphoras to nine.[96] The 'Latinization', which included adoption of Western vestments and exclusive use of unleavened bread, continued through the subsequent missal of the nineteenth and early twentieth century. In the twentieth century Maronite historians of the liturgy began to argue for a return to more indigenous usages, and this was finally given official encouragement after Vatican II by the Sacred Congregation for Oriental Churches. Experimental projects, including use of the Anaphora of the Twelve Apostles as the prime anaphora, culminated in the 1992 *The Book of Offering according to the Tradition of the Antiochene Syriac Maronite Church*, promulgated by Patriarch Nasrallah Sfeir. The rite is in Arabic with some parts in Syriac, including a common Institution Narrative used in the six West Syrian anaphoras contained in the book (Twelve Apostles, St Peter, St James, St John, St Mark and St Sixtus). The rite shows not only restoration of some older elements, but also the simplification that accompanied the Vatican II reforms in the Western Catholic rite. The anaphoras have a common Institution Narrative, which is still a left-over

92 Sebastian Brock, 'Some Early Witnesses to the East Syrian Liturgical Tradition', *Journal of Assyrian Academic Studies* 18 (2004), pp. 9–45.

93 Michel Hayek, *Liturgie Maronite: Histoire et texts eucharistiques*, Paris: Maison Mame, 1964, pp. 61–7.

94 The term is taken from the study edited by Jacob Vellian, *The Romanization Tendency*, Syrian Churches Series, vol. 8, Kottayam: K. P. Press, 1975. In that collection, see the essays by Elias el-Hayek (pp. 85–93) and P.-E. Gemayel (pp. 94–5).

95 Hayek, *Liturgie Maronite*, pp. 67–71, 319–33.

96 In addition to Hayek, *Liturgie Maronite*, p. 70, see Emmanuel Khoury, 'Genesis and Development of the Maronite Divine Liturgy', in Madey (ed.), *Eucharistic Liturgy in the Christian East*, pp. 1–31; Seely J. Beggiani, *The Divine Liturgy of the Maronite Church: History and Commentary*, New York: St Maron Publications, 1998.

symptom of Latin influence on the Maronites. However, the Patriarchal Liturgy Commission let it be known that it was investigating the reintroduction of *Sharar*.[97] Archbishop Youssif Soueif and other scholars worked on this project, and it was published in Arabic and Syriac in 2008. It is to be celebrated on the Sunday of the Consecration of the Church, the Sunday of the Priests, New Sunday, the Feast of Peter and Paul and the Feast of the Departure of the Virgin Mary. Thus the oldest anaphora of the Maronite Rite is once more in use.

Here we will consider the oldest manuscript with *Sharar*, the West Syrian and Latinized pre-1992 rite, and the post-1992 rite.

According to the extensive study by Pierre-Edmund Gemayel, the earliest forms we have are to be found in manuscripts Paris 71, Aleppo 619 and Vatican 309, and these manuscripts also contain *Sharar*.[98] They yield the following outline:

1 Preparation of the elements.
The priest, vested, prepares the bread and places it on the altar with a prayer. Then he prepares the wine and prays for himself.
2 Penitential Office.
Doxology, Proclamation of the deacon, Initial prayer, Psalm 51 and prayer, Sedro according to the metre of St Ephrem.
3 Trisagion and lections.
Trisagion, prayer of the Trisagion, Psalm, Pauline reading, Halleluia, imposition of incense, Gospel, Thanksgiving, dismissal of catechumens.
4 Pre-anaphora.
Hymns, Creed, prayer of faith (beginning with the Syriac word *Sharar*), prayer of preparation, prayer of peace, Kiss of Peace, commemorations and prayer of praise.
5 The Anaphora.
6 Lord's Prayer, *Sancta sanctis*, Fraction, Intinction and Commixture, Communion.
7 Prayers of Thanksgiving and Blessing.

Although the bread and wine were not unveiled until just prior to the anaphora, they were first prepared at the beginning of the liturgy. Although the eleventh-century *Book of Direction* mentions deacons preparing them at the beginning of the Liturgy of the Word, and therefore assuming a 'Great Entrance' of the elements just prior to the anaphora, Hayek has questioned whether in fact the Maronite tradition ever knew an 'offertory procession' and argues that the gifts were prepared at the altar at the beginning of the rite.[99] Whatever the earlier tradition or traditions may have been, the earliest manuscripts testify to the preparation on the altar at the beginning of the service.[100] There may have once

97 Beggiani, *Divine Liturgy of the Maronite Church*; http://www.stmaron.org/1qurbono.html.

98 P.-E. Gemayel, *Avant-Messe Maronite: Histoire et Structure*, Rome: Pontificium Institutum Orientalium Studiorum, 1965, p. 211.

99 Hayek, *Liturgie Maronite*, p. 175.

100 Paul F. Bradshaw and Maxwell E. Johnson, *The Eucharistic Liturgies: Their Evolution and Interpretation*, Collegeville: Liturgical Press, 2012, state the opposite, but they must have in mind the post-1992 rite.

been more lections, but by the time of our surviving manuscripts the lections consisted of Epistle, Psalm and Gospel.

The Maronites often lived alongside Syrian Orthodox communities and shared a common language; West Syrian influence is found in many manuscripts, which has been carried over into the printed missals. The preparation of the elements and the penitential office were assimilated to the First and Second Services as in the Syrian Orthodox rite, and the *Sedro*, *Qolo* and *Etro* chants and prayers were introduced. Though Chalcedonian, the Maronites used the Trisagion with insertions for certain seasons, including in Holy Week, 'Christ who was crucified for us', and claim that the Trisagion has both a trinitarian and a christological address, though the seasonal insertions show a clear christological preference.[101] In the pre-anaphora, as in the West Syrian rite, there are the three prayers – of peace, imposition of hands and of the veil. The pre-communion rites seem to have been overlaid by Western elevation ceremonies, giving rise to a sequence of consignation, Lord's Prayer, *Sancta sanctis* and manual acts.[102] A beautiful christological prayer is used for the Commixture:

> You have united, O Lord, your divinity with our humanity, and our humanity with your divinity, your life with our mortality, and our mortality with your life. You have assumed what is ours, and you have given us what is yours, for the life and salvation of our souls. To you, O Lord, be glory for ever.

The contemporary rite, which departs from other Eastern rites by being celebrated facing the people, shows streamlining associated with twentieth-century Western liturgical reform. A brief preparation and lighting of the candles precede the solemn entrance and service of the word which incorporates some of the older penitential service including Psalm 51. The bread and wine are received at the altar after the Liturgy of the Word, and offertory prayers are offered prior to the prayers of peace.

Sharar

Since the distinct anaphora of the Maronite Church, *Sharar*, has now been restored to use, it is useful to examine this anaphora as witnessing to a unique Maronite usage. Nearly all of the text of Addai and Mari is found in *Sharar*. The exception is the 'Institution–Anamnesis' paragraph, which is omitted, and instead *Sharar* has a quite distinct Institution Narrative and Anamnesis. It also has extensive intercessions, but these come before the Epiklesis, and thus *Sharar* has the distinctive East Syrian shape shared with the Anaphoras of Theodore and Nestorius.

Sharar, which is addressed to the Son, retains a quite distinct introductory dialogue which includes 'To you, O Lord, God of Abraham, Saviour of Isaac,

101 Emmanuel Khoury, 'Genesis and Development', p. 119.

102 Boutros Gemayel, 'Fraction, consignation, Commixtion dans la liturgie Syro-Maronite', in *Symposium Syriacum 1972*, Rome: Pontificium Institutum Orientalium Studiorum, 1974, pp. 163–81.

Comforter of Israel, glorious and holy King forever, it is fitting to give thanks, adore, and glorify'.[103] Whereas Addai and Mari, in the first intercession mentioning the upright and righteous fathers 'in the commemoration of the body and blood of your Christ which we offer to you upon the pure and holy altar as you have taught us', adds a petition for tranquility and peace, in *Sharar* a quotation from John 6 introduces the Institution and Anamnesis:

> We remember your Passion, Lord, as you taught us. In that night when you were handed over to the crucifiers, Lord, you took bread in your pure and holy hands, you looked to heaven toward your glorious Father, you blessed, signed, sanctified, you broke and gave to your disciples, the blessed Apostles, and you said to them: This bread is my body which is broken and given for the life of the world, for the pardon of debts and forgiveness of sins of those who partake of it. Take, eat it, and it shall be for eternal life for you.
>
> Also over the chalice, in the same manner you gave thanks and praise, Lord, and you said: This chalice is my blood, the new covenant, which is shed for many for the remission of sins. Take, drink of it, all of you, and it shall be for the pardon of debts, the remission of sins, and life forever and ever.
>
> Each time that you shall have eaten of this holy body and shall have drunk of this chalice of life and salvation, you will recall the death and resurrection of your Lord until the great day of his coming.
>
> (Congregation: We remember . . .)
>
> We prostrate before you, only-begotten of the Father, First-born of the Essence, Spiritual Lamb who descended from the heights to the depths to become a propitiatory sacrifice on behalf of all of humanity, to bear freely their sins, to pardon sinners by your blood, and to sanctify the impure by your immolation.

It is possible that *Sharar* represents an Antiochene expansion of the earlier anaphora, or it may be that we have Antiochene and Edessan versions of a common ancient anaphora. *Sharar* has a much more pronounced theology of eucharistic sacrifice than the East Syrian anaphora. However, what is interesting is that the Epiklesis of *Sharar* lacks the words found in Addai and Mari requesting that the Holy Spirit 'bless and sanctify' the elements. Whereas the other six anaphoras currently in use have a common Institution Narrative, the authentic narrative of *Sharar* has been retained, though the 'Romanization Tendency' is still to be seen in the larger print used for the narrative with signing of the elements, but not for the Epiklesis.[104] It is perhaps inevitable that a community in communion with Rome is unable to resist the Western hegemony regarding the function of the Institution Narrative. Unlike the East and West Syrians, the Maronites show no discomfort with the term 'transubstantiation'.

103 ET in Bryan D. Spinks, *Addai and Mari – The Anaphora of the Apostles: A Text for Students*, Bramcote: Grove Books 1982; Beggiani, *Divine Liturgy*, pp. 74–85.

104 The words of Consecration for the Anaphora of *Sharar* and of the Twelve Apostles chanted in Syriac are available on a single CD published by St Maron Publications, Virginia.

Concluding remarks

The three Syriac-speaking traditions share not only a common liturgical language; they also share some liturgical material, partly in their common claim on St Ephrem and the hymns and prayers that have been ascribed to him. The East Syrian tradition limited its anaphoras to three, but the West Syrian witnesses to a tradition of new compositions continuing until the Middle Ages. The Maronite rite witnesses to a synthesis between the East and West Syrian traditions, though subsequently having a Western theology and mentality imposed upon its rite. In the East Syrian and West Syrian tradition, the Epiklesis is an important moment in the anaphora, and given that the East Syrians use Addai and Mari which has no narrative, it is difficult to see how the narrative could be claimed to be 'consecratory' or even essential in that tradition – a fact now accepted by the Roman Catholic Church.[105] The Maronite printed texts show the Roman concern for the importance of the Words of Institution as 'consecratory'. The theme of sacrifice and concerns for Christology are reflected in the increasing complexity of the rites associated with Fraction and Commixture, with the Syrian Orthodox tradition perhaps being the most complex. These rituals, however, are a clergy-only concern, mostly taking place behind the drawn sanctuary curtain. The anaphoras of East and West Syria show a healthy eschatology reflected in the requests for the fruits of communion. All acknowledge in some way that the Eucharist is an offering, with *Sharar* using language of immolation. The East Syrian eucharistic theology, building on the work of Theodore of Mopsuestia, and reflected in the shape of the Anaphoras of Nestorius and Theodore, seems to emphasize the eucharistic presence as analogous to the resurrection. In contrast, following very strictly the teaching of Cyril of Alexandria, the West Syrian sees a parallel with the incarnation. Although the Maronite rite has inherited both these theologies, Western Catholic teaching has overlaid what might otherwise have been an interesting synthesis or juxtaposition.

105 Robert F. Taft, 'Mass without Consecration? The Historic Agreement on the Eucharist between the Catholic Church and the Assyrian Church of the East Promulgated 26 October 2001', *Worship* 77 (2003), pp. 68–88; Nicholas V. Russo, 'The Validity of the Anaphora of Addai and Mari: Critique of the Critiques', in Maxwell E. Johnson (ed.), *Issues in Eucharistic Praying in East and West*, Collegeville: Liturgical Press, 2010, pp. 21–62.

7

The Ethio-Eritrean ('Ge'ez') and Armenian Traditions

The Ethio-Eritrean and the Armenian Churches have two things in common: they are both non-Chalcedonian Churches and are therefore in communion with one another; both were founded from other Churches that have influenced their liturgical heritage. Apart from these things, they are two very different ecclesial communities and have quite different liturgical traditions.

The Orthodox *Täwahdo* ('united') Churches of Ethiopia and Eritrea

Christianity was adopted by the ancient kingdom of Askum in Ethiopia sometime in the fourth and fifth centuries. The tradition that seems to have a solid basis is that the Syrian Frumentius was appointed the first bishop by Athanasius. The Church appears to have had close ties with Egypt and Nubia, and the Metropolitan was provided by Egypt until 1951, with the Metropolitan becoming Patriarch (Catholicos) in 1959. Syrian influence in the earlier period can also be detected. The Church includes among its Scripture *1 Enoch*, *Jubilees*, *3 and 4 Ezra* and, at least at one time in some communities, the *Ascension of Isaiah* and the *Shepherd of Hermas*.[1] Either as a result of Jewish influence or a deliberate imitation of Israel, there are certain practices in the Ethiopian Church that give it a distinctly Jewish flavour, including circumcision and concern for the Sabbath.[2] With the Persian devastations and the rise of Islam, the Church's fortunes waned, but resurgence took place in the early Middle Ages. In the fourteenth and fifteenth centuries theological controversies over the Trinity, the form of God, the Sabbath and the Virgin Mary all had their impacts on the theological literature and on the liturgy. There is an Ethio-Eritrean Catholic Church, which is far more Latinized than the Orthodox. With Eritrean independence in 1993 the Eritrean Orthodox Church has become a separate church from the Ethiopian Orthodox Church but shares the same liturgical inheritance. The liturgical language is Ge'ez, especially for the hymnody, but the more modern language, Amharic, is also used. Tigriňňa replaces Amharic in Eritrea.

1 See Pierluigi Piovanelli, 'The Adventures of the Apocrypha in Ethiopia', in A. Bausi (ed.), *Languages and Cultures of Eastern Christianity: Ethiopia*, Aldershot: Ashgate, 2012, pp. 87–109.

2 For differing theories, see chs 8–10 in Bausi, *Languages and Cultures*.

The Ethiopian liturgical tradition is probably the least researched of all the classical traditions. The close ties with Egypt, including an Egyptian Metropolitan, would suggest very similar liturgical uses. This is true for much of the *Ordo communis*, but much less so for the anaphoras of this tradition. Paulos Tzadua observed:

> Structurally, and in some points also textually, the Ethiopian rite and the Coptic rite of Egypt, both having derived from the ancient Alexandrian liturgy, are equal. While the Ethiopian rite gets its origin from Alexandria, it underwent, nevertheless, such an evolution that the actual form of the liturgy seems to be very distant from the original to the point of assuming the dignity of an independent rite.[3]

The Ethiopian Anaphora of Basil is a late translation from the Arabic, and neither of the two Ethiopian anaphoras named St Gregory have any relationship with the Egyptian anaphora of that name. Hitherto, the Anaphora of St Mark/Cyril has been known only in a late translation from an Arabic version, and although this anaphora was included in the 1945 missal of the Ethiopian Catholics, it is not recognized or used by the Ethiopian Orthodox today. Egyptian influence seems more of the type represented by the White Monastery in Upper Egypt than of the Alexandrian uniformity of Pope Gabriel II Ibn Turaik. A clearer picture of the early Askumite period may emerge with the forthcoming publication of the important 'Askumite Collection', a recently discovered fifth- or sixth-century Ethiopic canonico-liturgical collection being edited by Alessandro Bausi.[4] It is already known to contain the Anaphora of the Apostles (derived from the so-called *Apostolic Tradition* (*AT*)) and a form of the Anaphora of St Mark.[5] Emmanuel Fritsch has pointed out that we would expect liturgical forms of the Askumite period to be in Greek, and so although this may be an early Euchologion, as it is in Ge'ez it may have been a translation made for a particular purpose other than strictly practical use.[6] Thus the current view of development is as follows. Among the ancient canonical and authoritative documents of the Ethiopian Church are translations of the Egyptian *Canons of Hippolytus*; the *Senodos*, one of the versions of the so-called *AT*, which, like the Latin recension, includes the Eucharistic Prayer recommended for a bishop to say at his ordination; and *Mashafa Kidan* (Ge'ez translation of *Testamentum Domini*), which also includes the Eucharistic Prayer of that Church Order. Whether these were used in that form in Ethiopia remains to be seen from what emerges from the 'Askumite Collection'. Ernst

3 P. Tzadua, 'The Divine Liturgy according to the Rite of the Ethiopian Church', in J. Madey (ed.), *The Eucharistic Liturgy in the Christian East*, Kottayam: Prakasam Publications, and Paderborn: Ostkirchendienst, 1982, p. 40.

4 For some preliminary observations, A. Bausi, 'The So-called Traditio Apostolicae: Preliminary Observations on the New Ethiopic Evidence', in Heike Grieser and Andreas Merkt (eds), *Volksglaube im antiken Christentum*, Darmstadt: Wissenschaftliche Buchgesellschaft, 2009, pp. 291–321.

5 Emmanuel Fritsch, 'The Anaphoras of the Ge'ez Churches: A Challenging Orthodoxy', forthcoming in the Addai and Mari Congress. I am grateful to Fr Fritsch for giving me a copy of his important paper and this advance information.

6 Fritsch, 'The Anaphoras of the Ge'ez Churches'.

Hammerschmidt listed 20 known anaphoras in the Ethiopic tradition, 14 of which are used by the Orthodox, and 17 used by the Catholics, printed in an amended way.[7] Of the remaining three he listed, one has been shown not to be an anaphora at all, and the other two are not in use.[8] It is generally agreed that the foundational anaphoras are the Anaphora of the Apostles, which is an expansion of the so-called Hippolytan Prayer, and the Anaphora of our Lord Jesus Christ, which is an expansion of the Eucharistic Prayer in *Testamentum Domini*. In other words, they are not simply the texts found in the *Senodos* and *Mashafa Kidan*. It is tempting to conclude with Bandrés that they are simply expansions of the once used earlier texts as contained in the *Senodos* and the *Mashafa Kidan*.[9] However, Reinard Meßner and Martin Lang have argued that the foundational Anaphoras of the Apostles and of Our Lord themselves are of a late date.[10] This position is based on the fact that the Ethiopic version of the *AT* is part of the *Senodos*, which was translated from the Arabic in the thirteenth or fourteenth century. They demonstrate how the current texts have been expanded with insertions from Coptic Gregory and Coptic Matthew (the White Monastery text). The Emperor Zar'a Ya'Eqob, in the *Mashafa berhan* deplored the creation of new texts:

> And they have even established the anaphora by their own authority, abandoning the *Anaphora of the Lord* which is written in the *Kidan* and the *Anaphora of the Apostles* which is written in the *Senodos*.[11]

Meßner and Lang concluded that both the Anaphora of the Apostles and of Our Lord Jesus Christ 'are to be considered late redactions of ancient literary, not of liturgically used texts'.[12] Though this conclusion may have to be revisited in the light of the 'Askumite Collection', the use of the two foundational anaphoras may perhaps date only from the time of Zar'a Ya'Eqob.

Of the remaining anaphoras, Ernst Hammerschmidt classed them thus:[13]

1. Translations, or based on foreign sources. This would include St Mark and St Basil, St James.
2. Indigenous anaphoras such as Jacob of Serug, Athanasius and Our Lady by Kyriakos.

---

7 Ernst Hammerschmidt, *Studies in the Ethiopic Anaphoras*, 2nd edn, Berlin: Akademie-Verlag, 1987/8.

8 Stefan Strelcyn, 'L'Action de Grâce de N.-D. Marie et l'anaphore de N.-D. Marie dit *Mä'aza Qeddase* dans le Liturgie Éthiopienne', *Journal of Semitic Studies* 24 (1979), pp. 241–9. Hammerschmidt acknowledges this in his 1987/88 edition. It is Anaphora 11 in Hammerschmidt.

9 José L. Bandrés, 'The Ethiopian Anaphora of the Apostles: Historical Considerations', *Proche-Orient Chretien* 34 (1986), pp. 3–13.

10 Reinhard Meßner and Martin Lang, 'Ethiopian Anaphoras Status and Tasks in Current Research via an Edition of the Ethiopian Anaphora of the Apostles', in Albert Gerhards and Clemens Leonhard (eds), *Jewish and Christian Liturgy and Worship: New Insights into Its History and Interaction*, Leiden: Brill, 2007, pp. 185–205.

11 From *The Book of the Light*, trans. Emmanuel Fritsch, in 'The Anaphoras of the Ge'ez Churches' (see note 5).

12 Meßner and Lang, 'Ethiopian Anaphoras', p. 194.

13 Hammerschmidt, *Studies in the Ethiopic Anaphoras*, pp. 43–4.

It would seem that many (and possibly all) of the anaphoras date from the fourteenth and fifteenth centuries and reflect religious controversy or the settling of controversy. Getatchew Haile suggests that in the writings of Emperor Zar'a Ya'Eqob (1434–48), in particular in the *Mashafa berhan*, *Mashafa milad* and *Ta'ammera Maryam*, we find evidence of the religious controversies he inherited over the ability to describe God, over the Trinity, Mary and the Sabbath.[14] He proposes that both dissidents and Orthodox composed anaphoras, or altered anaphoras, to express their views. Thus Athanasius is clearly centred on the question of the Sabbath, and the Anaphora of St John Son of Thunder takes the theme of John 1.18, 'No one has ever seen God', and some of its statements in Getatchew Haile's view seem to support the dissident Zamikael rather than the emperor.

The various anaphoras are appointed for use on certain festivals or seasons with the common invariable *Ordo communis*. The priests and deacons assigned to the service wash their feet and hands, usually near the 'Bethlehem'. The bread is baked in the Bethlehem, a small room at a certain distance from the church.[15] The *Ordo communis* is as follows, and in brackets we give the corresponding prayer or parallel material (cf.) in the Coptic rite as found in F. E. Brightman's *Liturgies Eastern and Western*:[16]

- Preparation of the priest.
- Psalms 25, 61, 102, 103, 130 and 131.
- Prayer of Gregory before entering the Veil.
- Prayer of John.
- Prayers over the vessels.
- Vesting and washing of hands and preparing the elements (Brightman, pp. 144–5).
- Prayer of St Basil (Brightman, p. 147).
- Covering of the bread and wine (Brightman, pp. 148–9).
- The Absolution of the Son (Brightman, pp. 148–9).
- Litany (cf. Brightman, p. 150).
- Rite of incense.
- Multiple prayers and petitions (cf. Brightman, p. 150).
- Pauline Epistle, Catholic Epistle, Acts of the Apostles, interspersed with prayers and chant (Brightman, p. 153).
- Trisagion (cf. Brightman, p. 155).
- Gospel (Brightman, p. 156).
- Dismissal of catechumens (cf. Brightman, p. 157).
- *Accessus ad Altare* (Coptic is different; Brightman, p. 158).

14 Getatchew Haile, 'Religious Controversies and the Growth of Ethiopic Literature in the Fourteenth and Fifteenth Centuries', *Oriens Christianus* 65 (1981), pp. 102–36.

15 For this and what follows on the *Ordo communis*, I am indebted to Emmanuel Fritsch, 'The Preparation of the Gifts and Pre-anaphora in the Ethiopian Eucharistic Liturgy in around 1100 A.D.', paper given at the SOL Congress, Louaize, Lebanon, 2012, forthcoming.

16 For the Ethiopian text I have followed Marcos Daoud, *The Liturgy of the Ethiopian Church*, reprint, London: Routledge, 2005.

- Prayers for peace (cf. Brightman, p. 160. The Ethiopian has the same themes but different texts).
- Creed.
- Uncovering of the bread and wine (different texts from the Coptic).
- Washing of hands.
- Prayer for the giving of the Kiss of Peace.
- (Variable Pre-Anaphora.)
- Anaphora.
- Prayer of the Fraction and Lord's Prayer.
- Prayer of Penitence and Commemorations.
- *Sancta sanctis.*
- Commixture (Declaration, 'This is the true holy body' etc.; Brightman, p. 185).
- Communion.
- Psalm 150.
- Thanksgiving ('Pilot of the Soul').
- Prayer of the Laying on of Hands.
- Blessing and Dismissal.

Without doubt this is the most complex and exotic of all of the Eastern rites, with nearly every unit becoming a 'soft point' and being elaborated with liturgical formulae and chant. Although a good many of the prayers of the Coptic rite are reproduced, they too have been augmented or replaced by variations on the theme. Much takes place behind the Veil, or curtain, and as Bandrés explains, the imagery of the Hebrew temple has been overlaid on Ethiopian church architecture and the ritual areas inside.[17] The preparation at the beginning is, as Phillip Tovey has shown, a rite of separation:

> The power of God must fall on the ministers afresh and thus make them worthy even to enter the sacred space of the sanctuary. The holiness of this space is viewed in Ethiopia by the use of the Old Testament analogy of the sanctuary of the church representing the Holy of Holies.[18]

Emmanuel Fritsch has outlined a reconstruction of the preparation as it might have been until 1100, when deacons prepared the bread and wine, bringing them in from the Bethlehem and placing them on a prothesis table in a separate room. The priest did his own preparations and selected the bread. Real wine was used until sometime before the tenth century, when Muslim opposition to alcohol and difficulty in obtaining wine led to the use of either soaked raisins or crushed grapes mixed with water. Fritsch suggests the following, based on liturgical sources and architectural evidence:

---

17 José L. Bandrés Urdániz, *A Glance behind the Curtain: Reflections of the Ethiopian Celebration of the Eucharist*, Adigrat: Master Printing Press, 2008. See also David Phillipson, *Ancient Churches of Ethiopia*, New Haven: Yale University Press, 2009.

18 Phillip Tovey, *Inculturation of Christian Worship: Exploring the Eucharist*, Aldershot: Ashgate, 2004, p. 65. Ch. 4 is specifically on the Ethiopian Eucharistic rite. Emmanuel Fritsch has pointed out to me that 'Holy of Holies' is reserved for the Old Testament Temple.

- Outside: washing of hands and feet.
- In the sanctuary: preparation of the priest and of the altar.
- In the northern Pastophorion: entrance of the offerings of the Pastophorion.
- Selection and preparation of the bread.
- Preparation of the chalice.
- Blessing of the offerings (possibly).
- Covering of the offerings.
- Prayer of the prothesis.

In the sanctuary: the public liturgy begins:

- Dialogue.
- Prayer of Thanksgiving of St Basil.
- Absolution.[19]

Fritsch surmises that the change came about as changes in Coptic Church space impacted the Ethiopian Church space:

> In 1100 A.D. we are therefore somewhat ahead of the major ritual changes which were originally triggered by the wish the Copts had to honour a larger number of saints by dedicating new altars to them at a time when it was no longer possible to build more churches. As a result, the *pastophoria*, and in particular for what regards the present study the *prothesis pastophorian*, were transformed into additional sanctuaries, in which additional altars would be dedicated to more saints. The initial process of that change was probably triggered between the 9th and 10th centuries since one altar only was dedicated in the churches until the 9th century and Pope Abraham the Syrian is first documented as having consecrated a 'central' altar in Cairo's church of Saint Mecurius. The preparations completed hitherto in the *prothesis* chamber were therefore done at the altar itself as the initial section of the public Eucharist, which entailed important modifications of the *ordo* and, eventually, of the architecture. The first Ethiopian clearly documented example of a church arranged for the new *ordo* is so far at Mikā'ēl Ambā, which was consecrated by Metropolitan Mikā'ēl in 1150 A.D., under the Zāgwē King Anbassā Wedem.[20]

As in all the Eastern preparations now at the beginning of the rite, there is a tendency in the liturgical formulas to 'pre-empt' the anaphora itself and in a prayer almost identical to the corresponding Coptic rite the priest says:

> O my Master, Jesus Christ, coeternal pure Word of the Father, and Word of the Holy Spirit, the life-giver, thou art the bread of life which didst come down from heaven, and didst foretell that thou wouldest be the Lamb without spot for the life of the world:

19 Fritsch, 'Preparation of the Gifts'.
20 Fritsch, 'Preparation of the Gifts', pp. 1–2.

> We pray and beseech of thine excellent goodness, O lover of man, make thy face to shine upon this (*pointing*) bread, and upon this (*pointing*) cup, which we have set upon this spiritual ark (*tabot*=altar) of thine:
>
> Bless this bread (*benediction over the bread*), and hallow this cup (*benediction over the cup*), and cleanse them both (*benediction over both*).
>
> And change this (*pointing*) bread to become thy pure body, and what is mingled in this (*pointing*) cup to become thy precious blood, let them be offered for us all for healing and for the salvation of our soul and our body and our spirit.
>
> Thou art the King of us all, Christ our God, and to thee we send up high praise and glory and worship, with thy good heavenly Father and the Holy Spirit, the life-giver, who is coequal with thee, both now and ever and world without end. Amen.[21]

Further Coptic parallels can be seen in the incensing prior to the lections, the lections with their prayers, and the position of the Trisagion prior to the Gospel.

Like all the classical rites, the Fraction and Commixture have become complex rites. The bread stamp of the Church has 13 crosses, and a particular manner of breaking the upper crust of the consecrated bread is followed while, formerly, chanting the Prayer of the Fraction.[22] Now the Fraction is performed at the end of the anaphora and before the Prayer of the Fraction.[23]

The Ethiopian anaphoras

As noted, there are at present 19 known anaphoras, and not all of these are in use.[24] They reflect mainly the West Syrian pattern, but have their own style and identity, and most are lengthy. The Anaphoras of the Apostles and of Our Lord Jesus Christ have been expanded to include the Sanctus (the texts in the Church Orders do not have the Sanctus), and Meßner and Lang note that some of the amplification has parallels in the Coptic Anaphoras of Cyril and Gregory. It is some of the most distinct features of some of these Eucharistic Prayers that are most interesting, and here we will consider four. Nearly all the anaphoras add 'bread' to the saying of Jesus, 'This bread is my body', though Roman Curial intervention removed this as being 'invalid' for its Uniate Church.[25]

---

21 Daoud, *Liturgy of the Ethiopian Church*, pp. 24–5.

22 José Bandrés, 'The Rite of the Fractio or the Breaking of the Bread in the Ethiopian Liturgy', *Ethiopian Review of Cultures* 4–5 (1994–95), pp. 101–11.

23 My thanks to Emmanuel Fritsch for this information.

24 See note 8 above. Until now most authorities List 20, but Bradshaw and Johnson find 22.

25 O. H. E. Burmester, 'A Comparative Study of the Form of the Words of Institution and the Epiclesis in the Anaphorae of the Ethiopic Church', *Eastern Churches Quarterly* 13 (1959), pp. 13–42.

St Athanasius[26]

The opening praise is less praise than an exhortation to the faithful about anger and sin:

> I will cause heaven and earth to bear witness against you so that you may stand in fear and trembling, none making any disturbance. Let no one remain here who is angry with his brother, like the vengeful Cain. Let no one remain here who is quarrelling with his brother like Dathan and Abiram who quarreled with Moses.

Immediately prior to the Sanctus it states:

> We, who were born in flesh like them [the saints], have three births: one is the holy baptism which makes us like Christ, one is the body and blood of Christ which forgive iniquity and sin, and one is the tears of penitence which flow from within like Jordan and bring us in purity before God.

Its most interesting feature, however, is that it celebrates the 'holy Sabbath of Christians', the 'first day of the week'.[27] A struggle in the fourteenth and fifteenth centuries centred on whether the Sabbath should be observed as well as Sunday. In fact, both are kept, but this anaphora clearly exalts Sunday over the Jewish Sabbath:

> Oh, this day was known by the prophets and was hidden from the people of the Jews, but to us it has been absolutely revealed; it alternates like the sun, it rules every week and reigns every week and is numbered every week.

The anaphora praises/describes the eschatological nature of the Christian first day of the week, and even links it with the Eucharist, and intercession:

> Today on this day the Sabbath of light, in which thy body and blood are prepared, we remember those whose names we know through the word of this deacon, and remember thou through thy mercy those whose names we do not know. Write their names in the book of life in free Jerusalem.

St John Son of Thunder[28]

Getatchew Haile believes this anaphora originated with the dissidents who argued that since no one has seen God at any time, God cannot be described, and that their sub-trinitarian belief that the Trinity is names and not hypostases or forms.[29] In the opening praise it declares:

---

26 Daoud, *Liturgy of the Ethiopian Church*, pp. 138–40.
27 Daoud, *Liturgy of the Ethiopian Church*, pp. 138, 144.
28 Daoud, *Liturgy of the Ethiopian Church*, p. 89.
29 Haile, 'Religious Controversies'.

> None knows thy beginning or end: infinite art thou, nor can any find thee, and none can know thee or see thee.

Later it declares:

> The Father is the witness of the Son and the Holy Spirit. And the Son preaches about the Father and the Holy Spirit. And the Holy Spirit teaches about the Father and the Son, in order that the three may be worshipped in one name.

After the Sanctus we find:

> Thou art unique and eternal, holy Father. Thou art unique and eternal, holy Son. Thou art unique and eternal, Holy Spirit. Three names and one God.

Getatchew Haile sees the dissidents' theology in the 'one name', and a refusal to say 'persons'.[30] The Epiklesis is quoted in the *Mashafa mestir*, and so established by the first quarter of the fifteenth century. The Epiklesis asks:

> let the gate of light be opened, and let the doors be unlocked, and let thy living Holy Spirit come, descend, light upon, linger and dwell upon and bless the offering of this bread, and sanctify the cup and make this bread the communion of thy body, giver of life and make this cup also the communion of thy blood, giver of mercy.

St Jacob of Serug[31]

This anaphora is addressed in part to the Father and in part direct to Christ. The post-Sanctus prays:

> Thou art the long cord which will not be severed from the Father, thou art the creator of heaven and earth. Thou didst come down from heaven by thy will. The womb of the Virgin contained thee. A little daughter, who was the daughter of the poor, carried thee. The Galilean (= Mary) embraced thee (= Jesus). Thou didst sanctify her soul, purify her body and strengthen her and she was not afraid of thee.
>
> Thou wast born at Bethehem and thou didst appear like a man. Thou wast baptized by John, didst walk on the sea, didst rebuke the winds and quicken souls.[32]

The Christology here may verge on adoptionism. However, the Words of Institution, addressed to Christ, have a particularly interesting form, where Christ

30 Haile, 'Religious Controversies', pp. 126–7.
31 Daoud, *Liturgy of the Ethiopian Church*, p. 221.
32 Daoud, *Liturgy of the Ethiopian Church*, p. 223.

becomes the agent of the celebration, juxtaposing the words 'at that time' (*ameha*) and 'now' (*ye'ezeni*):[33]

> Thou didst take bread in thy holy hands to give to thy pure disciples.
>
> People: We believe . . .
>
> O thou who didst bless at that time, now bless this (*pointing*) bread with blessing. (*benediction three times*)
> O thou who didst break at that time with thanksgiving, now break this (*pointing*) bread.
>
> People: Amen amen amen, we believe . . .
>
> Thou didst also mix the cup of wine with water to give to thy pure disciples. O thou who didst sanctify at that time, now sanctify this (*pointing*) cup. (*benediction three times*) O thou who didst grant at that time, now grant this cup. (*He shall then move the cup with his right hand in the sign of the cross.*)
>
> People: Amen amen amen.
>
> O thou who didst unite at that time, now unite this bread with this (*pointing*) cup to be thy body and blood.[34]

It also has a curious Epiklesis:

> Let the gate of light be opened and the doors of glory unlocked and the curtain before the face of the Father be withdrawn, and let the Lamb of God descend and sit on this (*pointing*) holy table prepared before me, thy servant. Let 'Melos' the fearful sword of fire be sent and appear over this (*pointing*) bread and cup: (*benediction once over the Bread, and once over the Cup, and once more over both*) to fulfil [*sic*] this offering.[35]

Much discussion has centred on the 'Melos'. Some have seen this as a magical word, and others have argued that it is a cipher for Solomon, read backwards, and according to the *Kebra Nagast* (The Glory of the Kings) Solomon is a secret name for Christ.[36] In a recent paper, Habtemichael Kidane has observed that in the Ethiopian philologists and in the ancient commentary, the *Andemta*, it is understood as the Holy Spirit, and that is how it should be understood.[37]

---

33 Habtemichael Kidane, 'The Institution Narrative–Anamnesis in the Ethiopian Anaphora of James of Sarug', in André Lossky and Manlo Sodi (eds), *Faire Memoire: L'anamnèse dans le liturgie*, Conférences Saint-Serge LVIe Semaine d'Études Liturgiques Paris 29 juin–2 juillet 2009, Vatican City: Libreria Editrice Vaticana, 2011, pp. 119–48.

34 Daoud, *Liturgy of the Ethiopian Church*, pp. 224–5.

35 Daoud, *Liturgy of the Ethiopian Church*, p. 225.

36 See Hammerschmidt, *Studies in the Ethiopic Anaphoras*, pp. 161–2.

37 Habtemichael Kidane, 'Apropos of the Epiclesis of the Ethiopian Anaphora of James of Sarug', paper presented at the Society of Oriental Liturgy congress, Louaize, Lebanon 2012. See also 'The Holy Spirit in the Ethiopian Orthodox Tawahedo Church Tradition', in Teresa

Our Lady Mary ascribed to Cyriacus of Bahnasah[38]

Getatchew Haile has argued that this anaphora was in fact most probably authored by Abba Sanu'el of Wali.[39] Whoever the author was, he drew on the Ge'ez translation of Psalm 103.22, which mistranslated the Septuagint and reads, 'All his works bless; his divinity is in all lands. My soul blesses.'[40] The author also knew the Ethiopian traditions about Mary, and the *Waddase Maryam*, the hymns of Mary, by heart.[41] The anaphora begins with a quote from Psalm 45.1, 'My heart is inditing a good matter'; it then addresses Mary for her part in salvation history and requests her intercession. The post-Sanctus prays:

> O Virgin, full of glory, with whom and with what likeness shall we liken thee? Thou art the loom from which Emmanuel took his ineffable garment of flesh. He made the warp from the same flesh as that of Adam, and the woof is thy flesh. The shuttle is the Word himself, Jesus Christ. The length of the warp is the shadow of God the Most High. The weaver is the Holy Spirit.

In his earlier article, Getatchew Haile draws attention to different manuscript readings that also reflect the trinitarian controversy and 'name' of God.[42] The *Textus Receptus* reads:

> The Father, the Son and the Holy Spirit think. The Father, the Son and the Holy Spirit speak. The Father, the Son and the Holy Spirit like.

However, some manuscripts read:

> The Father thinks, the Son speaks and the Holy Spirit is pleased.

Haile notes that the attributing special actions about the one thought of creation to each of the persons in the Trinity in this way, as though assigning them to the mind, the tongue and the heart of one person, was not acceptable to Zar'a Ya'Eqob. Haile suggests the second reading was the original, and that the anaphora, or this part of it, represents the struggle between the dissidents and the theology espoused by King Zar'a Ya'Eqob. It also reflects memories of religious disputes with the Jews and Muslims of Ethiopia, with reference to both religions wrongly teaching that God is one person and one body. The anaphora also addresses the bread and the cup as ultimately coming from Mary. After the Words of Institution, in words reminiscent of Jacob of Serug, the priest asks:

Berger and Bryan D. Spinks (eds), *The Spirit in Worship – Worship in the Spirit*, Collegeville: Liturgical Press, 2009, pp. 179–205.

38 Daoud, *Liturgy of the Ethiopian Church*, p. 104.

39 Getatchew Haile, 'On the Identity of Silondis and the Composition of the Anaphora Ascribed to Hereyaqos of Behensa', *Orientalia Christiana Periodica* 49 (1983), pp. 366–89.

40 Haile, 'On the Identity' p. 378.

41 Haile, 'On the Identity' p. 379.

42 Haile, 'Religious Controversies', p. 119.

> O our Lord, as it happened then bless, hallow and give this bread . . . O our Lord, as it happened then bless, hallow and give this cup.

This appears to serve as the Epiklesis.

Concluding remarks

The anaphoras are so profuse and so varied that it is difficult to give some overview. The theme of offering is reiterated at various points and not only in the anaphora. The Fraction in St Athanasius says:

> Again we supplicate the God of mercy and minister to him who is himself the minister; we sacrifice to him who is himself the sacrifice, and offer to him who is himself the offering, Let the Lamb come from the highest that we may see him with our eyes, slay him with our hands and rejoice in him.[43]

It is significant that these words are recited just after the Fraction. Both Fritsch and Bandrés draw attention to the importance of gestures in this tradition. Fritsch notes:

> One striking feature is the way the relationship between Jesus Christ and the celebrant is expressed. While the latter is praying all along, listing the actions Jesus Christ did once and for all in the past, he actually also repeats those same actions over the bread and the cup placed before him, re-presenting Jesus Christ in the act of blessing, breaking, pouring *now* through the agency of the celebrant's hand . . . the gestures are, in terms of the prayer, declared Christ's indeed, acting through the celebrant's hand.[44]

Likewise Bandrés, in his devotional and theological explanation of the Ethiopian rite, says:

> In the Eucharist we do not offer the Last Supper of Christ with his disciples; rather by repeating the gestures of Christ at the Last Supper we make remembrance of His death and resurrection now, i.e. we – or better the Spirit present in the assembly – actualise those past events at this very moment.[45]

Bandrés draws attention to the 'now' in Jacob of Serug and Our Lady Mary associated with the Narrative of Institution, and the Fraction and Commixture, and asserts:

> The sentence 'Join now this bread with this cup' makes a direct allusion to the rite of intinction of the consecrated bread with the consecrated wine, compul-

---

43 Daoud, *Liturgy of the Ethiopian Church*, p. 152.

44 Fritsche, 'Anaphoras', pp. 31–2 of unpublished ms. The ms has 'along' but the sense seems to demand 'alone'

45 Bandrés, *Glance Behind the Curtain*, p. 70.

> sory in the Ethiopian liturgy, which signifies the resurrection. It is, therefore, the risen Body of Christ who comes to us in the Eucharistic species.[46]

The anaphoras in this tradition do indeed have Words of Institution – even if in some it is more of a précis – and most have some form of Epiklesis. They also take the opportunity to reflect teachings on other things, often (at least to Western ears and minds) pushing the business of the Supper into the background with extended teaching on the eschatology of the Sabbath, the importance of Mary in spiritual life and devotion, and ancient long-forgotten local trinitarian disputes. It may be that the focus of eucharistic action – presence, sacrifice and fruits of communion – are, in this tradition, expressed in the prayers and gestures of the Fraction and Commixture, even though carried out behind the curtain. As Bandrés comments of the Ge'ez tradition:

> The deep mystery of the *fractio* reveals not only the real presence of Christ in the Eucharist; it does more than that. The eucharistic bread contains all the redemptive mysteries of the life of Christ, including His second coming. That is why those who share in this One, Unique Bread, participate in the full redemption brought by Christ and become the new creation, the new eschatological people of God, the first fruits of the Kingdom of Christ through the Spirit.[47]

The Armenian Apostolic rite

Armenia was evangelized from two distinct areas: from Edessa and Osrhoene from the south, and from Cappadocia in the west. Its great missionary and first bishop was St Gregory the Illuminator, who was consecrated in Caesarea, and Armenia itself was a Christian country by 314. The Greek influence of Caesarea was important, but Armenia was also aware of a tradition of St Thaddeus being its first missionary from Edessa, and the Syrian influence on the Armenian language, theology and liturgy is considerable. In 387 Armenia was divided between the Byzantine and Persian empires, the larger part being under the Persians. It was during this time that the Armenian alphabet was developed and classical Armenian, or Grabar, evolved, suitable for theological and liturgical use. Byzantine influence was enormous throughout the East and continued to exert an influence on the Armenians. The result was that there co-existed both a Chalcedonian group and a non-Chalcedonian group in the Church, though finally the non-Chalcedonian Christology prevailed. Later still, in Cilicia, the Armenians were brought into contact with the West through the Crusades, and for a time were in communion with Rome. The result was Latinization, and certain Western liturgical practices were adopted. Robert Taft summarizes the liturgical influence as follows:[48]

46 Bandrés, *Glance Behind the Curtain*, p. 72.

47 Bandrés, *Glance Behind the Curtain*, p. 105.

48 Robert Taft, 'The Armenian "Holy Sacrifice (*Surb Patarg*)" as a Mirror of Armenian Liturgical History', in Robert Taft (ed.), *The Armenian Christian Tradition: Scholarly Symposium in Honor of the Visit to the Pontifical Oriental Institute, Rome, of His Holiness Karekin I, Supreme Patriarch and Catholicos of All Armenians, December 12, 1996*, Rome: Pontificio Istituto Orientale, 1997, pp. 175–97.

1 In the formational period, the period of origins, there was Mesopotamian-Syriac and Cappadocian influence.
2 In the period of Late Antiquity, beginning with the fifth century, we observe considerable hagiopolite influence on the Armenian liturgy, especially in the lectionary and calendar of feasts and commemorations.
3 Later in the Middle Ages, from around the beginning of the second millennium, there was a strong wave of Byzantine influence.
4 Then, during the Crusades, contact with the Latin armies passing through Asia Minor resulted in a substantial influx of elements from the Latin liturgies.

It may be that the hagiopolite influence is even earlier than Taft suggests. These different influences account for the fact that although today, and probably since the tenth century, only one anaphora is used, the tradition once knew and used a number of anaphoras. The 'indigenous' Armenian anaphoras are St Gregory the Illuminator, which in fact is a very early version of St Basil (arm.Bas.1), Sahak, Gregory of Nazianzen, Cyril of Alexandria and the sole survivor in use, Athanasius. It also has the following 'imports': Byz.Bas (arm.Bas.2) and CHR, St James and Ignatius of Antioch, and the Roman *canon missae*. How widely any of these were ever used is debatable, and they may have been used only in the Byzantine borderlands or, in the case of the *canon missae*, only Cilicia.

Considerable work has appeared in recent decades to clarify what Gabriele Winkler has described as the multifaceted layers of origin and early evolution of this liturgical tradition, and she herself has been one of the main contributors.[49] A French translation of arm.Bas.1 was published by A. Renoux in 1970, and a critical text based on a Lyons codex was published in 2001 by Erich Renhart.[50] Winkler herself has edited critical editions of arm.Bas.1 and arm.Bas.2, as well as Sahak.[51] Hans-Jürgen Feulner has edited the Anaphora of Athanasius.[52] Important classical commentaries on the rite by Step̔anos Siwnec'i (eighth century), Xosrov Anjewac'i (*c.* 950) and Nerses Lambronac'i (twelfth century) have also been published, and assist in tracing the development of the rite.[53]

The Anaphora of St Gregory the Illuminator is proving to be important not only for the history of Armenian liturgy, but in the puzzle of the anaphoras named after St Basil. Arm.Bas.1 seems to preserve forms that suggest it pre-dates the Egyptian

49 Gabriele Winkler, 'Armenia's Liturgy at the Crossroads of Neighbouring Traditions', *Orientalia Christiana Periodica* 74 (2008), p. 363.

50 A. Renoux, 'L'Anaphore Arménienne de Saint Grégoire l'illumateur', in B. Botte et al. (eds), *Eucharisties d'Orient et l'Occident*, Paris: Cerf, 1970, pp. 83–108; Erich Renhart and Jasmine Dum-Tragut, *Armenische Liturgien*, Graz: Schnider, 2001. This also has useful essays on the Armenian rite.

51 Gabriele Winkler, *Die Basilius-Anaphora*, Anaphorae Orientales 2, Rome: Pontificio Istituto Orientale, 2005; *Die Armenische Liturgie des Sahak*, Anaphorae Orientales 3, Rome: Pontificio Istituto Orientale, 2011.

52 Hans-Jürgen Feulner, *Die Armenische Athanasius-Anaphora*, Anaphorae Orientales 1, Rome: Pontificio Istituto Orientale, 2001.

53 D. M. Findikyan, *The Commentary on the Armenian Daily Office by Bishop Step̔anos Siwnec'i (+735)*, Rome: Pontificio Istituto Orientale, 2004; Peter Cowe, *Commentary on the Divine Liturgy by Xosrov Anjewac'i*, New York: St Varten Press, Diocese of the Armenian Church in America, 1991; I. Kéchichian, *Nersès de Lambron (1153–1192): Explication de la Divine Liturgie*, Beirut: Dar El-Machreq, 2000.

Anaphora, or at least has elements that are equally old. Winkler suggests that the christological section of this anaphora reflects the Antiochene Creed of 341, and this, as with Byzantine Basil, accounts for the intercessions being for the dead and then the living as in the Creed with Christ judging the dead and the living.[54] She also suggests East Syrian influence in that the early Syrian way of describing the incarnation, 'putting on the body', is reflected in the allusion to Philippians 2.9, 'putting on the form of a slave'. On the other hand, unlike most other versions of Basil, the Epiklesis requests for the Spirit to be sent rather than 'come'. Parallels with the East Syrian Anaphora of Theodore the Interpreter are interesting, but one wonders whether some of the vocabulary and terms were mediated via the Peshitta and the translation of works of Ephrem rather than direct liturgical borrowing. Nonetheless, it would seem that arm.Bas.1 is the oldest of the Armenian anaphoras, and represents an interesting synthesis of the two original missions to Armenia – Edessa and Cappodocia – and not simply Cappadocia as some have claimed. Winkler finds allusions to this anaphora in the commentary of Step̔anos Siwnec'i, but Xosrov seems to know only Athanasius.

Sahak, according to Winkler, though undoubtedly inspired structurally by the arm.Bas.1, is a Eucharistic Prayer with its own characteristics.[55] Its opening praise gives a rehearsal of creation and the Fall, putting these before the Sanctus rather like the prayer of *Apostolic Constitutions* VIII. St Cyril of Alexandria, which has no relationship to other Eastern anaphoras of this name, opens with a long list of ascriptions of God, such as uncreated, timeless, infinite, unknowable, deathless, and so on. Winkler believes that the introduction to the Sanctus shows influence of the Targums.[56] Gregory of Nazianzen has a complex structure, and perhaps represents overlapping traditions. There is a post-Sanctus that is addressed to the Father, an Epiklesis to approach communion, followed by a consecratory Epiklesis, and after the Institution and Anamnesis returns to the theme of praise with a renewed recitation of the Institution and then intercessions. It prays:

> We beseech you, Lord, that this may be your commemoration and our new commemoration. And make this bread into the precious body of your Christ . . .

Winkler comments, 'this Anaphora poses major problems'.[57]

As already noted, only one anaphora is in use, and that is Athanasius. This will be discussed in the context of the outline of the current Armenian rite. The commentaries enable us to reconstruct the outline at earlier dates. Bold type indicates borrowing from the Byzantine rite, and bold italics indicates borrowing from the Latin rite.

- Hymn of Vesting.
- Psalm of Vesting.

54 Winkler, *Basilius-Anaphora, passim*; 'Armenia's Liturgy at the Crossroads'.

55 Winkler, *Die Armenische Liturgie des Sahak*; 'On the Formation of the Armenian Anaphoras: A Completely Revised and Updated Overview', *Studi sull'Oriente Cristiano* 11 (2007), p. 122.

56 Winkler, 'On the Formation', p. 125.

57 Winkler, 'On the Formation', p. 127.

- ***Vesting prayers.***
- Washing of Hands and Psalm.
- ***Confession and Absolution.***
- Psalms of Accession.
- Litany, prayers and Prayer of Gregory of Narek.
- Prothesis.
- Chant and prayer as elements are prepared (unleavened bread, unmixed chalice).
- Prayer of the Prothesis and Psalm of the Prothesis.
- Censing with prayers.
- Curtain opened.
- Initial Blessing.
- Introit. On Sundays **the Mongenes.**
- *Oremus.*
- Doxology.
- Peace to All.
- Inclination.
- **Prayer of the First Antiphon.**
- Psalm and Hymn of Jashou.
- **Prayer of the Second Antiphon.**
- **Prayer of the Third Antiphon.**
- **Prayer of Entrance.**
- Lifting of the Gospel Book.
- Trisagion (non-Chalcedonian).
- **Prayer of the Trisagion.**
- Litany.
- **Ektene Prayer.**
- Psalm.
- Prophecy reading (Old Testament).
- Apostle (Epistle).
- Gospel.
- Creed.
- Prayers and Litany.
- Dismissal of the catechumens.
- Hymn of the Great Entrance and Angelic Songs.
- **Prayer of the Great Entrance (in secret).**
- **Cherubicon (Deacon).**
- The laying of the gifts.
- Prayer of the offertory.
- The Kiss of Peace.
- Anaphora.
- Lord's Prayer.
- Prayer of the Paternal Name.
- Prayer of Inclination.
- *Sancta sanctis.*
- Prayer of Elevation.
- Blessing to the Trinity and Hymn of Doxology.
- Intinction and Fraction.

- Prayers before Communion.
- Communion.
- Thanksgiving.
- Hymns and prayers.
- Blessing and Dismissal.
- ***Last Gospel.***

The Liturgy of the Word, or Synaxis, is described by Step'anos Siwnec'i in his commentary on the Office of the Third Hour. Daniel Findikyan usefully summarizes the seventh/eighth-century content:

> In Stepanos' time the Synaxis began with the introit of the priest, and perhaps also the people, accompanied by Ps 92. The gospel was then elevated and carried in procession around the altar, accompanied by the Trisagion. The Liturgy of the Word seems to have corresponded exactly to its *déroulement* today. Readings from the prophets, from the Apostle Paul, and from the gospels are preceded respectively by the Midday Psalm, the *Mesedi*, and the Alleluia. The gospel is preceded by exhortations to attention. After the Liturgy of the Word, the Synaxis concludes with the Creed, followed by a proclamation and prayer.[58]

Findikyan observes that the term *Mesedi* is in fact a Palestinian term, which Stepanos misunderstands, but which again may indicate Jerusalem influence. He also suggests that although genetically the Trisagion is Byzantine, structurally it has a different function in the Armenian rite. Xosrov does not comment on the Synaxis, and by the time of Nerses Lambronac'i, further Byzantine elements as well as Latin rite elements had been incorporated into the rite.[59] Among the former are the Prayer of the Great Entrance and the Cherubicon; among the latter are the vesting prayers and Confiteor, and the Last Gospel.[60]

The Anaphora of St Athanasius has some clear borrowing from arm.Bas.1 in the phrasing of the Institution Narrative, the second part of the anamneses and some elements of the intercessions.[61] However, there are also echoes and parallels with the Syrian tradition in the post-Sanctus and Epiklesis, and Feulner concludes that it probably dates from the sixth century and was used in South-

58 Findikyan, *Commentary on the Armenian Daily Office*, pp. 467–8. For the text of the commentary, see pp. 140–50. See also Charles A. Renoux, 'La Célébration de la Parole dans le rite Arménien avant le Xe siècle', in A. M. Triacca and A. Pistoia (eds), *L'Eucharistie: Célébrations, Rites, Piétés*, Rome: CLV Edizioni Liturgiche, 1995, pp. 321–30.

59 For the complexity of relations with Byzantium and the Latin West, see Gabriele Winkler, 'Armenia and the Gradual Decline of its Traditional Liturgical Practices as a Result of the Expanding Influence of the Holy See from the 11th to the 14th Century', in A. M. Triacca (ed.), *Liturgie de l'Élise Particulière et Liturgie de l'Élise universelle*, Rome: Edizione Liturgiche, 1976, pp. 329–68.

60 Hans-Jürgen Feulner, 'On the "Preparatory Rites" of the Armenian Divine Liturgy: Some Remarks on the Ritual of Vesting', in Roberta R. Ervine (ed.), *Worship Traditions in Armenia and the Neighboring Christian East*, New York: St Vladimir's Seminary Press, 2006, pp. 93–117.

61 Feulner, *Armenische Athanasius-Anaphora*, pp. 306–36, 363, 446–50.

ern Armenia alongside others that it has eventually displaced.[62] Some of its characteristics include symmetry in the introduction to the Words of Institution, though not in the words of Jesus and mention of the true incarnation of Jesus. The atoning nature of Christ's work is summed up in the post-Sanctus:

> you gave us your only-begotten Son, both debtor and debt, immolation and anointed, lamb and heavenly bread, high priest and sacrifice; for he is distributor and he himself is distributed always in our midst without ever being consumed.[63]

This striking juxtapositioning of christological and eucharistic vocabulary beautifully encapsulates the eucharistic mystery that is also continued in the Anamnesis, 'bringing forth the saving mystery of the body and blood of your Only-begotten. We remember . . . and we offer to you yours of your own from all and for all.' Xosrov commented:

> *Offering* refers to placing on the altar the bread and cup which is the *mystery of the body and blood of* the *Son* of God. It is a *mystery* for the bread and wine are seen, but *the body and blood of the Son* of God are perceived. And the *mystery* is called *saving* because we were saved and continue to be saved by it in life and death.[64]

The Epiklesis asks that the Spirit be sent on the congregation as well as the bread and wine to 'make' (*arasc'es*) them the body and blood of Christ by 'changing' (*p'oxarkem*), and Feulner notes that these correspond to the Greek terms found in the Byzantine Anaphora of John Chrysostom. Xosrov gave an incarnational analogy in his commentary:

> The Holy Spirit sent by the Father took flesh from Mary's womb and mingled and united it to God the Word who was revealed as one Son and God, born from her. The Holy Spirit acts in the same way in church at the holy altar. Taking the bread He unites it to the Son of God and likewise the cup to become *truly Christ's* body and blood . . . He also effects such prodigious miracles, transforming the mere bread and wine into the incorruption of the body and blood of the Son of God.[65]

Isaac Kéchichian states that this is also the approach of Nerses.[66] However, there is a passage in Nerses that suggests that in fact he combined both an incarnational and resurrectional analogy to consecration:

---

62 See Feulner's summary of *Die Armenische Athansius-Anaphora*, in 'The Armenian Anaphora of St Athanasius', in Maxwell E. Johnson (ed.), *Issues in Eucharistic Praying in East and West*, Collegeville: Liturgical Press, 2011, pp. 189–218.

63 Feulner, 'Armenian Anaphora of St Athanasius', p. 212.

64 Cowe, *Commentary on the Divine Liturgy by Xosrov Anjewac'i*, p. 171.

65 Cowe, *Commentary on the Divine Liturgy by Xosrov Anjewac'i*, pp. 177–9.

66 Kéchichian, *Nersès de Lambron*, pp. 24–5.

> In the same way also, just now as the body and blood of Christ were placed as testimony before God by our priest, and the sign of confirmation of the spiritual sacrifice; but God the Father, taking with the spiritual sacrifice its figure also as God almighty, has breathed his life-giving Spirit into the inanimate body. He made it, which was beforehand a sensible body, now by the Holy Spirit, the body of Christ, and by the union of the Spirit with the wine, he has consecrated and made it his blood.[67]

The intercessions seem to have combined two different forms – perhaps anaphoral intercessions and the Diptychs read by the deacon – to yield a pattern of Living–Dead–Dead–Living. This eschatological section concludes by asking reward for those who remember us in prayer, and to make us fit temples to receive the body and blood of Christ. Xosrov commented, 'This means fit us by the saving sacrifice as a dwelling and house for *Your only-begotten Son*.'[68] Eucharistic belief is perhaps summed up in a modern commentary on the '*Soorp Badarak*':

> the transformation of both the congregation and of the elements of the Holy Eucharist is sought by the invocation of the Holy Spirit. The congregation becomes holy and united in one Lord, and the bread and wine are transformed into the living Body and Blood of our Lord, resurrected from the Tomb. The first is essential, because without holiness of heart and mind the faithful cannot be worthy to share in the Lord's resurrection and victory over death, the death which corresponds to our sins. At this point the Armenian and other Eastern churches believe the bread and wine become truly the Body and Blood of Jesus Christ and thereby an element which affects our communion with Him. During the Epiclesis, therefore, bread and wine change in nature and become communion, reconciliation with God through Christ's sacrifice. This is revealed in the following prayer said by the priest:
>
> Before Thee, O Lord, Son of God, who art sacrificed to the Father for (our) reconciliation, bread of Life broken among us, we implore Thee, through the shedding of Thy Holy Blood, have mercy upon the flock saved by Thy Blood.[69]

Concluding summary

In contrast with not only the Ethio-Eritrean but all other Eastern traditions, the Armenian rite has only a single anaphora now in use, though its earlier anaphoras have become important not only for the development of the anaphoras named 'St Basil', but also for how other indigenous anaphoras were compiled drawing on the Syrian and Cappadocian strands of Christian influence in Armenia. Characterized by use of unleavened bread (usually stamped with the crucifix and broken into four at the Fraction) and unmixed wine, this tradition shows a most interesting juxtaposition of christological and eucharistic terms in its post-Sanctus, which in some ways encapsulate the Eastern concern with the mystery of the Eucharist.

---

67 Kéchichian, *Nersès de Lambron*, p. 222.

68 Cowe, *Commentary on the Divine Liturgy by Xosrov Anjewac'i*, p. 197.

69 Gorun Shrikian, *An Interpretation of the Holy Liturgy or Soorp Badarak of the Armenian Apostolic Church*, New York: Armenian Apostolic Church of America, 1984, pp. 50–1.

8

The Classical Western Rites

The Classical Western rites usually listed are the Roman, the Hispano-Mozarabic (Visigothic), the Gallican, the Celtic and the Ambrosian. One difficulty in identifying all of these as distinct rites, rather than local versions or 'uses' of a rite, is that the process of synthesis and osmosis has blurred some of the distinctions. For example, the Stowe Missal may be less a witness to a quite distinct Celtic or Irish rite than a snapshot of the later Romano-Western synthesis at a particular point in time in Ireland. Likewise the Ambrosian rite, particularly the Eucharist, has so much in common with its powerful Roman sister as to appear as a variant rather than a distinct rite. What these different Western rites had in common was the Latin language.

The Hispano-Mozarabic rite

The origins of the Christian Church in Spain are, like most other places, shrouded in mystery. Paul, in the Letter to the Romans, desired to visit communities in Hispania in the 50s CE, and no doubt Christianity migrated there as elsewhere, through Jewish communities, traders and the military. Communities were well established by 254. The Visigothic settlements in the Roman Empire from the late fourth century led to their migration into the Iberian Peninsula, and they eventually established a kingdom over most of the Iberian Peninsula as well as part of Gaul. The Visigothic rulers had been converted by Arians, and thus Hispano-Roman Christian communities were at odds with the Arian Visigothic newcomers. King Reccared (586–601) adopted Catholic Nicene Christianity, and so a synthesis began to take place. There is evidence that under Bishops Isidore of Seville and Ildephonse of Toledo liturgical creativity flourished in order to bring unity and to provide sound teaching. Byzantine invasion and a short-lived kingdom brought some Eastern liturgical influence to Hispania. However, the eighth-century Muslim invasion meant that many Christians fled north, and those that remained lived with considerable restrictions. It appears that as a result of Muslim domination, or as a missionary sop, a form of Adoptionist Christology was taught. The eleventh century saw the final defeat and ejection of the Muslim rulers, sealed in 1085 with the recapture of Toledo. In the siege of Toledo, the Christians – the Mozarabs – played a distinctive part in defeating the Muslims, and for their Christian loyalty the Mozarabs were rewarded by being granted a special status, and their six parishes were allowed to keep their traditional indigenous rites. By this time the Romano-Western synthesis was already widely used throughout the rest of Hispania and, with the exception of these parishes, it now formally replaced any surviving indigenous use.

What was this 'indigenous' rite and where did it originate? Some of the *Ordo communis* is provided by Isidore of Seville in his *De Ecclesiasticis Officiis*, which dates between 598 and 615.[1] The fore-Mass is not precisely described, but the work suggests that there were antiphons, responsories, prayers, Scripture readings and alleluia.[2] The actual sacramental celebration is described in more detail:[3]

- *Offertorium* (mention of the sacrifice of the Eucharist).
- Prayer of Admonition.
- Prayer of Invocation.
- Prayer for those offering and the faithful departed.
- Eucharistic Prayer (*illatio*, Sanctus, Institution, Anamnesis and Consecration).
- Lord's Prayer.
- Nicene Creed.
- Blessing of the people.

In a section called 'The Sacrifice', Isidore explained:

> It is commanded that Christians celebrate this sacrifice, having left behind and finished the Jewish sacrificial offerings that had been commanded to be celebrated during the slavery of the former people. Therefore, that sacrifice is done by us which the Lord himself did for us.[4]

Of the bread and wine, he added:

> However, although these things are visible, nevertheless, sanctified through the Holy Spirit, they pass over into the sacrament of the divine body.[5]

For the prayers of this rite we are reliant on the *Liber Mozarabicus Sacramentorum* and the *Liber Ordinum*, edited from manuscripts that are eleventh and twelfth century.[6] Férotin believed that some of the texts went back to *c.* 400, on the grounds that certain feasts such as for St Jerome and St Martin appear in some rare manuscripts and are described as 'new comers'.

The rite has much in common with the Gallican, and this latter itself may have been characteristic of the eucharistic liturgy in much of the West at one time. Both rites show considerable variety and pluriformity, and may reflect a

1 Thomas L. Knoebel, *Isidore of Seville: De Ecclesiasticis Officiis*, New York: The Newman Press, 2008, p. 12.

2 Knoebel, *Isidore of Seville*, pp. 32–3.

3 Knoebel, *Isidore of Seville*, pp. 39–41.

4 Knoebel, *Isidore of Seville*, pp. 41–2.

5 Knoebel, *Isidore of Seville*, p. 42.

6 Marius Férotin, *Le Liber Mozarabicus Sacramentorum et Les Manuscrits Mozarabes*, reprint, Rome: CLV Edizioni Liturgiche, 1995; *Le Liber Ordinum. En usage dans L'Église Wisigothique et Mozarabe d'Espagne du Cinquième au Onzième siècle*, reprint, Rome: CLV Edizioni Liturgiche, 1996.

time when local bishops still regularly compiled new prayers.[7] Since both the Hispano-Mozarabic and Gallican rites have echoes of and slight parallels with some Eastern rites, the older view was that they originated in the East, either from Ephesus by way of Irenaeus of Lyons, or from the Ambrosian rite, introduced from Cappadocia by Auxentius who was the Arian Bishop of Milan. Others have suggested that the Hispano-Mozarabic rite was derived from the Gallican. The more common view at present is that both may be derived from Latin-speaking North Africa, though so little is known of the latter that it is difficult to find strong liturgical evidence.[8] Eastern symptoms probably witness to popular liturgical migrations and borrowings rather than some ancient genesis.

Pluriformity in the West meant that the Romano-Western synthesis liturgies were used alongside the older indigenous rites. The gradual Christian reconquest of the Iberian Peninsula coincided with the attempts of Gregory VII (1061–85) to assert authority over the Christian rulers of the West. Because certain Spanish bishops had espoused Adoptionism, Roman authorities were suspicious of the orthodoxy of the indigenous rite, and as a consequence Christian rulers and church authorities in Northern Spain were encouraged to use the Romano-Western synthesis. Raúl Gómez-Ruiz notes:

> In Gregory's attempts to assert his authority over the Christian rulers of the West, liturgy became the battleground and the Cluniac reform of monasticism became the agent. Cardinal Hugh Candidus, known as the White, was the first known papal legate in the peninsula from 1065–68 under Pope Alexander II (1061–73); he raised concerns about the Mozarabic liturgy with King Fernando I. Later, other legates were sent under Pope Gregory VII. The latter's efforts were most successful in terms of the replacement of the Mozarabic rite by the Roman rite in 1080.[9]

Toledo was captured by Alfonso VI, who already in 1076 had decreed the adoption of the Roman rite in his realm.[10] However, he allowed the Mozarabs who had assisted him to retain their old liturgies and it is the manuscripts from these parishes together with others that have survived that are our witnesses to the Hispano-Mozarabic rite.[11] Jordi Pinell found two distinct traditions represented in the manuscripts.[12] Tradition A manuscripts, the Northern tradition, are associated

7 See Allan Bouley, *From Freedom to Formula: The Evolution of the Eucharistic Prayer from Oral Improvisation to Written Texts*, Washington, DC: Catholic University of America, 1981.

8 Bouley, *From Freedom to Formula*, p. 169.

9 Raúl Gómez-Ruiz, *Mozarabs: Hispanics and the Cross*, New York: Orbis Books, 2007, p. 29.

10 Joseph F. O'Callaghan, 'The Integration of Christian Spain into Europe: The Role of Alfonso VI of León-Castile', in Bernard F. Reilly (ed.), *Santiago, Saint-Denis, and Saint Peter: The Reception of the Roman Liturgy in León-Castile in 1080*, New York: Fordham University Press, 1985, pp. 101–20.

11 Ramón Gonzálvez, 'The Persistence of the Mozarabic Liturgy in Toledo after 1080', in Reilly (ed.), *Santiago, Saint-Denis, and Saint Peter*, pp. 157–85.

12 Jordi Pinell, *Liturgia Hispánica*, Barcelona: Centre de Pastoral Litúrgica, 1998, pp. 39–40.

with the parishes of Santa Eulalia, San Lucas and San Sebastián. Dated by Pinell between the eighth and twelfth centuries, they represent Toledo use. Tradition B manuscripts, the Southern tradition, associated with the parishes of Santa Justa y Rufina, San Marcos and San Torcuato and dating from between the tenth and twelfth centuries, represent the use of Seville. It should be noted that Anscari Mundó has argued that all the manuscripts are much later and date at earliest from the eleventh century.[13] These two traditions have many common texts, but sometimes have a different order of prayers, and different Scripture readings. The *Ordo Missae* represented by these manuscripts is as follows:[14]

- [Preparatory prayers for the priest, for vesting, and preparation of the elements.]
- *Praelegendum* (Antiphon and Entrance Psalm).
- *Gloria in excelsis.*
- Trisagion – on festivals. Can be sung in Greek or Latin or both.
- Prayer after the Gloria.
- *Prophetia* (Old Testament).
- Psalm.
- (Feast days: a reading from the Acts of the Martyrs and *Benedicite.*)
- Epistle.
- Gospel.
- *Laudes* (chant with alleluia). cf. Isidore.
- *Sacrificium* (= Isidore's *offertoriam*).
- *Oratio Admonitionis* (prayer addressed to the assembly).
- *Oremus*; R. *Hagios, Hagios, Hagios, Domine Deus, Rex aeterne, tibi laudes et gratias.*
- *Alia orati.*
- Diptychs.
- *Oratio post nomina.*
- *Oratio ad pacem.*
- The Peace.
- Eucharistic Prayer (*Illatio*, Sanctus, *oratio post-Sanctus*, Institution, *oratio Post Pridie*, doxology).
- **Tradition A:** Fraction/**Tradition B:** Nicene Creed.
- Nicene Creed.
- Fraction.
- Lord's Prayer.
- Commixture with *Sancta Sanctis.*
- *Benedictio* (cf. Isidore).
- *Ad Accedentes* (Psalm 33).
- Communion.
- *Completuria.*
- Dismissal.

---

13 Anscari Mundó, 'La datación de los códices litúrgicos visigóticos toledanos', *Hispania Sacra* 38 (1965), pp. 1–25.

14 Pinell, *Liturgia Hispánica*, pp. 152–83; Raúl Gómez-Ruiz, *Mozarabs*, pp. 53–67; Archdale A. King, *Liturgies of the Primatial Sees*, London: Longman, Green and Co., 1957, pp. 457–628.

The priest's preparation of himself and of the elements reflect later developments, akin to the Eastern prothesis rites, and perhaps were added between the tenth and twelfth centuries, though no certain date can be given. The entrance retains a simplicity of an earlier period, though it may be that the Gloria was borrowed from the developing Romano-Western synthesis, and relegated the Trisagion to certain festivals.[15] The *oratio Admonitionis* is a prayer to prepare the assembly to exercise the gift of prayer in the solemn intercessions that follow (Diptychs). The Diptychs themselves did not migrate to the Eucharistic Prayer. The position of the Creed is unique to this rite, though the two manuscript traditions differ in whether it precedes or follows the Fraction. It may be that this was because the Creed was recited during the Fraction. The bread is arranged in the form of a cross. Just as the entrance has preserved a simplicity, so the dismissal too is brief and seems to have resisted growth.

The Eucharistic Prayer is totally variable according to the feast or Sunday, with only a fixed Introductory Dialogue, Sanctus with Benedictus and Institution Narrative. The opening dialogue begins with the Psalm verse, 'I will go unto the altar of God', in place of the *Dominus Vobiscum* of Rome, and includes two separate exhortations – ears to the Lord, and hearts to the Lord. Some of the Eucharistic Prayers are extremely brief, and others incredibly long, particularly the *illatio* (*inlatio*) or variable Preface:

> the length of the text varies as much as between the eleven lines of the *inlatio* for the Thursday of the fourth week of Lent and that for the Sunday after Ascension and the eighty-eight lines of the *inlatio* for the Mass for the Saturday after Easter; this can be compared to the variation of between twelve to fifteen lines in a Roman Preface.[16]

Díaz y Díaz argues that the variable parts of the Mass were used and developed as a means to educate and inform, which he finds rooted in the teachings of Isidore and Ildephonse. With the conviction that the Mass of the Ascension was the work of Ildephonse of Toledo, Díaz y Díaz writes:

> The *Missa* [= *oratio Admonitionis*] paraphrases at some length the account in Acts 1:9–11; the *Alia* amplifies Eph. 4:8; the *Inlatio*, divided into three parts, celebrates the Ascension as a triumph – regaining the celestial mansion after having regained for mankind the true possession of the earth – after a series of heroic acts marked by an anaphora of seven elements; a long development justifies the divine power which, after walking on the waters (Matt. 14:26 etc.), can ascend unaided above the clouds. This brings the author to a valuable example of the *cedat* topos: the wonders are less than the benefits conveyed by the God Man, a theme to which the *Post Sanctus* is devoted, while the *Post Pridie* develops the theme of the signs of the future coming of Christ, possibly because of his earlier ascension into Heaven. Thus a rich treatise on the benefits and the power of Christ and on the hope of the redeemed is

15 King, *Liturgies of the Primatial Sees*, p. 575.

16 M. C. Díaz y Díaz, 'Literary Aspects of the Visigothic Liturgy', in Edward James (ed.), *Visigothic Spain: New Approaches*, Oxford: Clarendon Press, 1980, pp. 61–76, p. 62.

> compressed into this Mass; the faithful arrive at an understanding of all its variety and transcendence only at the end of the office.[17]

Yet, although this was a means of teaching, Díaz y Díaz suggests that the length and the terminology were not designed for uneducated aural comprehension of the liturgical text, and on the whole the liturgical texts were designed for an ecclesiastical minority.[18]

Isidore had commented that after the Sanctus, 'there follows a sixth prayer, which is the confirmation of the sacrament, so that the oblation that is offered to God, sanctified through the Holy Spirit, might be conformed to the body and blood of Christ'.[19] He seems to have in mind the recitation of the Narrative, and the *Post Pridie*, and suggests that the latter had a petition for the Holy Spirit – an Epiklesis. In fact only some of the *Post Pridie* prayers invoke or mention the Spirit, and others are content to simply ask for God the Father, or the Son, to bless and hallow the elements. That for the Nativity prays:

> Observing, O Lord, these your gifts and precepts, we place on your altar these sacrifices (holocaust) of bread and wine, asking you in the abundance of your sacred mercy, that by the same Spirit by which uncorrupted Virginity conceived you in flesh, the undivided Trinity may sanctify these oblations; so that when they will be received by us with no less fear than veneration, whatever there is of life harmful to the soul may wither, and that which is withered shall not revive.[20]

In this instance this is an incarnational–pneumatological eucharistic theology, though with an eschatological request concerning the soul. On the other hand, the corresponding prayer for Epiphany simply asks for the Lord Jesus to manifest himself.[21] Not only is there no mention of the Holy Spirit, but in addition there is no request to hallow the elements, and there is no reference to sacrifice or oblations. There is such a wide range of petitions that it is impossible to extrapolate any single consistent theology of presence and offering.[22]

In 1500 Alfonso Ortíz was able to compile the necessary manuscripts to allow Cardinal Francisco Ximénez de Cisneros to publish the *Missale mixtum* in 1500, and Cisneros established the Chapel of Corpus Christ in Toledo Cathedral for this renaissance of the Hispano-Mozarabic rite. As Susan Boynton has noted, the Preface bespeaks 'a philological project in a humanist vein'.[23] Ortíz was allowed to edit, rewrite, exclude and reorder material as he felt fit. Twenty-five of the Mass formularies in the *Missale mixtum* were compiled and partly recomposed by Ortíz from various sources, and for seven further Masses he adapted

17 Díaz y Díaz, 'Literary Aspects', p. 69.

18 Díaz y Díaz, 'Literary Aspects', p. 75.

19 Knoebel, *De Ecclesiasticis Officiis*, p. 40.

20 Férotin, *Liber Mozarabicus*, p. 57.

21 Férotin, *Liber Mozarabicus*, p. 88.

22 See also the example in *PEER*, pp. 152–4.

23 Susan Boynton, 'Restoration or Invention? Archbishop Cisneros and the Mozarabic Rite in Toledo', forthcoming in Yale Institute of Sacred Music journal, *Colloquium* 6 (2013), pp. 125–39.

existing texts to create new formularies.[24] The resulting work was a humanist's rendering of the old rite for sixteenth-century use. A more authentic edition was published in 1755, and a missal was printed in Mexico in 1770, but neither represented the old Hispano-Mozarabic rite as it was in 1085. In the wake of Vatican II, new efforts to revitalize the rite led to a new *Missale Hispano-Mozarabicum* in 1991, which has utilized both traditions identified by Pinell.

The Gallican rite

Archdale King noted that the term 'Gallican' has been used in at least five different senses:

1 the rite existing in Gaul before the reforms of Pippin and Charlemagne;
2 the Roman rite altered and enriched in Gaul and Germany by the Carolingian school of liturgists;
3 a French use introduced by the Normans into Apulia and Sicily;
4 the Franco-Roman rite (Romano-Western synthesis), which, at the instigation of Gregory VII, replaced the Hispano-Mozarabic rite, and was referred to as Liturgia Gallicana; and
5 the French diocesan books of the eighteenth century.[25]

King reserved the term for the distinct rite that existed in Gaul prior to the ninth century, and it is used here in that sense.[26] It may have been used in parts of Britain and Ireland since a Gallican Eucharistic Prayer is preserved in a fragment of an Irish sacramentary (the book containing the prayers needed by the celebrant at the Eucharist), Munich Staatsbibl, CLM 14429, dated to the seventh century.[27] The early centres included Arles, Lyons, Marseilles and Lérins. Early traces are discussed by Bouley, and the sources listed by Smyth.[28] Important among the latter for the Eucharist include the so-called Masses of Mone, the *Missale Gothicum* and the *Missale Gallicanum Vetus*. There is also an exposition of the Mass attributed to Germanus of Paris (+576). Since the writer draws on the *De Ecclesiasticis officiis* of Isidore of Seville, it is not the work of Germanus, and the rite described seems already to betray signs of osmosis with the Roman rite.[29] It is nevertheless

24 Boynton, 'Restoration or Invention?'

25 Archdale A. King, *Liturgies of the Past*, Milwaukee: The Bruce Publishing Company, 1959, p. 77.

26 King, *Liturgies of the Past*, p. 77.

27 Matthieu Smyth, *La Liturgie Oubliée: La prière eucharistique en Gaul antique et dans l'Occident non romain*, Paris: Cerf, 2003, p. 55.

28 Bouley, *From Freedom to Formula*, 181–92; Smyth, *La Liturgie Oubliée*, 51–96.

29 Philippe Bernard, *Transitions liturgiques en Gaule carolingianne: Une traduction commentée des deux 'lettres' faussement atrribuées à l'évêque Germain de Paris*, Paris: Hora Decima, 2008; E. C. Ratcliff (ed.), *Expositio Antiquae Liturgiae Gallicanae*, London: Henry Bradshaw Society, 1971.

still an important source for the Gallican rite. The *Ordo communis* of this rite was as follows:[30]

- *Antiphona ad praelegendum* Psalm.
- Deacon's call for silence.
- Greeting.
- Trisagion and Kyrie.
- *Prophetia (Benedictus).*
- *Collectio post prophetiam.*
- *Prophetia* (Old Testament reading).
- Responsory.
- Epistle.
- *Benedicite.*
- *De Aius ante Evangelium* (Trisagion).
- Gospel.
- *Sanctus post Evangelium.*
- Homily.
- *Preces* (Litany).
- *Collectio post preces.*
- Dismissal of the Catechumens.
- Intercessions [?].
- Offertory with *Sonus* and *Laudes* (alleluias).
- *Praefatio missa* and *Collectio.*
- Recital of names and *collectio post nomina.*
- *Collectio ad pacem.*
- Peace.
- Eucharistic Prayer (*Contestatio* or *Immolatio*, Sanctus, Post Sanctus, Secreta (Institution), Post Secreta or Post-Mysterium, Doxology).
- Fraction with chant.
- Blessing by the bishop.
- Communion and communion chant (*trecanum*).
- *Post Eucharisticam* and *collection.*
- Dismissal [?].
- Distribution of blessed bread.

A number of elements correspond to those in the Hispano-Mozarabic rite, and thus may point to a common origin. The Trisagion, for example, is in the same position and can also be sung in Greek and Latin. The rite did not seem to include the recitation of the Creed until introduced in the Frankish dominions in the ninth century. King opined that the bread and wine had been prepared before the liturgy.[31] At the offertory the bread was brought to the altar by a deacon in a vessel shaped like a tower, while the wine was brought in a chalice, though pseudo-Germanus, like Theodore of Mopsuestia, referred to them

30 See King, *Liturgies of the Past*, pp. 152–83; Ratcliff (ed.), *Expositio Antiquae Liturgiae Gallicanae*; Henry Beck, *The Pastoral Care of Souls in South-East France during the Sixth Century*, Rome: Universitatis Gregorianae, 1950, pp. 134–54.

31 King, *Liturgies of the Past*, p. 165.

as the body and blood of Christ.[32] The *Prefatio missae* was an exhortation to prayer, as in the Hispano-Mozarabic rite. The Fraction was complex, and there is evidence that at one time, as in the Syrian Orthodox rite, the fragments were arranged in the shape of a human.[33] The blessing before communion again has a counterpart in the Hispano-Mozarabic rite.

In comparison with the Roman rite, the Latin style of both the Hispano-Mozarabic and Gallican rites has been characterized as florid and verbose. However, whereas Díaz y Díaz felt that the former would have been difficult for any but educated clerics to understand, Els Rose's examination of the Latin of the *Missale Gothicum* has noted the neologisms as well as syntax characterized by 'vulgar traits' and Greek and Hebrew elements, and many examples of everyday speech.[34] She also draws attention to the importance of the provision for celebrating the saints, and the use of hagiographies, and especially the *Acts of Andrew*.[35]

The Gallican Eucharistic Prayers are constructed on the same lines as the Hispano-Mozarabic prayers, with much creativity and verbosity in the *Contestiones* or Prefaces. The Masses of Mone have seven Gallican Eucharistic Prayers, but with alternative and extra *Contestationes,* giving 15 in number. A Sunday *Contestatio* begins:

> We . . . should unceasingly venerate you, both by prayer in public worship at your holy altar, and also, by reckoning all the unutterable things you have done, by the silent devotion of love in the secret depths of the heart. Righteous indeed are your ways, O King of the nations. Who shall not fear and magnify your name? Here indeed we have no resounding melodies: for the saints, who by sustained harmonies of their merits overcame the Beast of this world [. . .] but not for us, tossed upon the world's ocean, that song of Moses, nor yet angelic voices – save that perhaps angels are present here to extol our consecration of the Body and Blood of your dearly beloved Son.[36]

This *Contestatio* continues for nearly a further two pages before abruptly transitioning to the Sanctus. Two others are concerned with the prophet Elias (Elijah) and St Germanus of Auxerre. The former gives a graphic account of the prophet's ascent into heaven, and the latter gives thanks at great length for the life and detailed work of St Germanus. The *Contestatio* (*Immolatio*) in the *Missale Gothicum* for the feast of the Children in the Christmas octave reproduces words from a sermon of Caesarius of Arles:

32 'Corpus vero domini ideo defertur in turribus . . . sanguis vero Christi ideo specialiter offertur in calice', Ratcliff, *Expositio Antiquae Liturgiae Gallicanae*, p. 10.

33 King, *Liturgies of the Past*, p. 178.

34 Els Rose, *Missale Gothicum. e codice Vaticano Regienesi latino 317 editum*, Turnhout: Brepols, 2005, pp. 184–5.

35 Rose, *Missale Gothicum*, p. 328.

36 ET in Arthur Linton, *Twenty-Five Consecration Prayers, with Notes and Introduction*, London: SPCK, 1921, pp. 110–13. I have altered Linton's translation, taken from J. M. Neale and G. H. Forbes, *The Ancient Liturgies of the Gallican Church*, Burntisland: The Pitligo Press, 1855. The Masses are published under the title of the *Missale Richenovense*, and it was still thought there were eleven masses rather than seven. The text is fragmentary, indicated by [. . .].

> who were torn away by a servant of Herod from the breasts of the nursing mothers. They are rightly called the flowers among the martyrs, who born amid the cold of unbelief, broke a night frost of persecution, as it were, at the moment when they blossomed as the first flower buds of the church.[37]

Rose notes that the *Contestatio* for the Circumcision places the event in the wider context of the liturgical season:

> During these present days, which the commemoration of your deeds and gifts has marked with various reasons for ceremonies which are wholesome for us, we acknowledge – because joy renews both the time of past gladness and the time of eternal goodness – and rejoice all the more profusely because we live again through the commemoration of hallowed grace, as in the joy still fresh in mind. We therefore commemorate the present day, the eighth day after the redeeming birth, which is marked by the lawful circumcision of the Lord, born of the flesh, according to the appointed commemoration . . .[38]

As with the Hispano-Mozarabic prayers, there are so many and they are so varied that it is difficult to attempt some general overview. The study of John Frendo on the Gallican Post Secreta drew attention to the frequent request, 'Panis vero in corpus et vinum transformatur in sanguinem' and 'legitima eucharistia.'[39] Sometimes the Holy Spirit is mentioned in relation to consecration, but often is not. Frendo argued that the sense of transformation is putting the body of Christ in a condition of being edible, and his blood in a condition of being drinkable; to change the body of Christ into the eucharistic bread, and his blood into the eucharistic wine:

> in other words 'transformare' means: to change the form or the state of the Body and Blood of Christ (which in themselves are not edible and drinkable) and to give them the external form, the new state of Bread and Wine'; to make them present and visible (in a certain sense) to our eyes, in the state of bread and wine; to give them in the state of food (the bread) and drink (the wine) so that men may be able to eat and drink them. Finally they are 'transformati' into bread and wine.[40]

Frendo took 'legitimate' to mean that the prayers asked God to sanctify the offerings so that the bread and wine become a true, legitimate, fruitful and sanctifying Eucharist for the communicants, though Louise Batstone has argued that this has more to do with concern for correct ceremonial in an era that was demanding correct liturgical books and properly prepared clergy.[41] Frendo was

37 Rose, *Missale Gothicum*, p. 216; text, p. 369.

38 Rose, *Missale Gothicum*, p. 219; text, p. 372.

39 John A. Frendo, *The 'Post Secreta' of the 'Missale Gothicum' and the Eucharistic Theology of the Gallican Anaphora*, St Venera, Malta: St Joseph's Home, 1977.

40 Frendo, '*Post Secreta*', p. 77.

41 Frendo, '*Post Secreta*', p. 82; Louise Batstone, 'Doctrinal and Theological Themes in the Prayers of the Bobbio Missal', in Yitzak Hen and Rob Meens (eds), *The Bobbio Missal: Liturgy and Religious Culture in Merovingian Gaul*, Cambridge: Cambridge University Press, 2004, pp. 168–86.

concerned to suggest that the Gallican Eucharistic Prayers had a nuanced view of presence that was different from the *canon missae* of the received Romano-Western synthesis. Regardless of whether his arguments are valid, unlike the Hispano-Mozarabic rite, the Gallican rite as a separate rite, together with its many Eucharistic Prayers, perished.

The Roman rite

Paul Bradshaw has recently remarked that our knowledge of Roman liturgy unfortunately turns out to be no more than partial, and in most aspects quite late in time.[42] Justin Martyr gives some information for what one congregation did in *c.* 150, but how typical it was of other congregations in the city is anyone's guess. Now that the so-called *Apostolic Tradition* can no longer be counted as either third century or as 'Roman', it means that our first eucharistic sources of any substance are limited to possibly the Mai fragments, the Letter of Innocent I to Decentius of Gubbio, the Verona Sacramentary and *Ordo Romanus Primus*.[43] The Mai fragments (early fourth century) are the work of an Arian who quotes parts of the Catholic liturgy against the Catholics, including Prefaces (*praefatio*) of the Eucharistic Prayer. The Letter of Innocent I (fifth century) revealed something about the Roman position of the Peace, the naming of the offerers, and the Roman ceremony of the *fermentum*. The Verona Sacramentary (sixth century) is less a sacramentary than it is a collection of older *libelli* – shorter texts containing the prayers of one or two Masses. There is no Eucharistic Prayer in this collection, though a good many Proper Prefaces. Some of the material is thought by some to have been composed by Pope Leo.[44] *Ordo Romanus Primus* is a summary description of the papal Mass in Santa Maria Maggiore in the seventh or eighth century. In addition, most scholars acknowledge that the *canon missae*, the Roman Eucharistic Prayer, was fixed by the time of Gregory the Great, and the text that has come down in what is called the Old Gelasian Sacramentary gives us the text that Gregory would have known. This sacramentary is an eighth-century manuscript written at Chelles, and so already a 'Frankish edition' with Gallican additions, but it is regarded as representing a text from the seventh century for use by presbyters in the titular churches of Rome.[45] The Mass in this Old Gelasian lacks the Agnus Dei that was introduced by the Syrian Pope Sergius I (687–701).

42 Paul F. Bradshaw, 'What Do We Really Know about the Earliest Roman Liturgy?', paper given at the North American Academy of Liturgy 2010, p. 15.

43 For these texts, see Gordon Jeanes, *The Origins of the Roman Rite*, Alcuin/GROW Joint Liturgical Study 20, Bramcote: Grove Books, 1991; Martin F. Connell, *Church and Worship in Fifth-century Rome: The Letter of Innocent I to Decentius of Gubbio*, Alcuin/GROW Joint Liturgical Study 52, Cambridge: Grove Books, 2002; Alan Griffiths, *Ordo Romanus Primus: Latin Text and Translation with Introduction and Notes*, Alcuin/GROW Joint Liturgical Study 73, Norwich: Canterbury Press, 2012.

44 N. W. James, 'Was Leo the Great the Author of Liturgical Prayers?', *Studia Patristica* 26 (1991), pp. 35–40.

45 Hugo Brandenburg, *Ancient Churches of Rome from the Fourth to the Seventh Century*, Turnhout: Brepols, 2005.

Ordo Romanus Primus gives the following for the papal Mass:[46]

- [Procession from the Lateran. Pope on horseback. The Pope is met by the presbyters, sexton carrying a thurible, acolytes and counsellors. The Pope enters supported by deacons. Deacons and other clergy wore chasubles.]
- Signal for the singers.
- Introit antiphon. Pope enters preceded by incense and seven candlesticks.
- Kyries.
- *Gloria in excelsis* (if it is the season).
- Greeting: Peace be with you.
- Collect.
- Epistle.
- Responsory and Alleluia.
- Gospel.
- The schola sing (a psalm).

Deacons and acolytes prepare the altar and vessels. The pope receives the oblations of the principal citizens. The archdeacon receives the flasks of wine and pours them into a chalice, and when the chalice is full, the wine is poured into a bowl held by an acolyte. The loaves are received. The archdeacon washes his hands and arranges the offerings on the altar. Water is added to the wine. The pope signals the schola to stop singing.

- (Offertory Prayer – *oratio super oblate* – the final words are mentioned.)
- *Canon missae*, beginning *with Sursum corda*, and *Gratias agamus*, and includes the singing of the Sanctus.
- [Lord's Prayer.]
- Peace.
- Fraction.
- Agnus Dei.
- Psalmody during Communion.
- Post-Communion Prayer.
- Dismissal.
- Brief Blessing.

A psalm for the Introit seems to have been the common origin for all eucharistic traditions, but the Eastern rites underwent change because of the Stational liturgies and the psalmody and antiphons sung en route. The ninefold Kyrie eleison was once thought to be the remnant of a litany that had in turn replaced the Prayers of the People or Solemn Prayers which survived in the Good Friday liturgy. The litany was then moved earlier in the rite.[47] The detailed study of Paul de Clerck suggested that in fact this was not the case, since the litanies themselves fell into disuse. The Kyrie, he thought, was a deliberate independent chant

46 Griffiths, *Ordo Romanus Primus*.

47 G. G. Willis, *Essays in Early Roman Liturgy*, London: SPCK, 1964, pp. 3–48.

that was introduced at the beginning of the Mass because it was popular.[48] More recently Peter Jeffery has revisited the evidence and has suggested that they are indeed the remnant of a litany, in fact the Litany of the Saints, which was sung in procession to the stational church.[49] The *Gloria in excelsis* was used as a final canticle at Morning Prayer. It was used in the Roman Mass first only by the bishop on Sundays and feast days, but was later extended to presbyteral use. Jeffery suggests that the earliest form of ordination for the Bishop of Rome allows a glimpse of the Kyries and the Gloria in transition to the fore-Mass:

> The new pontiff entered during the psalmody, in a clerical procession led by seven candles. With the other bishops and priests he stopped at the confession or tomb of St. Peter for the litany, then proceeded up to his seat. There he was ordained, exchanged the peace, and had the honor of intoning the final canticle, the Gloria in excelsis. The opening of the Roman Mass followed a similar model: the pope's entrance procession was marked by the Introit. The litany was sung upon arrival at the altar area, where the confession [i.e. martyr's tomb] would be in a Roman basilica. The candles and other processional paraphernalia were put in their places. The pope intoned the Gloria, then greeted the people and said the collect.[50]

Jeffery points out that the Introit announced the pope's arrival, whereas the litany and its responses covered the whole procession, and thus dovetailing was the result at this soft point in the rite. Although some think that Rome once had an Old Testament reading, the later evidence provides only for an Epistle and Gospel reading. The single offertory prayer was said silently, hence its alternative name, *Secreta*. Kenneth Stevenson found three categories of this prayer. First, those that are imprecise and speak only of *vota* (vows) and *solemnia celebrare* (celebrate the solemnities), which 'offer' the entire celebration. Another category speaks of 'the gift offered' or 'these gifts', with overt sacrificial terminology. Third, some of these prayers speak of 'spiritual victim' and 'that have been placed on this altar', and refer quite explicitly to the eucharistic bread and wine.[51] The actual logistics of the offertory at the papal Mass were complex, due to the number of communicants and also because of social rank. However, unlike the Eastern tradition where the selection of bread and wine were made at the beginning of the rite by the deacons and only at what became the Great Entrance were they processed to or moved to the altar, at Rome the selection was made at the offertory. The Peace comes just prior to the Fraction and Communion, after the Eucharistic Prayer and the Lord's Prayer, though *Ordo Romanus Primus* does not mention the Lord's Prayer. The position of the Peace was one of the issues raised by Innocent I

---

48 Paul de Clerck, *La 'Prière universelle' dans les liturgies latines anciennes: Témoignages patristiques et texts liturgiques*, Münster: Aschendorff, 1977.

49 Peter Jeffery, 'The Meaning and Functions of Kyrie Eleison', in Bryan D. Spinks (ed.), *The Place of Christ in Liturgical Prayer: Trinity, Christology, and Liturgical Theology*, Collegeville: Liturgical Press, 2008, pp. 127–94.

50 Jeffery, 'Meaning and Functions of Kyrie Eleison', p. 193.

51 Kenneth Stevenson, *Eucharist and Offering*, New York: Pueblo Press, 1986, p. 86.

in the letter to Decentius, Innocent insisting that the Peace be given 'after all those things about which I must not speak', that is, in the Roman position after (and not prior) to the Eucharistic Prayer. Innocent also mentions the *fermentum*, the practice of sending part of the consecrated bread from the papal Mass to the presbyters presiding at the other titular churches (post-Constantinian churches, the property having been given and named after the benefactor) in the city of Rome, though he did not advise Decentius to follow suit, and made it clear that this only happened for the churches within the city and not those outside the city walls.[52] John Baldovin has suggested that the titular presbyters did not consecrate their own bread and wine, but consecration was by contact with the *fermentum*. He suggested that since the older place of the Kiss of Peace in Justin Martyr was before the Eucharistic Prayer, it may have been the *fermentum* that gave rise to the later Roman position, since in the titular churches there would have been a Liturgy of the Word, followed by the Kiss of Peace, and Communion.[53] The Fraction seems to have occurred after the Kiss of Peace.[54] The African and Roman tradition followed the maxim that surfaces in late fourth-century African councils that prayer at the altar should always be directed to the Father.[55] The Agnus Dei, addressed to the Son, is an Eastern import introduced by Pope Sergius I. A hallmark of this liturgy is its brief dismissal, with a request for the pope to bless, and the papal response, 'May the Lord bless us'.

It appears that by the fifth or sixth century Rome had moved to a single *canon missae* or Eucharistic Prayer.[56] The Old Gelasian entitled it *canon actionis* – the rule of the action, perhaps meaning fixed prayer. It is possible that this was a means of establishing unity among the different ethnic and linguistic groups in the city of Rome. The various sections of the canon are referred to by the opening Latin words: *Vere Dignum* (*Praefatio*), Sanctus and Benedictus, *Te igitur, Memento Domine, Communicantes, Hanc igitur, Quam oblationem, Qui pridie, Unde et memores, Supra quae, Supplices te, Memento etiam, Nobis quoque, Per quem.* Although a single prayer, it was not entirely fixed, since there are three variables: the *Praefatio*, variable according to feast and season; the *Communicantes* which can have insertions; and the *Hanc igitur*, which has some seasonal Propers. Jean Magne's claims that echoes of the *Supra quae* and *Te igitur* are to be found in Tertulian and Irenaeus respectively are not persuasive, though the echoes in Zeno of Verona (*c.* 370) identified by Gordon Jeanes are

52 Connell, *Church and Worship in Fifth-century Rome*, pp. 23, 39.

53 John F. Baldovin, 'The Fermentum at Rome in the Fifth Century: A Reconsideration', *Worship* 79 (2005), pp. 38–53.

54 Barry M. Craig, *Fractio Panis: A History of the Breaking of Bread in the Roman Rite*, Rome: Studia Anselmiana, 2011.

55 Edward Kilmartin, 'The Liturgical Prayer in Early African Legislation', *Ephemerides Liturgicae* 99 (1985), pp. 105–27.

56 What follows is based on my essay 'The Roman Canon Missae', in Albert Gerhards, Heinzgerd Brakmann and Martin Klöckener (eds), *Prex Eucharistica III/I. Ecclesia Antiqua et Occidentalis*, Fribourg: Academic Press, 2005, pp. 129–43. Critical text: Bernard Botte, *Le canon de la Messe Romaine*, Louvain: Abbaye du Mont César, 1935. *PEER*, pp. 163–7.

convincing.[57] A good section of the canon resembles a Eucharistic Prayer quoted by Ambrose in *De Sacramentis*. Although Ambrose claimed to follow Rome in many things, it might be best to see his text as a close Milanese cousin rather than the Roman canon in Ambrose's time. Michael Morton, Enrico Mazza and more recently Walter Ray have noted the similarities between the Roman prayer and the Egyptian anaphoral tradition.[58] Morton made an important observation: 'It is not however a matter of the Latin text being copied from the East, but of being formed from comparable Greek anaphoral prayers long used in Rome and Milan.'[59] At some stage Greek gave way to Latin as the liturgical language in Rome, and it may also be that the canon developed by amalgamation of a variety of earlier prayers used in Rome by different ethnic groups. However, Latin seems to have first been used as a liturgical language in North Africa, and thus a number of scholars refer to the Roman canon as the Romano-African *canon missae*. Influence of North Africa is perhaps seen in the Institution Narrative of the canon. It draws mainly on Matthew's account of the Last Supper, as does that quoted by Cyprian. It also uses the word *enim* – 'Hoc est enim Corpus meum'. Though *enim* is not found in the Vulgate Latin, it is found in the Old Latin Bible, which originated in North Africa.[60] The canon also describes Melchizedek as 'High Priest' and Abel as 'righteous', neither of which descriptions are found in the Old Testament. However, they are both so described in the Targums, which points to their antiquity in the canon.[61] Imperial court language and the language of votive offerings in the Roman pagan cults have also been pressed into Christian service.[62] These, together with the listing of Roman martyrs or saints and martyrs who had a large cult in Rome, point to this prayer as being honed specifically for the Church in Rome.[63]

The *Prefatio*, which corresponds to the *Illatio* and *Contestatio* of the Hispano-Mozarabic and Gallican rites, varies in number in different sacramentaries. The Verona Sacramentary has 267, whereas the Old Gelasian has 54. The tendency over time was to reduce them in number. They lead into the Sanctus. The Mai

57 J. Magne, 'Rites et prières latines et grecques aux deux premiers siècles', *Studia Ephemeridis Augustinianum* 42 (1993), pp. 325–49; Gordon Jeanes, 'Early Latin Parallels to the Roman Canon? Possible References to a Eucharistic Prayer in Zeno of Verona', *Journal of Theological Studies* 37 (1986), pp. 427–31.

58 Michael Morton, 'Rethinking the Origin of the Roman Canon', *Studia Patristica* 26 (1993), pp. 63–6; Enrico Mazza, *The Origins of the Eucharistic Prayer*, Collegeville: Liturgical Press, 1995, pp. 240–86; Walter Ray, 'Rome and Alexandria: Two Cities, One Anaphoral Tradition', in Maxwell E. Johnson (ed.), *Issues in Eucharistic Praying in East and West: Essays in Liturgical and Theological Analysis*, Collegeville: Liturgical Press, 201, pp. 99–127.

59 Morton, 'Rethinking the Origin of the Roman Canon', p. 65.

60 For details, see E. C. Ratcliff, 'The Institution Narrative of the Roman Canon Missae. Its Beginning and Early Background', *Studia Patristica* 2 (1957), pp. 64–82.

61 R. le Defaut, 'Le titre de Summus sacerdos donné à Melchisédech est-il d'origine juive?', *Recherches de Science Religieuse* 50 (1962), pp. 222–9.

62 A. Stuber, 'Die Diptychon-Formel für die Nomina offerentium im römischen Messkanon', *Ephemerides Liturgicae* 68 (1954), pp. 127–46; V. Fiala, 'Les prièrs d'acceptation de l'offrande et le genre littéraire du canon romain', *Eucharisties d'Orient et d'Occident I*, Paris: Cerf, 1970, pp. 117–33.

63 V. L. Kennedy, *The Saints of the Roman Canon*, 2nd edn, Vatican City: Pontificio Istituto de Archeologia Cristiana, 1963.

fragments point to the existence of written Prefaces already in the fourth century. The second of these two fragments, though, gives thanks to the Father for the gift of the Son, and has phrases similar to ones found in the *Te igitur* and *Supplices te*, and ends, 'through Jesus Christ our Lord, through whom we ask and pray'.[64] Not only does this echo Egyptian anaphoral use, but it also suggests that the Sanctus was either not in the Roman Eucharistic Prayer at this time or at least not used at every Eucharist. E. C. Ratcliff long ago argued that the *canon missae* makes better sense if the *Vere dignum* could move to *Te igitur* without being interrupted by the Sanctus.[65] A remark by Pseudo-Ambrose on the Holy Spirit mentions that not everywhere in the West used the Sanctus, and it may well be that, in contrast with Addai and Mari where the Sanctus seems integral, that of the Roman canon represents a later addition.[66] Most scholars seem to think that the two *Memento* prayers are later additions to the canon, perhaps once being recited by the deacon and, in his absence, by the priest, and thus came to be incorporated into the prayer. Seasonal additions to the *Communicantes* are found in the Verona and later sacramentaries, and 41 variable *Hanc igitur* prayers are found in the Old Gelasian.[67]

What is the theology of this ancient anaphora of the city of Rome? First, it seems to pattern itself on the concept of votive offering, and thus has a considerable amount of sacrificial terminology. Second, it has a petition for consecration in the *Quam oblationem* immediately before the Institution Narrative. The parallel in Ambrose asks for the bread and wine to be the 'figure' of the body and blood of Christ, whereas the *canon missae* asks:[68]

> Vouchsafe, we beseech you, O God, to make this offering wholly blessed, approved, ratified, reasonable, and acceptable; that it may become to us the body and blood of your dearly beloved Son Jesus Christ our Lord.

Though 'figure' may sound more 'primitive' it may be best to see here variant terminology rather than some significant development from 'figure' to 'become'. However, there is no invoking of the Holy Spirit in the Roman tradition, which some have seen as a sign of antiquity, pre-dating the fourth-century Trinitarian debates.[69] The recitation of the Narrative following this petition seems to echo the idea found in Cyprian, that if one does what Jesus did the bread and wine

64 Jeanes, 'Early Latin Parallels to the Roman Canon?', p. 428.

65 E. C. Ratcliff, 'Christian Worship and Liturgy', in K. E. Kirk (ed.), *The Study of Theology*, London: Hodder and Stoughton, 1939, p. 443.

66 L. Chavoutier, 'Un Libellus pseudo-ambrosien sur le Saint-esprit', *Sacris Erudiri* 11 (1960), pp. 136–91.

67 It has been suggested that part of a Hispano-Mozarabic *Post Pridie* represents the earliest Roman sequence *Te igitur-Quam oblationem*, and that by putting together a Mai fragment, this *Post Pridie* (but before the narrative!) and the material from Ambrose we can reconstruct an earlier form of the Roman Eucharistic Prayer. What this actually produces is a thoroughly ridiculous piece of scholarly speculation. *PEER*, pp. 156–8.

68 *PE*, pp. 426–47; *PEER*, pp. 162–7.

69 See Teresa Berger, '*Veni Creator Spiritus*: The Elusive Real Presence of the Spirit in the Catholic Tradition', in Teresa Berger and Bryan D. Spinks (eds), *The Spirit in Worship: Worship in the Spirit*, Collegeville: Liturgical Press, 2009, p. 152 and note 28.

will become what the Lord said they would. The Eucharist is an offering of the passion, and God is beseeched to accept this offering so that the communicants may feed on the body and blood of Christ. The eschatological dimension is articulated by uniting the Roman Church with the saints and martyrs and the heavenly worship at the altar in heaven. Neil Roy has recently suggested that the saints of the *Communicantes* headed by the Virgin Mary, and the martyrs of the *Nobis quoque* headed by the Baptist, function like a *Deëis* in Christian art, where they stand either side of Christ in prayer.[70] The *Communicantes* asks for the offerers to be in communion with the saints, headed by the Virgin Mary; after the Institution Narrative where Christ is central, the *Unde et memores* offers the unspotted victim 'the holy bread of eternal life and the cup of everlasting salvation'; the *Supra quae* asks God to look upon them favourably and accept them as he did the pre-Mosaic offering made by Abel, Abraham and Melchizedek; the *Supplices te* asks the gifts to be carried by 'your angel' (Jesus?) to the altar on high in the sight of God, and that those who partake of the body and blood at this altar may be filled with heavenly blessing and grace. The departed are named in the *Memento*, and in the *Nobis quoque* petition is made that the communicants may have some part in the fellowship of the Apostles and martyrs, 'into whose company we ask that you will admit us, not weighing our merits, but bounteously forgiving'. The saints and martyrs flank the communicants, and the body and blood of Christ, the acceptable sacrifice, allow the communicants to partake of this same fellowship. It was an indigenous prayer that made perfect sense in the culture of the city of Rome.

The Ambrosian or Milanese rite

The rite of Milan has distinct differences from the later Roman rite in the Divine Office and Baptism, but the eucharistic rite is very similar, and it may have assimilated its rite to Rome. The order shows some similarities with the Hispano-Mozarabic and Gallican rites.[71]

- [Preparatory prayers and Confiteor – beginning in the ninth century.]
- Ingressa (Introit chant – single verse).
- *Gloria in excelsis.*
- Threefold Kyrie eleison.
- *Oratio super populum.*
- Prophecy (OT reading).
- Psalm.
- Epistle.
- Alleluia.
- Antiphon before the Gospel (on certain festivals).
- Gospel.

70 Neil J. Roy, 'The Mother of God, the Forerunner, and the Saints of the Roman Canon: A Euchological *Deëis*', in Johnson (ed.), *Issues in Eucharistic Praying*, pp. 327–48.

71 Pre-Vatican II text: 'Order of Mass in the Ambrosian Rite', http://www.sanctamissa.org/en/resources/rites/ambrosian-rite.pdf.

- (Dismissal of the catechumens: collects contained in the ancient missals.)
- Kyrie and *Antiphona post Evangelium.*
- *Pacem habete* (original Milanese position of the Peace).
- *Oratio super sindonem* (offertory prayer over the cloths).
- Offertory and offertory prayers (latter from eleventh century).
- Creed.
- *Oratio super oblata.*
- Eucharistic Prayer.
- Fraction and Commixture.
- Lord's Prayer.
- Agnus Dei.
- Peace.
- [Communion Prayers.]
- Transitorium.
- *Oratio post comunionem.*
- Threefold Kyrie.
- Dismissal – Benedicat, Placeat and Blessing.
- [Last Gospel.]

The Ambrosian Missal had some 263 Proper Prefaces, but the *canon missae* is that of Rome with only minor textual variants. Archdale King classed these Prefaces in what are in fact five very broad and mixed groups: (a) in the form of collects, and ending with the doxology *per Dominum nostrum*; (b) narratives normally relating the lives of saints; (c) oratorical Prefaces, exhibiting high-flown rhetoric, rather like the Gallican prayers; (d) antithetical Prefaces where two subjects are opposed to each other such as heaven and hell; and (e) Prefaces with parallels between persons such as Eve and Mary.[72] It is these, as well as some of the components of the *Ordo Missae* that give it a distinctive form.

The rite has remained in use, and underwent some revision in the wake of the Second Vatican Council.[73] This revision has brought the rite into some conformity with the post-Vatican II Roman rite, though it still retains many Prefaces, and in addition to the four Eucharistic Prayers of the new Roman rite it has two additional Eucharistic Prayers.[74]

Celtic rite or tradition?

Although much is written about the Celtic rite, Hugh Kennedy has maintained that there is not sufficient evidence of a distinct and homogeneous rite as

72 King, *Liturgies of the Primatial Sees*, pp. 428–9.

73 *Missale Ambrosianum iuxta ritum Sanctae Ecclesiae Mediolanensis*, Milan: Centro Ambrosiano di Documentazione e Studi Religiosi, 1981.

74 Achille M. Triacca, 'Le déroulement de la Messe Ambrosienne', in A. M. Triacca and A. Pistoia (eds), *L'Eucharistie: Celebrations, Rites, Piétés*, Rome: CLV Edizioni Liturgiche, 1995, pp. 339–79; 'Le Preghiere Eucharistiche Ambrosiane', in Albert Gerhards, Heinzgerd Brakmann and Martin Klöckener (eds), *Prex Eucharistica III/I. Ecclesia Antiqua et Occidentalis*, Fribourg: Academic Press, 2005, pp. 145–202; Alan Griffiths, *We Give You Thanks and Praise: The Ambrosian Eucharistic Prefaces*, Norwich: Canterbury Press, 1999.

celebrated among the diverse people who shared Celtic roots.[75] What evidence there is comes from Ireland, and points to the existence of Gallican material alongside material deriving from the Romano-Western synthesis. The Reichenau fragment, written in Irish script and dated to the seventh century, has a form of Mass that follows the Gallican order. However, it is the Stowe Missal that is regarded as the most important Irish liturgical manuscript. It is written in at least two hands, and was probably written at Tallaght *c.* 792. Most of its prayers are in the concise Roman collect form, and it has the Roman *canon missae.* This latter does have some peculiarities, including a fixed trinitarian Preface, and *Memento etiam* in place of *Memento Domine,* but is still nevertheless the *canon missae.* At the same time there are Gallican elements. In his recent study, Neil O'Donoghue draws attention to the three elements that make the Stowe text different and distinct: (a) the eucharistic celebration begins with a long Litany of the Saints; (b) a hymn for the Fraction; and (c) a communion chant of a type not found elsewhere.[76] The question arises as to how specifically Irish these are. If Peter Jeffery is correct about the Kyries being a remnant of the Litany of Saints, then apart from the fact that the Stowe version includes some specifically Irish saints, this could be a snapshot of Roman use prior to the litany disappearing, leaving only the Kyries.[77] The chant used for the Fraction is a catena of Scripture verses concerning the reception of Christ in the Eucharist:

> They knew it was the Lord, Alleluia; in the breaking of the bread, Alleluia. The bread we break is the body of Jesus Christ, our Lord, Alleluia; the chalice we bless is the blood of Jesus Christ, our Lord, Alleluia. For the remission of our sins, Alleluia. Lord, let your mercy rest upon us, Alleluia; who put all our confidence in you, Alleluia. They knew it was the Lord, Alleluia; in the breaking of the bread, Alleluia. O Lord, we believe that in this breaking of your body and pouring out of your blood we become your redeemed people; We confess that in taking the gifts of this pledge here, we lay hold in hope of enjoying its true fruit in the heavenly places.[78]

O'Donoghue notes that the original text of this prayer has been changed by the Irish editor of the Stowe Missal, Móel Cáich, who has erased the last six lines and replaced them with the current ending.[79] The Missal includes a Mass Tract that describes a complex Fraction, when the bread may be broken into as many as 65 pieces and also laid out in the form of a cross. The third distinctive feature is the long series of prayers made up of antiphons and psalms for use during the Communion. It has been suggested that items in the Derrynavlan Hoard – a two-handled chalice of about 21 cm, a paten of about 36 cm in diameter, a strainer and a large bronze bowl – were the type of communion vessels designed

75 Hugh P. Kennedy, 'The Eucharistic Prayer in Early Irish Liturgical Practice', in Gerhards, Brakmann and Klöckener (eds), *Prex Eucharistica III/I*, p. 225.

76 Neil Xavier O'Donoghue, *The Eucharist in Pre-Norman Ireland*, South Bend: University of Notre Dame Press, 2011, p. 65.

77 Peter Jeffery, 'Meaning and Functions of Kyrie Eleison', pp. 187–8.

78 O'Donoghue, *Eucharist in Pre-Norman Ireland*, p. 68.

79 O'Donoghue, *Eucharist in Pre-Norman Ireland*, p. 69.

for distribution of communion as directed by the Stowe rubrics.[80] Whether the specific antiphons and psalms count as making it a distinct rite, though, is debatable. Rather than a Celtic rite, the Stowe Missal seems to represent a slightly Gallicanized form of the Roman rite – an Irish eighth-century contribution to the later Romano-Western synthesis, which perhaps came to Ireland via the same 'Gallican' tradition as produced the Bobbio Missal.[81] O'Donogue's recent study does, however, draw attention to what might be termed Old Irish contributions to eucharistic theology. First, the Antiphonary of Bangor, which was written between 680 and 691, has a special hymn to be sung while the priests receive communion, which O'Donoghue says is unprecedented in the whole of the West in the seventh century:

> Come, you holy ones, receive the body of Christ, drinking the holy Blood by which you were redeemed.
>
> You who were saved by the Body and Blood of Christ, let us praise God, by whom we are made anew.
>
> By this sacrament of the body and blood, all have escaped from the jaws of hell.
>
> Giver of salvation, Christ, the Son of God, has saved the world by his Cross and Blood.
>
> The Lord has been sacrificed for all, Himself both priest and victim.
>
> The law commanded the sacrifice of victims, foreshadowing the mysteries divine.
>
> Bestower of light and Saviour of all, He granted most noble grace to His holy people.
>
> Let all draw near with pure and faithful minds, let all receive the protection of eternal salvation.
>
> Guardian of the saints, you are leader, O Lord, and dispenser of life eternal to those who believe.
>
> He gives heavenly bread to the hungry, and to the thirsty water from the living spring.
>
> Christ the Lord himself comes, who is Alpha and Omega. He shall come again to judge us all.[82]

O'Donoghue points out the themes of holy fear, a eucharistic piety centred on the passion of Christ, and the Eucharist as being a protection from the Last

80 Próinséas Ní Chatháin, 'The Liturgical Background of the Derrynavlan Altar Service', *Journal of the Royal Antiquaries of Ireland* 110 (1980), pp. 127–48.

81 See Marc Schneiders, 'The Origins of the Early Irish Liturgy', in Próinséas Ní Chatháin and Michael Richter (eds), *Ireland and Europe in the Early Middle Ages*, Stuttgart: Klett-Cotta, 1996, pp. 76–98.

82 O'Donoghue, *Eucharist in Pre-Norman Ireland*, pp. 86–8.

Judgement. He also draws attention to the collection of homilies in the *Leabhar Breac*, many of which centre on the Eucharist as a representation of the Passion of Christ. One homily unfolds thus:

> it is He who, on the night before His crucifixion, offered up His blood and body, and gave them to His apostles to partake thereof. And He left with those Apostles, and with His whole church, to the end of time, the custom of making the same oblation to commemorate the first oblation when He subjected Himself to the cross and to death in obedience to the Heavenly Father, and to fulfil His will.
>
> This is the oblation in which is the full satisfying of God and the appeasing of His anger against the accurst seed of Adam; for in it was the full-growth of humility and lowliness, the full-growth of charity and heart-pity, and perfect sympathy for the wretchedness of the human race in general.[83]

The old Irish use, whether Gallican as in the Reichenau fragment, or in the synthesis as represented by the Stowe Missal, gave way to the later synthesis as mediated through the Norman Sarum Use. This latter is represented by the Irish Corpus Missal, though the Stowe *canon missae*, slightly emended, and the Fraction are reproduced in Brendan O'Malley's contemporary 'A Celtic Eucharist'.[84]

Concluding remarks

These Classical Western rites mutually influenced one another, with the prestige of Rome ensuring (and often without trying) that its rite was widely borrowed and adapted. Imported Roman books were combined with the Gallican material to produce a Romano-Western synthesis, with only the Hispano-Mozarabic and Ambrosian rites surviving rather like endangered species and generally confined to the Toledo parishes and the diocese of Milan respectively. Since the latter is so similar to its Roman sister, Vincent Lenti notes that it is only the Hispano-Mozarabic Mass that remains distinctive in its form and structure, and the greater variability of its texts is its strongest and most distinguishing feature.[85]

83 O'Donoghue, *Eucharist in Pre-Norman Ireland*, p. 126.

84 Brendan O'Malley (ed.), *A Celtic Primer: The Complete Celtic Worship Resource and Collection*, Harrisburg: Morehouse Publishing, 2002.

85 Vincent A. Lenti, 'Liturgical Reform and the Ambrosian and Mozarabic Rites', *Worship* 68 (1994), p. 426.

9

From the Romano-Western Synthesis to the Tridentine Reforms: Liturgy, Commentaries and Eucharistic Theologies

In the same way as there was mutual borrowing between Eastern rites, resulting for example in the Byzantine rite, so a similar process took place in the Latin West. The rite that evolved in the City of Rome – probably itself a process of synthesis – migrated north of the Alps and west, where it was supplemented with and adapted to local uses and came to dominate and displace most other earlier regional contenders, including older use in Rome itself. Often referred to as the Romano-Gallican or Romano-Frankish synthesis, it will be referred to here as the Romano-Western synthesis.

The Romano-Western synthesis

The prestige of the See of Rome, together with the fact that it possessed the tombs of St Peter and St Paul, made it a centre for pilgrims, visiting scholars and hierarchs, and ensured that its rites and customs were borrowed, copied and disseminated through the regions of the fast-crumbling Roman Empire. Imported Roman rites and uses tended to be used alongside more indigenous rites in Gaul, the Iberian Peninsula and elsewhere. It was books from Rome that were introduced into England with the mission of Augustine of Canterbury to Kent, and while older Uses of the British would have been used in the west and north and the Roman used in the south east, little trace has survived of the former. The resulting process of liturgical osmosis with ever-new permutations and syntheses based on the views of individual scribes and local needs is epitomized in the Merovingian and Carolingian kingdoms. Older textbooks have tended to suggest that the demise of the Gallican rites was the result of a deliberate policy of Charlemagne to impose the Roman rite throughout his kingdom, and this view is still sometimes repeated in recent books.[1] However, careful studies of this period reveal a much more complex process, with no evidence of any imperial edict to replace the older rites. Rosamond McKitterick argued that the contributions by Pippin and Charlemagne suggest that their encouragement of liturgy emphasized its more didactic elements that were aimed more directly at

1 For example, Martin D. Stringer, *A Sociological History of Christian Worship*, Cambridge: Cambridge University Press, 2005, p. 111.

the laity rather than any imposition.[2] Pippin's contribution was through establishing *scholae cantorum*, and he procured books for that end. The Roman method of chant supplanted the Gallican method. The Frankish kings' contribution to the evolution of the Romano-Western synthesis in sacramentaries was in their role as patrons who commissioned a particular text for a specific purpose rather than any comprehensive replacement.[3] This suggestion has been explored in more depth by Yitzak Hen.[4] He notes how the Merovingian King Dagobert heaped treasure and landed property on the Abbey of Saint-Denis. The king required monks to exhort the clemency of Christ for him, and this resulted in prayers *pro rege*, *pro regibus* or *in pace*. The royal munificence of such monasteries embraced also the work of copying and editing liturgical manuscripts.[5] But these manuscripts already included some representing the Roman rite and others representing the Gallican rite. Among the former is the Old Gelasian Sacramentary. Much of this sacramentary is Roman in origin for the use of the presbyters of the titular churches, but it has been supplemented by Gallican material and altered for use north of the alps. It gave rise to the later mixed Gelasians where again more, but different, osmosis takes place. The Bobbio Missal is dated *c.* 700 and at times has been classed as Gallican. In fact, it is a prime example of the evolving synthesis in Merovingian times. It contains only one Eucharistic Prayer, the *canon missae*, and so witnesses to Roman usage, though, as Yitzak Hen observes, since we do not have an instance of the 'Roman' canon outside later Frankish sources – Bobbio and Old Gelasian – it is impossible to be sure that this is in fact *the* Roman canon.[6] However, the canon has two important 'Gallican' saints added to the *Communicantes*, and the Sanctorale reflects Gallican interests. Furthermore, the Proper Prefaces are called *Contestatio* and many are in the florid style of the Gallican prayers in *Missale Gothicum* and similar Gallican collections. There are 76 in total, and some of them paraphrase the sermons of Augustine, Maximus the Confessor and Ambrose.[7] Rubrics and headings in the Bobbio reflect knowledge of and presuppose elements in the Gallican rite. The Old Gelasian, then, is a Frankish manuscript, and while it is far less Gallicanized than the Bobbio Missal, nevertheless, it is no less a Gallican manuscript. They are both examples of Merovingian vitality, diversity and richness. McKitterick writes:

> Enough is extant however to indicate that the production of liturgical texts continued to be a largely individual affair conducted by the different monasteries and dioceses, in which the clergy were left a good deal of freedom to

---

2 Rosamond McKitterick, *The Frankish Church and the Carolingian Reforms 789–895*, London: Royal Historical Society, 1977, p. 122.

3 McKitterick, *Frankish Church*, p. 134.

4 Yitzak Hen, *The Royal Patronage of Liturgy in Frankish Gaul*, London: Henry Bradshaw Society, 2001.

5 Hen, *Royal Patronage*, pp. 37–41.

6 Yitzak Hen, 'The Liturgy of the Bobbio Missal', in Yitzak Hen and Rob Meens (eds), *The Bobbio Missal: Liturgy and Religious Culture in Merovingian Gaul*, Cambridge: Cambridge University Press, 2004, pp. 140–53.

7 Louise Batstone, 'Doctrinal and Theological Themes in the Prayers of the Bobbio Missal', in Hen and Meens (eds), *Bobbio Missal*, p. 176.

determine by actual use the proportion in which Frankish and Roman elements were to be mingled.[8]

For the Carolingian period Hen notes that Charlemagne certainly showed interest in the liturgy and the manner in which it was celebrated, though this was part of a more general reinvigoration of the Church in his domain. In his *Admonitio generalis* Charlemagne advocated the introduction of the Roman place for the Kiss of Peace and the recitation of the names of the dead during the Mass and was concerned with authority, orthodoxy and correctness. He had enlisted Paul the Deacon to prepare a new corrected homiliary for the clergy and, taking advantage of Paul's visit to Rome in the 780s, asked him to request Pope Hadrian for a copy of an authentic sacramentary put together by Pope Gregory the Great. After some delay a copy of the so-called Gregorian Sacramentary arrived at the court at Aachen, and is referred to as the Hadrianum. It was certainly not by Gregory and was of only limited usefulness to the Frankish Church. In order to make it usable, a supplement was added, once thought to be the work of Alcuin of York, but now regarded as the work of Benedict of Aniane, and this included new Masses *pro rege*.[9] Though the Carolingian scholar Walahfrid Strabo wrote that 'the prerogative of the Roman see was observed and the reasoned consistency of its arrangements persuaded all churches of the Latin speaking world to follow its custom and authority', the reality was different, and Charlemagne's concern was that priests celebrate the liturgy properly, and not impose a particular standard text.[10] The Hadrianum with Supplement did not circulate widely until the time of his successor, Louis the Pious, and it existed alongside new manuscripts of the mixed Gelasian type and Gallican. But from the mid-ninth century onwards, Hen notes, there was a growing tendency to fuse the Hadrianum and Supplement into one book, and through use at the royal court and through the influential monasteries this version of the synthesis spread and displaced older versions and rites, even being re-imported into Rome. However, the older Gallican Eucharistic Prayers were displaced, and the Roman *canon missae* in its form in the Hadrianum (other than minor variant readings) became the sole Eucharistic Prayer of most of the Western Church.

Carolingian commentaries on the Mass and theological debate

Walahfrid Strabo (*c.* 808–849) was a Frankish monk and tutor to Charles, the son of Louis the Pious, and he later became Abbot of Reichenau (838–849), though his *Libellus* was written in exile at Speyer (840–842).[11] Part of this work discusses the meaning of the Mass. He considered the concept of offerings to

8 McKitterick, *Frankish Church*, p. 129.

9 Hen, *Royal Patronage*, pp. 74–89.

10 Hen, *Royal Patronage*, p. 88.

11 For biography and the text, see Alice L. Harting-Correa, *Walahfrid Strabo's Libellus de Exordiis et Incrementis quarundam in observationibus ecclesiasticis rerum*, Leiden: Brill, 1996.

God in the Old Testament and stressed that Christ is the end of the law and, by his resurrection, affirms something new:

> At the supper with the disciples before His final surrender, after the ceremonies of the old Passover, He entrusted to them the sacraments of His body and blood in the substance of bread and wine (*in panis et vini substantia*). He taught them to celebrate them as a commemoration of his most holy passion.[12]

He used the term substance, though without any precise definition or meaning. Christ is a high priest of the order of Melchizedek and found a suitable sacrament for his body and blood, which he now transmits to his faithful. These very mysteries of our redemption 'are truly the body and blood of the Lord'.[13] Strabo acknowledged that once the Church offered corn, grapes, oil and other things alongside bread and wine, but intimates that this custom has been suppressed because some offered the flesh of a lamb to be consecrated.[14] When he turns to examine the Mass itself, Strabo gives a historical explanation, explaining when and who added various elements such as the Kyries and the Agnus Dei. However, Strabo's approach would be superseded by the adoption of the allegorical and typological approach that has already been encountered in the Eastern divines. Mary Schaefer notes that the commentaries 'utilize rememorative and moral allegory as well as typology to explain, primarily for the benefit of priests, the meaning of the parts of the Mass and of the ritual actions of the presider, other ministers, and assembly'.[15] They tended to explore the eucharistic offering in relation to the one sacrifice of Christ, and in later commentaries, the presence of Christ. One of the earliest and widely imitated even if controversial commentaries was the work of Amalarius of Metz (*c.* 780–850), *Liber officialis*. Amalarius taught that the Mass was a memorial, not a true sacrifice, and that the presence of Christ emphasized his role as victim rather than high priest. The presence can be described as the 'sensible nature of the bread and wine is changed (*verti*) into the rational nature, namely of the body and blood of Christ', and the sacrifice as 'one victim, Christ was offered for the just and the unjust. The same sacrifice, which was placed before, remains on the altar.'[16] Barbara Raw usefully summarizes Amalarius's allegorical explanation of the Mass:

> The early part of the mass, up to the gospel, represented Christ's birth and early life, the gospel represented his ministry and the canon his Passion and Resurrection. This drama was framed by the entrance procession and chant, which symbolized the patriarchs and prophets waiting for the Messiah, and by the blessing, which represented the risen Christ blessing his

12 Harting-Correa, *Walahfrid Strabo's Libellus*, pp. 100–1. I have slightly altered the translation.

13 Harting-Correa, *Walahfrid Strabo's Libellus*, pp. 104–5. Walahfrid Strabo uses *sacramenta*, but here the word is *mysteria*.

14 Harting-Correa, *Walahfrid Strabo's Libellus*, p. 109.

15 Mary M. Schaefer, 'Twelfth Century Latin Commentaries on the Mass: The Relationship of the Priest to Christ and the People', *Studia Liturgica* 15 (1982/83), pp. 77.

16 Edward J. Kilmartin, *The Eucharist in the West: History and Theology*, Collegeville: Liturgical Press, 1998, pp. 93–4.

> disciples before returning to heaven. The dramatic way in which the action was understood is shown particularly clearly in the interpretation of the canon. The deacons, who stand with bowed heads from the *Te igitur* to the beginning of the communion, play the role of the disciples, 'qui magna tribulatione erant oppressi' [who had been weighed down with great suffering]. The sub-deacons, who stand facing the celebrant across the altar, represent the holy women who remained with Christ during his sufferings. At the prayer *Supplices te rogamus* Christ commends his soul to God and dies and the sub-deacons raise their heads, 'aspicientes in dilectum sibi corpus, quousque pendet in cruce' [gazing at his beloved body as long as it hangs on the cross]. At the beginning of the prayer *Nobis quoque peccatoribus* the celebrant raises his voice and the congregation are invited to recall the centurion plunging the spear into Christ's side. The sense of being really present at the events of the past can be seen vividly at this point in the treatment of the chalice, which is placed to the right of the paten on the altar in order that it can catch the blood from Christ's side. As the prayer of consecration ends the celebrant and the archdeacon wrap the chalice and paten in two cloths and place them on the altar, enacting the parts of Joseph and Nicodemus placing Christ's body in the tomb. The mass reaches its climax at the communion when a particle of the host is placed in the chalice and the congregation relives the Resurrection of Christ.[17]

It is understandable how readers of Amalarius whose own gestures and ceremonial differed from his liturgy would change their rubrics to conform with his explanation.

A contemporary critic of Amalarius was Florus of Lyons (*c.* 810–*c.* 860), who expounded a different theology in his *De expositione missae*. Kilmartin wrote:

> Florus views the Mass as an activity, a sacrifice, in which an acceptable cultic offering is made to God. This offering takes place through the priest in the name of the Church and is intimately related to the bread and wine. These gifts become the body and blood of Christ through the consecration by Christ, in the power of the Spirit. As a consequence the Church now offers the body and blood of the Lord. This offering is a real offering of the body and blood of the Lord present *in mysterio*, but really at hand. This real offering repeats mysteriously the death of the Lord, the bloody offering of the cross that the sacrifice of the Church unfolds.[18]

The commentaries of Walahfrid Strabo, Amalarius and Florus were compiled against the backdrop of two theological approaches to the presence of Christ in the bread and wine, both written by monks at Corbie, Paschasius Radbertus and Ratramnus, and both entitled 'On the Lord's Body and Blood'. Paschasius wrote his treatise between 831 and 833, and he presented a revised version in *c.* 844 to Charles the Bald. It seems that it was originally written in response to

17 Barbara C. Raw, *Anglo-Saxon Crucifixion Iconography and the Art of the Monastic Revival*, Cambridge: Cambridge University Press, 1990, pp. 183–4.

18 Kilmartin, *Eucharist in the West*, p. 96.

a former student, Warin, and was probably designed to be a teaching aid for the many monks who were being ordained priests.[19] Paschasius taught that the body and blood of Christ in the Eucharist was the same body of Christ that was born of the Virgin Mary and crucified on the cross. It is so because the Creator willed it, and his will is power and wisdom, and the means by which God dwells in us so that we may remain members of his body.[20] There is a definite eschatological end:

> we only feed upon and drink the sacrament of the body and blood so that nourished from it we may be made one in Christ, that being invigorated by tasting him we may be prepared for things immortal and eternal.[21]

The unworthy, even if they eat, do not receive this.

Paschasius's explanation is based on his definition of a sacrament, and the distinction between a figure and truth. A sacrament is anything handed down to us in any divine celebration as a pledge of salvation when what is visibly done accomplished inwardly something far different, to be taken in a holy sense:

> They are called sacraments either because they are a secret in that in the visible act divinity inwardly accomplishes something secretly through the corporeal appearance, or from the sanctifying consecration, because the Holy Spirit, remaining in the body of Christ, latently accomplishes for the salvation of the faithful all these mystical sacraments under the cover of things visible.[22]

But he argued that because the sacrament is mystical, it is a figure, but also truth:

> But because he, after the flesh had to penetrate to heavens, so that, through faith, those reborn in him might with greater boldness seek, he has left us this sacrament, a visible figure and character of flesh and blood, so that through them our soul and our flesh are richly nourished for grasping things invisible and spiritual by faith. This which is outwardly sensed is, however, the figure or character but wholly truth and no shadow, because intrinsically perceived, and for this reason nothing else henceforth than truth and the sacrament of his flesh is apparent.[23]

He explained that what the priest does outwardly in memory of the passion is a figure, but the sacrament is truth in that the body and blood of Christ are created 'by the power of the Spirit in his word out of the substance of bread

19 Celia Chazelle, 'The Eucharist in Early Medieval Europe', in Ian Christopher Levy, Gary Macy and Kristen Van Ausdall (eds), *A Companion to the Eucharist in the Middle Ages*, Leiden: Brill, 2012, pp. 208–9.

20 ET of Paschasius and Ratramnus in G. E. McCraken and A. Cabaniss (eds), *Early Medieval Theology*, Library of Christian Classics vol. 11, Philadelphia: Westminster Press, 1957, pp. 94–108.

21 McCraken and Cabaniss (eds), *Early Medieval Theology*, p. 100.

22 McCraken and Cabaniss (eds), *Early Medieval Theology*, p. 98.

23 McCraken and Cabaniss (eds), *Early Medieval Theology*, p. 103.

and wine'.[24] Patricia Zirkel notes that the use of the term substance here is simply use of traditional nomenclature inherited from previous writers, and does not carry the Aristotelian definition used by the later scholastic theologians.[25] Paschasius's concern is to stress that the real body and blood of Christ are received in the sacrament. Thus he wrote:

> But because it is not right to devour Christ with the teeth, he willed in the mystery that this bread and wine be created truly his flesh and blood through consecration by the power of the Holy Spirit, by daily creating it so that it might be mystically sacrificed for the life of the world; so that as from the Virgin through the Spirit true flesh is created without union of sex, so through the same, out of the substance of bread and wine, the same body and blood of Christ may be mystically consecrated.[26]

In the figure of the bread there resides the truth, which is the flesh that 'was born of Mary, suffered on the cross, and rose again from the tomb'.[27] Yet, the 'method' or means of this is Christ's virtue, the knowledge of faith, the cause of power and the effect in will, which is beyond reason.

Paschasius seems to have drawn on the teaching of Ambrose of Milan as he understood it. A decade later, Charles requested Ratramnus to verify and comment on aspects of his confrere's theology. Ratramnus's work is mainly quotations from earlier writers, and although he cited Ambrose, he relied more on Augustine. He gave his particular understanding of figure and truth. Figure means a kind of overshadowing that reveals its intent under some sort of veil. Truth is representation of clear fact, not obscured by any shadowy images, but uttered in pure and open meaning. By the latter he seems to mean empirical truth or a demonstrable fact. The sacrament is a figure, with the result that:

> we see that a great difference separates the mystery of Christ's blood and body which now is taken by the faithful in the church from that which was born of the Virgin Mary, suffered, died, rose again, ascended to the heavens, sits on the right hand of the Father.[28]

For Ratramnus, the bread and wine exhibit one thing outwardly to human sense, but inwardly is something far different, something divine, which is revealed to the gaze of the believing soul, but which otherwise is not seen, received or consumed by fleshly senses. The bread and wine, through consecration, become the sacrament of Christ's body and blood. A change takes place, not in a corporeal sense but in a spiritual sense, 'figuratively, since under cover of the corporeal bread and of the corporeal wine Christ's spiritual body and blood do exist'. He wrote:

24 McCraken and Cabaniss (eds), *Early Medieval Theology*, p. 102.

25 Patrica McCormick Zirkel, 'The Ninth-Century Eucharistic Controversy: A Context for the Beginnings of Eucharistic Doctrine in the West', *Worship* 68 (1994), p. 9.

26 McCraken and Cabaniss (eds), *Early Medieval Theology*, p. 101.

27 McCraken and Cabaniss (eds), *Early Medieval Theology*, p. 94.

28 McCraken and Cabaniss (eds), *Early Medieval Theology*, p. 143.

> Not that they are actually two substances differing in themselves, namely body and spirit, but one and the same thing from one point of view has the appearance of bread and wine; from another however, it is Christ's body and blood. For as far as the physical appearances of both are concerned, the appearances are those of things created in a corporeal sense; but as far as their power is concerned, inasmuch as they have been spiritually made, they are the mysteries of Christ's body and blood.[29]

Ratramnus too speaks of substances, and behind his use of spiritual seems to be John 6.63, that the Spirit gives life, and the flesh (corporeal) counts for nothing; that is, the spiritual is more 'real' than the corporeal. The present heavenly body and blood of Christ are present under the veil of the corporeal bread and wine:

> From all that has thus far been said it has been shown that Christ's body and blood which are received in the mouth of the faithful in the church are figures according to their visible appearance, but according to their invisible substance, that is, the power of the divine Word, truly exist as Christ's body and blood. Therefore, with respect to visible creation, they feed the body; with reference to the power of a stronger substance, they feed and sanctify the souls of the faithful.[30]

Later post-Reformation polemic has tended to create a much wider gulf between Paschasius and Ratramnus than actually exists. Ratramnus, like some of the Church of the East writers, seems to lean towards a resurrected and ascended bodily presence (a 'spiritual' body according to Pauline teaching) over against the incarnational body taught by Paschasius, but both affirm a real divine presence and change, and Ratramnus agreed with Paschasius that the offering of the passion is daily enacted and offered in the Mass. Other contemporary divines joined the debate, with Hincmar of Reims giving a theology akin to that of Paschasius, and Gotteschalk taking an approach more akin to that of Ratramnus, though each having his own nuanced differences.[31] It would seem that the Paschasian incarnational approach became the prevailing theology in the Carolingian kingdoms, and this was perhaps understood to be supported more by the Roman *canon missae* than in some of the less direct petitions for consecration of the Gallican anaphoras.

Further commentary and doctrinal dispute

Ordo Romanus Primus gave ceremonial directions for a papal Mass. Some of the later *ordines* gave the developing ceremonial for Romano-Frankish celebrations. Ordo VII gives directions as to when the priest is to make signs of the cross over the bread and wine. The various *ordines*, and later the customaries,

29 McCraken and Cabaniss (eds), *Early Medieval Theology*, p. 123.
30 McCraken and Cabaniss (eds), *Early Medieval Theology*, p. 132.
31 Chazelle, 'The Eucharist in Early Medieval Europe'.

also included rubrics directing the priest's and other ministers' actions and ritual gestures. They were concerned to give the use of a particular cathedral or monastery, and it is unlikely that the complex rubrics were followed in small parish churches.[32] However, gestures at the Offertory, in the Eucharistic Prayer and at the Fraction and Communion were probably carefully observed, and these both inspired and in turn were developed from liturgical commentaries and theological writings and controversy on the Eucharist. Of the many later commentaries written, one of the more distinct and influential ones was Isaac of Stella's *Letter on the Mass.*[33]

Isaac of Stella (Étoile, *c.* 1100–69) studied in England and France and became Abbot of Étoile.[34] Isaac drew on the monastic ascent of the soul from *compunctio*, to *devotio*, to *contemplatio*. He appealed to the Old Testament tabernacle and Temple: the bronze altar which signifies a contrite heart, the gold altar where the heart is offered, and a third, the true altar, which is the throne of mercy, where there are angels, and the destiny of humanity's true vocation.[35] The first is true repentance, compunction, the second is holiness, or devotion, and the third is contemplation.[36] Isaac applied this to the *canon missae* which has three offerings:

> For the first offering separates us from the world; the second joins us to Christ; the third unites us to God. The first one does us to death; the second vivifies us; the third deifies us. The first action is the passion; the second is the resurrection; the third is the glorification.[37]

The first action is the offering of bread and wine (corresponding to the *Te igitur* to *Hanc igitur*), which is the killing of the entire physical life:

> Therefore, since bread and wine are the staple food and drink, without which physical life cannot persist, it is appropriate that the power of physical life be offered through the offering of these elements. For these staple elements make up part of this life, and they symbolize the whole of it. What more can a slave do, who desires to be reconciled to his Lord, than to offer out of his penury his whole sustenance, and thus make a sacrifice of his whole life?[38]

---

32 Richard W. Pfaff, 'Prescription and Reality in the Rubrics of Sarum Rite Service Books', in Lesley Smith and Benedicta Ward (eds), *Intellectual Life in the Middle Ages: Essays Presented to Margaret Gibson*, London: The Hambledon Press, 1992, pp. 197–205.

33 For the many later commentaries, see Gary Macy, 'Commentaries of the Mass during the Early Scholastic Period', in Lizette Larson-Miller (ed.), *Medieval Liturgy: A Book of Essays*, New York: Garland Science, 1997, pp. 25–59; Elizabeth Saxon, *The Eucharist in Romanesque France: Iconography and Theology*, Woodbridge: Boydell Press, 2006, pp. 128–47.

34 Text in Dániel Deme, *The Selected Works of Isaac of Stella: A Cistercian Voice from the Twelfth Century*, Aldershot: Ashgate, 2007, pp. 158–64.

35 Deme, *Selected Works*, pp. 159–60.

36 Deme, *Selected Works*, p. 160.

37 Deme, *Selected Works*, p. 163.

38 Deme, *Selected Works*, p. 161.

The *Quam oblationem* and *Qui pridie* is the second action; they vivify the bread and wine by adding the voice of power (Ps. 68.33), and this is an offering of the sacrifice of exultation and joy. In the *Supra quae* and *Supplices te*, the offering is taken to the altar in heaven:

> He (the priest) asks that, through the hands of the angel, namely his invisible minister, his sacrifice may be carried thither and be united to the body of Christ in heaven. For just as we partake of the bread and wine of the first altar by the fact that he looks down upon it, so he now asks that, by the power of the sacrament, he may communicate in the truth of that flesh and blood from this second altar, which is beyond the veil in heaven. This was the promise made to Abraham and realized by the grace given to Mary. So the priest asks to be united with the supreme head through the Spirit. For the head of Christ is God.[39]

The physical (bread and wine) is made spiritual (the body and blood of Christ), and the spiritual is made heavenly or divine (faithful reception and union with God). This is a devotional commentary, concerned with the soul.

This and many other commentaries were written against the backdrop of a growing theological discussion on the presence of Christ in the elements. The catalyst seems to have been the 'Beregarian' controversy. Berengar taught as a member of the cathedral chapter of Tours and was also Archdeacon of Angers. He promoted and extended selected teachings of Ratramnus which he believed to be the work of John Scottus Eriugena. A flamboyant personality who made many enemies, he was opposed by John, Abbot of Fécamp, and the controversy that resulted led to Berengar being summoned to appear before a synod, which condemned him *in absentia*, and then in 1059, before a Roman Synod. He was presented with the now famous oath drawn up by Humbert, Cardinal Bishop of Silva Candida, which stated:

> the bread and the wine that are set upon the altar, after consecration are not sacrament alone, but also are the true body and blood of our Lord Jesus Christ and in sensory fashion and not only as a sacrament but in truth are handled and broken by the hands of the priests, and ground between the teeth of the faithful . . .[40]

Once safely home, Berengar repudiated the oath (even Paschasius had rejected the idea of the body of Christ being chewed) and continued to teach what he had always taught. Claiming to cite Augustine he defined a sacrament as the visible form of an invisible grace – a definition that came to be widely adopted through its inclusion in Gratian's *Decretum*.[41] Berengar's concern was to honour the

39 Deme, *Selected Works*, p. 163.

40 Charles M. Radding and Francis Newton, *Theology, Rhetoric, and Politics in the Eucharistic Controversy, 1078–1079*, New York: Columbia University Press, 2003, p. 19, Latin text: p. 20.

41 N. M. Häring, 'Berengar's Definitions of *Sacramentum* and Their Influence on Mediaeval Sacramentology', *Mediaeval Studies* 10 (1948), pp. 109–46.

reality of the visible form as well as the invisible grace, which meant stressing the difference between the *signum* (sign) and the *res* (the reality). In reply to Humbert, he wrote, 'by consecration at the altar the bread and wine are made into religious sacraments, not so that they cease to be what they were, but so that they are that which is changed into something else'.[42] Berengar preferred the patristic terms of *figura*, *similitudo* and *pignus*, and held that whatever change there may be in the sacramental elements it cannot annihilate the bread and wine, for otherwise there can be no sacrament. The body of Christ must take up space, be seen and be tasted as a human body, but in fact this body of Christ exists only in heaven. The bread and wine are figures that point to the spiritual presence of Christ, though here again, spiritual does not mean less real, but simply not corporeal. Berengar's opponents regarded this as a denial that communicants received the true body and blood of Christ. He was answered by Lanfranc of Bec (later Archbishop of Canterbury) and Lanfranc's pupil, Guitmund of Aversa. Lanfranc asserted:

> We believe, therefore, that the earthly substances, which on the table of the Lord are divinely sanctified by the priestly ministry, are ineffably, incomprehensibly, miraculously converted by the workings of heavenly power into the essence of the Lord's body. The species and whatever other certain qualities of the earthly substances themselves, however, are preserved, so that those who see it may not be horrified at the sight of flesh and blood, and believers may have a greater reward for their faith at the sight. It is, nonetheless, the body of the Lord himself existing in heaven at the right side of the Father, immortal, inviolate, whole, uncontaminated, and unharmed. Truly it is possible to say, therefore, that it is the same body that was assumed from the Virgin, and also not the same body, which we receive. Indeed, it is the same body as far as it concerns its essence, true nature, and its own excellence. It is not the same body in its appearance, however, if one is considering the species of bread and wine and the rest of the qualities mentioned above.[43]

Lanfranc used the terms essence and substance to describe the reality of the body of Christ in the sacrament and a variety of words to convey change, including *converti*, *mutari*, *commutari*, *mutatio* and *transferri*.[44] The elements of bread and wine are the visible species that cover or envelop the invisible realities of the body and blood of Christ. He added:

> How the bread is converted into flesh, and the wine is converted into blood, and how the nature of each has essentially [*essentialiter*] changed, the just man who lives by faith does not scrutinize by argumentation and grasp by reason.[45]

42 Radding and Newton, *Theology, Rhetoric, and Politics*, p. 11.

43 Mark G. Vaillancourt, *Lanfranc of Canterbury on the Body and Blood of the Lord and Guitmund of Aversa on the Truth of the Body and Blood of Christ in the Eucharist*, Washington, DC: Catholic University of America Press, 2009, p. 66.

44 Vaillancourt, *Lanfranc*, p. 7.

45 Vaillancourt, *Lanfranc*, p. 61.

Guitmund was concerned to defend, and perhaps mitigate, the Humbert assertion of chewing (*atteri*) with the teeth. He argued that it meant to 'touch more closely', and just as Thomas touched the side of Christ, so the faithful can touch with their teeth the body of Christ, though Christ cannot be harmed or wounded.[46] Although the priest breaks the consecrated host, Christ cannot be broken into pieces. However, he also argued that the eucharistic presence was another post-resurrection appearance of the Lord. He wrote:

> But to us, however, that Eucharist, that divine manna, is the heavenly bread from God. For truly we receive from the sacred altars the flesh of the immaculate Lamb rendered incapable of suffering, through which we both live and are healed from corruption; this flesh can never be corrupted, nor perish, because, although from day to day it renews us, it itself never grows old.[47]

He asserted that although the change is difficult to comprehend since there is nothing remotely similar to the eucharistic change, it is a change of substance.[48] Alongside the use of substance, Guitmund also introduced the Aristotelian term 'accident' into his explanation, most probably drawing on Boethius.[49]

The scholarly debate and controversy continued to a point where Berengar was physically threatened at a council in Poitiers in 1075, which adopted the following statement of faith on the presence:

> that same bread and that same wine, after the consecration carried out there by the power of the Holy Spirit through the hand of the priest, is substantially transmuted [*substantialiter transmutatum*] into the true body and into the true blood of Christ – that is, into the very body that was born of the Virgin Mary, which suffered and was crucified for us, which rose from the dead, which sits at the right hand of God the Father, and into that same blood that flowed from his side as he hung on the cross, with no substance or nature of the bread and wine remaining beyond that likeness which we see with our bodily eyes, that we might not abhor the sacrament by reason of the horror of the blood.[50]

Berengar seemed to be on cordial terms with Pope Gregory VII, who was pressed to do something to stop the controversy, and he summoned Berengar to Rome in 1078/79, where Berengar was once again required to sign a confession of faith, though one that was far more careful in its language than was Humbert's oath. It was at this time that Alberic of Monte Cassino wrote his treatise against Berengar, affirming that the sacrament is not a figure, not a promise, not a signifying, but is truth. The bread and wine, 'losing their individual properties, are turned into Christ's flesh and blood'.[51] However, he ended by stressing that

46 Vaillancourt, *Lanfranc*, p. 12.

47 Vaillancourt, *Lanfranc*, p. 129.

48 Vaillancourt, *Lanfranc*, p. 117.

49 Vaillancourt, *Lanfranc*, p. 124, note 82.

50 The document was discovered in recent years by Robert Somerville and is cited in Radding and Newton, *Theology, Rhetoric, and Politics*, p. 27.

51 Vaillancourt, *Lanfranc*, p. 159.

although those who eat with the lips receive the body and blood of Christ, only its fruits are received by those who additionally eat with their hearts.[52] The 1079 confession that Berengar signed stated that the bread and wine placed on the altar,

> are through the mystery of the sacred prayer and the words of our Redeemer substantially changed into the true and proper and life-giving flesh and blood of Jesus Christ our Lord; and that after the consecration is the true body of Christ, which was born of the Virgin, as an offering for the salvation of the world hung on the cross, and sits at the right hand of the Father; and the true blood of Christ which flowed from his side; not only through the sign and power of the sacrament but in his proper nature and true substance.

The main concern was to insist that there were not several different bodies of Christ, but only one body, and that one body was truly received in the Eucharist as bread and wine.

One of the striking things about the works of this eleventh-century controversy was the virtual lack of reference to the liturgical rite itself. Another vocabulary and focus emerge, concerned with definitions and questions. Referring to the 1079 confession, Gary Macy commented:

> The oath demonstrated the technical expertise which had developed throughout the controversy. Here the technical terms of Aristotelian philosophy were introduced to describe the mode of presence which the Lord undertook in the sacrament. The sophistication which later theologians would develop as they rediscovered the use of Aristotelian concepts such as *substantia*, would continue to evolve new and more nuanced understandings of a sacramental terminology which would remain remarkably unchanged.[53]

The technical terms were used, but without agreed definition or full thought as to the possible philosophical ramifications. This growing sophistication may be illustrated by looking at the teachings of Hugh of St Victor and Peter Lombard.

Hugh of St Victor (1096–1141)

Hugh was a Paris theologian who wrote an extended work on the sacraments. Sacraments, he noted, were instituted by our first parents, since marriage itself is described as a *mysterion* in Scripture. According to Hugh, a sacrament is 'a corporeal or material element set before the senses without, representing by similitude and signifying by institution and containing by sanctification some invisible and spiritual grace'.[54] For something to be a sacrament, it must have a

52 Vaillancourt, *Lanfranc*, p. 169.

53 Gary Macy, *The Theologies of the Eucharist in the Early Scholastic Period*, Oxford: Clarendon Press, 1984, p. 37.

54 Roy J. Deferrari, *Hugh of Saint Victor on the Sacraments of the Christian Faith*, Cambridge, MA: Mediaeval Academy of America, 1951, p. 155.

similitude – something that makes it capable of representing the same thing; it must have an institution through which it is ordered to signify this thing; and it must have sanctification, through which it contains that thing and makes it efficacious. All divine sacraments are accomplished in threefold matter, namely, either in things or in deeds or in words.[55] For Hugh, and probably many of his contemporaries, there can be many sacraments and they include making the sign of the cross, blessing holy water and the ashes of Ash Wednesday. The Eucharist, Hugh noted, was instituted by Christ 'when after the supper of the old pasch, changing the bread and wine into His own body and blood by divine power, He gave it to His apostles to be eaten and He ordered that after this they should do the same in commemoration of Him'.[56] He asked whether at the supper this was his mortal or immortal body, and though he discussed each at length, noted that there is but one body of Christ. Probably with the Berengarian controversy in mind, he asserted that the sacrament can be both figure and truth, for 'although the sacrament is one, three distinct things are set forth there, namely, visible appearance, truth of body, and virtue of spiritual grace'.[57] He wrote:

> Through the words of sanctification the true substance of bread and the true substance of wine are changed into the true body and blood of Christ, the appearance of bread and wine alone remaining, substance passing over into substance. But the change itself is not to be believed to be according to union but according to transition, since by no means does essence add unto increase of essence, so that through what is added that to which is added becomes greater, but it happens by transition that what is added becomes one with that to which it is added.[58]

The fact that the bread is broken into parts does not mean that Christ is broken – for the whole is in each.[59] When you take it in your mouth, he is with the communicant corporeally, but Christ passes from the mouth to the heart.[60]

Peter Lombard (1100–60)

Peter Lombard became Archbishop of Paris and was a lasting influence in later medieval theology through his *Sententiae in IV Libris Distinctae*, which became the standard theological text of the thirteenth and fourteenth centuries. In the fourth book he turned to consider the nature of signs and sacraments. He combined the genuine Augustinian definition of a sacrament with that made popular by Berengar – it is a sign of a sacred thing and a visible form of an invisible grace.[61] He further defined it:

55 Deferrari, *Hugh of St Victor*, p. 163.
56 Deferrari, *Hugh of St Victor*, p. 304.
57 Deferrari, *Hugh of St Victor*, p. 308.
58 Deferrari, *Hugh of St Victor*, p. 310.
59 Deferrari, *Hugh of St Victor*, p. 312.
60 Deferrari, *Hugh of St Victor*, p. 314.
61 Peter Lombard, *Sentences*, Book 4.1.2, in Giulio Silano (trans.), *Peter Lombard: The Sentences. Book 4. On the Doctrine of Signs*, Toronto: Pontifical Institute of Mediaeval Studies,

> For a sacrament is properly so called because it is a sign of God's grace and a form of invisible grace in such a manner that it bears its image and is its cause. And so the sacraments were not instituted only for the sake of signifying, but also to sanctify.[62]

Although he was influenced by Hugh of St Victor, he departs from Hugh's insistence that there should be a 'corporeal or material element', and follows other contemporaries such as Master Simon of Flanders and Roland of Bologna in listing only seven sacraments.[63] For Lombard, a sacrament consists of words and things, and he makes a sharp distinction between sacraments of the Old Testament that promised and signified and those of the New that confer salvation.[64]

When discussing the sacrament of the altar, Lombard noted that it is called the Eucharist, 'because in this sacrament not only is there an increase of virtue and grace, but he who is the fount and origin of all grace is wholly received'.[65] In considering it further, he listed four things – its institution, form, sacrament and thing. It was instituted when, after the prefigured Paschal Lamb, he offered his body and blood to his disciples at the Supper. The form consists of the words of Jesus, 'This is my body, This is my blood', and 'when these words are pronounced, the change [*conversion*] of the bread and wine into the substance of the body and blood of Christ occurs; the rest [of the *canon missae*] is said to praise God'.[66] The bread and wine constitute the sacrament. The 'thing' is twofold. The thing contained and signified is the flesh of Christ, which he derived from the Virgin, and his blood; the thing signified and not contained is the unity of the Church. There are two ways of eating – sacramental, in which all those who receive partake, and the spiritual, which only the worthy partake of. Good and bad alike receive the sacramental body and blood, but only the good receive the 'mystical flesh'.[67] Lombard repudiated the idea that the body of Christ is only present in the sign; his body is invisible, veiled by the form of bread and wine.[68] Of the manner of the change, Lombard is cautious, suggesting he is not up to the task of defining it. It is not a formal but a substantial change. After considering different views on whether the substance of bread and wine still remain or change, he concluded that 'after the consecration the substance of bread and wine is not there, although the species remain, for the species of bread and wine are there, as indeed is their taste, so that one thing is seen and another is understood'.[69] On the fact that it is one sacrament but two species, he wrote:

2010, p. 3. See also Elizabeth Frances Rogers, *Peter Lombard and the Sacramental System*, Merrick: Richwood Publishing Company, [1917] 1976; Philipp W. Roseman, *Peter Lombard*, Oxford: Oxford University Press, 2004.

62 Lombard, 'Book 4.1.4', in Silano, *Lombard*, p. 4.

63 Marcia Colish, *Peter Lombard*, 2 vols, Leiden: Brill, 1994.

64 Lombard, 'Book 4.1.8', in Silano, *Lombard*, p. 6.

65 Lombard, 'Book 4.8.1', in Silano, *Lombard*, p. 41.

66 Lombard, 'Book 4.8.3', in Silano, *Lombard*, p. 42.

67 Lombard, 'Book 4.9.1–2', in Silano, *Lombard*, p. 47.

68 Lombard, 'Book 4.10.5–6', in Silano, *Lombard*, p. 51.

69 Lombard, 'Book 4.11.2', in Silano, *Lombard*, p. 57.

> And although the whole Christ is received under either species, yet the change of the bread is only into the flesh, and of the wine only into the blood. Nor are they to be called two sacraments, but one, because the same is received under both species; nor is the sacrament to be repeated, because the blessing is not repeated over the same species. Nor are other substances to be offered in the sacrifice of truth, because the body or blood of Christ cannot be consecrated from anything else.[70]

The 'accidents' or species are broken, but they are without subject; the subject, the body and blood of Christ, is impassible and is not broken; everyone receives the whole Christ.[71]

Lombard finally turned to the nature of the Eucharist as a sacrifice, and explained:

> what is offered and consecrated by the priest is called sacrifice and oblation, because it is a remembrance and representation of the true sacrifice and the holy immolation made on the altar of the cross. And indeed Christ died only once, namely on the cross, and there was immolated in himself; but he is daily immolated in the sacrament, because in the sacrament is made a remembrance of what was done once.[72]

The power of the sacrament is that it gives remission of sins and perfects virtue. Although, therefore, Lombard spent much time considering presence and change in the bread and wine, he also posits an eschatological and ecclesiological dimension to the sacrament, though again with little reference to the liturgy itself.

Women's voices

Liturgical texts and commentaries were something of a male monopoly, even if some were addressed to women.[73] A number of women did record their devotion to the Eucharist and the 'mystical' experience of communion. The Flemish mystic Hadewijch (*c.* 1220) wrote:

> Then he gave himself to me in the shape of the Sacrament, in its outward form, as the custom is; and then he gave me to drink from the chalice . . . After that he came himself to me, took me entirely in his arms, and pressed me to him; and all my members felt his in full felicity in accordance with the desire of my heart and my humanity. So I was outwardly satisfied and fully transported. And then, for a short while, I had the strength to bear this; but soon, after a short time, I lost that manly beauty outwardly in the sight of his form. I saw him completely come to nought and so fade and all at once dissolve that I could no

70 Lombard, 'Book 4.11.4', in Silano, *Lombard*, p. 58.

71 This is also the basis of concomitance, that the whole Christ is received in either of the elements. See James Megivern, *Concomitance and Communion: A Study in Eucharistic Doctrine and Practice*, New York: Herder Book Center, 1963.

72 Lombard, 'Book 4.12.5', in Silano, *Lombard*, p. 64.

73 Caroline Walker Bynum, *Fragmentation and Redemption: Essays on Gender and the Human Body in Medieval Religion*, New York: Zone Books, 1991, p. 124.

> longer recognize or perceive him outside me, and I could no longer distinguish him within me. Then it was to me as if we were one without difference.[74]

In the second part of the *Scivias*, Hildegard of Bingen (1098–1179) reflected more theologically using the analogy of the incarnation. God said to her:

> as Divinity displayed its wonders in the womb of the Virgin, it shows its secrets also in this oblation. How? Because here are manifested the body and blood of the Son of God . . . For as the body of my Son came about in the womb of the Virgin, so now the body of My Only-Begotten arises from the sanctification of the altar.[75]

She sees an analogy between Mary and the priest, and God interprets this to her:

> when the priest does his office as is appointed him, invoking Me in sacred words, I am there in power, just as I was there when My Only-Begotten, without discord or stain, became incarnate.[76]

Hildegard acknowledged that women cannot be ordained, but it is possible that in some religious orders women presided over an order of communion, probably communicating from previously consecrated elements. Jean Leclercq has drawn attention to a manuscript (*c.* 1100) from Monte Cassino, and some others that seem to have derived from it.[77] All the prayers are in the first person singular, and in one manuscript, they are all in the feminine. He concluded:

> What we have here is incorporation of communion in the Body and Blood of the Lord into a celebration during the course of which the eucharistic mystery, such as it was conceived by the piety of the tenth and eleventh centuries, is evoked in all its fullness.[78]

Though nowhere near as loud as the male hegemony, women's voices were not entirely drowned out in Western eucharistic thought and devotion.

The thirteenth-century consolidation

The commentaries and theologies of the thirteenth century need to be understood against the backdrop of a number of interrelated developments concerning the Eucharist.

---

74 Columba Hart, *Hadewijch: The Complete Works*, New York: Paulist Press, 1980, pp. 280–1.

75 Hildegard of Bingen, *Scivias*, trans. Columba Hart and Jane Bishop, New York: Paulist Press, 1990, 2.6.12–14.

76 Hildegard of Bingen, *Scivias*, 2.6.34.

77 Jean Leclercq, 'Eucharistic Celebrations without Priests in the Middle Ages', *Worship* 55 (1981), pp. 160–8.

78 Leclercq, 'Eucharistic Celebrations', p. 167; Gary Macy, *Treasures from the Storeroom: Medieval Religion and the Eucharist*, Collegeville: Liturgical Press, 1999, pp. 174–5.

1 The term substance had been used by an increasing number of theologians to describe the nature of Christ's presence in the Eucharist. It seems to have been one of those terms that many people 'understood', but without there being any precise doctrinal definition or explanation. The term came to be used in a confession drawn up by the Fourth Lateran Council in 1215, condemning the Albigensian heresy that denied the sacramental presence:

> There is one universal Church of the faithful, outside which, no one at all is in a state of salvation. In this Church, Jesus Christ Himself is both priest and sacrifice; and His body and blood are really contained in the Sacrament of the altar under the species of bread and wine, the bread being transubstantiated into the body and the wine into the blood by the power of God, so that, to effect the mystery of unity, we ourselves receive of that which is His what He Himself received of that which is ours. And, moreover, no one can consecrate this Sacrament except a priest who has been duly ordained to the keys of the Church, which Jesus Christ Himself gave to the Apostles and their successors.[79]

The term is not defined, but was perceived to have an official status.

2 The early liturgical texts were prayer texts, and gave few if any directions. It has already been noted how the *Ordines Romani* are documents that describe and prescribe gestures and ceremonial. One practice that arose was during the *canon missae* to elevate the bread and wine, which became inextricably linked with the question of precisely when did the consecration of the elements take place? V. L. Kennedy argued that three schools of thought can be identified between 1160 and 1210: those like Peter Manducator who refused to determine an exact moment of consecration; those such as Peter Cantor and Richard Cousin, who argued that consecration was complete only after the words spoken over both bread and cup; and the view expressed by those such as Peter of Poitiers, that the words over the bread were sufficient for the bread.[80] It was important to be exact, since people venerated the species, and it would be idolatry to venerate unconsecrated elements. A definition from Paris, usually attributed to Odo of Sully (Bishop of Paris, 1196–1208) confirmed and promoted the elevation of the Host to be made immediately after the recital of Christ's words concerning the bread.[81] It appears that a growing custom already in the twelfth century was to signal the consecration and elevation of the elements by ringing bells, raising lighted tapers and censing the elements. Whatever the precise date, these rituals became a growing practice in the thirteenth century.[82] By this time it was the practice to recite

79 As cited in Darwell Stone, *A History of the Doctrine of the Eucharist*, vol. I, London: Longmans, 1909, p. 313.

80 V. L. Kennedy, 'The Moment of Consecration and the Elevation of the Host', *Mediaeval Studies* 6 (1944), pp. 121–50.

81 For the problem of identifying this with Odo, see V. L. Kennedy, 'The Date of the Parisian Decree on the Elevation of the Host', *Mediaeval Studies* 8 (1946), pp. 87–96.

82 For further decrees, see Stone, *History of the Doctrine of the Eucharist*, pp. 353–6.

the *canon missae* silently – or at least so that the congregation could not hear it, other than for the recital or singing of the Sanctus. The elevation became the high point of the Mass, and given the medieval belief that sight was the most important sense for the soul, lay people preferred to see the consecrated elements rather than to receive them.[83] Even in the time of John Chrysostom, many lay people were reluctant to receive communion regularly, probably on account of the clergy insisting on worthy reception, which meant abstinence from sex and many other things. This was intensified in the medieval West, with communion being usually only three times a year, after receiving absolution through the sacrament of confession. Furthermore, for fear of spilling the wine, communion for the laity was restricted to bread only.

3 With growing devotion to the consecrated elements, miraculous stories of bleeding hosts and miracles brought about by the consecrated elements abounded. Doubters in the real presence were confronted with the bread turning into flesh.[84] These stories were impressed on the psyche of the laity, as typified by the mid-fifteenth-century miracle play, *The Croxton Play of the Sacrament*, in which the clerical Words of Institution are uttered by Jonathas the Jew as a gesture of profanity. The 'consecrated' host is then abused, only for the resurrected Christ to emerge and the doubters be converted.[85] This cumulative devotion together with the theological reflection had led to the institution of the feast of Corpus Christi. The feast is recorded as celebrated in 1246 in Liège, and was so popular that in 1264 Pope Urban IV ordered it to be kept throughout the Western Church.[86] The Bull ordering it stated:

> O most excellent Sacrament, to be adored, to be venerated, to be worshipped, to be glorified, to be extolled with highest praise, to be exalted by worthy oratory, to be honoured with all zeal, to be celebrated with devout observance, to be held fast by pure minds . . . This memorial ought to be continually celebrated, that we may be ever mindful of Him whose memorial we know it to be, because, the more often His gift is seen, the more firmly is the memory of Him retained. Therefore, although this memorial Sacrament is already celebrated in the daily observance of Mass, yet we think it fitting and worthy that at least once in the year, specially to overthrow the perfidy and madness of heretics, there be a more solemn and notable memory.[87]

83 Suzannah Biernoff, *Sight and Embodiment in the Middle Ages*, Basingstoke: Palgrave Macmillan, 2002, for the views of Bacon and Ockham on the eye and vision. Alexander of Hales articulated the two kinds of 'eating': eating by taste and eating by sight. One could touch and embrace the Saviour with one's bodily eyes.

84 See Miri Rubin, *Corpus Christ: The Eucharist in Late Medieval Culture*, Cambridge: Cambridge University Press, 1991; Caroline Walker Bynum, *Wonderful Blood: Theology and Practice in Late Medieval Germany and Beyond*, Philadelphia: University of Pennsylvania Press, 2007.

85 See Sarah Beckwith, 'Ritual, Church and Theatre: Medieval Dramas of the Sacramental Body', in David Aers (ed.), *Culture and History 1300–1600*, Wheatsheaf, NY: Harvester, 1992, pp. 65–89. For the text of the play, John C. Coldeway, *Early English Drama: An Anthology*, New York and London: Garland Publishing, Inc., 1993, pp. 274–305.

86 See Rubin, *Corpus Christi*; and Martin Dudley, 'Liturgy and Doctrine: Corpus Christi', *Worship* 66 (1992), pp. 417–26.

87 Cited in Stone, *History of the Doctrine of the Eucharist*, I, p. 345.

4 The growth of the Frankish Church coincided with a need for more monks to be ordained priest, and this helped fuel a devotional need for priests to celebrate the Mass daily, as their 'private Mass'. Linked with votive Masses – Masses celebrated, or offered for special intentions – the idea developed that the Mass, since it was a sacrifice, could be offered for many things, including the release of souls in purgatory. The concept of sacrifice in the Eucharist, as we have noted, seems to have been present very early, with reference to Malachi 1.11, though the details of how it was a sacrifice were left vague. The medieval Western theologians developed and defined the nature of sacrifice, so that Masses were offered and payment for such offerings became important clerical revenue.

All these factors are important in their own right, and cannot be developed in detail here, but they provide the backdrop for thirteenth-century reflections on the liturgy and the sacrament of the altar.

The development of the eucharistic liturgy from the sacramentary, which needed a variety of other books for the celebration of the liturgy, to the Missal, which contained everything a priest needed for saying Mass, was the result of the private need of ordained monks and other religious. The *Ordo Missae* seems to have evolved first by expansion with private prayers of the celebrant and then reformed by the removal of many of these towards a standardization under the pontificate of Pope Gregory VII (1073–85). Three types are generally identified: the Apology type, the Frankish type and the Rhenish type.[88] The last is regarded as a significant stage in the evolution of the rite.[89] Some of the features found in this type are as follows:

- Psalms 83, 84, 85 at the beginning, with prayers for vesting and handwashing.
- Prayer at the Introit: Psalm 42.
- Apologia during the Gloria.
- Prayer at the incense for the Gospel.
- Offertory prayers and *Orate fratres*.
- Psalms during the Sanctus and Canon (Psalms 19, 24, 50, 89, 90).
- Prayer during the Commixture.
- Prayer at the Peace.
- Prayer at Communion.
- Prayer and Post-Communion.
- Psalm 150 and Benedicite (Dan. 3).

Some standardization by removal of some of these was undertaken in the reforms of Pope Gregory VII. It would seem that later still, in 1243, the General of the Franciscans, Haymo of Faversham, submitted to his religious order an earlier *ordo* used by the Papal Curia which they adopted; through the Franciscans,

88 Joanne M. Pierce, 'The Evolution of the *Ordo Missae* in the Early Middle Ages', in Larson-Miller (ed.), *Medieval Liturgy*, pp. 3–24.

89 Andreas Odenthal, *Liturgie vom Frühen Mittelalter zum Zeitalter der Konfessionalisierung*, Tübingen: Mohr Siebeck, 2011, pp. 16–49. I am grateful to Professor Harald Buchinger for drawing my attention to this work.

Roman Curial Use was exported across Europe, and Curial Use would displace other Roman Uses.[90]

Further development and osmosis continued with additions and duplications, particularly at liturgical 'soft points' to produce the Romano-Western synthesis of the *Ordo Missae* which existed in a variety of diocesan, monastic and local Uses.[91] This can be illustrated from two of the primary late medieval English Uses, Sarum (Salisbury) and York.[92]

SARUM	YORK
Veni Creator Spiritus, and versicle and response.	*Grant to our understandings.*
O God to whom every heart.	
Antiphon and Psalm 43 antiphon.	
Kyrie, Lord's Prayer and Hail Mary.	
	Our actions, O Lord.
	Incline your holy ears.
Introit.	
Confessions and absolutions.	
Our help is in the Name of the Lord, etc.	
Kiss of Peace between ministers.	

90 S. J. P. Van Dijk and J. Hazelden Walker, *The Origins of the Modern Roman Liturgy*, London: Darton, Longman and Todd, 1960, esp. pp. 156–76; Joanne M. Pierce and John F. Romano, 'The Ordo Missae of the Roman Rite: Historical Background', in Edward Foley (ed.), *A Commentary on the Order of Mass of the Roman Missal*, Collegeville: Liturgical Press, 2011, pp. 3–33, esp. 23–5. By 1275 the city of Rome knew the liturgical uses or customs of the papal court, St Peter's in the Vatican, the reform of Cardinal Orsini, and the Lateran Basilica.

91 Edward Foley, 'A Tale of Two Sanctuaries: Late Medieval Eucharist and the Analogous', in Levy, Macy and Van Ausdall (eds), *Companion to the Eucharist in the Middle Ages*, pp. 327–63, contrasting Notre Dame, Paris, with the monastery of St Denis. For the development of the *Ordo Missae*, see Joanne M. Pierce, 'Evolution of the *Ordo Missae*'.

92 For the development of Uses in England, Richard W. Pfaff, *The Liturgy in Medieval England: A History*, Cambridge: Cambridge University Press, 2009. The Latin texts are in William Maskell, *The Ancient Liturgy of the Church of England*, Oxford: Clarendon Press, 1882 (reprint New York: AMS, 1973). ET: 'The Sarum Missal', http://justus.anglican.org/resources/bcp/Sarum/English.htm, and 'York Missal', http://anglicanhistory.org/liturgy/yorkmissal.pdf. See also Philip Baxter, *Sarum Use: The Ancient Customs of Salisbury*, Reading: Spire Books Ltd, 2008; P. S. Barnwell, Claire Cross, and Ann Rycraft, *Mass and Parish in Late Medieval England: The Use of York*, Reading: Spire Books Ltd, 2005.

Take away from us O Lord all iniquities.

In the name of the Father etc.

Kyrie.

Gloria in excelsis.

Collect.

Epistle.

Gradual.

Alleluia.

Gospel.

Creed.

Offertory is sung or said.

Accept O Holy Trinity.

May this [Sarum: 'new'] sacrifice.

Lavabo.

Cleanse me O Lord. *Veni creator spiritus.*

In the Spirit of humility.

In the name of the Father etc. May this sacrifice be signed.

Pray brothers and sisters.

May the grace of the Holy Spirit.

Canon missae.

Lord's Prayer.

Embolism.

Fraction.

Graciously grant peace.

Peace.

Agnus Dei.

Commixture.

O Lord, Holy Father.	

Passing the Peace (Pax board) [*different formulae*].

O God the father, the fountain and origin of all.	O Lord Holy Father of all.

O Lord Jesus Christ.

Various communion prayers.	Various communion prayers.

Communion.

Post-Communion.

Dismissal.

Closing Prayer.	Blessing of the people.
Last Gospel: John1.1–14.	Prayers and devotions including Benedicite, Ps.150 and Nunc Dimittis.

The comparison illustrates the considerable body of material in common, and the variations concentrated around the 'soft points'. The priest's private preparation at the beginning again has some material in common, but varied from Use to Use and also over time. Certain missals have a large number of private *apologiae* prayers for the priest prior to the public rite, and these proliferated in the eleventh century, but then declined and transmuted into a core preparation with a Confiteor and absolution.[93] The preparation was in some places recited in the sacristy, in others en route to the altar, and in others yet at the foot of the altar. The offertory prayers recited by the priest in these two English Uses are limited to two, whereas at Rome there were seven, which, apart from the old Roman secret, were mostly derived from Gallican and Hispano-Mozarabic sources.[94]

93 Adrien Nocent, 'Les apologies dans la celebration eucharistique', in A. Pistoia and A. M. Triacca (eds), *Liturgie et Rémission des Péchés*, Rome: Edizioni Liturgiche, 1975, pp. 179–96. The Sacramentary of Moissac has 43 apologiae.

94 For details, G. G. Willis, *Essays in Early Roman Liturgy*, London: SPCK, 1964, pp. 107–10; Paul Tirot, 'Histoire des Prières d'Offertoire dans la Liturgie Romaine du VIIè au XVIè siècle', *Ephemerides Liturgicae* 98 (1984), pp. 323–91.

They tended to pre-empt the *canon missae* itself, and came to be called the 'little canon'.[95] Rome was the last place in the West to include the Creed in its rite, Pope Benedict VIII ordering it to be sung at the instigation of Emperor Henry II. The private communion prayers of the priest were also variable, and the devotions after the dismissal. Sarum, as later Rome, had the Last Gospel, but this does not occur in the York Use. The York *canon missae* added 'atque omnium fidelium Christianorum' to the *Memento, Domine.*

Probably the most famous commentary on the Mass of this period was the *Rationale Divinorum Officiorum* of William Durandus (1230–96). He was an expert in both canon and civil law, and became a member of the papal court, and later Bishop of Mende. In his work on the symbolism of the church and its furnishings, he commented also on the Mass. For Durandus this sacrament represents the feast of the Church for which the Father killed the fatted calf in order to celebrate the return of the Son, 'wherein He offered Him the bread of life and the wine mixed with wisdom'.[96] Jesus being a priest according to the order of Melchizedek instituted the Mass when he transformed (*transmutavit*) the bread and wine into his body and blood by saying, 'This is my body', 'This is my blood', and by adding 'Do this in memory of me'. Like Isaac of Stella, he finds three sacrifices of the Church prefigured in the Old Testament, though they differ from Isaac's: of penitence, of justice and the Eucharist, and these are enacted in the Mass. Durandus explained:

> Now the priest offers these three sacrifices in the Mass: the first in the *Confiteor*, the second in the *Preface* and the third in the *Act of Grace* (or *Consecration*).[97]

The Mass makes present the passion, death, burial, resurrection and ascension of Christ, and every part of it represents something. Thus, the Introit is related to the choir of prophets, the Kyries with prophets such as Zachariah and John the Baptist, and the first Collect is connected with the incident of the child Jesus visiting the Temple and teaching the Jewish teachers. Of the Offertory to the canon he explained:

> The prayer which we call the *Secret* up to the *Nobis quoque peccatoribus* is designated as that prayer which Jesus said on the Mount of Olives. And what follows after signifies the time that our Lord spent lying in the sepulcher. When one puts the host in the wine, it shows that the soul of God returned to his body. The greeting which follows signifies the graces which Christ gave to His disciples. The breaking of the bread (*oblatae*) represents the breaking of the bread by Our Lord with the disciples at Emmaus.[98]

---

95 The theology is discussed in Kenneth Stevenson, *Eucharist and Offering*, New York: Pueblo Press, 1986, pp. 112–16.

96 Guilielmus Durandus, *The Rationale Divinorum Officiorum*, Louisville: Fons Vitae, 2007, p. 233.

97 Durandus, *Rationale Divinorum Officiorum*, p. 240.

98 Durandus, *Rationale Divinorum Officiorum*, p. 250.

The detailed commentary on the *canon missae* found meanings in the gestures of the celebrant as well as in the words of the prayer. The Eucharist is a sacrifice, the victim is consumed, and it brings the divine presence and forgiveness to the communicant.

Important contributions on sacraments and the Eucharist were made by Duns Scotus, William Ockham and Giles of Rome among others, though here we shall confine our consideration to Bonaventure and Thomas Aquinas.[99]

Bonaventure (1221–74)

Bonaventure became Cardinal Bishop of Albano and Minister General of the Friars Minor. As with other thirteenth-century theologians, we find much more precise use of Aristotelian terms and arguments. In Part VI of his *Breviloquium*, Bonaventure considered sacraments as remedies through which 'beneath the cloak of material species God's power operates in a hidden manner'; so that, 'being likenesses, they represent; from their mode of institution, they signify; being made holy, they are means of conferring a certain spiritual grace' by which the soul is healed of its weaknesses due to vice.[100] Furthermore:

> But because in themselves the sensible signs [of the sacraments] cannot produce any effect in the order of grace, although they are by nature distant representations of grace, it was necessary that the Author of grace INSTITUTE [appoint] them for the sake of signifying and BLESS them for the sake of sanctifying; so that through natural similitude they would represent, through conjoined institution they would signify, and through superadded benediction they would sanctify and prepare for grace, by which our soul is healed and cured.[101]

There are seven sacraments, instituted by God,

> in both material elements and words, in order to signify more clearly and to sanctify more effectively. For when, through sight and hearing – the most informative of the senses – these elements are seen and these words heard, they clearly reveal the meaning of the sign itself. Also, the words sanctify the material elements and make them more effective for the healing of man.[102]

It is against this definition that the Eucharist is expounded. Under two species of bread and wine, not only represented but also contained is the body and blood of Christ. Echoing Lombard, he stated:

99 See the detailed study of Aquinas, Scotus, Ockham and Giles in Marilyn McCord Adams, *Some Later Medieval Theories of the Eucharist*, Oxford: Oxford University Press, 2010. Aristotelian terms and analysis are ever deepened. See also Pierre-Marie Gy, 'La relation au Christ dans l'Eucharistie selon S. Bonaventure et S. Thomas d'Aquin', in Pierre-Marie Gy (ed.), *La Liturgie dans l'Histoire*, Paris: Cerf, 1990, pp. 247–83.

100 http://www.agnuz.info/tl_files/library/books/Bonaventure_breviloquium/.

101 http://www.agnuz.info/tl_files/library/books/Bonaventure_breviloquium/ (1.3).

102 http://www.agnuz.info/tl_files/library/books/Bonaventure_breviloquium/.

> This is brought about through consecration of the priest, using the vocal form instituted by the Lord: over the bread, '[For] this is My body'; over the wine, '[For] this is the chalice of My blood . . .' When these words are said by the priest with the intention of consecrating, the substance of the elements is transubstantiated into the body and the blood of Christ. While the species remain unchanged in their sensible form, both contain the whole Christ, not as confining Him in space, but sacramentally. Under these same species, He is offered to us as sustainment. Whoever receives it worthily, eating not merely in fact but also spiritually through faith and love, is more fully incorporated into the mystical body of Christ, being also refreshed and cleansed in himself.[103]

In the Eucharist God gave us this sacrament of the Holy Eucharist as a sacrificial offering, as a sacramental union and as sustainment on the way. The body and blood of Christ had to be present in this sacrament, not only figuratively but in reality, as a gift to suit the time. 'This sacrament contains the true body and immaculate flesh of Christ, in such a way that it penetrates our being, unites us to one another and transforms us into Him through that burning love by which He gave Himself to us [in the incarnation], offered Himself up for us [in the passion], and now gives Himself back to us, to remain with us until the end of the world.'[104] Bonaventure is less reticent than Lombard in explaining the nature of the change:

> And because Christ was to be present under these species by means of a change occurring not in Himself but in them, therefore when the two aforementioned formulas are pronounced, indicating the presence of Christ under the species, there occurs a change of substance of both into His body and blood, while the accidents alone remain as signs containing and expressing them.

His one reference to the liturgy concerned its solemnity in place, time, words, prayers and vestments, 'so that both the celebrating priests and the communicants may realize the gift of grace through which they are cleansed, enlightened, perfected, restored, vivified, and most ardently transformed into Christ by rapturous love'.[105]

Thomas Aquinas (1225–74)

Aquinas was the towering figure of medieval scholastic theology and later would have a crucial place in Roman Catholic theology. He gave full treatments to sacraments and the Eucharist in his *Summa Theologiae*. David Power writes:

> Thomas took some ritual developments for granted, for example, the silent recitation of the canon and the separation of the prefatory thanksgiving from

103 http://www.agnuz.info/tl_files/library/books/Bonaventure_breviloquium/ (9.1).
104 http://www.agnuz.info/tl_files/library/books/Bonaventure_breviloquium/ (9.5).
105 http://www.agnuz.info/tl_files/library/books/Bonaventure_breviloquium/ (9.7).

> the rest of the rest of the great prayer. He was familiar with the offering of Mass for the living and the dead. He explained the relative infrequency of communion by appealing to the difference in zeal and faith between his own time and that of the early church. He knew of the practice of giving communion in one kind only and of the use of spiritual communion as distinct from sacramental. One of his questions has to do with miraculous apparitions of Christ in the host, and he looked for reasons why other materials may not be substituted for wheaten bread and grape wine. Finally, in explaining the prayers and actions of the priest celebrating, he drew to a moderate extent on expositions of the Mass and on the canon that guided catechesis on the Mass for the people. Liturgical reform was not on his agenda. His interest was rather in a good explanation of the sacrament as known to his times, settling disputed theological questions, and explaining how all aspects of the sacrament and its celebration held together in an organic intelligibility.[106]

One of his concerns, shared by his other scholastic contemporaries, was with the question of place and space and how this related to Christ and the sacrament.[107]

For Aquinas, sacraments belong to the general category of signs. Sacraments can be considered, first, from the sanctifying cause which is the incarnate Word; second, from the aspect of humans who are sanctified by them; and third, from the aspect of the actual signification itself.[108] Establishing that the Eucharist is indeed a sacrament, there are three things to be considered, 'that which is sacrament only, and this is the bread and wine; that which is both reality and sacrament, to wit, Christ's true body; and lastly that which is reality only, namely the effect of the sacrament'.[109] The matter (material) are wheat unleavened bread and grape wine. On the question of presence, he asserted that the presence cannot be detected by sense, nor understanding, but by faith alone.[110] The presence does not begin by local motion, since Christ is present in several places in the sacrament, and so it has to be a change of substance and the substance of the bread and wine cannot remain.[111] The change is not like natural changes but is entirely supernatural, and effected by God's power alone:

> And this is done by Divine power in this sacrament; for the whole substance of the bread is changed into the whole substance of Christ's body, and the whole substance of the wine into the whole substance of Christ's blood. Hence this is not a formal, but a substantial conversion; nor is it a kind of natural movement: but, with a name of its own, it can be called 'transubstantiation'.[112]

---

106 David N. Power, *The Eucharistic Mystery: Revitalizing the Tradition*, New York: Crossroad, 1994, pp. 217–18.

107 See McCord Adams, *Some Later Medieval Theories*, pp. 19–20. The introductory chapter in this work is a very helpful explanation of the Aristotelian terminologies.

108 Thomas Aquinas, *Summa Theologica*, 3a.60.1, New Advent, http://www.newadvent.org/summa/index.html (Hereafter *ST*).

109 *ST* 3a.7.

110 *ST* 3a.75.1.

111 *ST* 3a.75.2.

112 *ST* 3a.75.4.

The accidents of the bread and wine remain after the consecration, by Divine providence. Indeed, for Aquinas, since in Aristotelian thought an accident cannot exist without its substance, what happens in the Eucharist is a miracle, by the active power of the Creator. The entire body of Christ is contained under the bread and wine.[113] He argued:

> The place in which Christ's body is, is not empty; nor yet is it properly filled with the substance of Christ's body, which is not there locally, as stated above; but it is filled with the sacramental species, which have to fill the place either because of the nature of dimensions, or at least miraculously, as they also subsist miraculously after the fashion of substance.[114]

The form of consecration are the words of Christ referring to the bread and wine, and the consecration of the bread is effected as soon as the words 'this is my body' are said. The sacrament works in humanity the effect that Christ's passion wrought in the world. Through instrumental causes – the signs, the priest and Christ – grace is mediated to the communicant. The reality of the sacrament is charity. The Eucharist is also a sacrifice, since it is commemorative of our Lord's passion, which was a true sacrifice. Aquinas appealed to the *canon missae* to show that the Eucharist is both offered as a sacrifice and consecrated and received as a sacrament:

> Then, regarding the consecration, performed by supernatural power, the people are first of all excited to devotion in the 'Preface,' hence they are admonished 'to lift up their hearts to the Lord,' and therefore when the 'Preface' is ended the people devoutly praise Christ's Godhead, saying with the angels: 'Holy, Holy, Holy'; and His humanity, saying with the children: 'Blessed is he that cometh.' In the next place the priest makes a 'commemoration,' first of those for whom this sacrifice is offered, namely, for the whole Church, and 'for those set in high places,' and, in a special manner, of them 'who offer, or for whom the mass is offered.' Secondly, he commemorates the saints, invoking their patronage for those mentioned above, when he says: 'Communicating with, and honoring the memory,' etc. Thirdly, he concludes the petition when he says: 'Wherefore that this oblation,' etc., in order that the oblation may be salutary to them for whom it is offered.
>
> Then he comes to the consecration itself. Here he asks first of all for the effect of the consecration, when he says: 'Which oblation do Thou, O God,' etc. Secondly, he performs the consecration using our Saviour's words, when he says: 'Who the day before,' etc. Thirdly, he makes excuse for his presumption in obeying Christ's command, saying: 'Wherefore, calling to mind,' etc. Fourthly, he asks that the sacrifice accomplished may find favor with God, when he says: 'Look down upon them with a propitious,' etc. Fifthly, he begs for the effect of this sacrifice and sacrament, first for the partakers, saying: 'We humbly beseech Thee'; then for the dead, who can no longer receive it, saying: 'Be mindful also, O Lord,' etc.; thirdly, for the

113 *ST* 3a.76.1.
114 *ST* 3a.76.5.

> priests themselves who offer, saying: 'And to us sinners,' etc. Then follows the act of receiving the sacrament.[115]

David Power usefully summarizes Aquinas's eschatological dimension of the Eucharist:

> The faithful are brought to join in Christ's offering through the prayers of the priest, but it is primarily in communion that they are made beneficiaries of the fruit of the passion. There they receive the grace that nourishes them in their lives of faith, offers a remedy for sin, uplifts them with the sweet inebriation of Christ's love, and joins them together in the one body in Christ, in foretaste of eternal communion with the Word.[116]

Dissident theologies and liturgies: Wyclif, Hus and the Utraquists

Not all theologians and clerics were privately convinced of the emerging official eucharistic beliefs. Guibert of Nogent (*c.* 1060–*c.* 1125), for example, questioned the Church's teachings on the eucharistic presence and originally wrote views that were heterodox. Subsequently he rewrote the offending sections portraying the heterodoxy as being not his own but the views of an unnamed adversary.[117] Later medieval philosophers knew that transubstantiation contravened Aristotelian thought and logic, and Aquinas justifies the accidents of bread and wine continuing to exist without their own substance by appealing to God's power and miracle. Other divines were prepared to explain the difficulty and to point out that 'consubstantiation' would be more logical. Duns Scotus had argued that it is possible in the abstract to hold that the substance of the body of Christ is present alongside the remaining substance of the bread and wine. This was also the case with the Franciscan Nominalist theologian William Ockham, who argued that it was more reasonable for the substance of the bread and wine to remain, 'apart from the decision of the Church to the contrary'. Both accepted the doctrine of transubstantiation on the grounds of church authority and teaching. However, the fourteenth-century Oxford theologian John Wyclif became an outspoken critic of the power of priests in confession, and became critical of the doctrine of transubstantiation. On philosophical grounds concerning real universals and that no real thing can be annihilated, he openly rejected the doctrine and retired from Oxford under a cloud in 1381. The Council of Blackfriars in 1382 accused him of holding three particular heretical views on the Eucharist:

115 *ST* 3a.83.4.

116 Power, *Eucharistic Mystery*, p. 236.

117 Guibert of Nogent, *Monodies and On the Relics of Saints*, ed. Joseph McAlhany, trans. Jay Rubenstein, New York: Penguin Books, 2011, p. xxi and pp. 227–36.

1 The sacrament of the Eucharist is, by its nature, a body of bread and of wine, which has within it, by virtue of the sacramental words, the true body of Christ at its every point.
2 The sacrament of the Eucharist is *figuratively* the body and blood of Christ, in which the bread and wine are transubstantiated, and of which something remains after consecration. But in the opinion of the faithful this is sophistry.
3 That there is an accident without a subject is without foundation. But if it were so, then God would be annihilated and an article of the Christian faith would perish.[118]

As Penn points out, the first avoids the term transubstantiation, the second uses the term figuratively without any hint of conversion, and the third makes it clear that the subject of the bread and wine must remain, though Wyclif himself never used the term consubstantiation.[119] In his *Trialogus*, he wrote: 'This venerable Sacrament is in its own nature real bread, and is sacramentally the body of Christ', and:

> It is not to be understood that the body of Christ comes down to the host which is consecrated in any Church, but it remains above in heaven fixed and unmoved; therefore it has spiritual being in the host and not dimensional being and the other accidents which are in heaven.[120]

Wyclif never denied the real presence and, although he had discussed the work of Berengar, was not a Berengarian. He retired to his rectory in Lutterworth and died two years later. Only in the fifteenth century was he condemned as a heretic and his remains were burnt. As far as it is known, Wyclif never advocated liturgical changes or reforms. It has been suggested that his later followers, the Lollards, did, and Anne Hudson has suggested that William Ramsbury, who was prosecuted before the Bishop of Salisbury for having undergone invalid ordination and illegally celebrating a form of Mass in the diocese of Salisbury, was a Lollard priest celebrating a Lollard Mass.[121] More recently, Richard Rex has suggested that in fact since Ramsbury was also accused of illicit sex, and the moral purity of clergy was a constant Lollard demand, the 'priest' Ramsbury was a con man, gaining money from saying illicit Masses, and far from being Lollard emendations of the Sarum Use, the omissions covered the man's lack of real knowledge of the rite.[122]

118 From the *Fasciculi Zizaniorum*, cited by Stephen Penn, 'Wyclif and the Sacraments', in Ian Christopher Levy (ed.), *A Companion to John Wyclif: Late Medieval Theologian*, Leiden: Brill, 2006, pp. 251–2.

119 Penn, 'Wyclif and the Sacraments', p. 252.

120 Cited in Stone, *History of the Doctrine of the Eucharist*, I, p. 367. See also the Confessions of Wyclif and the Lollard Confessions on the Eucharist in Anne Hudson, *English Wycliffite Writings*, Cambridge: Cambridge University Press, 1978.

121 Anne Hudson, 'A Lollard Mass', *Journal of Theological Studies* 23 (1972), pp. 407–19.

122 Richard Rex, 'Not a Lollard Mass after All?', *Journal of Theological Studies* 62 (2011), pp. 207–17.

If Wycliffite/Lollard eucharistic liturgies are elusive, the Hus connection and the Bohemian Ultraquists are less so. Jan Hus taught at Charles University, Prague, and eventually became rector. Jerome of Prague (a friend of Hus's) had brought back Wyclif's works, *Dialogus*, *Trialogus* and *De Eucharistia*, from Oxford, where he had studied from 1399 to 1401. Wyclif's works quickly spread throughout Bohemia and they grew in popularity. Hus himself was extremely critical of clerical power, was a proponent of reform and made himself unpopular. He was summoned to the Council of Constance, where he was condemned for heresy and burnt. He had defended some of Wyclif's teaching on authority and ecclesiastical power, though there is little evidence that he accepted Wyclif's eucharistic ideas. Out of Hus's condemnation came the Bohemian movement, which demanded communion in both kinds, with the chalice being restored to the laity; this coalesced with an earlier Bohemian movement for more frequent communion. Splits resulted in the more radical Toborite movement, which demanded radical reforms.

The studies of David Holeton on the much neglected Czech liturgies of the Utraquists do not suggest any immediate programme of liturgical reform, and until the sixteenth century all manuscript witnesses point to a continuing fidelity to medieval liturgical use with very few innovations.[123] Some parishes continued to use the Catholic rite in Latin, others in Latin and Czech, and others still all in Czech. One main innovation was the use of hymnody – again, both in Latin and in Czech. However, in the sixteenth-century transcription of the *Altar Book of Adam Táborský*, there are three Masses: High Mass, in Latin and in Czech, and an abbreviated sung Mass for an early celebration.[124] The deviation from the Catholic rite is concentrated in the offertory prayers. These have been moved forward in the service, after the singing of the prose and just before the Gospel. Just as the seven offertory prayers of the Roman rite anticipate the *canon missae*, so do these new compositions of the Utraquists. In the abbreviated Mass, the anticipation becomes replacement. After one of the new offertory prayers, 'Come, Almighty Sanctifier', the following rubric and text appear:

> *Once again, take the first sacrament in hand along with the ciborium; take the oblations – that is some of the small hosts – in hand and say:*
>
> Our Lord Jesus Christ, on the night he was betrayed took bread and when he had given + thanks, broke it and gave it to his disciples saying take and eat, this is my body which will be given for you. Whenever you eat this bread, you do it in memory of me.

123 David R. Holeton, 'Sacramental and Liturgical Reform in Late Mediaeval Bohemia', *Studia Liturgica* 17 (1987), pp. 87–96; David R. Holeton, 'The Evolution of Utraquist Liturgy: A Precursor of Western Liturgical Reform', *Studia Liturgica* 25 (1995), pp. 51–67; David R. Holeton, 'The Bohemian Eucharistic Movement in its European Context', *The Bohemian Reformation and Religious Practice* 1 (1996), pp. 23–47.

124 David R. Holeton, 'The Evolution of Utraquist Eucharistic Liturgy: Baumstark Confirmed', in Robert F. Taft and Gabriele Winkler (eds), *Comparative Liturgy Fifty Years after Anton Baumstark (1872–1948)*, Rome: Pontificio Istituto Orientale, 2001, pp. 777–85.

Having replaced the ciborium [on the corporal] say: We all believe together that this is + the Body of our Lord Jesus Christ.

A parallel consecration of the cup follows. The Gospel is read, the Creed recited, a sermon preached, and during a hymn the sacrament is carried in procession to the high altar with lights and the ringing of bells, and then people come up to receive. The offertory prayers plus recital of just the Institution Narrative replace the *canon missae*.

The Teaching of Gabriel Biel (d. 1495) and of the Council of Trent

Gabriel Biel taught theology at Tübingen. His exposition of the Mass was a text read and mastered by Martin Luther and thus forms a useful backdrop to at least one Reformation divine's theology. Though of the school of Duns Scotus, Biel's theology of the Eucharist represents an excellent summary of theology on the eve of the Reformations of the sixteenth century. After the consecration of the elements, 'the body of Christ, which was taken from the Virgin Mary, which suffered and was buried, which rose and ascended into heaven and sitteth at the right hand of God the Father, in which the Son of God will come to judge the living and the dead, is really and actually contained under the species of bread'.[125] The substance of the bread does not remain, but is transubstantiated, and the accidents of the bread and wine remain without a subject: 'the real body of Christ by real presence comes into the place of the substance of the bread under the same accidents, so that the bread is no longer there'.[126] This mystical food kindles love, renews the memory of the Lord's passion, sustains the performance of good, strengthens holy desire, cleanses venial sins and sometimes mortal sins, gives the life of grace and union with Christ.[127] On the eucharistic sacrifice, Biel wrote:

> In the service of the Mass there is the same sacrifice and oblation [i.e. as the Cross], not by a repeated death but by the commemorative representation of the once suffered death . . . Wherefore He suffered only once; and yet we daily present this memorial of His one death in this sacramental sacrifice . . . The Mass is not of equal value with the passion and death of Christ as regards merit, because in the sacrifice of the Mass Christ does not again die, though His death, and therefore all its merit, is specially commemorated in it . . . If the Mass were of equal value with the passion and death, then, as Christ suffered once only for the redemption of the whole world, so also one Mass would suffice for the redemption of all souls from the pains of purgatory, and for obtaining from God all good, which is not to be said.[128]

125 *Exposition of the Sacred Canon of the Mass*, cited in Stone, *History of the Doctrine of the Eucharist*, I, p. 389.

126 Stone, *History*, p. 389.

127 Stone, *History*, p. 389.

128 Stone, *History*, pp. 390–1.

The Mass can be offered for the living and the departed, and it can remove both venial and mortal sin.[129]

It was this teaching – by now regarded as 'traditional' – that came under attack from the Protestant Reformers and that the Council of Trent defended. The Council met on and off from December 1545 to December 1563, and during Session VII (1547) it defined Catholic teaching on sacraments, reiterating the number as seven and that they convey grace to those who receive them rightly.[130] It condemned those who omitted or changed things in the received liturgies. Session XIII (1551) reaffirmed transubstantiation:

> In the first place, the holy Synod teaches, and openly and simply professes, that, in the august sacrament of the holy Eucharist, after the consecration of the bread and wine, our Lord Jesus Christ, true God and man, is truly, really, and substantially contained under the species of those sensible things. For neither are these things mutually repugnant, – that our Saviour Himself always sitteth at the right hand of the Father in heaven, according to the natural mode of existing, and that, nevertheless, He be, in many other places, sacramentally present to us in his own substance, by a manner of existing, which, though we can scarcely express it in words, yet can we, by the understanding illuminated by faith, conceive, and we ought most firmly to believe, to be possible unto God: for thus all our forefathers, as many as were in the true Church of Christ, who have treated of this most holy Sacrament, have most openly professed, that our Redeemer instituted this so admirable a sacrament at the last supper, when, after the blessing of the bread and wine, He testified, in express and clear words, that He gave them His own very Body, and His own Blood; words which, – recorded by the holy Evangelists, and afterwards repeated by Saint Paul, whereas they carry with them that proper and most manifest meaning in which they were understood by the Fathers, – it is indeed a crime the most unworthy that they should be wrested, by certain contentions and wicked men, to fictitious and imaginary tropes, whereby the verity of the flesh and blood of Christ is denied, contrary to the universal sense of the Church, which, as the pillar and ground of truth, has detested, as satanical, these inventions devised by impious men; she recognising, with a mind ever grateful and unforgetting, this most excellent benefit of Christ. . .
>
> And because that Christ, our Redeemer, declared that which He offered under the species of bread to be truly His own body, therefore has it ever been a firm belief in the Church of God, and this holy Synod doth now declare it anew, that, by the consecration of the bread and of the wine, a conversion is made of the whole substance of the bread into the substance of the body of Christ our Lord, and of the whole substance of the wine into the substance of His blood; which conversion is, by the holy Catholic Church, suitably and properly called Transubstantiation.[131]

---

129 Stone, *History*, pp. 390–1.

130 'The Council of Trent: The Seventh Session', http://history.hanover.edu/texts/trent/ct07.html.

131 'The Council of Trent: The Thirteenth Session', http://history.hanover.edu/texts/trent/ct13.html.

The Council defended communion in one kind and adoration/veneration of the consecrated host. Session XXII (1562) defined the sacrifice of the Mass:

> Forasmuch as, under the former Testament, according to the testimony of the Apostle Paul, there was no perfection, because of the weakness of the Levitical priesthood; there was need, God, the Father of mercies, so ordaining, that another priest should rise, according to the order of Melchisedech, our Lord Jesus Christ, who might consummate, and lead to what is perfect, as many as were to be sanctified. He, therefore, our God and Lord, though He was about to offer Himself once on the altar of the cross unto God the Father, by means of his death, there to operate an eternal redemption; nevertheless, because that His priesthood was not to be extinguished by His death, in the last supper, on the night in which He was betrayed, – that He might leave, to His own beloved Spouse the Church, a visible sacrifice, such as the nature of man requires, whereby that bloody sacrifice, once to be accomplished on the cross, might be represented, and the memory thereof remain even unto the end of the world, and its salutary virtue be applied to the remission of those sins which we daily commit, – declaring Himself constituted a priest for ever, according to the order of Melchisedech, He offered up to God the Father His own body and blood under the species of bread and wine; and, under the symbols of those same things, He delivered (His own body and blood) to be received by His apostles, whom He then constituted priests of the New Testament; and by those words, Do this in commemoration of me, He commanded them and their successors in the priesthood, to offer (them); even as the Catholic Church has always understood and taught. For, having celebrated the ancient Passover, which the multitude of the children of Israel immolated in memory of their going out of Egypt, He instituted the new Passover, (to wit) Himself to be immolated, under visible signs, by the Church through (the ministry of) priests, in memory of His own passage from this world unto the Father, when by the effusion of His own blood He redeemed us, and delivered us from the power of darkness, and translated us into his kingdom.[132]

The Council defended the *canon missae* which had come under criticism from the Reformers:

> And whereas it beseemeth, that holy things be administered in a holy manner, and of all holy things this sacrifice is the most holy; to the end that it might be worthily and reverently offered and received, the Catholic Church instituted, many years ago, the sacred Canon, so pure from every error, that nothing is contained therein which does not in the highest degree savour of a certain holiness and piety, and raise up unto God the minds of those that offer. For it is composed, out of the very words of the Lord, the traditions of the apostles, and the pious institutions also of holy pontiffs.[133]

---

132 'The Council of Trent: The Twenty-Second Session', http://history.hanover.edu/texts/trent/ct22.html.

133 'The Council of Trent: The Twenty-Second Session', http://history.hanover.edu/texts/trent/ct22.html.

However, the Council itself did not undertake any liturgical reforms and handed this task to the Pope. Pope Pius IV appointed a Commission, but it was his successor Pius V who issued a missal and regulations for the Mass in 1570. Though the intention was to revise the missal in accordance with ancient rites and the Fathers, knowledge of the development was such that the rite was simply the Romano-Western synthesis, in its Roman Use, with, for example, saints' days centring very much on Italian interests. Robert Carbié notes:

> As a result, many of the elements added in the Carolingian period were kept in the new Order of Mass; they were kept, moreover, in the form that they had taken at Rome and in Italy where, in particular, the private prayers of the priest at the offertory and communion had become more extensive than in other regions.[134]

He aptly observed that it represented both the end result and a critical revision of medieval developments.[135] In fact, it differed only slightly from the first printed missal of the Roman Curia of 1474, which in turn was based on Haymo of Faversham's Missal and the earlier Roman Curial Use. The Bull *Quo primum* made the Roman Missal normative unless a diocese or religious order could prove its use was more than 200 years old. Many dioceses, though, simply adopted the 1570 Roman Use, and this gave a new uniformity to the Western Catholic Church, as well as serving as a liturgical text that was regarded as safeguarding orthodoxy and orthopraxis. Centralized at Rome, organic evolution of the Western rite was regulated and restricted by curial control. This Roman rite received only minor revisions to its 1962 format, had restricted use under Paul VI, but has seen a limited revival under the Pontificates of John Paul II and Benedict XVI.

Concluding remarks

For a variety of reasons to do with the prestige of the Roman see, it seems that its rite, though amalgamated with material from Gaul and the Frankish lands, finally emerged in a synthesis as the template for the entire Western Church. During this long period, debate escalated about the meaning of presence in the eucharistic elements, with the term transubstantiation emerging as the accepted and mandated term. The explanation of the term was and has continued to be not without problems, especially when the philosophical definitions of substance and accidents were explored with strict logic. The more the Western Church made this its official doctrine, so there arose individuals and movements dissenting from all or some of the doctrinal explanations.

134 Robert Carbié, *The Church at Prayer*, ed. A. G. Martmort, vol. 2: The Eucharist, London: Geoffrey Chapman, 1986, p. 176.

135 Carbié, *The Church at Prayer*, p. 149.

10

Luther and Lutheran Eucharistic Liturgies

Martin Luther's theology and eucharistic rites

The more or less universal Romano-Western rite, with local variants throughout the West, and the accepted teaching of scholastic methods of theology, were brought to an abrupt end in the sixteenth century with the Reformation. The rise of what historians term the Renaissance and Humanism led to a quest for original texts and sources, and this entailed a new appraisal of Holy Scripture as the prime text – to use Thomas Cranmer's words, 'the most precious jewel and most holy relic that remaineth on the earth'.[1] This led to a more historical assessment of the Scriptures and a concern for their original languages. Though many divines quietly worked for renewal inside the structures of the late medieval Western Church, some would demand immediate reformation, and initiated Reformation. The Reformers challenged much in the inherited ritual, and much of the prevailing theology of the Eucharist, though of course the Reformers differed among themselves as to the nature and extent of change needed in both. In Germany the Reformation was sparked by the Wittenberg professor, Martin Luther. Many of the more recent Luther studies have been concerned with a developmental approach, and have tended to trace the growth and change in his theology from his early works through to his more mature writings. Three phases are helpful in considering his eucharistic theology: the Young (pre-1519) Luther, the anti-Roman and anti-Fanatics Luther, and the Mature Luther.

The Young Luther

Luther was an Augustinian friar and priest, but as a theologian he was primarily an exegete and preacher, and his theology was basically an attempt to interpret Scripture, for it 'alone is the true Lord and master of all writings and doctrine on earth'.[2] That is because the Scriptures reveal the Lord and Author of Scripture, namely, Jesus Christ.[3] Thus it was that by 1517 Luther had come to a new

1 Thomas Cranmer, 'Preface to the Great Bible', http://www.bible-researcher.com/cranmer.html.

2 Martin Luther, *Luther's Works: American Edition*, ed. J. Pelikan and H. T. Lehman, 55 vols, St Louis and Philadelphia: Concordia and Fortress Press, 1955, vol. 32, pp. 11–12. (Hereafter cited as *LW*.)

3 *LW* 2, p. 295.

understanding of justification, and so later in the Schmalkald Articles of 1537 he could assert:

> The first and chief article is this, that Jesus Christ, our God and Lord, 'was put to death for our trespasses and raised again for our justification' (Rom. 4:24) ... Nothing in this article can be given up or compromised, even if heaven and earth and things temporal should be destroyed ... On this article rests all that we teach and practice against the pope, the devil, and the world.[4]

For Luther, the Word, Jesus Christ, justification, forgiveness of sins and the gospel are all synonymous, and all theology and liturgical rites are weighed and judged in the light of this. In his 1517/18 lectures on Hebrews 8.6, Luther broke new ground in explaining the promise as being the forgiveness of sins as well as the traditional interpretation of eternal life. In discussing the Eucharist in the context of Hebrews 9.17, he interpreted it not as sacrifice but as testament. On 9.14 he wrote:

> Accordingly, to this purity no law, no works, and nothing at all except this blood of Christ alone can contribute; nor indeed can the blood itself do this unless the heart of man believes that this blood has been shed for the remission of sins. For one must believe Him who makes the *testament* when he says (Matt. 26:28; Luke 22:20): 'This is the blood which is shed for you and for many for the remission of sins.'[5]

The anti-Roman and anti-Schwärmerei Luther

In his sermons preached on the Eucharist in 1519 and 1520, Luther emphasized that the sacramental sign or form is the bread and wine and he was critical that only one species was distributed. He also emphasized the communal aspect of the Eucharist.[6] However, his main concern was the need for worthy reception and faith so that the full fruits of communion might be received:

> For just as the bread is changed into his true natural body and the wine into his natural true blood, so truly are we also drawn and changed into the spiritual body, that is, into the fellowship of Christ and all saints and by this sacrament put into possession of all the virtues and mercies of Christ and his saints ...[7]

4 T. G. Tappert, *The Book of Concord*, Philadelphia: Fortress Press, 1959, p. 292.

5 *LW* 2, p. 209. I have changed the word 'covenant' in *LW* to 'testament', which is quite clearly signified in the Latin original, '*Oportet enim testatori credere*', Weimar edition of Luther's Works, Band 57, p. 208.

6 'The Blessed Sacrament of the Holy and True Body of Christ, and the Brotherhoods', 1519, *LW* 35, pp. 49–50.

7 *LW* 35, pp. 59–60.

In *The Babylonian Captivity of the Church* (1520), Luther attacked head-on the traditional Roman teaching on the sacraments and the Mass. He would accept only three sacraments – Baptism, Eucharist and Penance.[8] Of the 'captivities' of the Mass, the first was communion in bread only, and the second, transubstantiation. He appealed to Pierre d'Ailly (a pupil of William Ockham) that it would require fewer superfluous miracles to hold that real bread and wine remained with the substance of the body and blood of Christ and not their mere accidents, and became critical of the 'Aristotelian Church'.[9] Luther was not attacking the presence of Christ in the elements, but simply the formal defined doctrine of how and what. He wrote:

> I rejoice greatly that the simple faith of this sacrament is still to be found, at least among the common people. For as they do not understand, neither do they dispute whether accidents are present without substance, but believe with a simple faith that Christ's body and blood are truly contained there, and leave to those who have nothing else to do the argument about what contains them.[10]

The third 'captivity' was the idea that the Mass was a sacrifice that could be offered for something. For Luther, the Eucharist was a testament and a promise, grounded in the Words of Institution:

> We must turn our eyes and hearts simply to the institution of Christ and this alone, and set nothing before us but the very word of Christ by which he instituted the sacrament, made it perfect, and committed it to us. For in that word, and in that word alone, reside the power, the nature, and the whole substance of the mass. All the rest is the work of man, added to the word of Christ, and the mass can be held and remain a mass just as well without them.[11]

Indeed, for Luther the Institution Narrative was the substance of the Mass, and when Christ said 'Take and eat', it was as though he was saying:

> Behold, O sinful and condemned man, out of the pure and unmerited love with which I love you, and by the will of the Father of mercies (II Cor. 1:3), apart from any merit or desire of yours, I promise you in these words the forgiveness of all your sins and life everlasting. And that you may be absolutely certain of this irrevocable promise of mine, I shall give you my body and pour out my blood, confirming this promise by my very death, and leaving you my body and blood as a sign and memorial of this same promise. As often as you partake of them, remember me, proclaim and praise my love and bounty towards you, and give thanks.[12]

8 *LW* 36, p. 18.
9 *LW* 36, p. 29.
10 *LW* 36, p. 32.
11 *LW* 36, p. 36.
12 *LW* 36, p. 40.

Important for Luther was Augustine's dictum that when the Word is added to the elements it becomes a sacrament.[13] Later, in 1522, Luther would write:

> For if you ask: what is the gospel? You can give no better answer than these words of the New Testament, namely, that Christ gave his body and poured out his blood for us for the forgiveness of sins . . . Therefore these words, as a short summary of the whole gospel, are to be taught and instilled into every Christian's heart, so that he may contemplate them continuously and without ceasing, and with them exercise, strengthen, and sustain his faith in Christ, especially when he goes to the sacrament.[14]

For Luther the Words of Institution are the gospel in a nutshell. However, since they are the testament and promise of a gift, the Eucharist is something to be received as gift, not something that can be offered to God. Thus in *The Babylonian Captivity*, Luther was critical of some of the prayers of the *canon missae*, which supported the idea that the Mass was a sacrifice, and suggested that the priest should omit both the prayers of the 'Little Canon' and the *canon missae*, which by this time meant the prayers of the *Te igitur* onwards.

On his return from the Diet of Worms in 1521, Luther was 'detained' and hidden in Wartburg Castle, and the reforming cause of Wittenberg temporarily fell to others. Luther had suggested that the *canon missae* should be omitted, but he had made no liturgical provision. Others did so, namely Kaspar Kantz, the prior of the Carmelite brothers at Nördlingen, and at Wittenberg, Andreas Bodenstein von Karlstadt. Kantz provided a German rite with an exhortation on communion, a confession, the *Veni Sancte Spiritus* with a prayer for the grace of the Holy Spirit. This was followed by the common Preface with Sanctus and Benedictus, a paraphrase of the *Quam oblationem* and the Words of Institution (*verba*), followed by the Lord's Prayer, Agnus Dei and a Communion Prayer. All reference to offering had been removed.[15]

More disturbing as far as Luther was concerned was Karlstadt's Mass and subsequent teaching. Karlstadt issued a pamphlet in June 1521, entitled *On the Recipients, Signs and Promise of the Holy Sacrament of Christ's Flesh and Blood*, which in many ways reiterated much of what Luther taught.[16] However, Amy Burnett has noted some significant differences – less interest in the term testament and a sharp separation between sign and thing signified, reflecting the influence of a Neoplatonic/Augustinian and Erasmian dualism that Luther did not share.[17] Karlstadt also argued that it was a sin not to have communion in both kinds. In his later writings he indicated that the substances of bread and wine remain in the Eucharist, using the Aristotelian logic that Luther rejected, and, possibly with some knowledge of Cornelius Hoen's teachings, more and

13 For Augustine, see Chapter 3.

14 'The Misuse of the Mass', 1522, *LW* 36, p. 183.

15 Text in E. Sehling, *Die Evangelischen Kirchenordnungen des XVI. Jahrhunderts*, 5 vols, Leipzig, 1902–13, vol. 1, p. 697.

16 English text in Amy Nelson Burnett, *The Eucharistic Pamphlets of Andreas Bodenstein von Karlstadt*, Kirksville: Trueman State University Press, 2011.

17 Amy Nelson Burnett, *Karlstadt and the Origins of the Eucharistic Controversy*, New York: Oxford University Press, 2011, p. 14.

more severed the link between sign and the thing signified.[18] By the end of 1521 Karlstadt announced that he would celebrate an evangelical Mass, simply reciting the Words of Institution, omitting the *canon missae*, and without wearing the traditional vestments. The new order was adopted on 24 January.

Luther returned to Wittenberg in March, and denounced the changes since they had been ushered in without thought for tender consciences. There ensued a bitter controversy between Luther and Karlstadt, with Luther placing Karlstadt alongside Müntzer and Zwingli of Zurich as fanatics or *Schwärmer*. Luther thus found himself fighting on two fronts. Luther refused to sunder sign and thing signified, and it was disagreement over the meaning of 'This is my body' that led to division among the Reformers. The work of Cornelius Hoen, who had argued that 'is' means signifies, and that one must distinguish between the bread received in the mouth and Christ received by faith, seems to have been known to Karlstadt before its general publication in 1525.[19] Luther dismissed transubstantiation as an unnecessary and unscriptural explanation of the presence, and though he thought 'consubstantiation' more reasonable, never taught such a doctrine. Rather, he simply insisted that Christ was bodily present in the elements. At the Colloquy at Marburg in 1529, in the discussion about the place of Christ's body, Luther stated:

> 'This is my body' is enough for me. I confess that the body is in heaven, I also confess that it is in the sacrament. I am not concerned about what is contrary to nature but only what is contrary to faith.[20]

Luther published his first evangelical Mass, the *Formula Missae*, in 1523.[21] He retained Latin mainly, as he argued later in the *Deutsche Messe* (1526),[22] for the sake of educating the youth, though he also was adamant that simply translating Latin forms into German would not result in a good vernacular liturgy. He retained most of the first part of the Mass:

> First, we approve and retain the introits for the Lord's days and the festivals of Christ, such as Easter, Pentecost, and the Nativity, although we prefer the Psalms from which they were taken as of old. But for the time being we permit the accepted use . . .
>
> Second, we accept the Kyrie eleison in the form in which it has been used until now, with the various melodies for different seasons, together with the Angelic Hymn, Gloria in Excelsis, which follows it. However, the bishop [pastor] may decide to omit the latter as often as he wishes.
>
> Third, the prayer or collect which follows, if it is evangelical (and those for Sunday usually are), should be retained in its accepted form; but there should be only one. After this the Epistle is read. Certainly the time has not yet come to attempt revision here, as nothing unevangelical is read, except

18 See Burnett, *Karlstadt*, pp. 16–35.
19 Burnett, *Karlstadt*, pp. 16–35.
20 *LW* 38, p. 58.
21 *CD*, pp. 33–6; *PEER*, pp. 191–5.
22 *CD*, pp. 36–9; *PEER*, pp. 195–9.

> that those parts from the Epistles of Paul in which faith is taught are read only rarely, while the exhortations to morality are most frequently read. The Epistles seem to have been chosen by a singularly unlearned and superstitious advocate of works . . .
>
> Fourth, the gradual of two verses shall be sung, either together with the Alleluia, or one of the two, as the bishop may decide. But the Quadragesima graduals and others like them that exceed two verses may be sung at home by whoever wants them. In church we do not want to quench the spirit of the faithful with tedium. Nor is it proper to distinguish Lent, Holy Week, or Good Friday from other days, lest we seem to mock and ridicule Christ with half of a mass and the one part of the sacrament. For the Alleluia is the perpetual voice of the church, just as the memorial of His passion and victory is perpetual.
>
> Fifth, we allow no sequences or proses unless the bishop wishes to use the short one for the Nativity of Christ: 'Grates nunc omnes.' There are hardly any which smack of the Spirit, save those of the Holy Spirit: 'Sancti Spiritus' and 'Veni sancte spiritus' . . .
>
> Sixth, the Gospel lesson follows, for which we neither prohibit nor prescribe candles or incense. Let these things be free.[23]

Luther also retained the Creed. However, as regards the Little Canon and *canon missae*, he stated:

> Eighth, that utter abomination follows which forces all that precedes in the mass into its service and is, therefore, called the offertory. From here on almost everything smacks and savors of sacrifice . . . Let us, therefore, repudiate everything that smacks of sacrifice, together with the entire canon and retain only that which is pure and holy, and so order our Mass.

His work of 1525, *The Abomination of the Secret Canon*, was a scathing analysis of each part of the *canon missae*, mocking its concern for offering and mention of the saints, and it is clear that Luther had no attachment to it whatsoever. Though many commentators have followed Yngve Brilioth in seeing Luther as hacking the *canon missae* to pieces, it is probably better to see him as removing the entire *canon missae*, and replacing it with a more scriptural version of the Words of Institution.[24] His Reformed canon thus had:

- *Sursum corda* and common Preface.
- Words of Institution.
- Sanctus with Benedictus and the elevation of the elements.

Whereas in the old Mass, the Words of Institution were whispered, Luther desired them to be intoned to the same chant as the Lord's Prayer. Since the

---

23 *LW* 53, pp. 22–5.

24 Yngve Brilioth, *Eucharistic Faith and Practice, Evangelical and Catholic*, trans. Arthur Gabriel Herbert, London: SPCK, 1930; Bryan D. Spinks, *Luther's Liturgical Criteria and His Reform of the Canon of the Mass*, Grove Liturgical Study 30, Bramcote: Grove Books, 1982.

printed missals regarded the *canon missae* as beginning with *Te igitur* and that it was recited in silence, and sometimes the priest elevated the elements while the choir was still singing the Sanctus, this was not such an innovation. The 'new' element was the chanting of the Words of Institution. The remainder of this rite was as follows:

- Lord's Prayer.
- *Agnus Dei* and Communion (use of the prayer 'O Lord Jesus Christ').
- If the priest desires to have the communion sung, let it be sung. But instead of the *complenda* or final collect, because it sounds almost like a sacrifice, let the following prayer be read in the same tone: 'What we have taken with our lips, O Lord . . .' The following one may also be read: 'May thy body which we have received . . . The Lord be with you, etc.' In place of the *Ita missa* let the Benedicamus domino be said, adding Alleluia according to its own melodies where and when it is desired. Or the Benedicamus may be borrowed from Vespers.
- Customary blessing or Numbers 6.24–7, or Psalm 67.6–7.

Luther suggested that celebrants might want to sing the words over the bread and distribute it prior to the words over the wine and the giving of the cup.

He published his vernacular *Deutsche Messe* in 1526. It had an Introit with a hymn or German psalm, the German Kyries, Collect and Epistle and Gospel separated by a German hymn. The Apostles' Creed in hymnic form in German was sung, and after the sermon there was a paraphrase of the Lord's Prayer and an admonition. The Words of Institution were then intoned – to the same tone as the Gospel. Paul Nettl writes:

> As with other texts which deeply stirred him, this too begins with a high note, 'C', stressing the first syllable, *Unser*. Then the voice, as though in humility, drops a third and plays around with 'A', then to sink down to the 'F' at the second syllable of the word *verraten*, as though expressing deep despair at the misdeeds of His disciple. There, where Jesus himself speaks, *Nempt*, the melody starts in with a low 'F' with concise simplicity, moves around this repercussion tone, to rise at the phrase, *für euch*, as if to give melodious expression to salvation by the Saviour's death. What we experience in this simple sequence of tones, full of symbolism, is the deeply personal, sorrowful, yet consoling devotion which radiates from the mystery of the communion as Luther felt it.[25]

As far as Luther was concerned, in emphasizing the Words of Institution, he was replacing the *canon missae* with the Gospel itself, and in the Gospel it is God in Christ who does something for humanity and offers us something, namely, himself. This was not a remnant of the canon prayed to God, but the gospel in a nutshell offering Christ and his forgiveness. As in the *Formula Missae*, he

25 Paul Nettl, *Luther and Music*, Philadelphia: Muhlenberg Press, 1948, p. 79; cf. Robin A. Leaver, *Luther's Liturgical Music*, Grand Rapids: Eerdmans, 2007, pp. 180–8; recording on the CD, Praetorius, *Mass for Christmas Morning*, Archiv Produktion 439250.

suggested that the bread might be distributed before the words over the wine and a German paraphrase of the Sanctus or the hymn *Gott sei gelobet* or the hymn by Jan Hus, *Jesus Christus unser Heiland*, sung while the bread was distributed, and the Agnus Dei during the giving of the cup.

In this work Luther also mentioned another rite – of deeply committed Christians who would gather in homes to pray and celebrate the Lord's Supper. However, he wrote, 'But as yet I neither can nor desire to begin such a congregation or assembly or to make rules for it.' He never did.

The Mature Luther

Luther continued to battle the fanatics in defending the real presence of Christ in the sacrament, though endorsing their mutual rejection of the sacrificial nature of the Eucharist. His mature statements are to be found in his Large Catechism of 1529 and in the Schmalkald Articles of 1537. The 1529 Catechism asserted that the Sacrament of the Altar 'is the true body and blood of the Lord Christ in and under the bread and wine which we Christians are commanded by Christ's word to eat and drink'.[26] The words 'in' and 'under' are key here. Citing Augustine, he affirmed that when the word (Words of Institution) is joined to the element, the bread and wine 'are truly the body and blood of Christ. For as we have it from the lips of Christ, so it is; he cannot lie or deceive.'[27] The essence of the sacrament is in the words 'for you', and this food for the soul both strengthens and sustains us, and offers us all the treasures of heaven to us. 'The treasure is opened and placed at everyone's door, yes, upon everyone's table, but it is also your responsibility to take it and confidently believe that it is just as the words tell you.'[28]

The Schmalkald Articles reject the Mass as a sacrifice, but affirm that the bread and wine 'are the true body and blood of Christ and that these are given and received not only by godly but also wicked Christians'.[29] However, 'As for transubstantiation, we have no regard for the subtle sophistry of those who teach that bread and wine surrender or lose their natural substance and retain only the appearance of and shape of bread . . .'[30]

Other Lutherans and Lutheran liturgies

As crucial as Luther's name and theology is to the Lutheran tradition, he did not work alone but was assisted by close colleagues. When detained at Wartburg, leadership of the new evangelical movement in Wittenberg fell to Andreas Karlstadt and Phillip Melanchthon; whereas the former parted company with Luther, the latter played a leading role in the German Reformation. Other prominent figures were Johannas Bugenhagen, Johann Brenz, Justus Jonas and

26 Tappert, *Book of Concord*, p. 447.
27 Tappert, *Book of Concord*, p. 448.
28 Tappert, *Book of Concord*, p. 450.
29 Tappert, *Book of Concord*, p. 310.
30 Tappert, *Book of Concord*, p. 311.

Andreas Osiander.[31] It was Melanchthon's contribution that would become controversial after Luther's death. His *Loci Communes* of 1521 were regarded as a first systematic statement of Lutheran theology. However, the *Loci* continued to be modified and, as Harold Lentz noted, became less polemical towards scholastic theology and more respectful of the church Fathers, evincing a deeper respect for philosophical method in theology; 'there became ever more evident an independent spirit which held a varying viewpoint from Luther'.[32] In the *Loci Communes*, Melanchthon argued that the gospel is the promise of grace and signs are closely connected to the promises.[33] He preferred the term sign to sacrament; they are instituted to excite faith.[34] The thing is the sign, the words are the promise of grace; although he referred to Luther's *Babylonian Captivity*, Melanchthon listed only two divinely appointed signs, baptism and the Table of the Lord.[35] He referred to chewing Christ's body and drinking his blood at the table, and the focus is forgiveness of sins that comes not by participation but by faith.[36] Denying that the Eucharist is a sacrifice he asserted that its significance lies in its function of confirming us as often as our consciences waver.[37] It was Melanchthon who drew up the Augsburg Confession of 1530, approved by Luther, where the German text stated:

> It is taught among us that the true body and blood of Christ are really present in the Supper of our Lord under the form of bread and wine and are there distributed and received. The contrary doctrine is therefore rejected.[38]

The list of disagreements included communion in two kinds. In rejecting that the Mass was a sacrifice offered to God, the Confession nevertheless insisted that 'the Mass is observed among us with greater devotion and more earnestness than among our opponents'.[39] Melanchthon also wrote *The Apology of the Augsburg Confession*, where some topics received considerable expansion. Eucharistic presence is reasserted, 'but to make it clear to all our readers that we defend the doctrine received by the whole church – that in the Lord's Supper the body and blood of Christ are truly and substantially present and are truly offered with those things that are seen, bread and wine'.[40] The belief that the Mass gives grace *ex opere operato* is rejected, alongside the belief that the Mass can be offered for the living and the dead. The Lutheran abolition of private Masses was justified by appeal to the Eastern Church, and the use of German

31 See David C. Steinmetz, *Reformers in the Wings*, Philadelphia: Fortress Press, 1971.

32 Harold H. Lentz, *Reformation Crossroads*, Minneapolis: Augsburg Publishing House, 1958, p. 5.

33 Charles Alexander Hill, *The Loci Communes of Philip Melanchthon*, Boston: Meador Publishing Company, 1944, p. 238.

34 Hill, *Loci Communes*, p. 241.

35 Hill, *Loci Communes*, p. 242.

36 Hill, *Loci Communes*, p. 258.

37 Hill, *Loci Communes*, p. 259.

38 Tappert, *Book of Concord*, p. 34.

39 Tappert, *Book of Concord*, p. 56.

40 Tappert, *Book of Concord*, pp. 179–80.

hymns in an evangelical Latin Mass was also defended. Two types of sacrifice are identified:

> One is the propitiatory sacrifice; this is a work of satisfaction for guilt and punishment that reconciles God or placates his wrath or merits the forgiveness of sins for others. The other type is the eucharistic sacrifice; this does not merit the forgiveness of sins or reconciliation but by it those who have been reconciled give thanks or show their gratitude for the forgiveness of sins and other blessings received.[41]

Melanchthon hoped that he might succeed in uniting Lutherans and Reformed, and after 1530 seemed to some of his contemporaries to depart from a pure Lutheran stance. In discussion with Bucer and in dialogue with Oecolampadius, Melanchthon shifted from using *distribuere* to *exhiberi*.[42] In his *Loci* of 1535 he moved towards a general sacramental presence rather than viewing it specifically in the bread and wine.[43] The term 'exhibit', offered, was used in his modification of the Augsburg Confession, which enabled Calvin and others to sign the Augustana Variata (1540). Article X read, 'Concerning the Supper of the Lord they teach that with the bread and wine are truly exhibited the body and blood of Christ to those who eat the Lord's Supper.' Here 'with' (*cum*) replaced the German 'under' (*unter*), and exhibited (*exhibeantur*) replaced 'distributed'. Although 'with' might be understood as in and under, it also allowed for the idea that the presence was only as the bread and wine were consumed. Quere observes that over against Luther's stress on the *body* present *in* the bread, Melanchthon's doctrine of Christ's presence *in usu* becomes the corollary and even the locus of the *personal* presence.[44]

Lutherans such as Mathias Flacius Illyricus regarded Melanchthon as a crypto-Calvinist and developed a strict (and to outsiders, fundamentalist) reading of Luther's works as 'canonical' Lutheran teaching. Luther's idea of *adiaphora*, things indifferent, had meant that with regard to vestments, for example, it didn't matter whether they were worn or not. For the 'Gnesio-Lutherans' anything *adiaphora* that someone tried to enforce ceased to be *adiaphora* and was to be rejected. This would have some effect on the ritual of the Fraction. The Reformed Churches began to insist on a deliberate Fraction of the bread as part of the essential eucharistic action, and the Lutheran congregation at Antwerp was pressured to bring their rite into conformity with the Reformed. Although they made concessions such as giving up singing the Kyries and wearing vestments, they refused to have a ceremonial Fraction. Flacius was one of their consultants, and arguing that 'breaking of bread' was a Hebrew idiom and not the basis of an obligatory rule, he wrote:

---

41 Tappert, *Book of Concord*, p. 252. For discussion of Melanchthon's concept of sacrifice, D. Richard Stuckwisch, *Philip Melanchthon and the Lutheran Confession of Eucharistic Sacrifice*, Bynum: Repristination Press, 1997, 2011.

42 Ralph Walter Quere, *Melanchthon's Christum Cognoscere: Christ's Efficacious Presence in the Eucharistic Theology of Melanchthon*, Nieuwkoop: B. De Graaf, 1977, p. 307.

43 Quere, *Melanchthon's Christum Cognoscere*, p. 356.

44 Quere, *Melanchthon's Christum Cognoscere*, p. 385.

> 'This do' refers only to the preceding command to accept and eat the bread and wine, the body and blood of the Lord, and reciting the words of Christ. And not to everything preceding, to the circumstances, which are not essential things, commanded by Christ, but are clearly free matters . . .[45]

What of the eucharistic liturgy? Between 1523 and 1555 some 135 *Kirchenordnungen* were produced for Lutheran cities. Frank Senn observed:

> They differ considerably in minor details, and yet their liturgical provisions show a remarkable similarity. This was due to the far-reaching influence of Luther and the fact that many of the church orders were prepared by the same authors (Bugenhagen seven, Brenz five, Jonas four, Melanchthon four, Bucer three or four, etc.).[46]

Important here are the words with which Luther ended his 1523 Latin Mass:

> But in all these matters we will want to beware lest we make binding what should be free, or make sinners of those who may do some things differently or omit others. All that matters is that the Words of Institution should be kept intact and that everything should be done by faith.

This freedom resulted in a great variety of 'uses' among Lutherans. Luther D. Reed classified the *Kirchenordnungen* in three groups:[47]

1 The Saxo-Lutheran group of central and North Germany. This group included Johannes Bugenhagen's orders for Brunswick, Hamburg, Lübeck, Pomerania, Denmark, Schleswig-Holstein and Hildesheim, as well as the orders compiled by Justus Jonas, Andrea Osiander and Johannes Brenz.
2 The ultra-conservative group, retaining many pre-Reformation traits, including Brandenburg, Pfalz-Neuburg and Austria.
3 The radical or mediating group such as Württemberg, where concessions were made to the Reformed tradition.

German Reformation cities tended to base their reforms on either the *Formula Missae* or the *Deutsche Messe*, or a combination of them, with adaptation to the local needs or tastes. Hans-Christoph Schmidt-Lauber has noted some that follow the *Deutsche Messe* with the Words of Institution juxtaposed with communion and those that follow the *Formula Missae*, where the Words of Institution are followed by the Sanctus, Lord's Prayer and Agnus Dei, and then

45 *Confessio Ministrorum Jesu Christi*, 1567. Cited in Oliver K. Olson, 'The "Fractio Panis" in Heidelberg and Antwerp', in Derk Visser (ed.), *Controversy and Conciliation: The Reformation and the Palatinate 1559–1583*, Alison Park: Pickwick Publications, 1986, pp. 147–53, 150–1. See also Oliver K. Olson, *Matthias Flacius and the Survival of Luther's Reform*, Wiesbaden: Harrassowitz Verlag, 2002.

46 Frank C. Senn, *Christian Liturgy: Catholic and Evangelical*, Minneapolis: Fortress Press, 1997, p. 332.

47 Luther D. Reed, *The Lutheran Liturgy*, Philadelphia: Fortress Press, 1947, pp. 89–90.

communion.[48] Most do not depart radically from Luther's models, as evidenced by Bugenhagen's rites.[49] Susan Karant-Nunn has observed that one feature of Bugenhagen's programme is the explicitly incorporated admonitions, prior to the *verba* and in the form of a collective confession before communion itself.[50] A contemporary account of Mass in Nürnberg in 1532 was given by Sir Thomas Elyot, who was a member of a party of diplomats:

> Although I had a chaplain, yet could not I be suffered to have him to sing Mass, but was constrained to hear their Mass, which is but one in a church, and that is celebrated in form following. The priest, in vestments after our manner, singeth everything in Latin, as we use, omitting suffrages. The Epistle he readeth in Latin. In the meantime the sub-deacon goeth into the pulpit and readeth to the people the Epistle in their vulgar; after, they peruse other things as our priests do. Then the priest readeth softly the Gospel in Latin. In the mean space the deacon goeth into the pulpit and readeth aloud the Gospel in the Almaigne tongue. Mr. Cranmer saith it was shewed to him in the Epistles and Gospels they kept not the order we do, but do peruse every day one chapter of the New Testament. Afterwards, the priest and the quire do sing the *Credo* as we do; the secrets and preface they omit, and the priest singeth with a high voice the words of the consecration; and after the levation the deacon turneth to the people, telling them in the Almaigne tongue a long process how they should prepare themselves to the communion of the flesh and blood of Christ; and then may every man come that listeth, without going to any confession.[51]

Here, as in many orders, the elevation was retained, and continued to survive for some time in certain areas. The traditional vestments also continued in many places until the late eighteenth century.[52]

Some of the more obvious departures from Luther's recommendations include the Württemberg 1553 order, where a preaching service – Introit, German psalm-paraphrase, sermon, Ten Commandments, Creed, Lord's Prayer, General Prayers of the Church, psalm or hymn – could have the Lord's Supper appended,

48 Hans-Christoph Schmidt-Lauber, 'The Lutheran Tradition in German Lands', in Geoffrey Wainwright and Karen B. Westerfield Tucker (eds), *The Oxford History of Christian Worship*, Oxford: Oxford University Press, 2006, p. 403. See also James Ambrose Lee II, 'Tracing Wittenberg's Liturgical Lineage: Mecklenburg's Reception of Luther's Reforms of the Mass', thesis for the STM, Yale Divinity School, 2012.

49 Johannes H. Bergsma, *Die Reform der Messliturgie durch Johannes Bugenhagen (1485–1558)*, Kevelaer: Verlag Butzon and Bercker, 1966, which gives outlines and discusses Bugenhagen's rites of Braunschweig–Hamburg–Lübeck, Wittenberg, Pomerania, 1535; Denmark and Schleswig-Holstein, Hildesheim and Braunschweig–Wolfenbüttel, 1543. See also Walter Göbell, *Die Schleswig-Holsteinische Kirchenordnung von 1542*, Neumünster: Karl Wachholtz Verlag, 1986.

50 Susan Karant-Nunn, *The Reformation of Ritual: An Interpretation of Early Modern Germany*, London: Routledge, 1997, p. 119.

51 Nicholas Pocock (ed.), *Records of the Reformation: The Divorce 1527–1533*, vol. 2, Oxford: Clarendon Press, 1870, pp. 229–30.

52 Ernst Walter Zeeden, *Faith and Act: The Survival of Medieval Ceremonies in the Lutheran Reformation*, St Louis: Concordia Publishing House, 2012, pp. 31–4.

which included a confession with absolution, a prayer for right reception, the Lord's Prayer and the Words of Institution.[53] Reformed influence is evident.

One of the most evident features is that the new 'canon' consisted of mainly the Words of Institution, though in the *Formula Missae* family, the *Sursum corda*, Preface and Sanctus. Though some inferred that the *verba* of Christ should not be enclosed by or be attached to any prayers, not all of Luther's contemporaries shared this conclusion. The Mark Brandenburg rite of 1540 had prayers for the emperor and rulers, for clergy, for unity and for forgiveness recited quietly by the priest before the *verba*, in addition to retaining other prayers from its former Catholic liturgy.[54] The Pfalz-Neuberg order (1543), prepared by Osiander, had the following prayer before the *verba*:

> O Lord Jesu Christ, the only true Son of the living God, who hast given thy body for us all in the bitter pains of death, and hast shed thy blood for the forgiveness of our sins, and who, moreover, hast commanded all thy disciples to eat and to drink the same thy body and thy blood, and thereby to commemorate thy death; we bring before thy divine Majesty these thy gifts of bread and wine; and we pray thee by thy divine grace, goodness, and might, to hallow, bless, and create, that this bread may be thy body and this wine thy blood, and that all who eat and drink thereof may attain to everlasting life; who with the Father, in the unity of the Holy Spirit, livest and reignest for ever and ever. Amen.[55]

Also of interest is the rite prepared for Archbishop Hermann von Wied of Cologne.[56] Prepared for a reforming Catholic archbishop by Martin Bucer, thought by the Reformed as too Lutheran, and Philip Melanchthon, regarded by the Gnesio-Lutherans as being a Crypto-Calvinist, the liturgy represents an interesting ecumenical experiment. It was bilingual, and provided lengthy exhortations, and a confession with absolution, some of which was adopted by Thomas Cranmer in his rite. The *Sursum corda* 'shall be handled in the traditional manner', and was followed by an extended Preface giving thanks for salvation history and especially the work of Christ,

> who through the cross and death delivered us from sins and the power of the devil, and brought us again into thy favor by his holy Spirit whom he sent unto us from thee; and gave his body and blood to be the food of a new and eternal life, that, being more confirmed through the trust of thy mercy and love, we should ever go forward to all that that is thy pleasure by renewing

53 Schmidt-Lauber, 'Lutheran Tradition', p. 404.

54 Zeeden, *Faith and Act*, p. 16. See also the important essays by Margrit Thøfner, 'Framing the Sacred: Lutheran Church Furnishings in the Holy Roman Empire', and Evelin Wetter, '"On Sundays for the laity . . . we allow mass vestments, altars and candles to remain": The Role of Pre-Reformation Ecclesiastical Vestments in the Formation of Confessional, Corporate and "National Identities"', in Andrew Spicer (ed.), *Lutheran Churches in Early Modern Europe*, Farnham: Ashgate, 2012, pp. 97–131 and 165–95.

55 Cited in G. J. Cuming, *A History of Anglican Liturgy*, London: Macmillan and Co., 1969, p. 333.

56 *PEER*, pp. 221–5.

> and sanctifying of ourselves; and that we should glorify and exalt thee here and evermore in all our words and deeds, and sing unto thee without end with all thy holy angels and beloved children.

This led into the Sanctus, and then came the *verba*, Lord's Prayer, Peace and Communion. The Prayer after Communion is of some interest:

> Almighty, everlasting God, we give thanks to thy exceeding goodness, because thou hast fed us with the body of thy only-begotten Son <our Lord> and given us his blood to drink. We humbly beseech thee, work in us with thy Spirit, that, as we have received this divine sacrament with our mouths, so we may also receive and ever hold fast with true faith thy grace, remission of sins, and communion with Christ thy Son. All which things thou has exhibited unto us in these sacraments through our Lord Jesus Christ thy Son, which liveth and reigneth with thee in unity of the Holy Ghost, very God and very man, for ever. Amen.

The prayer asks for the fruits of communion, though in Luther's thought this happens with those who believe, and therefore no further request is necessary. The prayer seems to reflect the sacramental parallelism associated with Bucer – that the fruits may not be conterminous with the reception. The term 'exhibited' was (as we shall note later) a favourite Bucerian term, but one that Melanchthon had used in the 1540 Latin version of the Augsburg Confession.

Martin Chemnitz

The mature confession of faith subscribed to by most Lutherans was the *Formula of Concord* (1577). Drawn up by a number of theologians, it is generally acknowledged that much of the drafting was done by Martin Chemnitz. Chemnitz's many works included a theology of the Lord's Supper, *De Coena Domini*, written in 1569. In other writings he had rejected Roman Catholic teachings on the sacrifice of the Mass, and apparently sided with those who rejected any prayers of the Eucharist other than the *verba*, asserting that 'he acts wickedly who takes away the consecration of the Eucharist from the Words of Divine Institution and transfers it to the prayers of the Canon which have been patched together by men out of unsound and sound, or rather, mostly out of unsound materials'.[57] *De Coena Domini* was a defence of the Lutheran teaching against the Reformed, the 'Sacramentarians'. Throughout the work, Chemnitz repeatedly insists on the 'proper and natural meaning' of the *verba*:

57 *The Examination of the Council of Trent*, Part II, trans. Fred Kramer, cited in Bjarne Wollan Teigen, *The Lord's Supper in the Theology of Martin Chemnitz*, Brewster, MA: Trinity Lutheran Press, 1986, p. 79.

> When the words of the Supper are taken in their proper and natural sense, then we have the one sure meaning regarding the substantial presence, distribution, and reception of the body and blood of the Lord.[58]

He reiterated the early Luther's concern that the *verba* are the last will and testament of the Son of God: 'when the last will and testament of a man has been executed, we are required under the law to observe the words with special care so that nothing be done which is either beside or contrary to the final will of the testator'.[59] Chemnitz rejected a local enclosing of the body of Christ or a crass physical commingling of the body of Christ with the elements, but the word *est* in the *verba* means that the body of Christ is in, with and under the elements. He wrote:

> It is not one body which was sacrificed for us on the cross and another which is distributed and received in the Supper; but the same substance of the body of Christ which was given for us on the cross is broken in the Supper with the bread for those who eat it, that is, it is offered and distributed.[60]

An examination of Scripture passages demonstrates, proves and confirms the proper and natural meaning, namely,

> that the Lord's Supper consists not only of the external symbols of bread and wine but also of the very body and blood of the Lord, and that in the celebration of this Supper there is distributed and received by the mouth of the partakers not only bread and wine but at the same time also the true and substantial body and blood of Christ. But how this takes place or can happen is not mine to ask.[61]

He appealed to the teaching of Cyril of Alexandria regarding the analogy between the incarnation and the Eucharist. Consecration is effected by the recitation of the *verba*:

> Therefore the words of institution are spoken in our Lord's Supper, not merely for the sake of history but to show to the church that Christ himself, through His Word, according to His command and promise, is present in the action of the Supper and by the power of this word offers His body and blood to those who eat. For it is He who distributes, though it be through the minister; it is He who says: 'This is my body.' It is He who is efficacious through His Word, so that the bread is His body and the wine His blood. In this way, and because of this, we are sure and believe that in the Lord's Supper we eat, not ordinary bread and wine, but the body and blood of Christ.[62]

58 Martin Chemnitz, *The Lord's Supper*, trans. J. A. O. Preus, St Louis: Concordia Publishing House, 1979, p. 86.

59 Chemnitz, *Lord's Supper*, p. 27.

60 Chemnitz, *Lord's Supper*, pp. 123–4.

61 Chemnitz, *Lord's Supper*, p. 148.

62 *Examination of the Council of Trent II*, cited in Teigen, *Lord's Supper*, p. 81.

To modern exegetes it seems strange that Chemnitz interpreted the word 'bless' in the Institution Narratives as meaning the words 'This is my body' – 'the special power of the divine Word' – rather than the obvious meaning of blessing God in prayer, which he explicitly denied.[63] Though he conceded that the elements might be adored since Christ is present, the object is to receive not parade around the elements. The fruits for believers include the merits of Christ for reconciliation, salvation, eternal life and fellowship.[64]

The Formula of Concord was a statement of Saxon Lutheran theology framed against the Council of Trent and the Reformed confessions ('Sacramentarians'). Article VII was concerned with the Lord's Supper. After a review of the earlier Reformation controversies and Luther's teaching, it asserted:

> We are therefore bound to interpret and explain these words of the eternal, truthful, and almighty Son of God, Jesus Christ, our Lord, Creator, and Redeemer, not as flowery, figurative, or metaphorical expressions, as they appear to our reason, but we must accept them in simple faith and due obedience in their strict and clear sense, just as they read . . . He was not speaking of a symbol of his body, or of a representation . . . He was speaking of his true, essential body.[65]

It asserted that all who partake receive the true, essential body and blood of Christ, but for believers it is a pledge and assurance of sins forgiven, and for the unbeliever, judgement and damnation, but it rejected 'papistic transubstantiation' and denied that the sacrament was an offering. The meaning of 'Do this' was listed as taking bread and wine, consecrating it (by recital of the *verba*) and distributing and receiving the bread and wine, quite deliberately omitting any reference to 'breaking'. Breaking was regarded as utilitarian.

Some later theological and liturgical issues

It has been noted that Brandenburg's sixteenth-century Lutheran Reformation was liturgically quite conservative, and as Bodo Nischan says, 'looked like the least evangelical among Germany's Protestant churches'.[66] However, Elector Johann Sigismund embraced Reformed theology and so attempted to bring a second Reformation to Brandenburg in the early seventeenth century. Margrave Johann Georg had told the staunchly Lutheran Simon Gedicke in 1613, 'Your communion contains still many papal superstitions, yet does not observe the things Christ instituted and ordered us to do.'[67] The Reformed court chaplains wanted to abolish candles, pictures, albs, chasubles and wafer communion bread, as well as genuflecting and ringing bells at the consecration. The Elector

63 Chemnitz, *Lord's Supper*, p. 104.

64 Chemnitz, *Lord's Supper*, pp. 38, 193.

65 Tappert, *Book of Concord*, pp. 577, 578.

66 Bodo Nischan, *Prince, People, and Confession: The Second Reformation in Brandenburg*, Philadelphia: University of Pennsylvania Press, 1994, p. 134.

67 Cited in Nischan, *Prince, People, and Confession*, p. 138.

openly declared his Reformed commitment at a communion service at Christmas 1613. His former Lutheran chaplain described the scene:

> Not far from the altar a communion table, covered with white velvet cloth, had been placed . . . On the table lay a long cake, already cut, so that Füssel [the officiating minister] could easily break off one piece after another and place it into the hands of each communicant . . . There was no consecration, as we know it. No Lutheran hymns were sung . . . About fifty people communed.[68]

Gedicke paid particular attention here to the breaking of the bread, which in Lutheran practice was utilitarian and not a deliberate symbolic ceremony. The Heidelberg Reformed theologian, Thomas Erastus, had listed three reasons for the necessity of a deliberate Fraction ceremony: (1) the obligation of imitating Christ; (2) the command implied in the term 'breaking of bread' used in Acts 2 and 20; and (3) the necessity of visual symbols of Christ's passion and death and of the unity of the Church represented by the 'one loaf'.[69] It became an important element in Reformed eucharistic rites and was interpreted as indicating that the sacrament was an analogy or commemoration of the cross and passion and did not entail the bodily presence in the elements. Gedicke explained the Lutheran position:

> Breaking bread means in the Bible the same as distributing the bread. For if a loaf of bread is to be divided among many it has to be broken . . . However, it is the Calvinists' own invention when they claim that the bread has to be broken to symbolize the crucifixion of Christ's sacrificial body. Never in all eternity will they be able to prove that this was the reason why Christ instituted the bread.[70]

The outcome in Brandenburg was that the Court was Reformed, but most of the citizens remained Lutheran, and two churches – Reformed and Lutheran – were now recognized in the territory. The Fraction thus became a sign of whether one believed the Lutheran bodily presence or the Reformed personal presence.

The seventeenth century also saw the rise of both Lutheran Orthodoxy and of Lutheran Pietism. Martin Chemnitz is often seen as a precursor to theologians such as Johann Konig, Johann Quenstedt and Johann Gerhard. These theologians freely used scholastic methodology to codify Lutheran theology. They distinguished between the earthly element (*materia terrestris*) and the essence (*forma*) of the sacrament. The administration of the Lord's Supper consists (1) in blessing the bread and cup (by the *verba*), (2) in distributing the blessed

68 Cited in Bodo Nischan, 'The "Fractio Panis": A Reformed Communion Practice in Late Reformation Germany', *Church History* 53 (1984), p. 22.

69 Nischan, 'The "Fractio Panis"', p. 20.

70 Nischan, 'The "Fractio Panis"', p. 27.

bread and cup, and (3) in eating and drinking the consecrated elements.[71] A Fraction is conspicuously absent. Quenstedt stated:

> The breaking of the bread may be necessary for its distribution, yet it is not an act essential to this sacrament, nor need it necessarily be performed in the very celebration of the Holy Supper. It is a free act, since it may be done also beforehand.[72]

In his work on the Lord's Supper (1610), Johann Gerhard (1582–1637) stated:

> Even though we indeed receive bread and wine in the holy Lord's Supper, yet it is not ordinary bread and wine. Rather, the bread that we bless (received and eaten) is the fellowship of the body of Christ; the chalice which we consecrate in the holy Lord's Supper (received and drunk) is the fellowship of the blood of Christ, 1 Cor. 10:16. Therefore, no less than the bread and wine, the body and blood of Christ are present in the holy Lord's Supper.[73]

His favourite term was 'essential presence'. The bread and wine do not change, but 'the body of Christ is received and eaten in, with, and under the consecrated bread [and] the blood of Christ is received and drunk in, with, and under the consecrated wine'; Christ is no more spatially contained in the elements than the Holy Spirit is spatially locked up in our souls.[74] He followed Chemnitz in insisting that it is not mere historical recital of the Institution. Schmeling points out that Gerhard has been understood to teach that Christ's body and blood are present only at the eating and not before, but he wrote:

> If it is asked regarding the order of nature, we state that the presence is prior to the eating, for unless the body of Christ is present in the bread it is not able to be eaten sacramentally. [*Si de ordine naturae quaeritur, praesentiam priorem statuimus manducatione, quia nisi corpus Christi in pane praesens adesset, non posset a nobis sacramentaliter manducari.*][75]

With the Reformed concern for a ceremonial fraction in mind he affirmed, 'it is not necessary that a large bread be used, and in the midst of the action of the holy Supper it be broken into pieces, or that the wine be poured out, to thereby indicate one thing or another. Rather, it is sufficient that the bread be eaten and

71 See Friedrich Kalb, *Theology of Worship in 17th-Century Lutheranism*, St Louis: Concordia Publishing House, 1965, p. 97.

72 Theologia IV, p. 216, cited in Kalb, *Theology of Worship*, p. 98.

73 Johannes Gerhard, *A Comprehensive Explanation of Holy Baptism and the Lord's Supper*, 1610, trans. Elmer Hohle, Malone: Repristination Press, 2000, p. 258.

74 Gerhard, *Comprehensive Explanation*, pp. 295–6.

75 Loci Theologici, Locus 21, Para. 195, cited in Gaylin R. Schmeling, *Gerhard – Theologian and Pastor*, http://www.blts.edu/wp-content/uploads/2011/06/GRS-Gerhard.pdf. Loci theologici cum pro adstruenda veritate . . . opus praecilissimum novum tomis comprehensum denuo . . . curavit adjectis notis ipsius Gerhardi posthumis a filio collectis paginis editionis Cottae in margine diligenter notatis. Praefationem, indices generales post G. H. Mullerum adauctos ac vitam Io. Gerhardi adjecit Ed. Preuss. Berolini, sumtibus Gust. Schlawitz, 1863–85.

the wine be drunk'.[76] The main fruit of communion for Gerhard is forgiveness of sins, and we are made partakers of Christ's own body – union and communion with Christ through his own body and blood. In his *Sacred Meditations* he taught:

> Thus this Holy Supper will transform our souls; this most divine sacrament will make us divine men, until finally we shall enter upon the fullness of the blessedness that is to come, filled with all the fullness of God, and wholly like Him.[77]

Gerhard was a representative of Lutheran Orthodoxy, but had also been a student of one of the precursors of Pietism, Johann Arndt. In his *True Christianity* (1605), Arndt had challenged the developing Lutheran Orthodoxy and instead taught the importance of the godly life, heartfelt faith and union of the soul with God, the *unio mystica*. In *True Christianity*, he wrote:

> But take care that Christ himself pray within thee, and the Holy Spirit groan within thee (Rom. 8:26); for as he is 'the Spirit of grace and of supplications' (Zech. 12:10), so, in order to make thy prayers effectual, it is necessary that he also pray in thy heart, the temple of spirit and truth. John 4:23. If this be not done, thy prayers are all of little avail. – Thou believest that in Baptism thou receivest remission of sins, the new birth, and adoption as a child of God. Thou believest aright. But unless thou find in thyself the fruit of baptism, the new birth, the unction of the Spirit, and divine illumination, thy baptism shall avail thee nothing. – Thou believest, according to the words of St Matthew (Matt. 26:26), that in the external Sacrament of the Lord's Supper, thou receivest the true, essential body and the blood of Christ. Thou believest aright. But if thou dost not also eat it inwardly and spiritually, thou wilt not only lose all the benefits of that institution, but dost also eat and drink condemnation to thyself. 1 Cor. 11:29. – Thou believest that Christ was the true Lamb of God offered for us upon the cross. John 1:29. Yet consider: What good can this do thee, unless the same [pg 381] Lamb of God become the daily food and nourishment of thy inward man? 1 Cor. 5:7. It appears, therefore, that thy treasure ought to be *within* thee, and that unless thou seek it there, thou shalt never find it.[78]

The emphasis here is on the inward. Although Arndt was a precursor, Lutheran Pietism flowered with the writings of Philipp Jakob Spener (1635–1705). For Lutheran Orthodoxy, Spener's emphasis on regeneration and the inward working of the Spirit implied a downgrading of the sacraments. Spener himself spoke highly of the sacraments, teaching that the Word is the divine letter of grace and the sacraments are the seal on the letter. Baptism brings new birth, and the Supper is the means of renewal. Outwardly he followed Lutheran teaching,

76 Gerhard, *Comprehensive Explanation*, p. 232.

77 Johann Gerhard, *Sacred Meditations*, trans. C. W. Heisler, Philadelphia: Lutheran Publication Society, 1896, p. 111.

78 *True Christianity* II.I.4, http://www.gutenberg.org/files/34736/34736-h/34736-h.html.

namely that the sacrament consists of an earthly visible element and a heavenly spiritual element. There is both a sacramental and a spiritual eating. The latter is 'the truly essential body of Christ, who was given and crucified for us', 'his very essence'.[79] The Supper is Christ's last will and testament, offering assurance of our salvation and the forgiveness of sins. He wrote:

> We know and believe out of Christ's words that he is really there. How he is there, we do not understand. We need not understand it, for if we had to understand it, then it would happen when we ourselves should provide it. However, Christ does this and it is enough for us that he knows how he does it and is supposed to do it. We only know that it is not spatial or natural, but divine and supernatural, again real presence.[80]

Spener attacked what he regarded as the prevailing *opus operatum* attitude to the Supper that he detected in many of his Lutheran co-religionists:

> There are extraordinarily many people who think only of discharging this holy work and of how often they do it. But they hardly consider whether their spiritual life may be strengthened thereby, whether they proclaim the Lord's death with their hearts, lips, and life, whether the Lord works in and rules over them or they have left the old Adam on his throne.[81]

He stressed the need for proper preparation and heartfelt confession and at the same time encouraged more frequent communion. His emphasis on the Holy Spirit's power to give the sacraments vitality drew suspicion that he was denying the objective presence of Christ. In his defence, James Stein suggests that Spener was concerned with the practical side of the sacrament rather than scholarly academic explanation.[82] The intimacy of Pietism is seen in the devotional prayers of Johann Starck (1680–1756), where the communicant confesses that she receives from Jesus, 'Bridegroom of my soul', 'your true body and your true blood' and also that 'My soul is now restored, for I have been united with Jesus . . . O Jesus, live in me.'[83]

Christian Gerber, the Pietist pastor of Lockwitz, near Dresden, wrote an account of worship in Saxony, which was published in 1732:

> Before we approach the Holy Supper, we first make our confession in the confessional, and after receiving the absolution we proceed to the Holy Table of our most bountiful Savior. This most sacred Supper . . . we celebrate according to the order and institution of our Lord with the greatest devotion and reverence, and during it the servants of God exercise the greatest care so

79 Philipp Spener, *Die Evangelische Glaubenslehre*, 1687, cited in K. James Stein, *Philipp Jakob Spener: Pietist Patriarch*, Chicago: Covenant Press, 1986, p. 222.

80 Spener, *Die Evangelische Glaubenslehre*, cited in Stein, *Philipp Jakob Spener*, p. 223.

81 Philip Spener, *Pia Desideria*, 1675, ET in Theodore G. Tappet, *Introduction to Pia Desideria*, Philadelphia: Fortress Press, 1964, p. 67.

82 Stein, *Spener*, p. 225.

83 Johannes F. Starck, *Tägliches Handbuch in guten wie in bösen Tagen 1728*, ET Starck's *Prayer Book*, St Louis: Concordia Publishing House, 2009, pp. 255–6, 258.

> that in the distribution of it neither any of the consecrated bread nor any of the wine is dropped or falls to the earth. In the ancient church the priest addressed the communicants as they approached the Holy Supper with this thought-provoking formula: 'Lift up your hearts to God,' a formula even today still in use in various places at Holy Communion. After this, the Lord's Prayer . . . and the Words of Institution are read or sung . . . Throughout the reception of Holy Communion the congregation keeps on praising and glorifying the Lord our God with spiritual and devotional hymns and songs of praise. In most localities also wax candles are lit in this celebration, and the officients who distributed this most worthy meal are clad in white surplices and beautiful chasubles.[84]

One place where the formula and much more of the traditional rite and ceremonies was still in use was Leipzig during the time of Bach's residency (1723–50). The city was a bastion of Lutheran Orthodoxy and anti-Pietistic, and its liturgy combined elements of both Luther's *Formula Missae* and the *Deutsche Messe*, according to the festivals and times of service. The archives of this period were diligent in their listing of details which suggest the following order of the Mass:[85]

- Organ prelude or German hymn.
- Introit sung by the choir.
- Organ piece.
- Kyries by choir or German version by congregation.
- Gloria by choir or German version by congregation.
- Salutation and Collect.
- Epistle.
- Hymn.
- Gospel.
- Cantata.
- Creed.
- Pulpit Service: admonition to prayer, a prayer-hymn, Lord's Prayer, Gospel read again, sermon, intercessions and announcements.
- Hymn or Cantata.
- Chanted Latin Preface.
- Sanctus by choir.
- Lord's Prayer chanted by the celebrant.
- Words of Institution chanted by the celebrant.
- Communion, during which hymns were sung.
- Post-Communion Collect.
- Blessing.
- Closing hymn.

84 Christian Gerber, *Historie der Kirchen Ceremonien in Sachsen*, 1732, cited in Günther Stiller, *Johann Sebastian Bach and Liturgical Life in Leipzig*, St Louis: Concordia Publishing House, 1984, p. 263.

85 Stiller, *Johann Sebastian Bach*, pp. 118–31, though the summary here does not do justice to Stiller's rich description.

The celebrant wore an alb and chasuble, assistant ministers wore surplices and during the Words of Institution a consecration bell was rung by the sexton.

Bach himself was no Pietist, but Arndt's *True Christianity* was a book that he owned, and this, together with the eucharistic writings of August Pfeiffer (1640–98), seem to have partly accounted for the mystical element some have detected in some of his compositions.[86] The Words of Institution in the St Matthew Passion are set within a wider textual and musical meditation on the love of God and union with God. Contrasting the way that earlier in this Passion Bach differentiates between the Evangelist and the words of Christ, and reminding us that the work was set for use within the liturgy of Good Friday, Markus Rathey writes:

> This is now different in the setting of the words of institution. The meter switches into triple meter and the melodic line is much more song-like than the damnatory recitative sung by the evangelist. We also see that the vocal bass and the basso continuo move in beautiful parallel motion. And even where Bach gives up the parallel movement of the two voices, he tries to create as many harmonious intervals as possible between the vocal and the instrumental basses. The result is a beautiful, harmonious setting of the words of institution. But it is more than that. The highly melodic, diatonic voice leading, the parallel movement between two voices (which is accentuated by the unusual fact that two bass voices move in parallels), and the sometimes dialogical interplay between the vocal and instrumental bass voices, are typical features of love duets at this time. Bach sets the words of institution as a love song![87]

Thus the Lutheran Orthodoxy of Leipzig and the *unio mystica* tradition so loved by the Pietists (and many Lutheran Orthodox too) unite in Bach's music for the *verba* in the Matthew Passion.

The Lutheran Orthodoxy of Bach's Leipzig was not to endure for long as Enlightenment influences arrived in the form of Superintendent Johann Georg Rosenmüller's term of office (1785–1815). In 1787 he abolished the ringing of the consecration bell. In 1788 he wrote:

> Whether the Words of Institution are chanted or spoken is basically immaterial. But the money spent on wax candles, chasubles and other vestments for the Mass could be spent more profitably. I hope that in our day a person will not easily find a clergyman for whom such things would be so important that he would rather leave the ministry than exchange his cope and chasuble for

86 Mark P. Bangert, '"This is my Blood of the New Testament". The Institution of the Lord's Supper in Bach's Matthew Passion: An Exemplar for Hearing the Passion', in A. A. Clement (ed.), *Das Blut Jesu und die Lehre von der Versöhnung im Werk Johann Sebastian Bach*, Amsterdam: Royal Netherlands Academy of Arts and Sciences, 1995, pp. 215–32.

87 Markus Rathey, 'St Matthew', Colloquium Presentation, Yale Institute of Sacred Music 2011, p. 14.

> a gown, as happened in Prussia, Pomerania, Magdeburg, and Halberstadt about 50 years ago.[88]

In 1787 he introduced a public confession in preparation for communion, and German hymns were to replace the Latin hymns. In 1795 the wearing of chasubles was abolished, and Latin Prefaces were limited until finally disappearing in 1812. He also abolished the holding of a small napkin up to the communicants so that no consecrated element should fall on the ground – a practice he regarded as teaching transubstantiation. He published new prayer formulas more in keeping with Enlightenment sensibilities. The extreme to which some Enlightenment liturgical compilers went is given in an essay by Jeremiah Ohl. From the 1808 Agenda of Christian Sintentis:

> An Invitation to Communion:
>
> Let us do as the Apostles did, and not come to the Altar to receive a sacrament, but to bring our sacrament thither (!), viz., the obligation to hold fast His teachings, which bring us so much happiness, and always and everywhere to show public spirit, as He did.
>
> Verba.
>
> Let all hear the invitation of Jesus Himself to His Supper! After this manner spake the Lord when He took bread, brake it praying, and distributed it: Take, eat, this is my Body, which shall soon be offered for your benefit. Repeat this in remembrance of Me! Thus spoke the Lord when he afterward also prayerfully passed the cup around: Take, drink, this is my Blood; which shall soon be shed for your benefit. Repeat this in remembrance of Me![89]

A prayer of thanksgiving after communion began with these words:

> Before you, the Omnipresent One, have these admirers of Jesus professed their sacrament of the Altar. To you, Omnipresent One, do they appeal with all confidence and joy, that they have done so with truly upright hearts.

The words of administration in another Enlightenment Agenda had:

> Eat this bread; may the spirit of devotion rest upon you with all its blessings. Drink a little wine; moral power does not reside in this wine, but in you, in the teachings of God, and in God.

Or,

---

88 *Pastoralanweisung* 1788, cited in Stiller, *Johann Sebastian Bach*, p. 108.

89 Jeremiah F. Ohl, 'The Liturgical Deteriorization of the Seventeenth and Eighteenth Centuries', *Memoirs of the Lutheran Liturgical Association IV* (1901–2), pp. 75–8.

> Use this bread in remembrance of Jesus Christ; he that hungers after pure and noble virtue shall be fulfilled. Drink a little wine; he that thirsts after pure and noble virtue shall not long for it in vain.[90]

More sober and traditional forms of liturgy were championed in the nineteenth century by figures such as Theodore Kliefoth and Wilhelm Löhe, who both attempted a distillation of earlier forms to produce an 'authentic' Lutheran *ordo*.[91]

Scandinavia: some Danish and Swedish variations

Luther was concerned with the gospel, but there is a sense in which his concern was mainly with the German nation and the German people.[92] It was left to Bugenhagen, for example, to establish church polity and worship in Denmark. The first reform was by Claus Mortensen in 1529, the Malmø Mass. It combined traditional Latin forms on the lines of the *Formula Missae* with some Danish forms. The sermon was followed by a psalm and an admonition to say the Lord's Prayer. Then the Sanctus in Danish was given, with musical notation, followed by the Words of Institution. The *Sursum corda* and Preface were in an appendix as optional, but a Sanctus trope in Danish was also given, so that the Sanctus appears to have been used twice.[93] The main reform was to come with Bugenhagen's 1537 rite. Bugenhagen wrote of the consecration:

> Examine the institution of Christ which says This my bread is my body; this my cup is my blood, etc. How do we have all this? Through the institution of Christ. He Himself thus instituted, ordained, and desired it. Christians embrace this institution and give thanks [to Him]. Therefore it would be folly to omit these words of institution, and a sin not to trust in them. For without these [words], I ask, what would we look for in the bread and the cup?[94]

90 Ohl, 'Liturgical Deteriorization', from Hufnagel, *Liturgische Blätter*.

91 John Klenig, 'The Liturgical Heritage of Theodor Kliefoth', in Bart J. Day et al. (eds), *Lord Jesus Christ, Will You Not Stay: Essays in Honor of Ronald Feuerhahn on the Occasion of His Sixty-Fifth Birthday*, Houston: Feuerhahn Festschrift Committee, 2002, pp. 105–20; Naomichi Masaki, *He Alone is Worthy: The Vitality of the Lord's Supper in Theodor Kliefoth and in the Swedish Liturgy of the Nineteenth Century*, Församlingsförlaget, Göteborg, 2013; Thomas Schattauer, 'The Reconstruction of Rite: The Liturgical Legacy of Wilhelm Löhe', in Nathan Mitchell and John F. Baldovin (eds), *Rule of Prayer, Rule of Faith: Essays in Honor of Aidan Kavanagh, OSB*, Collegeville: Pueblo Press, 1996, pp. 243–77. D. Richard Stuckwisch, *Johann Konrad Wilhelm Löhe: Portrait of a Confessional Lutheran*, Malone: Repristination Press, 1994. For the development in America, see D. M. Kemerer, 'Early American Liturgies', *Memoirs of the Lutheran Liturgical Association* IV (1901–2), pp. 85–94.

92 Bryan D. Spinks, 'Evaluating Liturgical Continuity and Change at the Reformation: A Case Study of Thomas Müntzer, Martin Luther, and Thomas Cranmer', in R. N. Swanson (ed.), *Continuity and Change in Christian Worship*, Woodbridge: Boydell and Brewer, 1999, pp. 165–6.

93 Bugenhagen, *Danske Messebøger Fra Reformationstiden*, Copenhagen: J. H. Schultz Forlag, 1959.

94 Cited in Teigen, *Lord's Supper in the Theology of Martin Chemnitz*, p. 71.

Bugenhagen's order omitted *Sursum corda*, Preface and Sanctus from the text, but offered them as an option on festivals. Of more interest, however, was the Swedish development. The Reformation was a gradual process, and although Olavus Petri studied in Wittenberg, the reformation was tied to an emerging Swedish national consciousness, and it is perhaps not surprising that rites and ceremonies dear to Sweden were retained. The Mass Petri published in 1531 began with a preparation, confession and absolution.[95] The Introit, Kyries and Gloria followed, then Collect and traditional lections with a gradual hymn. The Apostles' or Nicene Creed could be used. The *Sursum corda* was followed by a lengthy Preface, recounting the salvific work of Christ, which, without a break, continues into the Institution Narrative. The Sanctus followed, the Lord's Prayer, and communion with Agnus Dei, a communion exhortation and then administration of the elements. A brief post-communion prayer was followed by the Aaronic blessing. It was a conservative revision based on the *Formula Missae* and a revision made by Andreas Döber in 1525 at Nuremberg. The Church Order of Archbishop Laurentius Petri of 1571 asserted that '[t]he right understanding of this sacrament is that one here receiveth with bread and wine the very Body and Blood of our Lord Jesus Christ', and one wonders what the force of the old Swedish *medh* (with) actually implied.[96] However, the major interest was the so-called 'Red-Book' of King John III. John had a Catholic wife, and seems genuinely concerned to find some ecumenical rapprochement with Rome. In an attempt to have an independent Swedish church recognized by Rome, he published a liturgy that reintroduced a number of prayers reworked from the Latin Mass. It provided a priest's preparation and prayers for vesting, and the old preparation on the way to the altar. The traditional *Ordo Missae* followed. At the offertory, three offertory prayers were provided, the second being a modified version of the *Te igitur* of the *canon missae*. The third, reminiscent of the Pfalz-Neuburg prayer (above), included a petition for the Spirit to bless the elements:

> Bless and sanctify with the power of your Holy Spirit that which is prepared and set apart for this holy use, bread and wine, that rightly used it may be unto us the body and blood of your Son, the food of eternal life, which we may desire and seek with greatest longing.[97]

The Preface and Proper Preface was followed with the Words of Institution and Sanctus, but this was followed by other parts of the *canon missae*, emended – the *Memores igitur*, *Supplices te* and *Nobis quoque*. In many ways this was a brilliant and enterprising transposing of Catholic material into an evangelical key. However, Rome would not make concessions, and the Swedish church

95 Text in Eric E. Yelverton, *The Mass in Sweden: Its Development from the Latin Rite from 1531 to 1917*, London: Henry Bradshaw Society, 1920. *PEER*, pp. 201–3; see also Frank C. Senn, 'The Mass in Sweden: From Swedish to Latin?', in Karen Maag and John D. Witvliet (eds), *Worship in Medieval and Early Modern Europe: Change and Continuity in Religious Practice*, Notre Dame: University of Notre Dame Press, 2004, pp. 63–83.

96 Yelverton, *Mass in Sweden*, p. 58.

97 Senn, *Christian Liturgy*, p. 432.

found it too Catholic, and so it did not survive the king's death. His successor, Charles IX, was Reformed by conviction, and so introduced a Communion Office, which would have led the Church in the very opposite direction to that of John III. Yelverton commented:

> The words of institution of the Lord's Supper are repeated *five* times, four times in succession in the introductory exhortation, and once again in the preface: they are treated purely as a record of an historical event in the earthly life of Our Lord, evidently for the purpose of annulling the Lutheran doctrine of the 'ubiquitas carnis Christ'. Furthermore the communion address (*nattvards förmaning*), which includes the ten commandments with a running commentary, is framed in words which exclude all conception of an objective presence of Christ in the sacrament of the altar even at its reception.[98]

This rite was also rejected by the Church in Sweden. The new rite of 1614 dropped the use of Latin, and the service was called *Kyrkotienst*, Church Service. The sermon, as in Bach's Leipzig, was surrounded with a hymn, the Lord's Prayer, a confession and absolution, as well as general intercessions and a further hymn. Any future innovations were to be taken only from Lutheran sources. As Yelverton's texts show, little change was made up to 1917.

Concluding remarks

Although Luther allowed much leeway in reform, few Lutheran rites strayed far from Luther's textual paradigms. Sixteenth-century biblical hermeneutics allowed Luther to see the *canon missae*, as explained in the commentaries and backed by scholastic theology and official pronouncements, in direct contradiction to the teaching of Scripture. Although he was aware of the Eucharistic Prayers of the Eastern rites, they seem to have played no part in his dogmatic reformulations of the liturgy. It is difficult for modern scholars to understand how the Words of Institution – a latecomer into the Eucharistic Prayer – should take the place of any Eucharistic *Prayer* at all, and how the words that Jesus 'gave thanks' or blessed were seemingly either ignored or subsumed by dogmatics into the *verba* alone. However, the most significant shift is that, at the Reformation, theology now leads to major liturgical rewriting in a far more obvious, conscious and deliberate way than appears to have been the case in previous centuries.

98 Yelverton, *Mass in Sweden*, p. 123.

11

The Reformed Tradition: From Ulrich Zwingli to Eugène Bersier[1]

The Reformed tradition embraces a wide variety of churches that derive their theologies from prominent Swiss, French and German theologians of the sixteenth century, whose ideas were embraced and developed in some of the Swiss Cantons, Huguenot France, the German Palatinate, Hungary, Poland, the Netherlands and Scotland. It is often named 'Calvinist', but even if John Calvin was the most outstanding theologian of this tradition, he was not the only voice. The early formative eucharistic rites and theological developments came from Zurich, Basel and Strasbourg as much as from Calvin's Geneva. In trying to differentiate the sacramental teaching of the various Reformed theologians, Brian Gerrish has usefully used three categories – symbolic memorialism, symbolic parallelism and sacramental instrumentalism – and these will be utilized here.[2]

Zurich: Zwingli and Bullinger

Ulrich Zwingli had been educated in the Universities of Vienna and Basel and in 1519 was called to be a pastor in Zurich. Trained in the new humanist learning, by 1522 he had openly adopted Reformation principles, and called for the abolition of indulgences, fasting, veneration of saints, clerical celibacy and pilgrimage. His understanding of the Eucharist rested on two basic fundamental theological convictions.[3] First, that nothing that is not warranted by Scripture is necessary; indeed, it is to add to the Gospel. Whereas Luther accepted things not forbidden as *adiaphora*, for Zwingli everything needed to be mandated or otherwise it must be discarded. Second, he believed in the immediacy of grace through faith in Christ, which is mediated by the Holy Spirit and is spiritual. It cannot be mediated by a physical rite or ceremony. This latter belief was a result of his Neoplatonism; he drove a sharp wedge between the physical and

1 Some material in this chapter is adapted from Chapter 2 of Bryan D. Spinks, *Reformation and Modern Rituals and Theologies of Baptism: From Luther to Contemporary Practices*, Aldershot: Ashgate Publishing, 2006, and Chapter 1 of Bryan D. Spinks, *Sacraments, Ceremonies and the Stuart Divines*, Aldershot: Ashgate Publishing, 2002.

2 Brian Gerrish, 'The Lord's Supper in the Reformed Confessions', in Donald McKim (ed.), *Major Themes in the Reformed Tradition*, Grand Rapids: Eerdmans, 1992, pp. 245–58.

3 See Peter Stephens, 'Zwingli's Sacramental Views', in E. J. Furcha and H. Wayne Pipkin (eds), *Prophet, Pastor, Protestant*, Allison Park: Pickwick Publications, 1984, pp. 155–69; *The Theology of Huldrych Zwingli*, Oxford: Clarendon Press, 1986.

fleshly, and the spiritual. He preferred to speak of the immortality of the soul than of the resurrection of the body, and although he professed a Chalcedonian Christology, he seems to have seen the humanity of Christ as only necessary for the suffering on the cross.

In the list of Articles published in 1523 Zwingli defined the word sacrament according to the old Latin meaning, as an oath taken by soldiers.[4] He thus regarded the sacraments like tokens or badges that we wear, just as a monk might wear a habit, or a soldier wear the emblem of his Swiss canton. Sacraments become ecclesial events or signs, not signs mediating something from God. Zwingli wrote:

> If a man sews on a white cross, he proclaims that he wishes to be a confederate. And if he makes the pilgrimage to Nähenfels and gives God praise and thanksgiving for the victory vouchsafed to our forefathers, he testifies that he is a confederate indeed. Similarly the man who receives the mark of baptism is the one who is resolved to hear what God says to him, to learn the divine precepts and to live his life in accordance with them.[5]

In his 1523 Articles he rejected the idea that the Eucharist was a sacrifice, stressing instead that it was a memorial of a sacrifice and a seal of our redemption.[6] However, sometime in 1524, prior to its widespread publication in 1525, Zwingli had read and accepted the teaching of the Dutch lawyer Cornelius Hoen.[7] Hoen argued that Christ instituted the Eucharist in order to give those who are his own a sure pledge (*pignus*) for the forgiveness of sins, and compared the bread and wine to the ring that a bridegroom gives as a pledge or token to his bride. The words of Christ, 'Hoc est Corpus meum' should be understood figuratively, and 'est' had the force of 'signifies'. Eating and drinking is not in the elements of bread and wine, but is a spiritual eating governed by John 6, and an opportunity to remember the one salvific sacrifice of Christ. Zwingli also read a work of Karlstadt, who himself had read Hoen, and so in his letter to Matthew Alber of November 1524, Zwingli explained that John 6 is the key to understanding the Eucharist, and suggested with regard to the words 'This is my body',

> Put 'signifies' for 'is' here and you have, 'Take, eat; this signifies my body which is given for you.' Then the meaning will certainly be, 'Take, eat, for this which I bid you do will signify to you or remind you of my body which presently to be given for you.'. . . Since, therefore, this Lord's Feast, or in Paul's words, Lord's Supper, was instituted that we might call to remembrance the death of Christ, which he suffered for us, it is clear that it is the sign itself by

4 *Huldrych Zwingli Writings*, trans. E. J. Furcha, vol. 1, Allison Park: Pickwick Publications, 1984, p. 99.

5 *Corpus Reformatorum*, IV.217, cited in Stephens, 'Zwingli's Sacramental Views', p. 159.

6 *Huldrych Zwingli Writings*, vol. 1, p. 98.

7 See the recent study by Bart Jan Spruyt, *Cornelius Henrici Hoen (Honius) and His Epistle on the Eucharist (1525)*, Leiden: Brill, 2006. It was shown to Zwingli by Hinne Rode. Spruyt, p. 116.

> which those who rely upon the death and blood of Christ mutually prove to their brethren that they have the faith.[8]

It is possible to exaggerate the influence of Hoen, but that work seems to have assisted Zwingli in clarifying his own thoughts on the Eucharist. In *A Commentary Concerning True and False Religion*, 1525, Zwingli outlined the following beliefs:

1. It is a mistake to understand a sacrament as having any inherent power either to convey forgiveness or to strengthen faith; for this ties the freedom of God's Spirit to human performance.
2. A sacrament can accordingly only have the character of an *initiatio*, a ceremony of initiation, or an *oppignoratio*, a *publica consignatio*, an oath, a public confession of allegiance. Here Zwingli takes up the ancient Latin meaning of *sacramentum* (seemingly allowing the Latin to interpret the Greek *mysterion*), which makes a sacrament a sign and badge of commitment. So far as the Eucharist is concerned, this makes it a visible, public affirmation and demonstration of faith.
3. The worth and value of the flesh of Christ is not that it is eaten by us, but that it was slain for us. To eat his flesh is simply to believe that he was sacrificed for us.
4. The point and purpose of the contrast between 'flesh' and 'spirit' in John 6 is that the Spirit of God raises our hearts above all earthly and material things and brings our faith to bear on Jesus Christ, to the strengthening of our soul and spirit.
5. The risen and glorified body of Christ is in heaven, where he sits at the right hand of the Father; it cannot at the same time be present on earth in bread and wine. Otherwise his human nature would be utterly unlike any other, which would contradict the incarnation.
6. Christ's Words of Institution have to be interpreted in the light of all these considerations. That is precisely the task and responsibility of authentic faith, which can by no means take them literally. 'That is' means, as elsewhere in the Bible, 'signifies'. Genuine faith is not credulous literalism or superstition; and it must exclude any notion of 'real presence' which involves confusing the divine and human natures of Christ, and so divinizes what is and remains creaturely, namely Christ's truly human body and human nature.

In a work of 1526, *The Lord's Supper*, he rejected the argument that the Words of Institution should be taken literally and reproduced Hoen's illustration of the wedding ring. In a work addressed to Luther, *A Friendly Exegesis*, published early in 1527, Zwingli pinpointed their main difference, namely, over the meaning of the Words of Institution, Zwingli denying that there is any physical presence of Christ in the elements. Their failure in agreement at Marburg in 1529 was precisely over the issue of presence and the interpretation of Christ's

8 *Huldrych Zwingli Writings*, trans. H. Wayne Pipkin, vol. 2, Allison Park: Pickwick Publications, 1984, p. 139.

words.[9] Zwingli's teaching is neatly summarized in *An Exposition of the Faith*, 1531, the same year that he was to die in battle at Cappel. Sacraments (Baptism and the Lord's Supper) are sacred things that testify to historical facts, represent high things and augment faith. Rejecting that Christ is eaten in the Supper physically, naturally, essentially or even quantitatively, Zwingli insisted that Christ was eaten spiritually and sacramentally:

> To eat the body of Christ spiritually is equivalent to trusting with heart and soul upon the mercy and goodness of God through Christ, that is, to have the assurance of an unbroken faith that God will give us the forgiveness of sins and the joy of eternal salvation for the sake of his Son, who gave himself for us and reconciled the divine righteousness to us. For what can he withhold from us when he delivered up his only begotten Son?
>
> If I may put it more precisely, to eat the body of Christ sacramentally is to eat the body of Christ with the heart and the mind in conjunction with the sacrament . . . So then when you come to the Lord's Supper to feed spiritually upon Christ, and when you thank the Lord for his great favour, for the redemption whereby you are delivered from despair, and for the pledge whereby you are assured of eternal salvation, when you join with your brethren in partaking of the bread and wine which are the tokens of the body of Christ, then in the true sense of the word you eat him sacramentally. You do inwardly that which you represent outwardly, your soul being strengthened by the faith which you attest in the tokens.[10]

Summarizing Zwingli's thought, Peter Stephens suggested that he saw it as a thanksgiving for and memorial of Christ's death, a confessing of one's faith in that death and a pledging of oneself in response to Christ's death; compared with much medieval practice, Zwingli's was a strongly corporate and ethical emphasis.[11] His emphasis on the communicant's subjective remembering led Gerrish to class this as symbolic memorialism.

How did this play out liturgically? In 1523, Zwingli published an attack on the Mass entitled *De canone missae epicheiresis*.[12] He did not accept the authenticity of Ambrose's *De Sacramentis* and so dismissed its witness. He regarded the *canon missae* as a *congeries*, a result of various writers making additions that took its final form after the time of Gregory the Great. Had it existed in the time of Gregory, he would have corrected the barbarous and coarse Latin; apparently it did not occur to the humanist scholar that the style of Latin witnessed to the canon's antiquity. However, his main attack is on the idea of the Mass as sacrifice. Yet whereas Luther removed the canon, Zwingli offered a Reformed canon. Indeed, this rite of 1523 is quite conservative in terms of its structure. The work is in Latin, though it is not clear whether this was for

9 *Huldrych Zwingli Writings*, vol. 2, p. 238; for the Colloquy texts, Herman Sasse, *This Is My Body*, Adelaide: Lutheran Publishing House, 1977.

10 In G. W. Bromily, *Zwingli and Bullinger*, Library of Christian Classics, vol. XXIV, Philadelphia: Westminster Press, 1953, pp. 258–9.

11 Stephens, *Theology of Huldrych Zwingli*, p. 254.

12 *PEER*, pp. 183–8.

scholarly convention or usage. Nearly the whole of the first part of the Mass is retained, except that the saints' days Collects, proses and sequences disappear, as also the offertory prayers. The lections were in German, but not the canon. *Sursum corda*, Preface and Sanctus were retained – probably because, as with the case of Luther, no one regarded these as being part of the canon. Four prayers took the place of the traditional canon:

1 Rehearsal of redemption history, not unlike that encountered in the classical Greek anaphoras. It ends with an offering, not of bread and wine but of prayer and praise in the form of the Lord's Prayer.
2 Beseeching God to feed the hungry soul. In this prayer Zwingli shows his theological hand – it is our souls that are made in the image of God, and these must be fed with spiritual food, that is given by the word. It is a prayer to be fed by God's word.
3 A prayer that takes up the theme of the one offering Christ. The language in this prayer is ambiguous, and scholars have argued that this takes us far beyond the usual characterization of Zwinglianism, though this does not account for the fact that Zwingli made further reforms of a less ambiguous nature.
4 A prayer that incorporated the Agnus Dei, requesting forgiveness because of the passion, and then the Words of Institution.

He provided words of administration, 'The body/blood of our Lord Jesus Christ preserve you to everlasting life', and the rite was to end with a brief thanksgiving, the Nunc dimittis and a blessing.

Zwingli was attacked by conservatives and progressives alike, and in his *Defense* addressed to Theobald von Geroldseck urged that vestments must be abolished, but as to the complaint of the prayers of his new canon, they can be omitted, and if they are at variance with Christ, this must be demonstrated from Scripture.[13] In April 1525 a much more radical reform was carried through. The normal Sunday service was no longer the Mass, or Eucharist. It was a preaching service, based on the vernacular preaching service called Prone. Such a service had been very popular in Basel, introduced by John Surgant in 1502. Surgant had used it to supplement the Mass; Zwingli used it to replace the Mass. Its structure was as follows:[14]

- Bidding prayer.
- Lord's Prayer.
- Ave Maria.
- Sermon.
- Remembrance of those who had died in the week.
- General confession.
- Pardon.

13 *Defense of the Pamphlet on the Canon of the Mass*, 1523, ET by Henry Prebles, typescript, p. 9.

14 Text in Bard Thompson, *Liturgies of the Western Church*, New York: Meridian Books, 1961, pp. 147–8.

It is clear that by 1525 Zwingli had developed his doctrine to a point where preaching the word was the most important feature, and the Eucharist was limited to four times a year. We should remember that most medieval laity were used only to communicating once or at most three times a year. Given that for the Reformers a Mass must be a communicating Mass, one can understand the reduction. With this reform, both vestments and music were abolished.

The order for the Eucharist was to be used at Easter, Pentecost, 11 September – the feast of the patronal saints of Zurich – and Christmas.[15] A Preface to the service notes that the Eucharist is a thanksgiving to God and a memorial. After the preaching service, there came a prayer for assistance at this service, a fixed Epistle from 1 Corinthians 11.20–29, *Gloria in excelsis* recited by the people. In fact, part of Zwingli's theology was the importance of the civic authorities in things sacred and secular, and he had to bow to the demands of the City Council that this would be recited by two deacons and not by the people. There was a fixed Gospel – from John 6. The kissing of the Gospel book was retained. There followed the Creed, exhortation, Lord's Prayer, a Prayer of Approach and then the Words of Institution. It is interesting to note that this ends with the words, 'For as often as you eat this bread and drink this cup, you proclaim and *glorify* the Lord's death.' After communion comes Psalm 112 (113), a brief thanksgiving and the Dismissal. The reformed canon of 1523 has gone; but the summary given in Jasper and Cuming is misleading: just as Luther did in 1526, the *Sursum corda* Preface is replaced by an exhortation, which emphasized that the Eucharist is a subjective commemoration with praise and thanksgiving. The prayer stressed the unity of the body of Christ, the fact that the body has the task of giving praise and thanks for redemption, and the death of Christ. There is a case for saying that the exhortation, Lord's Prayer, this prayer and the narrative together constituted a more radical canon. The Eucharist is an expression of ecclesiological solidarity and witness to the world rather than the presence of Christ in the community through the bread and wine.

Zwingli's 'memorialism' has on the whole been regarded as inadequate – by many of his contemporaries in the Reformed tradition, as well as by many subsequent theologians. Since he died in battle, it is impossible to know whether he might have nuanced his position in more tranquil times. Bruce Gordon, however, has drawn attention to another aspect of Zwingli's liturgy:

> The Zwinglian liturgy was moulded as a narrative; it was the narrative of the Last Supper, and the Passion of Christ, and those attending this service were not spectators, but disciples. This drama did not lack movement, for each of the images culled from Scripture was intended to serve the believer in the imitation of Christ. This was Zwingli's concept of recollection, for memory is movement and through the liturgy the community comes to its defining memory, that Christ offered himself as the bread of life. Hence the centrality of John 6 to Zwinglian worship. Within this drama Zwingli employed a range of images and formulations which would have been familiar to the people; these images were not static; and in themselves had no purpose other than to

15 German text in Fritz Schmidt-Clausing, *Zwinglis liturgische Formulare*, Frankfurt am Main: Verlag Otto Lembeck, 1970, pp. 32–9; ET in Thompson, *Liturgies*, pp. 140–55.

> serve as stimulants to individual and collective consciences in their journey of recollection.[16]

Gordon drew attention to the title of the rite – *Aktion* – and argued that the minister acted as prophet in the sermon, but as host at the table: 'It was the minister's voice which was heard at the feast . . . For whilst these words might have no effect upon the substantial nature of the bread and wine, they were the essential catalyst for the community's recollection of its true nature.'[17] Christ is present not in the elements but, as the historical narrative is retold, he is present in his divinity in the community. Zwingli read the Words of Institution as the people received the elements; it was his successor, Bullinger, who insisted they be read prior to the elements being received. The liturgy and its enactment seem to have been intended to be more dynamic than some liturgical scholars have hitherto concluded.

Zwingli died on the battlefield in 1531, and his successor at Zurich was Heinrich Bullinger, who felt duty bound to uphold Zwingli's teaching. Later he was in dialogue with John Calvin of Geneva, since there were fundamental differences between the Zurich–Basel–Berne theologians and Geneva on the question of sacraments. Bullinger modified the Zurich position, and his views were set forth succinctly in the *Decades* and in the *Second Helvetic Confession* (1566). Whereas Calvin (following Martin Bucer) could speak of sacraments as being instruments (*instrumenta*) and of exhibiting (*exhibent*) the grace they signify, Bullinger declined to use such language, allowing only that sacraments might be implements (*organa*), but his preferred terms were sign and signify. A sacrament is a witnessing to God's will, and is a remembrance and renewing of the benefits and promises of God.[18] Of the Lord's words at the Last Supper, he wrote:

> those words of the Lord are not roughly to be expounded according to the letter, as though bread and wine were the body and blood of Christ substantially and corporally, but mystically and sacramentally: so that the body and blood of Christ do abide in their substance and nature, and in their place, I mean, in some certain place of heaven; but the bread and wine are a sign or sacrament, a witness or sealing, and a lively memory of the body given and his blood shed for us.[19]

Bullinger distinguished sharply between the sign and the thing signified. Grace, which is the favour and good will of God, is mediated by the Holy Spirit, and therefore the sacraments are not themselves channels of grace.[20]

---

16 Bruce Gordon, 'Transcendence and Community in Zwinglian Worship', in Swanson (ed.), *Continuity and Change*, Woodbridge: Boydell and Brewer, 1999, pp. 128–50, pp. 130–1.

17 Gordon, 'Transcendence and Community', p. 140.

18 Heinrich Bullinger, *Decades*, vol. 5, Parker Society, Cambridge: Cambridge University Press, 1850, p. 251.

19 Bullinger, *Decades*, vol. 5, pp. 253–4.

20 Bullinger, *Decades*, vol. 5, p. 309.

> Christ's body is eaten and his blood drunken spiritually; it is also eaten and drunken sacramentally. The spiritual manner [is] accomplished by faith, whereby being united to Christ, we be made partakers of all his goodness. The sacramental manner is only performed in celebrating the Lord's supper. The spiritual eating is perpetual unto the godly, because faith is to them perpetual. They communicate with Christ both without the supper and in the supper.[21]

Thus the *Second Helvetic Confession* put it:

> We do not approve of the doctrine of those who teach that grace and the things signified are so bound to and included in the signs that whoever participate outwardly in the signs, no matter what sort of persons they be, also inwardly participate in the grace and things signified.[22]

This dualism, where the inward grace and outward sign do not necessarily coincide, has aptly been termed symbolic parallelism by Gerrish; the two may happen at the same time, but are not so joined that this must be so. In this respect, Bullinger seems to differ from Zwingli. As to the eucharistic liturgy, Bullinger's *Agenda* of 1532 and 1535 reproduced most of Zwingli's 1525 rite, though with some explicatory material added.[23]

Strasbourg: Diobald Schwartz and Martin Bucer

The key Reformer of Strasbourg was Martin Bucer, a former Dominican priest. He initially aligned himself with Wittenberg, for which he was excommunicated by the Bishop of Speyer. He came to Strasbourg in 1524 and remained there until the Interim of 1548. He attempted to find agreement between Zurich and Wittenberg, and was later involved in dialogue with Catholic theologians, with the result that many on the Protestant side mistrusted him. By 1524 he had adopted the sacramental views of Zwingli, but in subsequent years, in his role as a sixteenth-century ecumenist, ever hopeful of finding unity and agreement, he developed his own particular eucharistic theology. René Bornert and Peter Stephens divide his sacramental thinking into two periods, though Stephens also posits a later period of consolidation.[24] From 1524 until 1530 there is a sharp dualism (as in Zwingli and Bullinger), but between 1530 and 1551 the inward

21 Bullinger, *Decades*, vol. 5, p. 463.

22 Ch. 19, Latin text in Philip Schaff, *The Creeds of Christendom*, vol. 3, Grand Rapids: Baker Books, [1876] 1998, p. 289; ET. 'The Second Helvetic Confession', http://www.ccel.org/creeds/helvetic.htm.

23 See Leo Weisz, 'Heinrich Bullinger's Agenda', *Zwingliana* 10 (1954–58), pp. 1–23; comparative table in Markus Jenny, *Die Einheit des Abendmahlsgottesdienstes bei den elsässischen und schweizerischen Reformatoren*, Zürich–Stuttgart: Zwingli Verlag, 1968, pp. 54–6.

24 René Bornert, *La Réforme Protestante du Culte à Strasbourg au XVIe siècle (1523–1598)*, Leiden: Brill, 1981, p. 309; Peter Stephens, *The Holy Spirit in the Theology of Martin Bucer*, Cambridge: Cambridge University Press, 1970.

and outward are brought into closer union. In his *Grund und Ursach* (1524), he said of the Lord's Supper:

> The Lord commanded the bread to be eaten and the cup to be drunk, and directed and commanded [to go] at once from the bodily to the spirit, to remember him . . . the Lord has given nothing bodily in holy communion except eating and drinking, and that for the sake of the spiritual, that is, his remembrance.[25]

Yet, by 1527 he had started to use the term *exhibere/fürtragen*, which became a key term and which David Wright notes can only mean 'confer', 'impart' and 'bestow'.[26] Bornert commented:

> The sacraments, he says, are not only external signs but also 'instruments', 'channels', 'implements' of the interior reality which they signify. They 'present' (*praesentare, zustellen*), they 'offer' (*offere, anbieten*), they 'give' (*dare, reichen, darreichen, dargeben, schenken*), they 'communicate' (*communicare, übergeben*) the spiritual gift which the faithful receive (*recipere, empfangen*) by faith.[27]

In the *Gospels* (1536) he wrote that sacraments are the visible gospels, instituted by Christ 'so that he may communicate his redemption to us through them. Thus it is quite clear that they are in a certain way instruments and channels of the Spirit and of his grace.'[28] In the same year, he endorsed the Wittenberg Concordat and he explained its statement on the Eucharist:

> the body and blood of Christ himself are truly present, not just effective, powerfully, effectively, spiritually, but *vere, substantilaiter, essentialiter*, essentially, and truly, and are given and received with bread and wine.[29]

Unlike Luther, for Bucer 'with' the bread and wine was not interchangeable with 'under' and 'in', and thus Gerrish placed Bucer also in the category of symbolic parallelism.

All the Reformers rejected the teaching that the Mass was a sacrifice, and in 1524 Bucer recalled his early unease with the *canon missae*: 'often I celebrated Mass and read the Canon, and my intention in doing so was equally devout, but at the time, I could not assess the meaning of the words, "these offerings", "these gifts", and similar expressions found in the Canon. Thus I recited them and did not even know why.'[30] This unease became open condemnation in a

25 Cited in Bornert, *La Réforme*, p. 242.

26 David Wright, 'Infant Baptism and the Christian Community in Bucer', in *Martin Bucer: Reforming Church and Community*, Cambridge: Cambridge University Press, 1994, pp. 95–106, p. 99.

27 Bornert, *La Réforme*, p. 317.

28 Stephens, *Theology of Huldrych Zwingli*, p. 217.

29 Stephens, *Theology of Huldrych Zwingli*, p. 257.

30 *Ein kurtzer warhafftiger bericht* 1524, cited in Nicholas Thompson, *Eucharistic Sacrifice and Patristic Tradition in the Theology of Martin Bucer 1534–1546*, Leiden: Brill, 2005, p. 93.

report by the Strasbourg preachers in 1526, of which Bucer seems to have been the principal author:

> See what a blasphemy it is: before the consecration he offers up a bit of bread and wine to God for his own sins and those of all Christians, living and dead, for their salvation and eternal life. The death of Christ alone has effected and provided for this.[31]

However, as Thompson has demonstrated, in later conversations with Catholic theologians in the hope of finding some agreement, Bucer was prepared to accept that the term 'offer' might be applied to the Eucharist, and in his *Psalms Commentary* wrote:

> There is the one and only blood of Christ, which makes expiation for our offences and reconciles us to the Father (Hebrews 9:[12]). For this we, too, give solemn thanks in the sacred Eucharist, and with our commemoration and thanksgiving we, as it were, repeat it.[32]

He seems to have been prepared to allow the use of the Roman *canon missae* by others provided it was understood in an 'evangelical' manner, as part of allowing different liturgical usages to co-exist as part of a united Church. This certainly did not mean reintroducing it into the liturgical reforms of Strasbourg.[33] Those reforms began with the *Teutsche Messe* of Diobald Schwartz in 1524. After the invocation, the final verse of Psalm 100 was used for an invitation to prayer, a Confiteor was said, and 1 John 1.9 and Mark 9.24 served as an absolution. Another invocation – Psalm 124.8 – was given (this was common in a number of German and Swiss medieval rites) and then the Introit. The ninefold Kyrie was reduced to three. The Gradual was omitted. The prayers of the 'Little Canon' were replaced by a version of the *Orate fratres*, exhorting the congregation to pray to the Father through the Son for the gift of the Spirit so that the Church might be a reasonable offering to God. After *Sursum corda*, Preface and Sanctus came a prayer of intercession for the Christian people, city and magistrates, and was followed by the recitation of the Words of Institution and a prayer of thanks. Clearly it was the Catholic idea of eucharistic sacrifice that was the target of this reform.

It was shortly after the publication of this liturgy that Bucer published his *Grund und Ursach* (1524), which included his idea of the reform of the Mass:

> When the congregation comes together on Sunday, the minister admonishes them to make confession of their sins and to pray for pardon; and he confesses to God on behalf of the whole congregation, prays for pardon, and proclaims

31 Cited in Thompson, *Eucharistic Sacrifice*, p. 113.

32 Cited in Thompson, *Eucharistic Sacrifice*, p. 120.

33 See the discussion in Bornert, *La Réforme*. For the texts, see Friedrich Hubert, *Die Strasburger liturgischen Ordnungen im Zeitalter der Reformation*, Göttingen: Vandenhoek und Ruprecht, 1900; L. Büchsenschütz, *Histoire des Liturgies en Langue Allmande dans l'Église de Strasbourg au XVIe siècle*, Cahors, 1900.

> the remission of sins to those that believe. Then the whole congregation sings several short psalms or hymns of praise, after which the minister makes a brief prayer and reads to the congregation a passage from the writings of the Apostles, expounding the same as briefly as possible. Thereupon the congregation sings again: the Ten Commandments or something else. The priest then proclaims the Gospel and delivers the sermon proper. After this the congregation sings the Articles of our Faith. The priest then offers a prayer for the civil authority, in which he prays for an increase of faith and love, and grace to keep the remembrance of Christ's death with profit.
>
> Then he admonishes those who wish to observe the Lord's Supper with him, that they would do so in remembrance of Christ, to die to their sins, bear their cross willingly, and love their neighbor truly, being strengthened in faith, which must then come to pass when we consider with believing hearts what unlimited grace and goodness Christ hath shown us, in that He offered His body and blood to the Father on our behalf. After the exhortation he proclaims the Gospel of the Lord's Supper, as the three evangelists, Matthew, Mark, and Luke, have described it, together with Paul in 1 Cor. 11. Then the priest divides the bread and cup of the Lord amongst them, and also partakes of it himself. Presently the congregation sings another hymn of praise. After that the minister closes the Supper with a short prayer, blesses the people, and bids them go in the peace of the Lord. This is the manner and custom with which we now celebrate Christ's Supper on Sundays only.[34]

New orders of service quickly flowed from the printing presses in the following months, each one having some changes, some minor and some major, responding to Bucer's ideas. H. O. Old observes that finally, with the Strasbourg Psalter of 1526, the liturgy reaches a form which it maintains for more than a decade.[35] Vestments were discarded, versicles and responses were eliminated, the Sanctus and Benedictus disappeared, and the Kyries and *Gloria in excelsis* may be replaced by a psalm. More psalmody was used, and the lectionary readings were replaced by a Gospel reading that was read chapter by chapter. Yet, in spite of the stabilization, between 1524 and 1539 some 18 editions were published. That of 1539 illustrates how often the later additions to the medieval service were the ones liked and developed by the Reformers. The rite began with a confession, with a choice of three, with an absolution from 1 Timothy 1 or some other of four suggested scriptural quotations. A hymn or psalm was sung, with the possibility of the Kyries and *Gloria in excelsis*. A short prayer was offered for illumination in the sermon, a psalm sung, and then the Gospel reading and sermon. A lengthy exhortation on the sacrament followed, including the words, 'the Lord truly offers and gives His holy and sanctifying flesh and blood to us in the Holy Supper, with the visible things of bread and wine . . .'.[36] Here again we find Bucer using 'with' (*mit*), but not 'in'. The Creed was sung and the minister

---

34 Cited in Thompson, *Liturgies*, pp. 161–2.

35 H. O. Old, *The Patristic Roots of Reformed Worship*, Zurich: Theologischer Verlag, 1970, p. 39.

36 Text in Thompson, *Liturgies*, p. 171; German text in Hubert, *Strasburger liturgischen Ordnungen*, p. 98. Thompson has 'body' whereas I have followed the German, *fleysch*.

then prayed a prayer from behind the altar. A choice of three was given. They were of an intercessory nature and each concluded with the Lord's Prayer, and in a sense they represent a Reformed canon. The first included a request that 'we verily receive and enjoy the true communion of His body and blood, of our Saviour Himself, who is the only saving bread of heaven'. The second included the words, 'draw our hearts and souls to this thy Son, so that as He presents Himself to us in His holy Gospel and sacraments, and bestows His body and blood that we who are corrupt in ourselves may live in Him – we may receive such a love as His with living faith'. The third asked that we 'with right faith receive and enjoy His true body and true blood, yea Himself our Saviour'. If an exhortation was not given after the sermon, one could be given at this point, and the Words of Institution followed. Then came the administration. After singing a psalm, the rite ended with a thanksgiving prayer (choice of two) and a blessing from Numbers and a dismissal, 'Depart! The Spirit of the Lord go with you unto eternal life. Amen.'

With the Interim of 1548, Strasbourg became Lutheran with a Lutheran liturgy and teaching.

Basel, Berne and Neuchâtel and the Liturgies of Oecolampadius and Farel

One of the principal Reformers at Basel was Johannes Oecolampadius (1482–1531). He studied at Heidelberg and then at Tübingen, where he met Melanchthon. He entered a monastery in 1520 and in 1523 became the priest at St Ulrich's in Basel. By this time he had adopted evangelical views, and by November 1524 it was widely known that he shared similar views on the Eucharist to Zwingli.[37] In 1523 he published *Das Testament Jesu Christi*, which was designed to be a private prayer book for lay people to follow the Mass and understand it in an evangelical manner. Smend noted that it was based on the Mass for Maundy Thursday.[38] Old usefully summarizes the evangelical canon:

> First we have a prayer of self oblation, asking God to accept the gift of our souls and bodies, which God himself has created, and that he sanctify them through his divine grace. The prayer continues with a very free paraphrase of the whole of the story of the institution of the Lord's Supper according to Luke. After the Canon we find a collect that God should not regard the sin of the worshiper but the faith of the Church. A third prayer confesses faith in the presence of Christ in the sacrament, in the Incarnation of the Son of God for the redemption of man and in the sacrificial death of the Savior of the world.

37 Diane Poythress, *Reformer of Basel: The Life, Thought, and Influence of Johannes Oecolampadius*, Grand Rapids: Reformation Heritage Books, 2011; see also Amy Nelson Burnett, *Teaching the Reformation: Ministers and Their Message in Basel, 1529–1629*, Oxford: Oxford University Press, 2006.

38 Julius Smend, *Die Evangelischen Deutschen Messen bis zu Luthers Deutscher Messe*, Göttingen: Vandenhoek and Ruprecht, 1896, p. 57, 'ist der einer freien Verdeutschung der Missa in coena Domini'. For the text, see pp. 51–7.

> The prayer then turns to the testament or covenant which Christ has given us in this Holy Supper and gives thanks to God that we have been included in the covenant.[39]

This was a devotional guide, and not a public liturgy, but its emphases indicated the direction of the Basel Reformer's theology. In his 1525 work *On the Genuine Words of the Lord*, he wrote, 'I freely confess the body of Christ to be present in the bread in that mode in which he is present in the Word itself', which certainly was a repudiation of a corporeal presence.[40] In the same work he wrote:

> I set forth the body of Christ and say it is a sacrament or sacred figure of the body of Christ or a mystery which is the same. And similarly you find the blood of Christ explained as a mystic cup or a mystery or as a sacrament of his blood.[41]

Like Zwingli, Oecolampadius stressed the difference between sign and signified, arguing that the words 'This is my body' are to be understood as a trope. In the First Confession of Basel, drafted by Oecolampadius and Myconius, the Eucharist was likened to the water in baptism – just as the water is not changed, so neither are the bread and wine:

> But we do not include in the Lord's food and drink the natural and real and substantial body of Christ, which was born of the pure Virgin Mary and suffered for us and ascended into heaven. Therefore we do not adore Christ in the signs of bread and wine, which we commonly call the Sacraments of the body and blood of Christ, but in heaven at the right hand of God the Father, whence He will come to judge the living and the dead.[42]

Oecolampadius drew up a eucharistic liturgy for use in Basel *c.* 1525, *Form und gestalt Wie das Herren Nachtmal*, though it was not until 1529 that a revised form was made the official liturgy.[43] It assumed a worship service of the word with a sermon.[44] After the sermon an admonition is given that provides evangelical teaching on the Eucharist, since those who desire to receive must 'understand and hold the mystery of the sacrament'. The mystery is 'that Christ is for us the bread of life; which we attest with thanksgiving by this sacramental bread'. The Creed is recited, and then a lengthy list of categories of sinners is named that are excluded from the Supper – such as idolaters, sorcerers, blasphemers. This 'fencing of the table' would become a hallmark of many of the

39 Old, *Patristic Roots*, p. 16.

40 Poythress, *Reformer of Basel*, p. 105.

41 Cited in Ralph Walter Quere, *Melanchthon's Christum Cognoscere: Christ's Efficacious Presence in the Eucharistic Theology of Melanchthon*, Nieuwkoop: B. De Graaf, 1977, p. 180.

42 Cited in Stone, *A History of the Doctrine of the Holy Eucharist*, London: Longmans, 1909, vol. 2, p. 48.

43 Smend, *Die Evangelischen Deutschen Messen*, pp. 214–19; Pahl, *CD*, pp. 199–225, ET Thompson, *Liturgies*, p. 211–15.

44 See Jenny, *Einheit*, pp. 75–88.

latter Reformed rites. A prayer for those in authority was followed by the Lord's Prayer. As in the Strasbourg rite, this seems to be an evangelical reinterpretation of the *canon missae*, this part being suggested by the *Te igitur*. A confession followed, with a Psalm (130.1–8) and an absolution. Readings from Isaiah 53.1–7 and Matthew 27.25–50 were followed by a reflection on the readings concerning the sacrifice of Christ, concluding with the words, 'Wherefore we remember with thanksgiving the benefit of His body and blood, even as He hath willed us to recall by the holiest of all services – His Supper. Think upon it now, as you sit near Christ and hear of Him.' The Words of Institution were read and the Lord's Prayer and another short admonition to worthy reception. The words of administration avoided any suggestion that the bread and wine conveyed the body and blood of Christ: 'The undoubted faith, which you have in the death of Christ, lead you into eternal life. The faith, which you have in the spilt blood of Jesus Christ, lead you into eternal life.'

The rite ended by commending the communicants to love, especially of the poor, which was a very powerful reminder of the mission of the Church. However, the emphasis on remembering the passion, and the lack of association of the bread and wine with the body and blood of Christ, illustrate a liturgy of symbolic memorialism.

Berne was in the orbit of Basel and Zurich, and both Zwingli and Oecolampadius were involved in bringing the Reformation to Berne and its territories. The Berne Disputation led to the Ten Conclusions, which included Point IV that it was not possible to demonstrate from Scripture that the corporeal and essential body and blood of Christ were contained in the bread and wine of the Eucharist, and Point V rejected the belief that the Mass could be offered for the living and the dead.[45] A eucharistic liturgy was published in 1529. This was modelled on the Zurich rite, though with echoes of Basel too. It provided for invocation, a confession of sin, the Creed and intercessions, rather like the Zurich word service. There is a communion admonition, which explains the Supper as a spiritual food and the need for worthiness. The Words of Institution are read, and there is a post-communion admonition.[46]

After the Berne Disputation, Guillaume Farel (1489–1565) was charged with making the German texts available to the French-speaking areas around Berne. If these were ever published, they have not survived. However, he did publish his liturgy for Neuchâtel, *La Maniere et fasson* (1533), which is thought to be a more polished version of his earlier French forms. He studied in Paris and was influenced by the humanist Jacque Lefèvre d'Etaples. He became a preacher in Meaux under Bishop Guillaume Briçonnet, and by that date had already espoused many of the Reformation tenets. By 1524 he had relocated to Basel, and then worked for the Reformation in the area of Montbéliard. According to Elfriede Jacobs, Farel held his own particular sacramental theology, and it changed over time.[47] While this is correct, his earlier views which he held when

45 Philip Schaff, *The Creeds of Christendom*, vol. 3, Grand Rapids: Baker Books, 1998, p. 209.

46 *CD*, pp. 227–36.

47 Elfriede Jacobs, *Die Sakramentslehre Wilhelm Farels*, Zurich: Theologischer Verlag, 1978.

he composed this liturgy were very much in line with Zwingli and Oecolampadius. His earlier sacramental teaching was set out in his *Sommaire* of 1529. In this work sacraments were described as 'signs and public attestations of that which ought to be in the faithful'.[48] Salvation cannot derive from exterior practice, and so in the sacraments we have assurance and guarantee of divine grace, but they themselves do not convey that grace. The Roman Mass together with vestments and candles are all condemned. Instead:

> In remembrance of our Lord Jesus who once was offered for us to cleanse our sins, they all take and eat from one bread and drink from one cup, waiting for the triumphant and marvelous coming of Jesus which will be like his ascension to Heaven, where he is presently sitting at the right hand of his Father until his enemies are put under his feet. For the coming of the Saviour will not be invisible, but will be seen by all like lightning which comes from the East and is seen all the way to the West.[49]

The eschatological focus here is directly related to the Reformed conviction, over against Luther, that the body of Christ is in heaven where it remains until his coming again, and so cannot be 'in' or 'under', and for the early Farel, even 'with' the elements. A little more of Farel's theology of the Eucharist was contained in the long Preface to his liturgy. The Supper is a visible communion with the members of Jesus Christ and signifies the fellowship and union among Christians and with Christ. The heart of many does not get beyond the bread and cup presented to them, and there is a need for communicants to be worthy and to understand the meaning of the Supper. The service itself was preceded by a word service in the manner of Zurich and Basel, with a bidding prayer and Lord's Prayer, proclamation of the word with intercessions, the Ten Commandments, confession of sins, Apostles' Creed and further intercession. An exhortation outlined the saving work of Christ, including that the Supper was instituted 'in remembrance of his very great love by which he gave his body on the cross and poured out his blood for the forgiveness of sins'. All were exhorted to examine themselves, with a lengthy list of those who are excluded, as at Basel and Zurich. The call is made for humble hearts and contrition, with an assurance of God's forgiveness. The Lord's Prayer was recited and the Apostles' Creed. Yet another exhortation followed, leading into the Words of Institution from 1 Corinthians with an explanation, including the words:

> He commands that eating and drinking be done at his table in remembrance of him, that is, as often as we take the bread and drink from the cup, we announce the death of our Lord Jesus Christ – how he died for us, presenting his body under the sign of the bread and poured out his blood for us, as the cup signifies.[50]

---

48 ET in Jason Zuidema and Theodore Van Raalte, *Early French Reform: The Theology and Spirituality of Guillaume Farel*, Farnham: Ashgate Publishing, 2011, p. 134.

49 Zuidema and Van Raalte, *Early French Reform*, p. 137.

50 Zuidema and Van Raalte, *Early French Reform*, p. 215.

This is followed by what would become Farel's gift to the Reformed liturgical tradition. In his *De genuine verborum*, Oecolampadius had urged that the *Sursum corda* in the Mass should be interpreted as lifting our hearts up to Christ at the right hand of the Father and not to the bread and wine of the altar. Farel put this teaching into his communion exhortation:

> Therefore lift up your hearts on high, seeking the things that are above in heaven where Jesus Christ is seated at the right hand of the Father. Do not let yourselves be held back by visible things which become corrupt through use. Let all of you come with joyful heart in brotherly unity to take from the table of our Lord, returning thanks to him for the very great love which he has shown us. Have the death of this good Saviour written in your hearts as an eternal memory so that your heart will be inflamed and you will also move others to the love of God by following his holy word.[51]

It has become known as the 'Reformed *Sursum corda*', and in contrast to calling down the presence of Christ in the bread and wine, exhorts the worshippers to ascend to the presence of Christ in heaven.

The administration followed, where the 'Reformed *Sursum corda*' was reinforced:

> May Jesus, the true Saviour of the world, who died for us and ascended in glory to the right hand of the Father, live in your hearts by his Holy Spirit, causing all of you to be alive in him through a living faith and perfect love. Amen.[52]

The rite concluded with a post-communion bidding prayer, and a final admonition with a brief blessing. What is striking is just how little prayer remains in this rite, and how the minister is constantly exhorting and giving explication on the Supper; other than receiving the elements, the people have little role. Farel moved on to Geneva, and this rite was in use in Geneva when John Calvin arrived in 1536.

Calvin in Strasbourg and Geneva

After studies in law, and then turning to divinity and espousing Reformation principles, Calvin had fled France and during his stay in Basel completed the first edition of his *Institutes* (1536). He gave the following definition of sacraments:

> On the nature of sacraments, it is very important for us that some definite doctrine be taught, to learn from it both the purpose for which they were instituted and their present use. First, what is a sacrament? An outward sign by which the Lord represents and attests to us his good will toward us to sustain the weak-

51 Zuidema and Van Raalte, *Early French Reform*, p. 215.
52 Zuidema and Van Raalte, *Early French Reform*, p. 216.

> ness of our faith. Another definition: a testimony of God's grace, declared to us by an outward sign. From this we also understand a sacrament never lacks a preceding promise but is rather joined to it by way of appendix, to confirm and seal the promise itself, and to make it as it were more evident to us.[53]

It would seem that Calvin took over Luther's idea of promise, and combined it with Zwingli's emphasis on sacrament as sign, seal and confirmation. In the Lord's Supper we are spiritually fed by the Lord's goodness, and give thanks for his kindness. The body and blood are 'represented under bread and wine', and they exhibit to us the body of Christ.[54] However, the chief function is to seal and confirm the promise by which he testifies that his flesh is food and his blood is drink. Calvin accepted Luther's concept of promise, but he rejected the idea of ubiquity, since Christ's body is in heaven. He also rejected as subtle (with the idea of being erroneous) those who spoke of Christ as being 'really' or 'substantially' present. Probably with the liturgy of Basel in mind (though not its frequency), he described the ideal eucharistic liturgy thus:

> As far as the Sacred Supper is concerned, it could have been administered most becomingly if it were set before the church very often, and at least once a week. First, then, it should begin with public prayers. After this a sermon should be given. Then, when bread and wine have been placed on the Table, the minister should repeat the words of institution of the Supper. Next, he should recite the promises which were left to us in it; at the same time, he should excommunicate all who are debarred from it by the Lord's prohibition. Afterward, he should pray that the Lord, with the kindness wherewith he has bestowed this sacred food upon us also teach and form us to receive it with faith and thankfulness of heart, and, inasmuch as we are not so of ourselves, by his mercy make us worthy of such a feast. But here either psalms should be sung or something read, and in becoming order the believers should partake of the most holy banquet, the ministers breaking the bread and giving the cup. When the Supper is finished, there should be an exhortation to sincere faith and confession of faith, to love and behavior worthy of Christians. At the last, thanks should be given, and praises sung to God. When these things are ended, the church should be dismissed in peace.[55]

In the same year (1536) Calvin passed through Geneva, intending to stay one night only. Guillaume Farel, by now pastor of Geneva, persuaded him – with threats of punishment – to stay as teacher and assist the programme of reformation. Farel's liturgy was in use, and it may be Farel's influence that accounts for a more Oecolampadian/Farelian separation of the outward and the inward in sacraments found in his 1539 edition of the *Institutes*. Both Farel and Calvin were expelled from Geneva in 1538, and Calvin became pastor to the French congregation in Strasbourg. It is here that he came under the influence of Bucer,

53 John Calvin, *Institutes of the Christian Religion: 1536 edition*, trans. Ford Lewis Battles, Grand Rapids: Eerdmans, 1975, p. 87.

54 Calvin, *Institutes*, p. 103.

55 Calvin, *Institutes*, pp. 122–3.

and adopted and extended Bucer's terminology of exhibit and instrument, which was to be his mature doctrine, and is described by Gerrish as symbolic instrumentalism. In the 1559 *Institutes* he explained:

> God uses the means and instruments which he sees to be expedient, in order that all things may be subservient to his glory, he being the Lord and disposer of all. Therefore, as by bread and other aliment he feeds our bodies, as by the sun he illumines, and by fire gives warmth to the world, and yet bread, sun, and fire are nothing, save inasmuch as they are instruments under which he dispenses his blessings to us; so in like manner he spiritually nourishes our faith by means of the sacraments, whose only office is to make his promises visible to our eye, or rather to be pledges of his promises.[56]

In his important study of the Calvinist doctrine of the Eucharist, Christopher Elwood observed:

> In the notion that the sacraments are instruments of God's grace we have the real hallmark of the Calvinist doctrine. Calvin invokes instrumentality as a way of distinguishing sacramental signs from the communicative power that proceeds from and is the exclusive prerogative of God. The signs are efficacious not because of an inherent capacity but in the sense that they are instruments God has chosen to attest to the genuine operation of the Spirit's power to unite believers with the body of Christ. In keeping with traditional conceptions of the sacrament, then, the notion of divine power remains a prominent feature, while every hint of the physical sign being imbued with power is removed. With such a dynamic understanding of the relationship of signs to their efficacy, Calvin intended to maintain the notion of the Supper as an efficacious symbol in which the body of Christ is truly offered to the faithful, while safeguarding the idea of the Spirit's transcendent power as the efficient cause of this communication.[57]

Calvin used various forms of *exhibere* no fewer than 17 times in Book 4.17 of the 1559 *Institutes*. Joseph Tylenda observed that he used it in the sense of not bringing about a presence, but presupposing a presence that the signs manifest.[58] For Calvin, though Christ's risen body is in heaven, the Holy Spirit works as a channel to overcome the barrier of space so that he could speak of 'a true and substantial communication of the body and blood of the Lord'.[59] At the

56 Calvin, 1559, *Institutes* 4.14.12. Cf. *Tracts and Treatises* 2:506, 'the flesh and blood of Christ are substantially offered and exhibited to us in the Supper', trans. Henry Beveridge, 3 vols, Grand Rapids: Eerdmans, 1958.

57 Christopher Elwood, *The Body Broken: The Calvinist Doctrine of the Eucharist and the Symbolization of Power in Sixteenth-Century France*, Oxford: Oxford University Press, 1999, p. 71. See also B. A. Gerrish, *Grace and Gratitude: The Eucharistic Theology of John Calvin*, Edinburgh: T & T Clark, 1993, and Lee Palmer Wandel, *The Eucharist in the Reformation: Incarnation and Liturgy*, Cambridge: Cambridge University Press, 2006, ch. 4.

58 Joseph N. Tylenda, 'The Ecumenical Intention of Calvin's Early Eucharistic Teaching', in Brian A. Gerrish (ed.), *Reformatio Perennis: Essays on Calvin and the Reformation in Honor of Ford Lewis Battles*, Pittsburgh: Pickwick Press, 1981, pp. 27–47, 31–2.

59 *Institutes*, 1559, 4.17.19.

Colloquy of Regensburg, he and Melanchthon had signed an emended version of the Augsburg Confession (the *Augustana variata*), with Article 10 reading, 'the body and blood of Christ are truly exhibited with the bread and wine to those who eat in the Supper of the Lord'.[60] For the sake of political expediency, Calvin did sign the Zurich Consensus (1551), worked out with Bullinger, and that document was regarded as representative of the wider Swiss Reformed theology.[61] Bullinger would not use the term *instrumenta*, but only *organa*, implement, for sacraments. However, the Calvin who signed the Consensus was not the Calvin of his writings, and his teaching of the 1559 *Institutes* allows us to see his interpretation of the Consensus. His mature doctrine is expressed in the *Confessio Fidei Gallicana* (1559), where Article XXXVI taught that by a secret and incomprehensible power of his Spirit Christ feeds and strengthens us with the substance (*de la substance*) of his body and blood. Article XXXVII explained:

> We believe, as has been said, that in the Lord's Supper, as well as in baptism, God gives us really and in fact that which he there sets forth to us; and that consequently with these signs is given the true possession and enjoyment of that which they present to us. And thus all who bring a pure faith, like a vessel, to the sacred table of Christ, receive truly that of which it is a sign; for the body and the blood of Jesus Christ give food and drink to the soul, no less than bread and wine nourish the body.[62]

Calvin's liturgy, however, was drawn up *c.* 1540 for use in Strasbourg, and then later adapted for Geneva on his return there in 1542.[63] Although a brilliant biblical exegete and systematician, Calvin does not appear to have been particularly gifted as a liturgiographer, and his Sunday morning service and rite for the Lord's Supper were an amalgamation of Bucer's Strasbourg rite and Farel's rite for Neuchâtel/Geneva. His own contributions mostly took the form of explication and exhortation, and very little in the way of euchology. Whereas Zwingli had excluded music from worship, Calvin included the metrical psalms of Clément Marot, which were an integral part of his worship.[64]

No copy of the first edition of his Strasbourg rite has survived, and it is known only through the 1542 edition, so some scholars speculate as to whether changes were made for the second edition. The order of Sunday morning worship was based on Bucer and thus is ultimately derived from the Mass via Schwarz. When there was a communion, the eucharistic material was inserted after the Apostles' Creed.

---

60 Sasse, *This is My Body*, pp. 252–60.

61 For the Zurich (Tigurinus) Consensus, see Timothy George, 'John Calvin and the Agreement of Zurich', in Timothy George (ed.), *John Calvin and the Church*, Louisville: Westminster John Knox Press, 1990, pp. 42–58; Paul Rorem, *Calvin and Bullinger on the Lord's Supper*, Alcuin/Grow Liturgical Study 12, Bramcote: Grove Books, 1989.

62 Schaff, *Creeds of Christendom*, vol. 3, pp. 380–1.

63 The most recent and exhaustive study is Christian Grosse, *Les Rituels de la Cène: Le culte eucharistique réformé à Genéve (XVIe –XVIIe siècles)*, Geneva: Librairie Droz, 2008.

64 Catherine Reuben, *La Traduction des Psaumes de David par Clément Marot: Aspects poétiques et théologiques*, Paris: H. Champion, 2001.

- Opening Call to Worship: 'Our help is in the name of the Lord, who made heaven and earth.'
- Bidding to confession.
- Confession.
- Scripture sentence of remission of sins.
- Absolution.
- First Table of the Decalogue sung in metre.
- Prayer of Instruction in the Law.
- Second Table of the Decalogue.
- Prayer for Illumination.
- Lection.
- Sermon.
- Long Prayer.
- Apostles' Creed sung in metre.
- [When communion, bread and wine prepared during the Creed.]
- Reformed Eucharistic Prayer.
- Lord's Prayer.
- Exhortation with Words of Institution and excommunication of unworthy groups.
- Breaking of bread and delivery.
- Words of Administration.
- Psalm 138.
- Thanksgiving.
- Nunc dimittis.
- Psalm, when no communion.
- Aaronic blessing.

The call to worship is that found in a number of Reformed orders and, as noted, is found in medieval Catholic sources too. Calvin borrowed the second of Bucer's confessions, and the Scripture sentence and absolution is from the same source.[65] The Decalogue is suggested by Farel's rite, though dividing the commandments and singing them to metre seems to be Calvin's idea. A prayer of illumination comes from earlier Swiss Reformed rites. The Long Prayer was adapted from Bucer's third long prayer of intercession. What is termed a Reformed Eucharistic Prayer has no resemblance to the ancient anaphoras, but is a prayer to God asking among other things that, 'In steadfast faith may we receive His body and blood, yea Christ Himself entire, who being true God and true man, is verily the holy bread of heaven which gives us life', and requests that 'we may truly become partakers of the new and eternal testament, the covenant of grace'. It gives thanks and praise, and describes the Eucharist as 'the blessed memorial and remembrance (*memoire et recordation*) of thy dear Son'.

---

65 Text in P. Barth and G. Niesel (eds), *Joannis Calvini Opera Selecta*, vol. 2, reprint: Eugene, OR: Wipf and Stock, 2011, pp. 18–26, 39–50; ET Thompson, *Liturgies*, pp. 197–210. *CD*, pp. 355–62; *PEER*, pp. 215–18. It is discussed in more detail in Bryan D. Spinks, *From the Lord and 'The Best Reformed Churches': A Study of the Eucharistic Liturgy in the English Puritan and Separatist Traditions 1550–1633*, Rome: CLV Edizioni Liturgiche, 1984, pp. 54–66.

Jean Cardier argued that the prayer stresses the double grace of justification and sanctification by participation in the whole Christ.[66] The exhortation begins with the Words of Institution and has been inspired by Farel's exhortation, though Calvin has changed the sequence and has expanded it. Farel's 'Reformed *Sursum corda*' was rendered thus:

> [To do so,] let us lift our spirits and hearts on high where Jesus Christ is in the glory of His Father, whence we expect Him at our redemption. Let us not be fascinated by these earthly and corruptible elements which we see with our eyes and touch with our hands, seeking Him there as though He were enclosed in the bread or wine. Then shall our souls be disposed to be nourished and vivified by His substance when they are lifted up above all earthly things, attaining even to heaven, and entering the Kingdom of God where He dwells. Therefore let us be content to have the bread and wine as signs and witnesses, seeking the truth spiritually where the Word of God promises that we shall find it.[67]

In his commentary on the Gospels, Calvin suggests that when Christ gave thanks it was a 'preparation and transition to consider the mystery', which is precisely the purpose of the exhortation.[68] The words of administration were, 'take, eat, the body of Jesus which has been delivered unto death for you; This is the cup of the new testament in the blood of Jesus which has been shed for you.'

On his return to Geneva, Calvin was allowed to celebrate the Eucharist only quarterly, in spite of his protests. Whereas in Strasbourg he drastically modified Farel's rite to bring it into line with Bucer's Strasbourg usage, in Geneva he had to modify the Strasbourg rite to bring it more in line with Farel's rite, which had, one may assume, continued in use even after the two Reformers had left the city. The absolution was removed in the Sunday morning service, and when the Eucharist was celebrated a paragraph was added to the Long Prayer after the sermon, incorporating much of his Strasbourg Reformed Eucharistic Prayer. The Genevan edition also allowed psalms to be sung or Scripture to be read during communion, and no words of administration were provided. The material composed by Calvin moved Geneva beyond the early Farel, but it expressed Calvin's doctrinal understanding of 1542; it is possible that the Calvin of the 1559 *Institutes* might have had more to say about what was received in this sacrament.[69]

John Knox, Geneva and Scotland

The Reformation took much longer to achieve in Scotland than in many countries, and for two or three decades of the latter part of the sixteenth century

66 Jean Cardier, 'La Prière Eucharistique de Calvin', in B. Botte et al. (eds), *Eucharisties d'Orient et d'Occident*, Paris: Cerf, 1970, pp. 171–80.

67 Thompson, *Liturgies*, p. 207.

68 *Commentary on a Harmony of the Evangelists*, ET W. Pringle, 3 vols, Edinburgh, 1846, vol. 3, p. 204.

69 Farel seems to have shifted his views to nearer those of Calvin. See Christopher Elwood, *The Body Broken*.

many places in Scotland were still Catholic and unreformed. The most prominent Reformer was John Knox. Knox had been minister at Berwick on Tweed, on the English side of the border, and was supposed to use the 1549 *Book of Common Prayer* (*BCP*). In fact he drew up his own communion liturgy for Berwick in 1550, of which we have a fragment:[70]

- Sermons of the benefits of God.
- John 13–16.
- Trinitarian invocation.
- Prayer – praise for creation and redemption, together with petition for faith and thanksgiving.
- 1 Corinthians 11.20–31.
- (Declaration of the apostles' mind upon the same place.)
- Excommunication.
- Confession.
- Scriptural assurance of forgiveness.
- Prayer for the congregation.
- A prayer for the Queen's Majesty.
- Communion was administered sitting at the altar table or at tables set up for the occasion.

Also in 1550 Knox wrote a summary of Scripture teaching on the Eucharist:

> First, we confess that it is a holy action, ordained of God, in the which the Lord Jesus, by earthly and visible things set before us, lifts us up unto heavenly and invisible things. And that when he had prepared his spiritual banquet, he witnessed that he himself was the lively bread wherewith our souls are fed unto everlasting life.
>
> And therefore, in setting forth bread and wine to eat and drink, he confirms and seals up to us his promise and communion (that is, that we shall be partakers with him in his kingdom); and he represents unto us, and makes plain to our senses, his heavenly gifts; and also gives unto us himself, to be received with faith, and not with mouth, nor yet by transfusion of substance; but so, through the virtue [*power*] of the Holy Ghost, that we, being fed with his flesh, and refreshed with his blood, may be renewed both unto true godliness and to immortality.
>
> And also [we confess] that herewith the Lord Jesus gathered us unto one visible body, so that we are members one of another, and make altogether one body, whereof Jesus Christ is the only Head; and, finally, that by the same sacrament, the Lord calls us to remembrance of his death and passion, to stir up our hearts to praise his most holy name.
>
> Furthermore, we acknowledge that this sacrament ought to be come unto reverently, considering there is exhibited and given a testimony of the wonderful society and knitting together of the Lord Jesus and of the receivers; and also, that there is included and contained in this sacrament, [a testimony] that

70 In D. Laing (ed.), *The Works of John Knox*, 6 vols, Edinburgh, 1864, vol. 1.

> he will preserve his kirk. For herein we are commanded to show the Lord's death until he come (1 Cor. 11:26).
>
> Also we believe that it is a confession, wherein we show what kind of doctrine we profess; and what congregation we join ourselves unto; and likewise, that it is a bond of mutual love amongst us. And, finally, we believe that all the comers unto this holy Supper must bring with them their conversion unto the Lord, by unfeigned repentance in faith; and in this sacrament receive the seals and confirmation of their faith; and yet must in nowise think that for this work's sake their sins are forgiven.[71]

On Mary's accession to the throne, Knox fled to Europe, first to Frankfurt and then to Geneva. In Frankfurt he was one of a number of English exiles who wanted to use a Reformed liturgy rather than the English *BCP*, and they had with them an English translation of Calvin's Genevan liturgy. Not succeeding, they left and journeyed to Geneva where John Knox, William Whittingam, Anthony Gilby, John Fox and Thomas Cole drew up *The Genevan Form of Prayers* 1556, for the use of the English exiles.[72] On Knox's return to Scotland this liturgy was adopted as part of the *Book of Common Order* in 1562 and 1564, though its use was not regarded as mandatory.[73] Knox was a prominent figure in drawing up the Scottish Confession (1560), which set forth the following on the Eucharist in Article XXI:

> we utterly condemn the vanity of those who affirm the sacraments to be nothing else than naked and bare signs . . . we assuredly believe . . . that in the Supper rightly used, Christ Jesus is so joined with us that He becomes the very nourishment and food of our souls. Not that we imagine any transubstantiation of bread into the Christ's body, and of wine into His natural blood, as the Romanists have perniciously taught and wrongly believed; but this union and conjunction which we have with the body and blood of Christ Jesus in the right use of the sacraments is wrought by means of the Holy Ghost, who by true faith carries us above all things that are visible, carnal, and earthly, and makes us feed upon the body and blood of Christ Jesus, once broken and shed for us but now in heaven, and appearing for us in the presence of His Father. Notwithstanding the distance between His glorified body in heaven and mortal men on earth, yet we must assuredly believe that the bread we break is the communion of Christ's body and the cup which we bless the communion of His blood.

This Article appears to reject the symbolic memorialism of Zwingli, espousing something akin to symbolic parallelism. It makes it clear that the real Christ is

71 *A Summary, According to the Holy Scriptures, of the Sacrament of the Lord's Supper 1550*, http://www.swrb.com/newslett/actualNLs/summarls.htm.

72 The classic study is William D. Maxwell, *The Liturgical Portions of the Genevan Service Book*, Edinburgh: Oliver and Boyd, 1931, 2nd impression, London: Faith Press Ltd, 1965.

73 For the Scottish Reformation, Alan R. MacDonald, *The Jacobean Kirk 1567–1625: Sovereignty, Polity and Liturgy*, Aldershot: Ashgate, 1998. For Knox's theology, see Thomas F. Torrance, *Scottish Theology from John Knox to John McLeod Campbell*, Edinburgh: T & T Clark, 1996.

received, through the Holy Spirit. However, the liturgy that Knox helped compile did not explicitly express such a rich doctrine.

The 1556 liturgy was closely modelled on Calvin, but with material from the *BCP* 1552 and material from Knox's Berwick liturgy.[74]

The Sunday morning service consisted of a confession, with a choice of two, a psalm, prayer for illumination, Scripture reading and sermon, a prayer for the whole estate of Christ's Church, the Lord's Prayer, Creed, psalm and ended with the Aaronic blessing and Grace. When the Lord's Supper was celebrated, it began after the Creed and psalm with the recitation of the Institution Narrative, which was recited before and not as the beginning of the exhortation. Like Calvin and Farel, it included excommunication of various categories of sinners. The rendering of the 'Reformed *Sursum corda*' was thus:

> let us not suffer our minds to wander about the consideration of these earthly and corruptible things (which we see present to our eyes and feel with our hands) to seek Christ bodily present in them as if he were enclosed in the bread or wine, or as if these elements were turned and changed into the substance, of his flesh and blood. For the only way to dispose our souls to receive nourishment, relief, and quickening of his substance, is to lift up our minds by faith above all things worldly and sensible, and thereby to enter into heaven, that we may find, and receive Christ, where he dwelleth, undoubtedly very God, and very man, in the incomprehensible glory of his Father . . .[75]

There followed a Reformed Eucharistic Prayer, the first part of which was from Knox's Berwick liturgy. Here Knox and his fellow compilers took seriously the need to give thanks as part of 'do this' in the Institution. The prayer is not modelled on the classical anaphoras, but did give thanks for salvation history. A rubric required the minister to break the bread. In later English Puritan editions of this liturgy, the Fraction rubric would be expanded, perhaps reflecting Calvin's words:

> We ought carefully to observe, that the chief, and almost the whole energy of the sacrament, consists in these words, It is broken for you: It is shed for you. It would not be of much importance to us that the body and blood of the Lord are now distributed, had they not once been set forth for our redemption and salvation. Wherefore they are represented under bread and wine.[76]

Whereas for Luther the elevation may have been a pictorial Anamnesis, for the Reformed it was the Fraction. This rite concluded with a thanksgiving, asking that the benefits of communion may be imprinted and fastened to our hearts, and Psalm 130 or some other suitable thanksgiving with a blessing. Having its liturgical antecedents in Berne, Neuchâtel, Strasbourg and Geneva, with

74 G. J. Cuming, 'John Knox and the Book of Common Prayer: A Short Note', *Liturgical Review* 10 (1980), pp. 80–1.

75 Thompson, *Liturgies*, pp. 302–3, spelling modernized.

76 *Institutes* 4.17.3.

additions from the *BCP* and Knox's Berwick liturgy, it is a striking example of Reformed liturgical synthesis.

Zacharius Ursinus, the Heidelberg Catechism and the German Palatinate liturgy of 1563

The chief architects of the German Reformed tradition were Zachariah Ursinus and Caspar Olevianus. Ursinus had studied at Wittenberg but he was regarded by the Lutherans as a crypto-Calvinist. In 1560 he moved to Zurich, and in 1561 was appointed professor at Heidelberg, which under Frederick III had espoused the Reformed tradition in place of Lutheranism. Ursinus drew up the Heidelberg Catechism, and assisted in preparing the 1563 Palatine liturgy.[77] The Catechism defined sacraments as 'visible, holy signs and seals appointed by God' to seal the promise of the gospel.[78] In answer to the question of how this is signified in the Supper, it taught:

> Thus, that Christ has commanded me and all believers to eat of this broken bread, and to drink of this cup, and has joined therewith these promises: First, that his body was offered and broken on the cross for me, and his blood shed for me, as certainly as I see with my eyes the bread of the *Lord* broken for me, and the cup communicated to me; and, further, that with his crucified body and shed blood he himself feeds and nourishes my soul to everlasting life, as certainly as I receive from the hand of the minister, and taste with my mouth, the bread and cup of the *Lord*, which are given me as certain tokens of the body and blood of Christ.[79]

The stress on the broken bread reinforces the importance of the Fraction of the bread in this tradition. Lee Palmer Wandel notes that in contrast to Calvin's complex formulation of the sign, the far more circumscribed 'token' was employed.[80] The Catechism rejected change in the elements, but nevertheless insisted that 'we are as really partakers of his true body and blood, through the working of the Holy Ghost, as we receive by the mouth of the body these holy tokens in remembrance of him'.[81] The Supper testified that we have full forgiveness of all our sins by Christ's one sacrifice.[82] Ursinus's detailed commentary on the Catechism gave much more elucidation on the various questions and answers. There is a sacramental union, and Christ did not take his body in, with

77 For the view that it was the work solely of Ursinus, see Fred H. Klooster, 'The Priority of Ursinus in the Composition of the Heidelberg Catechism', in Derk Visser (ed.), *Controversy and Conciliation: The Reformation of the Palatinate 1559–1583*, Allison Park: Pickwick Publications, 1986, pp. 73–100. Lyle Bierma, 'The Purpose and Authorship of the Heidelberg Catechism', in *An Introduction to the Heidelberg Catechism: Sources, History, and Theology*, Grand Rapids: Baker Books, 2005.

78 Schaff, *Creeds of Christendom*, vol. 3, p. 328.

79 Schaff, *Creeds of Christendom*, vol. 3, p. 332.

80 Wandel, *Eucharist in the Reformation*, p. 206.

81 Wandel, *Eucharist in the Reformation*, p. 335.

82 Wandel, *Eucharist in the Reformation*, p. 335.

or under the bread except in a sacramental sense. It is a sign of grace on the part of God, 'who exhibits unto us certain benefits which we receive by faith'.[83]

Olevianus seems to have had oversight of the formulation of the liturgy that was published with the Catechism.[84] For Sunday worship the service began with psalmody and then a prayer before the sermon, with the Lord's Prayer, lection and sermon. A confession based on that of the 1536 Lutheran Württemberg order followed, with absolution, and then a prayer of intercession ending with the Lord's Prayer, or a paraphrase of the Lord's Prayer. A psalm was sung and the service ended with the Aaronic blessing. An instruction noted that the Lord's Supper be celebrated at least once a month in the town, every two months in the villages and everywhere on Easter, Pentecost and Christmas. A preparation service was provided to be used on the Saturday before the celebration of the Supper. This included an exhortation that, echoing the Catechism, explained of Christ's promise,

> that His body was as surely offered for you on the Cross, and His blood shed for you, as you see with your eyes that the bread which the Lord calls his body is broken for you, and the cup of thanksgiving is offered unto you; second, that by the operation of the Holy Spirit, the Lord Christ feeds and nourishes your hungry and contrite heart and weary soul with His crucified body and shed blood unto eternal life, as surely as you do receive from the Minister's hand, and do eat and drink by mouth, of the holy bread and cup of the Lord's remembrance of Him.[85]

The eucharistic liturgy commenced with the Words of Institution and exhortation, drawn from Calvin and the Dutch version of the liturgy of Jan Laski (see later). A prayer followed, which functioned as a Eucharistic Prayer. It asked that 'through the power of the Holy Spirit our weary and contrite hearts may be fed and quickened by His true body and blood, yea of Him who is true God and man, the only bread of heaven'. The Lord's Prayer was recited, and then the Creed, and a version of the 'Reformed *Sursum corda*':

> That we may now be fed with Christ, the true bread of heaven, let us not cleave with our hearts to this external bread and wine, but lift up our hearts and faith into heaven, where Christ Jesus is our Intercessor at the right hand of His heavenly Father (where the articles of our Christian faith also direct us) and doubt not that through the action of the Holy Spirit our souls shall be fed and nourished with His body and blood, as truly we receive the holy bread and cup in remembrance of Him.[86]

---

83 *The Commentary of Dr. Zacharias Ursinus on the Heidelberg Catechism*, trans. G. W. Williard, Grand Rapids: Eerdmans, [1852] 1954, pp. 377–440.

84 Kenneth E. Rowe, 'The Palatinate Liturgy and the Pennsylvania Germans', in Heather Murray Elkins and Edward C. Zaraoza (eds), *Pulpit, Table, and Song: Essays in Celebration of Howard G. Hageman*, Lanham: Scarecrow Press, 1996, p. 56. *CD*, pp. 509–23. ET of the liturgy by Bard Thompson, 'The Palatinate Liturgy Heidelberg, 1563', *Theology and Life* 6, 1963, pp. 49–67.

85 Thompson, 'Palatinate Liturgy', p. 58.

86 Thompson, 'Palatinate Liturgy', pp. 64–5.

It would seem that the Heidelberg theologians' prayer for the Holy Spirit, the Lord's Prayer and the articles of faith (Creed) were to have the effect of directing the heart to heaven. Then came the words of administration from 1 Corinthians 9, the bread which we break, the cup of blessing etc., and then the minister was to break off a piece of bread for each communicant. During communion there was singing or reading of the passion or Isaiah 53. Two alternative prayers of thanks were given, the first weaving together Psalm 103.1–4 with passages from Romans. The service concluded with a psalm and a blessing as in the Sunday morning service. It changed very little prior to the nineteenth century and was exported to the USA by German Reformed immigrants.[87]

Jan Laski and Petrus Datheen: the Polish and Dutch rites

Jan Laski (John à Lasco) was Polish and was described by his contemporaries as a nobleman. He had been prepared for the Catholic Church under the guidance of his uncle who was the Primate of Poland. However, his sojourns in Basel meant that he came under the influence of Oecolampadius and also Bullinger. Though he remained an independent thinker, his sacramental views are nearer Basel and Zurich than Strasbourg and Geneva. He settled in Emden as Superintendent of the Church of East Friesland. The Augsburg Interim of 1548 forced him to flee, and he eventually came to England, where he was appointed Superintendent to the immigrant churches in London – French, Dutch and Italian, the so-called 'Stranger Churches'. The French Church in Glastonbury, under Valerand Poullain, used Calvin's Strasbourg rite.[88] In 1551, Laski indicated that he had started work on a manual for governing the London foreign churches and their worship. His work perhaps circulated in drafts for comment by the ministers of the various congregations, but was not published until 1555 under the title *Forma ac Ratio*.[89] Versions exist in French, Italian and Dutch. The Dutch version appeared in 1554 – prior to Laski's final version, and was the work of Marten Micron. It appears to be based on an earlier version or was Micron's own adaptation.[90] Micron's version was used by the Dutch Reformed Church at Austin Friars from 1558 and was also in use in the Netherlands, until it was finally supplanted by the 1566 rite by Petrus Datheen.

Laski's rite had its genesis during his time in Emden and elements of the East Friesland rite appear in his *Forma ac Ratio*.[91] Laski's own eucharistic doctrine seems to have hovered somewhere between symbolic memorialism and symbolic parallelism. Dirk Rodgers observes that Laski attempted to redefine the notion of 'exhibition' used by Bucer and Calvin, when he wrote, 'We do not exclude

87 See further in Rowe, 'Palatinate Liturgy'.

88 A. C. Honders, *Valerandus Pollanus Liturgia Sacra (1551–1555)*, Leiden: Brill, 1970.

89 Spinks, *From the Lord and 'The Best Reformed Churches'*; Michael S. Springer, *Restoring Christ's Church: John a Lasco and the Forma ac Ratio*, Aldershot: Ashgate Publishing, 2007.

90 W. F. Dankbaar, *Martin Micron De Christlicke Ordinancien der Nederlantscher Ghemeinten Te Londen (1554)*, S'Gravenhage: Martinus Nijhoff, 1956.

91 Anneliese Sprengler-Ruppenthal, *Mysterium und Riten nach der Londoner Kirchenordnung der Niederländer*, Köln–Graz: Böhlau Verlag, 1967.

from the sacraments a true and salvific exhibition of Christ's body and blood, although we say that this exhibition does not consist in any real connection with the elements, nor in any work of the minister.'[92] Annaliese Sprengler-Ruppenthal notes that whereas Calvin used *communicatio*, Laski used *communio*, carrying a different emphasis.[93] Petkūnas also argues that Laski's Christology, where the human and divine natures do not seem to be a true hypostatic union, did not permit the bodily presence of Christ in the sacrament.[94] Some features of his eucharistic liturgy in *Forma ac Ratio* that are also found in Micron's version include a detailed instruction on carrying out the Fraction, and Communion was by sitting at the communion table.[95] Pettegree comments:

> The mode of celebration demonstrates both Lasco's determination to return to the pure model of the apostolic church and the practicality which runs through the whole order. Communion was to be taken seated round the communion table as a faithful re-enactment of the Last Supper, but as each group came to the table a gap was to be left opposite the minister so that the whole congregation might see. The celebration was preceded by a lengthy process of self-examination, repentance, and reconciliation.[96]

His rite provided for the following:

- Public reminder of those who are excluded.
- Prayer from the pulpit that we may testify publicly the communion in the body and blood of Christ.
- Words of Institution.
- Exhortation on worthiness, including his version of the 'Reformed *Sursum corda*'.
- 1 Corinthians 5.7–8 (from the communion table).
- Fraction and Administration: 'The bread which we break is the communion in the body of Christ. Take, eat and remember that the body of our Lord Jesus Christ was for us given up to death on the beam of the cross (*in crucis patibulo*) for the remission of all our sins. The cup of blessing which we bless is the communion in the blood of Christ. Take, drink and remember that the blood of our Lord Jesus Christ was for us poured out on the beam of the cross for the remission of all our sins.'
- During the Administration one of the ministers may read John 6, 13, 14 or 15.

---

92 Dirk W. Rodgers, *John à Lasco in England*, New York and Frankfurt: Peter Lang, 1994, p. 121, citing Laski's *Brevis et Dilucida*.

93 Sprengler-Ruppenthal, *Mysterium und Riten*, p. 160.

94 Darius Petkūnas, *Holy Communion Rites in the Polish and Lithuanian Reformed Agendas of the 16th and Early 17th Centuries*, Klaipėda: Klaipėdos Universiteto Leidykla, 2007, p. 83.

95 ET by D. G. Lane in Spinks, *From the Lord, and The 'Best Reformed Churches'*, pp. 157–76.

96 Andrew Pettegree, *Foreign Protestant Communities in Sixteenth-Century London*, Oxford: Clarendon Press, 1986, p. 60.

- Words of Assurance: 'Be sure and do not doubt, all of you who have participated in this Lord's Supper and mediated on its divine Mystery, that you have a sure and health-giving communion with him in his body and blood to eternal life. Amen.'
- Exhortation on the fruits of communion.
- Thanksgiving.
- Admonition.
- Psalm.
- Blessing.

Laski finally settled back in Poland and assisted in the organization of the Protestant communities there, which consisted of Bohemians (Hussites), Lutherans and Reformed, and was compounded by an anti-trinitarian movement.[97] His *Forma ac Ratio* was used in modified form by some groups, and it was influential in two further Polish liturgies, the 1581 *Forma albo porządek* and Krzyztof Kraiński's *Porządek nabożeństwa*, 1599. The latter began with an invocation of the Holy Spirit, retained the Agnus Dei, and had the administration of the bread before the wine.[98] Laski's influence was still discernible in the unifying Agenda of 1637.[99] The Hungarian Reformed rite was also derived from Laski's *Forma ac Ratio*.

In the Netherlands, Micron's liturgical forms were gradually replaced by the less cumbersome liturgy of Petrus Datheen, the minister of the exiled Dutch congregation in Frankenthal. Recognizing Elector Frederick's desire for harmony, Datheen translated and adapted the 1563 Palatinate rite.[100] Micron's Fraction was retained in the earlier editions of the 1566 Dutch rite, but in later editions of 1568 and 1610 his formulae were removed. Thus Micron's translation of Laski's liturgy was replaced by Datheen's translation of the German Reformed Church.[101]

Reformed orthodoxy and the Lord's Supper

Towards the end of the sixteenth century and continuing through the seventeenth century, Reformed theology, like Lutheran theology, entered a period

97 Petkūnas, *Holy Communion Rites*, p. 35.

98 For the details of both these rites, see Petkūnas, *Holy Communion Rites*, pp. 197–202, 206–12.

99 Kazimierz Bem, 'The Formation of the Polish and Lithuanian Reformed Liturgy', STM Thesis, Yale Divinity School, 2012, which in addition to taking issue with some of Petkūnas's views has an English translation of the 1637 *Agenda albo Forma porzadku*. See also '"From Many Different Sources": The Formation of the Polish and Lithuanian Reformed Liturgy', in Teresa Berger (ed.), *Liturgy in Migration: From the Upper Room to Cyberspace*, Collegeville: Liturgical Press, 2012, pp. 101–30.

100 Lee Palmer Wandel seems not to have been aware of this derivation, and suggests that Datheen is dependent on Calvin's rite. *Eucharist in the Reformation*, p. 197.

101 For Datheen's liturgy, *CD*, pp. 526–35; see also Spinks, *From the Lord and The 'Best Reformed Churches'*, pp. 135–9, Daniel James Meeter, *'Bless the Lord, O my soul'. The New-York Liturgy of the Dutch Reformed Church 1767*, Lanham: Scarecrow Press, 1998, pp. 3–25.

of scholasticism, or orthodoxy, when the tenets of the faith were codified. Richard Muller lists divines beginning with Theodore Beza who worked with Calvin and was his successor in Geneva, to Thomas Ridgley in England who died in 1734.[102] Methodological hallmarks of this included the acceptance and use of Aristotelian terminology, and the tendency to summarize theology by a series of propositions. Beza had studied at Orleans with Melchior Wolmar, and eventually accepted the Reformed faith and fled to Switzerland, where he became professor of Greek at Lausanne. In 1558 he was called to be rector of the new Academy of Geneva. Jill Raitt's study of Beza's teaching on the Eucharist shows a development over time, and a tendency of increasing use of Aristotelian terms.[103] In his Confession of Faith in 1556, Beza argued as Calvin that sacraments, like the Word, are instruments of the Holy Spirit. They are channels or conduits used by the Holy Spirit to join us to Christ and increase our union with him. Raitt notes that in this work he begins to elaborate his understanding and use of the term *analogia*, where he explains that the Fraction of the bread represented the suffering of Christ, the distribution taught that the benefits are given to individuals, and the bread, being made from many grains, and the wine from grapes, express the unity of the Church.[104] By 1567 he could call sacraments 'effective causes' due to their nature as analogous signs and as their use as instruments of the Holy Spirit.[105] By the 1570s and 1580s he uses the four causes of scholastic theology – Christ is the efficient cause, the bread and wine are the material cause, the action of the Holy Spirit is the formal cause, and the final cause is the giving of Christ and his gifts.[106] The English theologian William Ames who, on account of his habitual Nonconformity fled England to the University of Franekar, published his work *The Marrow of Sacred Theology* in 1623. His system of theology could be summarized in chart form in accordance with Ramist methodology. Ames defined a sacrament as a sign, and held that a sign served three functions: it informs (*notificans*), it reminds (*commonefaciens*) and it seals (*obsignans*).[107] Baptism and the Lord's Supper were discussed in a series of 31 terse propositions. Ames held a theology more akin to Bullinger and Laski than Calvin and Beza, and asserted of the Eucharist:

> The spiritual nourishment in this sacrament does not require that the bread and wine be changed into the body and blood of Christ, or that Christ be corporally present with them. It is required only that they be changed in their application and use, and that Christ be spiritually present with those who receive them in faith.[108]

---

102 Richard Muller, *Post-Reformation Dogmatics*, vol. 1: Prolegomena to Theology, Grand Rapids: Baker Books, 1997.

103 Jill Raitt, *The Eucharistic Theology of Theodore Beza: Development of the Reformed Doctrine*, Chambersburg: AAR Studies in Religion, 1972.

104 Raitt, *Eucharistic Theology*, p. 28.

105 Raitt, *Eucharistic Theology*, p. 41.

106 Raitt, *Eucharistic Theology*, pp. 45–6.

107 William Ames, *The Marrow of Sacred Theology*, trans. John Dykstra Eusden, Grand Rapids: Baker Books, 1997, pp. 196–7.

108 Ames, *Marrow*, p. 212.

Johannes Wollebius (1556–1629) studied at Basel and was later Old Testament professor there. His *Compendium Theologicae Christianae* (1626) exemplifies the Reformed scholastic method. In Chapter XXII, sacraments are discussed as seals of the covenant of grace, and the word sacrament was defined as an oath and then, second, as a mystery that 'signifies something hidden and supernatural [*divinis*] set forth in signs or types'.[109] The efficient cause is the entire Holy Trinity, especially Christ; the agents are legitimately called ministers; and the means of which a sacrament is performed is the Word of Institution, which does not change substance or quality, but only use.[110] There is an internal heavenly matter (Christ and his benefits) and an external form (legitimate administration).[111] In the Eucharist Christ is present by his body and blood in sacramental presence, which Wollebius explained as:

> (1) symbolic, because he is not in the bread, but rather is represented by the bread as by a symbol; (2) a presence of faith, by which we apply Christ and his merit to ourselves, and (3) a presence of power and result.[112]

On the question of sacrifice, Wollebius insisted that whereas the papal Mass is a sacrifice, the Supper is in fact in memory of the sacrifice. The purpose of the Supper, above all, 'is to confirm spiritual nourishment or preservation to eternal life by the merit of the death and obedience of Christ. On this the union of the faithful with Christ and with one another depends'.[113]

Francis Turretin (1623–87) studied at Geneva, Leiden, Utrecht, Paris, Samur, Montauban and Nîmes, and became professor of theology at Geneva in 1653. His wide knowledge of international Reformed theology as well as Lutheran and Catholic writings allowed him to publish his lengthy *Institutes of Elenctic Theology* between 1679 and 1685. The section on sacraments was the nineteenth topic extended over 31 questions. He represented the quintessence of Reformed orthodox method illustrated by the following passage that discussed the relationship of sign and signified:

> Now they are not one in genus or species and number, but by analogy. Hence it follows that this union is not natural (formed by a physical contact), or local (by lack of nearness and nonexistence, or by the coexistence of one in the other), or hypostatical; but analogical, relative and sacramental. This consists principally in three things: (1) in signification, by which the external symbols are as representative and commemorative signs, but the internal things are represented and commemorated signs; (2) in the sealing of the thing signified and sealed, by which the elements are as a seal, pledge and token; the body and blood of Christ, as the thing sealed; (3) in the exhibition of the thing signified and sealed, inasmuch as the external thing is the moral instrument by

109 ET in John W. Beardslee III, *Reformed Dogmatics*, New York: Oxford University Press, 1965, p. 120.

110 Beardslee III, *Reformed Dogmatics*, p. 121.

111 Beardslee III, *Reformed Dogmatics*, p. 122.

112 Beardslee III, *Reformed Dogmatics*, p. 134.

113 Beardslee III, *Reformed Dogmatics*, p. 134.

> and with which God wishes to be efficacious and to communicate really the internal thing to the believer. The signification is placed in the similitude of properties and effects of the sign and thing sealed (which have a close connection with each other). As the bread and wine are the most sufficient and efficacious means of sustaining and conserving the life of the body, so the body and blood of Christ afford nourishment to the soul and are the most sufficient and efficacious means of cherishing and supporting the spiritual life. As the bread and wine are separated in the Supper, so the body and blood of Christ were separated on the cross. As the bread is broken and the wine poured out, so the body of Christ was broken on the cross by pains and torments; when his heart was lacerated by a sense of the wrath of God and his hands and feet were transfixed by nails; his side was pierced with a spear and his blood poured out there. As the bread and wine do not nourish unless they are received into the mouth, so the body and blood of Christ do not nourish the mind when they are only considered speculatively, but when they are practically received by faith and applied to us. Finally, as the communicants are all partakers of one bread, so believers partake of one Christ and with him and in turn with each other coalesce into one body by faith and love (1 Cor. 10:16, 17).[114]

On the whole, during this period few or no changes were made to most of the foundational liturgies. However, the increasing complexity of Reformed orthodoxy is perhaps mirrored in the 1616–17 draft liturgy for Scotland prepared by William Cowper, who became Bishop of Galloway. In his theological works Cowper described the bread of the Eucharist as 'an exhibiting instrument of Christ's body', and he simply lifted this into his proposed liturgy: 'Lord blesse it that it may be unto us ane effectual exhibiting instrument of the Lord Jesus.'[115] A particular expression of Reformed orthodoxy is represented by the English *Westminster Confession and Catechisms* (1647) together with their liturgical counterpart, *A Directory for the Public Worship of God* (1644). These documents stem from the period of the English Civil War when the Episcopal Church of England had been replaced by a loose Presbyterian system of church government. They were drawn up by selected clergy of the Church of England together with some Scottish Commissioners who together formed the Westminster Assembly of Divines, appointed by Parliament, and they reflect the prevailing theology of the time. At the Restoration they were disowned by the Church of England but became foundational documents for the Church of Scotland and later English-speaking Presbyterianism.[116]

Chapter XXVII of the *Westminster Confession* defined sacraments as 'holy signs and seals of the covenant of grace', instituted by God, representing Christ and his benefits, and to confirm our interest in him. The grace that is exhibited

---

114 Francis Turretin, *Institutes of Elenctic Theology*, trans. George Giger, James T. Dennison, 3 vols, Phillipsburg: Presbyterian and Reformed Publishing Company, 1997, vol. 3, pp. 434–5.

115 Spinks, *Sacraments, Ceremonies and the Stuart Divines*, pp. 58–60. The text of the eucharistic liturgy is on pp. 191–7.

116 Bryan D. Spinks, 'The Westminster Confession: The "Bastard Child" of the Church of England', in David M. Loades (ed.), *Word and Worship*, Oxford: The Davenant Press, 2005, pp. 151–61.

in or by sacraments is not conferred by any power in them but 'upon the work of the Spirit and the Word of Institution, which contains, together with a precept authorizing the use thereof, a promise of benefit to worthy receivers'.[117] Chapter XXIX expounded the Lord's Supper, noting that Christ in this ordinance has appointed ministers 'to declare his word of institution to the people, to pray, and bless the elements of bread and wine, and thereby to set them apart from a common to an holy use; and to take and break the bread'. Worthy receivers in partaking of the visible elements receive Christ, not carnally in, with, or under the bread and wine, but spiritually and really.[118] 'Spiritually' here is regarded as superior to, and more real than 'in, with, or under'.

The *Directory* appeared earlier, and was a compromise between those who wanted to adopt Knox's Form of Prayers, and the Independents and 'Radical party' members of the Church of Scotland who refused to have any written liturgical text.[119] The service of the Lord's Supper of the latter is represented by the account given by John Cotton in New England in his *The Way of the Churches of Christ in New England*, published in 1645. The order was not significantly different from other Reformed rites, other than any prayer was extemporary, communion was given to people where they were seated and there were separate blessings over the bread and the wine.[120] The *Directory* was drawn up by a sub-committee, the majority of whom did not espouse set forms of worship, but whose theology was certainly Reformed orthodoxy. The order suggested what might be in the prayers rather than actual prayers. The recommended order, following on from the usual Sunday service, was: exhortation on the benefit of the sacrament, excommunication of the unworthy and encouragement to repentance; the recital of the Words of Institution; optional explanation of the Words of Institution; Prayer of Thanksgiving or blessing of the elements; Fraction and delivery; exhortation; solemn thanksgiving. A rubric directed the minister 'to begin the action of sanctifying and blessing the elements of bread and wine', and in the prayer after the Institution Narrative to pray God 'to vouchsafe his gracious presence, and the effectual working of his Spirit in us; and so to sanctify these elements both of bread and wine, and to bless his own ordinance, that we may receive by faith the body and blood of Jesus Christ, crucified for us'. Communion could be at the table or around it. The Minutes show that the compilation was a contentious process, and the Independents continued to use

117 Text in Schaff, *Creeds of Christendom*, vol. 3, p. 661.

118 Schaff, *Creeds of Christendom*, pp. 665–6.

119 See Bryan D. Spinks, *Freedom or Order?: The Eucharistic Liturgy in English Congregationalism 1645–1980*, Allison Park: Pickwick Publications, 1984, ch. 2; *Sacraments, Ceremonies and the Stuart Divines*, pp. 119–29; Richard A. Muller and Rowland S. Ward, *Scripture and Worship: Biblical Interpretation and the Directory for Public Worship*, Phillipsburg: P. & R. Publishing, 2007; Samuel Rutherford, a Radical party member of the Church of Scotland, remarked of Knox's liturgy, 'we will not owne this liturgy. Nor are we tyed unto it'; Bryan D. Spinks, 'The Origin of the Antipathy to Set Liturgical Forms in the English-Speaking Reformed Tradition', in Lukas Vischer (ed.), *Christian Worship in Reformed Churches Past and Present*, Grand Rapids: Eerdmans, 2003, p. 79, citing manuscript Minutes of the Westminster Assembly, Dr Williams Library, London, vol. 2, p. 492.

120 John Cotton, *The Way of the Churches of New England*, 1645, p. 68.

separate blessings for the bread and wine. However, what is of note is the highly technical phraseology recommended for the minister to use in prayer.

Symptoms of the eighteenth-century 'Enlightenment'

According to Bruno Bürki, Jean-Frédèric Ostervald (1663–1747) who was pastor of Neuchâtel represents 'a reasoned orthodoxy touched by the early Enlightenment', having acquired his theological and philosophical orientation from England and the Netherlands.[121] The influence of Enlightenment thinkers such as John Locke and Isaac Newton can be seen in the sacramental theology of Benjamin Hoadly (1676–1761), where the bodily absence of Christ is emphasized and the Eucharist is a moral duty, requiring faith, repentance, thankfulness and charity, and is a rite of subjective remembrance.[122] A similar emphasis is found in Ostervald's *A Compendium of Christian Theology*. Sacraments are public pledges and seals of the divine covenant. On the Lord's Supper he questioned the *Second Helvetic Confession*'s assertion (from Calvin) that we receive the substance of the body of Christ since, for Enlightenment thought, this was nonsense. As he noted, 'It opposes right reason, which does not admit our conceiving a body, without extension, visibility, &c.'[123] The sacramental rite shows forth the death of Christ, and this act invites us to the most perfect discharge of all the duties of a grateful mind, and of piety.[124] Reason, mind, duty and piety are crucial words here.

Ostervald was attracted to the *BCP* of the Church of England, and he used material from it for the rite he compiled for Neuchâtel in 1713.[125] It began with an invocation of the Trinity and a prayer, after which came the Institution Narrative, an excommunication of sinful groups, and a call for worthy reception. His Enlightenment convictions were expressed in the final paragraph:

> And that we might have continual remembrance of the tremendous love of our blessed Saviour, who thus died for us, and of those infinite good things which he has provided for us, he instituted this holy sacrament to be for us a pledge of his love and a perpetual memorial of his death to our great and everlasting comfort. Let us then offer today and at all times to our loving Redeemer, as well as to the Father and to the Holy Spirit, our praises and thanksgivings, which is our bounded duty.[126]

121 Bruno Bürki, 'Reformed Worship in Continental Europe since the Seventeenth Century', in Vischer (ed.), *Christian Worship in Reformed Churches*, p. 37; Bruno Bürki, 'Beispielhaft reformierte Form der Liturgie in Neuchâtel', in Martin Klöckener and Benedikt Kranemann (eds), *Liturgiereformen*, Münster: Aschendorff, 2001, vol. 1, pp. 417–35.

122 Bryan D. Spinks, *Liturgy in the Age of Reason: Worship and Sacraments in England and Scotland 1662–c.1800*, Farnham: Ashgate, 2008, pp. 146–52.

123 J. F. Ostervald, *A Compendium of Christian Theology*, trans. John McMains, Hartford, CT: Nathaniel Patten Publishing, 1788, p. 360.

124 Ostervald, *Compendium*, pp. 364–5.

125 Text in Bruno Bürki, *Cène du Seigneur – eucharistie de l'Église*, 2 vols, Fribourg: Éditions Universitaires Fribourg Suisse, 1985, vol. 1, pp. 14–24; *PEER*, pp. 283–9.

126 *PEER*, p. 286.

There then follows a eucharistic Preface adapted from the 1662 *BCP* Prayer of Consecration, including special Prefaces for Christmas, Easter, Pentecost and in September. Intercessions followed, with a confession and absolution, and then, at the table, an adaptation of the 1662 Prayer of Consecration. His memorialist beliefs are reinforced in the words of administration: 'Remember (*souvenez vous*) that Jesus Christ your Saviour died for you and give him thanks; Remember that Jesus Christ your Saviour shed his blood for you and give him thanks.'[127] The Nunc dimittis was sung, and then he provided a prayer of thanksgiving that emphasized that we should not forget his many benefits, and having grave hearts, believe and continually advance in the faith. The rite ended with the *Gloria in excelsis* (again, from 1662), an exhortation that reminded worshippers that this was a public profession of faith (cf. Zwingli), and a final blessing. Similar Enlightenment concerns are to be found in the Genevan liturgy of 1743, where Calvin's words of receiving Christ's body and blood, 'Christ Himself entire', were omitted, and a new invitation to communion stressed humility, repentance, faith, piety and charity, for communion was 'one of the most solemn duties of Religion'.[128]

Some nineteenth-century fruits of liberalism and Romanticism

The Enlightenment concern for reasonable religion coalesced with pietism in the theology of Friedrich Schleiermacher (1768–1834). He found traditional Christian doctrine difficult to believe, though he regarded being religious an essential part of being human. He characterized this religious feeling as being a feeling of absolute dependency which he termed 'God-consciousness', and the supreme manifestation of this God-consciousness was revealed in Jesus. He wrote:

> If it is the essence of redemption that the God-consciousness already present in human nature, though feeble and repressed, becomes stimulated and made dominant by the entrance of the living influence of Christ, the individual on whom this influence is exercised attains a religious personality not his before.[129]

Schleiermacher rejected traditional Chalcedonian Christology and suggested that Jesus had perfect God-consciousness through the indwelling of the Holy Spirit. God-consciousness is activated when Christ, or the Spirit, enters a person. However, for Schleiermacher, perhaps more indebted to Zwingli than he wished to acknowledge, external things such as sacraments have little value other than as ecclesial expressions of faith. He only reluctantly used the term 'sacrament'.[130] As regards the Lord's Supper, the Words of Institution are central because from them flow 'the redeeming and fellowship-forming love of Christ',

---

127 *PEER*, p. 288; Bürki, *Cène du Seigneur*, p. 23.

128 Bürki, *Cène du Seigneur*, pp. 25–42.

129 Friedrich Schleiermacher, *The Christian Faith*, ET: Edinburgh: T & T Clark, [1821, 1830] 1989, p. 476.

130 Schleiermacher, *Christian Faith*, pp. 657–9.

which is not only represented but newly made active.[131] The words of John 6 are interpreted as meaning that Christ must become our being and well-being, and the effect of the Supper is that as a simultaneous act of many, the consciousness of benefit in each is accompanied by a sympathetic sense that the same thing is happening to others.[132] Schleiermacher was of the Reformed tradition, but in the Union Church of Lutherans and Reformed, and he outlined the teachings of Luther, Zwingli and Calvin, without any adjudication, other than stressing that it was the effects of participation that were important, the main one being fellowship with Christ, 'for living faith in Christ is simply the consciousness of our union with Him'.[133] Sin disturbs the union, and the Supper reminds us of sins forgiven:

> And for this the representation of the whole body of believers natural in the action of the Supper is an important factor. For it cannot but give rise in each individual to a strong excitation of the common Spirit, as well as to a heightened consciousness both of his general and his special vocation within this fellowship; and this cannot but be accompanied by a new impulse to develop his gifts.[134]

This seems to be an elaborate way of saying the Supper enhances group identity. The idea that the elements might be instruments of grace was foreign to Schleiermacher's theology. Although it is difficult to pinpoint any liturgy compiled as a direct result of this theology, Bürki has noted how place for extempore prayer allowed for the articulation of such beliefs among liberal-minded ministers.[135] It certainly did not call for any elaborate rite.

Quite the reverse was true for the influence of the nineteenth-century Romantic Movement, which led to a renewed interest in the medieval and the ancient. As will be noted in a later chapter, a new church came into being, the Catholic Apostolic Church, which developed a very elaborate liturgy inspired by that of the Church of England, the Roman Catholic rite and certain of the Eastern rites. This liturgy in turn influenced publications in at least three Reformed traditions.[136]

The German Reformed Church in the USA: Mercersburg

The Mercersburg theology is associated with the names of John Williamson Nevin (1803–86) and Philip Schaff (1819–83) as developed at Mercersburg

131 Schleiermacher, *Christian Faith*, p. 641.

132 Schleiermacher, *Christian Faith*, p. 641.

133 Schleiermacher, *Christian Faith*, p. 652.

134 Schleiermacher, *Christian Faith*, p. 652.

135 Bürki, 'Reformed Worship in Continental Europe', pp. 42–4.

136 For two of the three discussed here, see Gregg Alan Mast, *The Eucharistic Service of the Catholic Apostolic Church and Its Influence on Reformed Liturgical Renewals of the Nineteenth Century*, Lanham: Scarecrow Press, 1999. The fact that this liturgy was not Roman Catholic, Lutheran or Anglican commended itself to some of the 'high church' Reformed liturgical leaders.

Seminary, Pennsylvania. Nevin was formerly a Presbyterian, but moved away from what he perceived to be its liberalism, individualism and subjectivism, migrating to the German Reformed Church which was more confessional. Both he and Schaff were also influenced by the English Tractarian movement which emphasized the catholic heritage of the Church of England. They recalled the German Reformed Church in the USA to its Calvinist and catholic heritage, which they expressed in their writings, and in their 'provisional' or 'Mercersburg' Liturgy of 1857. In his work *The Mystical Presence*, Nevin attacked the prevailing 'Puritan' memorialist interpretation of the Supper, and restated what he believed to be Calvin's position. He wrote of the Eucharist:

> The sign and the thing signified are, by Christ's institution, mysteriously bound together, so as to form in the sacramental transaction one and the same presence. Not as though the last were in any way included in the first as its local or material receptacle. The conjunction is in no sense such as to change at all the nature of the sensible sign, in itself considered or to bring it into any physical union with the grace it represents. But still the two form one presence. Along with the outward sign is exhibited always at the same time the represented grace. The union of the one with the other is mystical and peculiar altogether to the nature of a sacrament; but it is not for this reason *less* real but only a great deal *more* real than it could be possibly under any natural and local forms. The invisible grace thus made present by sensible signs in the sacraments, is 'Christ *and* the benefits of the new covenant'. Not the *benefits* of the new covenant only; but Christ himself also in a real way, as the only medium of a real communication with the benefits. Christ first and *then* and *therefore* all his benefits; as inhering only in his person and carrying with them no reality under any different view.[137]

A mystical sacrament required a mystical rite. Schaff visited England in 1854 and wrote enthusiastically to his wife about the Catholic Apostolic Church, or 'Irvingites', and we may assume he acquired a copy of the liturgy. Brenner commented, 'It is as though Schaff seated himself at an organ with the score of the catholic Apostolic Liturgy before him and began to improvise.'[138] In the 'provisional' liturgy Schaff and Nevin attempted to reintroduce to the Reformed tradition a eucharistic liturgy more in keeping with the Classical Western shape, which included a full Eucharistic Prayer.[139] Thus it began with an invocation, Collect for Purity, Scripture sentences and *Gloria in excelsis*, followed by the readings, Collect of the Day, sermon and Creed. It provided an exhortation, confession and absolution, Eucharistic Prayer (*sursum corda*, Long Preface, Sanctus

137 John Williamson Nevin, *The Mystical Presence and the Doctrine of the Reformed Church on the Lord's Supper*, ed. Linden J. DeBie, Eugene, OR: Wipf and Stock, 2012, p. 158. The ensuing battle between Charles Hodge of Princeton and Nevin over his interpretation serves as a reminder that there have always been different ways of reading Calvin, though Hodge never replied to Nevin's demolition of Hodge's review.

138 Scott F. Brenner, 'Philip Schaff the Liturgist', *Christendom* 11, 1946, p. 450.

139 For the text and full discussion of the making of this rite, see Jack Martin Maxwell, *Worship and Reformed Theology: The Liturgical Lessons of Mercersburg*, Pittsburgh: Pickwick Press, 1976.

and Benedictus, Words of Institution with Fraction and Elevation, Epiklesis, Anamnesis and intercessions). There were some blessings prior to the Peace and reception of the elements. The Epiklesis prayed:

> Almighty God, our heavenly Father, send down, we beseech Thee, the powerful benediction of Thy Holy Spirit upon these elements of bread and wine, that being set apart now from a common to a sacred and mystical use, they may exhibit and represent to us with true effect the Body and Blood of Thy Son, Jesus Christ; so that in the use of them we may be made, through the power of the Holy Ghost, to partake really and truly of His blessed life, whereby only we can be saved from death, and raised to immortality at the last day.[140]

Gregg Mast draws attention to the Anamnesis, which he describes as 'a remarkable piece of writing in a Reformed document'.[141] Not only are the person and merits of Christ presented to God, but so are 'the reasonable sacrifice of our own persons; consecrating ourselves, on the altar of the gospel, in soul and body, property and life, to Thy most blessed service and praise'.[142]

Scotland

The Church of Scotland worshipped with the memory of the Westminster *Directory*, but no official new denominational rite had been published, with ministers being content with free prayer. Communion had become quarterly, and in many areas congregations came together outdoors for 'communion seasons' with preparatory sermons and communion and post-communion services extended over two or three days, a practice that fed into the American Holy Fairs and revival meetings.[143] Some individuals did write down summaries of their services, and some ministers did write prayers for communion, a few of which have survived.[144] The nineteenth century saw the rise of individual publications to assist ministers, in an attempt to improve the standard of worship and curb rambling and bad extempore prayer. In 1865, three young ministers, Robert Story of Rosneath, J. Cameron Lees of Paisley Abbey and George Campbell of Eastwood, with the encouragement of older established ministers of a 'high church' persuasion, founded the Church Service Society. Other leading members included G. W. Sprott and Robert Lee. Story would later write:

---

140 In Maxwell, *Worship and Reformed Theology*, p. 449. It is odd that both Holy Spirit and Holy Ghost are used.

141 Mast, *Eucharistic Service*, p. 73.

142 Maxwell, *Worship and Reformed Theology*, p. 449.

143 For Scotland, see Spinks, *Liturgy in the Age of Reason*, pp. 21–30, 67–78, 216–35; Robin A. Leaver, *A Communion Sunday in Scotland ca.1780: Liturgies and Sermons*, Lanham: Scarecrow Press, 2010. For Scotland and America, see Leigh Eric Schmidt, *Holy Fairs: Scotland and the Making of American Revivalism*, 2nd edn, Grand Rapids: Eerdmans, 2001; Kimberly Bracken Long, *The Eucharistic Theology of the American Holy Fairs*, Louisville: Westminster/John Knox Press, 2011.

144 See Spinks, *Liturgy in the Age of Reason*, and Leaver, *Communion Sunday*.

> The public services of the Church of Scotland had become probably the baldest and rudest in Christendom. The parish kirks, owing to the niggardliness of the heritors, were comfortless and coarsely furnished. The music was rough and untrained; only in a few of the town churches was it rendered with any attempt at taste and skill. The Bible was scarcely read. The prayers were reduced in number to two at the most, and were drearily long and uninteresting. The Lord's Prayer [and Creed] were never heard. The sermon was the great feature of the service; and it was too often a 'screed of dull doctrine or of cold morality'.[145]

The aim of the society was to study liturgies with a view to preparing and publishing forms for public worship. The *Euchologion* was published in 1867, with a further six editions in the following 30 years, each edition being refined and expanded in some way or other. In the second edition (1869), for example, the eucharistic liturgy was entitled 'The Sacrament of the Lord's Supper', and provided an optional exhortation after the prayer that followed the sermon at the morning service and a confession. After a hymn came the Grace, then the Words of Institution and an 'Address' inspired by the Westminster *Directory*, including the words 'Setting apart these elements by the Word and prayer to be sacramentally the body and blood of Christ'. The Creed followed and a Prayer of Approach and the Prayer of the Veil from the Catholic Apostolic Church. The Eucharistic Prayer (but without introductory *Sursum corda*) followed, large sections of which were from the Catholic Apostolic rite. The Words of Institution had already been recited, and they were repeated at the distribution, and so did not feature in the Eucharistic Prayer. An Epiklesis came after the Sanctus:

> And we most humbly beseech Thee, O merciful Father, to vouchsafe unto us Thy gracious presence, as we now make that memorial of His most blessed sacrifice which Thy Son hath commanded us to make: and to bless and sanctify with Thy Word and Spirit these Thine own gifts of bread and wine which we set before Thee: that we, receiving them, according to our Saviour's institution, in thankful remembrance of His death and passion, may, through the power of the Holy Ghost, be very partakers of His body and blood, with all His benefits, to our salvation and the glory of Thy most holy name.[146]

This Epiklesis has affinities with the 'provisional' liturgy which was well known to the compilers of the *Euchologion*. In the sixth edition (1890), the prayer of humble access of the Church of England was included, together with the Agnus Dei, before the Eucharistic Prayer. This latter was now introduced with 'lift up your hearts' with congregational response. The final words of the Epiklesis were changed to 'with all His benefits, to our spiritual nourishment and growth in grace', suggesting that sacraments did give grace. In the final edition this paragraph would be further expanded. Although opponents referred to members of the Society as 'Scoto-Catholics', the eucharistic rite was popular, and used at the

145 R. H. Story, *Reformed Ritual in Scotland*, 1890, p. 36, cited in J. M. Barkley, *The Worship of the Reformed Church*, London: Lutterworth Press, 1966, pp. 32–3.

146 *Euchologion*, 2nd edn, Edinburgh: William Blackwood, 1869, p. 234.

General Assembly from 1890 to 1923. The Eucharistic Prayer would influence the official Church of Scotland rite in 1923, *Prayers for Divine Service.*

Eugène Bersier

Bersier (1831–89) was Anglo-Swiss by birth, and he became minister of L'Église de l'Étoile, Paris. This was an independent evangelical church, and Bersier brought it into the French Reformed Church. He created a liturgy for his congregation that in his view expressed the best of the Reformed tradition, but also its older Catholic heritage. He knew the *BCP* of the Church of England, but he too was influenced by the Catholic Apostolic Liturgy. Bürki writes:

> In contrast to the rational or 'liberal' development within Protestantism, he aimed to uphold the heritage of Reformed theology. The Trinitarian faith, confessing the divinity of Jesus Christ, was fundamental for him. His emphasis on redemption through the sacrificed blood of the Crucified One came from his Awakening-style piety. Rather than individual conversion, however, he stressed praise for God as holy and transcendent. The social-ethical commitment of this representative of nineteenth-century Protestantism is noteworthy.[147]

His 1874 liturgy included the *Gloria in excelsis* near the beginning of the rite. The main interest is the Eucharistic Prayer, which has Proper Prefaces, and asked, 'O God, send upon us your Holy Spirit so that in participating in this bread and cup, we may receive the body and blood of your Son.'[148] The liturgy he prepared for submission to the official General Synod at their invitation in 1888 was rather more 'Reformed', and a rather different 'Eucharistic' Prayer, without Preface and Sanctus, came before the consecration which was by recitation of the Institution Narrative, and this was followed by an invitation to communion.

English Congregationalist contributions

The English Independents, or Congregationalists, followed no set liturgical text, but glimpses of their order of celebrating the Lord's Supper were recorded by John Cotton (*c.* 1633), and subsequently for Richard Davis of Rothwell (*c.* 1700) and Isaac Watts (*c.* 1723).[149] Important contributions came from Davis and Watts in the form of hymns to be sung at the Lord's Supper.[150] Watts, for example, in the third book of his *Hymns and Spiritual Songs*, originally published in 1707, contained hymns 'Prepared for the holy Ordinance of the

147 Bürki, 'Reformed Worship in Continental Europe', p. 47.

148 Both the 1874 and 1888 communion rites are in Bürki, *Cène du Seigneur*, vol. 1, pp. 70–100.

149 For Cotton, see Spinks, *Freedom or Order?*. For Davis and Watts, see Spinks, *Liturgy in the Age of Reason*, pp. 87–8, 239–40.

150 For the hymns of Davis, see Spinks, *Liturgy in the Age of Reason*, p. 89.

Lord's Supper'. There are 25 hymns including: 'Twas on that dark, that doleful night', 'Jesus invites his saints to meet around his Board', 'When I survey the wond'rous Cross', and 'Nature with open volume stands'. The nineteenth century saw fashionable English Congregational congregations preparing set liturgical forms, mainly based on the Church of England's *BCP*. However, in the nineteenth century, with John Hunter (1849–1917), Congregationalism found a worthy liturgiographer, and his several editions of *Devotional Services* became immensely popular.[151] Perhaps his most famous legacy was his exhortation/invitation to communion, which included the following words:

> Come to this sacred Table, not because you must, but because you may: come to testify, not that you are righteous, but that you sincerely love our Lord Jesus Christ, and desire to be His true disciples: come, not because you are strong, but because you are weak, not because you have any claim on Heaven's rewards, but because in your frailty and sin you stand in constant need of Heaven's mercy and help: come, not to express an opinion, but to seek a Presence and pray for a Spirit.

Concluding remarks

There were fundamental differences to be found among the foundational Reformed theologians on the Eucharist, particularly on how and in what manner one received the body and blood of Christ, and Gerrish's threefold categories of symbolic memorialism, parallelism and instrumentalism are well founded. However, those differences were rarely expressed very strongly liturgically. Perhaps the greatest disappointment here is with Calvin, who certainly in later writings emphasized the reality of what (or who) was received in communion, and Nevin was not wrong in seeing in Calvin a 'mystical' union. The main difference in the liturgy was the historic derivation, with Zurich 1525 and Strasbourg–Geneva–Knox being derived from the Mass, and Basel–the Palatinate–Netherlands–Poland being derived more from an independent application of New Testament ideas to liturgical compilation. H. O. Old has shown how many of the Reformers really believed that they had the Fathers on their side.[152] It is difficult to understand why, in the process, prayer was so often replaced by exhortation and explication, making the rite almost into an instructed ritual. The use of exhortation and explication opened the way to 'modernization' to keep up with theological trends, which allowed for erosion of orthodoxy in the eighteenth and nineteenth centuries. Yet, by the mid-nineteenth century at least some figures in some of the Churches were beginning to try to reclaim more classical patterns and forms and to re-appropriate and promote the teaching of Calvin as normative for the Reformed tradition.

151 The English Congregationalist communion tradition is treated at length in my *Freedom or Order?*, see ch. 6 for details of the communion rite in the various editions of Hunter's *Devotional Services*.

152 Old, *The Patristic Roots of Reformed Worship*.

12

The Anglican Tradition: From Thomas Cranmer to the Tractarian Disputes

The English Reformation began in the 1530s as a judicial separation of the English Church from the authority of Rome, and only later did it become a liturgical and theological separation. Under Henry VIII the reforms were more of a liberal humanism, with the English Great Bible to be read in churches, the suppression of the cult of the saints, and in 1544, a litany in English in place of all other litanies. Henry promoted a number of evangelically minded clergy to bishoprics, including his archbishop, and after Henry's death, together with the Protestant Council that ruled on behalf of the young King Edward, they pursued a Protestant reform. As Gordon Jeanes has recently remarked, 'What was unusual in England was the use of the liturgy as the central plank in reform . . . The use of the printed book as an agent of reform was very much a feature of the time, and a novelty historically.'[1] In 1548 an English vernacular communion preparation was issued that was to be inserted prior to the place of communion in the Latin Mass. In 1549 a *Book of Common Prayer* (*BCP*), with an Act of Uniformity, replaced all Latin rites other than for ordination. The latter were replaced in 1550. The 1549 Prayer Book, some of the services of which seemed little more than vernacular translations, was replaced in 1552, with a new Act of Uniformity, by a more obviously Protestant book. The chief architect and primary liturgiographer of these liturgical projects was Archbishop Thomas Cranmer.

The Order of the Communion was prefaced by a Royal Proclamation that asked the new order to be accepted:

- An exhortation giving notice of communion and the need for preparation.
- Directions for preparation of sufficient bread and wine.
- An exhortation to worthiness.
- A warning not to communicate if unworthy.
- Invitation to Confession.
- General Confession.
- Absolution.
- Comfortable Words of Scripture.
- Prayer of Approach – 'We do not presume to come to this thy table'.

1 Gordon Jeanes, 'The Tudor Prayer Books: That "The Whole Realme Shall Have but One Use"', in Stephen Platten and Christopher Woods (eds), *Comfortable Words, Polity, Piety and the Book of Common Prayer*, London: SCM Press, 2012, p. 22.

- Directions for Communion and Words of Delivery – bread and wine.
- A blessing.

Much of this is taken from one of Cranmer's favourite sources – *Simplex ac pia Deliberatio* – prepared by Martin Bucer and Phillip Melanchthon for Archbishop Hermann von Wied of Cologne. The copy of the Latin translation from Cranmer's library is preserved at Chichester Cathedral, and the notations show that he not only owned it, but read and studied it in detail. Although this German work was by Bucer and Melanchthon, it was published under Hermann's name, and Cranmer's use of it is interesting. As Archbishop, he seems to have been very selective about his sources. He could still draw on his experience of Lutheran worship in Nürnberg, even though his relationship with Osiander had cooled. But two of his main sources of inspiration were by a cardinal and by a fellow archbishop. It would seem that Cranmer was keen to use sources from his peers rather than those of a lesser rank.

A close comparison of the phraseology of the *Deliberatio* and Cranmer's 1548 order was undertaken by Geoffrey Cuming.[2] The minutiae of textual comparisons are not irrelevant – they confirm the dependence. Of the ten items in Cranmer's order listed, numbers 1, 3, 5, 8 are all based on the German source. He wove other elements into his sources, and even added something entirely new, such as the prayer that came to be known as the Prayer of Humble Access. According to Cuming, this latter begins with a phrase from a priest's private preparation prayer found in two printed missals before 1548, but on the whole this is Cranmer inspired by the vision of Isaiah and the story of the Syro-Phoenician woman.

What were the doctrinal implications? The exhortations used the word 'spiritual', but this was not itself at this time a word solely used by Protestants. It restored communion in two kinds, but beyond that there is little that anyone could object to. What later would be called the Prayer of Humble Access included the words 'so to eat the flesh of thy dear Son Jesus Christ, and to drink his blood, in these holy mysteries', which seemed traditional Catholic teaching. Some hint of direction, however, is given in the Royal Proclamation, which requested that the devotion be received quietly and that such a reception would encourage those in authority 'further to travail for the Reformation and setting forth of such godly orders'. A rubric also explained that this order would stand only for a time 'until other order shall be provided'. These words implied that further godly orders were planned and would appear, and that these would be part of a Reformation. Since whatever doctrine was enshrined in this devotion, and in the subsequent 'godly orders' of 1549 and 1552, was unlikely to be incompatible with that of their chief author, it is Cranmer's eucharistic doctrine that is important here.

Cranmer never had the time or leisure to write extensively on the sacraments. He did write *A Defence of the True and Catholic Doctrine of the Sacrament* in 1550, which seems to have included material he had written earlier, and in 1551

2 G. J. Cuming, *The Godly Order: Texts and Studies Relating to the Book of Common Prayer*, London: SPCK, 1983, pp. 76–80. See also F. E. Brightman, *The English Rite*, 2 vols, London: Rivingtons, 1915.

he wrote an answer to the imprisoned Stephen Gardiner's *Reply* to his *Defence*. The style of both, though, is polemical and mainly concerned with the Eucharist. However, as chief architect of the Prayer Books it is reasonable to conclude that he would not compile a liturgy that conflicted with his own theological convictions. And the liturgy that he bequeathed to Anglicanism does express doctrine, even if many English divines had rather different eucharistic theologies.

In the past, attempts have been made to identify or label Cranmer's sacramental theology, and the attempts have not been helped by his own words at his trial in 1555. He was accused of teaching three different doctrines of the Eucharist, but he replied that he had taught only two. The three have been perceived to be the Roman, Lutheran and Reformed; the two as Roman and Reformed. It might be assumed that he knew his own mind, and if he said he taught only two, that is so. However, most scholars feel that there was a transition, from the Roman through the Lutheran view. When or what the 'Lutheran' phase may have been, the theology he set out on the sacraments certainly placed him in the Reformed ambit rather than the Lutheran.

If the final view was Reformed, which Reformed doctrine, or whose? According to C. H. Smyth, he was a Bucerian, whereas Brilioth and Timms labelled him as a Calvinist.[3] According to Gregory Dix and C. C. Richardson he was a Zwinglian.[4] Diarmaid MacCulloch notes many similarities with Zwingli but also a few concepts that he thinks approximate to Calvin.[5] The recent extensive survey by Brian Douglas attempts to place all Anglican eucharistic theologies in one of four broad categories of Immoderate Realism, Moderate Realism, Immoderate Nominalism or Moderate Nominalism. Cranmer is placed as a Moderate Nominalist, but these categories are far too broad and 'catch all' to be particularly helpful.[6] Gerrish's threefold division is more helpful, and Cranmer seems to hover between symbolic memorialism and symbolic parallelism.[7] At times he echoes Zwingli, Oecolampadius and Bullinger (even though in a letter of 1537 to Vadianus he rejected the teaching of Zwingli and Oecolampadius), and at other times he seems to echo Bucer. Part of the problem is that Cranmer's ideas did undergo development, and what he affirmed in the *King's Book* of 1543 was not what he taught in 1550. In addition, he used ambiguous language which can be interpreted in a number of ways.[8] His favourite expression is spiritual presence, or spiritually exhibited, but 'spiritual' is a qualifying term found in all Reformation writers. Also, in 1548 he published in English translation the Lutheran Catechism of Justus Jonas. It went through three editions, each one

3 C. H. Smyth, *Cranmer and the Reformation under Edward VI*, London: SPCK, 1926; Y. Brilioth and Arthur Gabriel Herbert, *Eucharistic Faith and Practice: Evangelical and Catholic*, London: SPCK, 1930; George Timms, *Dixit Cranmer*, London: A. R. Mowbray, 1947.

4 Gregory Dix, *The Shape of the Liturgy*, London: Dacre Press, 1945; *Dixit Cranmer et Non Timuit*, London: Dacre Press, 1948; C. C. Richardson, *Zwingli and Cranmer on the Eucharist: Cranmer Dixit et Contradixit*, Evanston: Seabury-Weston Theological Seminary, 1949.

5 Diarmaid MacCulloch, *Thomas Cranmer*, New Haven: Yale University Press, 1996.

6 Brian Douglas, *A Companion to Anglican Eucharistic Theology. Volume 1: The Reformation to the 19th Century*, Leiden: Brill, 2012.

7 For Gerrish, see the previous chapter.

8 Alan Bartlett, 'How Protestant was Cranmer's 1552 Prayer Book?', in David M. Loades (ed.), *Word and Worship*, Oxford: The Davenant Press, 2005, pp. 65–74.

being revised in places to try to make it consistent. What we find is that phrases that attest to the Lutheran Real Presence are translated in a way that interprets the doctrine in a Reformed manner. However, such renderings were not consistent the whole way through, which has led to ambiguity. It is probably correct to conclude that by 1548 Cranmer had reached a view of the sacraments that was Reformed, and this was consistent throughout the revision of the Prayer Book. Cranmer wrote: 'I have not trusted any man or friend . . . but I have diligently expended and weighed the matter myself.[9] Thus, ultimately, Cranmer's doctrine of the sacraments, even if it has a Swiss German flavour, is 'Cranmerian'.

Cranmer made his opposition to the traditional teaching of the Catholic Church quite clear:

> But what availeth it to take away beads, pardons, pilgrimages, and such other like popery, so long as the two chief roots remain unpulled up? . . . The rest is but branches and leaves . . . but the very body of the tree, or rather the roots of the weeds, is the popish doctrine of transubstantiation, of the real presence of Christ's flesh and blood in the sacrament of the altar (as they call it), and of the sacrifice and oblation of Christ made by the priest, for the salvation of the quick and the dead.[10]

He saw no need to treat baptism and the Eucharist differently, whereas the medieval Catholic Church did. Thus, just as the water in baptism was applied to a holy use, but didn't change into something else, so the bread and wine were applied to a holy use, but didn't change. In Book III of *A Defence*, Cranmer wrote:

> Consecration is the separation of any thing from a profane and worldly use unto a spiritual and godly use. And therefore when usual and common water is taken from other uses, and put to the use of baptism, in the name of the Father, and of the Son, and of the Holy Ghost, then it may rightly be called consecrated water, that is to say, water put to an holy use.[11]

And in his Preface to his *Answer* to Gardiner's Explication he had written:

> And sometimes by this word 'sacrament' I mean the whole ministration and receiving of the sacraments, either of baptism, or of the Lord's supper: and so the old writers many times do say, that Christ and the Holy Ghost be present in the sacraments; not meaning by that manner of speech, that Christ and the Holy Ghost be present in the water, bread or wine, (which be only the outward visible sacraments) but that in the due ministration of the sacraments according to Christ's ordinance and institution, Christ and his holy Spirit be

9 J. E. Cox (ed.), *Writings and Disputations of Thomas Cranmer Relative to the Sacrament of the Lord's Supper*, Oxford: Parker Society, 1844, p. 223.

10 J. I. Packer and G. E Duffield (eds), *The Work of Thomas Cranmer*, Philadelphia: Fortress Press, 1965, p. 57.

11 Packer and Duffield (eds), *Work of Thomas Cranmer*, p. 181.

> truly and indeed present by their mighty and sanctifying power, virtue, and grace, in all them that worthily receive the same.[12]

In his recent exhaustive survey of Cranmer's sacramental theology, Gordon Jeanes notes that in his mature theology Cranmer selected the words sign, signify and figure for his sacramental discourse.[13] He distinguished three modes of Christ's presence – the corporal, the sacramental and the spiritual:

> And although Christ in his human nature substantially, really, corporally, naturally and sensibly, be present with his Father in heaven, yet sacramentally and spiritually he is here present. For in water, bread, and wine, he is present as in signs and sacraments, but he is indeed spiritually in the faithful Christian people, which according to Christ's ordinance be baptized, or receive the holy communion, or unfeignedly believe in him.[14]

In the sacraments God works inwardly in the heart by the Holy Spirit. In one instance in answering Gardiner, he picks up Bucer's phraseology but qualifies it:

> But in this place he easeth you nothing at all; for he saith no more but that the body and blood of Christ be exhibited unto the worthy receivers of the sacrament, which is true, but yet spiritually, not corporally. And I never said that Christ is utterly absent, but I ever affirmed that he is truly and spiritually present, and truly and spiritually exhibited unto the godly receivers: but corporally is he neither in the receivers, nor in or under the forms of bread or wine, as you do teach clearly without the consent of Master Bucer, who writeth no such thing.[15]

Jeanes notes that Cranmer does use the Bucerian/Calvinist term 'exhibit', but 'only very rarely, and then very carefully'.[16] Yet, Cranmer can echo Oecolampadius and Farel:

> as we see with our eyes and eat with our mouths very bread, and see also and drink very wine, so we lift our hearts unto heaven, and with our faith we see Christ crucified with our spiritual eyes, and eat his flesh thrust through with the spear, and drink his blood springing out of his side with our spiritual mouths of our faith . . . So that although we see and eat sensibly very bread and drink very wine, and spiritually eat and drink Christ's very flesh and blood, yet may we not rest there, but lift up our minds to his Deity, without the which his flesh availeth nothing, as he saith himself.[17]

12 Cox (ed.), *Writings and Disputations*, p. 3.

13 Gordon P. Jeanes, *Signs of God's Promise: Thomas Cranmer's Sacramental Theology and the Book of Common Prayer*, London: T & T Clark, 2008, p. 136.

14 Packer and Duffield, *Work of Thomas Cranmer*, p. 79. Jeanes, *Signs of God's Promise*, p. 140.

15 Answer, in Cox, *Writings and Disputaions*, pp. 126–7; Jeanes, *Signs of God's Promise*, pp. 145–6.

16 Jeanes, *Signs of God's Promise*, p. 145.

17 Answer, in Cox, *Writings and Disputations*, p. 317.

Jeanes draws attention to the importance of the abortive *Reformatio Legum* of 1552, which condemned transubstantiation and the Lutheran view of presence, and stated that sacraments do not contain in themselves what they signify. The section on the Eucharist mentions sitting at the Lord's Table, as in Laski, and not in the *BCP*s, which require kneeling for communion. The Eucharist is described as a sacrament that seals the grace of the Holy Spirit and the pardon of sins for those who receive the bread and wine and who by faith understand it to be the body and blood of Christ.[18] This might suggest either that influence of other divines is reflected in this document, or that Cranmer had continued to develop his own understanding and had adopted the term 'seal' rather than 'signify'. In summary, Brian Douglas observes that for Cranmer there is bread and wine on earth and the carnal body and blood of Christ in heaven, without any realist link between the two. Jeanes concludes that the elements and actions of the sacrament are left somewhat exterior and incidental to the private engagement of faith between God and the recipient.[19] When this teaching is taken in conjunction with the argument that Cranmer had a planned series of liturgical reforms in mind, then we may assume that his views were most perfectly expressed in 1552, which is implied by the 1552 Act of Uniformity. It explained that 1549 had had to be replaced because of 'the curiosity of the minister and mistakers', and 1552 is 1549 'godly persued, explained and made fully perfect'.

The making of the 1549 book, and the part played by a committee, is not fully clear, and some texts in the Wanley part books suggest that a provisionally agreed text was revised at the last minute after a committee had finished its work.[20] The Communion Service of 1549 is a simplified Sarum Mass, composed in a vernacular Protestant key and incorporating much of the material from the 1548 order. The structure is still recognizably that of the Sarum Mass, which had been a major source. Entitled 'The Supper of the Lorde and Holy Communion, commonly called the Masse', it represented structurally a conservative revision of the Mass. The liturgical Calendar was greatly pruned of saints' days, but the traditional Sunday sequence of the Calendar was left, and the Eucharist was to be celebrated on Sundays and on some weekdays. It was still celebrated with vestments and certain ceremonial – though here the contemporary accounts show a division between the declared Reformers who simplified the ceremonial and vesture, and the more traditional who celebrated it as though it were the old Mass in English.

All that remained of the preparation was the Lord's Prayer and final Sarum preparation prayer, the Collect for Purity, now said by the priest at the altar. A full psalm – as Luther suggested – was recited for the Introit, with the Kyries, *Gloria in excelsis* and Collect for the Day and for the monarch. Luther had

18 Jeanes, *Signs of God's Promise*, p. 138. See Gerald Bray, *Tudor Church Reform: The Henrician Canons of 1535 and the Reformatio Legum Ecclesiasticarum*, Woodbridge: Boydell Press, 2000.

19 Douglas, *Companion to Anglican Eucharistic Theology*, vol. 1, p. 89; Jeanes, *Signs of God's Promise*, p. 184.

20 W. H. Frere, 'Edwardine Vernacular Services before the First Prayer Book', *Journal of Theological Studies* 1 (1900), pp. 229–46; Gordon Jeanes, 'Early Steps in the English Liturgy: The Witness of the Wanley Part Books', unpublished paper given at Society for Liturgical Study, 2010.

abolished sequences, and so did Cranmer. After the Epistle and Gospel, Creed and homily, we find the exhortations inspired by Hermann. Luther, as all serious Reformers, abolished the offertory prayers or 'Little Canon', and Cranmer replaced these prayers with Scripture sentences relating to almsgiving. Cranmer then provided a new canon or Eucharistic Prayer, with *Sursum corda*, Preface, Sanctus and Benedictus, prayers of intercession, the setting apart of the bread and wine, and a prayer celebrating the memorial, requesting benefits of communion, and a self-oblation. Jeanes rightly comments: 'The Eucharistic Prayer in 1549 is totally unlike any provision in the Lutheran or Reformed churches.'[21]

The Lord's Prayer, the Peace and a reference to Christ as the Paschal Lamb is followed by the other elements from Hermann – the invitation to confession, confession, absolution and scriptural words of assurance. The post-communion thanksgiving was, in the view of Jacobs, inspired by the opening words of a prayer from the Nürnberg 1533 rite.[22] The overall shape of the rite has more affinities with Lutheran orders – particularly those based on the *Formula Missae* – than Reformed orders, because, like Luther, Cranmer here retained many parts of the Ordinary of the Mass. The rite also retains much of the devotional material taken from Hermann. Richard Hilles, a London merchant, wrote to Bullinger thus:

> we have an uniform celebration of the Eucharist throughout the whole kingdom, but after the manner of the Nuremberg churches and some of those in Saxony; for they do not yet feel inclined to adopt your rites respecting the administration of the sacraments . . . our bishops and governors seem, for the present at least, to be acting rightly; while, for the preservation of the public peace, they afford no cause of offence to the Lutherans, pay attention to your very learned German divines, submit their judgment to them, and also retain some popish ceremonies.[23]

What eucharistic theology was expressed in this rite? The second part of the rite began with the offertory, but not of bread and wine. The prayers of the 'Little Canon' have gone and been replaced by Scripture sentences relating to alms and money – charity. A rubric mentions that bread and wine are prepared, but it is utilitarian with no ceremonial direction.

The Eucharistic Prayer or canon begins with the traditional *Sursum corda*, Preface, Proper Preface, Sanctus and Benedictus. The remainder of the canon had been rewritten in three sections:

---

21 Jeanes, *Signs of God's Promise*, p. 196.

22 H. E. Jacobs, *The Lutheran Movement in England*, Philadelphia: General Council Publication House, 1916, p. 243. See also Bryan D. Spinks, 'German Influence on Edwardian Liturgies', in Dorothea Wendebourg (ed.), *Sister Reformations: The Reformation in Germany and in England*, Tübingen: Mohr Siebeck, 2010, pp. 175–89.

23 *Letter* 'CXXI', in Hastings Robinson (ed.), *Original letters relative to the English reformation, written during the reigns of King Henry VIII, King Edward VI, and Queen Mary: chiefly from the archives of Zurich. Translated from authenticated copies of the autographs, and edited for the Parker Society*, Cambridge: Cambridge University Press, 1846–7, p. 266.

1 Corresponding to *Te igitur–Hanc igitur*, the offering of the gifts and prayer for the pope and king were replaced by offering prayer for the Church and world, and those in need. The offering of prayers replaced the Roman offering of the elements.
2 Corresponding to *Quam oblationem* and *Qui pridie*. It emphasized the single and complete offering and sacrifice of Calvary, echoing phraseology already found in the *King's Book*, and it speaks of the Eucharist as a memorial – a significant Protestant word, but used equally by Catholic commentators. It asked:

> and with thy holy spirit and word, vouchsafe to bl + ess and sanc + tify these thy gifts and creatures of bread and wine, that they may be unto us the body and blood of thy most dearly beloved son Jesus Christ.

Many scholars have looked for signs that here Cranmer had used an Epiklesis from Eastern liturgies, but there are reasons, however, why this might not be the case. Though Cranmer had access to the liturgies of Basil and Chrysostom, he does not appear to have used them anywhere else. The prayer of Chrysostom in Morning Prayer is from a Latin translation. The verbal parallels, listed in Brightman, *The English Rite*, are minimal. At that time (1915), Brightman was persuaded that Cranmer had used the Eastern sources. In Basil and Chrysostom, having Eucharistic Prayers of the West Syrian or Syro-Byzantine type, the Epiklesis comes after the Narrative of Institution and not before as here. In the Egyptian anaphoras there is precedent, but Cranmer does not appear to have had access to those. Brightman changed his mind on this in 1927, but few are aware of this retraction.[24]

The petition is for thy Holy Spirit and word. Word almost certainly means, as in medieval sermons, and Reformation writings, the Institution Narrative. In the sermon for Corpus Christi, John Myrc (Mirk) wrote: 'Christ's body that is made in the altar by virtue of the Holy words that the priest saith there and by the working of the Holy Ghost.'[25]

Both F. E. Brightman and E. C. Ratcliff gave examples from medieval writings and Benedictionals which included 'Holy Spirit and word' and the manual actions indicated by crosses. They concluded that medieval Western devotional sources were behind it. However, elsewhere I have argued that inspiration might also have come from Peter Martyr Vermigli, the Italian Reformer, who lodged with Cranmer during the compilation of the 1549 Prayer Book, and with whom Cranmer acknowledged having had conversations on the Eucharist.[26] Martyr later became Regius Professor of Divinity at Oxford, and in his writings he taught that consecration or

24 F. E. Brightman, 'The New Prayer Book Examined', *Church Quarterly Review* 104 (1927), pp. 219–52.

25 John Myrc, *Mirk's Festial: A Collection of Homilies, Early English Texts*, London: Kegan Paul, French: Trübner: 1906, p. 168. Sermon for Corpus Christi.

26 Bryan D. Spinks, '"And with Thy Holy Spirite and Worde": Further Thoughts on the Source of Cranmer's Petition for Sanctification in the 1549 Communion Service', in Margot Johnson (ed.), *Thomas Cranmer: Essays in Commemoration of the 500th Anniversary of his Birth*, Durham: Turnstone Ventures, 1990, pp. 94–102. See for references to Ratcliff and Brightman.

hallowing is by faith, the operation of the Holy Spirit, and the reciting of the word from Christ – the narrative. Gordon Jeanes has drawn attention to the use of word and Spirit in the Catholic Encheiridion of Cologne, as well as Cranmer's interpretation of John Damascene where word and Holy Spirit are linked, and concludes that with the phrase 'Holy Spirit and word' 'we are as close to [sixteenth-century] ecumenical consensus as we could possibly be'.[27]

Of more subtlety is the clause 'that they may be unto us the body and blood of thy most dearly beloved son Jesus Christ'. Surely this is an English translation of the words of the Roman *Quam oblationem*, 'ut nobis corpus et sanguis fiat dilectissimi Filii tui Domini Dei nostri Jesu Christi'. Bishop Stephen Gardiner thought so, and so he asserted that 1549 taught the real presence. We may note Cranmer's reply:

> And therefore, in the book of the holy communion, we do not pray absolutely that the bread and wine may be made the body and blood of Christ, but that unto us in that holy mystery they may be so.[28]

The words were removed in 1552, and the elevation of the host (retained by Luther) was prohibited by rubric.

3 The final paragraph replaced the corresponding Latin prayers, and is a petition to God for the benefits of communion, self-oblation of the communicants, their prayers and supplications. Of interest are the words 'that whosoever shall be partakers of this holy communion, may worthily receive the most precious body and blood of thy Son Jesus Christ'. This carefully changes the sense of the Roman prayer which assumes that those who receive, receive the body and blood of Christ. Cranmer makes a distinction between partaking of communion, that is, receiving the elements, and receiving the body and blood of Christ, which only the worthy do.

After the canon came the Lord's Prayer, a communion sentence, the devotion from 1548 with the Agnus Dei. The 1548 words of administration were used with slight modification. After a post-communion, which included the words 'for that thou hast vouchsafed to feed us in these holy mysteries, with the spiritual food of the most precious body and blood of thy sonne, our saviour Jesus Christ', the service ended with a blessing.

What understanding of the Eucharist is or is not expressed here? Any notion of the eucharistic elements being offered is removed. Sacrifice and oblation is limited to there on the cross once for all, and here we offer prayers, our alms and oblations, thanksgiving and ourselves. What of presence? Words that suggested the presence of Christ included:

- The *Benedictus qui venit* – 'blessed is the one who comes' – the coming of Christ in the bread.
- Several prayers speak of the bread and wine as 'these holy mysteries'.

27 Jeanes, *Signs of God's Promise*, pp. 212–15.
28 Answer in Cox, *Writings and Disputations*, p. 79.

- The petition 'that they may be unto us the body and blood'.
- The words of administration call the elements the body and blood of Christ.
- The rubric for the Fraction (at the end of the service) said that 'men must not think less to be received in part than in the whole, but in each of them the whole body of our saviour Jesu Christ'.

These were all removed in the 'fully perfect' rite of 1552.

The 1552 communion rite

The 1549 *BCP* had a short shelf life. It was regarded by radical Protestants as too Catholic, and by conservative Catholics as too Protestant. Bucer wrote home to say that he understood that it made concessions to the weak, and was only for a time. Cuming offers some evidence to show that revision had already begun in 1549.[29] The revision was designed to exclude conservative Catholic interpretations of the rite, and the rubrics were carefully framed to exclude the possibility of disguising the service as a Mass in English. The altar was replaced by a table, which was set up in the chancel for communion, lengthwise, East–West. Traditional eucharistic vestments disappeared, though the surplice and academic dress were retained. Singing was excluded other than the *Gloria in excelsis*, which was repositioned at the conclusion of the service.

The 1552 service divided neatly into two distinct services, just as in most of the Reformed Churches. The first service, which was weekly, was based on the ante-communion or Liturgy of the Word. The Kyries were replaced by the Ten Commandments (cf. the Reformed Liturgies), with a response, 'Lord have mercy upon us and incline our hearts to keep thy law.' There is no Introit psalm. The first part of the 1549 canon, the intercessory section, was modified, and placed immediately after the offertory sentences. Then came a series of exhortations which required those who are going to communicate to move into the chancel, and those who are not, to depart. No one could gaze at the elements without partaking. When there was no communion, the service ended after this prayer for the Church militant (the departed were no longer mentioned) with a collect and blessing.

The second part of the service began with a physical move into the chancel, which was to have great effect on Anglican reordering of churches. The first verbal part was the invitation to confession, absolution and comfortable words, recycled from 1548 and 1549. We may note the following points:

1. There is no rubric requiring the bread and wine to be placed on the table. The practice seems to have been to put them on the table at the beginning of the service when it was a communion.

29 Geoffrey J. Cuming, *A History of Anglican Liturgy*, London: Macmillan and Co., 1969, pp. 101–2.

2 The offering of prayer for the Church – the Church militant prayer – is brought into the first part of the service. Intercession is no longer made in the vicinity of the bread and wine.
3 The *Benedictus qui venit* and the Agnus Dei were removed so that there is no hint of addressing Christ as though he was coming into or was present in the elements.
4 The *Sursum corda*, Preface, Proper Preface and Sanctus were retained.
5 The so-called Humble Access Prayer, 'We do not presume to come to this thy table', now came after the Sanctus, being moved from the position it had had in both 1548 and 1549. The reference to 'in these holy mysteries' was removed. The thought behind the move seems to be that just as Isaiah was overcome with unworthiness after hearing the Sanctus, so also is the communicant.
6 A prayer followed with the Narrative of Institution, being similar to the second paragraph in 1549. Later it would be called a Prayer of Consecration, but it did not have any such title in 1552. A rubric allowed any bread and wine used in the service but not eaten to be taken home and used by the minister, suggesting no real distinction between elements used in the service and any other bread and wine. There were no rubrics requiring the minister to take or touch the elements during this prayer.
7 The petition for the Spirit and word has gone, and the petition in 1549, 'that they may be unto us the body and blood', is rephrased: 'grant that we, receiving these thy creatures of bread and wine, according to thy Son our Saviour Jesus Christ's holy institution, in remembrance of his death and passion, may be partakers of his most blessed body and blood'. The receiving of the elements and receiving the body and blood of Christ are separated, suggesting a symbolic parallelism.
8 There was no Amen at the end of the prayer, but rather an action – immediate communion. The 1552 words of administration had no reference to the body and blood of Christ: 'Take and eat this in remembrance'; 'Drink this in remembrance'. In other words, for Cranmer to do this in remembrance is to eat and drink. You don't gaze at and play around with your food – you get straight on and eat it.
9 The third part of the 1549 canon is modified, and becomes an alternative post-communion prayer. The words of 1549, 'that whosoever shall be partakers of this holy communion, may worthily receive the most precious body and blood of thy son Jesus Christ; and be fulfilled with thy grace and heavenly benediction', were now rendered more subjectively: 'that all we which be partakers of this Holy Communion may be fulfilled with thy grace and heavenly benediction' – again no reference to the body and blood.
10 In the thanksgiving, the words 'for that thou hast vouchsafed to feed us in these holy mysteries with the spiritual food of the most precious body and blood' became: 'vouchsafe to feed us, which have duly received these holy mysteries with the spiritual food of the most precious body and blood' – again disassociating the presence of Christ from the bread and wine. A final rubric – the 'Black' rubric – repudiated any 'real and essential presence' of Christ in the bread and wine.

There is no hint of presence in the elements in this rite. It does, however, have a doctrine of sacrifice, but not in association with the elements. It offers money; it offers prayers; it offers thanks; and it offers 'ourselves'. Communicants are prepared – invitation, confession, absolution; they plead for worthiness, 'we do not presume', and then receive; and then they 'offer ourselves, our souls and bodies'. Communicants, the body of Christ, have replaced the bread and wine or Christ as the oblation.

1559–1637

The 1552 book was even more short-lived than 1549. In 1553 the young sickly King Edward died and, after an unsuccessful attempt to bypass her, Henry's Catholic daughter Mary ascended the throne. Over the next five years the Reformation legislation was repealed, the Latin services restored, a number of bishops burnt for heresy, and the Kingdom was reconciled to Rome. But events on the Continent, and the death of Mary in 1558, meant that 1552 re-emerged to be the foundation liturgy for the Church of England and later Anglican Communion. English exiles in Frankfurt published an emended version of 1552, making it conform a little more to the Reformed usage of that city. The communion rite omitted the Collect for the Day and the lections, as well as the *Sursum corda*, Preface and Sanctus. However, with Mary's death in 1558 and the accession of Elizabeth, the Church of England was once more separated from Rome. Elizabeth's intentions for the Church are not clear, and there is some evidence that she wanted to restore the 1549 *BCP*; for example, some musicians composed music using the 1549 texts.[30] However, only one of the Marian bishops was prepared to co-operate, and Elizabeth had to rely on many churchmen who had spent time in exile and had absorbed ideas of continental reform. The rite that was eventually enacted with an Act of Uniformity was mainly the text of 1552, with some minor but not unimportant amendments. Before Morning Prayer a rubric required church furnishings and the layout of the interior, together with vesture and ceremonies, to be that which was in use in the second year of Edward VI. In theory this meant candles on the altar, and eucharistic vestments; in practice, the traditional eucharistic vestments were collected and removed. The Queen and her advisers expected the surplice and cope to be worn in parish churches for communion, but eventually this was confined to cathedrals, and in parish churches it proved difficult to enforce the use of the surplice, many clergy preferring to wear a black gown. The second change was that the words of administration from the 1549 Prayer Book were reintroduced and prefixed to those of 1552. Now the bread and wine were associated with the body and blood of Christ. Third, the 'Black Rubric' concerning kneeling, which rejected any real or essential presence, was removed. In her own chapel,

30 Bryan D. Spinks, 'From Elizabeth I to Charles II', in Charles Heffling and Cythia Shattuck (eds), *The Oxford Guide to The Book of Common Prayer*, New York: Oxford University Press, 2006, pp. 44–55; 'The Elizabethan Primers: Symptoms of an Ambiguous Settlement or Devotional Weaning?', in Natalie Mears and Alec Ryrie (eds), *Worship and the Parish Church in Early Modern Britain*, Farnham: Ashgate, 2013, pp. 73–87.

Elizabeth retained a table in the altar position and adorned with candles and crucifix. There continued to be complaints that some clergy tried to celebrate the Holy Communion as if it was a Mass, but as the older Catholic-trained clergy died, so the memory of Catholic style of celebration died out, and a Prayer Book piety established itself in England.[31]

What of eucharistic belief? Cranmer's text was compromised by the new words of administration, but otherwise the liturgical text that expressed his beliefs remained intact. However, no one thought that Cranmer's doctrinal views were foundational or sacrosanct. In terms of official or semi-official doctrine, we may cite the Articles of Religion set forth in 1563, which had been revised from articles prepared in 1553, and the catechism of Alexander Nowell, which was drawn up to be bound with the Articles of Religion, but failed to gain official status. In the former, Article XXV defined sacraments as badges and tokens, and described them as 'sure witnesses and effectual signes of grace and Gods good wyll towards us'. Article XXVIII, 'Of the Lordes Supper', was shorter than its 1553 counterpart, omitting discussion on the location of Christ's body and asserting that the body of Christ is given, taken and eaten only after a heavenly and spiritual manner, and received by faith. The wicked carnally press with their teeth the sacrament of the body and blood of Christ, but do not partake of Christ. The Articles, by their nature, were broad enough to embrace a wide range of beliefs. Nowell rewrote his catechism, and it was the most widely used catechism in the English Church.[32] It was based on an earlier catechism by Bishop John Poynet, and Calvin's catechism. Ian Green notes that Nowell frequently added the word 'grace' to sacraments, and given the popularity of the catechism it may have played the largest part in spreading the association of sacraments with grace in the English Church.[33] On the bread and wine at the Supper, Nowell explained:

> the word of God and heavenly grace coming to them, there is such efficacy, that as by baptism we are once regenerate in Christ, and are first, as it were, joined and grafted into his body; so, when we rightly receive the Lord's Supper, with the very divine nourishment of his body and blood, most full of health and immortality, given to us by the work of the Holy Ghost, and received of us by faith, as the mouth of our soul, we are continually fed and sustained to eternal life, growing together in them both into one body with Christ.[34]

Dudley Fenner, a Cambridge-trained theologian who because of his nonconformity fled to Holland to escape the jurisdiction of Archbishop Whitgift, came close to Cranmer's theology of sacraments. He argued that both the human senses and the sacramental elements become instruments of the Holy Spirit.

---

31 For the latter, see Judith Maltby, *Prayer Book and People in Elizabethan and Early Stuart England*, Cambridge: Cambridge University Press, 1998.

32 See Ian Green, *The Christian's ABC: Catechisms and Catechizing in England c. 1530–1740*, Oxford: Clarendon Press, 1996.

33 Green, *The Christian's ABC*, pp. 512–13.

34 G. E. Corrie, *A Catechism Written in Latin by Alexander Nowell, Dean of St. Paul's: Together with the Same Catechism Translated into English by Thomas Norton*, Parker Society, Cambridge: Cambridge University Press, 1853, p. 214.

Sacramental signs offer, represent and seal up. In the Eucharist, Christ is present, but not in or even with the bread and wine, and the bread is not turned into his body. The bread, so argued Fenner, is

> an instrument whereby truly is communicated by the working of the H. Ghost to our faith, the very bodye and blood of Christ: so the words, *This is my body*, that is, an instrument which offereth and representeth to all, one body, and sealeth up the true receiving of his very body and blood.[35]

They become 'sacramentally' his body and blood, and he dwells in us and we in him by the virtue and power of his divine working. William Perkins (1558–1602) was the best-known international theologian of the Elizabethan Church and the most widely published. He explained sacraments as 'an outward seale or instrument to confirme faith, not as a medicine restores and confirmes health'.[36] Sacraments were instruments, but moral instruments. Perkins (long before Gregory Dix!) argued that there was a fourfold action in the Supper – of taking, giving thanks, breaking and eating. Of the presence of Christ in the sacrament, he wrote:

> For the first, we hold and teach that Christs body and blood, are truly present with the bread and wine, being signes in the sacrament: but how? not in respect of place or coexistence: but by Sacramentall relation on this manner. When a word is uttered, the sound comes to the eare; and at the same instant, the thing signified comes to the minde; and thus by relation the word and the thing spoken of, are both present together. Even so at the Lords table bread & wine must not be considered barely, as substances and creatures, but as outward signes in relation to the body and blood of Christ.[37]

The emphasis on the mind raises the question as to how far Perkins is steeped in symbolic memorialism. He admitted that there was a sacrificial dimension to the Supper, 'because it is a commemoration, and also a representation unto God the Father of the sacrifice of Christ offered upon the crosse'.[38] The Supper is the sacramental offering of Christ, which is symbolized in Perkins's third action of the rite, the Fraction.[39] Although he spoke of the sacraments as instruments of grace, he always qualified this in such a manner as to place him closer to Bullinger than to Calvin. This is partly because his teaching on predestination and the priority of God's will left little room for manoeuvre in sacraments. His contemporary, Richard Hooker (1554–1600), had been part of a group of Reformed churchmen who gathered around John Rainolds at Oxford, but later aligned himself with those who gave full support to the Elizabethan Settlement. Although he dismissed Calvin as simply a teacher in the smallish city of Geneva, he was obviously very well acquainted with Calvin's

---

35 Dudley Fenner, *The Whole Doctrine of the Sacraments*, Middleburgh: np, 1588, Section E.
36 William Perkins, *Works* 1, Cambridge, 1616, p. 547.
37 Perkins, *Works* 1, 1, p. 590.
38 Perkins, *Works* 1, 2, p. 551.
39 Perkins, *Works* 1, 1, p. 593.

writings, and put forward his own version of symbolic instrumentalism. This is because, in contrast to Perkins, for Hooker God's love has priority, and his will is always an expression of his love – leaving room for God to manoeuvre in the sacraments.[40] In Book 5 of his monumental work, *Of the Lawes of Ecclesiasticall Politie*, Hooker wrote:

> When sacraments are said to be visible signes of invisible grace, wee thereby conceive how grace is indeede the verie ende for which these heavenlie mysteries were instituted, and besides sundrie other properties observed in them the matter whereof they consist is such as signifieth, figureth, and representeth theire ende. But still theire efficacie resteth obscure to our understanding, except wee search somewhat more distinctly what grace in particular that is whereunto they are referred, and what manner of operation they have towards it . . . Sacramentes are the powerfull instruments of God to eternall life.[41]

Hooker taught that sacraments are powerful instruments of God in which God may and does give grace. They have a moral element, but also an ecclesiastical and, more importantly, a mystical element. Their main purpose is to allow a mystical union with God. He rejected transubstantiation, consubstantiation and the 'sacramentarian' (Zwinglian) view and insisted instead on a personal presence. He wrote that the Words of Institution should be understood thus:

> This hallowed foode, through concurrence of divine power, is in veririe and truth, unto faithful receivers, instrumentallie a cause of that mysticall participation, whereby as I make my self wholly theirs, so I give them in hande an actuall possession of all such saving grace as my sacrificed bodie can yield, and as theire soules do presently need, this is 'to them and in them' my bodie.[42]

Hooker's insistence that sacraments are instruments through which God conveys grace, and his emphasis on personal presence and mystical union and participation, place him close to various aspects of Calvin's teaching. What the Articles, Nowell's catechism, Fenner, Perkins and Hooker all illustrate is a wide Reformed understanding of sacraments and the Eucharist, but none felt the need to cite Cranmer as their authority.

Hooker gave a robust defence of the National Church and its liturgy. However, a good many of the Elizabethan Church did not think that the *BCP* expressed sound theology and were critical of the survival of popish forms and ceremonies, and urged further reform as evidenced in *An Admonition to the Parliament* (1572). In earlier historiography such churchmen were labelled

40 For full discussion on Perkins and Hooker, see Bryan D. Spinks, *Two Faces of Elizabethan Anglican Theology: Sacraments and Salvation in the Thought of William Perkins and Richard Hooker*, Drew University Studies in Liturgy 9, Lanham: Scarecrow Press, 1999.

41 Richard Hooker, *Of the Lawes of Ecclesiasticall Politie*, Book 5:50.3, London: John Windet, 1597.

42 Hooker, *Lawes*, Book 5:67.12.

'Puritan', as opposed to something called 'Anglican'. Nearly all those labelled as 'Puritan' were members of the Church of England and conformed, and were as 'Anglican' as any other Church of England cleric. Even those few who were convicted of nonconformity remained in the National Church. More recent historians have preferred to label them as the 'godly', though this too brings its own problems. It was from this wide constituency that in 1584 and 1587 attempts were made through Parliament to replace the Cranmerian liturgy with the Genevan *Form of Prayers*.[43] On Elizabeth's death and the succession of James VI of Scotland to the throne, the aspirations of the 'godly' were renewed, and they hoped that James would conform the Church of England to the Reformed Church of Scotland. In fact, the opposite occurred. However, in James's progression south to be crowned, he was presented with the Millenary Petition which requested further reform. The immediate outcome was the Hampton Court Conference of 1604, and the *BCP* of 1604. The concessions made to the 'godly' were minimal, and no alterations were made in the communion rite. However, one significant addition was that the catechism in the book was extended to include the sacraments. This was the work of John Overall, Dean of St Paul's and later Bishop of Coventry and Lichfield and then of Norwich, though his source was Nowell's catechism. This addition taught that the Lord's Supper was ordained for the continual remembrance of the sacrifice of the death of Christ and the benefits we receive. The outward sign is the bread and wine, but the inward which is signified is 'The body and blood of Christ, which are verily, and indeed taken and received of the faithful in the Lord's Supper'.

Another important addition was made in the Canons of 1604. Canon 21 stated:

> Furthermore, no Bread or Wine newly brought shall be used; but first the words of Institution shall be rehearsed, when the said Bread and Wine be present upon the Communion-table.[44]

This may have been in response to the case of Robert Johnson in 1573.[45] During communion the wine gave out, and Johnson, who was often in trouble with authority, sent for more and immediately poured it into the cup and continued giving communion. He was prosecuted on the grounds that he should have recited the words of consecration over the new wine. His defence was that there was no rubric that required this. He was found guilty and sent to prison, where he subsequently died. It is difficult to know how widely the case was known, and no rubric was added at the time. Although there was still no rubric, 'reconsecration' was now required by canon law.

The 1604 book left Cranmer's 1552 rite in its Elizabethan refinement intact. However, the Jacobean period saw considerable development and division

43 Bryan D. Spinks, *From the Lord and the Best Reformed Churches*, Rome: CLV, 1984.

44 C. H. Davis (ed.), *The English Church Canons 1604*, London, 1869.

45 E. C. Ratcliff, 'The English Usage of Eucharistic Consecration 1548–1662 –II', *Theology* 60 (1957), pp. 273–80; Richard Buxton, *Eucharist and Institution Narrative*, London: SPCK, 1976, pp. 89–92.

among English divines over sacramental theology. There was the 'avant-garde conformists' or 'patristic reformed churchmen', who were disciples of Lancelot Andrewes and John Overall. Andrewes made some private additions to the communion service, and had his own ceremonial in his chapel, which included burning incense.[46] John Overall used the first of the two post-communion thanksgivings in its 1549 position, immediately after the prayer with the Words of Institution, and before communion. Technically this was nonconformist, but the liturgical practices and accompanying interest in patristic theology flowered in their protégés, who were known as the Durham House Group, or 'Laudians'. Among the latter, Francis White, who became Bishop of Carlisle, wrote that sacraments are 'conduiets of life, and conveiancies of heavenly grace to us', and the body and blood of Christ are 'now represented, made present, communicated, and received in a mystical manner, in the lawful use of this Sacrament'.[47] Another member of this group, Richard Montagu, stressed that in the Eucharist the body and blood of Christ 'is *really* participated & communicated; and by means of that *reall participation, life from him and in him conveid into our soules*'. He cited the Epiklesis of the Anaphora of St Basil to support his belief that there was a change in the elements – they have 'Sacramentall Being'.[48] The Durham House Group looked back to the 1549 communion rite as the ideal, and sought decency and ceremonial in worship, and appealed to Elizabethan Articles that had fallen into abeyance.[49] They also taught a mystical presence in the eucharistic elements, and regarded the Eucharist as having a sacrificial dimension, it being a commemoration or a representation of the one sacrifice of Christ.[50] Among the 'godly' divines, many followed the approach of Perkins and regarded sacraments as obsignatory signs. William Ames, a nonconformist who represents Reformed scholasticism, was nevertheless a Church of England priest. Archbishop Ussher of Armagh held views on sacraments not very different from Ames, teaching that they were seals for confirming the gospel. Bishop John Thornborough (who, though a bishop, divorced his wife and remarried) described sacraments as signs and seals of the covenant, and they exhibit and seal to us all grace and promises of Christ. However, we also find another group represented by Samuel Ward of Sidney Sussex, Cambridge, who felt that unless sacraments accomplished something, there was little point in celebrating them. After

46 See Bryan D. Spinks, *Sacraments, Ceremonies and the Stuart Divines*, Aldershot: Ashgate, 2002, pp. 45–7; for an excellent discussion of Andrewes' liturgical innovations, see Peter McCullough, 'Absent Presence: Lancelot Andrewes and 1662', in Platten and Woods (eds), *Comfortable Words*, pp. 49–68. Also Kenneth Stevenson, *Liturgy and Interpretation*, London: SCM Press, 2011, pp. 137–205.

47 Francis White, *The Orthodox Faith and Way to the Church Explained and Justified*, London, 1617, pp. 161–2.

48 Richard Montagu, *A Gagg for the New Gospell? No: A New Gagg for an Old Goose*, London, 1624, p. 296; *Appello Caesarem. A Just Appeale from Two Unjust Informers*, London, 1625, p. 290.

49 Calvin Lane, *The Laudians and the Elizabethan Church*, London: Pickering and Chatto, 2013.

50 For more detail, see Spinks, *Sacraments, Ceremonies and the Stuart Divines*.

reading Hooker, he wrote to Ussher arguing that it was insufficient simply to call sacraments obsignatory signs or seals:

> For God doth offer and exhibit grace promised in the sacrament; then we exercise our faith in relying upon God, promising, offering, and exhibiting on his part; and so according to the tenure of the covenant, receive the grace promised, and then sacraments in the second place do assure us of the grace received.[51]

Ward's views on sacramental efficacy were developed by his pupil Thomas Bedford, for whom sacraments are real instruments that confer grace, and in the Lord's Supper the primary grace is incorporation into Christ and remission of sins.[52] Ward and Bedford gave no indication that their views were in conflict with the liturgical rites they used, but the Durham House Group did. Their theology came to flower not in England but in Scotland, when Charles I's Scottish bishops attempted to introduce a new liturgy. As noted in the previous chapter, Knox's liturgy was the paradigm, though a growing number of ministers declined to use it word for word. Furthermore, the attempts of 1618–19 at revision came to nothing. Under Bishop James Wedderburn, who was sympathetic to the Durham House Group, and with the encouragement of Archbishop Laud, a new prayer book was drawn up for Scotland, and the communion rite was patterned after that of 1549.

The book was rejected, and a riot was instigated at its use in St Giles Cathedral, Edinburgh. This has been perceived as 'Low Church' Presbyterians rejecting a High Church liturgy, and there may be some grain of truth in that. However, the book was primarily rejected for three reasons. First, because it was the English book, or former English book, being imposed on the Scots. Second, it was not so much which liturgy as whose; it was the bishops' book and, during the reign of Charles, Scottish bishops had begun to attempt to impose more authority on the parish ministers and were unpopular. Third, there was a growing radical group in the Church of Scotland that rejected any set liturgical forms, be they Cranmerian, Knoxian or Calvinian. The book failed, but was not forgotten.

How, though, did it express the theology of the Durham House or 'Laudian' Group?

1 Among the opening rubrics is the following:

> The holy Table, having at the Communion time a carpet and a fair white linen cloth upon it, with other decent furniture meet for the high mysteries there to be celebrated, shall stand at the uppermost part of the Chancel or Church, where the Presbyter, standing at the north side or end thereof, shall say the Lord's Prayer with this Collect following for due preparation.

---

51 James Ussher, *The Whole Works of the Most Rev. James Ussher, DD*, ed. C. R. Erlington, vol. 15, Dublin: Hodge and Smith and Co., 1864, pp. 505–6.

52 Thomas Bedford, *A Treatise of the Sacraments*, London, 1638.

The Laudian ideal was decency and order, with the Holy Table railed in and furnished with throw-over frontal and if possible two candlesticks – though not necessarily lighted candles. And the table stood in use and out of use where the old altar had stood. Laud's diocesan and provincial policy was to attempt to enforce this in place of the former practice of moving the table into the chancel when there was a communion.

2 The Laudians believed that the gifts of bread and wine, while in no way a sacrifice, were nevertheless used as a memorial of a sacrifice, and therefore wished to say more about the elements. Thus the rubric for the offering of alms was extended thus:

> And when all have offered, he shall reverently bring the said bason with the oblations therein, and deliver it to the Presbyter, who shall humbly present it before the Lord, and set it upon the holy Table. And the Presbyter shall then offer up and place the bread and wine prepared for the Sacrament upon the Lord's Table, that it may be ready for that service.

3 Reference to the departed was reintroduced into the Church militant prayer.

4 The *Sursum corda*, Preface, Sanctus are reunited with the prayer having the Words of Institution by the prayer 'We do not presume' being put back to its 1549 position.

5 The Laudians did believe in consecration. They rejected transubstantiation in language as strong as Cranmer; they regarded their view as Protestant, and Laud himself claimed that his view was endorsed by Calvin. In 1637, after the Sanctus we have this rubric:

> Then the Presbyter, standing up, shall say the Prayer of Consecration, as followeth. But then, during the time of Consecration, he shall stand at such a part of the holy Table, where he may with the more ease and decency use both hands.

The prayer is called – for the first time in Anglican history – a Prayer of Consecration. Also the minister is directed to take the paten in his hands, and the cup or flagon. As already noted, the words 'vouchsafe to bless and sanctify with thy word and Holy Spirit these thy gifts of creatures of bread and wine' are utilized before the Words of Institution. The words of administration were those of 1549. Any consecrated elements are to be covered over, and in the final rubrics we find:

> And if any of the bread and wine remain which is consecrated, it shall be reverently eaten and drunk by such of the communicants only, as the Presbyter which celebrates shall take unto him; but it shall not be carried out of the church.

Cranmer's permission for the curate to have the elements for his own purpose was removed. There is an explicit concept of presence in association with the elements, and there is an understated idea of offering, and thus no longer explaining and making fully perfect Cranmer's eucharistic theology.

Jeremy Taylor, Richard Baxter and the 1662 Prayer Book: eucharistic theologies and liturgies

The Scottish protests of 1637 snowballed to end in the English Civil War, and Parliament replaced the *BCP* with the Westminster *Directory*, and imposed fines for the use of the former. Recent scholarship has shown that the *BCP* was used in some form or other much more widely than was once supposed. Some ministers knew it off by heart, and made suitable alterations so that it sounded different. Others used parts and left other parts out. An example of this is Robert Sanderson's *A Liturgy in Times of Rebellion*, which was a shortened and adapted form of the *BCP*, but sufficiently different for it not to be classed as the *BCP*.

Two interesting liturgies were produced during this period which illustrate where the creative minds of Episcopalians and the 'godly' might have gone if allowed. In 1658 Jeremy Taylor published his *Collection of Offices*. This was an Episcopalian Anglican attempt to offer a liturgy that was different from the *BCP* but that had an eye on liturgical tradition and history; and since it was not the *BCP*, it could be used without fine. It was the *BCP* that was outlawed, not use of a set liturgy.

In 1661, before the Restoration had made up its liturgical mind, the Presbyterian Anglicans were asked to submit their objections to the *BCP*, and in addition to this they appended a liturgy called *A Reformed Liturgy*, or the Savoy Liturgy. Its main author was Richard Baxter; it shows Presbyterian Anglican theology, and acquaintance with the Westminster Directory, turned into a set liturgy.

Taylor (1613–67) wrote on the Eucharist in a number of his works, including *The Worthy Communicant*, *The Real Presence and Spiritual of Christ in the Blessed Sacrament*, *Clerus Domini* and the *Great Exemplar*. He explained why the Eucharist could be understood as a sacrifice:

> Now what Christ does always in a proper and most glorious manner, the ministers of the gospel also do in theirs: commemorating the sacrifice upon the cross, 'giving thanks', and celebrating a perpetual eucharist for it, and by 'declaring the death of Christ;' and praying to God in the virtue of it, for all the members if the church, and all persons capable; it is *in genere orationis* a sacrifice, and an instrument of propitiation, as all holy prayers are in their several proportions.[53]

Taylor's preferred terms are 'representing' and 'commemorating' the death and sacrifice of the cross. In *The Worthy Communicant* he wrote:

> he became infinitely gracious in the eyes of God, and was admitted to the celestial and eternal priesthood in heaven; where in the virtue of the cross he intercedes for us, and represents an eternal sacrifice in the heavens on our behalf . . . He hath commanded us to do on earth, that is, to represent His death, to commemorate this sacrifice, by humble prayer and thankful record . . .

53 *Clerus Domini*, in R. Heber and C. P. Eden (eds), *The Works of Jeremy Taylor*, 10 vols, London: Longmans, 1847–52, vol. 1, p. 33.

> the holy table being a copy of the celestial altar, and the eternal sacrifice of the lamb slain from the beginning of the world being always the same; it bleeds no more after the finishing of it on the cross; but it is wonderfully represented in heaven, and graciously represented here; by Christ's action there, by His commandment here.[54]

Taylor taught that the bread and wine are a communication, exhibition and donation of Christ's body and blood, not formally, but virtually and effectually, and referred to the presence as in a 'spiritual real manner'. Consecration was by solemn prayer and invocation. For his communion rite, Taylor made an adaptation of the Liturgy of St James with some borrowing from St Basil.

He divided his rite into three: Ante-Communion, Communion and Post-Communion. In the Ante-Communion, after the Lord's Prayer, there were two prayers borrowed from the Prayer of Incense and the *Proskomide* of the Liturgy of St James. Where the Greek prayed for confidence to offer a fearful and unbloody sacrifice, Taylor rephrased it to become 'to represent a holy, venerable and unbloody sacrifice'. From the same source he introduced the liturgical use of the Beatitudes. There was an Epistle and Gospel, commination, General Confession, Absolution, Offering of Alms, *Sursum corda*, Preface and Sanctus.

Communion consisted of the Lord's Prayer, cherubic hymn, invocation, thanksgiving and Institution Narrative, oblation, communion prayers and distribution. Large sections were direct from St James, though with free adaptation and repositioning and again with a nuanced translation of the sacrificial terminology. In his Prayer of Consecration Taylor began with the introduction to the Epiklesis of James, which he abbreviates but also expands to express his theology. It asks:

> send thy Holy Ghost upon our hearts, and let him also descend upon these gifts, that by his good, his holy, his glorious presence, he may sanctifie and enlighten our hearts, and he may bless and sanctifie these gifts.
>
> *That this Bread may become the Holy Body of Christ.*
>
> Amen.
>
> *And this Chalice may become the life-giving Blood of Christ.*
>
> Amen.
>
> That it may become unto us all that partake of it this day, a Blessed instrument of Union with Christ, of pardon and peace, of health and blessing, of holiness and life Eternal, through Jesus Christ our Lord. *Amen.*[55]

The Post-Communion consisted of the Lord's Prayer, Prayer for the Catholic Church, 'Eucharistical' Prayers (post-communion thanksgivings) and Blessing.

54 Heber and Eden (eds), *Works*, vol. 8, pp. 37–8.

55 Text in W. Jardine Grisbrooke, *Anglican Liturgies of the Seventeenth and Eighteenth Centuries*, London: SPCK, 1958, pp. 193–4.

Richard Baxter (1615–91) was Taylor's contemporary. Both were chaplains in the Civil War, though on different sides, and both were imprisoned at some stage in their lives. At the Restoration both were offered bishoprics, but whereas Taylor accepted, Baxter declined and preferred dissent to conformity. Prior to the final Restoration Settlement, and as a contribution to it, he drew up an alternative liturgy to the *BCP*. It was based on the *BCP* and also his own use and interpretation of the Westminster *Directory* when minister at Kidderminster.[56] Baxter's eucharistic theology had a trinitarian base and was founded upon the concepts of consecration, commemoration and communication. He explained it succinctly in a work entitled *A Saint or a Brute*:

> We have here communion with the blessed Trinity, in the three parts of this eucharistical sacrament! As the Father is both our Creator and the offended majesty, and yet he hath sent his Son to be our Redeemer; so in the first part which is the CONSECRATION, we present to our Creator the creatures of bread and wine, acknowledging that from him we receive them and all, and we desire that upon our dedication, by his acceptance that they may be made sacramentally and representatively the body and blood of Jesus Christ.
>
> In the second part of the eucharist, which is the COMMEMORATION of the sacrifice offered on the cross, we break the bread and pour forth the wine, to represent the breaking of Christ's body, and shedding of his blood for the sin of man; and we beseech the Father to be reconciled to us on his Son's account, and to accept us in his beloved, and to accept all our sacrifices through him. So that as Christ now in heaven is representing his sacrifice to the Father, which he once offered on the cross for sin, so must the minister of Christ represent and plead to the Father the same sacrifice, by way of commemoration, and such intercession as belongeth to his office.
>
> The third part of the eucharist is to OFFER and PARTICIPATION; in which the minister representing Christ, doth by commission deliver his body and blood to the penitent, hungry, believing soul: and with Christ is delivered a sealed pardon of all sin, and a sealed gift of life eternal. All which are received by the true believer.[57]

Although Baxter speaks of consecration, his main interest seems to be the eucharistic actions as they relate to the one sacrifice of the cross. Like Taylor, he calls it a representation, and in addition sees the Eucharist as pleading the sacrifice of Christ. He explained this further in another of his works:

> The commemoration chiefly (but not only) respecteth God the Son. For he hath ordained, that these consecrated representations should in their manner and measure, supply the room of his bodily presence, where his body is in heaven: and that thus, as it were, in effigy, in representation, he might be

56 The fullest recent treatment is Glen Segger, 'Petition for Peace: A Theological Analysis of Richard Baxter's Reformed Liturgy in its Ecclesiological Context', PhD dissertation, Drew University, 2008. Revised version forthcoming in the Ashgate Liturgy series.

57 W. Orme (ed.), *The Practical Works of the Rev. Richard Baxter*, 20 vols, vol. 10, London, 1830, pp. 317–18.

> still crucified before the church's eyes; and they might be affected, as if they had seen him on the cross. And that by faith and prayer, they might, as it were, offer him up to God; that is, might shew the Father that sacrifice, once made for sin, in which they trust, and for which it is that they expect all the acceptance of their person with God, and hope for audience when they beg for mercy, and offer up prayer or praise to him.[58]

This idea of 'pictorial re-enactment' is given considerable emphasis in his communion rite.[59] This rite was designed to follow the morning service on those occasions when the sacrament was celebrated. Glen Segger has noted the chiastic structure of the communion rite:

> In this scheme, the opening exhortation matches together with the closing exhortation, the prayer of confession relates to the prayer of thanksgiving, the receiving of the bread and wine mirrors the communion, and the words of institution are connected with the fraction . . . According to this model, the liturgy reaches its zenith with the Eucharistic ritual actions of consecration, commemoration and communion, culminating in the minister's declaration:
>
> This Bread and Wine, being set apart, and consecrated to this Holy use by God's appointment, are not now Common Bread and Wine, but Sacramentally the Body and Blood of Christ.[60]

In the opening explication, Baxter gave a summary of his doctrine: the Eucharist was instituted 'to be a continued representation and remembrance of his death'. Consecration makes the bread and wine 'sacramentally, or representatively, the body and blood of Christ'; the breaking of the bread and the pouring of the wine 'represent and commemorate the sacrifice of Christ's body and blood upon the cross once offered up to God for sin'. In the opening exhortation, Baxter wrote: 'see here Christ dying in this holy representation! Behold the sacrifice Lamb of God, that taketh away the sins of the world! It is his will to be thus frequently crucified before our eyes . . . Receive now a crucified Christ here represented.' Baxter was a self-taught theologian and found Aquinas, Scotus and Durandus particularly congenial, and it may be that he absorbed some of their terminology and ideas on eucharistic sacrifice, since his terminology is quite different from the majority of his fellow 'godly' divines. His threefold action was expressed in his rite. The Eucharistic Prayer could be prayed as one prayer, or as three prayers with actions, and directed in turn to the Father, Son and Spirit. Consecration had a prayer addressed to God as Creator, asking him to 'sanctify these thy creatures of bread and wine, which, according to thy institution and command, we set apart to this holy use, that they may be sacramentally the body and blood of thy Son Jesus Christ'. The Institution Narrative was read, with a declaration that the elements were now set apart and were 'Sacramentally the Body and Blood of Christ'. This was followed by a prayer to Christ that 'through the

58 Orme (ed.), *Practical Works*, vol. 4, p. 316.

59 *CD*, pp. 490–3; *PEER*, pp. 270–6, summary only; full text in Bard Thompson, *Liturgies of the Western Church*, New York: Meridian Books, 1961, pp. 375–405.

60 Segger, 'Petition for Peace', pp. 96–7.

sacrifice of thy body and blood' we may gain pardon and reconciliation. The minister then performed a dramatic Fraction and Libation:

> *Then let the Minister take the Bread, and break it in the sight of the people, saying:*
>
> The body of Christ was broken for us, and offered once for all to sanctify us: behold the sacrificed Lamb of God that taketh away the sins of the world.
>
> *In like manner let him take the Cup, and pour out the Wine in the sight of the congregation, saying:*
>
> We were redeemed with the precious blood of Christ, as of a Lamb without blemish and without spot.

Then there was a prayer addressed to the Holy Spirit, which asked for the fruits of communion, including softening of the heart, humility for our sins and growth in grace.

Theologically, Taylor and Baxter had considerable agreement, especially on commemoration and sacrifice. Liturgically, they had very different ideas. However, taken with 1637, it becomes apparent that many found the liturgical text of Cranmer no longer an ideal expression of doctrinal and liturgical thinking in the mid-seventeenth century. However, the Restoration Settlement led to the 1662 *BCP*, which showed little interest in 1549 and no interest in the creativity of Taylor and Baxter. William Sancroft's marginal note on the placing of the Prayer of Oblation summed up the whole of the 1662 enterprise: 'My LL. ye BB. at Elie house Ordered all in ye old Method.' The communion rite was basically the Cranmerian text as nuanced in 1559, with some changes in rubrics and headings. These may be summarized as follows:

1. When there is a communion, the priest is required to place so much bread and wine as will be sufficient on the table. A preparation of the elements – an offertory – is restored. The evidence of seventeenth-century commentators was that the rubric was often ignored, and the common practice was to continue to place bread and wine on the table before the service began.
2. The word 'oblations' was added to the prayer for the Church militant, though it was never made clear what this meant.
3. The prayer with the Words of Institution is now called – as in 1637 – the Prayer of Consecration, though the wording was not altered from Cranmer's prayer and so still had no petition for sanctification in the prayer text. It is consecration by prayer title. However, the title indicates that the Church of England did now believe that the elements were consecrated.
4. Manual acts are introduced. The minister is directed to take the paten into his hand, and to break the bread, and take the cup, and touch other flagons and chalices. This is a clumsy concession to the Puritans who wanted a deliberate taking, and a deliberate Fraction and Libation, though as illustrated by Baxter.
5. 'Amen' was placed at the end of the Prayer of Consecration, thus signalling that it was a complete prayer in its own right.

6 Rubrics distinguished between consecrated and unconsecrated bread and wine, and there are directions for reconsecration if the bread and wine should run out.
7 The 'Black Rubric' was restored, but significantly altered. It no longer referred to the excluding of any 'real and essential presence of Christ's natural flesh and blood' in the bread and wine, but instead, of 'any Corporal Presence of Christ's natural Flesh and Blood', since too many Reformed theologians had insisted that there was a real and essential presence but not substantial corporal presence. It may be that in this alteration Cranmer's doctrine is quietly dropped.

Colin Buchanan pointed out that whereas for Cranmer there is one high point – the receiving of the elements – in 1662 there is now another high point, a consecration of the bread and wine.[61] The repudiation of sacrifice remained, and the ideas on this matter of the Durham House Group, Taylor and Baxter were given no liturgical consideration or expression.

From the Liturgy of Comprehension, 1689, to the Deposited Book of 1928

A good number of clergy, like Richard Baxter, felt unable to accept the Restoration Settlement and opted for dissent. Some of the Presbyterian-minded had hoped for comprehension, whereas others, such as Baptists and Independents, had no wish for comprehension. The political uncertainty of the Catholic King James II, and his imprisonment of some bishops, together with the fear of a Catholic restoration, led to talks aimed to bring the Presbyterians back into the Established Church.[62] Included in the scheme was a revision of the liturgy, and the proposals, known as the Liturgy of Comprehension, included omission of the ante-communion, which normally followed Morning Prayer and the Litany of Sunday, unless there was a communion. The Beatitudes were substituted for the Ten Commandments (cf. Taylor), and a new prayer of preparation was inserted before the prayer for the Church militant. A prayer formula was to introduce the Words of Institution in case further consecration was needed, and kneeling for communion could be dispensed with for those who had scruples against kneeling.[63] The political crisis ended with the flight of James and the accession of William and Mary, and the comprehension talks came to an end. Immediately, though, another crisis arose – the problem of the oath of suprem-

61 Colin Buchanan, *What Did Cranmer Think He Was Doing?*, Bramcote: Grove Books, 1976.

62 Steve Pincus, *1688: The First Modern Revolution*, New Haven: Yale University Press, 2009.

63 *Copy of the Alterations in the Book of Common Prayer Prepared by the Royal Commissioners for the Revision of the Liturgy in 1689*, Printed by Order of the House of Commons, London, 1854; Timothy J. Fawcett, *The Liturgy of Comprehension 1689*, Southend-on-Sea: Mayhew-McCrimmon, 1973; Bryan D. Spinks, *Liturgy in the Age of Reason: Worship and Sacraments in England and Scotland 1662–c. 1800*, Farnham: Ashgate, 2008. Much of this section is based on the latter study.

acy and succession, which led to the Nonjuring secession and Jacobite resistance to first William and Mary and then to the Hanovarian dynasty. Many of the Nonjurors were High Churchmen, and retained friendship with many High Churchmen who remained with the Established Church.[64] Some were Jacobite sympathizers, and others were not. The three great waves of Jacobite activity, 1689–96, 1714–23 and 1745–53, were marked by High Church and Nonjuring liturgical enterprises.

One very influential High Churchman was John Johnson of Cranbrook (1662–1725), who published *The Propitiatory Oblation in the Holy Eucharist* in 1710, and in 1714 and 1718 a two-part work, *The Unbloody Sacrifice and Altar, Unvail'd and Supported.* In Part I he accepted without argument that when the ancient liturgies referred to the unbloody sacrifice they were referring to the sacrifice of the sacramental bread and wine. Johnson wrote:

> the Bread and Wine, or, which is the same thing, the Sacramental Body and Blood, were by the Ancients esteemed, not only the Representation of a Sacrifice, but a real sacrifice; and that the sacred Symbols were thus offer'd to God, the Liturgies are a Demonstration; in every one of which a solemn Tender of the Symbols is made to God, after the Words of Institution have first been pronounced over them . . .[65]

On eucharistic presence, he argued:

> Tho' Bread and Wine in themselves can be no more than Figures; yet when the Holy Ghost has bless'd and sanctify'd them, they are in Power and effect to us the same, that the Archetypes would be: And tho' we cannot apprehend this by our Taste, or Sight; yet we may, by our Reason, inform'd by a right Faith.[66]

Johnson appealed to the ancient liturgies to stress that there was an offering of the elements after the consecration, and also an invocation of the Spirit so that the elements became the body and blood of Christ. Though he seemed to think that these were somehow reflected in the 1662 communion rite, other High Churchmen and many Nonjurors did not. Two High Churchmen, Edward Stephens and Johannes Grabe, produced liturgies that were basically the Church of England *ordo*, but with particular eucharistic and other prayers that stressed offering and included an Epiklesis upon the elements. Stephens crafted two communion rites. That of 1696 was closely modelled on 1549, though he made his own additions. In the rite of *c.* 1700, the Eucharistic Prayer was inspired by that of *Apostolic Constitutions* VIII, St Basil and St James.[67] The Epiklesis prayed:

---

64 For more detail, see Spinks, *Liturgy in the Age of Reason.*

65 John Johnson, *The Unbloody Sacrifice and Altar, Unvail'd and Supported*, Part I, London, 1714, p. 44.

66 Johnson, *Unbloody Sacrifice and Altar*, p. 177.

67 See Grisbrooke, *Anglican Liturgies*; and Spinks, *Liturgy in the Age of Reason*, pp. 110–16.

> and send down thy Holy Spirit upon these Proposited Elements, to sanctify and Bless them, that to us who partake thereof, this *Bread* may be made the Precious Body of thy *Christ*, and this *Wine* the Precious Blood of thy *Christ*, to the Remission of all our Sins, and to the mighty Confirmation of us in all Grace, and to Eternal Life.[68]

Stephens used this liturgy in his Oratory, which was frequently attended by Dr Johannes Grabe, a former Lutheran who had found refuge at Christ Church, Oxford. Grabe believed that the *BCP*'s consecration prayer was defective, and he too insisted that the elements became the flesh and blood of Christ by 'Spiritual Energy, Valor, Grace and Virtue'. He compiled two liturgies, one in English and one in Greek, both modelled on the 1549 rite and drawing upon Stephens.[69]

Of more interest is the work of the Nonjurors, though it is important to note that their congregations were very small, and the exotic liturgies that were composed were never widely used.

The Nonjurors agreed that as a matter of conscience, having taken oaths to the House of Stuart, they could not take new oaths to William and Mary and then to the Hanoverians and had either been deprived or had voluntarily left the Established Church. Beyond this, they had little agreement and soon split over liturgical practice and then over liturgies themselves. Three of the original Nonjuring bishops had died in 1689, and Archbishop Sancroft handed authority over his fellow Nonjurors to Bishop Lloyd. Lloyd, with encouragement from George Hickes, determined to keep the succession alive, and Hickes and Thomas Wagstaffe were consecrated bishops. All the Scottish bishops had become Nonjurors, and Hickes, with Scottish Archbishop Campbell and James Gadderar, consecrated Jeremy Collier, Nathaniel Spinckes and Samuel Hawes as 'bishops at large'. In 1716 a dispute erupted about liturgical practices.[70] Hicks held doctrinal views similar to John Johnson, and like Johnson believed that the 1662 rite expressed such beliefs, and for Hickes, part of representing the true Church as it was in 1689 included adherence to the liturgy then in place. Hickes did use the 1549 rite in private, and soon some Nonjurors raised the possibility of reintroducing that rite into their congregations. In particular this group, the 'Usagers', wanted the invariable use of the mixed chalice, prayers for the faithful departed, an explicit petition for consecration, and the prayer of oblation to come immediately after the Prayer of Consecration. Whereas Spinckes saw no need to reintroduce 1549, Collier did, and he appealed to Grabe on the invocation, that it 'procur'd the Descent of the Holy Ghost. And thus the Bread, tho' remaining in its former Substance, had supernatural Qualities, and a new Force, for the benefit of the unworthy receiver, conve'd into it.'[71] The Usagers

68 Text in Grisbrooke, *Anglican Liturgies*, p. 227.

69 See Spinks, *Liturgy in the Age of Reason*, pp. 113–16; Gunther Thomann, *John Ernest Grabe's Liturgies: Two Unknown Anglican Liturgies of the Seventeenth Century*, Nürnberg: privately printed, 1989. Expanded as *Studies in English Church History*, Stoke on Trent: privately printed, 1995.

70 Spinks, *Liturgy in the Age of Reason*, pp. 119–29; James David Smith, *The Eucharistic Doctrine of the Later Nonjurors*, Cambridge: Grove Books, 2000.

71 Jeremy Collier, *A Vindication of the Reasons and Defence*, Part II, London, 1719, p. 131.

split from the Non-usagers and in 1717 adopted the four practices, and in 1718 a text for the Eucharist was issued. This latter followed the outline of much of the 1549 rite, but with a Eucharistic Prayer inspired by *Apostolic Constitutions* VIII, St Basil and St James.[72] The Anamnesis/oblation and Epiklesis read:

> we Offer to Thee, our King and our God, according to his holy Institution, this Bread and this Cup; giving thanks to thee through him, that thou hast vouchsafed us the honour to stand before thee, and to Sacrifice unto thee. And we beseech thee to look favourably on these thy Gifts, which are here set before thee, O thou self-sufficient God: And do thou Accept them to the honour of thy Christ; and send down thine Holy Spirit, the witness of the passion of our Lord Jesus, upon this Sacrifice, that he may make this (f) Bread the Body of thy Christ, and this (g) Cup the Blood of thy Christ; that they who are partakers thereof, may be confirmed in godliness, may obtain remission of their sins, may be delivered from the Devil and his snares, may be replenished with the Holy Ghost, may be made worthy of thy Christ, and may obtain everlasting life, Thou, O Lord Almighty, being reconciled unto them through the merits and mediation of thy Son our Saviour Jesus Christ; who, with Thee and the Holy Ghost, liveth and reigneth ever one God, world without end. Amen.[73]

Although a reunion was attempted in 1732, with the 1718 liturgy being laid aside, some on each side refused to enter the union, resulting in three factions. Among the continuing Usagers, Thomas Deacon became the leading liturgical pioneer and published a communion rite in 1734, which followed the Prayer Book rite, but made liberal use of *Apostolic Constitutions* VIII.

In England the Nonjurors atrophied to extinction, but in Scotland they persisted as a separate minority Episcopal Church alongside the Presbyterian Church of Scotland, and when the last heir of James II had died, they ceased to be Nonjuring. In the early years after 1689 their services were little different from their Scottish Presbyterian eucharistic celebrations, but through the eighteenth century they adopted the 1662 rite, and then some, such as Bishop Rattray, experimented with the liturgy of St James. In 1764 the Scottish Episcopalians adopted the second part of the 1637 communion rite, which in turn had looked back to 1549.

High Churchmen and the Nonjurors looked back to the Durham House Group and beyond that to the early Church for their theological rationale. More liberal churchmen looked to the new learning of the Enlightenment and to reason. John Locke advocated a reasonable reading of Scripture, which for him meant a 'Low Church' Protestant reading with little or no dogma, and he questioned the received teaching on Christology and the Trinity. This was true also of his contemporary, Isaac Newton, who carefully examined Scripture, and in his notes underlined those passages that he thought undermined trinitarian doctrine. Locke considered the words 'This is my Body', and presented four different views, he

72 For the influence of the first of these, see Leonel L. Mitchell, 'The Influence of the Rediscovery of the Liturgy of Apostolic Constitutions on the Nonjurors', *Ecclesia Orans* 13 (1996), pp. 207–21.

73 Text in Grisbrooke, *Anglican Liturgies*, pp. 289–90.

himself preferring that the bread and wine are 'only' a representation of the body and blood, which suggests a different understanding of the word 'represent' than found in Taylor and Baxter. This new learning is seen in the work of William Whiston and Samuel Clarke, both students of Newton and their friend Bishop Benjamin Hoadly, who had imbibed Locke while at Cambridge.

William Whiston (1667–1752) was a polymath, who succeeded Newton as Lucasian Professor at Cambridge. He shared Newton's suspicion of Athanasian Christology and trinitarian doctrine, and for publishing his views was dismissed from his post. He believed that the *Apostolic Constitutions* was apostolic, and that its Eunomian Christology was apostolic. In 1713 he published the Church of England liturgy reduced to his idea of primitive doctrine, which meant eliminating full-blown trinitarian references, and subordinating the Son. However, his convictions concerning *Apostolic Constitutions* meant that he rewrote the 1662 Prayer of Consecration according to the 1549 rite, with its petition for consecration 'with thy holy spirit and Word', and he included an Anamnesis, offering and presenting the gifts 'as memorials of the precious body and blood of thy dear Son'.[74] Samuel Clarke (1675–1729) was denied further preferment in the Church because of his sub-orthodox views on the Trinity. His recommendations for liturgical reform were expressed in his *Scripture–Doctrine of the Trinity* (1712) and are also preserved in an interleaved 1724 edition of the *BCP*, now in the British Library.[75] His concern was to rephrase trinitarian references, to subordinate the Son and avoid referring to the Son as divine. This had little effect on eucharistic doctrine, other than to emphasize the memorial aspect (after all, Jesus was not fully divine), and in his catechism, which was published posthumously in 1730, he taught that sacraments have no physical efficacy, but only moral qualification. Clarke was mainly concerned with spiritual benefits and moral qualifications for participation.[76] Hoadly (1676–1761) caused uproar among High Churchmen in his 1735 work, *A Plain Account of the Nature and End of the Sacrament of the Lord's Supper*, which is an expression of Lockean theology. The act of remembrance, argued Hoadly, implied bodily absence and 'This strongly implies the Belief of his *Bodily Absence* to be even necessary to this Duty: and that his *Bodily Presence* is utterly inconsistent with it'. The elements are not represented as things offered or sacrificed to God. What is required is faith, repentance, thankfulness and charity, and not concepts of presence or offering. Communion is a federal rite, a covenant and a remembrance of a covenant, but above all it is a moral obligation or duty:

> This is that personal *Appropriation* of the *Bread* and *Wine* to the Serious and Religious *Remembrance* of the *Body* and *Blood* of *Christ*, which alone can make this *Rite* of any Benefit to a Believer, by making it acceptable to God. It is, if I may use the word, a sort of *Consecration* of them, which is the Duty of

74 Text in Grisbrooke, *Anglican Liturgies*, p. 257. See Spinks, *Liturgy in the Age of Reason*, pp. 136–9.

75 Interleaved Book of Common Prayer, 1724, British Library C.24.b.21.

76 Samuel Clarke, *An Exposition of the Church–Catechism*, Dublin, 1730.

> Every *Communicant* himself; and without which all other *Consecrations* that have gone before, will do *Him* No service at all.[77]

Hoadly's doctrine was an extreme example of symbolic memorialism. He appears, though, to have been quite content with the 1662 text.

The views of the High Churchmen and Nonjurors, and these Newtonian and Lockean divines, came together in a blending in the making of the first *BCP* for America (1789/90). Some of Clarke's ideas were taken up in John Jones's *Free and Candid Disquisitions Relating to the Church of England* (1749), and in 1774 Theophilus Lindsey published *The Book of Common Prayer Reformed according to the Plan of the Late Dr. Samuel Clarke*. The latter was certainly known to Benjamin Franklin and Sir Francis Dashwood, who published an abridgement of the Prayer Book in 1773. The Lord's Supper in this work omitted references to Christ in the Preface, had no Prayer of Consecration and administered the bread and wine with the words of 1552 – an extreme memorialism! This book in turn was one of those used by William White, one of the authors of the *Philadelphia Book of Common Prayer* (1786).[78] Thanks to the intervention of the newly consecrated Bishop Samuel Seabury, this book was not adopted without some considerable, and more orthodox, revision. The most notable feature of the 1789/90 American *BCP* was the borrowing of the petition for consecration and words of offering from the Scottish 1764 communion office:

> we thy humble servants, do celebrate and make here before thy divine Majesty, with these thy holy gifts, WHICH WE NOW OFFER UNTO THEE, the memorial thy Son hath commanded us to make . . . And we most humbly beseech thee, O merciful father, to hear us; and, of thy almighty goodness, vouchsafe to bless and sanctify, with thy Word and Holy Spirit, these they gifts and creatures of bread and wine . . .

The words of offering were in capitals and accentuated the recovery of a concept of offering of the gifts in this newly formed independent Anglican Church. In England, though, the 1662 rite remained the only rite in use, until the doctrinal and liturgical impacts of nineteenth-century Tractarianism and the Ecclesiologists.

The older Reformed strain of theology in the Church of England that survived the Restoration was mainly subsumed into the eighteenth-century Evangelical Revival.[79] One of its nineteenth-century offspring, Edward Bickersteth, who was a fierce opponent of the Tractarian Movement, wrote a hugely popular

77 B. Hoadly, *A Plain Account of the Nature and End of the Sacrament of the Lord's Supper*, London, 1735, p. 121.

78 For the details behind the American book, see Paul V. Marshall, *One, Catholic, and Apostolic: Samuel and the Early Episcopal Church*, New York: Church Publishing Corporation, 2004. Marion J. Hatchett, *The Making of the First American Book of Common Prayer*, New York: Seabury Press, 1982.

79 For the continuation of the Reformed, see Stephen Hampton, *Anti-Arminians: The Anglican Reformed Tradition from Charles II to George I*, Oxford: Oxford University Press, 2008; Grayson Carter, *Anglican Evangelicals: Protestant Secessions from the Via Media, c. 1800–1850*, Oxford: Oxford University Press, 2001; Peter Toon, *Evangelical Theology 1833–1856: A Response to Tractarianism*, Atlanta: John Knox Press, 1979.

A Treastise on the Lord's Supper (1822), which is representative of Evangelical doctrine at that time.[80] The book was primarily to serve as an encouragement and preparation for receiving communion, but the first chapters unfold Bickersteth's understanding of the Eucharist. It was instituted at the paschal supper which contained 'so lively a resemblance and picture' of Jesus' own immediate sufferings.[81] Whereas Passover prefigured, by shedding blood, the redemption of Christ, the supper would exhibit, by striking emblems, the redemption of Christ.[82] Bread was chosen because it is the ordinary support of man, and a wholesome food; wine was appointed because of its strengthening and exhilarating properties.[83] The wine represents the separation of the blood from the body. However, argued Bickersteth, common sense alone dictates the rejection of transubstantiation and consubstantiation. The elements are emblems, figures or tokens; 'Just as seeing the bust of the king, we should say, "This is the King!" so does our Saviour say, "*This is my body!*"'[84] The atonement gives forgiveness, justification and sanctification, and the Eucharist is designed as a perpetual exhibition and commemoration of the atoning sacrifice of Christ.[85] It also declares aspects of Christ's death which he listed as declaring the fact of Christ's death, the manner of his death, and the true cause of his death, and quoting from Mr Scott's *Letters* with full agreement, he asserted that as the prayer ended with the words 'through Jesus Christ our Lord', 'we more fully and forcibly represent in the celebration of the Holy Eucharist, wherein we plead the virtue and merits of the same sacrifice here, that our great High Priest is continually urging for us in heaven'.[86] Although he is unclear on how Christ is present, he affirms his presence, and convicts those who do not distinguish the sacrament from any common meal as an unworthy receiver. In the remainder of his manual, he included large sections from the 1662 communion, indicating his satisfaction.

Rather different was the estimation of the Tractarians.[87] They attacked Erastianism and Protestantism, arguing that the Church of England was part of the ancient Catholic Church. They retrieved both patristic and medieval doctrine and liturgical practices. The Ecclesiologists promoted Gothic revival architecture, and ceremonial to match.[88] Both led to a Catholic revival within the Anglican Church, and unofficial liturgical innovations. Edward Pusey, for example, defended language of real presence in the elements and of the sacrificial

80 See Christopher J. Cocksworth, *Evangelical Eucharistic Thought in the Church of England*, Cambridge: Cambridge University Press, 1993; Douglas, *A Companion to Anglican Eucharistic Theology*, vol. 1, ch. 4, *passim*.

81 Edward Bickersteth, *A Treatise on the Lord's Supper*, 6th edn, London: Seeley, 1825, p. 2.

82 Bickersteth, *Treatise*, p. 3.

83 Bickersteth, *Treatise*, p. 9.

84 Bickersteth, *Treatise*, p. 13.

85 Bickersteth, *Treatise*, p. 53.

86 Bickersteth, *Treatise*, p. 61. I have been unable to identify the source.

87 For the wide range of beliefs among English theologians in the nineteenth century, see Douglas, *Companion to Anglican Eucharistic Theology*, vol. 1, pp. 451–624.

88 For an overview, see Bryan D. Spinks, 'The Transition from "Excellent Liturgy" to Being "Too Narrow for the Religious Life of the Present Generation"', in Platten and Woods (eds), *Comfortable Words*, pp. 98–120.

dimension of the Eucharist. In his 1843 sermon on the Holy Eucharist, Pusey wrote:

> I believe the consecrated elements to become, by virtue of his consecrating Words, truly and really, yet spiritually and in an ineffable way, His Body and Blood, I learnt also to withhold my thoughts as to the *mode* of this great Mystery, but 'as a Mystery' to 'adore it.' With the Fathers, then, and our own great Divines, (explaining, as I believe, the true meaning of our Church,) I could not but speak of the consecrated elements, as being, what, since He has so called them, I believe them to become, His Body and Blood; and I feared not, that, using their language, I should, when speaking of the Divine and 'spiritual' things, be thought to mean otherwise than 'spiritually,' or having disclaimed all thoughts as to the *mode* of their being, that any should suppose I meant a *mode* which our Church disallows.[89]

In an appendix to his Sermon *Will ye also go away?* (1867), he wrote:

> I believe that in the Holy Eucharist the body and blood of Christ are sacramentally, supernaturally, ineffably, but verily and indeed, present 'under the form of bread and wine', and that, 'where his body is, there is Christ' . . . in the celebration of the Holy Eucharist the priest presents and pleads to the Father that same body which was broken for us, and the blood which was shed for us, therein sacramentally present by virtue of the consecration, which our great High Priest in His perpetual intercession for us, locally present in His natural body at the right hand of the Father, evermore exhibits before the Father for us.[90]

Like Bickersteth, Pusey can speak of pleading the sacrifice, though as this became a favourite term of the Tractarian party, so Evangelicals increasingly backed away from their patrimony which went back to Baxter. The resulting conflict brought forth certain Evangelical emended rite suggestions that would rule out a Tractarian reading of the liturgy; and as Tractarianism grew into Anglo-Catholicism, unofficial supplemental texts, the Sarum Mass and even the current Roman rite were used in some Church of England churches.[91] Officially sponsored reform brought forth the Convocation Prayer Book (1880), which had few revisions of any worth and came to nothing. The result of a report of a Royal Commission in 1906 set in motion the long and painful process that

89 Edward Pusey, 'The Holy Eucharist a Comfort to the Penitent', http://anglicanhistory.org/pusey/pusey4.html.

90 Cited in Darwell Stone, *A History of the Doctrine of the Eucharist*, vol. 2, London: Longmans, 1909, p. 542. See Alf Härdelin, *The Tractarian Understanding of the Eucharist*, Uppsala: University of Uppsala, 1965. Teresa Berger, *Liturgie – Spiegel der Kirche: Eine systematische-theologische Analyse des liturgischen Gedankenguts im Traktarianism*, Forschungen zur systematischen und ökumenischen Theologie 52, Göttingen: Vandenhoeck and Ruprecht, 1986.

91 A. Elliott Peaston, *The Prayer Book Revisions of the Victorian Evangelicals*, Dublin: APCK, 1963; Mark Dalby, *Anglican Missals and their Canons: 1549, Interim Rite and Roman*, Alcuin/GROW Joint Liturgical Study 41, Cambridge: Grove Books, 1998.

culminated in the proposed *BCP* 1927, which failed to gain parliamentary sanction, as was also the case of its revision in 1928.[92] The proposed Eucharistic Prayer followed the Scottish and American model of repositioning the prayer of oblation immediately after the Prayer of Consecration, and it introduced a petition for consecration:

> Hear us, O merciful Father, we most humbly beseech thee, and with thy Holy and Life-giving Spirit vouchsafe to bless and sanctify both us and these thy gifts of Bread and Wine, that they may be unto us the Body and Blood of thy Son, our Saviour Jesus Christ, to the end that we, receiving the same, may be strengthened and refreshed both in body and soul.

Noting how much a role Bishop Walter Howard Frere had played in the formulation of this Eucharistic Prayer, Louis Bouyer observed:

> Wishing to provide the Anglican Church with an ideal eucharist, he found nothing better than to propose to it a neo- or pseudo-Syrian Eucharist, constructed with previously selected elements and then put together again in quite a different order, taken from the Roman canon as passed through Cranmer's Zwinglian rolling press . . . Any commentary would be a needless cruelty.[93]

Other Anglican provinces adopted new Prayer Books *c.* 1928/29, but none moved away from the basic Cranmerian material in its 1549, 1552, 1559, 1637 and 1662 manifestations.

Concluding remarks

The history of Anglicanism until the last decades of the twentieth century is a history of extremely varied theologies of the Eucharist, all kept together and affirmed, or marginalized and ignored, or totally contradicted by a strange adherence to the Cranmerian text. That text began life as a Protestant reform of the Sarum Use of the Romano-Western synthesis, with insights from Lutheran sources. Its revision revised the liturgical text in a more Reformed manner. Some

92 For this long, tedious and ultimately futile process, see J. D. Martell, 'The Prayer Book Controversy 1927–28', MA thesis, University of Durham, 1974; Donald Gray, *The 1927–28 Prayer Book Crisis. 1. Ritual, Royal Commissions, and Reply to the Royal Letters of Business*, Alcuin/GROW Liturgical Study 60, Norwich: Canterbury Press, 2005; *The 1927–28 Prayer Book Crisis. 2. The Cul-de-sac of the 'Deposited Book . . . until further order be taken*, Norwich: Canterbury Press, 2006; Bryan D. Spinks, 'The Prayer Book "Crisis" in England', in Hefling and Shattuck (eds), *The Book of Common Prayer*, pp. 239–43; John Maiden, *National Religion and the Prayer Book Controversy, 1927–1928*, Woodbridge: The Boydell Press, 2009.

93 Louis Bouyer, *Eucharist: Theology and Spirituality of the Eucharistic Prayer*, Notre Dame: University of Notre Dame Press, 1968, pp. 428–9. An excellent observation, though Frere and his fellow revisers could only do what could be done in 1927. Bouyer's views on the evolution of the Eucharistic Prayer, cutting edge in 1968, are today as embarrassing as the 1928 Eucharistic Prayer. A humble reminder that most scholarly views have a limited shelf-life!

have seen the final Cranmerian Eucharist of 1552 as 'Zwinglian' memorialism, though in fact it is probably more accurate to class it as Cranmerian symbolic parallelism. The 1552 book was compiled at a time when Cranmer hoped to invite international Protestant scholars to England to confer as a rival council to Trent. It failed, but it may be that 1552 could be construed as some Protestant ecumenical rite. It affirmed what all agreed, and (e.g. the words of administration) avoided those things that were controversial. Whatever Cranmer's intent, although subsequent divines referred to his writings, very few in the English Church held Cranmer in the same authoritative position as Lutherans held Luther, or the Reformed came to revere Calvin. Subsequent Church of England divines, whether 'godly' or avant-garde conformists, wrote richer and very different theologies of the Eucharist than Cranmer. Yet the changes and chances of English church life meant that his liturgical text, which expressed Cranmer's own theology, with only minor change, remained the liturgical text of the Church of England and most Anglican provinces well into the twentieth century.

13

The Radical Reformation and Some New Churches of the Eighteenth and Nineteenth Centuries

This chapter reviews the Eucharist as it was conceived and practised in some of the more radical groups that emerged in the Reformation, together with some new ecclesial groups that had their origins in the various revivals of the eighteenth-century Enlightenment period and the subsequent nineteenth-century Romantic era.

Thomas Müntzer and the Anabaptists

Luther made recommendations for reform, but hesitated in implementing them, and became annoyed when others did so before him. Karlstadt was one, and Luther regarded him as an extremist and dangerous. Another was Thomas Müntzer, whom Luther regarded as even more extreme and more dangerous.

Little is known of Müntzer's early life. Born in Stolberg, probably *c.* 1488/89, he began studies in Leipzig, but by 1512 was at the new university of Frankfurt. He had been ordained priest by 1514, and between 1516 and 1517, when confessor to the nuns at the convent of Frohse, he drafted an Office for the patron saint Cyriacus. It drew on familiar breviaries and books of hours. By 1517/18 we know that he was in association with the Wittenbergers and considered himself a disciple of Luther. However, he was fiercely anti-clerical, preached polemical sermons and lacked diplomacy, and his career then became one of a series of expulsions. In 1523 he arrived in Allstedt, where he became pastor in the main church of St John in New Town. It was during this time that he compiled Reformation liturgies in the German tongue. He wrote:

> This attribution to the Latin words of a power like the incantations of the magicians cannot be tolerated any longer, for the poor people leave the churches more ignorant than they entered them, contrary to what God has declared in Isaiah 54, Jeremiah 31 and John 6, that all the elect should be instructed by God.[1]

1 Peter Matheson (ed.), *The Collected Works of Thomas Müntzer*, Edinburgh: T & T Clark, 1988, p. 168.

He provided a German form of Morning Prayer and Vespers. In his German Mass (outlined in 1523, and a full text in 1524) we encounter a fairly traditional structure.[2] The Introit is a whole psalm – Psalm 45 being provided, though he also provided Isaiah 45.8, *Rorate Coeli*, and Psalm 19.2, *Coeli ennarrant*. Müntzer defended the Kyrie eleison liturgical unit on the grounds that 'the friends of God, realizing his eternal mercy, may praise and glorify his name'.[3] Likewise the *Gloria in excelsis* was retained, with the greeting 'Der Herr sey mit euch', the Collect, Epistle, Alleluia, Gospel and Creed. An *Offertorium* was also provided, but gone are the prayers of the so-called 'Little Canon'. Yet, Müntzer retained the *Sursum corda*, with Preface, Proper Preface, Sanctus and Benedictus. Then came the Words of Institution, the Lord's Prayer, the Peace, Agnus Dei, Collect and Blessing. Müntzer provided a general Preface, and then Proper Prefaces for Passiontide, Christmas, Easter and Pentecost. Following Luther's suggestions, Müntzer had removed the *canon missae* because of its pronounced supplicatory and sacrificial terminology, and replaced it simply with the Words of Institution.

Luther was critical of the fact that the German style was not good enough and also that Müntzer had retained plainsong, which was not suited to the German language. However, Luther was alarmed by Müntzer's radical social agenda. Müntzer attacked the Wittenbergers for having trapped the Spirit in the text of Scripture. Rather, the Spirit resides in the Church and ministers. He was influenced by the German mystical tradition, which set great store on suffering. He also gave Scripture an apocalyptic interpretation. The combination of mystical piety and suffering with the birth pangs of an apocalyptic upheaval led to his conviction that the princes to whom Luther could appeal had forfeited their role in the struggle for the Kingdom, and power was to be given to the people. This was expressed liturgically not so much in his German Mass as in his services for morning and evening, and in his translation of the psalms. The end result was the peasant uprising, the slaughter at Frankenhausen and Müntzer's execution as ringleader.

Müntzer was acquainted with some of the future leaders of the Anabaptist movement, and although he himself did not abandon infant baptism, he advocated an Anabaptist position. A eucharistic hymn attributed to him was included in a hymn book associated with the Anabaptist Hans Hutt.[4] Anabaptism does not have one single origin, and emerged in Switzerland, South Germany and the Netherlands. Among the more prominent leaders of Anabaptism, many of whom squabbled with each other, was Balthasar Hubmaier.

Hubmaier (born *c.* 1480) was a Catholic priest and taught at the University of Ingolstadt. He read the works of Luther, Zwingli and Erasmus, and this changed his life. He aligned himself with Zwingli, but they parted company when Zwingli would not accept Hubmaier's ideas on baptism. Hubmaier was rebaptized with a number of others in 1525 and became pastor of the new Anabaptist congregation in Waldshut. He was burnt at the stake in Vienna in 1528.

---

2 *CD*, pp. 9–13; ET in Matheson, *Collected Works of Thomas Müntzer*, pp. 166–77.

3 Textually it appears as if the ninefold Kyrie is reduced to a fourfold Kyrie. In fact it was ninefold – the 'fourth' kyrie is there to denote a different musical ending. I am grateful to Professor Robin Leaver for pointing this out.

4 Matheson, *Collected Works of Thomas Müntzer*, pp. 399–400.

On the Lord's Supper Hubmaier seems to intensify some of Zwingli's insights, particularly in the belief that the Supper is a memorial, manifesting the Church as the body of Christ, and a means of Christian communion with one another and a pledge to one's neighbour. In his 1525 *Summa of the Entire Christian Life*, he wrote:

> Here it is obvious that the bread is not the body of Christ but only a reminder thereof. Likewise, the wine is not the blood of Christ but also a memorial that he shed his blood and distributed it on the cross to all believers for the washing away of our sins, as the hoop in front of the tavern is not wine, but a remembrance thereof.[5]

In *A Christian Catechism* (1526), he explained of the Supper:

> It is a public sign and testimonial of the love in which one brother obligates himself to another before the congregation that just as they now break and eat the bread with each other and share and drink the cup, likewise they wish now to sacrifice and shed their body and blood for one another; this they will do in the strength of our Lord Jesus Christ, whose suffering they are now commemorating in the Supper with the breaking of bread and the sharing of the wine, and proclaiming his death until he comes. Precisely this is the pledge of love in Christ's Supper that one Christian performs toward the other, in order that every brother may know what good deed to expect from the other. . . . the bread and wine are nothing but memorial symbols of Christ's suffering and death for the forgiveness of our sins.[6]

In his 1527 *A Form for Christ's Supper*, Hubmaier outlined the order that should be followed. The priest should kneel and make a confession on behalf of everyone, and then he should sit and discuss Luke 24.31, after which:

> The priest shall also rebuke those who are foolish and slow to believe all the things that Moses and the prophets have spoken, that he may kindle and make fervent and warm the hearts of those at the table, that they may be afire in fervent meditation of his bitter suffering and death in contemplation, love, and thanksgiving, so that the congregation with its whole heart, soul, and strength calls out to him:
>
> Stay with us, O Christ! It is toward evening and the day is now far spent. Abide with us, O Jesus, abide with us. For where thou art not, there everything is darkness, night, and shadow, but thou art the true Sun, light, and shining brightness, John 8:12. He to whom thou dost light the way, cannot go astray.[7]

---

5 H. Wayne Pipkin and John H. Yoder (eds), *Balthasar Hubmaier: Theologian of Anabaptism*, Scottdale: Herald Press, 1989, pp. 87–8.

6 Pipkin and Yoder (eds), *Balthasar Hubmaier*, pp. 354–5.

7 Balthasar Hubmaier, 'A Form for Christ's Supper' (1527), http://www.anabaptistnetwork.com/book/export/html/252.

Other chapters of Scripture could also be used: 'the 10th or 11th chapter of Paul's First Epistle to the Corinthians, or the 13th, 14th, 15th, 16th, or 17th chapter of John. Or Matthew 3 or Luke 3 on changing one's life, Sirach 2 on the fear of God'. The priest is to read 1 Corinthians 11 and discuss worthy reception, and then all say the Lord's Prayer, which was followed by a covenant called the Pledge of Love. The order continued thus:

> The bishop takes the bread and with the church lifts his eyes to heaven, praises God and says:
>
> We praise and thank thee, Lord God, Creator of the heavens and earth, for all thy goodness toward us. Especially hast thou so sincerely loved us that thou didst give thy most beloved Son for us unto death so that each one who believes in him may not be lost but have eternal life, John 3:16; 1 John 4:9; Rom. 8:32. Be thou honoured, praised and magnified now, forever, always and eternally. Amen.
>
> Now the priest takes the bread, breaks it, and offers it to the hands of those present, saying:
>
> The Lord Jesus, in the night in which he was betrayed, took the bread, gave thanks, and broke it, and said: 'Take, eat. This is my body, which is broken for you. Do this in my memory.' Therefore, take and eat also, dear brothers and sisters, this bread in the memory of the body of our Lord Jesus Christ, which he gave unto death for us.
>
> Now when everyone has been fed, the priest likewise takes the cup with the wine and speaks with lifted eyes:
>
> 'God! Praise be to thee!'
>
> and offers it into their hands, saying:
>
> Likewise the Lord Jesus took the vessel after the Supper and spoke: 'This cup is a new testament in my blood. Do this, as often as you drink, in memory of me.' Take therefore also the vessel and all drink from it in the memory of the blood of our Lord Jesus Christ, which was shed for us for the forgiveness of our sins.
>
> When they have all drunk, the priest says:
>
> As often as you eat the bread and drink of the drink, you shall proclaim the death of the Lord, until he comes, 1 Cor. 11:26.
>
> Now the church is seated to hear the conclusion.
>
> Most dearly beloved brethren and sisters in the Lord. As we now, by thus eating the bread and drinking the drink in memory of the suffering and shed blood of our Lord Jesus Christ for the remission of our sins have had fellowship one with another, 1 Cor. 10:17; 12:12; Eph. 4:4; Col. 1:3; Eph. 1; 4; 5, and have all become one loaf and one body, and our Head is Christ, we should properly become conformed to our Head and as his members follow after him, love one another, do good, give counsel, and be helpful to one

another, each offering up his flesh and blood for the other. Under our Head Christ we should all also live, speak, and act honourably and circumspectly, so that we give no offence or provocation to anyone, Matt. 18; Mark 9; Luke 17; 1 Cor. 8; Rom. 14. So that also those who are outside the church might not have reason to blaspheme our head, our faith, and church, and to say: 'Does your head Christ teach you such an evil life? Is that your faith? Is that your baptism? Is that your Christian church, Supper, and gospel, that you should lead such an ungodly and shameful life in gluttony, drunkenness, gambling, dancing, usury, gossip, reviling, cursing, blasphemy, pride, avarice, envy, hate and wrath, unchastity, luxury, laziness, and frivolity?' Matt. 18:6. Woe, woe to him who gives offence! It would be better for him that a millstone should be hung around his neck and he should be cast into the depth of the sea. Let us rather take upon ourselves a righteous, honourable, and serious life, through which God our Father who is in heaven may be praised.

Since our brotherly love requires that one member of the body be also concerned for the other, therefore we have the earnest behest of Christ, Matt. 18:14ff., that whenever henceforth a brother sees another erring or sinning, that he once and again should fraternally admonish him in brotherly love. Should he not be willing to reform nor to desist from his sin, he shall be reported to the church. The church shall then exhort him a third time. When this also does no good, she shall exclude him from her fellowship. Unless it should be the case that the sin is quite public and scandalous; then he should be admonished also publicly and before all, so that the others may fear, 1 Cor. 5:1; 1 Tim. 5:20; Gal. 2:11.

Whereupon I pray and exhort you once more, most dearly beloved in Christ, that henceforth as table companions of Christ Jesus, Luke 22:15, you henceforth lead a Christian walk before God and before men. Be mindful of your baptismal commitment and of your pledge of love which you made to God and the church publicly and certainly not unwittingly when receiving the water and in breaking bread. See to it that you bear fruit worthy of the baptism and the Supper of Christ, that you may in the power of God satisfy your pledge, promise, sacrament, and sworn commitment, Matt. 18; Luke 3:8. God sees it and knows your hearts. May our Lord Jesus Christ, ever and eternally praised, grant us the same. Amen.

Dear brothers and sisters, watch and pray lest you wander away and fall into temptation, Matt. 24:42; 25:13; Luke 16. You know neither the day nor the hour when the Lord is coming and will demand of you an accounting of your life. Therefore watch and pray, I commend you to God. May each of you say to himself, 'Praise, praise, praise to the Lord eternally!' Amen.

Arise and go forth in the peace of Christ Jesus. The grace of God be with us all. Amen.[8]

John Rempel concluded:

8 Hubmaier, 'A Form for Christ's Supper'.

> Hubmaier makes it clear that bread and wine are outer signs of an inner essence here on earth. This essence is the Christian covenant of love. The Lord's Supper is still a sacrament in the formal sense: it has an outward symbolic part and an inward reality. That reality is the church's covenant of love. But the role of a sacrament as a bridge between the human and the divine has been rejected.[9]

Remple examined the teaching of two other Anabaptist leasers, Pilgram Marpeck and Dirk Philips, as well as Hubmaier. Though there are many differences between them, he notes a number of commonalties that belong to the heart of this tradition.[10] For them all, the Christian life inseparably consisted of a relationship with God and the Church. The Lord's Supper was based not only on the memory of Christ's self-sacrifice but also on the communicant's pledge to imitate Christ in living with sister, brother, neighbour and enemy. They all stressed the humanity of Christ, and since spiritually he could only be in one place, it was impossible for his physical body to be in the elements. Like Zwingli, they used John 6 to interpret the narratives of the Last Supper. They characterized the Supper as primarily ethical.

Remple cites a communion prayer of Leenaerdt Clock which prayed that, through the gift of the Spirit, believers may be fed with the body and blood of Christ, and that they may have assurance of this feeding through the breaking of the bread.[11] However, no liturgical documents that may be deemed normative prior to the nineteenth century seem to have survived.[12] The conservative Amish community may preserve an order that goes back to its late seventeenth-century origins.

The separation of Amish from the wider movement took place in 1694 in Switzerland and South Germany, when followers of Jacob Ammann excommunicated those who in Ammann's opinion were too lax over the *Meidung* (shunning of those who had lapsed), as well as in their ideas of salvation.[13] On account of religious wars, poverty and persecution, large groups of Amish and Mennonites emigrated to the USA in the eighteenth century, and although Mennonites are still found in their native Europe, the Amish there became extinct and exist now only in the USA and Canada.

One of the reasons for the Amish split in 1694 was over the frequency of the Lord's Supper, and foot-washing. The Mennonites thought that once a year was sufficient for the Lord's Supper and thought that foot-washing had to be part of the celebration. Ammann insisted on two celebrations a year that would include foot-washing. Some of the formulae/prayers said at communion have been handed down in ministers' manuals. The nineteenth-century Unzicker manuscript, which records an older tradition, has the following:

9 John D. Rempel, *The Lord's Supper in Anabaptism: A Study in the Christology of Balthasar Hubmaier, Pilgram Marpeck and Dirk Philips*, Waterloo and Scottdale: Herald Press, 1992, p. 56.

10 Rempel, *The Lord's Supper in Anabaptism*, p. 199.

11 Rempel, *The Lord's Supper in Anabaptism*, p. 202.

12 Rempel, *The Lord's Supper in Anabaptism*, p. 202.

13 See Milton Gascho, 'The Amish Division of 1693–1697 in Switzerland and Alsace', *The Mennonite Quarterly Review* 11 (1937), pp. 235–66.

> After one has narrated the account of the death of our Lord until the Ascension, then he reads from the Gospel the usual part of the sixth chapter of John. Then also afterward an explanation is made of what the communion signifies, how a person is to prepare himself for it and so on and that one [the presiding bishop] intends to make the beginning with the breaking of bread.
>
> Then one says, 'Our Lord Jesus in the night when he was betrayed took the bread and thanked his Heavenly Father. We wish to do likewise with an earnest prayer'.
>
> After the prayer of thanksgiving then one says
>
> After he had given thanks he broke the bread and gave it to his disciples and said, 'Take and eat, this is my body which is given for you. This do in remembrance of me'. Accordingly I also intend to make a beginning with this bread and this in the hope and in the belief that he through his bitter suffering and death has purchased and redeemed us from the curse and fall of Adam. Also in the hope and in the confidence that he will be thanked for this by us and our posterity forever. Also in the hope and in the faith that he will raise us up at the last day and lead us with him into his everlasting kingdom. And whoever stands with me in such a hope let him also come after me and eat of this bread and this in memory of the bitter suffering and death of our Lord and Saviour Jesus Christ as has been set forth in your hearing.
>
> With the cup one says
>
> After he had broken bread he took the cup and thanked his Heavenly Father. Let us also thank him with an earnest prayer!
>
> After the thanksgiving one says
>
> After he had given thanks, he gave the cup to his disciples and said, 'Take it and drink all ye of it. This is the cup of the New Testament in my blood which was shed for you for the forgiveness of sins'. Accordingly, I also intend to make a beginning with this drink and this in the hope and in the faith that he by his bitter suffering and death and by the shedding of his innocent blood has purchased and redeemed us from the curse and fall of Adam. Also in the hope and in the confidence that he will be thanked for this by us and our posterity forever. Also in the hope and in the faith that he will raise us up at the last day and lead us with him into his everlasting kingdom. And whoever stands with me in such a hope let him come after me and drink of this drink and this in memory of the bitter suffering and death and innocent shedding of the blood of our Lord and Saviour Jesus Christ as has been set forth in your hearing.[14]

The reference to 'earnest prayers' seems to be to those provided in *Die ernsthafte Christenpflicht*.[15]

---

14 John Umble, (ed.), 'An Amish Minister's Manual', *Mennonite Quarterly Review* 15 (1941), p. 107.

15 Leonard Gross (ed.), *Prayer Book for Earnest Christians*, Scottdale: Herald Press, 1997, pp. 101–3.

After the final prayer, a hymn is announced and each member of the assembly is invited to wash the feet of the person nearest to her/him and exchange a Kiss of Peace.

The hymn sung during this is 'Von Herzen woll'n wir singen' from the *Ausbund*, the Amish hymn book.[16]

The English Separatist and early Baptist groups

A number of more reforming-minded clergy and lay persons in the Church of England found themselves convicted of nonconformity in church courts. Most of these wished to stay in the National Church, but had problems with its ceremonies and polity. A few among these left the Church and began their own 'true' churches. For these a National Church was a contradiction since their reading of the New Testament led them to believe that each congregation was independent and could elect and ordain their own pastor. Some of these additionally believed in believers' baptism only. They all agreed that written prayers were to be eschewed, for public prayer was an extemporary gift of ministry through the Spirit.

The most prominent among the former in sixteenth-century England were the followers of Robert Browne and Henry Barrow, respectively called Brownists and Barrowists. Since they were persecuted by the authorities, and since they had no written prayers, we know little about their beliefs and worship other than from the polemical writings of some of the leaders, and some eyewitness accounts of the worship. According to Browne, who had been ordained in the Church of England, their services included prayer, thanksgiving, reading of Scripture, exhortation and edifying, with provision for discussion on subjects that were 'doubtful & hard'.[17] For the Lord's Supper Browne insisted on adequate preparation:

> There must be a separation frō those which are none of the church, or be vnmeete to receaue, that the worthie may be onely receaued.
> All open offences and faulting must be redressed.
> All must proue and examine them selues, that their consciences be cleare by faith and reprentance, before they receaue.[18]

There was to be preaching on the 'death and tormentes of Christ' and on the spiritual use of the body and blood of Christ. The eucharistic action followed:

> The preacher must take breade and blesse and geue thankes, and thē must he breake it and pronounce it to be the body of Christ, which was broken for thē, that by fayth they might feede thereon spirituallie & growe into one

16 Charles Burkhart, 'The Church Music of the Old Order Amish and Old Colony Mennonites', *Mennonite Quarterly Review* 27 (1953), p. 36.

17 Robert Browne, *A True and Short Declaration*, in A. Peel and Leland H. Carlson (eds), *The Writings of Robert Harrison and Robert Browne*, London: George Allen and Unwin Ltd, 1953, p. 422.

18 Robert Browne, *A Booke which sheweth the life and manners*, in Peel and Carlson (eds), *Writings of Robert Harrison and Robert Browne*, p. 280.

spiritual bodie of Christ, and so he eating thereof himself, must bidd them take and eate it among them, & feede on Christ in their consciences.

Likewise also must he take the cuppe and blesse and geue thankes, and so pronounce it to be the bloud of Christ in the newe Testament, which was shedd for remission of sinnes, that by fayth we might drinke it spirituallie, and so be nourished in one spirituall bodie of Christ, all sinne being clensed away, and then he drinking thereof himself must bydd them drinke thereof likewise and diuide it amōg them, and feede on Christe in their consciences.

Then must they all giue thankes praying for their further profiting in godlines & vowing their obedience.[19]

Browne later returned to the Church of England and conformed. Henry Barrow refused all persuasion and was executed for sedition. Barrow himself gave the following directions for the Supper:

> Unto the supper of the Lord are required the elements of bread and wine: which bread (after thankes giving) is to be broken and to be delivered with such words of exhortation as are thereunto prescribed, and the cup delivered in like manner.[20]

A description is given in a deposition to the magistrates by a Daniel Bucke of the Lord's Supper celebrated by Francis Johnson who led one of the London Barrowist congregations:

> Beinge further demaunded the manner of the Lord's Supper administred emongst them, he saith that five whight loves or more were sett uppon the table and that the pastor did breake the bread and then delivered yt unto some of them, and the deacons delivered to the rest, some of the said congregacion sittinge and some standing aboute the table and that the pastor delivered the cupp unto one and he an other, and soe from one to another till they had all dronken, usinge the words at the deliverye therof according as it is sett downe in the eleventh of the Corinthes the xxiiiith verse.[21]

The Separatists were isolated congregations, but their radical separation from the National Church set a precedent for others to follow. By the seventeenth century a number of groups had seceded to covenant together and advocate believers' baptism. The two main groups were the General Baptists and the Particular Baptists.

The Leaders of the General Baptists included John Smyth, Henry Denne, Thomas Grantham and Joseph Wright. The name 'General' reflects their belief that Christ's redemption extended to all, and humans have not lost the faculty of willing the good. John Smyth was a Cambridge graduate and was ordained

---

19 Browne, *A Booke*, p. 284.

20 Henry Barrow, *A Brief Discoverie of the False Church*, in Leland H. Carlson (ed.), *The Writings of John Greenwood and Henry Barrow 1592–1593*, London: George Allen and Unwin Ltd, 1970, pp. 418–19.

21 Carlson, *Writings of John Greenwood and Henry Barrow 1592–1593*, p. 307.

in the Church of England, but fell foul of the authorities. At Gainsborough the parish priest was neglectful of his duties, and Smyth attempted to upstage and replace him in the parish, but without a licence, so he came under episcopal displeasure. He then separated from the church, and gathered his own congregation which eventually settled in the Netherlands.

The leaders of the Particular or Calvinist Baptists included John Tombes and Henry Jessey. Like Smyth, they tended to be clergy of the Church of England who eventually came to reject infant baptism, though they also rejected the episcopal hierarchy and other elements of the English Church such as written forms of prayer. They held firmly to a doctrine of election. Tombes of Bewdley sparked off considerable controversy over baptism during the first days of the Westminster Assembly.[22] Henry Jessey seems to have left the Church of England *c.* 1635 to pastor the separatist congregation of Samuel Eaton (d. 1639). In 1638 the question of the validity of infant baptism surfaced, and the congregation split. One spin-off from this was the group of John Spilsbury and William Kiffin.

On the understanding of the Lord's Supper, and its celebration, the groups do not seem to have had major differences. Theology as articulated in the earliest Confessions was minimal. In a *Short Confession* of 1610, drawn up by Smyth and his supporters, it stated:

> 31. The Holy Supper, according to the institution of Christ, is to be administered to the baptized; as the Lord Jesus hath commanded that whatsoever he hath appointed should be taught to be observed.
>
> 32. The whole dealing in the outward visible supper, setteth before the eye, witnesseth and signifyeth, that Christ's body was broken upon the cross and his holy blood spilt for the remission of our sins. That the being glorified in his heavenly Being, is the alive-making bread, meat, and drink of our souls: it setteth before our eyes Christ's office and ministry in glory and majesty, by holding his spiritual supper, which the believing soul, feeding and . . . the soul with spiritual food: it teacheth us by the outward handling to mount upwards with the heart in holy prayer, to beg at Christ's hands the true signified food; and it admonisheth us of thankfulness to God, and of verity and love one with another.[23]

The *Particular Baptist London Confession* of 1644 only mentioned observing the Supper with no explanation of it. The *Second London Confession* of 1677 was based on the Westminster Confession, though the words 'sacrament' and 'seal' were removed and 'sacramentally' was replaced by 'figuratively', arguably moving more towards a symbolic memorialist understanding.[24] The General Baptist Thomas Grantham (1634–92) insisted that the words 'body' and 'blood' must be understood 'to be mystically, spiritually, or figuratively in the *Bread*

22 Bryan D. Spinks, *Sacraments, Ceremonies and the Stuart Divines*, Aldershot: Ashgate, 2002, p. 114.

23 William L. Lumpkin, *Baptist Confessions of Faith*, second revised edition, Valley Forge: Judson Press, 2011, p. 103.

24 Lumpkin, *Baptist Confessions of Faith*, pp. 292–5.

and *Wine*, and not the Bread and Wine to be mystically, spiritually, or figuratively, in the *Body* and *Blood* of Christ'.[25] He described the manner of celebration. The table being decently prepared and the bread and wine being set on it in a decent manner,

> The Messenger, or Elder does excite the People to due Humility, and Reverence in their approaching to the Holy Table of the Lord, shewing the occasion and Authority by, and upon which it was instituted for a perpetual Ministry in the Church of God. The great Use and Mystical signification of it, as Christ is evidently set forth in his Crucifixion, or bitter Death upon the Cross, as the alone Sacrifice, once offered for the Sins of Men, and that there is no more Offering for Sin, but the Offering up of Christ once for all.
>
> Then he putteth them in mind of the qualifications, necessary on their part to the due Reception of that Divine Ordinance, without which they will come together for the worse, and not for the better.
>
> Then *taking the Bread into his hands*, he calleth upon God in the Mediation of Jesus Christ, for a Blessing upon the Bread, that it may be Sanctified for that holy use for which it was ordained by Christ, and that by Faith, all that are to partake of that Bread, thereby may feed upon the Body of Christ, *which is the true Bread, and by him live for ever.*
>
> Then he breaketh the Bread, pronouncing the words of Christ, *This is my Body, &c.* willeth the People *to receive it in remembrance of Christ*, and as shewing forth the Death of Christ till he come the second time without sin to Salvation.
>
> In like manner *he taketh the Cup*, after the People have received the Bread, and with Prayer suitable to that great Mystery, it being sanctified, he poureth out of the Wine, remembering the words of Christ, *This Cup is the New Testament in my Blood, &c.* partakes of it himself (as he did also of the Bread) and gives it to the Deacons to Communicate to all the Congregation, and they all drink of it.
>
> Then some word of *Exhortation is given to the People* under the consideration of the unspeakable Mercy of God in the gift of his Son to dye for us, that we might live Eternally with him: all is concluded *with Prayers to the Lord* for all his Blessings, in the most joyful manner that the Minister is able to express them, and then usually something is given to the Poor, as every mans heart maketh him willing, being not constrained thereunto, but as the love of Christ constraineth him.[26]

This summary can be compared with the account from the Stone Yard Meeting House, Cambridge, in 1761. This congregation had seceded from a Congregational Church in *c.* 1720:

> As soon as the afternoon public service was concluded, such as chose to go home went. Such as chose to be spectators went up the galleries. The outer

25 Thomas Grantham, *Hear the Church, or, An Appeal to the mother of us all*, London, 1687, p. 12.

26 Grantham, *Hear the Church*, pp. 28–30.

gate was fastened for the avoiding interruption; always hurtful in public worship, particularly so in the Lord's-supper-time. Mary Norris, the servant of the church, uncovered the table with a clean linen cloth, and sat thereon bread in a basket, the crust being taken off: two borrowed silver cups: and three pints of red port wine. The pastor took his seat at the upper end of the table. The deacons next to him, two on each hand. The elder men-members at the table. The younger in the pews on the pastor's right hand. The women in pews at his left. The pastor began with a short discourse on the occasion, nature, benefits, etc. of this ordinance.

Then he read I Cor.xi.23 till he came at the words '*took bread*', then, taking the bread in his hand, he read '*and when he had given thanks*' and said, 'Let us do likewise', on which, the congregation rising, he gave thanks. This ended, and the church sat down again, he added, '*When he had given thanks, he brake it*:' and broke the bread. During which he spoke of the sufferings of Christ, etc. Then, delivering the plates of bread to the deacons, he said, '*Take eat; this is my body, which is broke for you: do this in remembrance of me.*' The deacons then carried the bread round to the members: during which the pastor and all the church sat silent. The deacons at their return took bread and ate: the pastor last of all because the servant of all. After he had eaten the bread he rose again and added, taking the cups into his hands, '*After the same manner also he took the cup*.' The congregation rising again he gave thanks again. Then he poured the wine from the bottles into the cups, discoursing as while he broke the bread. The deacons rising at the close, he gave them the cups saying '*This cup*' and so on to the end of the 26th verse. After the deacons returned, and were seated, they drank, and last the pastor: all sitting silent from the delivery of the cup to the deacon. The pastor rising subjoined, Our Saviour and his disciples '*sang a hymn and went out*,' let us do likewise. An hymn or psalm was then sung: after which a collection for the poor was made: the blessing added: and the assembly dismissed. The whole time was about three quarters of an hour.[27]

This latter is very close to the Westminster *Directory* as used by Independents (cf. John Cotton), with a separate consecration and administration of each element, and comparable to the order followed by the Independent minister Richard Davis of Rothwell, Northamptonshire.[28] It should be noted that Davis's congregation was already singing hymns composed for the Lord's Supper in the 1690s, as were the Baptist congregations of Benjamin Keach and Joseph Stennett, and these hymns carried much of the theology that supplemented the meagre Confessional statements.[29]

27 L. E. Addicott and L. G. Champion (eds), *Church Book: St. Andrew's Street Baptist Church, Cambridge 1720–1832*, Didcot: Baptist Historical Society, 1991, pp. 27–8. For other Baptist traditions and eucharistic theologies, see Dale R. Stoffer (ed.), *The Lord's Supper: Believers Church Perspectives*, Scottdale: Herald Press, 1997.

28 See Bryan D. Spinks, *Liturgy in the Age of Reason: Worship and Sacraments in England and Scotland 1662–c.1800*, Farnham: Ashgate, 2008. pp. 87–8.

29 See Spinks, *Liturgy in the Age of Reason*, pp. 89–104. For some nineteenth-century developments and controversies, see Michael Walker, *Baptists at the Table*, Didcot: Baptist Historical Society, 1992.

Some new Churches of the eighteenth century

The Moravians

The Moravian Church traces its roots to a subgroup of the Bohemian Brethren, or Hussites, called the *Unitas Fratrum*. The Thirty Years' War erupted in Europe in 1618, when Frederick, the Elector Palatine, accepted the throne of Bohemia after Protestants had deposed the Catholic Hapsburg ruler. In 1620 Imperial Catholic forces defeated the Protestants at the Battle of White Mountain, and thereafter the Hussites were persecuted. In 1722 a German-speaking remnant made its way to Saxony and found refuge on the estate of Count Nikolaus Ludwig von Zinzendorf at Herrnhut. Zinzendorf, who was a Lutheran Pietist, refounded and remodelled the Brethren or Moravians. They became involved in missionary work in the New World and, to assist that, founded a settlement in Fetter Lane, London. John Wesley had encountered Moravians on his voyage to Georgia in his early years; he translated their hymns and joined in their worship. Zinzendorf's piety found its expression in the hymns of the Brotherhood, where we find considerable preoccupation with the blood of the Lamb and the wounds of Jesus.[30] Zinzendorf wrote: 'From the Moment that a Man is converted, and a warm Thunderbolt from our Saviour's Wounds pierces his Heart, a Reflection takes place, how much we have sinned, to cost our Creator his Life.'[31] He did not, apparently, write at any length on the Eucharist, but made references to it in passing. Thus, for example, he wrote:

> He has indeed instituted Bread and Wine to be vehicles, whereby that heavenly Drink and Food, which during his Torments was prepar'd within Him in a View to us, is (like some strong Elixir, which nakedly might be too penetrating for the Tongue or Palate) yet farther adapted to our weak Mind and Body, when the Church will jointly and solemnly partake of it: But still, this is to be look'd on only as the *second* Condescension or Qualifying. The Corpse of Jesus is *itself* a *Vehicle*, a Temperament or Accommodation: For 'tis with his Body and Blood the Divine Nature enters into us, and 'tis thus we communicate with the Father, Son and Holy Ghost, as Creatures who stand in the nearest Relation of any to their Creator.[32]

In *Discourse Eighteen on the Augsburg Confession*, he wrote:

> We demand of our communicants faith in the *reale* [real], substantial presence; the *transubstantiations-idèe* [idea of transubstantiation] is sufficiently

30 Arthur J. Freeman, *An Ecumenical Theology of the Heart: The Theology of Count Nicholas Ludwig von Zinzendorf*, Bethlehem, PA: The Moravian Church in America, 1998. See also Colin Podmore, *The Moravian Church in England, 1728–1760*, Oxford: Clarendon Press, 1998.

31 N. Zinzendorf, *Maxims, Theological Ideas and Sentences, out of the Present Ordinary of the Brethren's Churches. His Dissertations and Discourses from the Year 1738 till 1747*, London, 1751, p. 103.

32 Zinzendorf, *Maxims*, pp. 164–5.

> removed in that the bread, out of the time of its use, is no Sacrament; this clears away all difficulties arising from that quarter at once.[33]

Article X of the Brethren's beliefs stated:

> Concerning the Supper of the Lord, we teach thus, that the true body and blood of Christ are really present in the Lord's Supper with the visible bread and wine, and are imparted and received.[34]

The rite for the Lord's Supper as contained in the *Liturgienbüchlein* of 1755 consisted of the following.[35] Hymn verses were sung in turn by the congregation, the liturgist and the choir. The bread was brought, and a hymn verse sung and then the Words of Institution regarding the bread were read, followed by the distribution and the 'Holy Kiss'. Then the wine was brought, accompanied by a hymn verse, and the Words of Institution relating to the wine were spoken. During the distribution a litany of the wounds was sung. The rite ended with a hymn verse. In a 1757 book, instructions were given for the administration.[36] Immediately after the general public confession and absolution, the consecration of the bread took place with the words relating to the bread. The method of administration, for decorum, was that a priest and deacon administer to the brothers and a priest and deaconesses to the sisters. The bread was in baskets, and the deacons were to break the bread and give it to two people at a time. During the administration, the hymn 'O that Jesus' faithful wife' was sung. All ate their pieces of bread at the same time with the celebrant saying 'Do this in remembrance of me'. There was a prayer during which the congregation knelt or prostrated. When all had stood up, the Holy Kiss was given with the words 'The unblemished Passover flesh that will make your body and soul pure'. Then sitting, a liturgy was sung concerning the body (corpse) of Christ, 'which cannot be described'. Then came the consecration of the wine, with words of St John concerning the two thieves having their legs broken, but Jesus having his side pierced, and blood and water flowing out. Songs of the passion were sung of the holy blood. A collect was prayed, and the Kiss of Peace was given again; the rite ended with an appropriate blessing depending on whether it is morning or evening. What is interesting is the separate consecrations and administration – as suggested by Luther but not generally followed by Lutheran churches – and the fact that most of the rite was sung. The emphasis was on the passion and suffering of Christ. A fine engraving of the Fetter Lane administration of the bread shows the priest and deacons wearing albs.[37]

---

33 Cited in Freeman, *Ecumenical Theology*, p. 289.

34 Contained in *Liturgic Hymns of the United Brethren, Revised and Enlarged, Translated from the German*, London, 1793.

35 Nicole Schatull, *Die Liturgie in der Herrnhuter Brüdergemeine Zinzendorfs*, Tübingen: Francke Verlag, 2005, pp. 227–9. My thanks to Professor Markus Rathey for help with some of the eighteenth-century German.

36 Schatull, *Die Liturgie*, p. 230.

37 Plate IX, Distributio, reprinted in Nikolaus Ludwig von Zinzendorf, *Ergänzungsband* VI, Hildesheim: Georg Olms Verlagsbuchhandlung, 965. See the front cover of this book.

Methodism

Methodism has become largely associated with John and Charles Wesley. However, the term 'methodist' when first coined in the eighteenth century was a pejorative term used to describe those who embraced the zeal of the wider Evangelical Revival. In England George Whitefield was equally a methodist, but on the question of salvation he was a Calvinist Methodist whereas the Wesleys were Arminian in theology. Although Whitefield and John Wesley were itinerant preachers, they were Church of England clergy, and many of their equally zealous brethren remained in their parishes, and were also in the early years deemed to be 'methodists'.

It was over the question of salvation and predestination that Whitefield split from the Wesleys. Whitefield found a powerful patroness in Selina, Countess of Huntingdon, and she staffed her private chapels with Calvinist-minded Evangelicals. Legal objections over her chapel at Spa Fields led to her secession from the Established Church, and her chapels formed the Countess of Huntingdon's Connexion. In the early years these chapels used the *Book of Common Prayer* suitably modified. Selina herself indicated how she wished Morning Prayer should be modified, but she did not suggest any revisions for the communion.[38] It is not known exactly how her ministers used the Prayer Book communion service, and any modifications were ad hoc. John Wesley, however, did publish an emended Prayer Book, and the eucharistic theology he shared with his brother Charles was expressed in the latter's hymns.

Hymn singing in public worship in the eighteenth-century Church of England was uncommon, most parishes using only the metrical psalms of Sternhold and Hopkins or Tate and Brady. The first evangelical collections of hymns were composed for more private meetings. Charles Wesley published *Hymns on the Lord's Supper* in 1745, and these were clearly intended for use in public worship. The Preface was written by John Wesley, and was abbreviated from Daniel Brevint's *The Christian Sacrament and Sacrifice* (1673); the hymns roughly followed Brevint's theological sequence with certain adaptations. In his recent study of these hymns, Daniel Stevick explains thus:

> As to the organization of the collection, Wesley presents his *Hymns on the Lord's Supper* in six parts of unequal size. They speak of the Lord's Supper:
>
> Part I. 'As it is a Memorial of the Sufferings and Death of Christ' (27 hymns).
>
> Part II. 'As it is a Sign and a Means of Grace' (65 hymns).
>
> Part III. 'The Sacrament a Pledge of Heaven' (23 hymns).
>
> Part IV. 'The Holy Eucharist as it Implies a Sacrifice' (12 hymns).
>
> Part V. 'Concerning the Sacrifice of our Persons' (30 hymns).
>
> 'After the Sacrament' (9 hymns).[39]

38 See further in Spinks, *Liturgy in the Age of Reason*, pp. 172–8.

39 Daniel B. Stevick, *The Altar's Fire: Charles Wesley's Hymns on the Lord's Supper, 1745 Introduction and Exposition*, Peterborough: Epworth Press, 2004, p. 29. See also Ole E. Borgen, *John Wesley on the Sacraments*, Grand Rapids: Francis Asbury Press, 1986; Lorna Khoo, *Wesleyan Eucharistic Spirituality*, Adelaide: ATF Press, 2005.

The sacramental elements are effectual and communicating signs and instruments (Hymn 28.2–3; 73.2), and:

> JESU, my LORD and GOD, bestow
> All which thy sacrament doth shew,
> And make the real sign
> A sure effectual means of grace. (Hymn 66.1–4)

The communicants feed on Christ:

> Now on the sacred Table laid
> Thy Flesh becomes our Food,
> Thy Life is to our Souls convey'd
> In Sacramental Blood. (Hymn 65.3–4)

Though the 1662 communion rite had no petition for consecration, the Wesleys saw a place for the Holy Spirit – an Epiklesis:

> Come, Holy Ghost, thine Influence shed,
> And realize the Sign,
> Thy Life infuse into the Bread,
> Thy Power into the Wine.
>
> Effectual let the Tokens prove,
> And made by Heavenly Art
> Fit Channels to convey thy Love
> To every Faithful Heart. (Hymn 72)

The Wesleys emphasized the one sacrifice of the cross, but were able to express also the sacrificial overtones of the Eucharist:

> Yet may we celebrate below,
> And daily thus thine Offering shew
> Expos'd before thy Father's Eyes;
> In this tremendous Mystery
> Present Thee bleeding on the Tree
> Our everlasting Sacrifice. (Hymn 124.2.1–6)

Many other themes and sub-themes of eucharistic belief were given expression through this collection and represent a rich tapestry of eucharistic theology and reflection.

John Wesley's own suggested liturgical reforms came later in 1784 in his *The Sunday Service*, prepared for America and subsequently modified for use in England. In a letter of 1784 to the American Methodists, which was usually printed as a Preface to the book, Wesley stated:

> And I have prepared a liturgy little differing from that of the church of England (I think, the best constituted national church in the world) which I advise

> all the travelling-preachers to use, on the Lord's day, in all their congregations, reading the litany only on Wednesdays and Fridays, and praying extempore on all other days. I also advise the elders to administer the supper of the Lord on every Lord's day.[40]

His work was mainly simplification by omission – of rubrics, of reference to the monarchy, collects and material for when there was no communion, and exhortations. Only four Proper Prefaces were retained, the rubric for kneeling at communion was removed, but apart from the deletion of the word 'one' before 'oblation', the 1662 Prayer of Consecration remained intact. Some copies lack the manual acts, and these pages seem to have been printed in the United States. The word 'Elder' replaced priest, and if more consecrated elements were needed, a rubric required the whole Prayer of Consecration to be recited.

As might be expected from Wesley's remarks about the Church of England liturgy, there are no radical changes in the text. However, whereas the Nonjurors and the Newtonians (John Wesley was acquainted with the works of both) published emendations of the liturgy to express their theological beliefs, the Wesleys expressed their theological interests by supplementation through hymns. By a quirk of history, what was to become the main Methodist hymnal, the 1780 Collection, was originally designed for private societal use, not public worship, and so did not contain the rich eucharistic hymns of Charles Wesley.[41]

Swedenborg and the New Church

Emmanuel Swedenborg (1688–1772) was the son of a Pietist bishop in the Lutheran Church of Sweden. He was a Latin scholar and a mineralogist, and published works on physiology and anatomy. He was a frequent visitor to England and met with the Moravians and with John Wesley. From the 1740s he began to write religious works under an assumed name. His name was appended to his 1768 work, *Conjugal Love*, which became controversial. He moved first to Amsterdam and then to London. In his religious writings, he developed the idea of a visible 'New Church', which was revealed to him in special revelations and visions. He never left the Church of Sweden (his body is in Uppsala Cathedral) and he never attempted to found the 'New Church'. Some of those who read his works did, particularly James and Robert Hindmarsh and John Clowes, Rector of St John's Deansgate, Manchester. A division arose between them as to whether the 'New Church' could be contained in an existing church or needed to be entirely separate. The Hindmarshes believed the latter, and in 1788 Robert Hindmarsh was chosen as priest and ordained by

40 James F. White (ed.), *John Wesley's Prayer Book: The Sunday Service of the Methodists in North America*, Akron: OSL Publications, 1991, facsimile, no pagination.

41 For the theology of the 1780 collection, see Teresa Berger, *Theology in Hymns? A Study of the Relationship of Doxology and Theology According to A Collection of Hymns for the Use of the People Called Methodists (1780)*, Nashville: Kingswood Books, 1995.

his congregation, and he in turn ordained his father, James, and Samuel Smith. So the New Church came into being, founded on the visions of Swedenborg.

Swedenborg had taught that God is single and a unity, and the Trinity is a trinity of activities not persons. He also taught that God and humanity are completely united in Jesus. The atonement means bringing back the lost, with a reformation of character, and that humans are capable of co-operating in their salvation. On sacraments he taught that hitherto they had been interpreted by a literal understanding of the word, but now a new heavenly meaning was revealed. In his *The True Christian Religion Containing the Universal Theology of the New Church* (1771) he recorded:

> After this, that assembly of Englishmen, ardently desirous of being wise, said to the angels, 'They speak such various things concerning the Holy Supper; tell us what the truth is.' The angels replied, 'The truth is, that the man who looks to the Lord and repents, is by that most holy thing conjoined with the Lord and introduced into heaven.' But they said from the assembly, 'This is a mystery'. And the angels answered, 'It is a mystery, but yet such as can be understood. The bread and wine do not effect this; there is nothing holy from them; but material bread and spiritual bread correspond to each other, and material wine and spiritual wine; and spiritual bread is the holy of love, and spiritual wine is the holy faith, both of them from the Lord; and both, the Lord: hence is conjunction of the Lord with man, and of man with the Lord; not with the bread and the wine, but with the love and faith of the man who has repented; and conjunction with the Lord is also introduction to heaven.' And after the angels had taught them something concerning correspondence, they said from the assembly, 'Now for the first time we can understand this also.' And when they said this, behold a flame descending from heaven with light consociated them with the angels, and they loved one another.[42]

Like much 'mystical' writing, this conceals more than it reveals, though union with the divine and love seem important goals of the Lord's Supper. 'Flesh' means charity and 'blood' means truth.

The liturgies issued by the New Church reveal a little more as to its beliefs about the Eucharist. Two of the earliest liturgical books were *The Liturgy of the New Church* (published in London in 1790 and printed by Robert Hindmarsh) and *The Liturgy of the Lord's New Church* (Manchester, 1793, possibly drawn up by Clowes). The Form for the Holy Supper in the Hindmarsh rite began with the bread and wine being placed on the table and the recitation of the Lord's Prayer. An exhortation followed, which included the statement, 'Yea, the Lord himself is now present in his DIVINE HUMANITY, and waiteth to open Heaven to all those who approach his Holy Supper worthily.'

The minister then recited a prayer inspired in part by the Anglican Collect for Purity, which included the petition, 'humbly praying that thou wouldst be pleased to communicate that spiritual and substantial Food, the Good and Truth

---

42 Emmanuel Swedenborg, *The True Christian Religion containing the Universal Theology of the New Church*, Amsterdam, 1771, ET: vol. II, Boston and New York: Houghton Mifflin Company, 1907, p. 791.

proceeding from thy GLORIFIED HUMANITY, which can alone nourish and preserve us to eternal Life'. There followed a lengthy explication outlining the eucharistic belief of the New Church, stressing the difference between a 'natural Sense' and the 'spiritual Sense'. This explication concluded:

> Thus Eating and Drinking are Acts of a spiritual Nature; and thus the Holy Supper becomes a Signing, Sealing, Certifying, and Witnessing, even before the Angels, that the worthy Receivers thereof are the Sons of God, and moreover as a Key to their House in Heaven, where they shall dwell to all Eternity.[43]

A prayer followed, rehearsing some of salvation history through the eyes of Swedenborg, and it included the petition:

> consecrate, we humbly beseech thee, with the Presence of thy DIVINE HUMANITY, these natural Elements of Bread and Wine, that they being received by our Bodies in the Spirit of Love to Thee, and Charity towards our Neighbour, we may at the same Time with our Souls feed upon that Divine Good which is thy Flesh and Body, and the Divine Truth which is thy Blood. Amen.

The rehearsal of the Words of Institution followed, and then the administration with the words:

> The Body of our Lord Jesus Christ, which is the Divine Good of his Divine Love, nourish and preserve you unto eternal Life. Take and eat this, in Remembrance that the Lord GLORIFIED his HUMANITY, and thereby became the God of Heaven and Earth.

The words for the cup began, 'The Blood of our Lord Jesus Christ, which is the Divine Truth of his Divine Wisdom, nourish and preserve you unto eternal Life.' The rite concluded with the Lord's Prayer, a psalm or hymn, a prayer of thanksgiving addressed to Christ which referred to his presence 'under the Forms of Bread and Wine to communicate, by Influx, the Divine Good and Truth', a short doxology and the Grace.

The rite of 1793 is more reminiscent of the Anglican rite, which might be expected if Clowes was the author. An exhortation giving notice of the Supper was to be read the previous Sunday. It began with offertory sentences suggested by 1662, the reading of the Institution Narrative, with manual actions. More Scripture sentences followed, and then an explication/exhortation, including the words:

> ye in (sic) will *eat this Bread of life*, and in understanding *drink this Blood of the New Covenant*, ye shall have *eternal life* – the seeds of immortal happiness implanted within you; and thereby obtain conjunction with the Lord, *He dwelling in you* by the good and truth proceeding from His Glorified Body,

43 *The Liturgy of the New Church*, London, 1790, 3rd edn, p. 104.

> and *ye in Him* by your being immediately within the sphere of His Holy Spirit, when living within the boundaries of His Divine laws of order – the precepts of His Word.[44]

A prayer followed, and then the Lord's Prayer, and communion with words of administration very similar to those of the 1662 book but with Swedenborgian additions. A hymn was sung, then a prayer of 'Thanksgiving and Glorification', mentioning being fed from 'Thy Glorified Body' (the final part of which is identical to that in Hindmarsh), and the Aaronic blessing. Another book, *Order of Worship of the Society of the New Church Meeting in Red Cross Street, London* (1794), shows similarities to these, and differences, showing pluriformity during the early years of the New Church.[45]

Some new Churches of the nineteenth century

The Catholic Apostolic Church

The origins of the Catholic Apostolic Church can be traced to a series of meetings held at Albury Park, the home of the wealthy banker and MP, Henry Drummond (1786–1860). Drummond brought together clergy and laity of different denominations to discuss biblical passages about prophecy; most were of the opinion that the return of Christ would precede a millennium, and the Parousia was imminent. One of the signs of the approaching Parousia would be the outpouring of prophecy and gifts of the Spirit. Among the group was Edward Irving, minister of a Scottish congregation at Cross Street, Hatton Garden, London, which later relocated to Regent Square, and several of the Albury Park group were members of his church.

In 1830 reports of the miraculous healing of Mary Campbell in Port Glasgow, and of the prophecies that accompanied it, reached the Albury group, and delegates were sent to investigate. Mary Campbell moved to London and became a member of Irving's congregation. They prayed for the manifestations of the Spirit, and in 1831 'tongues' and other gifts of the Spirit became part of public worship at Irving's church. Not all members of the church were enthusiastic about this, and Irving, already under suspicion for holding unorthodox christological views, was declared unfit to be a minister of the Church of Scotland. He and some 800 of the congregation left the Regent Square building. In 1833 the Church of Scotland deposed Irving from the ministry. He never held high office in the Church he had helped to found, and his death in 1834 ended any further contribution to it, even though members of this new Church were often referred to as 'Irvingites'.

As a result of the London manifestations and prophecies, prayer meetings were held at Albury Park, and John Cardale and Henry Drummond emerged as leaders of what would become the Catholic Apostolic Church. Prophecies led

44 *The Liturgy of the Lord's New Church*, Manchester, 1793, no pagination.

45 This church was pastored by the Revd Manoah Sibly, who differed from Hindmarsh on some issues of belief. Liturgies of 1800 and 1805 show a move towards a more uniform rite.

to the calling and setting apart of 12 Apostles who in turn instituted a ministry of Angels (bishops), Elders (priests) and Deacons, and the founding of the new Church.[46] As the community believed that they were living in the last days, no provision was made for filling the places of the Apostles as they died. With the death of the last Apostle in 1901, there could be no further ordinations, and the Church wound down to extinction. Its liturgy was to be influential in the Church of Scotland and in the Mercersberg Movement.

Initially this Church inherited a Church of Scotland pattern of worship.[47] Further directions for eucharistic worship were issued in 1838. However, under the direction of the Apostles, a liturgy with increasing ceremonial began to evolve. The first printed rite was published in 1843, and it continued to evolve until 1880. The liturgiographer of the Church was John Cardale, who also wrote a commentary on the liturgical rites.[48]

As a worshipping congregation rather than a meeting of delegates interested in prophecy, the Catholic Apostolic Church had its roots in Edward Irving's Church of Scotland congregation in London, and its theological foundations were Irving's. Irving published homilies on the Lord's Supper that reproduce a standard Presbyterian theology. He referred to the bread and wine as 'emblems', and the rite was a 'commemorative act'. The Eucharist was an ordinance for calling to remembrance, and likewise an ordinance for 'exciting unto hope and desire'.[49] Expounding John 6, where he interpreted the flesh of Christ/bread of life as Christ's doctrine and teaching, he wrote:

> The reason why He put the truth in this symbolical form to the Jews was, doubtless, because they required a sign similar to the manna in the wilderness, which He told them they had in His own person, which was the bread that came down from heaven. But to us it serves the more important purpose of ascertaining what it is which He hath embodied to all ages under the symbols of bread and wine, or of His body and blood. For He hath spoken so unequivocally and so repeatedly of His flesh and blood as meaning the spirit of His doctrine, then in that sense He must be understood when, under these emblems of body and blood, He handeth down some mysterious significance to His disciples in all future ages.[50]

He rejected the Roman and Lutheran understanding of presence, and insisted that the only transubstantiation that would take place was that of human nature

46 See Columba Flegg, *Gathered under Apostles: A Study of the Catholic Apostolic Church*, Oxford: Clarendon Press, 1992.

47 Kenneth W. Stevenson, 'The Catholic Apostolic Church – Its History and Its Eucharist', *Studia Liturgica* 13 (1979), pp. 21–45. For the development of this rite, see Gregg Alan Mast, *The Eucharistic Service of the Catholic Apostolic Church and Its Influence on Reformed Liturgical Renewals of the Nineteenth Century*, Lanham: Scarecrow Press, 1999.

48 John Cardale, *Readings in the Liturgy and Divine Offices of the Church*, 2 vols, London: Thomas Bosworth, 1874–75.

49 G. Carlyle (ed.), *The Collected Works of Edward Irving*, vol. 2, London: Alexander Strahan and Co., 1864, p. 603.

50 Carlyle, *Collected Works of Edward Irving*, p. 488.

at the resurrection. He nevertheless quoted from the *Scots' Confession* that the elements were not naked and bare signs, asserting:

> Christ doth as it were let down His body in this sacred symbol from its regal dignity to the capacity of the present weakness of man, and present it under a figure to all who have believed upon Him . . . In the sacrament we receive the seal and the pledge of that holy union which we already have through faith.[51]

The foundational Reformed liturgy and theology of Irving was to be superseded by the studies and work of John Cardale. In 1838 an order for communion was issued, which included the deacons bringing the elements to the table, a confession of unworthiness and absolution, and a prayer of intercessions for Church and world. The bread was then consecrated in a prayer that concluded with the Sanctus, and the communion in bread was given. Then came the consecration of the cup that included a petition for the Spirit upon the elements, followed by distribution of the cup. The service concluded with a psalm and a blessing.[52] Of note is the separate consecration and distribution of the elements. The Apostles of the Church researched worship in different traditions and Cardale embarked upon a historical study. The new liturgy evolved with a distinctly 'Catholic' flavour with liberal Eastern borrowings. Cardale outlined the theological basis and rationale in his *Readings upon the Liturgy and Other Divine Offices of the Church*, published in 1878. In the introductory section he considered the theological meaning of the Last Supper, deciding:

> The Lord, who had fulfilled and summed up the Law, became the author and the finisher of salvation, accomplishing His work by the willing offering to the death of that body, and the shedding forth of that blood, which He received from the Blessed Virgin, His mother: and in that same body raised from the grave, He hath received the new, the resurrection life and glory, of which He calls us to be partakers.
>
> In the sacrament which the Lord now instituted, He not only showed forth commemoratively His death upon the cross, and the blessings which flow to us therefrom, by the blessing and breaking of bread, the consecration of the material elements of bread and wine to be the Sacrament of His body and blood, and the making His disciples communicants thereof.[53]

Cardale concluded from his researches that there was a fivefold action in the eucharistic liturgy: oblation of bread and wine, which have already been set apart for holy use; solemn thanksgiving unto Almighty God for his goodness; solemn blessing, breaking and consecration of the bread, and blessing and con-

51 Carlyle, *Collected Works of Edward Irving*, pp. 494 and 498.

52 The document is to be found in P. E. Shaw, *The Catholic Apostolic Church, Sometimes Called Irvingite: A Historical Study*, Morning Heights, New York: King's Crown Press, 1946, pp. 104–5.

53 John Cardale, *Readings upon the Liturgy and Other Divine Offices of the Church*, 2 vols, London: Thomas Bosworth, 1878, vol. 1, p. 33.

secration of the wine; solemn presentation of the memorial; and consuming of the sacrament.[54] These were clearly articulated in the liturgy. The Liturgy of the Word followed the Western pattern, ending with the Creed. At the offertory there were prayers of offering of money/gifts, and a quite separate 'oblation' prayer, introduced by the *Orate fratres*, offering the bread and wine to God. Next came the *Sursum corda* and lengthy Preface. Proper insertions into the Preface for the various feasts and seasons were provided, and they were inserted at different but appropriate places in the lengthy common Preface. This section ended with the Sanctus, followed by the Lord's Prayer. The Preface and Sanctus were, for Cardale, 'our sacrifice of Eucharist', and he regarded 'giving thanks' as being a quite separate component from 'consecration'. The 'consecration' came after the Lord's Prayer, with what might be termed a 'compromise' regarding separate blessing of the elements. The celebrant prayed over the bread:

> Look upon us, O God, and bless and sanctify this bread.
>
> In the name of the FATHER, and of the SON, and of the HOLY GHOST, we bless + this bread; and we beseech Thee, heavenly Father, to send down Thy Holy Spirit, and make it unto us the Body of Thy Son Jesus Christ: WHO, THE SAME NIGHT etc.

A similar formula was provided for the cup. After this consecration – by the celebrant's blessing, the sending and making of the Holy Spirit, and recital of the words of Jesus, and concluded by an Amen – came the prayer of oblation. This differed from the oblation first offering the gifts to God and corresponds in the *Readings* to the solemn presentation of the memorial. It used the words, 'we Thy servants . . . do present unto Thee this reasonable and unbloody sacrifice which Thou hast instituted in Thy Church, the holy bread of life, and the cup of eternal salvation'. This prayer also had seasonal insertions. It was followed by the anthem of incense, and then the Commemoration of the Living followed by the Commemoration of the Departed. Each of these consisted of a considerable number of quite separate prayers. This whole anaphoric series of prayers concluded with a preparatory prayer for communion. The administration followed as a distinct section of the rite with Anglican and Roman Catholic material. The rite ended with the Te Deum and a Benediction.

This rite was quite a remarkable creation, using the best history the nineteenth century could give. Cardale's achievements, which were incredibly ecumenical, were aptly summed up by Kenneth Stevenson:

> He attempts to work out a doctrinal synthesis on matters he saw were divisive issues among the Churches. On the eucharistic presence, he stresses both 'real-ness' and communion of the faithful, by phrases like 'make it unto us' in the Consecration, and 'under the veil of earthly things we have now communion with him' in the Concluding Prayer before Communion. His formulations on the eucharistic sacrifice in the Prayer of Oblation are similarly comprehensive: he stresses both the 'once-and-for-all' offering of

54 Cardale, *Readings*, vol. 1, p. 34.

Christ ('have respect unto that Sacrifice once offered upon the cross') and the Church's participation in it ('we do . . . present unto Thee this reasonable and unbloody sacrifice'). Further, on the question of prayer and the departed he clothes his language with a like care, giving emphasis to the resurrection of the faithful – 'until our . . . perfecting . . . in the . . . resurrection' (Commemoration of the Departed).[55]

The Church of Jesus Christ of Latter-Day Saints

The Church popularly called the Mormon Church was, as its proper name suggests, one of the nineteenth-century Restorationist Churches, and, like the Catholic Apostolic Church, was founded on Pre-millennial beliefs.[56] The prophet Joseph Smith is purported to have received his first vision (cf. Swedenborg) in 1820:

> I saw a pillar of light exactly over my head, above the brightness of the sun, which descended gradually until it fell upon me.
>
> It no sooner appeared than I found myself delivered from the enemy which held me bound. When the light rested upon me I saw two personages, whose brightness and glory defy all description, standing above me in the air. One of them spake unto me, calling me by name, and said – pointing to the other – THIS IS MY BELOVED SON, HEAR HIM.[57]

The subsequent visions of an angel and the delivery to Smith of the *Book of Mormon* were regarded as a fulfilment of Revelation 14.6–7, and the Latter-Day Saints believed that they were living on the eve of the Second Coming. Prophecy held an important place in the life of the new Church, and the Restoration included the Aaronic and Melchizedek priesthoods. In 1835 Smith appointed Twelve Apostles and 'the Seventies'. The former, unlike the Twelve of the Catholic Apostolic Church, could have successors. The New Testament texts are important for understanding the Supper, but the *Book of Mormon* is regarded as canonical and explains the New Testament and Mormon practices. Third Nephi is an important book for establishing eucharistic practice. Chapter 18 tells of how the resurrected Jesus established the Supper among a group of peoples in the Americas called the Nephites:

> 5 And when the multitude had eaten and were filled, he said unto the disciples: Behold there shall one be ordained among you, and to him will I give power that he shall break bread and bless it and give it unto the people of my church, unto all those who shall believe and be baptized in my name.
>
> 6 And this shall ye always observe to do even as I have done, even as I have broken bread and blessed it and given it unto you.

---

55 Stevenson, 'Catholic Apostolic Church', p. 40.

56 Grant Underwood, *The Millenarian World of Early Mormonism*, Urbana and Chicago: University of Illinois, 1993. See also Douglas J. Davies, *An Introduction to Mormonism*, Cambridge: Cambridge University Press, 2003.

57 Cited in Ivan J. Barrett, *Joseph Smith and the Restoration*, Provo: Brigham Young University Press, 1973, p. 48.

> 7 And this shall ye do in remembrance of my body which I have shown unto you. And it shall be a testimony unto the Father that ye do always remember me. And if ye do always remember me ye shall have my Spirit to be with you.
>
> 8 And it came to pass that when he said these words, he commanded his disciples that they should take of the wine of the cup and drink of it, and that they should also give unto the multitude that they might drink of it.
>
> 9 And it came to pass that they did so, and did drink of it and were filled; and they gave unto the multitude, and they did drink, and they were filled.
>
> 10 And when the disciples had done this, Jesus said unto them: Blessed are ye for this thing which ye have done, for this is fulfilling my commandments, and this doth witness unto the Father that ye are willing to do that which I have commanded you.

Chapter 20.1–10 describes another gathering in which Jesus administers (this time miraculously) bread and wine, and may have served as the model for parts of the sacrament prayer in *Moroni* 4 and 5. In 26.11–21 Mormon gives additional details about how Christ administered the bread and wine during his resurrected appearance. *Moroni* 4.1–3 recounts the institution and gives a prayer over the bread that is used verbatim in the liturgy:

> 1 The manner of their elders and priests administering the flesh and blood of Christ unto the church; and they administered it according to the commandments of Christ; wherefore we know the manner to be true; and the elder or priest did minister it –
>
> 2 And they did kneel down with the church, and pray to the Father in the name of Christ, saying:
>
> 3 O God, the Eternal Father, we ask thee in the name of thy Son, Jesus Christ, to bless and sanctify this bread to the souls of all those who partake of it; that they may eat in remembrance of the body of thy Son, and witness unto thee, O God, the Eternal Father, that they are willing to take upon them the name of thy Son, and always remember him, and keep his commandments which he hath given them, that they may always have his Spirit to be with them. Amen.

Chapter 5 gives the prayer for the wine:

> 1 The manner of administering the wine – Behold, they took the cup, and said:
>
> 2 O God, the Eternal Father, we ask thee, in the name of thy Son, Jesus Christ, to bless and sanctify this wine to the souls of all those who drink of it, that they may do it in remembrance of the blood of thy Son, which was shed for them; that they may witness unto thee, O God, the Eternal Father, that they do always remember him, that they may have his Spirit to be with them. Amen.

These foundational texts serve as a blueprint for Mormon celebration of the Sacrament (applied specifically to the Eucharist), though in 1830, with the publication of the *Book of Mormon* and the Church's incorporation as a church, water was substituted for wine. The elements used are thus bread and water. The Sacrament Meeting is usually held every Sunday. Bradley Kramer describes the rite thus:

> The actual ordinance of the Sacrament begins with the collective singing of a hymn, during which members of the lay, all male priesthood (in most cases 'priests', usually young men ages 16 to 19) prepare the emblems by breaking the bread. Following the singing, sacrament prayers are offered, according to a prescribed pattern with pre-scripted wording, by the same men who prepared the emblems. The prayers, pronounced separately but almost identically for the bread and water, supplicate God the Father, in the name of Jesus Christ, to bless the emblems to the spiritual wellbeing of those who eat and drink, articulate a willingness on the part of all participants to take upon themselves the name of Jesus Christ, to hold him in remembrance, and to strictly keep his commandments, in return for which they ask that God bless them with the continued presence of the Holy Spirit. The bread and water are passed to all, usually by deacons (the entry-level office of the LDS priesthood, conferred upon most young men at age 12). During the passing and partaking portion of the ordinance, silence prevails. The ordinance typically lasts 10 to 15 minutes and takes place early in the Sacrament Meetings. The remainder of the meeting usually includes talks and musical performances by ward members, as well as congregational singing and a benediction.[58]

The Sacrament is regarded as a renewal of the covenant of baptism, and worthiness is required by the members. As far as theological belief is concerned, though no presence is associated with the elements, the presence of Christ is presupposed, and general beliefs about the Supper are not so different from many Protestant groups. In an article on the Sacrament, Matthew Bowman wrote:

> Thus, the Lord's Supper is not only a type of what has happened but also what is happening and, ultimately, what will happen. It gives us the entire scope of salvation history, from our fall to our redemption, wrapped up in the barest of actions, because all of those things are bound together in Christ's exodus through mortality.[59]

The Peculiar People of Essex and Kent

Among the smaller regional new Churches in nineteenth-century England was the Peculiar People, located in parts of Essex and Kent.[60] Its beginnings were in 1837 in Rochford, Essex, with James Banyard, who was a Wesleyan local

58 Article in W. Paul Reeve and Ardis E. Parshall (eds), *Mormonism: A Historical Encyclopedia*, Santa Barbara: ABC-CLIO, 2010, p. 252.

59 Matthew Bowman, 'This is my body: A Mormon Sacrament', *Dialogue: A Journal of Mormon Thought* 44 (2011), p. 213.

60 The details here are from Mark Sorrell, *The Peculiar People*, Exeter: Paternoster Press, 1979. The present writer remembers the surviving members of the Harrodite 'originals' of Cressing, Essex, in the 1960s, who still wore the traditional attire for church.

preacher. He was influenced by William Bridges, a London Wesleyan local preacher, and the Revd Robert Aitken. Aitken had seceded from the Church of England and preached among Methodist congregations. After a visit to Bridges in 1837, Banyard felt 'born again' in the Spirit and eventually left the Rochford Methodists to set up his own congregation.[61] As his movement spread in other Essex towns and villages, it adopted a strict code with abstention from alcohol and tobacco and the wearing of a dark suit and bowler hat for men and black capes and bonnets for the women for worship. It included the belief that healing was in the hands of the elders, and members should shun professional medical assistance. In early 1852 the Church was constituted with bishops and elders, with James Banyard, Samuel Harrod, John Thorogood and David Handley being made bishops. The name 'The Peculiar People' was chosen at that time. Banyard later broke his own rule, when he called a doctor to attend his child, and the Church deposed him. Bishop Samuel Harrod became the new leader. In 1890 a split occurred over rumours concerning the 70-year-old Harrod and a young married woman of the Church. Daniel Tansley was elected bishop of those who subsequently rejected the ministry of Harrod. There were thus the Harrodites and Tansleyites, though the Harrodites called themselves 'The Original Peculiar People'. After the death of Harrod and another prominent leader of the 'Originals', the Tansleyite Bishop William Heddle managed to heal the schism in 1913.

Under Samuel Harrod communion was celebrated for the first time in 1865 at the chapel at Daws Heath and then subsequently in the other chapels. Bishop Heddle tidied up the rules for the Supper, establishing celebrations at three-monthly intervals. Rules for celebration are given in *Church Order and Order of Advancing of Members into the Ministry,* which, although dating from *c.* 1926, given the conservative nature of The Peculiars, preserves the rite as observed by Heddle in the nineteenth century. It stated that the Presiding Elder was to give notice of celebration the previous Sunday. All services were to begin with a hymn, prayer and hymn, and to close with a hymn and benediction. When the Supper was celebrated, the morning service was to have Scripture expounded to show the need for self-examination 'previous to the partaking of the sacred ordinance'. The Supper was to be celebrated in the following manner:

> 83. *Before the afternoon service commences, a table to be placed in front of the Desk with the Wine and Glasses thereon, together with the Bread cut in finger portions, all to be placed upon the table and covered with a clean white cloth.*
>
> Sacrament Sunday Afternoon.
>
> 84. All the available time to be occupied solely for the purpose of reviewing the infinite grace of God, and the mysterious and matchless love, and extreme suffering of our Lord Jesus Christ, to procure our pardon and purchase our redemption.

61 The Rochford Wesleyan Church held that it ejected Banyard for refusing to obey instructions. Email from Dave Dobbin, Rochford Methodist Church, 21 January 2013.

85. Preaching being ended, a verse to be sung, then all Elders to descend from the Desk. The officiating Elder to wash his hands (solely for cleanliness). A suitable Hymn to be sung, the officiating Elder to uncover the elements and read I Cor. 11, 23–24, or Matt. 26, 26; Mark 14, 22; Luke 22, 19; then to offer thanks for such love, suffering and salvation, then break the bread, recalling the Saviour's words: This is my body which is given for you, &c. Then partake of the bread, first himself saying, after this manner: That he fully believes that Jesus Christ's body was broken for him, and that he partakes of this with the prayer that he may feed on Him, the Bread of Life, by faith in his heart, till He come. Then hand it to any Elders present and then to the brothers and sisters, commencing at the first seat, saying: The body of our Lord Jesus Christ was broken for thee, partake of this in commemoration thereof, and feed on Him, the Bread of Life, by faith in thy heart till He come.

86. A suitable Hymn may now be sung.

87. The Elder to read I Cor. 11, 25–26, or Matt. 26, 27–28; Mark 14, 23–24; Luke 22, 20. Then offer thanks for the all-atoning and cleansing blood of the Crucified One. The Elder then first partakes of the Wine, saying after this manner: 'I partake of this in commemoration of the blood which was shed for my sin, my pardon and cleansing, fully believing that the precious blood of Jesus Christ streamed from His Body on the Cross for me, &c. Praying that I may feed on Him by faith till He come.' Then hand it to the Elders, afterwards to the Brothers and Sisters commencing at the front seat – saying after this manner: 'The blood of the Lord Jesus Christ was shed to wash thy spirit white and to make you fit for Heaven, partake of this in commemoration thereof, and feed on Him by faith till He come.'

88. During the administration a suitable Hymn may be sung.

89. Close with a Hymn, Prayer and Benediction.[62]

This order of service is directory-style, and the separate thanksgivings and administrations of the bread and wine are akin to the Independents and Baptist celebrations. Methodism, though, was the backdrop to the Peculiars, and hymnody was important. The first hymn book was compiled in 1860 by Samuel Harrod and David Handley with the assistance of one other.[63] It drew upon a hymn book called *The Stirling* and on the *Methodist Hymn Book*.[64] Later revisions of the book included hymns suitable for the Lord's Supper, and these perhaps give some insight into the eucharistic piety of the late nineteenth-century Peculiars. The 1891 book, and that of 1900, contains 14 hymns for the Lord's Supper, numbered 452–65. Isaac Watts supplied 452, 453, 454, 458 and 462; Charles Wesley, 455, 456, 457 and 464.[65] Number 461 is by

62 *The Peculiar People, Church Order and Order of Advancing of Members into the Ministry*, Southend-on-Sea: The Peculiar People, no date, pp. 16–17. I am indebted to Howard Gardner, Company Secretary to the Union of Evangelical Churches (the successors to the Peculiars), for this information and the text of the communion hymns.

63 Sorrell, *Peculiar People*, p. 30.

64 Sorrell, *Peculiar People*, p. 30.

65 I am indebted to Professor Robin Leaver for information on the sources of these communion hymns.

'W.S', and the earliest source Robin Leaver could find is in a New York 1844 Primitive Methodist collection, and it may be that *The Stirling* provided this hymn.[66] Number 465 appeared anonymously in *Covenant Hymns*, 1849.[67] Number 459, by Mary Ann Moreton first appeared in the first editions of *The Latter-day Saints' Psalmody* (1889), and all references known to Robin Leaver are Mormon.

Number 452, 'Twas on that dark, that doleful night', speaks of the love of Christ's actions of taking and breaking, and the grace of his words. This feast shows forth his death, and if faithful, 'we all shall eat The marriage supper of the LAMB'.[68] Number 455 speaks of 'Thy mysterious supper' shared by the Lord's servants, who are fed and, although many, are one undivided bread. Number 458 describes the Eucharist as 'His testament of love', of which Christ's life is the seal. Number 460 describes the Eucharist as a celestial feast at which the communicants receive the body and blood of the Lord entirely free. The communicant confesses, 'I eat His flesh, and drink His blood, In signs of bread and wine.' The last of the selection has that piety of seeing the sacrifice of Christ in the eucharistic action, though the word 'sacrifice' is not used:

By faith, my Lord, I now behold,
Expiring on the tree;
Muse on the wondrous scene of love,
He dies, my soul, for thee.

Stretch'd on the cross, thy SAVIOUR hung,
Sustained thy heavy load;
Wash'd all thy dreadful crimes away,
In streams of richest blood.

Survey, my soul, the wondrous LAMB,
Slain for the chosen seed:
Oh! the amazing, matchless grace,
That moved Him thus to bleed!

Deeply affecting 'tis to see
My JESUS bath'd in blood;
To view in Him the crimson path
That leads my soul to GOD.

Given the bare bones of the order, it is in these hymns that The Peculiars' eucharistic theology was mediated.

---

66 *A Collection of Hymns: for Camp Meetings, Revivals, &c., for the Use of Primitive Methodists*, New York, 1844. Information from Professor Robin Leaver.

67 *Covenant Hymns, Being a Collection of Psalms, Hymns and Spiritual Songs to the Praise and Glory of Jehovah, Father, Son, and Holy Ghost in Covenant*, London, 1849. Information from Robin Leaver.

68 *The Peculiar People's Hymn Book*, revised by Samuel Harrod and Others, Daws Heath: A. Chalk, 1891.

Concluding remarks

Although this chapter examines some very different groups from different centuries, it is interesting how several of these read the New Testament accounts and took them as the basis for separate consecration of the elements and, in some cases, separate administrations. On the whole they represent a minimalist approach, though the Moravians showed some creativity, and with the Catholic Apostolic Church we see a remarkable compilation inspired by the various classical Eastern and Western traditions and nineteenth-century liturgical scholarship.

14

The Twentieth-Century Liturgical and Ecumenical Movements: From Vatican II to 'Lima' 1982

The mid to the late decades of the twentieth century were marked by an unprecedented industry of liturgical revision in the major Churches of the West, stimulated by two intertwining movements that began much earlier, the Liturgical Movement and the Ecumenical Movement. The first was (and perhaps still is) a movement that strictly speaking began within the Roman Catholic Church as a renaissance and renewal of liturgical piety, though it had parallels in, and certainly became an influence upon, the Western main-line Protestant Churches.[1]

Although precursors may be found in the nineteenth century, the Liturgical Movement has become mainly associated with Dom Lambert Beauduin of the Abbey of Mont César, Louvain, in Belgium, Abbot Ildefons Herwegen of Maria Laach and Pius Parsch of the Abbey of Klosterneuburg.[2] At a parish and convent level, women played an important part in this renewal.[3] The renewal was accompanied by scholarly research, which in turn gave rise to a desire among some for reform. The movement was given recognition in the papal encyclical *Mediator Dei* of 1947, which also acknowledged that elements in the liturgy could and might be changed. Liturgy congresses were held in the 1950s with frank exchanges among scholars on the directions that reforms should take, if this was ever to come about. There was particular discussion about reform of the main Catholic service, the Mass. With the calling of the Second Vatican Council, initiated by Pope John XXIII and brought to fruition by Pope Paul VI, a wide-ranging renewal and reform of the Roman Church came about. The first major document stemming from the Council was the Constitution on the Sacred

---

1 Ernest B. Koenker, *The Liturgical Renaissance in the Roman Catholic Church*, St Louis: Concordia Press, 1966; John Fenwick and Bryan Spinks, *Worship in Transition: The Liturgical Movement in the Twentieth Century*, Edinburgh: T & T Clark, 1995.

2 Cuthbert Johnson, *Prosper Gueranger (1805–1875): A Liturgical Theologian*, Rome: Pontificio Ateneo S. Anselmo, 1984; Fenwick and Spinks, *Worship in Transition*; Bernard Botte, *From Silence to Participation: An Insider's View of Liturgical Renewal*, Washington: The Pastoral Press, 1988; Sonya A. Quitslund, *Beauduin: A Prophet Vindicated*, New York: Newman Press, 1983; Keith F. Pecklers, *The Unread Vision: The Liturgical Movement in the United States of America 1926–1955*, Collegeville: Liturgical Press, 1998.

3 Teresa Berger, *Women's Ways of Worship*, Collegeville: Pueblo Press, 1999, ch. 4; Katharine E. Harmon, *There Were Also Many Women There: Lay Women in the Liturgical Movement in the United States 1926–59*, Collegeville: Liturgical Press, 2012.

Liturgy (*Sacrosanctum Concilium*, *SC*), which led to revision of the Roman liturgical rites and ceremonies, including the Mass.

The Ecumenical Movement traces its origins to the Edinburgh World Missionary Conference in 1910, from which came the Faith and Order Movement, subsequently to become the World Council of Churches (WCC). Many Orthodox Churches have been and are full participants. The Roman Catholic Church has never become a full member of the WCC but is a member of Faith and Order. In 1937 a committee was appointed to study the traditions of worship of the various member churches as a way to assist co-operation, and the report, delayed by the War, was published in 1951 as *Ways of Worship*. The document recognized many similar pastoral concerns in worship, and noted that there was a 'liturgical movement' to be found in Churches of widely differing traditions. It noted that the liturgical scholars of the various Churches were looking back to their 'classic' periods, and there was a common desire to recover the 'original pattern'.[4] In the opinion of contemporary liturgical scholars, this latter idea was wishful thinking – there was no original pattern – but the practical implications were that Churches had similar pastoral liturgical needs, and were finding common pastoral liturgical solutions. In addition, the Churches shared the fruits of liturgical scholarship, which in the twentieth century lacked much of the partisanship that had marked previous eras. The net result was a broadly shared liturgical consensus among the main-line Western Churches concerning liturgical reforms, particularly as relating to the shape of the eucharistic *ordo* and the Eucharistic Prayer.

Vatican II and the Roman Catholic Mass

Sacrosanctum Concilium was promulgated on 4 December 1963. In addition to important statements about liturgy in general, it set out a programme for reform. Since the liturgy is made up of elements of change, these 'not only may but ought to be changed with the passage of time if they have suffered from the intrusion of anything out of harmony with the inner nature of the liturgy'.[5] In the restoration, texts and rites should be drawn up to express more clearly what they signify and to allow active participation. Scripture readings and scriptural songs are important ingredients (*SC* 24); the rites should be distinguished by a noble simplicity, and be short, clear and unencumbered by useless repetitions (*SC* 34). Latin is still important, but the limits of using the vernacular are to be extended (*SC* 36). As regards the Eucharist, the people

> should be instructed by God's word and nourished at the table of the Lord's body; they should give thanks to God; by offering the Immaculate Victim, not only through the hands of the priest, but also with him, they should learn also to offer themselves; through Christ the Mediator, they should be drawn day

4 P. Edwall, E. Hayman and W. D. Maxwell (eds), *Ways of Worship*, London: SCM Press, 1951, p. 16.

5 *SC* 21, http://www,vatican.va/archive/hist_councils/ii_vatican_council/documents/vat-ii_const_19631204_sacrosanctum-concilium_en.html.

by day into ever more perfect union with God and with each other, so that finally God may be all in all. (*SC* 48)

The Mass is to be revised so that its nature and purpose, and the connection between the various parts, is clearly seen, and the rite is to be simplified and duplications removed (*SC* 50). More Scripture is to be read, and the common prayers ('prayers of the people') are to be restored (*SC* 54). The faithful are to be encouraged to receive communion more regularly (*SC* 55).

Some interim measures followed, but the major work, which was put into the hands of liturgical experts (*periti*) and then revised and approved by curial groups, resulted in the Missal of 1969, known as the Missal of Paul VI. The rites were composed in Latin, and then subsequently Bishops' Conferences of the various linguistic areas arranged and approved (though with final approval from Rome) the translations.[6] On the whole, Latin celebrations became rare, and most celebrations were in the new vernacular translations. The new forms were not without their critics, who have increased in number in more recent years as a conservative longing for a supposed earlier golden era has been given some official encouragement.[7] Similarly the English translations were criticized. The translating was in the hands of ICEL (International Commission on English in the Liturgy), with its headquarters in the USA. The task of translating the Latin texts into English for the whole English-speaking world was a formidable task given how the language differs widely over the globe. British English is quite different from American English, which in turn differs from the English spoken in Australia.[8] The method used has been called 'dynamic equivalence', as opposed to literal translation.[9] There have been criticisms that the resulting texts were too bland, lacking cadence and beauty, and, perhaps more importantly, paraphrasing, rephrasing and deliberately mistranslating the Latin original.[10] Some perceived these latter tendencies to be traits of liberalism and the influence of Protestantism. The English texts were revised in 2010 for use from 2011 (see Chapter 16), but in this chapter the earlier ICEL translations are the focus.

In response to the directives concerning the removal of duplications and redundancies, a new *ordo* was set forth in the 1969 Missal:

- **Introductory rites**: Entrance Antiphon/song. Greeting. Penitential Rite with Kyries. *Gloria in excelsis* (except Advent and Lent). Collect.

6 Only the briefest of summaries can be given here. For details, see Annibale Bugnini, *The Reform of the Liturgy 1948–1975*; ET Collegeville: Liturgical Press, 1990; Piero Marini, *A Challenging Reform: Realizing the Vision of the Liturgical Movement*, Collegeville: Liturgical Press, 2007.

7 For fuller discussion, see John Baldovin, *Reforming the Liturgy: A Response to the Critics*, Collegeville: Liturgical Press, 2008; Bryan D. Spinks, *The Worship Mall: Contemporary Responses to Contemporary Culture*, New York: Church Publishing, 2010, pp. 183–203.

8 A problem raised by John McHugh, *On Englishing the Liturgy: An Open Letter to the Bishop of Shrewsbury*, Durham: Ushaw College, 1983.

9 Keith F. Pecklers, *Dynamic Equivalence: The Living Language of Christian Worship*, Collegeville: Liturgical Press, 2003.

10 Uwe Michael Lang, *The Voice of the Church at Prayer: Reflections on Liturgy and Language*, San Francisco: Ignatius Press, 2012.

- **Liturgy of the Word:** Old Testament. Responsorial Psalm. Epistle. Gospel Acclamation. Gospel. Homily. Prayers of the Faithful.
- **Eucharist:** Offertory antiphon. Prayers over the gifts. Eucharistic Prayer (choice). Lord's Prayer. Kiss of Peace. Fraction. Agnus Dei. Commixture. Communion. Communion antiphon.
- **Concluding rites:** Post-Communion Prayer. Blessing. Dismissal.

For the first time a confession and absolution were contained within the eucharistic *ordo*, since in the older rite it was in the private preparatory prayers. The Kyries were reformulated to be part of the penitential section.[11] The Scriptures were 'opened up' by providing a three-year lectionary, with an Old Testament reading and psalm, as well as Epistle/New Testament reading and a Gospel reading. A three-year lectionary was compiled, with some *lectio continua* readings of the Epistles, and particular years given over to the Gospel of Matthew and of Luke, with Mark supplemented with readings from John in the third year. This lectionary proved very attractive to other Churches, and in the English-speaking world has led to the Revised Common Lectionary. A homily is expected to be given at the principal Sunday Mass. Intercessions for Church and world have been 'restored' in the position given by Justin Martyr, and these are the most variable part of the rite.

In the eucharistic part of the rite, the prayers of the offertory, the so-called 'Little Canon', were completely revised.[12] A prayer over the gifts, *Oratio super oblata*, was retained, but the other prayers were replaced by two *berakah*-style prayers of offering relating to the bread and wine. Earlier schemes of revision had provided words from the *Didache* to be said quietly while holding the paten, and raising the cup the priest was to say: 'Wisdom has built a house for herself, she has mixed her wine, she has set her table. Glory to you, God, for ever.' The priest was to say the *In spiritu humilitatis* silently, and then recite the *Oratio super oblata*. The idea was not to draw attention to the 'laying of the table' or anticipate the offering made in the Eucharistic Prayer. However, the final text included the two *berakah*-style prayers, which were rendered in English as:

> Blessed are you, Lord, God of all creation. Through your goodness we have this bread to offer, which earth has given and human hands have made. It will become for us the bread of life. Blessed be God for ever.

> Blessed are you, Lord, God of all creation. Through your goodness we have this wine to offer, fruit of the vine and work of human hands. It will become our spiritual drink. Blessed be God for ever.

11 See Peter Jeffery, 'The Meanings and Functions of *Kyrie eleison*', in Bryan D. Spinks (ed.), *The Place of Christ in Liturgical Prayer: Trinity, Christology, and Liturgical Theology*, Collegeville: Liturgical Press, 2008. For the introductory section, see Mark Searle, 'Semper Reformanda: The Opening and Closing Rites of the Mass', in Peter C. Finn and James M. Schellman (eds), *Shaping English Liturgy*, Washington: Pastoral Press, 1990, pp. 53–92; James J. McFarland, *Announcing the Feast: The Entrance Song in the Mass of the Roman Rite*, Collegeville: Liturgical Press, 2012.

12 See Frederick R. McManus, 'The Roman Order of the Mass from 1964 to 1969: The Preparation of the Gifts', in Finn and Schellman (eds), *Shaping English Liturgy*, pp. 107–38.

These were to be said inaudibly when there was an offertory song, and may be said aloud when there is no song, though their popularity means that they have come to be recited, song or no song, and have been borrowed by other denominations. However, as Stevenson observed, together with the other rubrical directions, they gave the preparation of the table an importance that the authors of the earlier scheme had not intended.[13]

It is the Eucharistic Prayers that rightly draw most attention. At the beginning of the revision process it was thought that there would simply be a revision of the *canon missae*, and among proposals for that revision those of Hans Küng and Karl Amon were notable. In 1963 Küng suggested that revision was an ecumenical opportunity, and that the intercessions and mention of saints should be removed, and the Anamnesis rephrased with words from St Basil and St John Chrysostom, 'offer to your sovereign majesty from the gifts which you yourself have given us', making it more acceptable to Protestant concerns.[14] Amon's suggestion, published in 1965, included a new thanksgiving Preface covering creation and redemption in Christ, and leaving a reduced intercession until after the Institution Narrative. He omitted any petition for consecration.[15] Cipriano Vagaggini suggested only minor revisions to the canon and advocated adding two additional Eucharistic Prayers, one with a variable Preface and one with a fixed Preface.[16] Revision proceeded along the lines proposed by Vagaggini, though some also proposed that a fourth prayer of the Eastern type be added, and that it should be St Basil. The simple adoption of St Basil – already used by the Catholic Eastern rite congregations – was resisted by Vagaggini on the grounds that a consecratory Epiklesis after the Words of Institution would undermine traditional Western Catholic teaching. The Roman *canon missae*, with minimal stylistic emendation, remained as Eucharistic Prayer 1.[17] Three new prayers were compiled, but to meet the concern that had been raised by Vagaggini the new prayers, including that inspired by St Basil, followed a structure that has come to be called the *ingenium romanum*:

- Opening praise to the Father.
- Statement of motives for thanksgiving (variable or invariable).
- Sanctus.
- Post-Sanctus.
- Consecratory Epiklesis on the gifts.
- Institution Narrative.
- Anamnesis or memorial prayer with acclamations.
- Communion Epiklesis on/for the people.

13 Kenneth Stevenson, *Eucharist and Offering*, New York: Pueblo Press, 1986, p. 203.

14 ET in Cipriano Vagaggini, *The Canon of the Mass and Liturgical Reform*, London: Geoffrey Chapman, 1967, pp. 76–9.

15 Vagaggini, *Canon of the Mass*, pp. 79–83.

16 Vagaggini, *Canon of the Mass*, pp. 122–3.

17 A. M. Roguet and Lancelot Sheppard, 'Translation of the Roman Canon', in Lancelot Sheppard (ed.). *The New Liturgy: A Comprehensive Introduction*, London: Darton, Longman and Todd, 1970, pp. 161–73; Enrico Mazza, *The Eucharistic Prayers of the Roman Rite*, New York: Pueblo Publishing, 1986, pp. 49–87.

- Intercession.
- Closing Doxology.

The precedent that was claimed for this was the Egyptian *Deir Balyzeh* and Louvain fragments (Barcelona now also, but not available in the 1960s), which are indeed precedents, though many would regard them as obscure and weak precedents. The pre-narrative consecratory Epiklesis insured that the consecratory effects of the Words of Institution would not be undermined by subsequent consecratory petitions. The compilation, Kavanagh noted, produced tensions of conflicting expert opinions that even Solomon could not have resolved.[18]

Prayer II was modelled directly on the Anaphora of the *Apostolic Tradition* (*AT*). It should be recalled that in the 1960s all serious liturgical scholars were of the opinion that this anaphora was by Hippolytus of Rome (*c.* 215), representing Roman tradition, and was the oldest authentic anaphora that had come down to us. One of the experts involved in the new compilations was Dom Bernard Botte, who had prepared a critical edition of the so-called *AT*.[19] Even if it was *c.* 215, it purports to be a Eucharistic Prayer recited at an ordination, and not a typical Sunday Eucharistic Prayer, but somehow scholarship of the 1960s became blind to this, and, as will be noted, it became the basis for Eucharistic Prayers in a number of denominations. Current scholarship suggests that today this would not be the case. In the case of the Roman Prayer II, since the Anaphora of *AT* lacks Sanctus and intercessions and has only an embryonic Epiklesis after the narrative, the prayer had to be revised to fit the *ingenium romanum* structure, with the addition of a Sanctus with Post-Sanctus, a consecratory Epiklesis (ICEL: 'Let your Spirit come upon these gifts to make them holy, so that they may become for us the body and blood of our Lord, Jesus Christ'), a communion Epiklesis (ICEL: 'May all of us who share in the body and blood of Christ be brought together in unity by the Holy Spirit'), and intercessions. Aidan Kavanagh astutely observed that the result was that the intercessory/consecratory section is greater than the section devoted to thanksgiving, rather making it 'a prayer for consecration of the elements more than anything else'.[20] The Anamnesis/offering slightly expanded the *AT* text, 'we offer you, Father, this life-giving bread, this saving cup'. The fruits of communion were reduced from the original text, though the overall eschatology is strengthened by the addition of intercessions with mention of the hope of resurrection.

The inspiration for Prayer III is disputed. Louis Bouyer was certain that it was based on the Gallican/Visigothic models, and had used the *Vere Sanctus* from a Visigothic feast of the Circumcision.[21] Adrian Nocent believed it to be inspired by an Egyptian model, but the Dutch Scholar Herman Wegman, supported by Enrico Mazza, believed it to be based on the model of the Roman

18 Aidan Kavanagh, 'Thoughts on the New Eucharistic Prayers', reprinted in R. Kevin Seasoltz (ed.), *Living Bread, Saving Cup*, Collegeville: Liturgical Press, 1982, p. 103.

19 Bernard Botte, *La Tradition Apostolique de saint Hippolyte*, LQF 39, Münster: Aschendorff, 1963.

20 Kavanagh, 'Thoughts on the New Eucharistic Prayers', p. 107.

21 Louis Bouyer, 'The Third Eucharistic Prayer', in Sheppard (ed.), *New Liturgy*, pp. 203–12.

canon missae, and was a response to Vagaggini's proposals.[22] It has no Preface and so any Preface or Proper Preface in the Missal can be used to begin this prayer. The *Vere Sanctus* echoes Malachi 1.11: 'From age to age you gather a people to yourself, so that from east to west a perfect offering may be made to the glory of your name.' The first Epiklesis has the request: 'We ask you to make [the gifts] holy by the power of your Spirit, that they may become the body and blood of your Son, our Lord Jesus Christ, at whose command we celebrate this eucharist.' The Anamnesis/offering has 'we offer you in thanksgiving this holy and living sacrifice. Look with favour on your Church's offering, and see the Victim whose death has reconciled us to yourself' (cf. *SC* 48).

Prayer IV echoes the Syro-Byzantine pattern of prayer, other than placing the consecratory Epiklesis before the Institution Narrative. It has been regarded as an extremely rich prayer in its theology. Aidan Kavanagh, though, regarded its offering terminology as novel. The ICEL text read: 'we offer you his body and blood, the acceptable sacrifice which brings salvation to the whole world. Lord, look upon this sacrifice which you have given to your Church . . .' Kavanagh commented:

> The meaning is clear: what is offered is understood to be the real presence of Christ's body and blood, which is the acceptable offering *given* to the church through the extraordinary power of the Spirit and the *verba Domini*. This is quite different from the other Prayers since here we find an offering of the Blessed Sacrament rather than of the church. This is novel, and can hardly be said to retain 'a most definitely traditional character.' One who has some acquaintance with the medieval and reformation history of eucharistic controversy will recognize the inadequacy of such a position, and may be forgiven his disappointment that its tendentiousness has got into a Catholic formulary precisely at a time when it could have been diagnosed and avoided most easily.[23]

The prayer does have a forceful eschatological vision. After mention of the pope and clergy, it prayed:

> Remember those who take part in this offering, those here present and all your people, and all who seek you with a sincere heart. Remember those who have died in the peace of Christ and all the dead whose faith is known to you alone. Father, in your mercy grant also to us, your children, to enter into our heavenly inheritance in the company of the Virgin Mary, the Mother of God, and your apostles and saints. Then, in your kingdom, freed from the corruption of sin and death, we shall sing your glory with every creature through Christ our Lord, through whom you give us everything that is good.

Whatever the problem over the phraseology of the eucharistic sacrifice, the prayer was regarded as a paradigm for an ecumenical Eucharistic Prayer in North America, and in revised form is found in some Protestant worship books.

22 For Nocent, Wegman and Mazza, see Mazza, *Eucharistic Prayers of the Roman Rite*, p. 123.

23 Kavanagh, 'Thoughts on the New Eucharistic Prayers', pp. 108–9.

Whereas the Eastern Churches and the other non-Roman Western traditions had enjoyed a number of anaphoras, Rome had only the *canon missae*, and that became the sole Eucharistic Prayer of the Western Church. Even Reformation Churches tended to give only one reformed version of 'consecration'. The provision of new prayers was to open up an industry of composition of new Eucharistic Prayers in most Western main-line Churches. With the euphoria of reform, a number of individual Catholics began publishing Eucharistic Prayers, and some of these gained semi-official status for a time. The prime example was the Dutch Church. The 1970 Missal published by the Dutch bishops contained the official Eucharistic Prayers, and in an appendix provided a further 11 by different authors. Among the authors listed, which included the Dutch liturgical scholar Herman Wegman, two (XII and XIII) were by the well-known priest-poet Huub Oosterhuis, whose Table Prayers have been translated into many languages including English. These two particular prayers shared Proper Prefaces, and XIII gave thanks for creation, for the work of Jesus Christ, leading into the Institution Narrative. The Anamnesis read, 'Therefore we set before you this sign of our faith', which is rather a different theology from that of Eucharistic Prayer IV.[24]

The Prayers of Oosterhuis, along with those of Thierry Maertens and American authors such as Robert F. Hoey, were the subject of a detailed study by John Barry Ryan, showing their virtues and faults.[25] One of the great attractions was the fresh, direct and more intimate language, though sometimes the theology was questionable. They had a modern feel about them, or a 'Sixties feel', and were not simply new prayers copying classical fourth-century prayers and vocabulary.[26] Bugnini notes, 'As a result of uncontrolled production, over a hundred models were in circulation, some of them clearly deficient.'[27] The result was that the Congregation for Divine Worship called upon Episcopal Conferences to brand such prayers as illicit. After careful study of some of the new compositions, it was concluded that new Eucharistic Prayers might be submitted by Synods or Episcopal Conferences for scrutiny by Rome, but authorization for use could only be given by the appropriate authority in Rome. However, in 1973, the Pope did authorize the Congregation for Divine Worship to prepare two or three formularies for the entire Church. In November 1973 it was decided to compose three Eucharistic Prayers for Masses with Children and two for the Holy Year, which were constructed on the theme of reconciliation.

24 'Daarom stellen wij dit teken van ons geloof', Nederlandse Commissie voor Liturgie, *Missaal, deel 1. Ordo Missae*, Hilversum: N. V. Gooi en Sticht, 1970, p. 131. ET in Huub Oosterhuis, *Open Your Hearts*, New York: Herder and Herder, 1971, p. 17.

25 John Barry Ryan, *The Eucharistic Prayer: A Study in Contemporary Liturgy*, New York: Paulist Press, 1974. For further on the Dutch experiments, see H. A. J. Wegman, *Goed of niet goed? Het eucharistisch gebed in Nederland* (Deel 1), Hilversum: Gooi en Sticht, 1976 and H. Manders and H. Wegman (eds), *Goed of niet goed? Het eucharistisch gebed in Nederland*, Deel 2, Hilversum: Gooi en Sticht, 1978.

26 Hugh McLeod, *The Religious Crisis of the 1960s*, Oxford: Oxford University Press, 2007. The direct style of the private prayers of Michel Quoist were also popular at this time. See also Bryan D. Spinks, 'Christian Worship or Cultural Incantations?', *Studia Liturgica* 12 (1977), pp. 1–19.

27 Bugnini, *Reform of the Liturgy 1948–1975*, p. 465.

All five were promulgated in 1975.[28] They were approved for experimental use and were not to be included in the Roman Missal.

The Eucharistic Prayers for children are marked by a simpler and more direct language style. All three are interspersed with congregational acclamations – Sanctus and Benedictus in 1; 'Glory to God in the highest' or 'Hosanna in the highest', and 'We praise you, we bless you, we thank you' in 2; and 'Glory to God in the highest' or some other suitable acclamation of praise in two places in the post-Anamnesis in 3. The consecratory Epiklesis in 1 prayed, 'We bring you bread and wine and ask you to send your Holy Spirit to make these gifts the body and blood of Jesus your Son. Then we can offer to you what you have given to us.' There is no further offering in this prayer. Prayer 2 requested God to send the Holy Spirit 'to change these gifts of bread and wine into the body and blood of Jesus Christ, our Lord', and had the Anamnesis, 'And so, loving Father, we remember that Jesus died and rose again to save the world. He put himself into our hands to be the sacrifice we offer you.' The eschatology unfolds in the post-narrative Epiklesis, asking the Spirit to bring us closer together in the family of God, and remembering family, friends, the departed, and asks:

> Gather us all together into your kingdom. There we shall be happy for ever with the Virgin Mary, Mother of God and our mother. There all the friends of Jesus the Lord will sing a song of joy.

Prayer 3 requested the Father to bless the gifts and make them holy and change them, and the Anamnesis affirmed, 'In this holy sacrifice, which he gave as a gift to his Church, we remember his death and resurrection.'

The less formal style of these prayers, necessary for children, was also extended for an adult register of language in the two prayers for reconciliation.[29] The Preface of Prayer 2, for example, which had originally been composed in German, read in the ICEL version:

> Father, all-powerful and ever-living God, we praise and thank you through Jesus Christ our Lord for your presence and action in the world. In the midst of conflict and division, we know it is you who turn our minds to thoughts of peace. Your Spirit changes our hearts: enemies begin to speak to one another, those who were estranged join hands in friendship, and nations seek the way of peace together. Your Spirit is at work when understanding puts an end to strife, when hatred is quenched by mercy, and vengeance gives way to forgiveness.

The Anamnesis prayed:

> Lord our God, your Son has entrusted to us this pledge of his love. We celebrate the memory of his death and resurrection and bring you the gift you

---

28 Details in Bugnini, *Reform of the Liturgy*, p. 476; Marini, *Challenging Reform*, p. 147.

29 For detailed discussion of these prayers, see Richard E. McCarron, 'EP RI and II. History of the Latin Text and Rite', in Edward Foley (ed.), *A Commentary on the Order of Mass of the Roman Missal*, Collegeville: Liturgical Press, 2011, pp. 453–63.

> have given us, the sacrifice of reconciliation. Therefore, we ask you, Father, to accept us, together with your Son. Fill us with his Spirit through our sharing in this meal. May he take away all that divides us.

The eschatological vision is again powerful:

> You have gathered us here around the table of your Son, in fellowship with the Virgin Mary, Mother of God, and all the saints. In that new world where the fullness of your peace will be revealed gather people of every race, language, and way of life to share in the one eternal banquet with Jesus Christ the Lord.

Joyce Ann Zimmerman has commented that this particular prayer might function as a sort of 'truth and reconciliation commission' for the liturgical assembly.[30]

Bishops' Conferences were able to submit prayers for approval for particular occasions or for their nation. That submitted by the Swiss Synod was approved for use, and subsequently approved for other countries, under the title 'Eucharistic Prayer for Use in Masses for Various Needs'. The original prayer in German, French and Italian was approved in 1974, and an English interim translation for use in the USA was issued in 1994. The prayer has variable Prefaces, and intercessory sections, recalling the Gallican and Hispano-Mozarabic Anaphoras.[31] Prayers submitted by India and the English-speaking world were not approved, but among those approved for a particular occasion and for a particular country are the Aboriginal Prayer and the Eucharistic Prayer for Zaire. The former, approved for use at a congress in 1973, was a short prayer, almost all constructed as a call-and-response prayer. The preamble explained that traditions, myths and religious beliefs are handed down by the use of the spoken word, in song or formal ceremonial conversation. Thus the Preface began:

> Cel: May the Father in heaven make you good in your hearts.
>
> All: May he make you good in your heart.
>
> Cel: Listen to the word of the Lord Jesus.
>
> All: We will listen.
>
> Cel: Father in heaven, you love us. You made all things.
>
> All: Father, you are good.

30 Joyce Ann Zimmerman, 'EP RII. The Mystagogical Implications', in Foley (ed.), *A Commentary*, p. 503.

31 Richard E. McCarron, 'History of the Text' and 'Theology of the Latin Text and Rite', in Foley (ed.), *A Commentary*, pp. 549–56 and 557–70. For problems with the Epiklesis in the original French version, see Paul de Clerk, 'Epiclèse et formulation du mystère eucharistique', in Andreas Heinz and Heinrich Rennings (eds), *Gratias Agamus: Studien zum eucharistischen Hochgebet: Für Balthasar Fischer*, Freiburg: Herder, 1992, pp. 53–6.

The Narrative of Institution was in the continuous present tense, 'he calls you good, Father. He breaks bread. And he says to his friends . . .'.[32]

The Zaire Mass was composed in 1973, though not finally approved until 1988. It was concerned to express certain traditional African values, such as the active presence of God as creator of the world, life as an ultimate gift, the family and community, and the nature and role of the Ancestors.[33] The Eucharistic Prayer, which, like the Aboriginal Prayer, is peppered with congregational acclamations, describes God as 'the sun too bright for our gaze' and thanksgiving includes for 'our river the Zaire, our forests, our rivers, our lakes'.

The removal of accretions, the fuller use of Scripture, the restoration of prayers of the faithful, and the plurality of Eucharistic Prayers have all had an impact on other Churches and the emergence of an 'ecumenical *ordo*'. The emerging similarity in structures across the Churches can be illustrated by the following chart comparing the Episcopal rite (1979), the British Methodist rite (1975), the Lutheran *Book of Worship* (1978) and the British United Reformed Church (1980).

Meth. 1975	Epis. 1979 (Rite II)	URC 1980	LBW 1978
Hymn Collect for Purity	[Hymn] Greeting	Call to Worship Prayer of Approach	Hymn Greeting
	Collect for Purity	Hymn	Kyrie, Gloria, or 'This is the feast'
[Commandments]	Kyries, Trisagion or Gloria	Confession	
		Assurance of Pardon	Collect of the day
Confession Declaration of Pardon		*Gloria in exclesis*	
Collect of Day (or other prayer)	Collect of the Day	or Kyries Prayer for Grace	
Gloria in excelsis		Theme of the day	
Old Testament reading, or Epistle, or both	Old Testament reading Psalm	Old Testament Psalm, hymn or canticle	First reading Psalm

32 Max Thurian and Geoffrey Wainwright (eds), *Baptism and Eucharist: Ecumenical Convergence in Celebration*, Geneva: WCC, and Grand Rapids: Eerdmans, 1983, pp. 198–201.

33 Chris Nwaka Egbulem, 'An African Interpretation of Liturgical Inculturation: The Rite Zairois', in Michael Downey and Richard Fragomeni (eds), *A Promise of Presence*, Washington: Pastoral Press, 1992, pp. 227–50. Edouard Kabongo, *Le Rite Zaïrois*, Frankfurt am Main: Peter Lang, 2008. Experimental text in English in Thurian and Wainwright, *Baptism and Eucharist*, pp. 205–9.

Gospel	Epistle	New Testament reading	Second reading
Sermon	Gospel or Epistle and Gospel		Alleluia Gospel
Intercessions	Homily	Sermon	Sermon
Peace	Creed	Hymn	Hymn of the day
Creed	Intercessions	Intercessions	Creed
Hymn	Confession		Intercessions
Eucharistic Prayer	Absolution	Peace	Peace
Fraction			
	Peace	Offertory and Hymn	Offertory
Pre-communion prayer	Eucharistic Prayer	Reading of Institution	Offertory prayer
Communion	Lord's Prayer		
	Fraction	Taking of bread and wine	
Silence	Invitation and Communion	Eucharistic Prayer	Eucharistic Prayer
Prayer	Post-communion	Lord's Prayer	Lord's Prayer
Hymn		Fraction	[optional Fraction]
Blessing and dismissal	Blessing and dismissal	Communion	Communion
		Post-communion	Post-communion
		Hymn	Blessing and dismissal
		Blessing and dismissal	

Given that more Eucharistic Prayers have been compiled in the twentieth century than in all previous centuries, it is simply impossible to comment upon all but a small sample from a small number of denominations.

As the WCC 1951 report had noted, the insights and aims of the Roman Catholic Church had spread to, or were shared by, other Churches, and often first steps can be traced prior to Vatican II, though all Churches were influenced by the Vatican II liturgies. In 1947 the Anglican Church in South India joined in a union with Methodists, Congregationalists and Presbyterians to form the Church of South India. The first synod of the new Church appointed a committee, with Leslie Brown as the Convenor, an Anglican who had been a friend of A. G. Hebert, a proponent of the ideals of the Catholic Liturgical Movement, and he drew on the insights of Hebert's writings. Under Brown's convenorship, the committee compiled a eucharistic liturgy that drew on earlier Anglican, Presbyterian and Methodist traditions, on the Syrian liturgy of St James, which was used by many of the Syrian Church Indians, and was also inspired by *AT*. Revisions of drafts and trial uses resulted in the *Book of Common Worship* (1963). The Liturgy of the Word was to be capable of standing as a complete service to be celebrated when no presbyter was available. Full congregational participation was another basic principle, and responses and acclamations were hallmarks of this. The Peace was another feature, strange at the time, and the westward position of the celebrant at the Eucharist. The confession and absolution came at the beginning. At the offertory, presbyter and people prayed together: 'Be present, be present, O Jesus, our good High Priest, as you were with your disciples, and make yourself known to us in the breaking of the bread.'

A Eucharistic Prayer was compiled giving thanks for creation and the whole salvific work of Christ. It articulated a concept of offering and presence, which in its 1972 edition prayed:

> And we humbly ask you Father, to take us and this bread and wine, that we offer to you, and make them your own by your Holy Spirit, so that our breaking of the bread will be a sharing in Christ's body and the cup we bless a sharing in his blood.

What was most significant was that here was a Church with a close relationship with the Anglican Communion having a liturgy that departed more from Cranmer than any previous official Anglican rite.

The place of the Prayer Book was the subject of the 1958 Lambeth Conference. Its report challenged Anglicans to recover primitive elements for the communion service – the use of an Old Testament lesson and, in the Eucharistic Prayer, thanksgiving for the mighty works of God and provision for more lay participation. It practically endorsed the structure of the Church of South India liturgy, which is perhaps not surprising given that the secretary of this sub-committee at Lambeth was Dr Leslie Brown, by then Archbishop of Uganda. It was also noted that there were two strains of eucharistic liturgy in Anglicanism – one based on 1549/1637 and the other based on 1552/1662. Between these was a tension on the idea of presence and sacrifice. It was suggested that the idea of the eternal sacrifice of Christ into which we enter might be a way forward for all parties. As different provinces embarked upon liturgical revision, two later documents, the so-called Pan Anglican Documents, were issued in 1965 and 1969, in order to give some common principles and goals of revision. The 1969 document outlined eight basic elements of the Eucharist: preparation, ministry of the word, the prayers (i.e. intercessions), offertory, thanksgiving over bread and wine, breaking of the bread, communion and dismissal. The content of the thanksgiving was outlined as follows:

> The basic elements and progression of this eucharistic prayer are:
>
> (a) *Sursum Corda*.
> (b) The proclamation and recital of the mighty acts of God in creation, redemption, and sanctification.
> (c) The Narrative of the Institution.
> (d) The Anamnesis of the work of Christ in Death, Resurrection, and Ascension 'until he come'. It is recognized that this is the most difficult section of the prayer in view of the different doctrinal emphases which are expressed and recognized within the Anglican Communion. The whole

concept of anamnesis is, however, so rich in meaning that it should not be impossible to express it in such a way that the needs of everyone are met. Whatever language is adopted should, however, avoid any idea of a propitiatory sacrifice or a repetition of Christ's sacrifice. The 'once for all' character of his work must not be obscured.

(e) The prayer that through the sharing of the bread and wine and through the power of the Holy Spirit we may be made one with our Lord and so renewed in the Body of Christ.

The whole prayer is rightly set in the context of praise, for example *Sursum corda* and Sanctus.[34]

The resulting liturgical revision across the Anglican Communion was profuse, and those between 1958 and 1984 (and not taking account of various trial liturgies) are collected in three volumes edited by Colin Buchanan. Only three provinces are selected for mention here.[35]

In England a Liturgical Commission had been appointed in 1954. It was reshaped in 1964 under Archbishop Michael Ramsey, and embarked upon experimental liturgical forms which eventually would form a book to be used alongside the 1662 *BCP*. Small booklets listed as Series 1, 2 and 3 were issued over the next few years. Series 1 was basically 1662 and 1928 material rearranged. The Eucharistic Prayer was unified by joining up the *Sursum corda*, Preface and Sanctus with the Prayer of Consecration and the Prayer of Oblation. The Church militant prayer was separated into paragraphs and made responsorial. Series 2 was a new compilation, but still in Tudor/Stuart language. The Eucharist was more streamlined, with new prayers and a new Eucharistic Prayer inspired by the writings of Justin Martyr and *AT*. It was mainly the work of E. C. Ratcliff and Arthur Couratin. It became controversial for Evangelicals, because it offered the bread and cup, and the final approved version was altered to 'make the memorial', leading to the resignation of Couratin from the Commission.[36] In the wake of Vatican II's adoption of the modern vernacular, Series 3 services were compiled in contemporary English.[37] Although Series 3 had contained only one Eucharistic Prayer, the final liturgical book, entitled *The Alternative Service Book 1980*, had four Eucharistic Prayers in its contemporary English rite. The division over eucharistic sacrifice in the Anglican Communion identified by the 1958 Lambeth Conference report was intensified in the Church of England between the Anglo-Catholic and Evangelical parties. Since the idea was that all clergy should be able to use the Eucharistic Prayers with a good conscience, the final texts had to be acceptable to all. All four had a similar structure with a consecratory petition coming

34 Colin O. Buchanan (ed.), *Further Anglican Liturgies 1968–1975*, Bramcote: Grove Books, 1975, p. 30.

35 Colin Buchanan (ed.), *Modern Anglican Liturgies 1958–68*, Oxford: Oxford University Press, 1968; *Further Anglican Liturgies 1968–75*; *Latest Anglican Liturgies 1976–1984*, London: SPCK, 1985.

36 For the exchanges over this, see the articles in *Theology* 69 (1966) and 70 (1967). Ratcliff was by then deceased.

37 R. C. D. Jasper (ed.), *The Eucharist Today: Studies on Series 3*, London: SPCK, 1974.

prior to the Institution Narrative.[38] Prayers 1 and 2 had the same phraseology, 'grant that by the power of your Holy Spirit these gifts of bread and wine may be to us his body and blood'. Prayer 3 was very similar, whereas Prayer 4 used Cranmerian wording:

> grant that by the power of your Holy Spirit we who receive these gifts of your creation, this bread and this wine, according to your Son our Saviour Jesus Christ's holy institution, in remembrance of the death that he suffered, may be partakers of his most blessed body and blood.

Prayer 1, the direct descendant of Series 3, requested in the Anamnesis, 'As we look for his coming in glory, we celebrate with this bread and this cup his one perfect sacrifice.'[39] Prayer 2 retained the old Series 2 phraseology, 'we make with this bread and this cup the memorial of Christ your Son our Lord'. Prayer 3 had 'we bring before you this bread and this cup', which represented a more benign English rendering of the Latin *offerimus* of *AT*. Prayer 4 offered the sacrifice of praise and thanksgiving. All four had the same Institution Narrative, which apparently had been insisted upon by Archbishop Michael Ramsey, on the grounds that he liked to pray these by memory looking heavenward, and thus needed a single version to memorize.

The Episcopal Church in the USA had started revision also in the 1950s, but its eventual new liturgy emerged in stages in the late 1960s and early 1970s. As it had already, since 1789/90, contained the word 'offer', and had a petition for the Spirit to come upon the elements, these could hardly be controversial as they had been in the Church of England. Its *Book of Common Prayer*, published in 1976, was adopted by General Convention in 1979. It too contained four Eucharistic Prayers in its modern version.[40] The first two, which had Proper Prefaces, were inspired by *AT* and the older 1789 prayer. Prayer A offered the gifts and requested that God would 'Sanctify them by your Holy Spirit to be for your people the Body and Blood of your Son'; Prayer B 'presents' the bread and wine, and requests the sending of the Spirit upon the gifts so that 'they may be the Sacrament of the Body of Christ and his Blood of the new Covenant'. The eschatological section of this prayer echoes some of the Roman prayers: 'in the fullness of time, put all things in subjection under your Christ where with [provision for listing saints' names] . . . all your saints, we may enter the everlasting heritage of your sons and daughters'. Prayer C, which has come to be called 'star-trek' because of its mention of 'vast expanse of interstellar space, galaxies, suns, the planets in their courses', was composed by Captain Howard Galley of the Church Army. It allowed congregational participation, and has a consecratory Epiklesis before

---

38 R. C. D. Jasper and Paul F. Bradshaw (eds), *A Companion to the Alternative Service Book 1980*, London: SPCK, 1986, pp. 213–31, for commentary and background history to the compilation of each Eucharistic Prayer.

39 See Paul Bradshaw, 'Celebrate', in *The Eucharist Today*.

40 H. B. Porter, 'An American Assembly of Anaphoral Prayers', in Bryan D. Spinks (ed.), *The Sacrifice of Praise: Studies on the Themes of Thanksgiving and Redemption in the Central Prayers of the Eucharistic and Baptismal Liturgies: In Honour of Arthur Hubert Couratin*, Rome: CLV Edizioni Liturgiche, 1981, pp. 181–96; Marion J. Hatchett, *Commentary on the American Prayer Book*, New York: HarperCollins, 1995.

the Narrative of Institution, 'we . . . now bring before you these gifts. Sanctify them by your Holy Spirit to be the Body and Blood of Jesus Christ our Lord.' It links the Church with its Jewish roots, calling on God of our Fathers, 'God of Abraham, Isaac, and Jacob'. Prayer D is 'A Common Eucharistic Prayer', compiled in 1975 by a group of liturgical scholars representing Lutheran, Episcopal, Methodist, Presbyterian and Roman Catholic traditions, and was based directly on Roman Catholic Eucharistic Prayer IV, 'recognizing this prayer as having a style and spirit of great beauty and spiritual depth, and deriving from the ancient and justly respected anaphora attributed to St. Basil'.[41]

Finally in this Anglican selection, *An Australian Prayer Book 1978* had to balance a variety of churchmanship including the Anglo-Catholic diocese of Ballerat and the ultra-conservative Evangelical diocese of Sydney. It was Australia's first liturgy since becoming an independent province and having hitherto the exclusive use of the 1662 *BCP*. The Eucharistic Prayer in the Second Order, which was a new compilation, prayed before the Institution Narrative:

> Merciful Father, we thank you for these gifts of your creation, this bread and this wine, and we pray that we who eat and drink them in the fellowship of the Holy Spirit in obedience to our Saviour Christ in remembrance of his death and passion may be partakers of his body and his blood.

The Anamnesis prayed:

> Father, with this bread and this cup, we do as our Saviour has commanded; we celebrate the redemption he has won for us; we proclaim his perfect sacrifice made once for all upon the cross, his mighty resurrection and glorious ascension; and we look for his coming to fulfil all things according to your will. Renew us by your Holy Spirit, unite us in the body of your Son, and bring us with all your people into the joy of your eternal kingdom.

The phraseology seems to meet any (diocese of Sydney?) Low Church sensibilities in that both the pre-narrative and post-narrative Epikleses associate the Spirit with the assembly only and not the elements. Though adopted for use in the diocese of Sydney, the latter's constant move to an extreme caricature of Reformation doctrine means the prayer was not widely used there. The three provinces chosen illustrate the wider Anglican sensibilities and breadth of eucharistic belief.

The Lutheran tradition inherited the German patterns that were modelled closely on Luther with the Words of Institution being the heart of the Eucharist, with only a Preface and Sanctus or no prayer at all; and the Swedish tradition that had retained a longer eucharistic section prior to the Institution. Certain High Church movements in Germany had authored eucharistic rites with something approaching the classical Eucharistic Prayer.[42] However, the rite of 1955 as revised in 1977 represented a halfway approach. A number of options were

---

41 Porter, 'American Assembly of Anaphoral Prayers', p. 192.

42 Arne Giewald and Günther Thoman, *The Lutheran High Church Movement in Germany and Its Liturgical Work: An Introduction*, Lulu.com, Raleigh, nd (2012?).

offered, varying from a short Preface, Sanctus, Lord's Prayer and the narrative, to a pre-narrative petition, 'Lord, send down upon us the Holy Spirit, sanctify and renew us in body and soul, and grant that under this bread and wine, we receive in true faith the very body and blood of your Son to our salvation', with an Anamnesis after the narrative, linking the remembering in the Eucharist with the intercession of Christ in heaven and the marriage feast of the Lamb.[43] The Church of Sweden's rite of 1975 introduced a much fuller Eucharistic Prayer which asked God to send the Spirit to create in us a living faith, and also to sanctify the bread and wine, 'so that we, through them, partake of the true body and blood of our Lord Jesus Christ'. More remarkable was the Anamnesis, which asked God (with some deliberate ambiguity) to 'look upon the perfect and everlasting sacrifice through which you reconciled us to yourself in Christ'. However, it was in the USA, where the Lutheran Churches came from different synods and ethnic groups that the concept of a Eucharistic Prayer was hotly debated. The Confessional Lutheran Church–Missouri Synod had invited the larger Lutheran Church of America and the American Lutheran Church (the two latter would later merge as the Evangelical Lutheran Church in America) to embark on liturgical revision to produce a common liturgy for American Lutherans.[44] In the course of proposals for a fuller Eucharistic Prayer, scholars such as Oliver Olsen, Paul Rorem and Gottfried G. Krodel were fiercely critical of any attempt to enclose the Institution Narrative within a prayer, suggesting that it totally contradicted Luther's clear teaching on the Mass.[45] Frank Senn's appeal to the Church of Sweden's canon in the 1576 'Red Book' of King Johan III fell on unreceptive descendants of German Confessionalism and Norwegian pietism.[46] Over this and many other doctrinal issues the Lutheran Church–Missouri Synod withdrew at the moment of publication from the 1978 *Lutheran Book of Worship* and compiled its own book, *Lutheran Worship*, in 1982. The former provided a Preface and Sanctus with provision for either a full Eucharistic Prayer, the Institution Narrative alone, or the Institution Narrative introduced with a very brief prayer. The post-narrative Epiklesis in the first option avoided any reference to the Spirit upon the elements, and simply asked for the Spirit, 'that we may receive the Lord's body and blood'. The latter included a reprint of the older Common Service, which was based upon a classical Lutheran rite;[47] a second order with *Sursum corda*, Preface, Sanctus and Benedictus, and a short introductory prayer to the narrative; and a third

43 Text in Thurian and Wainwright, *Baptism and Eucharist*, pp. 136–40.

44 Ralph W. Quere, *In the Context of Unity: A History of the Development of Lutheran Book of Worship*, Minneapolis: Lutheran University Press of Minneapolis, 2003, for the historical details.

45 Oliver K. Olsen, 'Contemporary Trends in Liturgy Viewed from the Perspective of Classical Lutheran Theology', *Lutheran Quarterly* 26 (1974), pp. 101–57; Paul Rorem, 'Luther's Objections to a Eucharistic Prayer', *The Cresset* 38:5 (1975), pp. 12–16; Gottfried G. Krodel, 'The Great Thanksgiving of the Inter-Lutheran Commission on Worship: It is the Christian's Supper and not the Lord's Supper', *The Cresset Occasional Paper* 1, 1976.

46 Frank C. Senn, 'Liturgia Svecanae Ecclesiae: An Attempt at Eucharistic Restoration During the Swedish Reformation', *Studia Liturgica* 14 (1980–1), pp. 20–36.

47 For the Common Service, see Luther Reed, *The Lutheran Liturgy*, Philadelphia: Fortress Press, 1947; Ralph W. Quere, *In the Context of Unity*.

rite which claimed to be inspired by Luther's *Deutsch Messe*, with an admonition, Lord's Prayer, recitation of the *verba*, and Hymn 214, a hymn version of the Sanctus. Luther's forms and theology dominated, though the corollary of this was that Luther's teaching is not directly reinforced in liturgical prayer, but only indirectly by refusal to use a Eucharistic Prayer and refusal to use an Epiklesis. However, it is by no means evident to all that Luther's teaching is incompatible with a Eucharistic Prayer and an Epiklesis.[48]

The French Reformed Church published a revised liturgy in 1963, with a Eucharistic Prayer in which the Words of Institution were read as a warrant after a Preface and Sanctus, and after the narrative the celebrant says 'Let us pray' before continuing in prayer. The offering was of ourselves, and the Holy Spirit too was invoked upon 'us', suggesting that the Spirit changes us so that we may receive Christ's body and blood in the elements. This section of prayer ended with words from *Didache* 9 for the ingathering of the Church. An interesting invitation to communion was provided:[49]

> Blessed are they that hunger and thirst after righteousness, for they shall be filled! Blessed are they whom Thou dost take with Thee to feed them with the blessings of Thy house! Blessed are they that are invited to the marriage feast of the Lamb! Come, says Jesus, for everything is prepared!

Words from 1 Corinthians 10 were recited at the Fraction, and a dismissal in peace was given after each 'serving' of communion. In the United Kingdom, the Church of Scotland produced a new communion rite in 1979 and the United Reformed Church a new rite in 1980.[50] Each had three communion orders and thus three prayers. The first Scottish order followed the tradition of the nineteenth-century *Euchologion*, with a Eucharistic Prayer that contained the Words of Institution, but the intercessions for living and dead came after the prayer, echoing the Catholic Apostolic influence from the nineteenth century. The Anamnesis came before the Institution Narrative and used terminology that first came into the Church of Scotland liturgy via Canada in 1940:

> Wherefore, having in remembrance the work and passion of our Saviour Jesus Christ, and pleading his eternal sacrifice, we thy servants set forth this memorial, which he hath commanded us to make, who in the same night . . . [institution narrative][51]

The phrase 'pleading his eternal sacrifice' occurred also in the other two prayers, though after the narrative. All three prayers invoked God for the Spirit

48 Bryan D. Spinks, 'Berakah, Anaphoral Theory and Luther', *Lutheran Quarterly* 3 (1989), pp. 267–80.

49 Thurian and Wainwright, *Baptism and Eucharist*, p. 151.

50 *The Book of Common Order (1979)*, Edinburgh: St Andrew Press, 1979; *A Book of Services*, Edinburgh: St Andrew Press, 1980.

51 For the background of 'pleading his eternal sacrifice', see Bryan D. Spinks, 'The Ascension and the Vicarious Humanity of Christ: The Christology and Soteriology behind the Church of Scotland's Anamnesis and Epiklesis', in J. Neil Alexander (ed.), *Time and Community: In Honor of Thomas Julian Talley*, Washington: Pastoral Press, 1990, pp. 185–201.

to sanctify or consecrate both the gifts and the people. Only the third order was in contemporary English, which probably accounted for the short shelf life this book had. The 1980 United Reformed rite represents the definitive liturgical text for the original union of the Congregational Church in England and Wales with the Presbyterian Church of England, and prior to further unions which then required a new liturgy. The first order, reflecting an older Church of Scotland usage, had the Words of Institution read as a warrant, a formula for taking the bread and wine, and then a short Eucharistic Prayer, with Proper Prefaces and Sanctus, but without further recitation of the Institution Narrative unless it was to be used at the Fraction. The second prayer, which used part of the Te Deum, was the ecumenical Eucharistic Prayer compiled by the British Joint Liturgical Group, and the third was one of Huub Oosterhuis's Table Prayers.

Finally, two Methodist Eucharistic Prayers may be mentioned. The British Methodist Church published a new eucharistic liturgy in 1975. It contained only a single Eucharistic Prayer, without Proper Prefaces. The post-Sanctus transitioned almost immediately to the Institution Narrative. The offering was our sacrifice of praise and thanksgiving, and ourselves (very Cranmerian!), and the petition for the Spirit was indirect: 'Grant that by the power of the Holy Spirit we who receive your gifts of bread and wine may share in the body and blood of Christ.' The United Methodist Church, USA, published *We Gather Together* (1980). The Eucharistic Prayer in the alternative rite, like its British counterpart, swiftly transitioned to the Institution Narrative. It had a more subtle Anamnesis, 'asking you to accept this our sacrifice of praise and thanksgiving, which we offer in union with Christ's offering for us', and the petition for the Spirit was for both 'us' and 'on these gifts'.[52]

In summary, it may be said that on the whole the 'new' Eucharistic Prayers were new versions of fourth- and fifth-century models. Only in a few, such as the unofficial Table Prayers of Oosterhuis, and in the Roman Catholic Eucharistic Prayers for Reconciliation, do we find a more contemporary style of composition. Two main 'families' emerged – the *ingenium romanum*, imitated by the Church of England 1980 rites and Eucharistic Prayer C of the Episcopal Church, and the 'Syro-Byzantine' model, though without the prolific intercessions found in these anaphoras. There was a division between those Churches that invoked the Spirit on the communicants only and those who invoked the Spirit on both the gifts and the communicants. There was also division in the articulation of offering – the gifts, and/or the communicants.

52 A. H. Couratin, 'The Methodist Sunday Service', *Church Quarterly Review* 2 (1969), pp. 31–8; A. Raymond George, 'From the Sunday Service to "The Sunday Service": Sunday Morning Worship in British Methodism', in Karen B. Westerfield Tucker (ed.), *The Sunday Service of the Methodists: Twentieth-Century Worship in Worldwide Methodism. Studies in Honor of James F. White*, Nashville: Kingswood Books, 1996, pp. 31–52; James F. White, 'United Methodist Eucharistic Prayers', in Frank C. Senn (ed.), *New Eucharistic Prayers: An Ecumenical Study of their Development and Structure*, Mahwah, New Jersey: Paulist Press, 1987, pp. 80–95.

Theologians and agreed statements

The Liturgical Movement and liturgical revision proceeded against the backdrop of some significant developments by certain theologians concerning the understanding of sacraments and the Eucharist for twentieth-century thought. Maurice de la Taille was one distinguished Catholic theologian who in his 1921 study attempted to address the concept of eucharistic sacrifice, arguing for a unity between the self-offering of Christ at the Last Supper, consummated on the cross, and that continued in the Mass.[53] He distinguished between immolation, the destruction of a victim, and oblation, offering, which is the central, gift-oriented action of sacrifice. On the Protestant side, F. J. Leenhardt argued that in the context of Hebraic thought, the words of Jesus indicate that the bread is associated with an end that transcends it, and argued that the term transubstantiation expressed that transformation. The substance of things is not in their empirical data, but in the will of God who upholds them, and substance should be understood as the final reality. Leenhardt objected to some of de la Taille's views on sacrifice, but nevertheless argued that there was a sacrificial dimension to the Lord's Supper:

> The same intention which made ready the Cross now inspires this apparently commonplace action. The gift of the bread is, in the final analysis, the same thing as the sacrifice of His life. Jesus does the one, because He has done the other. Both are the point where the same ministry, one entirely of service, that is of sacrifice, terminates and culminates.[54]

Theological giants Karl Rahner and Karl Barth agreed that ultimately there is only one sacrament, that is, Jesus Christ, and all other 'sacraments' or ordinances are derivative of the one foundational sacrament.[55] Catholic theologians, most notably Piet Schoonenberg and Edward Schillebeeckx, argued that transubstantiation, if tied to Aristotelian concepts, was outmoded for contemporary thought, and they championed instead the terms transignification and transfinalization, which if correctly understood better conveyed what transubstantiation had originally intended.[56] Lutheran theologians Gustav Aulén and Regin Prenter explored the concept of eucharistic sacrifice that was consistent with a

53 The original French was in three volumes, 1921, 1924 and 1931. ET, *The Mystery of Faith: Regarding the Most August Sacrament and Sacrifice of the Body and Blood of Christ*, two vols, New York: Sheed and Ward, 1940 and 1950. Michon M. Matthiesen, *Sacrifice as Gift:Eucharist, Grace, and Contemplative Prayer in Maurice de la Taille*, Washington: Catholic University Press, 2013.

54 ET in Oscar Cullman and F. J. Leenhardt, *Essays on the Lord's Supper*, Virginia: John Knox Press, 1958, p. 61.

55 Karl Rahner, *Theological Investigations IV*, Baltimore: Helicon Press, 1966, p. 221; Karl Barth, *Church Dogmatics, passim*; Paul D. Molnar, *Karl Barth and the Theology of the Lord's Supper*, New York: Peter Lang, 1996.

56 Piet Schoonenberg, 'Transubstantiation: How Far is this Doctrine Historically Determined?', in Hans Küng (ed.), *The Sacraments: An Ecumenical Dilemma*, New York: Paulist Press, 1967; Edward Schillebeeckx, *The Eucharist*, New York: Sheed and Ward, 1967; Joseph M. Powers, *Eucharistic Theology*, New York: Seabury Press, 1967.

Lutheran theology.[57] Important contributions were also made by Thomas F. Torrance of the Church of Scotland. Churches also entered upon bilateral conversations, many resulting in agreed statements on belief, including the Eucharist.[58] Here discussion will be limited to Aulén, Schillebeeckx, Torrance and a collection of essays from the Church of England, together with statements from the Anglican–Roman Catholic and Lutheran–Roman Catholic dialogues.

Aulén (1879–1977), a bishop in the Church of Sweden, took it for granted that in the New Testament the Supper is clearly associated with sacrifice; 'given for you', 'shed for you' interpret both the event at the table and the act of sacrifice in death. The words in the Supper connect with other verses about Jesus offering his life.[59] The sacrifice Jesus makes is on behalf of humanity, but it is also accepted by God on behalf of humanity. He not only offered himself, but God also gave him as a sacrifice.[60] As our great High Priest, the sacrifice is made once for all, but it is eternally valid and is continually relevant. It is the heavenly Christ who is invisibly present in the Supper, and whose coming is also hoped for. The Eucharist of the Last Supper was not itself a sacrifice, but it had a sacrificial character, because everything is concentrated around that final, self-giving sacrifice that immediately followed. Since the heavenly Christ is present, the sacrifice fulfilled once is effectively present in the sacrament: 'This sacrifice is present because the living Lord is present. But the living Lord cannot be present without actualizing his sacrifice.'[61] Although our offering is on a different plane than the sacrifice of Christ, his sacrifice is the foundation and is present in the Supper which we do.

If Aulén as a Lutheran explored what a Lutheran might say on sacrifice, Schillebeeckx as a Catholic explored presence and transubstantiation. Schillebeeckx noted that although the dogma of transubstantiation was expressed in Aristotelian categories, the Aristotelian content of these categories was not included in what the dogma intended to say, and in the world of quantum physics, 'substance' in Aristotelian terms as applied to material reality is untenable. He advocated the approach from anthropology and phenomenology. A fundamental question is, for whom is Christ present? He is present, argued Schillebeeckx, for the individual Christian and the Christian community. Christ gives himself as gift, and the elements mediate his personal presence. 'The host is Christ's gift of himself, and Christ's presence is that of the giver in the gift.'[62] He gives his death and resurrection in this sacramental meal. He wrote:

> The Eucharist is the sacramental form of this [the cross and resurrection] event, Christ's giving of himself to the Father and to men. It takes the form of a commemorative meal in which the usual secular significance of the bread and

57 Gustav Aulén, *Eucharist and Sacrifice*, Philadelphia: Muhlenberg Press, 1958; Regin Prenter, *Theologie und Gottesdienst/Theology and Liturgy*, Århus: Forlaget Aros, 1977.

58 John Reumann, *The Supper of the Lord: The New Testament, Ecumenical Dialogues, and Faith and Order on the Eucharist*, Philadelphia: Fortress Press, 1985.

59 Aulén, *Eucharist and Sacrifice*, p. 139.

60 Aulén, *Eucharist and Sacrifice*, p. 143.

61 Aulén, *Eucharist and Sacrifice*, p. 193.

62 Schillebeeckx, *Eucharist*, p. 120.

> wine is withdrawn and these become bearers of Christ's gift of himself – 'Take and eat, this is my body.' Christ's gift of himself, however, is not ultimately directed towards bread and wine, but towards the faithful. The real presence is intended for believers, but through the medium of and *in* this gift of bread and wine. In other words, the Lord who gives himself thus is *sacramentally* present. In this commemorative meal, bread and wine become the subject of a new *establishment of meaning*, not by men, but by the living Lord *in* the Church, though which they become the *sign* of the real presence of Christ giving himself to us. This establishment of meaning by Christ is accomplished in the Church and thus presupposes the real presence of the Lord in the Church, in the assembled community of believers and in the one who officiates in the Eucharist.[63]

For Schillebeeckx, terms coined by theologians such as J. de Baciocchi in the 1950s, transfunctionalism, transfinalization and transsignification, providing they were understood to convey what transubstantiation has been meant to convey, were helpful terms for the contemporary world.[64]

T. F. Torrance, from the perspective of the Church of Scotland's Reformed tradition, approached the Eucharist first of all from the more general supposition that all worship is properly a form of the life of Jesus Christ ascending to the Father in the life of those who are so intimately related to him through the Spirit that when they pray to the Father through Christ, it is Christ the incarnate Son who honours, worships and glorifies the Father in them. The Eucharist is the paschal mystery of Christ which he set forth for the participation of all who believe in him.[65] As instituted, the Supper is both an act of Christ and the act of the Church in his name.

> It is Christ himself, in his paschal mystery, who constitutes the living content, reality and power of the Eucharist (i.e., the *Lord's* Supper) and who gives meaning and efficacy to its celebration in the Church by being savingly and creatively present in his mediatorial agency as often as we '*do this in anamnesis*' of him, blessing what we do on earth at his command and accepting it as his own act done in heaven.[66]

It is not an independent act in response to what God in Christ has done, but 'an act towards the Father already fulfilled in the humanity of Christ in our place and on our behalf, to which our acts in his name are assimilated and identified through the Spirit'. For Torrance, it is being in Christ or 'Christ in us' that is vital:

> It is in this union and communion with Christ the incarnate Son who represents God to us and us to God that the real import of the Lord's Supper

63 Schillebeeckx, *Eucharist*, pp. 137–38.

64 Schillebeeckx, *Eucharist*, p. 109.

65 T. F. Torrance, 'The Paschal Mystery of Christ and the Eucharist', in *Theology in Reconciliation*, London: Geoffrey Chapman, 1975, pp. 106–38.

66 Torrance, 'Paschal Mystery', p. 109.

> becomes disclosed, for in eating his body and in drinking his blood we are given participation in his vicarious self-offering to the Father. As we feed upon Christ, the bread of life who comes down from above, eating his flesh and drinking his blood, thereby receiving his eternal life into our actual life, and living by Christ as he lives by the Father who sent him, he unites us and our worship with his own self-consecration and so offers us to the Father in the identity of himself as Offerer and Offering.[67]

Two lengthy passages illustrate what Torrance thought about both presence and sacrifice. Christ is present through

> the same kind of inexplicable creative activity whereby he was born of the Virgin Mary and rose again from the grave. Because it really is the presence of the Lord Jesus Christ in his living, creative reality, in his personal self-giving to us, it is a presence over which we have no kind of control, ecclesiastical, liturgical or intellectual. It is the same kind of presence that confronted the disciples on the first Easter morning at Emmaus or in the upper room at Jerusalem, and indeed it is the same presence except that now it takes another form, the eucharistic form specifically appointed by Jesus as the particular empirical form in which he has promised as the risen and glorified Christ to meet his people in the closest and most intimate way, throughout all history, in anticipation of his unveiled form when he will come again in great power and glory. It is the whole Jesus Christ who makes himself specifically and intensely present to us in this eucharistic form in his oneness as Gift and Giver, the whole Jesus Christ in the fulness of his deity and in the fulness of his humanity, crucified and risen, not a bare or naked Christ, far less only his body and blood, but Jesus Christ clothed with his Gospel and clothed with the power of his Spirit, who cannot be separated from what he did or taught or was in the whole course of his historical existence in the flesh. What he has done once and for all in history has the power of permanent presence in him. He is present in the unique reality of his incarnate Person, in whom Word and Work and Person are indissolubly one, personally present therefore in such a way that he creatively effects what he declares, and what he promises actually takes place: 'This is my body broken for you', 'This is my blood shed for many for the remission of sins'. The real presence is the presence of the Saviour in his personal being and atoning self-sacrifice, who once and for all gave himself up on the Cross for our sakes but who is risen from the dead as the Lamb who has been slain but is alive for ever more, and now appears for us in the presence of the Father as himself prevalent eternally propitiation.[68]

In his critique of Torrance, Robert Stamps suggests he held no notion of bodily presence in the Eucharist, holding instead a kind of 'transinstrumentation'.[69] However, it is clear from the quotation above that Torrance sees the whole

67 Torrance, 'Paschal Mystery', p. 111.

68 Torrance, 'Paschal Mystery', p. 120.

69 Robert J. Stamps, *The Sacrament of the Word Made Flesh: The Eucharistic Theology of Thomas F. Torrance*, Edinburgh: Rutherford House, 2007, p. 242, note 9.

Christ present in the elements, even though he does not use any term to describe the 'how' of the presence in the elements. As Torrance noted, 'the real presence which Christ grants to us in the Eucharist is objectively grounded in the presence of God to himself, and as such is the profoundest and most intensive kind of presence there could ever be'.[70] As to the manner in which the Eucharist is a sacrifice, Torrance wrote:

> that we *through the Spirit* are so intimately united to Christ, by communion in his body and blood, that we participate in his self-consecration and self-offering to the Father and thus appear with him and in him and through him before the Majesty of God in worship, praise and adoration with no other sacrifice than the sacrifice of Christ Jesus our Mediator and High Priest. Conversely, the eucharistic sacrifice is the self-consecration and self-offering of Jesus Christ in our nature ascending to the Father from the Church in which he dwells through the Spirit he has poured out upon it, uniting it to himself as his Body, so that when the Church worships, praises and adores the Father through Christ and celebrates the Eucharist in his name, it is Christ himself who worships, praises and adores the Father in and through his members, taking up, moulding and sanctifying the prayers of his people as they are united to him through communion in his body and blood.[71]

Christ has put himself in our place so that we may be put in his place, and through the Spirit we participate in his vicarious self-offering as the real agent of our worship, and through our prayers and thanksgivings in the Eucharist we offer Christ to the Father. It should be recalled that Torrance was able to draw on the Eucharistic Prayer of the 1940 (and 1979) *Book of Common Order*, which had the phrase 'pleading his eternal sacrifice', and in many ways Torrance's theology is an exegesis of those words.

The Church of England Doctrine Commission outlined English Anglican eucharistic theology in the 1972 collection, *Thinking about the Eucharist*. This collection appeared after the Liturgical Commission had compiled the Series 3 trial Eucharist report in 1971, in response to certain questions posed by the latter to the former.[72] The essays covered a broad spectrum, including the philosophical background, matter in theological and scientific perspectives, as well as the meaning of the Institution Narratives in their New Testament context. Since like other Reformation Churches, the original Anglican formularies had rejected the traditional Catholic teachings on eucharistic sacrifice and presence, it is the essays on these topics by J. L. Holden and H. E. W. Turner that are significant. Both approached their topic historically – in stark contrast to Torrance. Holden acknowledged that the Passover context of the Last Supper suggested some sacrificial connotation: 'The underlying logic was simple: reconciliation had taken place, sacrifices reconcile, so Christ's work, the occasion and basis

70 Torrance, 'Paschal Mystery', p. 121.

71 Torrance, 'Paschal Mystery', p. 134.

72 Archbishop's Commission on Christian Doctrine, *Thinking about the Eucharist*, London: SCM Press, 1972, p. iv. It is significant that the Liturgical Commission and the Doctrine Commission are distinct bodies who hardly, if ever, meet together!

of the reconciliation, must be interpreted sacrificially', and it was natural for the Eucharist to attract sacrificial language.[73] He acknowledged that Malachi 1.11 was quickly pressed into service and then outlined a developmental history from the offering of gifts (*1 Clement*), offering firstfruits (Irenaeus), to a shift in Cyprian to offering Christ's body and blood and the 'Anselmic' idea of offering the Eucharist for propitiation and satisfaction. The marriage between sacrificial language and the language of body and blood he regarded as a mistake. One of the difficulties with most of the commonest formulations involving sacrificial language, so he opined, is that they 'start too far up the conceptual ladder'. Yet, for all its limitations, Holden believed the idea of sacrifice to be indispensable, since it encapsulates the 'totality of self-offering'.[74] He was content with Augustine's statement that a true sacrifice is any act that is done in order that we may cleave in holy union to God.[75] Holden concluded somewhat ambivalently:

> But through all vicissitudes of theology, the eucharist remains the outstanding means by which God's people bring to a focus their total corporate and individual self-offering to him, because of Jesus, who both showed us the way and gave us the rite by which to grow in it. God's gift 'in Christ' and our response 'in Christ' meet and fuse in a single act.[76]

This seems to say in a rather anaemic manner what Torrance said much more forcefully.

Turner asserted that most Christians accept that Christ is present at the Eucharist, but noted that in the fourth century two main streams began to emerge: metabolism, asserting a change in the elements, and dualism, which emphasized co-presence of bread and wine and body and blood.[77] For Turner, the eucharistic presence of Christ is always a dynamic presence, and he detected a move to ontological or entitative terms, and to replace the question 'Who is present?' by the enquiry 'What is present?' Turner felt that the term 'substance', used by Catholics and Lutherans, was unhelpful, and preferred William Temple's term, 'transvaluation', which he thought was close to Schillebeeckx's use of transignification. He reviewed the use of the term 'sign' by Zwingli and the Council of Trent, and suggested that for Zwingli a sign was discontinuous with the thing signified, and so the sacraments are signs of what is absent, whereas in Catholic theology, a sign is continuous with what is signified.[78] Turner concluded that none of the categories proposed and discussed are free from difficulty, but:

> Perhaps the view that by consecration the elements become charged with a new and additional meaning as the media or vehicles of Christ's presence given in action, and that this meaning becomes henceforth part of their existence

73 Holden, 'Sacrifice and the Eucharist', in *Thinking about the Eucharist*, pp. 81–98, 83–4.

74 Holden, 'Sacrifice and the Eucharist', p. 95.

75 Holden, 'Sacrifice and the Eucharist', p. 97.

76 Holden, 'Sacrifice and the Eucharist', p. 98.

77 H. E. W. Turner, 'Eucharistic Presence', in *Thinking about the Eucharist*, pp. 99–114, 100.

78 Turner, 'Eucharistic Presence', p. 111.

> for the purposes for which the eucharist was instituted, is less exposed to difficulty than any other. The eucharist remains on any showing the sacrament of encounter with Christ, the action through which God's people are fed with the bread of life, which is also the bread of heaven.[79]

Thinking about the Eucharist was published in 1972, only months after the Anglican–Roman Catholic 1971 Windsor Statement on Eucharistic Doctrine, which had a wider Anglican representation.[80] The Report was in three sections of twelve paragraphs. It accepted that the identity of the Church as the body of Christ is 'both expressed and effectively proclaimed' by its being centred on the Eucharist (par. 3). There was no repetition of the one offering of Christ on the cross. The eucharistic memorial is no mere calling to mind of a past event, but 'the church's effectual proclamation of God's mighty acts' in which we enter into the movement of his self-offering (par. 5). Communion with Christ presupposes his true presence 'effectually signified by the bread and wine, which, in this mystery, become his body and blood' (par. 6). Christ is active and present in various ways in the entire eucharistic celebration, and he gives himself sacramentally in the body and blood of his paschal sacrifice. A footnote explained that the term transubstantiation should be seen as affirming the fact of Christ's presence and that a change takes place, but not as explaining how the change takes place. The eucharistic signs are the special gift of himself. In the Eucharistic Prayer, the bread and wine become the body and blood of Christ by the action of the Holy Spirit, so that in communion we eat the flesh of Christ and drink his blood (par. 10). By the transforming action of the Spirit of God, earthly bread and wine become the heavenly manna and the new wine, the eschatological banquet for the new man: elements of the first creation become pledges and firstfruits of the new heaven and the new earth (par. 11).[81]

A Lutheran–Roman Catholic statement on the Eucharist was published in 1967.[82] On the differences over eucharistic sacrifice, it acknowledged that the cross was once and for all, and that the Church offers praise and itself in the Eucharist. Each tradition was able to make the following its own:

> By him, with him and in him who is our great High Priest and Intercessor we offer to the Father, in the power of the Holy Spirit, our praise, thanksgiving and intercession. With contrite hearts we offer ourselves as a living and holy sacrifice, a sacrifice which must be expressed in the whole of our daily lives.[83]

---

79 Turner, 'Eucharistic Presence', p. 113.

80 Anglican/Roman Catholic Joint Preparatory Commission, 'The Final Report', http://www.anglicancommunion.org/ministry/ecumenical/dialogues/catholic/arcic/docs/pdf/final_report_arcic_1.pdf.

81 Comments and fears expressed about the Report were addressed in an Elucidation 1979 and are not elaborated here.

82 United States Conference of Catholic Bishops, 'The Eucharist: A Lutheran–Roman Catholic Statement', http://old.usccb.org/seia/luthrc_eucharist_1968.shtml.

83 US Conference of Catholic Bishops, 'The Eucharist'.

Remaining differences were noted. On the question of presence, it noted various forms of Christ's presence, such as in the people of God and in the reading of Scriptures. Both Churches agreed that in the sacrament of the Lord's Supper, Jesus Christ, true God and true man, is present 'wholly and entirely, in his body and blood, under the signs of bread and wine'. Both Churches used the terms really, truly and substantially present in the sacrament. Differences remain over reservation of the sacrament and adoration, and Lutherans reject the necessity of the term transubstantiation.

In summary, a good number of theological works and writings from this period suggested the possibility of convergence, and this optimism was strengthened by the bilateral conversations and agreed statements that resulted.

Baptism, Eucharist and Ministry and the Lima liturgy

The willingness of theologians to push boundaries in the search for ecumenical rapprochement took on a more official level through the WCC Faith and Order discussions. Whereas individual theologians spoke only for themselves, representatives of Faith and Order were spokespersons for their Churches. The fruit of many years of labour, the document *Baptism, Eucharist and Ministry* (*BEM*) was published by the WCC in 1982. Though not binding on any participating Church, it did represent the best that any ecumenical document could deliver on these subjects. It was adopted by the Faith and Order Commission of the WCC at its meeting in Lima, Peru, and a special eucharistic liturgy was drawn up to give liturgical expression to the consensus expressed in the section on the Eucharist.[84] Here an ecumenical *lex credendi* was given *lex orandi* expression.

The section on the Eucharist was divided into three parts – the Institution of the Eucharist, the Meaning of the Eucharist, and the Celebration of the Eucharist. Anchoring the Eucharist in the Pauline and Synoptic accounts of the Institution, it asserted that the Last Supper celebrated by Jesus was a liturgical meal employing symbolic words and actions: 'Consequently the eucharist is a sacramental meal which by visible signs communicates to us God's love in Jesus Christ, the love by which Jesus loved his own "to the end".'[85]

Its meaning is to be understood, first, by the fact that it is a gift from God. It includes thanksgiving, and it is a great sacrifice of praise in which Christ unites the faithful to himself and includes their own prayers within his own intercession. Bread and wine are presented to the Father, and they signify what the world is to become. It is a memorial, an Anamnesis, in which the Church is united with the Son, its great High Priest and intercessor. 'In the eucharist, Christ empowers us to live with him, to suffer with him and to pray through him as justified sinners, joyfully and freely fulfilling his will.'[86] In Christ we offer ourselves, and are united to the Lord and are in communion with the saints and martyrs. Strangely, in the light of Addai and Mari and other early prayers, it

84 For essays on the Report and on its background Max Thurian (ed.), *Ecumenical Perspectives on Baptism, Eucharist and Ministry*, Geneva: WCC, 1983.

85 *Baptism, Eucharist and Ministry*, p. 10.

86 *Baptism, Eucharist and Ministry*, p. 12.

stated that the Words of Institution are at the heart of the celebration. Without discussing how or terminology, it asserted that Christ's mode of presence at the Eucharist is unique. The commentary explained:

> *Many churches believe that by the words of Jesus and by the power of the Holy Spirit, the bread and wine of the eucharist become, in a real though mysterious manner, the body and blood of the risen Christ, i.e., of the living Christ present in all his fullness. Under the signs of bread and wine, the deepest reality is the total being of Christ who comes to us in order to feed us and transform our entire being. Some other churches, while affirming a real presence of Christ at the eucharist, do not link that presence so definitely with the signs of bread and wine. The decision remains for the churches whether this difference can be accommodated within the convergence formulated in the text itself.*[87]

The role of the Holy Spirit as invoked upon the bread and wine to be sacramental signs, and upon the Church, was emphasized. Equal emphasis was given to the Eucharist's eschatological nature, it being a foretaste of the Kingdom of God and gives communion with one another. Paragraph 22 stated:

> The eucharist opens up the vision of the divine rule which has been promised as the final renewal of creation, and is a foretaste of it. Signs of this renewal are present in the world wherever the grace of God is manifest and human beings work for justice, love and peace. The eucharist is the feast at which the Church gives thanks to God for these signs and joyfully celebrates and anticipates the coming of the Kingdom in Christ (I Cor. 11:26; Matt. 26:29).[88]

And in rather a beautiful passage:

> As it is entirely the gift of God, the eucharist brings into the present age a new reality which transforms Christians into the image of Christ and therefore makes them his effective witnesses. The eucharist is precious food for missionaries, bread and wine for pilgrims on their apostolic journey.[89]

The third section gave a summary of what has emerged as an ecumenical *Ordo Missae*:

- Hymns of praise.
- Act of repentance.
- Declaration of pardon.
- Proclamation of the Word of God, in various forms.
- Confession of faith (Creed).
- Intercession for the whole Church and for the world.
- Preparation of the bread and wine.

87 *Baptism, Eucharist and Ministry*, p. 12.
88 *Baptism, Eucharist and Ministry*, p. 14.
89 *Baptism, Eucharist and Ministry*, p. 15.

- Thanksgiving to the Father for the marvels of creation, redemption and sanctification (deriving from the Jewish tradition of the *berakah*).
- The words of Christ's Institution of the sacrament according to the New Testament tradition.
- The *Anamnesis* or memorial of the great acts of redemption, passion, death, resurrection, ascension and Pentecost, which brought the Church into being.
- The invocation of the Holy Spirit (*epiklesis*) on the community and the elements of bread and wine (either before the Words of Institution or after the Memorial, or both; or some other reference to the Holy Spirit which adequately expresses the 'epikletic' character of the Eucharist).
- Consecration of the faithful to God.
- Reference to the communion of saints.
- Prayer for the return of the Lord and the definitive manifestation of his Kingdom.
- The Amen of the whole community.
- The Lord's Prayer.
- Sign of reconciliation and peace.
- The breaking of the bread.
- Eating and drinking in communion with Christ and with each member of the church.
- Final act of praise.
- Blessing and sending.[90]

The eucharistic theology of this report was put into anaphoral form by Max Thurian for the Lima celebration, and it has come to be known as the 'Lima' liturgy. The Eucharistic Prayer was constructed on the *ingenium romanum* model, with the split Epikleses. It was also divided into sections and given a responsorial form. After the Sanctus the consecratory Epiklesis, reminiscent of that of the Anaphora of St James and echoes of Ephrem the Syrian, asked:

> Upon your eucharist send the life-giving Spirit, who spoke by Moses and the Prophets, who overshadowed the Virgin Mary with grace, who descended upon Jesus in the river Jordan and upon the Apostles on the day of Pentecost. May the outpouring of this Spirit of Fire transfigure this thanksgiving meal that this bread and wine may become for us the body and blood of Christ.

The congregation responded with *Veni Creator Spiritus!* The petition of the Epiklesis was continued in the introduction to the Words of Institution: 'May this Creator Spirit accomplish the words of your beloved Son, who, in the night . . .'. The Anamnesis tried to express *BEM*'s relating it to the priesthood of Christ and the heavenly intercession:

> Wherefore, O Lord, we celebrate today the memorial of our redemption: we recall the birth and life of your Son among us, his baptism by John, his last meal with the apostles, his death and descent to the abode of the dead; we

90 *Baptism, Eucharist and Ministry*, pp. 15–16.

> proclaim Christ's resurrection and ascension in glory, where as our Great High Priest he ever intercedes for all people; and we look for his coming at the last. United in Christ's priesthood, we present to you this memorial: Remember the sacrifice of your Son and grant to people everywhere the benefits of Christ's redemptive work.

Thurian explained the rationale behind this:

> By the eucharist as sacrifice of intercession, the Church unites with Christ's intercession founded on his sacrifice of the cross, and intercedes with the Father in favour of all persons, for the forgiveness of their sins, for their liberation and happiness, and implores the glorious manifestation of the kingdom.
>
> In communion with Christ's intercession and with his sacrifice on the cross, by setting before the Father the memorial of that sacrifice as praise and supplication, the Church offers itself, each of the faithful offers himself or herself, in an act of adoration and consecration. As Luther wrote: '. . . we present ourselves before God with our prayer, our praise and our sacrifice, only in the name of Christ and by his intermediary . . . He offers himself in heaven, and offers us with him.' And Calvin has this admirable image: Jesus Christ in the heavenly sanctuary 'is our altar, upon which we place our oblations, that whatever we venture to do, we may attempt in him.'[91]

After the communion Epiklesis, the anaphora made provision for mention of the saints and departed of the Church.

Concluding remarks

The *BEM* statement was a remarkable accomplishment. Together with the Lima Eucharist and its Eucharistic Prayer, it represents the high-water mark of the Liturgical Movement, of mid-twentieth-century liturgical scholarship and of ecumenical rapprochement. But by 1982 the tide was already on the turn. The optimism and vision of unity of modernity was replaced by the scepticism and plurality of the postmodern era.

91 Max Thurian, 'The Eucharistic Memorial, Sacrifice of Praise and Supplication', in Thurian (ed.), *Ecumenical Perspectives*, pp. 90–103, 101.

15

Some Trends in a Postmodern Era

There is nothing magical about 1982, and yet *Baptism, Eucharist and Ministry* and the Lima liturgy represent something of a watershed. Intellectuals and commentators on cultural trends discerned that the period of modernity, with a high tide in the 1960s and 1970s, had evolved or was morphing into late modernity or postmodernity.[1] The 'symptoms' of this cultural shift include a questioning of the idea of evolutionary and scientific progress, and a questioning of the hegemony of Euro-North Atlantic culture and values, as well as the monopoly of 'experts' in their respective disciplines. The idea that there is one right or correct solution/future/cultural norm has been replaced by new appreciation for plurality and differences. Lieven Boeve has summarized this cultural shift as follows:

> The fundamental plurality of the postmodern condition follows from the experience that each perspective seems to have equal legitimacy and worth, even if they are nonetheless incompatible. This basic experience presents itself across an extremely diverse range of domains in the human life-world: politics, economy, leisure, forms of personal and communal relationships, art, education, science, etc. There is no longer a universal perspective, no all-encompassing patterns of integration possessing universal and objectively determinable validity. Each claim to universality and totality is unmasked as the absolutisation of what is in reality a particular point of view.[2]

This went hand in hand with a growing concern for the extension of human rights and equal rights, which in turn led to social justice agendas gaining a higher profile in some Protestant Churches. Other Churches rediscovered some of their older and more conservative roots, and the cumulative result has been that the pace of ecumenism has slowed and new differences between Churches and within them have been clearly discernible. New megachurches came into being whereas main-line Western Churches have generally been in decline. These factors have had an impact on worship styles in many Churches, particularly language and the provision of multiple liturgical texts from which a selection

---

1 For readable introductions, see David Lyons, *Postmodernity*, 2nd edn, Minneapolis: University of Minneapolis Press, 2005; Steven Connor, *Postmodern Culture: An Introduction to Theories of the Contemporary*, 2nd edn, Oxford: Blackwell, 1997.

2 Lieven Boeve, 'Thinking Sacramental Presence in a Postmodern Context: A Playground for Renewal', in L. Boeve and L. Leijssen (eds), *Sacramental Presence in a Postmodern Context*, Leuven: Leuven University Press, 2001, p. 15.

may be made, as well as on theological method.[3] It is some of these that are explored further in this chapter.

In main-line Churches the 'ecumenical *ordo*' has gone largely unchallenged. The Church of Sweden's website gives the outline of its Sunday Mass (1986) as follows:[4]

> An outline of the order for Eucharist in the Church of Sweden follows, including one of the several possible Eucharistic Prayers. Hymns would normally be sung at several points.
> The Preparation
> Confession and Absolution
> Introit
> Kyrie
> Gloria
> The Ministry of the Word
> Collect
> Lessons (Old Testament, Epistle, Gospel)
> Sermon
> Creed
> Intercessions
> The Ministry of the Sacrament
> Offertory
> Thanksgiving
> Eucharistic Prayer
> Lord's Prayer
> Breaking of the Bread
> Peace
> Agnus Dei
> Communion
> Prayer (Post-Communion)
> Benedicamus
> Blessing.

In the Anglican Communion an International Anglican Liturgical Consultation (IALC) was established in 1985, and its meeting in Dublin in 1995 was devoted to the Eucharist.[5] The resulting statement recommended the following as the basic structure for the Sunday assembly:

3 Bryan D. Spinks, *The Worship Mall: Contemporary Responses to Contemporary Culture*, London: SPCK, 2010, and New York: Church Publishing, 2011; Stephen Burns, Nicola Slee and Michael N. Jagessar (eds), *The Edge of God: New Liturgical Texts and Contexts in Conversation*, London: Epworth Press, 2008; Michael N. Jagessar and Stephen Burns (eds), *Christian Worship: Postcolonial Perspectives*, London: Equinox Publishing, 2011.

4 Church of Sweden, 'Liturgy and Worship', http://www.svenskakyrkan.se/default.aspx?id=657790. See also Oloph Bexell (ed.), *The Meaning of Christian Liturgy: Recent Developments in the Church of Sweden*, Grand Rapids: Eerdmans, 2012.

5 David R. Holeton and Colin Buchanan, *A History of the International Anglican Liturgical Consultations 1983–2007*, Alcuin/GROW Joint Liturgical Study 63, Norwich: Canterbury Press, 2007; David Holeton (ed.), *Revising the Eucharist: Groundwork for the Anglican*

- Gathering of God's people.
- Proclaiming and receiving the Word of God.
- Prayers of the people.
- Celebrating at the Lord's Table.
- Going out as God's people.

It also considered the structure of the Eucharistic Prayer, giving a basic core that is developed or supplemented in various ways. The WCC publication *Eucharistic Worship in Ecumenical Contexts* (1998) posited a fourfold shape of Gathering, Word, Meal and Sending, and gave an outline similar to those above.[6] Many more recent eucharistic rites have extended the multiplicity of Eucharistic Prayers. The Church of Sweden's 1986 rite has eight, as does the Church of England's *Common Worship* modern-language rite. The Church of Scotland's *Common Order* (1994) provides three in its first communion order and one in each of the second and third orders. On the other hand, the Reformed Church of America's 2005 *Worship the Lord* provided only one. While many Eucharistic Prayers follow the outline of the classical anaphoras, there is a growing tendency to follow the trend found in the Roman Catholic Eucharistic Prayers for Children, and make the prayer more responsorial. However, not all follow the classical shape entirely. The Church of Scotland's 1979 order provided Eucharistic Prayers that included the Institution Narrative, whereas those of 1994 reverted to the pattern found in the 1940 *Book of Common Order*, with the narrative either read before the prayer or after the prayer and as part of the Fraction. The Lutheran Church–Missouri Synod's *Lutheran Service Book* (2006), in contrast to the Swedish Lutheran Church, still reflects a struggle over whether a Eucharistic Prayer subverts the words of the Institution Narrative. One form provides for prayer before and after the *verba* (a pattern found in the French Reformed rite), which looks like a Eucharistic Prayer and can be prayed as if it were, but which in fact is a prayer before and after the *verba*. The second form follows the old (German) Lutheran model of Preface, Sanctus, *verba* and Lord's Prayer. The Reformed Church of America's Prayer also has no Institution Narrative within the Prayer, but has it recited immediately after the Eucharistic Prayer.[7] The Presbyterian Church USA published an extremely rich *Book of Common Worship* in 1993, with the 'ecumenical ordo' and some very fine Eucharistic Prayers.[8]

Communion, Alcuin/GROW Joint Liturgical Study 27, Cambridge: Grove Books, 1994; David Holeton, *Our Thanks and Praise*, Toronto: Anglican Book Centre, 1998.

6 Thomas F. Best and Dagmar Heller (eds), *Eucharistic Worship in Ecumenical Contexts*, Geneva: WCC, 1998, pp. 142–6.

7 For this tradition, see Christopher Dorn, *The Lord's Supper in the Reformed Church in America: Tradition in Transformation*, New York: Peter Lang, 2007; James Hart Braum (ed.), *Liturgy among the Thorns: Essays on Worship in the Reformed Church of America*, Grand Rapids: Eerdmans, 2007.

8 Bryan D. Spinks and Iain R. Torrance (eds), *To Glorify God: Essays on Modern Reformed Liturgy*, Edinburgh: T & T Clark, 1999; Harold M. Daniels, *To God Alone Be Glory: The Story and Sources of the Book of Common Worship*, Louisville: Geneva Press, 2003; Peter C. Bower, *The Companion to the Book of Common Worship*, Louisville: Geneva Press, 2003;

Language

The concern for equal rights and the feminist movements of the 1960s were catalysts for feminist theologies and a concern for inclusive language in worship. Much of this has been an English-language concern, although its problems and concerns are not those of many other language areas of the world. The pre-1980s English liturgies used the older terms 'man', 'Man' and 'mankind' to refer to both men and women, and happily drew on only a small range of descriptors of God, mainly patriarchal – Lord, King, Shepherd, Almighty, for example. Some argued that this taught a picture of the 'maleness' of God, and more radical feminists have argued for replacing all male-gendered metaphors for God, as well as to speak inclusively – 'Let us pray for all people' rather than 'Let us pray for all men'. These concerns have been reflected in various ways and with various criteria in many newer English-language rites. In more recent eucharistic rites there has been a conscious effort to avoid, if possible, male and female pronouns, and to balance masculine and feminine imagery. One Eucharistic Prayer in the 1999 *Methodist Worship Book* (UK) begins 'God our Father and our Mother, we give thanks and praise'. The Eucharistic Prayers in some traditions have avoided addressing God as 'Father' and seem content with a sub-trinitarian theology, where God is addressed in differentiation from Jesus and the Holy Spirit. An example is found in the Second Order of Holy Communion for All Age Worship in *Worship: from the United Reformed Church*, (2003). The 'new' *Sursum corda* has:

> May God be blessed forever! **May God be blessed forever!** God is with us! **God is with us!** We give thanks and praise to God! **We give thanks and praise to God!**

The prayer addressed the 'Loving God', who gave us Jesus and gives us the Holy Spirit. The author, Susan Durber, has claimed that the prayer uses a trinitarian structure but without using Father/Son language, though without doubt Julian Templeton is correct to say that such prayers have loosed themselves from orthodox trinitarian moorings.[9] Similar trinitarian problems are found in the Eucharistic Prayers in *Enriching Our Worship* of the Episcopal Church of the USA.[10]

In many recent Eucharistic Prayers there has been a concern to follow the style found in the Roman Catholic Eucharistic Prayers for Reconciliation and, in Oosterhuis, with striking imagery and more poetic and memorable phraseology.

Arlo D. Duba, *Presbyterian Worship in the Twentieth Century with a Focus on the Book of Common Worship*, White Sulphur Springs: OSL Publications, 2012.

9 Susan Durber, 'An Inclusive Communion Order for a Denominational Worship Book', in Nicola Slee and Stephen Burns (eds), *Presiding Like a Woman*, London: SPCK, 2010, pp. 38–47; Julian Templeton, 'What's the Problem with God the Father? Some Implications of Impersonal References to God in Reformed Liturgy', in Julian Templeton and Keith Riglin (eds), *Reforming Worship: English Reformed Principles and Practice*, Eugene: Wipf and Stock, 2012, pp. 43–61.

10 Colin Buchanan (ed.), *Anglican Eucharistic Liturgies 1985–2010*, Norwich: Canterbury Press, 2011, pp. 96–9; Peter Nicholas Davies, *Alien Rites? A Critical Examination of Contemporary English in Anglican Liturgies*, Aldershot: Ashgate, 2005.

One of the Church of Sweden Eucharistic Prayers, picking up language from the Roman Catholic offertory prayers, prays:

> Let Your Holy Spirit come into our hearts
> to enlighten us with a living faith.
> Sanctify by your Spirit this bread and wine,
> which earth has given and human hands have made.
> Here we offer them to you,
> that through them we may partake
> of the true body and blood of our Lord Jesus Christ.

Eucharistic Prayer 3 of *Enriching Our Worship* prays:

> through Jesus Christ, your eternal Word, the Wisdom from on high by whom you created all things. You laid the foundations of the world and enclosed the sea when it burst from the womb; You brought forth all creatures of the earth and gave breath to humankind.
>
> Wondrous are you, Holy One of Blessing, all you create is a sign of hope for our journey.

Prayer G of the Church of England *Common Worship* (2000) borrowed from the ICEL English Eucharistic Prayer submitted to Rome but failed to be approved:

> Blessed are you, Lord God, our light and our salvation; to you be glory and praise for ever. From the beginning you have created all things and all your works echo the silent music of your praise.

Simpler but still 'poetic' language is found in the two new *Common Worship* Eucharistic Prayers for Children.[11] The Evangelical Lutheran Church of America's Eucharistic Prayer A in *This Far by Faith: An African American Resource for Worship*, prays, 'God of our weary years, God of our silent tears, you have brought us thus far along the way.'[12] Popular also in some circles is the neo-Celtic style and vocabulary in Ray Simpson's *Celtic Worship through the Year*.[13]

In some contrast to these trends is the new English translation of the Roman Missal, which began to be used in Advent 2011. A new English translation of the Missal was begun in 1981, but all the new proposals were rejected by the Congregation for Divine Worship and the Discipline of the Sacraments during 1997 and 1998, and ICEL itself underwent a complete restructuring, seen by many as a move in a more conservative direction. On 28 March 2001, the document *Liturgiam Authenticam* was published, which laid down new rules to govern translation, with a goal to keep the vernacular translations as near to

11 *Additional Eucharistic Prayers with Guidance on Celebrating the Eucharist with Children*, London: Church House Publishing, 2012.

12 *This Far by Faith: An African American Resource for Worship*, Minneapolis: Augsburg Fortress Press, 1999, p. 84.

13 Ray Simpson, *Celtic Worship through the Year: Prayers, Readings and Creative Activities for Ordinary Days and Saints' Days*, London: Hodder and Stoughton, 1998.

the Latin typical edition as possible. The changes are illustrated below by the opening of the *Gloria in excelsis* and part of Eucharistic Prayer 3:

ICEL/ICET 1970–73	ICEL 2010
Glory to God in the highest And peace to his people on earth.	Glory to God in the highest and on earth peace to people of good will.
Look with favor on your Church's offering,	Look, we pray, upon the oblation of your Church
and see the Victim whose death has reconciled us to yourself.	and, recognizing the sacrificial Victim by whose death you willed to reconcile us to yourself,
Grant that we, who are nourished by his body and blood,	grant that we, who are nourished by the Body and Blood of your Son
may be filled with his Holy Spirit,	and filled with his Holy Spirit,
and become one body, one spirit in Christ.	may become one body, one spirit in Christ.

The 2010 text has both ecumenical and linguistic implications. Many of the earlier texts of the Ordinary of the Mass – Gloria, Creed and Sanctus – were readily adopted by other English-speaking Churches and the texts became ecumenical. The new 2010 translations are quite different, and thus the English-speaking Roman Catholic Church has stepped away from its own original ecumenically shared texts. Linguistically, though a more literal translation certainly is more faithful to the Latin original, the result is a highly artificial and in places quite infelicitous English.

Another trend has been recognition of local and regional cultures, and therefore encouragement to inculturate the liturgy. This has freed many Western Churches in Africa, South America and Asia to break from a tradition of praying in European thought forms. The Anglican Province of Kenya begins its Eucharistic Prayer:[14]

> Is the Father with us? **He is.** Is Christ among us? **He is.** Is the Spirit here? **He is.** This is our God. **Father, Son and Holy Spirit.** We are his people. **We are redeemed.**

The Church of South India has a Eucharistic Prayer that begins:

14 Texts for these Anglican rites are in Buchanan, *Anglican Eucharistic Liturgies 1985–2010*.

Our Creator God is with us to bless us; **Saranam, saranam, saranam.** The risen Lord is with us to bless us; **Saranam, saranam, saranam.** The transforming Spirit is with us to bless us; **Saranam, saranam, saranam.**

Doctrine

The concern for inclusive language has, as noted above, sometimes given rise to a sub-orthodox trinitarian theology. In contrast, the Church of Ireland's Eucharist Prayer 3 in its 2004 liturgy addresses successive parts to the Father, to Christ and the Holy Spirit to give a robust Constantinopolitan trinitarianism. The work of John Paterson, it apparently took its cue from the IALC Dublin Statement and an essay by the present writer, which urged that the co-substantiality of the Trinity was best expressed by addressing each person of the Trinity as God.[15] The middle section of Eucharistic Prayer F in the Church of Sweden rite is addressed to Christ, having precedents in the Syrian Orthodox tradition.[16] However, it is the historical divisions from the Reformation over presence and sacrifice that still lurk in many rites and Eucharistic Prayers. In the Church of England's *Common Worship*, no Epiklesis asks specifically and directly for the Spirit upon the elements, seemingly to assuage Evangelical objections to invoking the Spirit on inanimate objects (surely in the Eucharist it is so the elements cease to be inanimate!) and Anglo-Catholics who believe that it is the Institution Narrative alone that consecrates.[17] Other Anglican provinces do have an Epiklesis on the elements. The Anamneses in two of the *Common Worship* Eucharistic Prayers use the term 'plead/pleading' the sacrifice made once for all. This term was used in the past by both Evangelical and High-Church divines, and so represents the recovery of past consensus. However, the original proposals voiced in the Liturgical Commission were to follow the Church of Scotland and have 'pleading the eternal sacrifice'. A number of Anglican Evangelicals were unable to understand 'eternal' as anything other than in a temporal meaning of 'continuous in time', and seemed unable or unwilling to embrace Calvin's understanding.[18] Other provinces, such as The Episcopal Church (USA) and

15 Kevin J. Maroney, 'The Church of Ireland's Eucharistic Prayer 3: Revision and Analysis', *Studia Liturgica* 39 (2009), pp. 171–84. See Bryan D. Spinks, 'Trinitarian Theology and the Eucharistic Prayer', *Studia Liturgica* 26 (1996), pp. 209–24. For an unsuccessful attempt in the Church of England, see Colin Buchanan and Trevor Lloyd, *Six Eucharistic Prayers as Proposed in 1996*, Cambridge: Grove Books, 1996. For the background to the 2004 Irish book, see Harold Miller, 'The Making of the Church of Ireland *Book of Common Prayer* 2004', Yale Institute of Sacred Music *Colloquium* 3 (2006), pp. 75–84; Harold Miller, *The Desire of our Souls*, Blackrock: Columba Press, 2004.

16 Discussed in Boel Hössjer Sundman, 'Interpretations of the Presence of God in Liturgy', in Oloph Bexell (ed.), *The Meaning of Christian Liturgy: Recent Developments in the Church of Sweden*, Grand Rapids: Eerdmans, 2012, pp. 53–90, 81.

17 See David J. Kennedy, *Eucharistic Sacramentality in an Ecumenical Context: The Anglican Epiclesis*, Aldershot: Ashgate, 2008, ch. 7. Bryan Spinks and Kenneth Stevenson, *Patterns for Worship: Essays on Eucharistic Prayers*, GSMisc 333, nd.

18 Bryan D. Spinks, 'The Ascension and the Vicarious Humanity of Christ: the Christology and Soteriology behind the Church of Scotland's Anamnesis and Epiklesis', in J. Neil Alexander (ed.), *Time and Community*, Washington: Pastoral Press, 1990, pp. 196–7.

South Africa have some prayers that 'offer' the gifts. The diocese of Sydney, which is ultra-Evangelical, issued its own eucharistic services in 2001 (as a counter-statement to those in *A Prayer Book for Australia*, 1995).[19] Form 1 focuses on the sacrifice of Christ on the cross, with a petition, 'Hear us, merciful Father, and grant that we, who eat and drink this bread and wine, may remember his death, and share in his body and blood.' Brian Douglas aptly observed:

> The act of eating and drinking the bread and wine does not necessarily have any link with the remembering and the sharing, apart from the fact that the act of eating and drinking seem to be occurring at the same period of time as the sharing in Christ's body and blood.[20]

The Narrative of Institution follows, with no Epiklesis or Anamnesis. Form 2 provides the following Eucharistic Prayer:

Lift up your hearts,
We lift them to the Lord.

Let us give thanks to the Lord our God.
Yes! he is worthy of our praise.

You are worthy, our Lord and God,
to receive glory and honour and power,
for you created all things
and by your will they existed and were created.
Therefore we lift our voices to praise you, saying
Holy, holy, holy is the Lord God almighty,
who was, and is, and is to come.

We praise you especially for your Son, our Saviour Jesus Christ,
who by his death on the cross
offered once and for all time,
the one true sacrifice for sin,
reconciling us to you
and satisfying your just demands.
By rising to new life
Jesus has secured eternal deliverance for his people.
Worthy is the Lamb, who was slain,
to receive praise and honour
and glory and power for ever and ever!
We thank you Father,
that on the night before he died, Jesus took bread;
and when he had given you thanks, he broke it,

19 'Sunday Services: A Contemporary Liturgical Resource', http://www.sundayservices.anglican.asn.au/lordssupper.html.

20 Brian Douglas, *A Companion to Anglican Eucharistic Theology*, vol. 2, The 20th Century to the Present, Leiden: Brill, 2012, p. 712.

and gave it to his disciples, saying,
'Take, and eat. This is my body given for you.
Do this in remembrance of me.'
After the meal, he took the cup,
and again giving you thanks he gave it to his disciples, saying,
'Drink from this, all of you.
This is my blood of the new covenant
which is shed for you and for many for the forgiveness of sins.
Do this, as often as you drink it, in remembrance of me.'
Therefore Father,
we thank you for these gifts of bread and wine,
and pray that we who eat and drink them,
believing our Saviour's word,
may share his body and blood. Amen.

15. *Turning to the people the minister says*

We eat the bread and drink the cup of the Lord
to proclaim our fellowship in his death.
We do this until he returns.
Come Lord Jesus, come!

Douglas suggests that, again, the eating and drinking is linked with proclamation, not the signs of bread and wine.[21] These liturgical differences across the Anglican Communion make it difficult to understand the statement in the Anglican–Orthodox Dialogue (2006), which stated:

> In taking bread and wine, giving thanks, breaking and giving, the priest is configured to Christ at the Last Supper. The president draws together the life and prayer of the baptised, and offers them to the Father with the bread and wine. In the Eucharistic Prayer, the offering of praise and thanksgiving for the mighty deeds of God, culminating in the sacrifice of the paschal mystery, is offered for all creation. Received by the Father, the gifts of bread and wine are returned in the Holy Spirit as Christ's risen life, his body and blood, the bread of heaven and the cup of salvation. In the eucharistic action, the Church is renewed in its prayer and self-offering as the priestly people of God.[22]

Such intra-denominational contradictions are found elsewhere too. Whereas the Church of Sweden can offer/present the gifts of bread and wine, and invoke the Spirit to sanctify the gifts, in the Lutheran Church–Missouri Synod, the Word and Spirit is invoked upon the people, and the gifts are given to us, not offered to God in any sense. In the Reformed tradition, four of the five Eucharistic Prayers in *Common Order* ask for the Spirit to come upon the people and the

21 Douglas, *Companion*, vol. 2, p. 715.

22 *The Church of the Triune God: The Cyprus Agreed Statement of the International Commission for Anglican–Orthodox Theological Dialogue 2006*, London: Anglican Communion Office, 2006, p. 72.

gifts of bread and wine, but the single Eucharistic Prayer of *Worship the Lord* asks for the Holy Spirit only on the people.

In a number of these prayers, though, there is a welcomed recovery of an eschatological dimension, usually anchored in ecclesiology. Eucharistic Prayer C of *Common Order* requests:

> Gather your Church together from the ends of the earth into your kingdom, where peace and justice are revealed, that we, with all your people, of every language, race, and nation, may share the banquet you have promised.

The Eucharistic Prayer in the Third Order has three paragraphs of remembering the Church, families and those with various needs, and a fourth remembers the departed. Eucharistic Prayer E of *Common Worship* prays:

> Lord of all life, help us to work together for that day when your kingdom comes and justice and mercy will be seen in all the earth. Look with favour on your people, gather us in your loving arms and bring us with [N *and*] all the saints to feast at your table in heaven.

The First Order in *Worship: From the United Reformed Church* prays:

> May we on earth be one with all Christ's people, and, when all things are complete, be raised up to be with him, [with . . . *the saints; those who have died*] and with all your faithful servants in the heavenly places, the homeland which we seek by faith.

Eucharistic Prayer B of the Church of South India prays: 'Restore the broken life of your creation; heal the disfigured body of your world; draw all creatures unto yourself through the cross and in the power of your risen life.'

Although the Roman Catholic Church has not authorized any new eucharistic liturgy or major revision since that of Vatican II, there have been papal encyclicals on the subject. Its theology has been stated succinctly in the 1994 (revised 1997) *Catechism of the Catholic Church*.[23] The Eucharist is the efficacious sign and sublime cause of the communion in the life and unity of the people of God (para. 1325). It unites us with the heavenly liturgy and anticipates eternal life, when God will be all in all. It is a sacrifice because it makes present the one sacrifice of Christ and includes the Church's offering (para. 1330). By celebrating the Last Supper in the course of Passover, Jesus gave the Jewish Passover its definitive meaning (para. 1340). The *Catechism* gives an important place to the Epiklesis in which 'the Church asks the Father to send his Holy Spirit (or the power of his blessing) on the bread and wine, so that by this power they may become the body and blood of Jesus Christ and so that those who take part in the Eucharist may be one body and one spirit' (para. 1353). Together with the Words of Institution the Spirit makes sacramentally present under the species of bread and wine Christ's body and blood (para. 1353). In celebrating

23 Catholic Church, *Catechism of the Catholic Church*, http://www.usccb.org/beliefs-and-teachings/what-we-believe/catechism/catechism-of-the-catholic-church/epub/index.cfm.

the Eucharist, we offer to the Father what he has himself given us, namely the gifts of his creation, bread and wine, which have become the body and blood of Christ. Christ is thus really and mysteriously made present (para. 1357). The presence is 'real', meaning in the fullest sense, and is a substantial presence, which has been fittingly called transubstantiation (paras. 1374 and 1376). Though traditional teaching in traditional language on presence and offering are in the *Catechism*, these are placed in a wider discussion including the actual liturgical context of the Eucharist and its ecclesiological dimension.

Postmodern eucharistic theologies

According to Lieven Boeve:

> In postmodern cultural–philosophical reflection, it may happen that the theologian finds a new impetus to interpret the Christian tradition in such a way that within the context of plurality it again inspires people who are searching for integration and orientation, but now without falling prey to the hegemonic schemes of master narratives.[24]

He argues that the Christian narrative which has become conscious of its own particularity and contingency can only adequately relate to the transcendent when it opens itself up, cultivating a contemplative openness into which the transcendent as interruptive event can enter and bear witness in a non-hegemonic way to the transcendent with the help of its own, always fragmentary words, images, stories, symbols and rituals.[25] In terms of sacramentental theology, there is a tendency among many theologians to speak of sacramentality rather than dwell on particular sacraments. This can be seen, for example, in the writings of the Anglican theologian David Brown, who in a range of interdisciplinary studies explores the divine disclosure in the human body (dance), classical music, pop music and opera.[26] This in some ways represents a return to Ephrem the Syrian, where potentially God may use any thing as a *raza*, a divine mystery of self-disclosure. In terms of the 'traditional sacraments', including the Eucharist, there is a move away from the idea of metaphysical prototypes in eternity to the particular in space–time, the *haecceitas* ('thisness') of this eucharistic celebration, which is not the same as last week's eucharistic celebration.[27] Here discussion will centre on the Eucharist in the work of Roman Catholic theologians Louis-Marie Chauvet and Jean-Luc Marion, and the Anglican theologian and former Archbishop of Canterbury Rowan Williams.

---

24 Boeve, 'Thinking Sacramental Presence', p. 17.

25 Boeve, 'Thinking Sacramental Presence', p. 21.

26 David Brown, *God and Grace of Body: Sacrament in Ordinary*, Oxford: Oxford University Press, 2007. See also David Brown and Ann Loades (eds), *Christ: The Sacramental Word. Incarnation, Sacrament and Poetry*, London: SPCK, 1996; David Brown and Ann Loades (eds), *The Sense of the Sacramental. Movement and Measure in Art and Music, Place and Time*, London: SPCK, 1995.

27 K. B. Osborne, *Christian Sacraments in a Postmodern World: A Theology for the Third Millennium*, New York: Paulist Press, 2000.

Chauvet (b. 1941) has developed a symbolic theology from within sacramental practices. He has been influenced by Heidegger's philosophy and rejects the notion of causality, preferring the relation of mutual and reciprocal gift or symbolic exchange as a better analogy for sacramental grace. Rejecting 'onto-theology', he appeals to the studies of language and ritual as the basis for understanding divine disclosure and presence. His methodology, which is certainly not without its critics, was set out in *Symbol and Sacrament* (ET 1995), but here his work more specifically on the Eucharist is the focus.[28] Rejecting or qualifying what he regards as older models, Chauvet's starting point is that the sacraments are expressions in word and rite proper to the particular group that Christians are.[29] They belong to language – in its verbal and in its gestures/symbolic forms. Language is not an instrument but a meditation, and its sense depends upon one's culture and desire. Sacraments are an important element in the mother tongue of Christians. Particularly important by way of illustration is the Emmaus road encounter (Luke 24.13–35) where God takes the initiative; the event is one of disclosure because of the Word (Scriptures) and the sacramental gesture of breaking the bread. What Luke tells us is that each time the Church takes the bread, pronounces the blessing, breaks it and gives it in memory of the Lord Jesus, it is Jesus that does this through the Church. 'The gestures the church makes, the words it pronounces are his gestures and his words – it is a "sacrament".'[30] Since Christ is ascended, the Church now occupies his place. The Scriptures testify that the Word wants to inhabit through the Spirit the very body of the people of God – as individuals, as the social body and as 'cosmic' body, such as bread and wine. Differentiating between a sign and a symbol, Chauvet notes that in language it is symbolic function that has priority. In order to hear what transpires in the liturgy (words and gestures) one has to enter into the type of language it employs. Liturgy belongs to the symbolic order, and its aim is to establish communication between the participants and God, and as a consequence among themselves. As already noted, Chauvet regards God's gift and grace in the Eucharist as being best understood as symbolic exchange (in contrast to market exchange), which elicits a return-gift:

> the *reception* of God's grace *as* grace, and not as anything else, requires (relation of implication) the *return-gift* of faith, love, conversion of heart, witness by one's life . . . The gift is received as such only if it elicits the return-gift of gratitude, thanksgiving, increase of love.[31]

He illustrates this with reference to Eucharistic Prayer 2 of the Roman rite. The Eucharistic Prayer divides into three narrative sub-programmes (NP). NP1 covers the initial thanksgiving and Sanctus; NP2 covers the Epiklesis on the

28 Louis-Marie Chauvet, *The Sacraments: The Word of God at the Mercy of the Body*, Collegeville: Liturgical Press, 2001. See also Philippe Bordeyne and Bruce Morrill (eds), *Sacraments, Revelation of the Humanity of God: Engaging the Fundamental Theology of Louis-Marie Chauvet*, Collegeville: Liturgical Press, 2008; Joseph Christopher Mudd, 'Eucharist and Critical Metaphysics: A Response to Louis-Marie Chauvet's Symbol and Sacrament Drawing on the Works of Bernard Lonergan', PhD dissertatiom, Boston College, 2010.

29 Chauvet, *Sacraments*, p. 3.

30 Chauvet, *Sacraments*, p. 26.

31 Chauvet, *Sacraments*, p. 124.

gifts, the Institution Narrative and Anamnesis; NP3 covers the remainder of the Prayer. In NP2, with the narrative,

> This sudden passage from a citation to a faraway past to its being used in the present, in the discourse of the Eucharistic Prayer, shows that *by citing Jesus at the Last Supper, the church sees itself in fact cited by him, its Lord, cited to act.*[32]

The Church cannot 'narrate' Jesus as Christ and Lord without being itself taken in the present into what it narrates in the past. The Church holds its identity by constantly receiving itself from him (a real presence).

And the Anamnesis:

> Because, as was forcefully emphasized above, the gratuitous and gracious gift of God is not in the order of value-objects, the church can appropriate it only by letting go of it, take it only by giving it back, giving it back with thanksgiving or, better still, giving back to God the very Grace of God, that is, Christ Jesus who continues to give himself up to the church in sacrament.[33]

According to Chauvet, the communion Epiklesis demonstrates that the sacramental offering of the body and blood of Christ is the ritual mediation which symbolically shows what the return-gift is – the existential offering of one's own life.[34] In terms similar to T. F. Torrance, Chauvet explains the 'we offer you' of the Anamnesis as objective – the offering of 'Christ-in-sacrament' by the Church, and subjective – the offering of the Church in, with and through Christ.[35] Citing Henri de Lubac (an important figure for a good number of recent writers on the Eucharist), Chauvet notes that the body of Christ was understood in a threefold sense – the risen and ascended Christ, the 'eucharistic' body and the ecclesial body – and the emphasis was once on the relationship between the latter two: the ecclesial body was the truth of the eucharistic body.[36] For Chauvet, the Eucharist makes the Church and the Church makes the Eucharist.

Chauvet manages to speak of presence and offering by reference to the eucharistic celebration itself, its words and gestures, and does so without using the term transubstantiation, which he certainly does not deny, but which is outdated onto-theology. By contrast, Jean-Luc Marion defends the term transubstantiation, though without endorsing the Aristotelian philosophical background. In his work *God without Being*, Marion is critical of the idea of God as 'being' and onto-theology, which results in an idol; he selects 'icon' as a preferable concept:

> The icon, which unbalances human sight in order to engulf it in infinite depth, marks such an advance of God that even in the times of the worst distress indifference cannot ruin it. For, to give itself to be seen, the icon needs only itself.[37]

---

32 Chauvet, *Sacraments*, p. 134.
33 Chauvet, *Sacraments*, p. 135.
34 Chauvet, *Sacraments*, p. 136.
35 Chauvet, *Sacraments*, p. 136.
36 Henri de Lubac, *Corpus Mysticum*, Notre Dame: Notre Dame University Press, 2006.
37 Jean-Luc Marion, *God without Being*, Chicago: University of Chicago Press, 1991, p. 24.

The cross becomes central and it subverts classical metaphysics; only the cross can signify pure gift whose name is love. Here, like Chauvet's symbolic exchange, Marion sees gift as only possible in the form of divine love where on the cross God 'crosses' out God. As with Chauvet, he considers the Emmaus road story as a key text to understanding the divine disclosure. The theologian finds his or her place in the Eucharist because the Eucharist offers itself as the place for a hermeneutic, and the Eucharist becomes the test of every theological systematization.

> The Christian assembly that celebrates the Eucharist unceasingly reproduces this hermeneutic site of theology. First the text: the prophets, the law, the writings, all of the Old Testament (as in Luke 24:27), then the *logia* of the Christ (as in Luke 24:17: *logoi* displaced in 24:18–24, through a sort of hypothetical kerygma, hypothecated by death) . . . the priest who presides over the Eucharist begins by 'carrying out the hermeneutic' . . . Finally the community: it hears the text, verbally passes through it in the direction of the referent Word, because the carnal Word comes to the community, and the community into him. The community therefore interprets the text in view of its referent only to the strict degree that it lets itself be called together and assimilated, hence converted and interpreted by the Word, sacramentally and therefore actually acting in the community.[38]

On the subject of 'presence', Marion notes that explanations always seem to end up in a 'eucharistic physics'. However, he also notes that the term transubstantiation, in Greek *metabole*, was introduced quite independently of any reading of Aristotle. Eucharistic presence must be understood starting from the present, but the present must be understood first as a gift that is given.[39]

> It is a question of making an appeal, in the name of a past event, to G⊠d, in order that he recall an engagement (a covenant) that determines the instant presently given to the believing community.[40]

According to Marion, the theology of transubstantiation alone offers the possibility of distance, since it strictly separates my consciousness from him who summons it. The bread and wine are the gift given without return – the gift of love:

> The Son took on the body of humanity only in order to play humanly the Trinitarian game of love; for this reason also, he loved 'to the end' (John 13:1), that is, to the Cross; in order that the irrefutable demonstration of the death and resurrection not cease to provoke us, he gives himself with insistence in a body and a blood that persist in each day that time imparts to us.[41]

The commitment of Christ as bread and wine is the outpouring of the 'trinitarian philanthropy':

---

38 Marion, *God without Being*, p. 152.
39 Marion, *God without Being*, p. 171.
40 Marion, *God without Being*, p. 172.
41 Marion, *God without Being*, p. 177.

> The consecrated bread and wine become the ultimate aspect in which charity delivers itself body and soul. If we remain incapable of recognizing in it the ultimate advance of love, the fault is not its responsibility – love gives itself, even if 'his own did not receive him' (John 1:11); love accomplishes the gift entirely, even if we scorn this gift: the fault returns to us, as the symptom of our impotence to read love, in other words, to love. Hence our tendency to reduce the eucharistic present to everything except to the love that ultimately assumes a body in it. Christ endures taking a sacramental body, venturing into the *here and now* that could blaspheme and/or idolize him, because already, he took a physical body, to the point of 'not resisting, not recoiling . . . not withdrawing (his) face from insults . . . rendering (his) face hard as stone' (Isaiah 50:5–7). The sacramental body completes the oblation of the body, oblation that incarnates the trinitarian oblation – 'You wanted neither sacrifice, nor oblation, but you fashioned me a body' (Psalms 40:7 according to the LXX, taken up again in Hebrews 10:5–10). In short, *the eucharistic present is deduced from the commitment of charity.*[42]

In consuming the food we do not assimilate Christ to us, but are assimilated through the sacramental body of the Christ to his ecclesiastical body. As Nathan Mitchell observes, Marion sees transubstantiation as a way to guarantee the 'irreducible exteriority' of Christ's presence in the Eucharist, and this exteriority makes intimacy possible by guaranteeing that otherness is not swallowed by the devouring self of a community's consciousness, will and attention.[43]

Rowan Williams's understanding of the Eucharist may be gleaned from a variety of his writings, though the summary here is mainly limited to two publications, *Eucharistic Sacrifice: The Roots of a Metaphor* and *On Christian Theology*.[44] Though aware of a renewed wider search for sacramentality, Williams stresses that Christian sacraments have their meaning in the understanding of signs within the Christian community. He has explained:

> Human creatures are summoned to relate to the world and to use its resources in such a way that God's self-offering in love comes through; and they are givenøøWord of God in human flesh, Jesus crucified and raised. When we engage in the action of the Eucharist, we show first what Jesus did and does, and then what humanity in Jesus may do: as he makes new meaning out of the bread and wine by his words, so we are enabled to make our world carry the truth of God's sacrificial love. Sacramentality is not a general principle that the world is full of 'sacredness': it is the very specific conviction that the world is full of the life of God whose nature is known in Christ and the Spirit. The meaning we make in all our creative activity has to be informed by this kind

42 Marion, *God without Being*, p. 178.

43 Nathan Mitchell, *Real Presence: The Work of the Eucharist*, South Bend: Notre Dame Center for Pastoral Liturgy, 2000, p. 121.

44 Rowan Williams, *Eucharistic Sacrifice: The Roots of a Metaphor*, Grove Liturgical Study 31, Bramcote: Grove Books, 1982; Rowan Williams, *On Christian Theology*, Oxford: Blackwell Publishing, 2000. For a deeper discussion, see Julie Gittoes, *Anamnesis and the Eucharist: Contemporary Anglican Approaches*, Aldershot: Ashgate, 2008.

of holiness. We live in a world alive with God, but that life comes to light fully only when seen in connection with 'Christ the Sacrament', to use the words of one modern theologian.[45]

Williams argues that sacraments are harder to explain the more we isolate them. Rather like Chauvet, he calls upon anthropology to explain that humans modify and transform their environment through signs; being human, being bodily and being a user of 'signs' are inseparable.[46] The inference is that the Christian community of faith makes use of signs to explain and transform its vocation, mission and self-understanding. Jesus took a 'sign' of the covenant of Israel and transformed it:

> The Last Supper is not a simple, primitive fellowship meal; as far back as we can go in the tradition about Jesus, it is seen as 'intending', meaning, the event that finally sets Jesus and his followers apart from the continuities of Israel and makes the beginnings of a new definition of God's people. Maundy Thursday *means* Good Friday and Easter, the sealing of the new and everlasting covenant. In the costly gift of his chosen and beloved to the risk of rejection and death, God uncovers the scope of his commitment in a way that alters the whole quality of human trust and commitment to him: he creates *faith* . . . The supper draws us into the event of the covenant's sealing, placing us with the unfaithful disciples at table whose unfaithfulness is to be both judged and set aside by God – for the supper is also celebrated as the meal shared with the risen Jesus.[47]

Williams stresses that Jesus in offering himself as the means of the new covenant is himself 'sacrament', and in celebrating the Supper the Church makes sense of itself. As with Chauvet and Marion, Williams stresses also that the signs are created by what Christ creates, 'his own self as a gift of God'. He suggests that the Anglican Article that rejected transubstantiation is intelligible against a background of devotional practice that seemed to 'immobilize' Christ. He notes that signs are always signs of what they are not, but are transformations of the world by reordering it. The Supper is a sign of the transfiguration of the world, of a God committed to drawing our lives into the order of healing and communion.[48] The harvest of the natural order becomes the harvest of God's action, and Christ becomes the visible sign of God's new order under the form of the first signs of fruition or fulfilment in the inanimate creation.[49] Williams writes of Jesus' institution of the Eucharist:

> By his surrender 'into' the passive forms of food and drink he makes void and powerless the impending betrayal, and, more, makes the betrayers his guests

45 Foreword to Geoffrey Rowell and Christine Hall (eds), *The Gestures of God: Explorations in Sacramentality*, London: Continuum, 2004, p. xiii.

46 Williams, *On Christian Theology*, p. 201.

47 Williams, *On Christian Theology*, pp. 203–4.

48 Williams, *On Christian Theology*, p. 207.

49 Williams, *On Christian Theology*, p. 215.

> and debtors, making with them the promise of divine fidelity, the covenant, that cannot be negated by their unfaithfulness.[50]

The 'other' becomes the object of love, and the elements are the medium of gift, not instruments of control.

In his earlier work, Williams argued that 'gift' is crucial in understanding how the Eucharist can be described as a sacrifice. Looking at the early evidence in Justin, Ignatius and Irenaeus, he considers their views to be an answer to the question, what do Christians do for the polis? The answer is, they 'sacrifice'. As applied to the Eucharist, it was seen as a thank-offering, not a sin-offering. Once we understand that no Christian 'sacrifice' can bribe God,

> we are free to consider the eucharist as a gift whose sole motive and purpose is gratitude – a gift which therefore shares the character of the Son's eternal praise of the Father in being an act of gratuitous love, and so may be called an offering of the Son to the Father. We give what we have been given – the flesh and blood of Jesus which opens to us the vision of eternal praise and glorification.[51]

The Church celebrates God's gratuitous love; through the sacrifice of the cross it is brought near to the holy to be made holy, and, as the temple, to offer the sacrifice of gratuitous love. Drawing upon Ignatius, Ephrem and J. Van Baal, Williams asserts:

> By the 'gift' of his presence – the presence in our world of an unreserved compassion and of an unrestricted hope – he establishes communion; but this can be clearly shown only in conditions of final rejection and dereliction. The gift is consummated on the cross . . . we, drawn into communion, into participation with God through the mutual giving of Jesus and his Father, have become part of a fellowship initiated and sustained by gift, and to abide in this fellowship is to learn how we can give, to each other and to God. That we can give at all rests on what we have *been* given, on the sense of receiving our very selves as gift. Yet we have been shown the cost of giving: the acceptable sacrifice is the one consumed by fire.[52]

Contemporary Pentecostal contributions

Pentecostalism has its origins in the late nineteenth and early twentieth centuries, and so is hardly a postmodern movement. However, as Albrecht rightly observes, although it came in obscurity, survived in inner-city missions, storefront assemblies and rural chapels on the margins of American (and British) society, it emerged as the largest Christian movement of the twentieth century,

50 Williams, *On Christian Theology*, p. 216.
51 Williams, *Eucharistic Sacrifice*, p. 12.
52 Williams, *Eucharistic Sacrifice*, pp. 28 and 29.

and it continues to expand.[53] The movement grew out of the Wesleyan holiness movement and, in Britain, the Congregationalist tradition, neither of which use set forms of liturgy. The older Pentecostal groups are those of the Assemblies of God, the International Church of the Four Square Gospel and, in Britain, the Elim Pentecostal Church. A typical communion service is described on a Pentecostal website thus:

> We normally have communion in the morning service, although sometimes in the evening too. We read from the Bible about how Jesus had some bread and wine with his disciples, and told us to think of him. We will pray, and then share the bread and wine. Sometimes some music is played, but at other times it is quiet, so we can talk to God ourselves and thank him for sending Jesus so we can be forgiven, and know him today.
>
> We stay sitting in our seats while the bread and wine are passed around. Anyone who loves Jesus, and wants to, can share the wine and bread. The wine is usually in special tiny glasses, so that everyone gets one each, but the bread is a broken up loaf that you break a small piece off.[54]

As the Churches became established and larger, so the formal theological training of their pastors and leaders developed, and theologians from the Pentecostal movement have made significant contributions in recent decades. Drawing on contemporary ecumenical scholarship and postmodern methodology, four recent notable studies on sacramental worship and the communion need to be noted.

Simon Chan is Professor of Systematics at Trinity College, Singapore, and his denominational allegiance is the Assemblies of God. His concern is the ecclesiological deficit among Evangelicals, as identified in the Chicago Call, issued by a group of Evangelical theologians in 1977. Chan noted the call to historic roots and continuity, to creedal identity and sacramental integrity, as well as authority and unity. However, he notes the weakness of ecclesiology, and it is this question that is addressed in his liturgical theology – subtitled 'The Church as Worshiping Community'.[55]

Chan contrasts two approaches to ecclesiology, the instrumental and the ontological. In the first, biblical history is understood in linear terms; the creation of humanity in the divine image and likeness is the ultimate divine purpose, with a rescue package of salvation history in which the Church is a covenant people of God and a means to fulfilling this original purpose. In this model, the Church derives its identity from the larger world. Chan prefers the ontological, where creation is the backdrop to the elective grace of God and covenant relationship.

---

53 Daniel E. Albrecht, *Rites in the Spirit: A Ritual Approach to Pentecostal/Charismatic Spirituality*, Sheffield: Sheffield Academic Press, 1999, p. 27.

54 Re:Quest, 'I Go to a Pentecostal Church', http://www.request.org.uk/main/churches/pentecostal/pentecostal02.htm. See also 'Pentecostal Communion Service – Pastor Andrew Evans', uploaded on 26 December 2010. http://www.youtube.com/watch?v=98fOIk8hDYk.

55 Simon Chan, *Liturgical Theology: The Church as Worshiping Community*, Downers Grove: InterVarsity Press, 2006.

Appealing to Ephesians 1.4, the Church precedes creation in that it is what God has in view from all eternity.

This in turn leads to exploration of the Church in relation to the Trinity and the Church as the people of God, the body of Christ and the temple of the Spirit. The Church is a communion, because its members are incorporated into the body of Christ; and the Church becomes one body by eating and drinking the body and blood of Christ. Echoing Henri de Lubac and John Zizioulas, Chan asserts, 'In sum, ecclesial communion is first and foremost an essentially eucharistic communion.'[56] The Church is called to be a worshipping community. From this ontological ecclesiology, Chan approaches worship. As a divine institution, to be the Church is to be the worshipping community making a normative response to the revelation of the triune God. It is worship that distinguishes the Church as the Church.[57] Chan is critical of both the common Evangelical service where worship is an add-on to the main business of the sermon, and the charismatic service which is more concerned to create an atmosphere. He suggests the *ordo* of true worship is incarnational or sacramental, in the sense that Christ is the primordial sacrament; it has a eucharistic orientation, an eschatological orientation and a missiological orientation. Appealing both to history and to noted Evangelical theologians, Chan reiterates that the Lord's Supper is the central service of the Church, for it makes us what we eat. Not only does the Word culminate in the sacrament, but unless preaching has a eucharistic orientation, it no longer qualifies as the proclamation of the gospel. Chan commends the ecumenical *ordo* as outlined by the WCC and a full Eucharistic Prayer of the classical shape. On presence, he notes a difference over the relationship of the physical elements to the spiritual body and blood of Christ, and whether 'conversion' is associated with the Words of Institution or the Epiklesis. For his own tradition, he cites 1 Timothy 4.4–5, arguing that there is no need to choose between the two.[58] The sharing of the elements is a powerful expression of manifesting the unity of the congregation. Furthermore, he suggests also an ecclesiological dimension for understanding eucharistic offering:

> The church in offering up the firstfruits of creation *becomes* the firstfruits of the new creation (cf. Jas 1:18) and shows what God intends for the world to become. The goal of creation is to become the church: the church is prior to creation. The church does most for the world when it is least like the world, whereas the church that tries very hard to be 'relevant' to the world spells doom for itself and for the world.[59]

Challenges can be made to Chan's thesis, and one weakness is the fact that he is unaware that the authorship and dating of *Apostolic Tradition* is now disputed. However, from the tradition of the Assemblies of God, this represents a serious attempt to engage with ecumenical theology and the wider liturgical tradition.

56 Chan, *Liturgical Theology*, p. 29.
57 Chan, *Liturgical Theology*, p. 42.
58 Chan, *Liturgical Theology*, pp. 144–5.
59 Chan, *Liturgical Theology*, p. 84.

Wolfgang Vondey, a professor of systematic theology, writes from within the Church of God Pentecostal tradition.[60] He too has recently been concerned with ecclesiology, and particularly as symbolized in bread throughout the biblical and Christian traditions. He regards bread as a neglected image/sign in ecclesiology and theology, and his study is concerned to bring out its fullest possible implications. Inevitably, the Last Supper and Lord's Supper have a crucial place. Vondey notes:

> Before his death, the Last Supper is the only meal where Jesus is recorded to explicitly take on the role of the host. Second, whereas Jesus taught and practiced unreserved and indiscriminate hospitality, on this occasion he seems to invite only his closest disciples to take part in the meal. With this the stage is set for an unprecedented and, as it were, final opportunity for Jesus to teach his disciples. Third, the occasion for this Last Supper is not any ordinary meal. The Gospels take great care to place this final meal in the explicit context of the Jewish Passover.[61]

Vondey appeals to Chauvet that the sacrificial aspect of the Supper/cross turns the sacrificial around and redirects it to ethical practice from which Vondey concludes that the bread must exhibit the characteristics that define the self-giving of the body of Christ in the service to the world.[62] In the Eucharist, the companionship celebrates the death, resurrection and ascension of Christ, who is recognized, despite his visible absence, in his continuing presence in the breaking of the bread.[63] 'The people of bread thereby acknowledge Christ as the continuing host of the meal and yearn for the recognition of his presence in the breaking of the bread.'[64]

Although this is a theology of 'bread', Vondey notes the implications for the celebration of communion. In its ideal form, the sharing of bread is a celebration of the fruitfulness and purpose of creation as part of human companionship, and therefore he is critical of the wafers and small biscuits used in his and many denominations for communion: 'As mere symbols, the "elements" distributed in the churches feed neither the faithful nor the poor and hungry.'[65] Though offering no euchological advice, Vondey does make a plea for better practice:

> Eucharistic theology has essentially collapsed in a large number of the Evangelical, Pentecostal, and Free Church traditions of North America. Separated from the realm of companionship, the eucharistic meal has become an autonomous and often optional entity. The breaking of the bread is no more

60 The Church of God traces itself to a nineteenth-century origin, but was clearly influenced by A. J. Tomlinson. See Cecil M. Robeck, Jr, *The Azusa Street Mission and Revival: The Birth of the Global Pentecostal Movement*, Memphis: Thomas Nelson, 2006, p. 219.

61 Wolfgang Vondey, *People of Bread: Rediscovering Ecclesiology*, New York: Paulist Press, 2008, p. 145.

62 Vondey, *People of Bread*, pp. 155, 154.

63 Vondey, *People of Bread*, p. 167.

64 Vondey, *People of Bread*, p. 187.

65 Vondey, *People of Bread*, p. 298.

> than an occasional add-on, a monthly, quarterly, or annual practice no longer essential to the life of the faithful.[66]

Implicit is a challenge to do better.

To do better is also the message of Daniel Tomberlin, also of the Church of God. Noting that the 'altar' in Pentecostal worship is central (in terms of an altar call, and healing), Tomberlin argues that the worship at Pentecostal altars is often ecstatic, that is, the worshipper is often lifted into 'heavenly places', and is thus a foretaste of heaven.[67] Furthermore, spiritual worship is expressed in sacraments, which includes being nourished at the table of the Lord and offering oneself with others as living sacrifices. Christ is our sanctifier, but he offered himself for our sanctification, and this is directed towards the whole human person, spirit, soul and body. Noting how the Spirit is essential as outpouring and gift for the Pentecostal tradition, ordinances or sacraments combine the Spirit with the physical. Since the Pentecostal tradition knows of anointed handkerchiefs as examples of tangible anointing, he suggests that the tradition should not have a problem with the idea that the Spirit moves and rests on physical objects such as bread and a cup at communion. He writes:

> The elements of the sacraments are material substances which the Spirit *touches*. In the observance of the sacraments, believers *touch* the elements and are *touched* by the Spirit. The elements of the sacraments are mediating gifts of grace because of the presence of the Spirit of grace.[68]

In discussing 1 Corinthians, Tomberlin observes that Paul insists that liturgy and charismata be governed by a dual concern for order and power, and Pentecostals often struggle to find a balance. As regards the Eucharist, because many Pentecostals have rejected the primacy of this ritual, there has been limited discussion on a serious sacramental theology and practice. Citing Pentecostal figures such as A. J. Tomlinson and J. Roswell Flower (Assemblies of God), he argues that they perceived a presence inherent in the Lord's Supper and regarded it much more than a memorial meal.[69] To partake of the holy meal is transformative. Tomberlin appeals to the idea of energies as found in Gregory Palamas as a concept that should appeal to Pentecostalists, and thus:

> With the Anabaptists, Pentecostals gladly affirm the presence of Christ and the witness of the Spirit in the worshipping community. With emphasis on the miraculous, it seems logical that Pentecostals would be willing to affirm the presence of Christ and the Spirit in the bread and cup of the holy meal. These two views are not mutually exclusive.[70]

---

66 Vondey, *People of Bread*, p. 300.

67 Daniel Tomberlin, *Pentecostal Sacraments: Encountering God at the Altar*, Cleveland, TN: Center for Pentecostal Leadership and Care, Pentecostal Theological Seminary, 2010, p. 26.

68 Tomberlin, *Pentecostal Sacraments*, p. 86.

69 Tomberlin, *Pentecostal Sacraments*, pp. 168, 171.

70 Tomberlin, *Pentecostal Sacraments*, p. 175.

He writes that the Lord's Supper is offered for the salvation of humanity, and champions the concept found in Ignatius and others that it is the medicine of immortality, or healing ointment. He suggests that the challenge for Pentecostal pastors who seek to conform to the New Testament pattern of worship is how to integrate the Lord's Supper into regular worship, and offers possible solutions:

> Frequent celebration of the Lord's Supper can be incorporated into Pentecostal worship in a variety of ways. One of which is to celebrate the Supper during the 'praise and worship' portion of a worship service. As worshipers sing, congregants are directed to move to the altar where elders serve the bread and cup. After receiving the Supper elements, congregants may return to their seats to conclude the service. In this manner, the celebration of the Lord's Supper is not an interruption of the worship service, but a natural movement and essential part of worship.
>
> Because the altar call is usually the climax of Pentecostal worship, a pastor may wish to incorporate the Lord's Supper as a closing altar call. After an invitation to sinners and/or those desiring prayer for healing or other needs, a pastor may call all worshipers to the altar for a time of prayer. The bread and cup may be offered to all worshipers who come forward to pray, or after worshipers have prayed. This option provides the opportunity to employ another way to celebrate the Lord's Supper.[71]

Tomberlin offers resources, including songs (which should reflect remembrance, atonement, nourishment, healing, confession, fellowship and the *parousia*) and sample liturgical forms, including some from the Episcopal *Book of Common Prayer* emended. He accepts that the denomination opted for grape juice because of alcoholism (at the period of its origins), but argues for the single loaf and cup, with individual cups being filled from the single cup. He notes, 'A congregation that expects commercially produced wafers and grape juice from a bottle, or a prepackage (sic) item, may project a low view of this sacred observance.'[72]

A final recent contribution comes from Chris E. W. Green, who is also from the Church of God and provides a historical overview of the theology of the Lord's Supper in the Pentecostal tradition. In conversation with contemporary theologians, he offers some suggestions for the Pentecostal Churches today. He writes:

> To take the Supper rightly, then, is to be drawn into a cruciformed life, to be stamped with the *character* or 'mind of Christ' (à la 1 Cor. 2:16 and Phil. 2.5–8). It is to receive the Christomorphic 'vision of life distributed with the bread'. To partake of Christ's body and blood is to be made like Christ in his life-giving death, to be empowered by the same Spirit to live as he lived, pray as he prayed, believe as he believed, obey as he obeyed until one's life like his is taken, blessed, broken, and given out for the world. Those who love him want nothing more and can accept nothing less.[73]

---

71 Tomberlin, *Pentecostal Sacraments*, pp. 184–5.

72 Tomberlin, *Pentecostal Sacraments*, p. 190.

73 Chris E. W. Green, *Toward a Pentecostal Theology of the Lord's Supper: Foretasting the Kingdom*, Cleveland: COPT Press, 2012, p. 206.

Discussing the Fourth Gospel, he observes that the 'eating' and 'drinking' of Christ's 'flesh' and 'blood' produces an excess of blessings. These benefits can be summed up in saying that to eat Christ is to receive nothing less than '*abiding intimacy with Christ himself*'.[74] With Lamar Williamson he can say that 'To eat Jesus' flesh is to take his humanity into our own, identifying with him in lowly service at the cost of life itself.'[75] Although expressed in different ways, he argues that the apostolic witnesses agree that in the Lord's Supper 'we are brought up together to participate in the Trinitarian life, a life of always-overflowing love and mutual delight. In Christ, who presents himself to us in this sacrament, we truly receive God and one another.'[76] The Supper pre-enacts Christ's life of sweeping, boundary-violating hospitality and his atoning death for the life of the world, while pre-enacting the future messianic feast as well. He writes:

> In the Eucharist-event, the Spirit 'broods over' the cosmically-enthroned Christ, the celebrating congregation, and the elements on the Table, opening the celebrants to the presence of the risen Jesus who the Spirit makes in that moment bodily present for them, with, in, and through the thereby-transfigured bread and wine.[77]

Appealing to the Catholic theologian Herbert McCabe, Green says that the bread, by the miraculous power of the Creator, does not need to become a new kind of thing in the world; it becomes only what it already is in the new world, the world of the eschaton.[78] The implications for his denomination are that the Eucharist needs to hold a more eminent place and be celebrated more frequently; like Tomberlin, he suggests that the symbolism requires a single loaf and cup.

Consciously postmodern Eucharists

While certainly not consciously drawing upon any of the particular theologians discussed above, others have compiled 'postmodern' liturgies for use by groups who reach out to youth or by particular emerging church groups. Here we consider Eucharistic Prayers from Simon Rundell of the alt.worship group 'blesséd', from Grace Church, Ealing, London, and from 'Rough Edge', a group of Christians based in the Durham area, all in the UK.[79]

Simon Rundell provides ideas and materials for alt.eucharistic worship, and a DVD is included as a coach. Though he recommends Eucharistic Prayer B from *Common Worship* or looking at alternative Eucharistic Prayers from sister Churches in the Anglican Communion, he provides a Eucharistic Prayer

74 Green, *Pentecostal Theology*, p. 235.

75 Green, *Pentecostal Theology*, p. 236, citing Lamar Williamson, *Preaching the Gospel of John: Proclaiming the Living Word*, Louisville: Westminster John Knox Press, 2004, p. 83.

76 Green, *Pentecostal Theology*, p. 240.

77 Green, *Pentecostal Theology*, p. 282.

78 Green, *Pentecostal Theology*, p. 284.

79 For further groups and discussion of emerging and alternative worship, see Spinks, *Worship Mall*.

with commentary in 'A Simple Mass'.[80] In an introductory explication Jesus is referred to as 'The Man', capital M. The *Sursum corda* is broken up with commentary, and so after the initial greeting, a reader says:

> For he is with us, now. Supporting, guiding, counselling and comforting. Stirring up the complacent and crying out for justice, transforming lives and making whole.[81]

After 'Let us give thanks to the Lord our God' and the response, either the celebrant or reader (it is not clear) says:

> In ways which we do not understand, or could ever hope to understand, Christ is present in our midst. The many thousands, millions of words of theologians, the prayers of saints, the witness of the apostles: *none* of them have ever got their heads around what happens here.

Readers give a commentary on and interpretation of the eucharistic mystery which takes the place of a Preface.

> 1: We can't see the wind, but we know what happens to the trees.
>
> 2: Look not for the wind, but the effect of the wind.
>
> 1: We can't see any outward change in the bread and wine, but we know that something is different.
>
> 2: Look not for God hiding under an ordinary piece of bread, as St. Francis once said, but look for the effect on those who share in the Body and Blood of Christ.
>
> Cel: Bread: simple, wholesome, good. The staple of life and proof in our hands of God's bountiful goodness to us all.
>
> Wine: source of joy and gladness, an example of God's love in a glistening drop of rich, dark sweetness.
>
> Our prayers echo the song of the angels, saints, prophets and patriarchs and whole company of heaven as they say; (Sanctus).[82]

The post Anamnesis acclamation is again an explication in prayer:

> It's good. It's changed. And through it we are changed.
>
> You won't find the Man wedged between the crumbs, but he is there.
>
> He gives himself to us in this way, so we can get our heads around the enormous idea of God stepping down into our world.

---

80 Simon Rundell, *Creative Ideas for Alternative Sacramental Worship*, Norwich: Canterbury Press, 2010, p. 74.

81 Rundell, *Creative Ideas*, p. 77.

82 Rundell, *Creative Ideas*, pp. 77–8.

He gives himself to us, so that we may become a part of him.

You eat food. It becomes part of you.

You eat of this, and you become a part of him. A Holy Communion, at one with God.

The only thing we can do is respond in love and joy, awe and wonder.

May all of us who taste this foretaste of heaven be brought together as your Church on this earth, empowered with the power of God.

May we remember all those not with us, and bring us all into your heavenly presence, though the powerful and mighty, saving work of our Saviour.[83]

Although the language at times is rather too instructional, it seems to express the gift of love and transformation that are important in Chauvet, Marion and Williams.

From the Grace Church Community in London comes the following Eucharistic Prayer:

lift up your hearts
we lift them up to god
lift up your heads
we lift them up to god
lift up your voices
we lift them up to god
lift up your hearts
we lift them up to god

we praise you for your unswerving love for us
though we are fragile
though we are wounded
though we are broken
you have never stopped loving us
and you have never forsaken us

greater love has no one than this that they lay down their life for their friends

you take what is broken and transform it through your death and love
what once was hurt
what once was friction
what left a mark
no longer stings
because grace makes beauty
out of ugly things

so we join with the angels singing
holy holy holy
holy holy holy

83 Rundell, *Creative Ideas*, p. 79.

lord god almighty
lord god almighty
heaven and earth are full of your glory
heaven and earth are full of your glory
hosanna in the highest
hosanna in the highest
in your last meal with your friends
before your betrayal
you took the bread and gave thanks
you broke it and shared it saying 'take and eat. this is my body broken for you'
christ's body is broken
we are christ's body, we are broken
may christ's broken body nourish you in all the right places

you took the cup of wine, gave thanks and shared it saying
'drink this, my blood shed for you'
christ's body is wounded
we are christ's body, we are wounded
may the blood that flowed from christ's wounds heal you in all the right places

send your holy spirit on us
heal our brokenness
by showing us our place in your community of faith
great is the mystery of faith
christ has died
christ is risen
christ will come again

this is the table of christ
today it is literally made of our brokenness
a sign that christ welcomes us all as we are
there is no need to pretend and no need to hide

so gather at this table
not because you are whole
but because you recognise your need for healing
not because you are good enough
but because you recognise these gifts of god[84]

The prayer seems to switch from addressing God to being an exhortation addressed to the community, and is concerned with the community understanding of itself as the wounded body of Christ.

Rather different is the Beat Mass from Rough Edge. 'Beat' is used in reference to the literary movement in the USA of the 1950s and 60s. It stretches words and language to create 'almost tangible word pictures', and it pulls words and language to breaking point. In addition, the introduction explains, 'it often speaks of stepping beyond the ordinary to find truth or purpose or worthwhile meaning'.[85]

84 'Wounded Eucharistic Prayer', http://www.freshworship.org/book/print/545.
85 Rough Edge, *The Beat Eucharist*, np: Rough Edge, 2010, p. 8.

It was written to be read at a fast rate ('ranted'), and music and videos that may accompany it are available from the website.[86] The Eucharistic Prayer has a paraphrase/interpretation of the traditional *Sursum corda*, and the following extract from the 'Preface' gives an indication of the claim to stretch language:

> Holier than all, you are God, faultless Father, all wonderful, Ever watching this earth of love and ashen pain, your vigilance does not falter. Poured out from the depths of your heart you shared with us, your very flesh, Jesus who walked and taught and died among us, To wrench death and all that decays us from pedestals steeped in time.[87]

The Words of Institution are paraphrased thus:

> Taking bread, thanking for bread and tearing bread he spoke, 'My body to be taken and torn for all as an offering for you all.' Jesus, who welcomed, invited and loved among us offered praise for the fruit of the vine, Taking wine and giving wine he spoke, 'My life blood emptied of myself to cleanse the depths of darkness and to break the rusted poisoned chains of sin.' 'Do this, and when you do this, remember, remember, remember me, Jesus.'[88]

The petition for consecration is centred very much on the communicants:

> Share with us the Eternal Holy Breath, So that with bread and wine, we as one can partake in Jesus, who walked and talked and died among us, with watchful eyes alert and hearts burning flames of expectation and acknowledgement. That, we as one, who share this feast, Will offer our meagre, broken, love-lacking, faith-fleeing, hurting, caked in chaos, decayed and decimated lives to you, you who accepts (sic) us as one, in your utter pure holiness . . .[89]

A striking weakness in this prayer is that throughout Jesus is spoken of in the past, and there is no hint that Christ is alive and reigns in glory, but simply that he lives on with the faultless Father. Christ seems to have been immobilized in heaven, and there is little hint of divine presence in the prayer. Much of the language is striking, but, in typical postmodern secular fashion, is concerned about 'us' and our ability to use evocative imagery. Beat seems to have got the better of divine mystery.

Very recently Stefan Böntert has said:

> Liturgy is by its very nature an open, ongoing project, bearing within itself openness toward ever-new forms of expression, including those generated by

86 'Engage Worship: Resources and Training for Innovative, Creative and World-Changing Worship', www.engageworship.org, under 'Beat Eucharist' and 'themes'.

87 Rough Edge, *Beat Eucharist*, p. 81.

88 Rough Edge, *Beat Eucharist*, p. 86.

89 Rough Edge, *Beat Eucharist*, pp. 88–9.

technological advances and new media. The internet has to be included in such liturgical openness toward new forms.[90]

Since hallmarks of the postmodern era are computers and cyberspace, it is no surprise that the question of digital liturgy has been raised. There are indeed 'online churches', though the questions about ecclesiology that this raises seem complex. But if there are online churches, can they have online sacraments? Paul Fiddes has suggested that an avatar can receive the bread and wine of the Eucharist within the logic of the virtual world, and it will still be a means of grace, but others hold that sacraments cannot be offered online because they are means of grace celebrated in the midst of the body of Christ, the living, breathing, touching, hearing, tasting and smelling human, incarnate, community.[91] What little research has been undertaken suggests an even split on the question among regular worshippers who also explore online churches.[92] Online communion is offered, for example, by AlphaChurch, which has music and the recitation of a liturgy, and provides the following instructions:

> **To prepare** for Holy Communion – Eucharist
> Gather your communion elements before you begin the service:
> 1.) get a small amount of **something to drink** like juice, water, soup, broth, tea or milk.
> 2.) get a small amount of **something to eat** like a cracker, a small piece of bread, a little piece of a tortilla, or a few grains of cooked rice.
>
> During the Communion–Eucharist service the elements will be blessed/sanctified and you will eat and drink them. You may light a candle nearby to represent the light of Christ. Background music is included with the service of Holy Communion. Turn your speaker volume to a medium level. Read aloud with the responses during the Service. You may take Holy Communion as often as you wish. The service is changed periodically.[93]

Many other websites provide a similar 'service', which includes a minister telling those online when to pick up their bread and cup, and the minister's recitation

---

90 Stefan Böntert, 'Liturgical Migrations into Cyberspace: Theological Reflections', in Teresa Berger (ed.), *Liturgy in Migration: From the Upper Room to Cyberspace*, Collegeville: Liturgical Press, 2012, pp. 279–95, 289. For a broader discussion, see Rachel Wagner, *Godwired: Religion, Ritual and Virtual Reality*, London: Routledge, 2012; Pauline Hope Cheong, Peter Fischer-Nielsen, Stefan Gelfgren and Charles Ess (eds), *Digital Religion, Social Media and Culture: Perspectives, Practices and Futures*, New York: Peter Lang, 2012.

91 Paul Fiddes, 'Sacraments in a Virtual World', summary at kateboardman.me.uk/blog/wp-content/.../virtual-communion.doc; Matthew Kelley, 'The Truth As Best I Know It: Sacraments in Cyper-Space', http://www.thetruthasbestiknowit.com/2009/07/sacraments-in-cyber-space.html; 'Digital bread and wine, anyone?' http://shipoffools.com/features/2012/online_sacraments.html.

92 Ally Ostrowski, 'Cyber Communion: Finding God in the Little Box', *Journal of Religion and Society* 8 (2006), pp. 1–8.

93 'Alpha Church Services of Holy Communion Eucharist', http://www.alphachurch.org/holycomm.htm.

of the Words of Institution.[94] As God is not confined by space–time, it can be argued that whether the Eucharist is perceived as a memorial or a metacosmic presence, it would seem not to matter since God is not confined, though whether such lack of physicality actually is 'Church' would seem to require a deeper consideration. It should be noted that an announcement that Pope Benedict XVI and Archbishop Rowan Williams had jointly recognized virtual sacraments was dated *April Fools' Day* 2012.[95]

Concluding remarks

Theologians such as Chauvet, Marion and Williams all share the concern that at the heart of the Eucharist is the sacrificial love of God given as gift. They share also a reluctance to 'isolate' the Eucharist in an older definition of sacrament, but explore a less rigid and more 'poetic' and 'metaphorical' understanding of the mystery, drawing upon anthropology of signs. None of them (to the author's knowledge) have penned new liturgies, believing that their theologies are expressed in the rites current in their respective Churches. The Pentecostal contributions witness to a rediscovery of a richer and deeper eucharistic theology with implications for liturgical renewal and enrichment. When taken with other mainline developments and the postmodern approach to theological discussion, there is indication of further cross-fertilization and mutual enrichment of Churches in what is a fast-changing contemporary world. Consciously postmodern rites can be very 'local' and group-conscious rather than Trinity-conscious, and the digital age raises many questions for the future, including what constitutes a meal with koinonia, and what 'presence' means in a material world.

94 International True Gospel Christian Ministry, 'Online Church Holy Communion Service', http://www.tgcm.org/communion.html.

95 Liturgy: Worship that Works – Spirituality that Connects, 'Pope & Archbishop of Caterbury recognize virtual sacraments', http://liturgy.co.nz/pope-archbishop-of-canterbury-recognise-virtual-sacraments/9224.

Afterword

Some Crumbs from Beneath the Table

This study has surveyed the New Testament background and setting of the Eucharist. Focusing mainly on the Eucharistic Prayer or anaphora, it has examined eucharistic liturgies, the development and theology of the anaphoras, and some of the developing eucharistic theologies in a number of traditions through the centuries to the present postmodern and digital age, as far as possible in dialogue with current scholarly opinion. It might be thought that after such a survey some grand conclusion should follow, setting forth the ideal Eucharistic Prayer and an impeccable ecumenical eucharistic theology. Anyone harbouring such expectations will be disappointed. The Eucharist is the 'ongoing feast',[1] and has no conclusion or perfection until it is fulfilled in the Kingdom of God. Instead, what follows are merely some personal musings on this ritual meal.

Meals, foodstuffs and meanings

Christmas 2006 was so far the most difficult and most painful time in my life. My wife Linda had been discharged from hospital at the beginning of December, since no further treatment for her aggressive leukaemia was possible. She had come home to die. This was to be the last Christmas dinner. We decorated the house as usual and set the table with festive ware, as usual, and I cooked what had been our traditional English Christmas dinner – roast turkey with stuffing, Yorkshire pudding, brussels sprouts, roast potatoes and parsnips, with English Christmas Pudding for dessert. Linda wanted us to be happy and joyful and celebrate as at previous Christmases, and we tried to do that. But we knew that there would be no Christmas dinner like this the following year. This was the Last Christmas dinner, and at times I was overwhelmed with tears. Any future Christmas dinner would be different, for however much the food and decorations might be the same, the meal would be marked by a real absence. Subsequent to her death it seemed best to me, or for me, not to try to replicate our version of the traditional English Christmas dinner, but to do something different, however little that 'different' might be. It could not be the same because it could never be the same again, but there still had to be Christmas dinner.

The Gospel accounts of the Last Supper do not make it clear whether or not the disciples understood that this was the Last Passover (or Passover-type) meal at which Jesus would be with them, but the narratives suggest that Jesus did.

1 Borrowed from Arthur Just's title, *The Ongoing Feast: Table Fellowship and Eschatology at Emmaus*, Collegeville: Liturgical Press, 1993.

It is perhaps not insignificant that of all the possible foods of the Passover, it was bread (unspecified whether leavened or unleavened) and wine (certainly fermented, and according to custom probably with water added) that Jesus selected to be central at what would later become the normative Lord's Supper. It is not that this was a new Passover, but 'another Passover'.[2] Instead of a real absence at future Passovers, which would have been only a sad memorial, this focus on bread and wine would allow a real presence, and a joyful remembrance with thanksgiving, a Eucharist; it would have a sameness and at the same time have a difference.

The histories of bread and bread-making, and wine-making, are fascinating. Einkorn was supplanted by emmer, and from emmer, club wheat was developed, which was capable of fermentation.[3] Grinding the grain and making the bread was laborious, and traditionally in women's hands.[4] Leon Kass observes:

> Human beings must discover that certain harvestable and storable but inedible seeds, if ground, will yield flour, which, if moistened, can be kneaded into dough, which, if baked, becomes an edible, relatively nonspoilable product . . . Next are the various arts of agriculture, from plowing, fertilizing, and sowing to irrigation, harvesting, and storing – many of which involve other arts, such as metalworking, toolmaking, and animal taming. Next, and vastly more important than these matters of know-how, are the disciplined changes in the human psyche and way of life that the practice of agriculture requires.[5]

The whole process is nothing more than a transmutation through destruction, or immolation, and yet is also a product of skill and art, a new creation. Fresh wholesome bread smells and tastes good, and in much of the world has been and continues to be the basic foodstuff.

Wine also is the product of the art of cultivation and selection, and then destruction. A single Eurasian grape species among some 100 that grow wild in temperate zones is the source of 99 per cent of the world's wine today.[6] There is evidence of Neolithic wine *c.* 5400–5000 BC, but it is possible that wine-making is even older.[7] McGovern notes:

---

2 Matthew Myer Boulton, 'Supercession or Subsession? Exodus Typology, the Christian Eucharist and the Jewish Passover', *Scottish Journal of Theology* 66 (2013), pp. 18–29, p. 28.

3 John Marchant, Bryan Reuben and Joan Alcock, *Bread: A Slice of History*, Stroud: The History Press, 2008; H. E. Jacob, *Six Thousand Years of Bread: Its Holy and Unholy History*, Garden City: Doubleday, Doran and Co., 1944; John Storck and Walter Dorwin Teague, *Flour for Man's Bread: A History of Milling*, Minneapolis: Minnesota University Press, 1952; Sergei Sveshnikov, *Break the Holy Bread, Master: A Theology of Communion Bread*, BookSurge.com, 2009.

4 Teresa Berger, *Gender Differences and the Making of Liturgical History: Lifting a Veil on Liturgy's Past*, Aldershot: Ashgate, 2011, ch. 4.

5 Leon R. Kass, *The Hungry Soul: Eating and the Perfecting of Our Nature*, New York: Free Press, 1994, p. 121.

6 Patrick E. McGovern, *Ancient Wine: The Search for the Origins of Viniculture*, Princeton: Princeton University Press, 2003, p. 1.

7 McGovern, *Ancient Wine*, p. 67.

> Winemaking implies a whole constellation of the techniques beyond taking the wild grapevine into cultivation. The plants must be tended year-round to ensure that they are adequately watered and protected from animals, which might trample them, graze on the vegetation, or eat the fruit. Pests, such as mites, louses, fungi, and bacteria that the vine is subject to, might have been invisible or just barely perceptible to Stone Age humans, but an early viticulturist would have observed the tell-tale signs of disease and have tried to find a solution. Perhaps, suspect plants were rooted up, or the healthy plants moved and segregated elsewhere. With increasing knowledge of horticulture and natural contingencies, growers established new plants with the desired characteristics. The magnitude of this accomplishment is accentuated by the fact that it takes five or six years before a young vine produces fruit.[8]

The art of cultivation is matched by the process of turning the fruit to wine:

> Grapes were first treaded in crushing vats to extract the juice or must. A bag press or a funnel and weight might have been used to squeeze out any remaining juice from the solid residue. Pottery jars were then filled with the juice, which quickly fermented to wine by natural processes.[9]

However, wine contains other properties that are not unimportant. McGovern continues:

> Early humans must have been astounded when they first experienced wine's tangible and seemingly other-worldly potency. Metaphorically, the lush, full-bodied clusters of the grapevine represented nature's fecundity, and it was not much of a leap to associate the juice of its fruit with the red liquid, blood, that filled and nourished the human body. If it was the preferred beverage of elite humans, wine must also be the drink of the gods. It was an elixir nonpareil.[10]

The 'spiritual' properties of wine are taken up by philosopher Roger Scruton. Wine, says Scruton, reminds the soul of its bodily origins, and the body of its spiritual meaning.[11] He writes:

> That first sip of a fine wine stirs, as it makes its way downwards, the rooted sense of my incarnation. I know that I am flesh, the by-product of bodily processes which are being brought to a heightened life by the drink that settles within me. But this very drink radiates the sense of self: it is addressed to the soul, not the body, and poses questions that can be formulated only in the first-person case, and only in the language of freedom: 'what am I, how am I, where now do I go?[12]

---

8 McGovern, *Ancient Wine*, p. 14.

9 McGovern, *Ancient Wine*, p. 59.

10 McGovern, *Ancient Wine*, p. 303.

11 Roger Scruton, *I Drink Therefore I Am: A Philosopher's Guide to Wine*, London: Continuum Press, 2010, p. 99.

12 Scruton, *I Drink Therefore I Am*, p. 106.

He regards wine as gift, but in terms of *agape* and not *eros:*

> Both come to fruition in a gift. But in *agape* the gift is repeatable, renewable, and always in search of some new recipient, while in *eros* the gift is focused on another, is jealously withheld until the moment is right and given only on condition of mutuality.[13]

It is an object of thought and a vehicle of reflection.[14]

In addition, wine was a prime medical agent, administered internally and externally (the Good Samaritan poured oil *and wine* on the wounded man), and those who drank wine were more likely to live longer than those who drank straight water (hence the advice in 1 Tim. 5.23). Furthermore, in addition to alcohol, wine has antioxidants. McGovern notes that the fermentation process made it more nutritious than grapes, and, 'more subtly, wine's preeminence in world history can be traced to its array of chemical compounds, which titillate the senses and challenge human imagination'.[15] Wine thus also represents a transmutation, giving rise to both pleasure and, in moderation, medicinal health benefits. It is, says Scruton, 'a living thing, the last result of other living things, and the progenitor of life in us'.[16]

Although a Passover setting might suggest unleavened bread, in the course of the history of the Church both leavened and unleavened bread have been used at the Eucharist, with certain Churches adopting the one and prohibiting the use of the other. The meaning of *artos* is such that in the New Testament context it could be either.[17] However, whether leavened or unleavened, Scripture assumes that it is bread and not, in the words of William Willimon, 'wafers and pellets that look more like fish food than bread of the world'.[18] Though pastoral concern may require provision for the gluten intolerant, bread for this feast should be bread-like in appearance and taste and be appetizing. An even greater problem is with the substitution *out of choice rather than of necessity* of something other than wine. It is true that in the Church in Kerala, unable to procure wine, raisins were soaked in water, and in Ethiopia crushed grapes were mixed with water. These instances are different from the nineteenth-century concern with alcoholism and hysteria over microbes that led to Thomas and Charles Welch's industry in grape juice and the use of individual communion cups.[19] The latter are absolutely

13 Scruton, *I Drink Therefore I Am*, p. 77.

14 Scruton, *I Drink Therefore I Am*, p. 123.

15 McGovern, *Ancient Wine*, p. 306.

16 Scruton, *I Drink Therefore I Am*, p. 131.

17 Interestingly, the Armenian Orthodox insist on unleavened bread, but are in communion with the Coptic, Syrian and Ethio-Eritrean Churches that use leavened bread.

18 William Willimon, 'Communion as a Culinary Art', *The Christian Century* (21 September, 1977), pp. 829–30.

19 William Chazonof, *Welch's Grape Juice: From Corporation to Co-operation*, Syracuse: Syracuse University Press, 1977; Susan J. White, *Christian Worship and Technological Change*, Nashville: Abingdon Press, 1994; Jennifer L. Woodruff Tait, *The Poisoned Chalice: Eucharistic Grape Juice and Common-Sense Realism in Victorian Methodism*, Tuscaloosa: University of Alabama Press, 2011. As far as the common cup and hygiene is concerned, the properties of alcohol, when combined with the quite amazing sterilizing properties of silver in a silver chalice or cup, make any contamination practically impossible.

necessary once the sterilizing properties of wine have been replaced by pasteurized grape juice, though some Church of Scotland churches retained a common cup but provided individual communion spoons.[20] It may be that grape juice should be available for those with alcoholic problems, but communion in one kind (and this would apply to the gluten intolerant also) has always been considered perfectly valid. The use of pre-packaged individual plastic containers of grape juice and a wafer speak more of fast food totally devoid of nutrition and flavour than of nourishing food and drink prefiguring the feast of the Kingdom. Good bread (leavened or unleavened) *and* good wine should be used for this 'other' Passover, since the food and drink should taste 'divine'.

These elements, selected from other possibilities of the Passover foods, seem already to prefigure the life, death and resurrection of Christ, and so are most apt for this 'other' Passover. Quite apart from whether 'transubstantiation' is an appropriate term for 'consecrated elements', Jesus' words concerning each element suggest at least some further transmutation in meaning, and the elements were intended to become in some way a vehicle for 'presence' instead of 'absence'. Roger Scruton writes of the Eucharist:

> Christ, holding the cup to his disciples, declares that 'this is my blood of the New Testament, shed for you and for the remission of sins'. The blood in question is not the physical stuff that goes by that name, but something intimately bound up with the 'I' of Christ. The bread just eaten at the altar – the body of Christ – is made conscious by the wine. Bread and wine stand to each other as body to soul, as object to subject, as the thing *in* the world to its reflection at the edge.[21]

Scruton, like Marion, sees the elements as meaning gift and self-less love. Whatever the 'transmutation', the bread and wine convey the 'I' of Christ, which is the gift of divine love. Angel Méndez Montoya argues that the gift's consumption carries an aspect of kenosis in order for the gift to be received.[22] The kenosis of the eucharistic gift is a self-immersion of Christ with the Holy Spirit into finite humanity; divinity takes the risk of becoming food because of a desire to indwell (or abide) in the beloved, just as food becomes part of the eater. He cites Gerard Loughlin:

> Gift and given, Christ and the donees who receive him, are one. To receive the gift of God is to be incorporated into the triune life, into the eternity of donation, of giving and receiving back again. Indeed, the unity of the body of Christ is the unity of giver, gift and given – of teller, story and listener; of playwright, play and player; of *host, meal and guest* – and the unity of the Body is the presence given in the present of the Eucharist.[23]

---

20 The Very Reverend Iain Torrance kindly gave me one of the small long-handled ladle-like, hall-marked silver spoons that came from Moffat Parish Church. The quality and design suggests a gravitas that disposable plastic spoons simply would not possess!

21 Scruton, *I Drink Therefore I Am*, p. 107.

22 Angel F. Méndez Montoya, *The Theology of Food: Eating and the Eucharist*, Chichester: Wiley-Blackwell, 2009, p. 143.

23 Méndez Montoya, *Theology of Food*, p. 155, citing Gerard Loughlin, *Telling God's Story: Bible, Church and Narrative Theology*, Cambridge: Cambridge University Press, 1996, p. 242.

Thanksgiving, sacrifice and presence

The saving work of Jesus Christ is pure thanksgiving, the perfect expression of praise to the Father, who through the Son pours out the divine love even to death on a cross. The whole passion is an unveiling of the Father's infinite love for the world.[24] Whenever the Church celebrates the Eucharist it recalls and receives again the gift of love through a ritual that represents the sacrifice of God and which is dramatically symbolized in the sharing of bread and wine. Ephrem expressed it perfectly:

> He broke the bread with his hands as a symbol for the sacrifice of his body. He mixed the cup with his hands as a symbol for the sacrifice of his blood. He sacrificed and offered himself, the priest of our atonement.[25]

Our gratitude is verbalized by recounting again the history of the gift, both in temporal history (then, there) as well as God's eternity (the alpha and omega, and to whom all ages belong). The classical anaphoras do this well, and by use of the Sanctus underline the eschatological nature of the liturgy. The praise of humanity is united with that of heaven, and in this ritual, time and eternity elide. The Spirit is invited to come upon the material and transcend the material to become spiritually fecund. The food and drink are earthly and heavenly, temporal and eternal. God's own institution of the ritual may be rehearsed, for the word goes forth and does not return empty. But the Institution Narrative is not itself the Church's thanksgiving, but only its permission and encouragement to make its thanksgiving. The Church unites in its prayer with the Church past, the Church present and the Church to come in the Kingdom. There is no reason why a Church need always or ever follow the structures of the classical anaphoras, but their substance is crucial. Since the prayer over the food voices to God before the world the gratitude for the gift, to abbreviate, truncate or hurry this prayer for the sake of time is bad practice and poor gratitude. Of course, where the meal resembles starvation rations and the worst of fast food, there is little incentive for prolonged thanksgiving. But a rich feast, the gift of divine love, requires an adequate thanksgiving. It should be, as in Justin Martyr's community, 'at some length' and prayed (said or chanted) with care, and not raced. The Lima Eucharistic Prayer, while like all anaphoras is not perfect, nevertheless deserves including in denominational books, or at least permitted even if only once a year, to express the unity that we supposedly already have.

H. E. W. Turner pointed out that our concern over presence should not be about the 'how' or 'what' but the 'who'.[26] Some extreme Protestant pastors take the opportunity to tell their congregations what they do not believe about the elements and presence, and almost plead for God to absent himself from the Supper, preferring to experience it as a memorial of an absent and departed

24 Peter Casarella, 'Eucharist: Presence of a Gift', in Roch A. Kereszty (ed.), *Rediscovering the Eucharist: Ecumenical Conversations*, New York: Paulist Press, 2003, p. 201.

25 'Paschal Hymn Unleaven Bread II.7', in J. Edward Walters (trans.), *Hymns on the Unleavened Bread*, Piscataway: Gorgias Press, 2012, p. 20.

26 H. E. W. Turner, 'The Eucharistic Presence', in *Thinking about the Eucharist*, London: SCM Press, 1972.

friend.[27] Perhaps you get what you do or don't pray for. Pseudo-Ephrem wrote: 'Take, eat in faith, and do not doubt that this is my body. Whoever eats it in faith, eats the Fire and Spirit in it. Whoever doubts and eats it, for him it is plain bread.'[28]

There is a difference between believing that Christ gives what he promises and having some technical explanation for the 'how'. What eucharistic doctrine gropes towards and strains to assert is the 'who'. It is not a shadow, or a memory, but the whole Christ, incarnate, crucified, dead and buried, risen, ascended and glorified – that one and only Christ, and not some substitute or some hologram. Matthew Levering notes with Bulgakov that Christ's glorified body is still a 'body' in the sense that all material things are created to manifest spirit:

> Christ's body is 'metacosmic', therefore, because his spirit can manifest itself in any matter and thereby unite such matter with his glorified 'body', making the matter to *be* his glorified body. The bread and wine manifest and are the glorified Lord. In terms of this world, the bread and wine are not changed; but in terms of the heavenly realm they are deified.[29]

The end or goal of the Eucharist is the consummation of our intimate union with the Person, Jesus Christ, in the glory of trinitarian communion.[30] Or, as the nineteenth-century Reformed theologian John Williamson Nevin put it, the real communication that believers have with Christ in the Holy Supper extends to his 'whole' person: 'We partake not of his divinity only, nor yet of his Spirit as separate from himself, but also of his true and proper humanity.'[31] Ephrem expressed it thus:

> His body was newly mixed with our bodies, and His pure blood has been poured out into our veins, and His voice into our ears, and His brightness into our eyes. All of Him has been mixed into all of us by His compassion, and since He loves His church very much, he did not give her the manna of her rival. He has living bread for her to eat.[32]

The one who is present and the one who is received is the one Lord Jesus Christ.

The one crucial sacrifice in Scripture is that of the cross, but the Supper expressed proleptically the sacrifice, and now the Eucharist both reclaims and

27 For an example, see Howard Dorgan, *Giving Glory to God in Appalachia: Worship Practices of Six Baptist Subdenominations*, Knoxville: University of Tennessee Press, 1987, p. 142.

28 'Sermones in Hebdomadam Sanctam IV.106–111', cited in Sidney H. Griffith, '"Spirit in the Bread; Fire in the Wine": The Eucharist as "Living Medicine" in Ephraem the Syrian', in Sarah Beckwith (ed.), *Catholicism and Catholicity: Eucharistic Communities in Historical and Contemporary Perspectives*, Oxford: Blackwell, 1999, pp. 113–34, p. 127.

29 Matthew Levering, *Sacrifice and Community: Jewish Offering and Christian Eucharist*, Oxford: Blackwell Publishing, 2005, p. 120.

30 Levering, *Sacrifice and Community*, p. 167.

31 John Williamson Nevin, *The Mystical Presence and the Doctrine of the Reformed Church on the Lord's Supper*, ed. Linden J. DeBie, Eugene, OR: Wipf and Stock, 2012, pp. 160–1.

32 'Hymns on Virginity 37', in Kathleen McVey, *Ephrem the Syrian: Hymns*, New York: Paulist Press, 1989, p. 425.

proclaims the sacrifice, and promises as gift him who was the sacrifice. It is difficult not to acknowledge that the theme of offering and sacrifice is bound up in some way with the Supper. In a sermon on the Lord's Supper, the eighteenth-century New England Congregationalist Jonathan Edwards wrote:

> What joy may it well cause in us when we see sensibly represented by Christ's own appointment Christ manifesting so great a love for us, to see Christ offering Himself slain for us, Himself to be our food for the relief of our poor, perishing souls.[33]

Discussing the Eastern Orthodox anaphoral phrase, 'offering your own of your own', D. Bentley Hart writes:

> Because God is Trinity, Christ's self-oblation for us is a naturally divine act; and the divinization of creation that it brings about is the perfect revelation of the *qurban* of God's Trinitarian being; and we see this in the Eucharist. We, in some real sense, taste and are nourished by the whole mystery of our redemption, our 'sacrificial' entry into the Trinity's life, and so in the drama of offering up and receiving, we gain some slight but true glimpse of the Trinity's infinite beauty.[34]

We are taken into Christ's sacrifice so that we may also offer a sacrificial way of life, imitating the divine love. Matthew Levering expresses it as follows:

> The sacrament of the Eucharist is a 'school' of charity; it builds the Church by enabling us to enact Christ's sacrifice with him. In the liturgy of the Eucharist, we learn 'Jesus Christ and him crucified' (1 Cor. 2:2) and thereby we '[p]ut on the whole armor of God' (Eph. 6:11) . . . Our cruciform communion, in the Eucharist, teaches us the path of the God-centered life by drawing us sacrificially out of ourselves and into the wondrous communion of Christ's Body.[35]

How to express this in the liturgy and in doctrine has and continues to be a cause of division.

From presence to eschatology

Levering's idea of a school of charity and his reference to Ephesians 6.1 connects well with the eschatological fruits and implications of this feast of bread and wine. The famous English chaplain of the First World War, Geoffrey Studdert Kennedy, reflected on the Eucharist and the broken, mutilated bodies of the men to whom he had tried to minister and then had to bury. He wrote:

33 Don Kistler (ed.), *Jonathan Edwards, Sermons on the Lord's Supper*, Orlando: Northampton Press, 2007, p. 53.

34 D. Bentley Hart, '"Thine Own of Thine Own": Eucharistic Sacrifice in the Orthodox Tradition', in Kereszty (ed.), *Rediscovering the Eucharist*, pp. 142–69, p. 165.

35 Levering, *Sacrifice and Community*, pp. 199–200.

> But here, broken bodies and pools of blood are the most ordinary things in life. So ghastly ordinary, always bodies, broken battered bodies, and always blood. Is it wrong to see in them His Body and His Blood – God's Body, God's Blood? They are His; He is their Father, their Lover, and His heart must bleed in them.[36]

He went on to apply this reflection to 'Christian soldiers':

> To be a man means to be a thinking creature, filled with the spirit of suffering and creative love which made him. The Sacrament is the means by which we become filled with that spirit. It is the heart, the blood centre, of the great army of men who, having seen and loved God in Christ, are resolved to fight for and suffer with Him unto death and beyond it. It is the appointed means and method of meeting God. We are ready to have our bodies broken and our blood shed in the great Christian warfare against wrong, and we come for the refreshing of our spirits that we may not shrink. That bread is the ration of a fearless, fiercely fighting army. That wine is the stirrup-cup of a band of knights who ride out to an endless war.[37]

In this meal many of the classical Eucharistic Prayers pray for forgiveness of sins, and life eternal, by means of the life-giving and absolving covenant-filled life of Christ – 'that he may dwell in us and we in him'. The implication is that we become involved and immersed in God's sacrificial love to and for the world, and are called to take up our cross and follow. It is this mutual indwelling whereby Christ dwells in and unites his Church as his body that also unites believers with one another not only of the present, but also of the past and the future. The classical anaphoras quickly developed prayers for the living and the dead. These lists today are often interminably long and full of long-forgotten names, and the pastoral wisdom of such lengthy lists of names is questionable. The principle, though, is absolutely sound. All are made present and alive in Christ because of this mutual indwelling, and we feast with and upon the same one whom others have in the past and more will do so in the future, until all will feast together in the Kingdom. John Koenig expresses it thus:

> In the strongest possible way Christ makes known to those who approach his table that he ardently desires their company, just as they are (John 14:18–23; 15:2; 17:2f; 21:12; see also Luke 22:15; Rom. 15:7). He welcomes believers with compassion, refreshment, and forgiveness (Matt. 11:28ff; 26:28). But then he also summons them to renewed discipleship (John 20:11–23; 21:9–22); for more than anything else the eucharistic Christ of the New Testament presents himself as a vigorous king, moving decisively toward the final appropriation of his rule over all creation.[38]

36 G. A. Studdert Kennedy, *The Hardest Part*, London: American YMCA, 1918, p. 134.

37 Studdert Kennedy, *The Hardest Part*, pp. 135–6.

38 John Koening, *The Feast of the World's Redemption: Eucharistic Origins and Christian Mission*, Harrisburg: Trinity Press International, 2000, p. 224.

This entails the transformation of this world until it becomes 'the kingdoms of our Lord and of his Christ', and the Lord of Hosts will provide that 'feast of rich food and choice wines'. In the meantime, he 'this wondrous banquet founded'. We do this in remembrance of him, celebrating in prayer, song and chant, and we receive the bread and wine, but (at least for this writer), like God's peace, its full meaning 'passes all understanding'.[39] After the act of communion the Church of Ireland eucharistic rite has something called 'the Great Silence'. That perhaps is a most fitting response to this sublime *mysterion*.

39 From the blessing at the Holy Communion 1662 rite of the Church of England.

Appendix 1

The Classical Anaphoral Families

East Syrian	West Syrian	Egyptian	Roman	Gallican/Mozarabic
Dialogue	Dialogue	Dialogue	Dialogue	Dialogue
Trinitarian praise	Praise/Thanksgiving	Brief praise	Preface	Preface (very variable in length)
Sanctus	Sanctus		Sanctus	Sanctus
		Intercessions	Intercession	
Christological Thanksgiving	Christological Thanksgiving	Sanctus and Epiklesis	Petition for Consecration	Transition Praise
Institution Narrative	Institution Narrative	(Anamnesis) Institution Narrative	Institution Narrative	Institution Narrative
Anamnesis	Anamnesis	Anamnesis	Anamnesis	Anamnesis
Intercessions	Epiklesis	Epiklesis	Intercessions	Epiklesis or Petition
Epiklesis	Intercessions			
Doxology	Doxology	Doxology	Doxology	Doxology

Bibliography

A Book of Services, Edinburgh: Saint Andrew Press, 1980.

A Collection of Hymns: for Camp Meetings, revivals, &c., for the Use of Primitive Methodists, New York, 1844.

'The Acts of Thomas', ET: *The Apocryphal Acts*, vol. II, ed. W. Wright, London: Williams and Norgate, 1871.

Addicott, L. E. and L. G. Champion (eds), *Church Book: St. Andrew's Street Baptist Church, Cambridge 1720–1832*, Didcot: Baptist Historical Society, 1991.

Additional Eucharistic Prayers with Guidance on Celebrating the Eucharist with Children, London: Church House Publishing, 2012.

Adisho, Mar, *The Book of Marganitha (The Pearl)*, trans. Mar Eshai Shimun XXIII, Ernakulam, Kerala: Mar Themotheus Memorial Printing, 1965.

Albrecht, Daniel E., *Rites in the Spirit: A Ritual Approach to Pentecostal/Charismatic Spirituality*, Sheffield: Sheffield Academic Press, 1999.

Alexopoulas, Stefanos, 'The Influence of Iconoclasm on Liturgy: A Case Study', in Roberta R. Ervine (ed.), *Worship Traditions in Armenia and the Neighboring Christian East*, Crestwood: St Vladimir's Press with St Nersses Seminary, 2006, pp. 127–37.

Alexopoulas, Stefanos, *Presanctified Liturgy in the Byzantine Rite: A Comparative Analysis of Its Origins, Evolution, and Structural Components*, Liturgia Condenda 21, Leuven: Peeters, 2009.

Alikin, Valeriy A., *The Earliest History of the Christian Gathering: Origin, Development and Content of the Christian Gathering in the First to the Third Centuries*, Leiden: Brill, 2010.

'Alpha Church Services of Holy Communion Eucharist', http://www.alphachurch.org/holycomm.htm.

Amar, Joseph P., 'Perspectives on the Eucharist in Ephrem the Syrian', *Worship* 61 (1987), pp. 441–54.

Ames, William, *The Marrow of Sacred Theology*, trans. John Dykstra Eusden, Grand Rapids: Baker Books, 1997.

Andrieu, M. and P. Collomp, 'Fragments sur papyrus de l'anaphore de saint Marc', *Revue ces sciences religieuses* 8 (1928), pp. 489–515.

Anglican/Roman Catholic Joint Preparatory Commission, 'The Final Report', http://www.anglicancommunion.org/ministry/ecumenical/dialogues/catholic/arcic/docs/pdf/final_report_arcic_1.pdf.

Antiochene Orthodox Christian Archdiocese of North America, *The Liturgikon: The Book of Divine Services for the Priest and Deacon*, Grand Rapids: Dickinson Press, 1989.

Archbishop's Commission on Christian Doctrine, *Thinking about the Eucharist*, London: SCM Press, 1972.

Artsruni, Vahan, CD, *Chants from the East, Sacred Episodes and Sacred Rituals*, music and documentary, Chicago: Assyrian Universal Alliance Foundation, 2007.

Assyrian Church of the East, *The Liturgy of the Holy Apostles Adai and Mari*, reprint, Piscataway: Gorgias Press, [1890] 2002.

Attridge, Harold W., 'The Original Language of the *Acts of Thomas*', in Harold W. Attridge, John J. Collins, and Thomas H. Tobin (eds), *Of Scribes and Scrolls: Studies on the Hebrew Bible, Intertestamental Judaism, and Christian Origins Presented to John Strugnell on the Occasion of His Sixtieth Birthday*, Lanham: University of America Press, 1990, pp. 241–50.

Attridge, Harold W., *The Acts of Thomas*, Salem: Polebridge Press, 2010.

Aulén, Gustav, *Eucharist and Sacrifice*, Philadelphia: Muhlenberg Press, 1958.

Aydin, Gabriel, *Jacob of Edessa: Commentary on the Holy Qurobo made to George the Stylite of Sarug from Ms. Berlin Sachau 218*, private translation.

Ayres, Lewis, *Nicaea and its Legacy: An approach to Fourth Century Trinitarian Theology*, New York: Oxford University Press, 2006.

Baldovin, John F. *The Urban Character of Christian Worship: The Origins, Development, and Meaning of Stational Liturgy*, Rome: Pontificorum Institutum Studiorum Orientalium, 1987.

Baldovin, John F., 'The Fermentum at Rome in the Fifth Century: A Reconsideration', *Worship* 79 (2005), pp. 38–53.

Baldovin, John, *Reforming the Liturgy: A Response to the Critics*, Collegeville: Liturgical Press, 2008.

Bandrés, José L., 'The Ethiopian Anaphora of the Apostles: historical considerations', *Proche-Orient Chretien* 34 (1986), pp. 3–13.

Bandrés, José L., *A Glance behind the Curtain: Reflections on the Ethiopian Celebration of the Eucharist*, Ethiopia: Master Printing Press, 2008.

Bandrés, José, 'The Rite of the Fractio or the Breaking of the Bread in the Ethiopian Liturgy', *Ethiopian Review of Cultures* 4–5 (1994–5), pp. 101–11.

Bangert, Mark P., '"This is my Blood of the New Testament": The Institution of the Lord's Supper in Bach's Matthew Passion: An Exemplar for Hearing the Passion', in A. A. Clement (ed.), *Das Blut Jesu und die Lehre von der Versöhnung im Werk Johann Sebastian Bachs*, Amsterdam: Royal Netherlands Academy of Arts and Sciences, 1995, pp. 215–32.

Barker, Margaret, *The Great High Priest: The Temple Roots of Christian Liturgy*, London: T & T Clark, 2003.

Barnwell, P. S., Claire Cross and Ann Rycraft, *Mass and Parish in Late Medieval England: The Use of York*, Reading, England: Spire Books Ltd, 2005.

Barrett, Ivan J., *Joseph Smith and the Restoration*, Provo: Brigham Young University Press, 1973.

Barrett-Leonard, R., *The Sacramentary of Sarapion of Thmuis: A Text for Students*, Alcuin/GROW Liturgical Study 25, Bramcote: Grove Books, 1993.

Barrow, Henry, 'A Brief Discoverie of the False Church', in Leland H. Carson (ed.), *The Writings of John Greenwood and Henry Barrow 1591–1593*, London: George Allen and Unwin Ltd, 1970, pp. 418–19.

Barth, Karl, *Church Dogmatics*, ed. T. F. Torrance, trans. G. W. Bromiley, originally published in German: Zollikon–Zürich: Evangelischer Verlag, 1932–59, London and New York: T & T Clark, 1936–77.

Barth, P. and G. Niesel (eds), *Joannis Calvini Opera Selecta*, vol. 2, reprint, Eugene, OR: Wipf and Stock, 2011.

Bartlett, Alan, 'How Protestant was Cranmer's 1552 Prayer Book?', in David M. Loades (ed.), *Word and Worship*, Oxford: The Davenant Press, 2005, pp. 65–74.

Bates, W. H., 'Thanksgiving in the Liturgy of St. Mark', in Bryan D. Spinks (ed.), *The Sacrifice of Praise*, Rome: CLV Edizioni Liturgiche, 1981, pp. 107–19.

Batstone, Louise, 'Doctrinal and Theological Themes in the Prayers of the Bobbio Missal', in Yitzak Hen and Rob Meens (eds), *The Bobbio Missal: Liturgy and Religious Culture in Merovingian Gaul*, Cambridge: Cambridge University Press, 2004, pp. 168–86.

Bauckham, Richard, *Jesus and the Eyewitnesses: The Gospels as Eyewitness Testimony*, Grand Rapids: Eerdmans, 2006.

Baum, Wilhelm and Dietmar Winkler, *The Church of the East: A Concise History*, London: Routledge, 2010.

Baumer, Christopher, *The Church of the East: An Illustrated History of Assyrian Christianity*, New York: I. B. Tauris, 2006.

Baumstark, Anton, 'Die Chrysostomosliturgie und die syrische Liturgie des Nestorios', *Chrysostomika* (1908), pp. 846–8.

Bausi, Alessandro, 'The So-called Traditio Apostolicae: Preliminary Observations on the New Ethiopic Evidence', in Heike Grieser and Andreas Merkt (eds), *Volksglaube im antiken Christentum*, Darmstadt: Wissenschaftliche Buchgesellschaft, 2009, pp. 291–321.

Baxter, Philip, *Sarum Use: The Ancient Customs of Salisbury*, Reading, England: Spire Books Ltd, 2008.

Beale, G. K., *The Temple and the Church's Mission*, Downers Grove: InterVarsity Press, 2004.

Beardslee III, John W. (trans.), *Reformed Dogmatics*, New York: Oxford University Press, 1965.

Beck, Edmund, *Ephraem Syrus: Sermones in Hebdomadam Sanctam*, Louvain: CSCO, 1979.

Beck, Henry, *The Pastoral Care of Souls in South-East France during the Sixth Century*, Rome: Universitatis Gregorianae, 1950.

Beckwith, Sarah, 'Ritual, Church and Theatre: Medieval Dramas of the Sacramental Body', in David Aers (ed.), *Culture and History 1300–1600*, New York: Harvester Wheatsheaf, 1992, pp. 65–89.

Bedford, Thomas, *A Treatise of the Sacraments*, London, 1638.

Beggiani, Seely J., *The Divine Liturgy of the Maronite Church: History and Commentary*, New York: St Maron Publications, 1998.

Bem, Kazimierz, '"From Many Different Sources": The Formation of the Polish and Lithuanian Reformed Liturgy', in Teresa Berger (ed.), *Liturgy in Migration: From the Upper Room to Cyberspace*, Collegeville: Liturgical Press, 2012, pp. 101–30.

Bem, Kazimierz, 'The Formation of the Polish and Lithuanian Reformed Liturgy', STM thesis, Yale Divinity School, 2012.

Berger, Teresa, *Liturgie–Spiegel der Kirche: Eine systematisch-theologische Analyse des liturgischen Gedankenguts im Traktarianism*, Forschungen zur Systematischen und ökumenischen Theologie 52, Göttingen: Vandenhoeck and Ruprecht, 1986.

Berger, Teresa, *Theology in Hymns? A Study of the Relationship of Doxology and Theology According to a Collection of Hymns for the Use of the People Called Methodists (1780)*, Nashville: Kingswood Books, 1995.

Berger, Teresa, *Women's Ways of Worship: Gender Analysis and Liturgical History*, Collegeville: Pueblo, 1999.

Berger, Teresa, '*Veni Creator Spiritus*: The Elusive Real Presence of the Spirit in the Catholic Tradition', in Teresa Berger and Bryan D. Spinks (eds), *The Spirit in Worship: Worship in the Spirit*, Collegeville: Liturgical Press, 2009, pp. 141–54.

Berger, Teresa, *Gender Differences and the Making of Liturgical History: Lifting a Veil on Liturgy's Past*, Aldershot: Ashgate, 2011.

Bergsma, Johannes H., *Die Reform der Messliturgie durch Johannes Bugenhagen (1485–1558)*, Kevelaer: Verlag Butzon and Bercker, 1966.

Bernard, Philippe, *Transitions liturgiques en Gaule carolingianne: Une traduction commentée des deux 'lettres' faussement atrribuées à l'évêque Germain de Paris*, Paris: Hora Decima, 2008.

Berthold, George C., *Maximus Confessor: Selected Writings*, New York: Paulist Press, 1985.

Best, Thomas F. and Dagmar Heller (eds), *Eucharistic Worship in Ecumenical Contexts*, Geneva: WCC, 1998.

Beukers, C. L., 'For our Emperors, Soldiers and Allies: An Attempt at Dating the Twenty-Third Catechesis by Cyrillus of Jerusalem', *Vigiliae Christianae* 15 (1961), pp. 177–84.

Bexell, Oloph (ed.), *The Meaning of Christian Liturgy: Recent Developments in the Church of Sweden*, Grand Rapids: Eerdmans, 2012.

Bickersteth, Edward, *A Treatise on the Lord's Supper*, 6th edn, London: Seeley, 1825.

Bierma, Lyle D., 'The Purpose and Authorship of the Heidelberg Catechism', in Lyle D. Bierma, Charles D. Gunnoe, Jr and Karin Maag, *An Introduction to the Heidelberg Catechism: Sources, History, and Theology*, Grand Rapids: Baker Books, 2005, pp. 49–74.

Biernoff, Suzannah, *Sight and Embodiment in the Middle Ages*, Basingstoke: Palgrave Macmillan, 2002.

Bindley, T. Herbert and F. W. Green, *The Oecumenical Documents of the Faith*, London: Methuen and Co., 1950.

Blond, George, 'Clement of Rome', in Willy Rordorf et al. (eds), *The Eucharist of the Early Christians*, New York: Pueblo Publishing, 1978, pp. 24–47.

Bloomberg, Craig L., *Contagious Holiness: Jesus' Meals with Sinners*, Downers Grove: InterVarsity Press, 2005.

Bobrinskoy, Boris, 'Liturgie et Ecclésiologie Trinitaire de Saint Basile', in B. Botte (ed.), *Eucharisities d'Orient et d'Occident*, vol. 2, Paris: Les Éditions du Cerf, 1970, pp. 197–240.

Boeve, Lieven, 'Thinking Sacramental Presence in a Postmodern Context: A Playground for Renewal', in L. Boeve and L. Leijssen (eds), *Sacramental*

Presence in a Postmodern Context, Leuven: Leuven University Press, 2001, pp. 3–35.

Bokser, Baruch M., *The Origins of the Seder: The Passover Rite and Early Rabbinic Judaism*, Berkeley: University of California Press, 1984.

Böntert, Stefan, 'Liturgical Migrations into Cyberspace: Theological Reflections', in Teresa Berger (ed.), *Liturgy in Migration: From the Upper Room to Cyberspace*, Collegeville: Liturgical Press, 2012.

The Book of Common Order (1979), Edinburgh: Saint Andrew Press, 1979.

Bordeyne, Philippe and Bruce Morrill (eds), *Sacraments, Revelation of the Humanity of God: Engaging the Fundamental Theology of Louis-Marie Chauvet*, Collegeville: Liturgical Press, 2008.

Borgen, Ole E., *John Wesley on the Sacraments*, Grand Rapids: Francis Asbury Press, 1986.

Bornert, René, *Les Commentaires Byzantins de la Divine Liturgie du VIIe au XVe siècle*, Paris: Institu Français d'Etudes Byzantines, 1966.

Bornet, René, *La Réforme Protestante du Culte à Strasbourg au XVIe siècle (1523–1598)*, Leiden: Brill, 1981.

Botte, Bernard, 'L'Anaphore Chaldéenne des Apôtres', *Orientalia Christiana Peridoica* 15 (1949), pp. 259–76.

Botte, Bernard, 'L'Eucologue de Sérapion est-il authentique'?', *Oriens Christianus* 48 (1964), pp. 50–6.

Botte, Bernard, *Le canon de la Messe Romaine*, Louvain: Abbaye du Mont César, 1935.

Botte, Bernard, *La Tradition Apostolique de saint Hippolyte*, LQF 39, Münster: Aschendorff, 1963.

Botte, Bernard, *From Silence to Participation: An Insider's View of Liturgical Renewal*, Washington: The Pastoral Press, 1988.

Bouley, Allan, *From Freedom to Formula: The Evolution of the Eucharistic Prayer from Oral Improvisation to Written Texts*, Washington: Catholic University of America, 1981.

Bouyer, Louis, *Eucharist: Theology and Spirituality of the Eucharistic Prayer*, Notre Dame: University of Notre Dame Press, 1968.

Bouyer, Louis, 'The Third Eucharistic Prayer', in Lancelot Sheppard (ed.), *The New Liturgy: A Comprehensive Introduction*, London: Darton, Longman and Todd, 1970, pp. 203–12.

Bower, Peter C., *The Companion to the Book of Common Worship*, Louisville: Geneva Press, 2003.

Bowman, Matthew, 'This is my Body: A Mormon Sacrament', *Dialogue: A Journal of Mormon Thought* 44 (2011), pp. 208–14.

Boynton, Susan, 'Restoration or Invention? Archbishop Cisneros and the Mozarabic Rite in Toledo', *Yale Institute of Sacred Music: Colloquium* 6 (2013), pp. 125–39.

Bracken Long, Kimberly, *The Eucharistic Theology of the American Holy Fairs*, Louisville: Westminster John Knox Press, 2011.

Bradshaw, Paul F., 'Zebah Todah and the Origins of the Eucharist', *Ecclesia Orans* 8 (1991), pp. 245–60.

Bradshaw, Paul F., 'Redating the Apostolic Tradition: Some Preliminary Steps', in Nathan Mitchell and John F. Baldovin (eds), *Rule of Prayer, Rule of Faith:*

Essays in Honor of Aidan Kavanagh OSB, Collegeville: Liturgical Press, 1996, pp. 3–17.

Bradshaw, Paul F., *The Search for the Origins of Christian Worship*, New York: Oxford University Press, 2002.

Bradshaw, Paul F., *Eucharistic Origins*, London: SPCK, 2004.

Bradshaw, Paul F., *Reconstructing Early Christian Worship*, London: SPCK, 2009.

Bradshaw, Paul F., 'The Barcelona Papyrus and the development of Early Eucharistic Prayers', in Maxwell. E. Johnson (ed.), *Issues in Eucharistic Praying in East and West: Essays in Liturgical and Theological Analysis*, Collegeville: Liturgical Press, 2010, pp. 129–38.

Bradshaw, Paul F., 'What Do We Really Know about the Earliest Roman Liturgy?', paper given at the North American Academy of Liturgy, 2010.

Bradshaw, Paul F. and Maxwell E. Johnson, *The Eucharistic Liturgies: Their Evolution and Interpretation*, Collegeville: Liturgical Press, 2012.

Bradshaw, Paul F., Maxwell E. Johnson and L. Edward Phillips, *The Apostolic Tradition: A Commentary*, Minneapolis: Fortress Press, 2002.

Brakmann, Heinzgerd, 'Le Déroulement de la Messe Copte: Structure et Histoire', in A. M. Triacca and A. Pistoia (eds), *L'Eucharistie: Célébrations, Rites, Piétés*, Rome: CLV Edizioni Liturgiche, 1995, pp. 107–32.

Brandenburg, Hugo, *Ancient Churches of Rome from the Fourth to the Seventh Century*, Turnhout: Brepols, 2005.

Braum, James Hart (ed.), *Liturgy among the Thorns: Essays on Worship in the Reformed Church of America*, Grand Rapids: Eerdmans, 2007.

Bray, Gerald, *Tudor Church Reform: The Henrician Canons of 1535 and the Reformatio Legum Ecclesiasticarum*, Woodbridge: Boydell Press, 2000.

Bremmer, Jan N., 'The Acts of Thomas: Place, Date and Women', in Jan N. Bremmer (ed.), *The Apocryphal Acts of Thomas*, Leuven: Peeters, 2001, pp. 74–90.

Bremmer, Jan N., 'The Apocryphal Acts: Authors, Place, Time, and Readership', in Jan N. Bremmer (ed.), *The Apocryphal Acts of Thomas*, Leuven: Peeters, 2001, pp. 149–70.

Brenner, Scott F., 'Philip Schaff the Liturgist', *Christendom* 11 (1946), pp. 443–56.

Brent, Allen, *Hippolytus and Roman Church in the Third Century: Communities in Tension before the Emergence of a Monarch–Bishop*, Leiden: Brill, 1995.

Brightman, F. E., *The English Rite*, two vols, London: Rivingtons, 1915.

Brightman, F. E., 'The New Prayer Book Examined', *Church Quarterly Review* 104 (1927), pp. 219–52.

Brightman, F. E., *Liturgies Eastern and Western*, Oxford: Oxford University Press, 1896 (1967 reprint).

Brilioth, Yngve, *Eucharistic Faith and Practice: Evangelical and Catholic*, trans. Arthur Gabriel Hebert, London: SPCK, 1930.

Brock, Sebastian, 'An Early Syriac Life of Maximus the Confessor', *Analecta Bollandiana* 91 (1973), pp. 299–346.

Brock, Sebastian, 'The Christology of the Church of the East in the Synods of the Fifth to Early Seventh Centuries: Preliminary Considerations and Materials', in G. D. Dragas (ed.), *Askum–Thyateira: A Festschrift for Archbishop*

Methodios of Thyateira and Great Britain, London: Thyateira House, 1985, pp. 125–42.

Brock, Sebastian, 'An Early Syriac Commentary on the Liturgy', *Journal of Theological Studies* 37 (1986), pp. 387–403.

Brock, Sebastian, 'Towards a Typology of the Epicleses in the West Syrian Anaphoras', in H.-J. Feulner, E. Velkovska and R. F. Taft (eds), *Crossroads of Cultures*, Rome: Pontificio Istituto Orientale, 2000, pp. 173–92.

Brock, Sebastian, 'Invocations to/for the Holy Spirit in Syriac Liturgical Texts: Some Comparative Approaches', in R. F. Taft and Gabriele Winkler (eds), *Comparative Liturgy Fifty Years after Anton Baumstark (1872–1948)*, Rome: Pontifical Oriental Institute, 2001, pp. 377–406.

Brock, Sebastian, 'Gabriel of Qatar's Commentary on the Liturgy', *Hugoye* 6:2 (2003), pp. 197–248.

Brock, Sebastian, 'Some Early Witnesses to the East Syriac Liturgical Tradition', *Journal of Assyrian Academic Studies* 18 (2004), pp. 9–45.

Brock, Sebastian, 'The Syriac Anaphora of the Twelve Apostles: An English translation', in J. Getcha and A. Lossky (eds), *Θυσία αἰνέσεως: Mélanges liturgiques offerts à la mémoire de l'archevêque Georges Wagner (1930–1993)*, Paris: Presses Saint Serge, 2005, pp. 345–51.

Brock, Sebastian, 'The Origins of the Qanona "Holy God, Holy Mighty, Holy Immortal" according to Gabriel of Qatar (Early 7th Century)', *The Harp* 21 (2006), pp. 173–85.

Brock, Sebastian and George Kiraz, *Ephrem the Syrian: Selected Poems*, Provo, UT: Brigham Young University Press, 2006.

Bromily, G. W. (ed.), *Zwingli and Bullinger*, Library of Christian Classics vol. 24, Philadelphia: Westminster Press, 1953.

Brooks, E. W., *The Sixth Book of the Select Letters of Severus*, London: Williams and Norgate, 1904.

Brooks, E. W., *A Collection of Letters of Severus of Antioch*, Patrologia Orientalis 12, Paris: Firmin-Dodot, 1919.

Brown, David, *God and Grace of Body: Sacrament in Ordinary*, Oxford: Oxford University Press, 2007.

Brown, David and Ann Loades (eds), *The Sense of the Sacramental: Movement and Measure in Art and Music, Place and Time*, London: SPCK, 1995.

Brown, David and Ann Loades (eds), *Christ: The Sacramental Word: Incarnation, Sacrament and Poetry*, London: SPCK, 1996.

Brown, Raymond, *The Gospel according to John*, two vols, Anchor Bible 29 and 29a, New York: Doubleday, 1966.

Browne, Robert, 'A Booke which sheweth the life and manners of all true Christians, 1582', in A. Peel and Leland H. Carlson (eds), *The Writings of Robert Harrison and Robert Browne*, London: George Allen and Unwin Ltd, 1953, pp. 221–395.

Browne, Robert, 'A True and Short Declaration, 1584', in A. Peel and Leland H. Carlson (eds), *The Writings of Robert Harrison and Robert Browne*, London: George Allen and Unwin Ltd, 1953, pp. 396–429.

Buchanan, Colin O. (ed.), *Modern Anglican Liturgies: 1958–1968*, Oxford: Oxford University Press, 1968.

Buchanan, Colin O. (ed.), *Further Anglican Liturgies: 1968–1975*, Bramcote: Grove Books, 1975.

Buchanan, Colin, *What Did Cranmer Think He Was Doing?*, Bramcote: Grove Books, 1976.

Buchanan, Colin O. (ed.), *Latest Anglican Liturgies: 1976–1984*, London: SPCK, 1985.

Buchanan, Colin O. (ed.), *Anglican Eucharistic Liturgies: 1985–2010*, Norwich: Canterbury Press, 2011.

Buchanan, Colin and Trevor Lloyd, *Six Eucharistic Prayers as Proposed in 1996*, Cambridge: Grove Books, 1996.

Buchinger, Harald, 'Early Eucharist in Transition? A Fresh Look at Origen', in Albert Gerhards and Clemens Leonhard (eds), *Jewish and Christian Liturgy and Worship: New Insights into Its History and Intersection*, Leiden: Brill, 2007, pp. 207–27.

Büchsenschütz, L., *Histoire des Liturgies en Langue Allmande dans l'Église de Strasbourg au XVIe siècle*, Cahors: A. Coueslant, 1900.

Budde, Achim, *Die ägyptische Basilios-Anaphora: Text–Kommentar–Geschichte*, Münster: Aschendorff, 2004.

Bugenhagen, Johann, *Danske Messebøger Fra Reformationstiden*, Copenhagen: J. H. Schultz Forlag, 1959.

Bugnini, Annibale, *The Reform of the Liturgy: 1948–1975*, Collegeville: Liturgical Press, 1990.

Bulcock, Harry, *A Modern Churchman's Manual*, London: Union of Modern Free Churchmen, 1941.

Bulgakov, Sergius, *The Holy Grail and the Eucharist*, Hudson: Lindisfarne Books, 1997.

Bullinger, Heinrich, 'The Second Helvetic Confession', http://www.ccel.org/creeds/helvetic.htm.

Bullinger, Heinrich, *Decades: Vol. 5*, Parker Society, Cambridge: Cambridge University Press, 1850.

Bultmann, Rudolph, *The Gospel of John*, Philadelphia: Westminster Press, 1964.

Burchard, Christopher, 'The Importance of Joseph and Aseneth for the Study of the New Testament: A General Survey and a Fresh Look at the Lord's Supper', *New Testament Studies* 33 (1987), pp. 102–34.

Burkhart, Charles, 'The Church Music of the Old Order Amish and Old Colony Mennonites', *Mennonite Quarterly Review* 27 (1953), pp. 34–54.

Bürki, Bruno, *Cène du Seigneur two – eucharistie de l'Église*, 2 vols, Fribourg: Éditions Universitaires Fribourg Suisse, 1985.

Bürki, Bruno, 'Beispielhaft reformierte Form der Liturgie in Neuchâtel', in Martin Klöckener and Benedikt Kranemann (eds), *Liturgiereformen*, vol. 1, Münster: Aschendorff, 2001, pp. 417–35.

Bürki, Bruno, 'Reformed Worship in Continental Europe since the Seventeenth Century', in Lukas Vischer (eds), *Christian Worship in Reformed Churches Past and Present*, Grand Rapids: Eerdmans, 2003, pp. 32–65.

Burmester, O. H. E. 'The Canons of Gabriel Ibn Turaik, LXX Patriarch of Alexandria', *Orientalia Christiana Periodica* 1 (1935), pp. 5–45.

Burmester, O. H. E., 'A Comparative Study of the Form of the Words of Institution and the Epiclesis in the Anaphorae of the Ethiopic Church', *The Eastern Churches Quarterly* 13 (1959), pp. 13–42.

Burns, Stephen, Nicola Slee and Michael N. Jagessar (eds), *The Edge of God: New Liturgical Texts and Contexts in Conversation*, Peterborough: Epworth Press, 2008.

Buxton, Richard, *Eucharist and Institution Narrative*, London: SPCK, 1976.

Cabaniss, Alan, *Pattern in Early Christian Worship*, Macon: Mercer University Press, 1989.

Cabasilas, Nicholas, *A Commentary on the Divine Liturgy*, trans. J. M. Hussey and P. A. McNulty, London: SPCK, 1960, and New York: St Vladimir's Seminary Press, 1997.

Calvin, John, *Commentary on a Harmony of the Evangelists*, trans. W. Pringle, three vols, Edinburgh, 1846.

Calvin, John, *Institutes of the Christian Religion* (1559), trans. Henry Beveridge, three vols, Grand Rapids: Eerdmans, 1958.

Calvin, John, *Institutes of the Christian Religion: 1536 edition*, trans. Ford Lewis Battles, Grand Rapids: Eerdmans, 1975.

Camelot, T., 'L'Eucharistie dans l'École d'Alexandrie', *Divinitas* 1 (1957), pp. 71–92.

Campbell, Thomas L., *Dionysius the Pseudo-Areopagite: The Ecclesiastical Hierarchy*, Lanham: University Press of America, 1981.

Capelle, B., 'Les liturgies "basiliennes" et S. Basile', in J. Doresse and E. Lanne (eds), *Un témoin archaïque de la liturgie copte de S. Basile*, Louvain: Publications Universitaires Louvain, 1960, pp. 45–74.

Capelle, Bernard, *Liturgies basiliennes et saint Basile*, vol. 47, Louvain: Institut orientaliste, 1960.

Carbié, Robert, *The Church at Prayer*, ed. A. G. Martmort, vol. 2, *The Eucharist*, London: Geoffrey Chapman, 1986.

Cardale, John, *Readings in the Liturgy and Divine Offices of the Church*, two vols, London: Thomas Bosworth, 1874–75, 1878.

Cardier, Jean, 'La Prière Eucharistique de Calvin', in B. Botte et al. (eds), *Eucharisties d'Orient et d'Occident*, Paris: Cerf, 1970, pp. 171–80.

Carlson, Leland H., *The Writings of John Greenwood and Henry Barrow 1592–1593*, London: George Allen and Unwin Ltd, 1970.

Carlyle, G. (ed.), *The Collected Works of Edward Irving*, vol. 2, London: Alexander Strahan & Co., 1864.

Caro, José Manuel Sánchez, *Eucharistia E Historia de la Salvacion*, Madrid: Biblioteca de Autores Cristianos, 1984.

Carter, Grayson, *Anglican Evangelicals: Protestant Secessions from the Via Media, c.1800–1850*, Oxford: Oxford University Press, 2001.

Casarella, Peter, 'Eucharist: Presence of a Gift', in Roch A. Kereszty (ed.), *Rediscovering the Eucharist: Ecumenical Conversations*, New York: Paulist Press, 2003, pp. 199–225.

Casey, Damien, 'Irenaeus: Touchstone of Catholicity', in B. Neil, G. D. Dunn and Lawrence Cross (eds), *Prayer and Spirituality in the Early Church, Vol. 3: Liturgy and Life*, Stathfield, Australia: St Pauls Publications, 2003, pp. 147–55.

'Catechism of the Catholic Church', http://www.usccb.org/beliefs-and-teachings/what-we-believe/catechism/catechism-of-the-catholic-church/epub/index.cfm.

Cerrato, J. A., 'The Association of the Name Hippolytus with a Church Order Now Known as The Apostolic Tradition', *St Vladimir's Theological Quarterly* 48:2 (2004), pp. 179–94.

Chalfoun, Khalil, 'Baptême et Eucharistie chez 'Ammār al-Başri', *Parole de L'Orient* 27 (2002), pp. 321–34.

Chan, Simon, *Liturgical Theology: The Church as Worshiping Community*, Downers Grove: InterVarsity Press, 2006.

Chatháin, Próinseás Ní., 'The Liturgical Background of the Derrynavlan Altar Service', *Journal of the Royal Antiquaries of Ireland* 110 (1980), pp. 127–48.

Chauvet, Louis-Marie, *The Sacraments: The Word of God at the Mercy of the Body*, Collegeville: Liturgical Press, 2001.

Chavoutier, L., 'Un Libellus pseudo-ambrosien sur le Saint-esprit', *Sacris Erudiri* 11 (1960), pp. 136–91.

Chazelle, Celia, 'The Eucharist in Early Medieval Europe', in Ian Christopher Levy, Gary Macy and Kristen Van Ausdall (eds), *A Companion to the Eucharist in the Middle Ages*, Leiden: Brill, 2012, pp. 205–49.

Chazonof, William, *Welch's Grape Juice: From Corporation to Co-operation*, Syracuse: Syracuse University Press, 1977.

Chemnitz, Martin, *The Lord's Supper*, trans. J. A. O. Preus, St Louis: Concordia Publishing House, 1979.

Cheong, Pauline Hope, Peter Fischer-Nieelsen, Stefan Gelgren and Charles Ess (eds), *Digital Religion, Social Media and Culture: Perspectives, Practices and Futures*, New York: Peter Lang, 2012.

Chilton, Bruce, *A Feast of Meanings: Eucharistic Theologies from Jesus through Johannine Circles*, Leiden: Brill, 1994.

Church of England, *Additional Eucharistic Prayers with Guidance on Celebrating the Eucharist with Children*, London: Church House Publishing, 2012.

The Church of the Triune God: The Cyprus Agreed Statement of the International Commission for Anglican–Orthodox Theological Dialogue 2006, London: Anglican Communion Office, 2006.

Clarke, Samuel, *An Exposition of the Church-Catechism*, Dublin, 1730.

Cocksworth, Christopher J., *Evangelical Eucharistic Thought in the Church of England*, Cambridge: Cambridge University Press, 1993.

Codrington, H. W., *Studies of the Syrian Liturgies*, London: Coldwell Ltd, 1952.

Coldeway, John C., *Early English Drama: An Anthology*, New York and London: Garland Publishing, 1993.

Colish, Marcia, *Peter Lombard*, 2 vols, Leiden: Brill, 1994.

Collier, Jeremy, *A Vindication of the Reasons and Defence.*, Part II, London, 1719.

Colombo, Giovanni, *Missale Ambrosianum iuxta ritum Sanctae Ecclesiae Mediolanensis*, Milan: Centro Ambrosiano di Documentazione e Studi Religiosi, 1981.

Connell, Martin F., *Church and Worship in Fifth-Century Rome: The Letter of Innocent I to Decentius of Gubbio*, Alcuin/GROW Joint Liturgical Study 52, Cambridge: Grove Books, 2002.

Connolly, R. H., *The Liturgical Homilies of Narsai*, Cambridge: Cambridge University Press, 1909.

Connolly, R. H., *Anonymi Autoris Expositio Officiorum Ecclesiae Georgio Arbelensi vulgo adscripta*, Rome: Corpus Scriptorum Christianorum Orientalium, and Paris: Gabalda, 1923.

Connolly, R. H., 'Sixth-Century Fragments of an East-Syrian Anaphora', *Oriens Christianus* 12–14 (1925), pp. 99–128.

Connolly, R. H., *Didascalia Apostolorum. The Syriac version translated and accompanied by the Verona Latin fragments, with an introduction and notes*, Oxford: Clarendon Press, 1929.

Connolly, R. H. (trans.), *A Commentary on the Mass by the Nestorian George, Bishop of Mosul and Arbel (10th century)*, OIRSI Publications 243, Vadavothoor, Kottayam, India: Pontifical Oriental Institute of Religious Studies, 2000.

Connolly, R. H. and H. W. Codrington, *Two Commentaries on the Jacobite Liturgy*, London: Williams and Norgate, 1913.

Connor, Steven, *Postmodern Culture: An Introduction to Theories of the Contemporary*, Oxford: Blackwell, 1997.

'Consecration for the Anaphora of *Sharar* and of the Twelve Apostles chanted in Syriac', CD, Virginia: St Maron Publications.

The Coptic Liturgy of Saint Mark the Apostle, Commonly known as the Liturgy of St. Cyril, http://www/saintmark.com.

Copy of the Alterations in the Book of Common Prayer Prepared by the Royal Commisioners for the Revision of the Liturgy in 1689, London: Order of the House of Commons, 1854.

Coquin, R.-G. 'L'anaphore alexandrine de saint Marc', *Le Museon* 82 (1969), pp. 307–56.

Corcoran, Simon and Benet Salway, 'A Newly Identified Greek Fragment of the *Testamentum Domini*', *Journal of Theological Studies* 62 (2011), pp. 118–35.

Corley, Kathleen E., *Maranatha: Women's Funerary Rituals and Christian Origins*, Minneapolis: Fortress Press, 2010.

Corrie, G. E., *A Catechism Written in Latin by Alexander Nowell, Dean of St. Paul's: Together with the same Catechism translated into English by Thomas Norton*, Parker Society, Cambridge: Cambridge University Press, 1853.

Costaz, Louis, *Syriac–English Dictionary*, Beirut: Éditions de l'Imprimerie Catholique, 1963.

Cotton, John, *The Way of the Churches of New England*, 1645.

Couratin, A. H., 'The Methodist Sunday Service', *Church Quarterly Review* 2 (1969), pp. 31–8.

Coutsoumpos, Panayotis, *Paul and the Lord's Supper: A Socio-Historical Investigation*, Frankfurt am Main: Peter Lang, 2005.

Covenant Hymns, Being a Collection of Psalms, Hymns and Spiritual Songs to the Praise and Glory of Jehovah, Father, Son, and Holy Ghost in Covenant, London, 1849.

Cowe, Peter, *Commentary on the Divine Liturgy by Xosrov Anjewac'i*, New York: St Varten Press, Diocese of the Armenian Church in America, 1991.

Cox, J. E. (ed.), *Writings and Disputations of Thomas Cranmer Relative to the Sacrament of the Lord's Supper*, Oxford: Parker Society, 1844.

Craig, Barry M., *Fractio Panis: A History of the Breaking of Bread in the Roman Rite*, Rome: Studia Anselmiana, 2011.

Cross, F. L., *St. Cyril of Jerusalem's Lectures on the Christian Sacraments*, London: SPCK, 1966.

Cross, S. H. and O. P. Sherbowitz-Weltzor, *The Russian Primary Chronicle: Laurention Text*, Cambridge, MA: The Medieval Academy of America, 1953.

Crossan, John D., *The Historical Jesus: The Life of a Mediterranean Jewish Peasant*, San Francisco: Harper, 1991.

Cullman, Oscar and F. J. Leenhardt, *Essays on the Lord's Supper*, Virginia: John Knox Press, 1958.

Cuming, Geoffrey J., *A History of Anglican Liturgy*, London: Macmillan and Co., 1969.

Cuming, Geoffrey J., 'Egyptian Elements in the Jerusalem Liturgy', *Journal of Theological Studies* 25 (1974), pp. 117–24.

Cuming, Geoffrey J., 'ΔΙ' ΕΥΧΗΣ ΛΟΓΟΥ', *Journal of Theological Studies* 31 (1980), pp. 80–2.

Cuming, Geoffrey J., 'John Knox and the Book of Common Prayer: A Short Note', *Liturgical Review* 10 (1980), pp. 80–1.

Cuming, Geoffrey J., 'Thmuis Revisited: Another Look at the Prayers of Bishop Sarapion', *Theological Studies* 41 (1980), pp. 568–75.

Cuming, Geoffrey J., 'The Anaphora of St. Mark: A Study in Development', *Le Muséon* 95 (1982), pp. 115–29.

Cuming, Geoffrey J., *The Godly Order: Texts and Studies Relating to the Book of Common Prayer*, London: SPCK, 1983.

Cuming, Geoffrey J., 'Pseudonymity and Authenticity, with Special Reference to the Liturgy of St. John Chrysostom', *Studia Patristica* 15 (1984), pp. 532–8.

Cuming, Geoffrey J., *The Liturgy of St. Mark Edited from the Manuscripts with a Commentary*, Rome: Ponificium Institutum Studiorum Orientalium, 1990.

Cutrone, E. C., 'Cyril's Mystagogical Catechesis and the Evolution of the Jerusalem Anaphora', *Orientalia Christiana Periodica* 44 (1978), pp. 52–64.

Cyril of Alexandria, 'Commentary on Luke (1859) Sermons 135–145 (Luke 20:19–22:38)', http://www.ccel.org/ccel/pearse/morefathers/files/cyril_on_luke_13_sermons_135_145.htm.

Dalby, Mark, *Anglican Missals and their Canons: 1549, Interim Rite and Roman*, Alcuin/GROW Joint Liturgical Study 41, Cambridge: Grove Books, 1998.

Danish National Church, *Danske Messebøger Fra Reformationstiden*, Copenhagen: J. H. Schultz Forlag, 1959.

Dankbaar, W. F., *Martin Micron De Christlicke Ordinancien der Nederlantscher Ghemeinten Te Londen (1554)*, S'Gravenhage: Martinus Nijhoff, 1956.

Daoud, Marcos (trans.), *The Liturgy of the Ethiopian Church*, revised by H. W. Blatta Marsie Hazen, 1954, reprint, London: Kegan Paul, 2005.

Darling Young, Robin, 'The Eucharist as Sacrifice According to Clement', in Roch A. Kereszty (ed.), *Rediscovering the Eucharist: Ecumenical Conversations*, New York: Paulist Press, 2003, pp. 63–91.

Davies, Douglas J., *An Introduction to Mormonism*, Cambridge: Cambridge University Press, 2003.

Davies, Peter Nicholas, *Alien Rites? A Critical Examination of Contemporary English in Anglican Liturgies*, Aldershot: Ashgate, 2005.

Davies, W. D., *Paul and Rabbinic Judaism*, 3rd edn, London: SPCK, 1970.

Davila, James R., *Liturgical Works: Eerdmans Commentaries on the Dead Sea Scrolls*, Grand Rapids: Eerdmans, 2000.

Davis, C. H. (ed.), *The English Church Canons 1604*, London, 1869.

Davis, Stephen J., *Coptic Christology in Practice: Incarnation and Divine Participation in Late Antique and Medieval Egypt*, Oxford: Oxford University Press, 2008.

Day, Juliette, *The Baptismal Liturgy of Jerusalem: Fourth- and Fifth-Century Evidence from Palestine, Syria and Egypt*, Aldershot: Ashgate, 2007.

Day, Juliette, 'The Catchetical Lectures of Cyril of Jerusalem: A Source for the Baptismal Liturgy of Mid-Fourth Century Jerusalem', in David Hellholm et al. (eds), *Ablution, Initiation, and Baptism: Late Antiquity, Early Judaism, and Early Christianity*, Berlin: De Gruyter, 2011, pp. 1175–200.

de Clerck, Paul, *La 'Prière universelle' dans les liturgies latines anciennes: Témoignages patristiques et texts liturgiques*, Münster: Aschendorff, 1977.

de Clerk, Paul, 'Epiclèse et formulation du mystère eucharistique', in Andreas Heinz and Heinrich Rennings (eds), *Gratias Agamus: Studien zum eucharistischen Hochgebet. Für Balthasar Fischer*, Freiburg: Herder, 1992, pp. 53–6.

de La Taille, Maurice, *The Mystery of Faith: Regarding the Most August Sacrament and Sacrifice of the Body and Blood of Christ*, two vols, New York: Sheed and Ward, 1940 and 1950.

de Lubac, Henri, *Corpus Mysticum*, Notre Dame: Notre Dame University Press, 2006.

Defense of the Pamphlet on the Canon of the Mass (1523), trans. Henry Prebles, typescript.

Deferrari, Roy J., *Hugh of Saint Victor on the Sacraments of the Christian Faith*, Cambridge: Mediaeval Academy of America, 1951.

Deme, Dániel, *The Selected Works of Isaac of Stella: A Cistercian Voice from the Twelfth Century*, Aldershot: Ashgate, 2007.

Díaz y Díaz, M. C., 'Literary Aspects of the Visigothic Liturgy', in Edward James (ed.), *Visigothic Spain: New Approaches*, Oxford: Clarendon Press, 1980, pp. 61–76.

'Digital bread and wine, anyone?', http://shipoffools.com/features/2012/online_sacraments.html.

Dimitrievskij, A., *Ein Euchologium aus 4 Jahrhundert, verfasst von Sarapion Bischoff von Thmuis*, Kiev, 1894.

Dix, Gregory, *The Treatise on The Apostolic Tradition*, London: SPCK, 1937.

Dix, Gregory, 'Primitive Consecration Prayers', *Theology* 37 (1938), pp. 261–83.

Dix, Gregory, *The Shape of the Liturgy*, London: Dacre Press, 1945.

Dix, Gregory, *Dixit Cranmer et Non Timuit*, London: Dacre Press, 1948.

Dodd, C. H., *The Interpretation of the Fourth Gospel*, Cambridge: Cambridge University Press, 1953.

Doig, Allan, *Liturgy and Architecture: From the Early Church to the Middle Ages*, Aldershot: Ashgate, 2008.

Dorgan, Howard, *Giving Glory to God in Appalachia: Worship Practices of Six Baptist Subdenominations*, Knoxville: University of Tennessee Press, 1987.

Dorn, Christopher, *The Lord's Supper in the Reformed Church in America: Tradition in Transformation*, New York: Peter Lang, 2007.

Douglas, Brian, *A Companion to Anglican Eucharistic Theology*, two vols, Leiden: Brill, 2012.

Doval, Alexis, *Cyril of Jerusalem Mystagogue*, Washington, DC: Catholic University of America, 2001.

Draper, Jonathan (ed.), *The Didache in Modern Research*, Leiden: Brill, 1996.

Draper, Jonathan, 'Ritual Process and Ritual Symbol in Didache', *Vigiliae Christianae* 54 (2000), pp. 121–58.

Drijvers, Jan Willem, *Cyril of Jerusalem: Bishop and City*, Leiden: Brill, 2004.

Drower, E. S., *Water into Wine: A Study of Ritual Idiom in the Middle East*, London: John Murray, 1956.

Duba, Arlo D. (ed.), *Presbyterian Worship in the Twentieth Century with a Focus on the Book of Common Worship*, White Sulphur Springs: OSL Publications, 2012.

Dudley, Martin, 'Liturgy and Doctrine: Corpus Christi', *Worship* 66 (1992), pp. 417–26.

Durandus, Guilielmus, *The Rationale Divinorum Officiorum*, Louisville: Fons Vitae, 2007.

Durber, Susan, 'An Inclusive Communion Order for a Denominational Worship Book', in N. Slee and S. Burns (eds), *Presiding Like a Woman*, London: SPCK, 2010, pp. 38–47.

Edwall, P., E. Hayman and W. D. Maxwell (eds), *Ways of Worship*, London: SCM Press, 1951.

Egbulem, Chris Nwaka, 'An African Interpretation of Liturgical Inculturation: The Rite Zairois', in Michael Downey and Richard Fragomeni (eds), *A Promise of Presence*, Washington, DC: Pastoral Press, 1992, pp. 227–50.

Ehrman, Bart D., 'The New Testament Canon of Didymus the Blind', *Vigiliae Christianae* 37 (1983), pp. 1–21.

Elior, Rachel, 'From Earthly Temple to Heavenly Shrines: Prayer and Sacred Song in the Hekhalot Literature and Its Relation to Temple Traditions', *Jewish Studies Quarterly* 4 (1997), pp. 217–67.

Elior, Rachel, *The Three Temples: On the Emergence of Jewish Mysticism*, Oxford: Littman Library of Jewish Civilization, 2004.

Elwood, Christopher, *The Body Broken: The Calvinist Doctrine of the Eucharist and the Symbolization of Power in Sixteenth-Century France*, Oxford: Oxford University Press, 1999.

'Engage Worship: Resources and Training for Innovative, Creative and World-Changing Worship', www.engageworship.org.

Engberding, H., *Das Eucharistische Hochgebet der Basileiosliturgie Textgeschichtliche Untersuchungen und kritische Ausgabe*, Theologie des christlichen Ostens 1, Münster: Aschendorff, 1931.

Engberding, H., 'Die syrische Anaphora der zwölf Apostel und ihre Paralleltexte', *Oriens Christianus* 12 (1937), pp. 213–47.

Ephrem, 'Hymns on Virginity 37', in Kathleen McVey, *Ephrem the Syrian: Hymns*, New York: Paulist Press, 1989.

Euchologion, 2nd edn, Edinburgh: William Blackwood, 1869.

Eusebius, 'Eusebius Church History X. 4. 69–72', in M. H. Shepherd, 'Eusebius and the Liturgy of St. James', *Yearbook of Liturgical Studies* 4 (1963), pp. 109–25.

Falk, Daniel K., *Daily, Sabbath, and Festival Prayers in the Dead Sea Scrolls*, Leiden: Brill, 1998.

Falk, Daniel K. and Philip Alexander, *The Mystical Texts*, London: T & T Clark, 2006.

Farag, Mary, 'Δύναμις Epicleses: An Athanasian Perspective', *Studia Liturgica* 39 (2009), pp. 63–79.

Farag, Mary, 'The Anaphora of St. Thomas the Apostle: Translation and Commentary', *Le Muséon* 123 (2010), pp. 317–61.

Fawcett, Timothy J., *The Liturgy of Comprehension 1689*, Southend-on-Sea: Mayhew-McCrimmon, 1973.

Fenner, Dudley, *The Whole Doctrine of the Sacraments*, Middleburgh, 1588.

Fenwick, John R. K., *'The Missing Oblation': The Contents of the Early Antiochene Anaphora*, Alcuin/GROW Liturgical Study 11, Bramcote: Grove Books, 1989.

Fenwick, John R. K., *The Anaphoras of St. Basil and St. James: An Investigation into Their Common Origin*, Rome: Pontificium Institutum Orientale, 1992.

Fenwick, John and Bryan Spinks (eds), *Worship in Transition: The Liturgical Movement in the Twentieth Century*, Edinburgh: T & T Clark, 1995.

Férotin, Marius, *Le Liber Mozarabicus Sacramentorum et Les Manuscrits Mozarabes*, reprint, with introduction by Anthony Ward and Cuthbert Johnson, Rome: CLV Edizioni Liturgiche, 1995.

Férotin, Marius, *Le Liber Ordinum: En usage dans L'Élise Wisigothique et Mozarabe D'Espagne du Cinquième au Onzième siècle*, reprint with introduction by Anthony Ward and Cuthbert Johnson, Rome: CLV Edizioni Liturgiche, 1996.

Feulner, Hans-Jürgen, 'Zu den Editionen orientalischer Anaphoren', in Hans-Jürgen Feulner, Elena Velkovska and Robert F. Taft (eds), *Crossroads of Cultures: Studies in Liturgy and Patristics in Honor of Gabriele Winkler*, Rome: Pontificio Istituto Orientale, 2000, pp. 251–82.

Feulner, Hans-Jürgen, *Die Armenische Athanasius-Anaphora*, Anaphorae Orientales 1, Rome: Pontificio Istituto Orientale, 2001.

Feulner, Hans-Jürgen, 'On the "Preparatory Rites" of the Armenian Divine Liturgy: Some Remarks on the Ritual of Vesting', in Roberta R. Ervine (ed.), *Worship Traditions in Armenia and the Neighboring Christian East*, New York: St Nersess Armenian Seminary, 2006, pp. 93–117.

Feulner, Hans-Jürgen, 'The Armenian Anaphora of St. Athanasius', in Maxwell Johnson (ed.), *Issues in Eucharistic Praying in East and West*, Collegeville: Liturgical Press, 2011, pp. 189–218.

Fiala, V., 'Les prières d'acceptation de l'offrande et le genre littéraire du canon romain', *Eucharisties d'Orient et d'Occident I* (1970), pp. 117–33.

Fiddes, Paul, 'Sacraments in a Virtual World' Summary at kateboardman.me.uk/blog/wp-content/.../virtual-communion.doc.

Findikyan, D. M., *The Commentary on the Armenian Daily Office by Bishop Step'anos Siwnec'i (+735)*, Rome: Pontificio Istituto Orientale, 2004.

Finkelstein, Louis, 'The Birkat Ha-mazon', *Jewish Quarterly Review* 19 (1928–29), pp. 211–62.

Flegg, Columba, *Gathered Under Apostles: A Study of the Catholic Apostolic Church*, Oxford: Clarendon Press, 1992.

Foley, Edward, 'A Tale of Two Sanctuaries: Late Medieval Eucharist and the Analogous', in Ian Christopher Levy, Gary Macy and Kristen Van Ausdall (eds), *A Companion to the Eucharist in the Middle Ages*, Leiden: Brill, 2012, pp. 327–63.

Fotheringham, J. K., 'The Evidence of Astronomy and Technical Chronology for the Date of the Crucifixion', *Journal of Theological Studies* 34 (1934), pp. 146–62.

Freedman, William, 'Literary Motif: A Definition and Evaluation', *Novel* 4 (1971), pp. 123–31.

Freeman, Arthur J., *An Ecumenical Theology of the Heart: The Theology of Count Nicholas Ludwig von Zinzendorf*, Bethlehem, PA: Moravian Church in America, 1998.

Frendo, John A., *The 'Post Secreta' of the 'Missale Gothicum' and the Eucharistic Theology of the Gallican Anaphora*, St Venera, Malta: St Joseph's Home, 1977.

Frere, W. H., 'Edwardine Vernacular Services before the First Prayer Book', *Journal of Theological Studies* 1 (1900), pp. 229–46.

Fritsch, Emmanuel, 'The Anaphoras of the Ge'ez Churches: A Challenging Orthodoxy', forthcoming in the Addai and Mari Congress papers.

Fritsch, Emmanuel, 'The Preparation of the Gifts and Pre-anaphora in the Ethiopoan Eucharistic liturgy in around 1100 A.D', paper presented at the SOL Congress, Louaize, Lebanon, 2012, forthcoming.

Frøyshov, Stig Simeon R., 'The Early Development of the Liturgical Eight-Mode System in Jerusalem', *St. Vladimir's Theological Quarterly* 51 (2007), pp. 139–78.

Frøyshov, Stig Symeon, 'The Georgian Witness to the Jerusalem Liturgy: New Sources and Studies', in Bert Groen et al. (eds), *Inquiries into Eastern Christian Worship*, Rome: Pontificio Istituto Orientale, 2008, pp. 227–67.

Fuchs, Hermann, *Die Anaphora des Monophysitischen Patriarch Jöhannan I.*, Münster: Aschendorff, 1926.

Garrow, Alan J. P., *The Gospel of Matthew's Dependence on the Didache*, London: T & T Clark, 2003.

Gascho, Milton, 'The Amish Division of 1693–1697 in Switzerland and Alsace', *Mennonite Quarterly Review* 11 (1937), pp. 235–66.

Gelston, Anthony, 'ΔΙ' ΕΥΧΗΣ ΛΟΓΟΥ', *Journal of Theological Studies* 33 (1982), pp. 172–5.

Gelston, Anthony, *The Eucharistic Prayer of Addai and Mari*, Oxford: Clarendon Press, 1992.

Gelston, Anthony, 'Theodore of Mopsuestia: The Anaphora and Mystagogical Catechesis 16', *Studia Patristica* 26 (1993), pp. 21–34.

Gelston, Anthony, 'The Relationship of the Anaphoras of Theodore and Nestorius to that of Addai and Mari', in George Karukaparampil (ed.), *Tuvaik: Studies in Honour of Rev. Jacob Vellian*, Syrian Church Series XVI, Kottayam: Manganam, 1995, pp. 20–6.

Gelston, Anthony, 'The Origin of the Anaphora of Nestorius: Greek or Syriac?', *Bulletin of John Rylands University Library of Manchester* 78 (1996), pp. 73–86.

Gelston, Anthony, 'Cyril of Jerusalem's Eucharistic Prayer: The Argument from Silence', *Studia Patristica* 46 (2010), pp. 301–5.

Gelston, Anthony, 'A Fragmentary Sixth Century East Syrian Anaphora', paper given at the Oxford Patristic Conference, August 2011, forthcoming in *Studia Patristica*.

Gemayel, Boutros, 'Fraction, consignation, Commixtion dans la liturgie Syro-Maronite', *Symposium Syriacum* 1972 (1974), pp. 163–81.

Gemayel, Pierre-Edmond, *Avant-Messe Maronite: Histoire et Structure*, Rome: Pontificium Institutum Orientalium Studiorum, 1965.

George, A. Raymond, 'From the Sunday Service to "The Sunday Service": Sunday Morning Worship in British Methodism', in Karen B. Westerfield Tucker (ed.), *The Sunday Service of the Methodists: Twentieth-Century Worship in Worldwide Methodism, Studies in Honor of James F. White*, Nashville: Kingswood Books, 1996, pp. 31–52.

George, Timothy, 'John Calvin and the Agreement of Zurich', in Timothy George (ed.), *John Calvin and the Church*, Louisville: Westminster John Knox Press, 1990, pp. 42–58.

Gerhard, Johann, 'Loci Theologici', in Gaylin R. Schmeling (ed.), *Gerhard – Theologian and Pastor*, http://www.blts.edu/wp-content/uploads/2011/06/GRS-Gerhard.pdf.

Gerhard, Johann, *Sacred Meditations*, trans. C. W. Heisler, Philadelphia: Lutheran Publication Society, 1896.

Gerhard, Johann, *The Comprehensive Explanation of Holy Baptism and the Lord's Supper*, trans. Elmer M. Hohle, Malone: Repristination Press, 2000.

Gerhards, Albert, *Die griechische Gregoriosanaphora: Ein Beitrag zur Geschichte des Eucharistichen Hochgebets*, Münster: Aschendorff, 1984.

Gerhardsson, Birger, *Memory and Manuscript: With Tradition and Transmission in Early Christianity*, Grand Rapids: Eerdmans, 1998.

Gerrish, B. A. 'The Lord's Supper in the Reformed Confessions', in Donald K. McKim (ed.), *Major Themes in the Reformed Tradition*, Grand Rapids: Eerdmans, 1992, pp. 245–58.

Gerrish, B. A., *Grace and Gratitude: The Eucharistic Theology of John Calvin*, Edinburgh: T & T Clark, 1993.

Giewald, Arne and Günther Thoman, *The Lutheran High Church Movement in Germany and Its Liturgical Work: An Introduction*, Raleigh: Lulu.com, 2011.

Ginsburg, Elliot K., '"The *neshamah* is always praying": Towards a Typology of Prayer in Jewish Mystical Tradition (a first offering)', in Bronwen Neil, Geoffrey D. Dunn and Lawrence Cross (eds), *Prayer and Spirituality in the Early Church, Vol. 3: Liturgy and Life*, Strathfield, Australia: St Pauls Publications, 2003, pp. 353–92.

Giraudo, Cesare, *La struttura letteraria della preghiera eucaristica: Saggio sulla genesi letteraria di una forma: toda veterotestamentaria, beraka giudaica, anafora Cristiana*, Analecta Biblica 92, Rome: Pontifico Istituto Biblico, 1981.

Gittoes, Julie, *Anamnesis and the Eucharist: Contemporary Anglican Approaches*, Aldershot: Ashgate, 2008.

Göbell, Walter, *Die Schleswig-Holsteinische Kirchenordnung von 1542*, Neumünster: Karl Wachholtz Verlag, 1986.

Gómez-Ruiz, Raúl, *Mozarabs, Hispanics and the Cross*, New York: Orbis Books, 2007.

Gonzálvez, Ramón, 'The Persistence of the Mozarabic Liturgy in Toledo after 1080', in Bernard F. Reilly (ed.), *Santiago, Saint-Denis, and Saint Peter: The Reception of the Roman Liturgy in Leon-Castile in 1080*, New York: Fordham University Press, 1985, pp. 157–85.

Gordon, Bruce, 'Transcendence and Community in Zwinglian Worship', in R. N. Swanson (ed.), *Continuity and Change in Christian Worship*, Woodbridge: Boydell and Brewer, 1999, pp. 128–50.

Grantham, Thomas, *Hear the Church, or, An Appeal to the mother of us all*, London, 1687.

Graves, Raphael, 'The Anaphora of the Eighth Book of the Apostolic Constitutions', in Paul F. Bradshaw (ed.), *Essays on Early Eastern Eucharistic Prayers*, Collegeville: Liturgical Press, 2002, pp. 173–94.

Gray, Donald, *The 1927–28 Prayer Book Crisis: 1. Ritual, Royal Commissions, and Reply to the Royal Letters of Business*, Alcuin/GROW Liturgical Study 60, Norwich: Canterbury Press, 2005.

Gray, Donald, *The 1927–28 Prayer Book Crisis. 2. The cul-de-sac of the 'Deposited Book' . . . until further order be taken*, Alcuin/GROW Liturgical Study 61, Norwich: Canterbury Press, 2006.

Gray, Patrick T. R., 'From Eucharist to Christology: The Life-Giving Body of Christ in Cyril of Alexandria, Eutyches and Julian of Halicarnassus', in István Perczel, Réka Forrai and György Geréby (eds), *The Eucharist in Theology and Philosophy: Issues of Doctrinal History in East and West from the Patristic Age to the Reformation*, Leuven: Leuven University Press, 2005, pp. 23–35.

Green, Chris E. W., *Toward a Pentecostal Theology of the Lord's Supper: Foretasting the Kingdom*, Cleveland, TN: COPT Press, 2012.

Green, Ian, *The Christian's ABC: Catechisms and Catechizing in England c.1530–1740*, Oxford: Clarendon Press, 1996.

Gregg, David, *Anamnesis in the Eucharist*, Bramcote: Grove Books, 1976.

Gregg, Robert C., 'Cyril of Jerusalem and the Arians', in Robert C. Gregg (ed.), *Arianism. Historical and Theological Reassessment*, Cambridge, MA: Philadelphia Patristic Foundation, Ltd, 1985, pp. 85–109.

Griffith, Sidney H., '"Spirit in the Bread; Fire in the Wine": The Eucharist as "Living Medicine" in Ephraem the Syrian', in Sarah Beckwith (ed.), *Catholicism and Catholicity: Eucharistic Communities in Historical and Contemporary Perspectives*, Oxford: Blackwell, 1999, pp. 113–34.

Griffiths, Alan, *Ordo Romanus Primus: Latin Text and Translation with Introduction and Notes*, Alcuin/GROW Joint Liturgical Study 73, Norwich: Hymns Ancient and Modern, 2012.

Griffiths, Alan, *We Give You Thanks and Praise: The Ambrosian Eucharistic Prefaces*, Norwich: Canterbury Press, 1999.

Grisbrooke, W. Jardine, *Anglican Liturgies of the Seventeenth and Eighteenth Centuries*, London: SPCK, 1958.

Grisbrooke, W. Jardine, *The Liturgical Portions of the Apostolic Constitutions: A Text for Students*, Alcuin/GROW Liturgical Study 13–14, Nottingham: Grove Books, 1990.

Gross, Leonard (ed.), *Prayer Book for Earnest Christians*, Scottdale: Herald Press, 1997.

Grosse, Christian, *Les Rituels de la Cène: Le culte eucharistique réformé à Genéve (XVIe–XVIIe siècles)*, Geneva: Librairie Droz, 2008.

Guibert of Nogent, *Monodies and On the Relics of Saints*, ed. Joseph McAlhany, trans. Jay Rubenstein, New York: Penguin Books, 2011.

Gy, Pierre-Marie, 'La relation au Christ dans l'Eucharistie selon S. Bonaventure et S. Thomas d'Aquin', in Pierre-Marie Gy (ed.), *La Liturgie dans l'Histoire*, Paris: Cerf, 1990, pp. 247–83.

Haile, Getatchew, 'Religious Controversies and the Growth of Ethiopic Literature in the Fourteenth and Fifteenth Centuries', *Oriens Christianus* 65 (1981), pp. 102–36.

Haile, Getatchew, 'On the Identity of Silondis and the Composition of the Anaphora Ascribed to Harayaqos of Bahansa', *Orientalia Christiana Periodica* 49 (1983), pp. 366–89.

Halperin, D. J., *The Faces of the Chariot*, Tübingen: J. C. B. Mohr, 1988.

Halteman Finger, Reta, *Of Widows and Meals: Communal Meals in the Book of Acts*, Grand Rapids: Eerdmans, 2007.

Hammerschmidt, Ernst, *Die Koptische Gregoriosanaphora: Syrische und Griechische Einflüsse auf eine Ägyptische Liturgie*, Berlin: Akademie Verlag, 1957.

Hammerschmidt, Ernst, *Studies in the Ethiopic Anaphoras*, 2nd edn, Berlin: Akademie-Verlag, 1987/88.

Hammerstaedt, Jürgen, *Griechische Anaphorenfragmente aus Ägypten und Nubien*, Opladen/Wisbaden: Westdeutscher Verlag GmbH, 1999.

Hampton, Stephen, *Anti-Arminians: The Anglican Reformed Tradition from Charles II to George I*, Oxford: Oxford University Press, 2008.

Hanseens, Jean Michel, *La Liturgie d'Hippolyte*, Rome: Pontifical Oriental Institute, 1965.

Härdelin, Alf, *The Tractarian Understanding of the Eucharist*, Uppsala: University of Uppsala, 1965.

Häring, N. M., 'Berengar's Definitions of *Sacramentum* and Their Influence on Mediaeval Sacramentology', *Mediaeval Studies* 10 (1948), pp. 109–46.

Harmon, Katharine E., *There Were Also Many Women There: Lay Women in the Liturgical Movement in the United States 1926–59*, Collegeville: Liturgical Press, 2012.

Harrod, Samuel et al. (eds), *The Peculiar People's Hymn Book*, London: A. Chalk, Daws Heath, 1891.

Hart, Columba, *Hadewijch: The Complete Works*, New York: Paulist Press, 1980.

Hart, Bentley D., '"Thine own of Thine own": Eucharistic Sacrifice in Orthodox Tradition', in Roch A. Kereszty (ed.), *Rediscovering the Eucharist*, New York: Paulist Press, 2003, pp. 142–69.

Harting-Correa, Alice L., *Walahfrid Strabo's Libellus de Eeordiis et Incrementis quarundam in observationibus ecclesiasticis rerum*, Leiden: Brill, 1996.

Hatchett, Marion J., *The Making of the First American Book of Common Prayer*, New York: Seabury Press, 1982.

Hatchett, Marion J., 'The Eucharistic Rite of the Stowe Missal', in J. Neil Alexander (ed.), *Time and Community: In Honor of Thomas Julian Talley*, Washington, DC: Pastoral Press, 1990, pp. 153–70.

Hatchett, Marion J., *Commentary on the American Prayer Book*, New York: HarperCollins, 1995.

Hawkes-Teeples, Steven, *St. Symeon of Thessalonika: The Liturgical Commentaries*, Toronto: Pontifical Institute of Medieval Studies, 2011.

Hayek, Micahel, *Liturgie Maronite: Histoire et texts eucharistiques*, Paris: Maison Mame, 1964.

Hazelden Walker, Joan, 'A Pre-Marcan Dating for the Didache: Further Thoughts of a Liturgist', *Studia Biblica* 3 (1978), pp. 403–11.

Heinmann, Joseph, *Prayer in the Talmud: Forms and Patterns*, New York and Berlin: De Gruyter, 1977.

Heintz, Michael, 'δι' εὐχῆς λόγου τοῦ παρ' αὐτοῦ (Justin Apology 1.66.2): Cuming and Gelston Revisited', *Studia Liturgica* 33 (2003), pp. 33–6.

Hen, Yitzak, *The Royal Patronage of Liturgy in Frankish Gaul*, London: Henry Bradshaw Society, 2001.

Hen, Yitzak, 'The Liturgy of the Bobbio Missal', in Yitzak Hen and Rob Meens (eds), *The Bobbio Missal: Liturgy and Religious Culture in Merovingian Gaul*, Cambridge: Cambridge University Press, 2004, pp. 140–53.

Herber, R. and C. P. Eden (eds), *The Works of Jeremy Taylor*, London: Longmans, 1847–52.

Hildegard of Bingen, *Scivias*, trans. Columba Hart and Jane Bishop, New York: Paulist Press, 1990.

Hill, Charles Alexander, *The Loci Communes of Philip Melanchthon*, Boston: Meador Publishing Company, 1944.

Himmelfarb, Martha, *Ascent to Heaven in Jewish and Christian Apocalypses*, New York: Oxford University Press, 1993.

Hoadly, B., *A Plain Account of the Nature and End of the Sacrament of the Lord's Supper*, London, 1735.

Holden, J. L., 'Sacrifice and the Eucharist', in Archbishop's Commission on Christian Doctrine (eds), *Thinking about the Eucharist*, London: SCM Press, 1972, pp. 81–98.

Holeton, David R., 'Sacramental and Liturgical Reform in Late Mediaeval Bohemia', *Studia Liturgica* 17 (1987), pp. 87–96.

Holeton, David R., 'The Bohemian Eucharistic Movement in its European Context', in *The Bohemian Reformation and Religious Practice. I, Papers from the XVIIth World Congress of the Czechoslovak Society of Arts and Sciences, Prague* (1994), pp. 23–47.

Holeton, David R. (ed.), *Revising the Eucharist: Groundwork for the Anglican Communion*, Alcuin/GROW Joint Liturgical Study 27, Cambridge: Grove Books, 1994.

Holeton, David R., 'The Evolution of Utraquist Liturgy: A Precursor of Western Liturgical Reform', *Studia Liturgica* 25 (1995), pp. 51–67.

Holeton, David R. (ed.) *Our Thanks and Praise*, Toronto: Anglican Book Centre, 1998.

Holeton, David R., 'The Evolution of Utraquist Eucharistic Liturgy: Baumstark Confirmed', in Robert F. Taft and Gabriele Winkler (eds), *Comparative Liturgy Fifty Years after Anton Baumstark (1872–1948)*, Rome: Pontificio Istituto Orientale, 2001, pp. 777–85.

Holeton, David R. and Colin Buchanan, *A History of the International Anglican Liturgical Consultations 1983–2007*, Alcuin/GROW Joint Liturgical Study 63, Norwich: Canterbury Press, 2007.

Holmes, Peter (trans.), *A Treatise on the Soul*, http://www.tertullian.org/anf/anf03/anf03-22.htm#P2560_840932.

Honders, A. C., *Valerandus Pollanus Lituria Sacra (1551–1555)*, Leiden: Brill, 1970.

Hooker, Richard, *Of the Lawes of Ecclesiastical Politie*, London: John Windet, 1597.

Houssiau, Albert, 'The Alexandrine Anaphora of St. Basil', in L. C. Sheppard (ed.), *The New Liturgy*, London: Darton, Longman and Todd, 1970, pp. 228–43.

Hubert, Friedrich, *Die Strasburger liturgischen Ordnungen im Zeitalter der Reformation*, Göttingen: Vandenhoeck und Ruprecht, 1900.

Hubmaier, Balthasar, 'A Form for Christ's Supper', http://www.anabaptistnetwork.com/book/export/html/252.

Hudson, Anne, 'A Lollard Mass', *Journal of Theological Studies* 23 (1972), pp. 407–19.

Hudson, Anne (ed.), *English Wycliffite Writings*, Cambridge: Cambridge University Press, 1978.

Humphreys, Colin J., *The Mystery of the Last Supper: Reconstructing the Final Days of Jesus*, Cambridge: Cambridge University Press, 2011.

Interleaved Book of Common Prayer 1724, British Library.

Internationale Kirchliche Zeitschrift 103: Heft 1–2 (January–June 2013).

Irenaeus, 'Adv.Haer', in David N. Power (ed.), *Irenaeus of Lyons on Baptism and Eucharist: Selected Texts with Introduction, Translation and Annotation*, Alcuin/GROW Liturgical Study 18, Bramcote: Grove Books, 1991.

Isaac, Jacques, *Taksa D-Hussaya: Le rite du Pardon dans l'Église syriaque orientale*, Rome: Pontificium Institutum Orientale, 1989, pp. 170–75.

Iskander, Athanasius, 'Article in March 1996', in Athanasius Iskander, *Understanding the Liturgy: A Series of Articles*, reprints of articles first published in *Parousia* September 1993–March 1997, Kitchener, Ontario: St Mary's Coptic Orthodox Church, 2001.

Jacob, A., 'La Tradition Manuscrite de la Liturgie de Saint Jean Chrysostome', in B. Botte et al. (eds), *Eucharisties d'orient et d'Occident*, vol. II, Paris: Les Éditions du Cerf, 1970, pp. 109–38.

Jacob, H. E., *Six Thousand Years of Bread: Its Holy and Unholy History*, Garden City: Doubleday, Doran and Co., 1944.

Jacobs, Elfriede, *Die Sakramentslehre Wilhelm Farels*, Zurich: Theologischer Verlag, 1978.

Jacobs, H. E., *The Lutheran Movement in England*, Philadelphia: General Council Publication House, 1916.

Jagessar, Michael N. and Stephen Burns (eds), *Christian Worship: Postcolonial Perspectives*, London: Equinox Publishing, 2011.

James, M. R. (trans.), 'The Acts of Peter', *The Apocryphal New Testament*, Oxford: Clarendon Press, 1924, http://www.earlychristianwritings.com/text/actspeter.html.

James, N. W., 'Was Leo the Great the Author of Liturgical Prayers?', *Studia Patristica* 26 (1991), pp. 35–40.

Jammo, Sarhad Y. Hermiz, *La Structue de la Messe Chaldéenne du Début jusq'à l'Anaphore. Gabriel of Qatar Etude Historique*, Rome: Pontificium Institutum Orientalium Studiorum, 1979.

Jammo, Sarhad, 'The Anaphora of the Apostles Addai and Mari: A Study of Structure and Historical Background', *Orientalia Christiana Periodica* 68 (2002), pp. 5–35.

Janeras, Sebastià, 'Le Trisagion: Une Formule Brève en Liturgie Comparée', in Robert F. Taft and Gabriele Winkler (eds), *Comparative Liturgy Fifty Years after Anton Baumstark (1872–1948)*, Rome: Pontificio Istituto Orientale, 2001, pp. 495–562.

Janeras, Sebastià, 'Sanctus et Post-Sanctus dans l'anaphore du *P.Monts.Roca inv.no.154b–155a*', *Studi sull Oriente Christiano* 11 (2007), pp. 9–13.

Jasper, R. C. D. (ed.), *The Eucharist Today*, Studies on Series 3, London: SPCK, 1974.

Jasper, R. C. D. and G. J. Cuming, *Prayers of the Eucharist: Early and Reformed*, New York: Pueblo Publishing, 1980.

Jasper, R. C. D. and Paul F. Bradshaw (eds), *A Companion to the Alternative Service Book 1980*, London: SPCK, 1986.

Jaubert, A., *La date de la Cène*, Paris: Gabalda, 1957.

Jaubert, A., *The Date of the Last Supper*, New York: Alba House, 1965.

Jeanes, Gordon, 'Early Latin Parallels to the Roman Canon? Possible References to a Eucharistic Prayer in Zeno of Verona', *Journal of Theological Studies* 37 (1986), pp. 427–31.

Jeanes, Gordon P., *The Origins of the Roman Rite*, Alcuin/GROW Joint Liturgical Study 20, Bramcote: Grove Books, 1991.

Jeanes, Gordon P., *Signs of God's Promise: Thomas Cranmer's Sacramental Theology and the Book of Common Prayer*, London: T & T Clark, 2008.

Jeanes, Gordon P., 'Early Steps in the English Liturgy: The Witness of the Wanley Part Books', unpublished paper at Society for Liturgical Study, 2010.

Jeanes, Gordon P., 'The Tudor Prayer Books: That "The Whole Realme Shall Have but One Use"', in Stephen Platten and Christopher Woods (eds), *Comfortable Words: Polity, Piety and the Book of Common Prayer*, London: SCM Press, 2012, pp. 20–34.

Jeffers, J. S., *Conflict at Rome: Social Order and Hierarchy in Early Christianity*, Minneapolis: Fortress Press, 1991.

Jeffery, Peter, 'The Meaning and Functions of Kyrie Eleison', in Bryan D. Spinks (ed.), *The Place of Christ in Liturgical Prayer: Christology, Trinity, and Liturgical Theology*, Collegeville: Liturgical Press, 2008, pp. 127–94.

Jefford, Clayton N. (ed.), *The Didache in Context*, Leiden: Brill, 1995.

Jenny, Markus, *Die Einheit des Abendmahlsgottesdienstes bei den elsässischen und schweizerischen Reformatoren*, Zürich–Stuttgart: Zwingli-Verlag, 1968.

Jeremias, Joachim, *The Eucharistic Words of Jesus*, London, SCM Press, 1966.

Johanny, Raymond, 'Ignatius of Antioch', in Raymond Johanny and Willy Rordorf (eds), *The Eucharist of the Early Christians*, trans. Matthew J. O'Connell, Collegeville: Liturgical Press, 2001, pp. 48–80.

Johnson, Cuthbert, *Prosper Gueranger (1805–1875): A Liturgical Theologian*, Rome: Pontificio Ateneo S. Anselmo, 1984.

Johnson, John, *The Unbloody Sacrifice and Altar, Unvail'd and Supported*, Part I, London, 1714.

Johnson, Laurence J. (ed.), *Worship in the Early Church: An Anthology of Historical Sources*, vol. 3, Collegeville: Liturgical Press, 2009.

Johnson, Maxwell E., *The Prayers of Sarapion of Thmuis: A Literary, Liturgical and Theological Analysis*, Rome: Pontificio Istituto Orientale, 1995.

Johnson, Maxwell E., 'The Archaic Nature of the Sanctus, Institution Narrative, and Epiclesis of the Logos in the Anaphora Ascribed to Sarapion of Thmuis', in Robert F. Taft (ed.), *The Christian East: Its Institutions and Its Thought: A Critical Reflection*, OCA 251, Rome: Pontificio Istituto Orientale, 1996, pp. 671–702.

Johnson, Maxwell E., 'Christian Initiation in Fourth-century Jerusalem and Recent Developments in the Study of the Sources', *Ecclesia Orans* 26 (2009), pp. 143–61.

Johnson, Maxwell E., 'Martyrs and the Mass: The Interpolation of the Narrative of Institution into the Anaphora', *Worship* 87 (2013), pp. 2–22.

Johnson, Maxwell E., 'Sharing "The Cup of Christ": The Cessation of Martyrdom and Anaphoral Development', in Steven Hawkes-Teeples, Bert Groen and Stefanos Alexopoulos (eds), *Studies on the Liturgies of the Christian East: Selected Papers of the Third International Congress of the Society of Oriental Liturgy, Volos, May 26–30, 2010*, Leuven: Peeters, 2013, pp. 109–26.

Johnson, Todd E., 'Recovering *Ägyptisches Heimatgut:* An Exercise in Liturgical Methodology', *Questiones Liturgique* 76 (1995), pp. 182–98.

Josephus, 'The Wars of the Jews or The History of The Destruction of Jerusalem: Book II', http://www.ccel.org/j/josephus/works/war-2.htm.

Jungmann, Josef, *The Place of Christ in Liturgical Prayer*, 2nd edn, London: Geoffrey Chapman, 1965.

Just, Arthur, *The Ongoing Feast: Table Fellowship and Eschatology at Emmaus*, Collegeville: Liturgical Press, 1993.

Kabongo, Edouard, *Le Rite Zaïrois*, Frankfurt am Main: Peter Lang, 2008.

Kalb, Friedrich, *Theology of Worship in 17th-Century Lutheranism*, St Louis: Concordia Publishing House, 1965.

Karant-Nunn, Susan, *The Reformation of Ritual: An Interpretation of Early Modern Germany*, London and New York: Routledge, 1997.

Karris, Robert J., *Eating Your Way through Luke's Gospel*, Collegeville: Liturgical Press, 2006.

Kass, Leon R., *The Hungry Soul: Eating and the Perfecting of Our Nature*, New York: Free Press, 1994.

Kavanagh, Aidan, 'Thoughts on the New Eucharistic Prayers', reprinted in R. Kevin Seasoltz (ed.), *Living Bread, Saving Cup*, Collegeville: Liturgical Press, 1982, pp. 102–13.

Kavanagh, Aidan, *Confirmation: Origins and Reform*, Collegeville: Pueblo Books, 1988.

Kazarian, Nicolas, 'The Sacramental Theology of Patriarch Jeremias II', 5th International Theological Conference of the Russian Orthodox Church, Moscow, 2007, http://theolcom.ru/ru/full_text.php?TEXT_ID=343.

Καζαμίας, Ἀλκιβιάδης, Ἡ Θεία Λειτουργία τοῦ Ἁγίου Ἰακώβου τοῦ Ἀδελφοθέου καὶ τὰ νέα σιναϊτικὰ χειρόγραφα, Θεσσαλονίκη, 2006.

Kéchichian, I., *Nersès de Lambron (1153–1192): Explication de la Divine Liturgie*, Beruit: Dar El-Machreq, 2000.

Kelley, Matthew, 'The Truth as Best I Know It: Sacraments in Cyper-Space', http://www.thetruthasbestiknowit.com/2009/07/sacraments-in-cyber-space.html.

Kemerer, D. M., 'Early American Liturgies', *Memoirs of the Lutheran Liturgical Association* IV (1901–2), pp. 85–94.

Kennedy, David J., *Eucharistic Sacramentality in an Ecumenical Context: The Anglican Epiclesis*, Aldershot: Ashgate, 2008.

Kennedy, Hugh P., 'The Eucharistic Prayer in Early Irish Liturgical Practice', in Albert Gerhards, Heinzgerd Brakmann and Martin Klöckener (eds), *Prex Eucharistica III. Ecclesia Antiqua et Occidentalis*, Fribourg: Academic Press, 2005, pp. 225–36.

Kennedy, V. L., 'The Moment of Consecration and the Elevation of the Host', *Mediaeval Studies* 6 (1944), pp. 121–50.

Kennedy, V. L., 'The Date of the Parisian Decree on the Elevation of the Host', *Mediaeval Studies* 8 (1946), pp. 87–96.

Kennedy, V. L., *The Saints of the Roman Canon*, 2nd edn, Vatican City: Pontificio Istituto de Archeologia Cristiana, 1963.

Khevsuriani, Lili et al., *Liturgia Ibero-Graeca Sancti Iacobi. Editio–translatio–retroversio–commentarii*, Münster: Aschendorff, 2011.

Khoo, Lorna, *Wesleyan Eucharistic Spirituality*, Adelaide: ATF Press, 2005.

Khoraiche, Albert, '"L'Explication de tous les Mysteres Divins" de Yohannan Bar Zo'bi seon le manuscript Borgianus Syriacus 90', *Euntes Docete* 19 (1966), pp. 386–426.

Khouri-Sarkis, G., 'L'Origine syrienne der l'anaphore byzantine de saint Jean Chrysostome', *L'Orient Syrien* 7 (1962), pp. 3–68.

Khoury, Emmanuel, 'Genesis and Development of the Maronite Divine Liturgy', in J. Madey (ed.), *The Eucharistic Liturgy in the Christian East*, Kottayam: Prakasam Publications, and Paderborn: Ostkirchendienst, 1982, pp. 101–31.

Kidane, Habtemichael, 'The Holy Spirit in the Ethiopian Orthodox Tawahedo Church Tradition', in Teresa Berger and Bryan D. Spinks (eds), *The Spirit in Worship – Worship in the Spirit*, Collegeville: Liturgical Press, 2009, pp. 179–205.

Kidane, Habtemichael, 'The Institution Narrative-Anamnesis in the Ethiopian Anaphora of James of Sarug', in André Lossky and Manlo Sodi (eds), *'Faire Memorie'. L'anamnèse dans le liturgie. Conférences Saint-Serge LVIe Semaine d'Etudes Liturgiques Paris 29 juin–2 juillet 2009*, Vatican City: Librereia Editrice Vaticana, 2011, pp. 119–48.

Kidane, Habtemichael, 'Apropos of the Epiclesis of the Ethiopian Anaphora of James of Sarug', paper presented at the Society of Oriental Liturgy Congress, Louaize, Lebanon, 2012.

Kilmartin, Edward J., 'Sacrificium Laudis: Content and Function of Early Eucharistic Prayers', *Theological Studies* 35 (1974), pp. 268–87.

Kilmartin, Edward J., 'John Chrysostom's Influence on Gabriel Qatraya's Theology of Eucharistic Consecration', in *Theological Studies* 42 (1981), pp. 444–57, p. 452.

Kilmartin, Edward, 'The Liturgical Prayer in Early African Legislation', *Ephemerides Liturgicae* 99 (1985), pp. 105–27.

Kilmartin, Edward J., *The Eucharist in the West: History and Theology*, Collegeville: Liturgical Press, 1998.

Kim, S., 'Jesus – The Son of God, the Stone, the Son of Man and the Servant: The Role of Zechariah in the Self-Identification of Jesus', in G. F. Hawthorne and O. Betz (eds), *Tradition and Interpretation in the New Testament: Essays in Honor of E. E. Ellis*, Tübingen, Mohr Siebeck, 1987, pp. 134–48.

King, Archdale A., *Liturgies of the Primatial Sees*, London: Longmans, Green and Co., 1957.

King, Archdale A., *Liturgies of the Past*, Milwaukee: Bruce Publishing Company, 1959.

King, Archdale A., *The Rites of Eastern Christendom*, vol. 1, reprint, Pisacataway: Gorgias Press, 2007.

King, Fergus J., *More than a Passover: Inculturation in the Supper Narratives of the New Testament*, Frankfurt am Main: Peter Lang, 2007.

Kirby, Peter, *Early Christian Writings*, http://www.earlychristianwritings.com/text/clement.html.

Kistler, Don (ed.), *Jonathan Edwards, Sermons on the Lord's Supper*, Orlando: Northampton Press, 2007.

Klawiter, Frederick C., 'The Eucharist and Sacramental Realism in the Thought of St. Ignatius of Antioch', *Studia Liturgica* 37 (2007), pp. 129–63.

Kleinig, Vernon P., 'Lutheran Liturgies from Martin Luther to Wilhelm Löhe', *Concordia Theological Quarterly* 62 (1998), pp. 125–64.

Klenig, John, 'The Liturgical Heritage of Theodor Kliefoth', in Bart J. Day et al. (eds), *Lord Jesus Christ, Will You Not Stay: Essays in Honor of Ronald Feuerhahn on the Occasion of His Sixty-Fifth Birthday*, Houston: Feuerhahn Festschrift Committee, 2002, pp. 105–20.

Klooster, Fred H., 'The Priority of Ursinus in the Composition of the Heidelberg Catechis', in Derk Visser (ed.), *Controversy and Conciliation: The Reformation of the Palatinate 1559–1583*, Allison Park: Pickwick Publications, 1986, pp. 73–100.

Knoebel, Thomas L., *Isidore of Seville: De Ecclesiasticis Officiis*, New York: Newman Press, 2008.

Knox, John, 'A Summary, According to the Holy Scriptures, of the Sacrament of the Lord's Supper 1550', http://www.swrb.com/newslett/actualNLs/summarls.htm.

Knox, John, *The Works of John Knox*, ed. David Laing, six vols, Edinburgh, 1864.

Kochuparampil, Jose (trans.), 'Eucharist in the Work on the Sacraments by Timothy II', dissertation, Rome, 2000.

Kochuparampil, Jose, 'Redemptive Economy in the Third East Syrian Anaphora Attributed to Mar Nestorius', forthcoming papers of the Fourth Congress of the Society of Oriental Liturgy, Notre Dame University, Louaize, Lebanon, 2012.

Kodell, Jerome, *The Eucharist in the New Testament*, Wilmington: Michael Glazier, 1988.

Koening, John, *The Feast of the World's Redemption: Eucharistic Origins and Christian Mission*, Harrisburg: Trinity Press International, 2000.

Koenker, Ernest B., *The Liturgical Renaissance in the Roman Catholic Church*, St Louis: Concordia Press, 1966.

Kopecek, T. A., *A History of Neo-Arianism*, Patristic Monograph Series 8, vol. 2, Cambridge, MA: Philadelphia Patristic Fundation Ltd, 1979.

Kopecek, T. A., 'Neo-Arian Religion: The Evidence of the Apostolic Constitutions', in Robert C. Gregg (ed.), *Arianism: Historical and Theological Reassessments: Papers from the Ninth International Conference on Patristic Studies, September 5–10, 1983, Oxford, England*, Cambridge, MA: The Philadelphia Patristic Foundation Ltd, 1985, pp. 153–79.

Kraemer, Ross S., *When Aseneth Met Joseph: A Late Antique Tale of the Biblical Patriarch and His Egyptian Wife, Reconsidered*, Oxford: Oxford University Press, 1998.

Kretschmar, G., *Stidien zur frühchristlichen Trinitätstheologie*, Tübingen: Mohr Siebeck, 1956.

Krodel, Gottfried G., 'The Great Thanksgiving of the Inter-Lutheran Commission on Worship: It is the Christian's Supper and Not the Lord's Supper', *The Cresset Occasional Paper* 1, Valparaiso: Valparaiso University Press, 1976.

Kropp, Angelicus M., 'Die Koptische Anaphora des Heiligen Evangelisten Matthäus', *Oriens Christianus* 29 (1932), pp. 111–25.

Kucharek, Casimir, *The Byzantine–Slav Liturgy of St. John Chrysostom: Its Origin and Evolution*, Allendale: Alleluia Press, 1971.

La Piana, George, 'Foreign Groups in Rome during the First Centuries of the Empire', *Harvard Theological Review* 20 (1927), pp. 183–403.

La Piana, George, 'The Roman Church at the End of the Second Century', *Harvard Theological Review* 18 (1925), pp. 201–77.

La Verdiere, Eugene, *Dining in the Kingdom of God: The Origin of the Eucharist According to Luke*, Chicago: Liturgy Training Publications, 1994.

La Verdiere, Eugene, *The Eucharist in the New Testament and the Early Church*, Collegeville: Liturgical Press, 1996.

Lalleman, Pieter J., *Acts of John*, Leuven: Peeters Publishers, 1998.

Lane, Calvin, *The Laudians and the Elizabethan Church*, London: Pickering and Cahato, 2013.

Lang, Bernhard, *Sacred Games: A History of Christian Worship*, New Haven: Yale University Press, 1997.

Lang, M. and R. Meßner, 'Ethiopian Anaphoras: Status and Tasks in Current Research Via an Edition of the Ethiopian Anaphora of the Apostles', in Albert Gerhards and Clemens Leonhard (eds), *Jewish and Christian Liturgy and Worship: New Insights into Its History and Interaction*, Leiden: Brill, 2007, pp. 185–205.

Lang, Uwe Michael, 'Eucharist without Institution Narrative? The Anaphora of Addai and Mari Revisited', in Uwe Michael Lang (ed.), *Die Anaphora von Addai und Mari: Studien zu Eucharistie und Einsetzungsworten*, Bonn: Nova and Vetera, 2007, pp. 31–65.

Lang, Uwe Michael, *The Voice of the Church at Prayer: Reflections on Liturgy and Language*, San Francisco: Ignatius Press, 2012.

Lanne, Emmanuel, 'Le Grand Euchologe du Monastère Blanc', *Patrologia Orientalis* 28.2 (1958), pp. 345–67.

Le Defaut, R., 'Le titre de Summus sacerdos donné à Melchisédech est-il d'origine juive?', *Recherches de Sciences Religieuses* 50 (1962), pp. 222–9.

Leaver, Robin A., *A Communion Sunday in Scotland ca.1780: Liturgies and Sermons*, Lanham: Scarecrow Press, 2010.

Leaver, Robin A., *Luther's Liturgical Music*, Grand Rapids: Eerdmans, 2007.

Leclercq, Jean, 'Eucharistic Celebrations without Priests in the Middle Ages', *Worship* 55 (1981), pp. 160–8.

Lee II, James Ambrose, 'Tracing Wittenberg's Liturgical Lineage: Mecklenburg's Reception of Luther's Reforms of the Mass', thesis for the STM, Yale Divinity School, 2012.

Lenti, Vincent A., 'Liturgical Reform and the Ambrosian and Mozarabic Rites', *Worship* 68 (1994), pp. 417–26.

Lentz, Harold H., *Reformation Crossroads*, Minneapolis: Augsburg Publishing House, 1958.

Léon-Dufour, Xavier, *Sharing the Eucharistic Bread: The Witness of the New Testament*, Mahwah: Paulist Press, 1987.

Leonhard, Clemens, 'Did Theodore of Mopsuestia Quote an Ancient "Ordo"?', *Studia Liturgica* 34 (2004), pp. 191–204.

'Letter CXXI', in *Original letters relative to the English reformation, written during the reigns of King Henry VIII, King Edward VI, and Queen Mary: Chiefly from the archives of Zurich*, translated from authenticated copies of the autographs, and edited for the Parker Society, ed. Hastings Robinson, Cambridge: Cambridge University Press, 1846–47.

Levering, Matthew, *Sacrifice and Community: Jewish Offering and Christian Eucharist*, Oxford: Blackwell Publishing, 2005.

Leyerle, Blake, 'Meal Customs in the Greco-Roman World', in Paul F. Bradshaw and Lawrence A. Hoffman (eds), *Passover and Easter: Origin and History in Modern Times*, Notre Dame: University of Notre Dame Press, 1999, pp. 29–61.

Lienhard, Joseph T., 'The "Arian" Controversy: Some Categories Reconsidered', *Theological Studies* 48 (1987), pp. 415–37.

Ligier, Louis, 'Anaphores orientales et prières juives', *Proche-Orient Chrétien* 13 (1963), pp. 3–20.

Ligier, Louis, 'The Origins of the Eucharistic Prayer: From the Last Supper to the Eucharist', *Studia Liturgica* 9 (1973), pp. 176–85.

Linton, Arthur, *Twenty-Five Consecration Prayers, with Notes and Introduction*, London: SPCK, 1921.

Liturgic Hymns of the United Brethren, Revised and Enlarged, Translated from the German, London, 1793.

The Liturgy of the New Church, 3rd edn, London, 1790.

Liturgy: Worship that Works – Spirituality that Connects, 'Pope & Archbishop of Caterbury recognize virtual sacraments', http://liturgy.co.nz/pope-archbishop-of-canterbury-recognise-virtual-sacraments/9224.

Logan, Alistair, *Gnostic Truth and Christian Heresy*, Edinburgh: T & T Clark, 1996.

Logan, Alistair, 'The Mystery of the Five Seals: Gnostic Initiation Reconsidered', *Vigiliae Christianae* 51 (1997), pp. 188–206.

Lombard, Peter, *The Sentences. Book 4: On the Doctrine of Signs*, trans. Giulio Silano, Toronto: Pontifical Institute of Mediaeval Studies, 2010.

Loughlin, Gerard, *Telling God's Story: Bible, Church and Narrative Theology*, Cambridge: Cambridge University Press, 1996.

Lumpkin, William L., *Baptist Confessions of Faith*, Valley Forge: Judson Press, 2011.

Lundhaug, Hugo, *Images of Rebirth: Cognitive Poetics and Transformational Soteriology in the Gospel of Philip and the Exegesis on the Soul*, Leiden: Brill, 2010.

Luther, Martin, *Luther's Works: American Edition*, ed. Jaroslav Pelikan and Helmut T. Lehman, 55 vols, St Louis and Philadelphia: Concordia and Fortress Press, 1955.

Lyons, David, *Postmodernity*, Minneapolis: University of Minneapolis Press, 2005.

MacCulloch, Diarmaid, *Thomas Cranmer*, New Haven: Yale University Press, 1996.

MacDonald, Alan R., *The Jacobean Kirk 1567–1625: Sovereignty, Polity and Liturgy*, Aldershot: Ashgate, 1998.

Mack, Burton L., *A Myth of Innocence: Mark and Christian Origins*, Philadelphia: Fortress Press, 1991.

MacMullen, Ramsay, *The Second Church: Popular Christianity* AD *200–400*, Atlanta: Society for Biblical Literature, 2009.

Macomber, W. F., 'A Theory on the Origins of the Syrian, Maronite and Chaldean Rites', *Orientalia Christiana Periodica* 39 (1973), pp. 235–42.

Macy, Gary, *The Theologies of the Eucharist in the Early Scholastic Period*, Oxford: Oxford University Press, 1984.

Macy, Gary, 'Commentaries of the Mass During the Early Scholastic Period', in Lizette Larson-Miller (ed.), *Medieval Liturgy: A Book of Essays*, New York: Garland Press, 1997, pp. 25–59.

Macy, Gary, *Treasures from the Storeroom: Medieval Religion and the Eucharist*, Collegeville: Liturgical Press, 1999.

Maestri, G., 'Un contributo alla conoscenza dell'antica liturgia egiziana: Studio dell'anafora del santo evangelista Matteo', in *Memoriam Sanctorum Venerantes Miscellanea in onore di Monsignor Victor Saxer*, Studi Di Antichita

Cristiana 48, Vatican City: Pontificio Istituto di Archeologia Cristiana (1992), pp. 525–37.

Magne, Jean, *Tradition Apostolique sur les Charismes et Diataxeis des Saints Apôtres*. Paris: np, 1975.

Magne, J., 'Rites et prières latines et grecques aux deux premiers siècles', *Studia ephemeridis Augustinianum* 42 (1993), pp. 325–49.

Maiden, John, *National Religion and the Prayer Book Controversy: 1927–1928*, Woodbridge: Boydell Press, 2009.

Malak, Ioannes, 'The Eucharistic Divine Liturgy According to the Rite of the Coptic Church of Alexandria', in J. Madey (ed.), *The Eucharistic Liturgy in the Christian East*, Kottayam: Prakasam Publications and Paderborn: Ostkirchendienst, 1982, pp. 3–34.

Malankara Mar Thoma Syrian Church, *Qurbana Thaksa in English*, np, 2006.

Malaty, Tadros Y., *Christ in the Eucharist*, Orange, CA: Coptic Orthodox Christian Center, 2001.

Maltby, Judith, *Prayer Book and People in Elizabethan and Early Stuart England*, Cambridge: Cambridge University Press, 1998.

Manders, H. and H. Wegman (eds), *Goed of niet goed? Het eucharistisch gebed in Nederland, Deel 2*, Hilversum: Gooi en Sticht, 1978.

Mani Rajan, K., *Queen of Sacraments*, Kottayam: Travancore Syriac Othodox Publishers, 2008.

Mannooramparampil, Thomas, *John Bar Zo'bi: Explanation of the Divine Mysteries*, Kottayam: OIRSI 157, 1992.

Marchant, John, Bryan Reuben and Joan Alcock, *Bread: A Slice of History*, Stroud: History Press, 2008.

Marini, Piero, *A Challenging Reform: Realizing the Vision of the Liturgical Movement*, Collegeville: Liturgical Press, 2007.

Marion, Jean-Luc, *God without Being*, Chicago: University of Chicago Press, 1991.

Markus, R. A., 'St. Augustine on Signs', *Phronesis* 2 (1957), pp. 60–83.

Maroney, Kevin J., 'The Church of Ireland's Eucharistic Prayer 3: Revision and Analysis', *Studia Liturgica* 39 (2009), pp. 171–84.

Marshall, Paul V., *One, Catholic, and Apostolic: Samuel Seabury and the Early Episcopal Church*, New York: Church Publishing Corporation, 2004.

Martell, J. D., 'The Prayer Book Controversy 1927–28', MA thesis, University of Durham, 1974.

Marxsen, Willi, *The Beginnings of Christology Together with The Lord's Supper as a Christological Problem*, Philadelphia: Fortress Press, 1979.

Masaki, Naomichi, *He Alone is Worthy. The Vitality of the Lord's Supper in Theodor Kliefoth and in the Swedish Liturgy of the Nineteenth Century*, Göteborg: Församlongförlaget, 2013.

Maskell, William, *The Ancient Liturgy of the Church of England*, 1882, reprint, New York: AMS, 1973.

Mast, Gregg Alan, *The Eucharistic Service of the Catholic Apostolic Church and Its Liturgical Renewals of the Nineteenth Century*, Lanham: Scarecrow Press, 1999.

Mateos, Juan, *La Célération de la Parole dans la Liturgie Byzantine: Étude historique*, Rome: Pontificorum Institutorum Studiorum Orientalium, 1971.

Matheson, Peter (ed.), *The Collected Works of Thomas Müntzer*, Edinburgh: T & T Clark, 1988.
Matheus, Robert (ed.), *A Commentary on the Mass by* [attributed to] *the Nestorian, George, Bishop of Mosul and Arbel*, trans. R. H. Connolly, Kottayam: OIRSI 243, 2000.
Matthiesen, Michon M., *Sacrifice as Gift: Eucharist, Grace, and Contemplative Prayer in Maurice de la Taille*, Washington: Catholic University Press, 2013.
Maxwell, Jack Martin, *Worship and Reformed Theology: The Liturgical Lessons of Mercersburg*, Pittsburgh: Pickwick Press, 1976.
Maxwell, William D., *The Liturgical Portions of the Genevan Service Book*, Edinburgh: Oliver and Boyd, 1931, reprint, London: Faith Press Ltd, 1965.
Mazza, Enrico, 'Una Anafora incomplete? Il Papiro Strasbourg Gr. 254', *Ephemerides Liturgicae* 99 (1985), pp. 425–36.
Mazza, Enrico, *The Eucharistic Prayers of the Roman Rite*, New York: Pueblo Publishing, 1986.
Mazza, Enrico, *The Origins of the Eucharistic Prayer*, Collegeville: Liturgical Press, 1995.
Mazza, Enrico, *The Celebration of the Eucharist*, Collegeville: Liturgical Press, 1999.
McCarron, Richard E., 'EP RI and II. History of the Latin Text and Rite', in Edward Foley, John F. Baldovin, Mary Collins and Joanne M. Pierce (eds), *A Commentary on the Order of Mass of The Roman Missal*, Collegeville: Liturgical Press, 2011, pp. 453–63.
McCarron, Richard E., 'History of the Text', in Edward Foley, John F. Baldovin, Mary Collins and Joanne M. Pierce (eds), *A Commentary on the Order of Mass of The Roman Missal*, Collegeville: Liturgical Press, 2011, pp. 549–56.
McCarron, Richard E., 'Theology of the Latin Text and Rite', in Edward Foley, John F. Baldovin, Mary Collins and Joanne M. Pierce (eds), *A Commentary on the Order of Mass of The Roman Missal*, Collegeville: Liturgical Press, 2011, pp. 557–70.
McCord Adams, Marilyn, *Some Later Medieval Theories of the Eucharist*, Oxford: Oxford University Press, 2010.
McCormick Zirkel, Patricia, 'The Ninth-Century Eucharistic Controversy: A Context for the Beginnings of Eucharistic Doctrine in the West', *Worship* 68 (1994), pp. 2–23.
McCraken, G. E. and A. Cabaniss (ed.), *Early Medieval Theology*, Library of Christian Classics, vol. 11, Philadelphia: Westminster Press, 1957.
McCullough, Peter, 'Absent Presence: Lancelot Andrewes and 1662', in Stephen Platten and Christopher Woods, *Comfortable Words: Polity, Piety and the Book of Common Prayer*, London: SCM Press, 2012, pp. 49–68.
McDonald, Lee Martin and James A. Sanders, *The Canon Debate*, Peabody: Henrickson, 2002.
McFarland, James J., *Announcing the Feast: The Entrance Song in the Mass of the Roman Rite*, Collegeville: Liturgical Press, 2012.
McGovern, Patrick E., *Ancient Wine: The Search for the Origins of Viniculture*, Princeton: Princeton University Press, 2003.

McGowan, Andrew, *Ascetic Eucharists: Food and Drink in Early Christian Ritual Meals*, Oxford: Clarendon Press, 1999.

McGowan, Andrew, 'Rethinking Agape and Eucharist in Early North African Christianity', *Studia Liturgica* 34 (2004), pp. 165–76.

McGowan, Andrew, 'Eucharist and Sacrifice: Cultic Tradition and Transformation in Early Christian Meals', in Matthias Klinghardt and Hal Taussig (eds), *Meals and Religious Identity in Early Christianity*, Tübingen: A. Francke, 2012, pp. 191–206.

McHugh, John, *On Englishing the Liturgy: An Open Letter to the Bishop of Shrewsbury*, Durham: Ushaw College, 1983.

McKitterick, Rosamond, *The Frankish Church and the Carolingian Reforms 789–895*, London: Royal Historical Society, 1977.

McKnight, Scot, *Jesus and His Death: Historiography, the Historical Jesus, and Atonement Theory*, Waco: Baylor University Press, 2005.

McLeod, Frederick G., 'The Christological Ramifications of Theodore of Mopsuestia's Understanding of Baptism and the Eucharist', *Journal of Early Christian Studies* 10 (2002), pp. 37–75.

McLeod, Hugh, *The Religious Crisis of the 1960s*, Oxford: Oxford University Press, 2007.

McManus, Frederick R., 'The Roman Order of the Mass from 1964 to 1969: The Preparation of the Gifts', in Peter C. Finn and James M. Schellman (eds), *Shaping English Liturgy*, Washington: Pastoral Press, 1990, pp. 107–38.

McVey, Kathleen E., *Ephrem the Syrian: Hymns*, Mahwah: Paulist Press, 1989.

Meeter, Daniel James, *'Bless the Lord, O my soul': The New York Liturgy of the Dutch Reformed Church 1767*, Lanham: Scarecrow Press, 1998.

Megivern, James, *Concomitance and Communion: A Study in Eucharistic Doctrine and Practice*, New York: Herder Book Center, 1963.

Méhat, André, 'Clement of Alexandria', in Raymond Johanny and Willy Rordorf (eds), *The Eucharist of the Early Christians*, trans. Matthew J. O'Connell, Collegeville: Liturgical Press, 2001, pp. 99–131.

Méndez Montoya, Angel F., *The Theology of Food: Eating and the Eucharist*, Chichester: Wiley-Blackwell, 2009.

Menze, Volker L., *Justinian and the Making of the Syrian Orthodox Church*, Oxford: Oxford University Press, 2008.

Mercier, B-Ch., *La Liturgie de Saint Jacques*, Paris: Firmin-Didot, 1946.

Meßner, Reinhard and Martin Lang, 'Ethiopian Anaphoras: Status and Tasks in Current Research via an Edition of the Ethiopian Anaphora of the Apostles', in Albert Gerhards and Clemens Leonhard (eds), *Jewish and Christian Liturgy and Worship: New Insights into Its History and Interaction*, Leiden: Brill, 2007, pp. 185–205.

Methuen, Charlotte, 'Widows, Bishops and the Struggle for Authority', *Journal of Ecclesiastical History* 46 (1995), pp. 197–213.

Methuen, Charlotte, 'For Pagans Laugh to Hear Women Teach: Gender Stereotypes in the *Didascalia Apostolorum*', *Studies in Church History* 34 (1998), pp. 23–35.

Metzger, Bruce M., *The Canon of the New Testament*, Oxford: Clarendon, 1987.

Metzger, Marcel, *Les Constitutions Apostoliques*, Sources Chretiennes 336, Paris: Les Éditions du Cerf (1987), pp. 52–4.
Metzger, Marcel, 'Nouvelles perspectives pour le prétendue Tradition apostolique', *Ecclesia Orans* 5 (1988), pp. 241–59.
Metzger, Marcel, 'Enquêtes autour de la prétendue Tradition apostolique', *Ecclesia Orans* 9 (1992), pp. 7–36.
Metzger, Marcel, 'The Didascalia and the Constitutiones Apostolorum', in Raymond Johanny and Willy Rordorf (eds), *The Eucharist of the Early Christians*, trans. Matthew J. O'Connell, Collegeville: Liturgical Press, 2001, pp. 194–219.
Meyendorff, Paul, *St. Germanus of Constantinople: On the Divine Liturgy*, Crestwood: St Vladimir's Seminary Press, 1984.
Milavec, Aaron, *The Didache: Faith, Hope, and Life of the Earliest Christian Communities, 50–70* CE, Mahwah: Newman Press, 2003.
Miller, Harold, *The Desire of our Souls*, Blackrock: The Columba Press, 2004.
Miller, Harold, 'The Making of the Church of Ireland *Book of Common Prayer* 2004', *Yale Institute of Sacred Music Colloquium* 3 (2006), pp. 75–84.
Mingana, Alphonse, *Commentary of Theodore of Mopsuestia on the Lord's Prayer and on the Sacraments of Baptism and the Eucharist*, Woodbrooke Studies 6, Cambridge: Heffers, 1933.
Mitchell, Leonel L., 'The Influence of the Rediscovery of the Liturgy of Apostolic Constitutions on the Nonjurors', *Ecclesia Orans* 13 (1996), pp. 207–21.
Mitchell, Nathan, *Real Presence: The Work of the Eucharist*, Notre Dame: Notre Dame Center for Pastoral Liturgy, 2000.
Molnar, Paul D., *Karl Barth and the Theology of the Lord's Supper*, New York: Peter Lang, 1996.
Montagu, Richard, *A Gagg for the New Gospell? No: A New Gagg for an old Goose*, London, 1624.
Montagu, Richard, *Appello Caesarem: A Just Appeale from Two Unjust Informers*, London, 1625.
Moosa, Matti, *The Maronites in History*, Piscataway: Gorgias Press, 2005.
Morton, Michael, 'Rethinking the Origin of the Roman Canon', *Studia Patristica* 26 (1993), pp. 63–6.
Mudd, Joseph Christopher, 'Eucharist and Critical Metaphysics: A Response to Louis-Marie Chauvet's Symbol and Sacrament Drawing on the Work of Bernard Lonergan', dissertation, Boston College, 2010.
Muller, Richard A., *Post-Reformation Dogmatics, Vol. 1: Prolegomena to Theology*, Grand Rapids: Baker Books, 1997.
Muller, Richard A. and Rowland S. Ward, *Scripture and Worship: Biblical Interpretation and the Directory for Public Worship*, Phillipsburg: P. & R. Publishing, 2007.
Mundó, Anscari, 'La datación de los códices litúrgicos visigóticos toledanos', *Hispania Sacra* 38 (1965), pp. 1–25.
Myer Boulton, Matthew, 'Supercession or Subsession? Exodus Typology, the Christian Eucharist and the Jewish Passover', *Scottish Journal of Theology* 66 (2013), pp. 18–29.
Myers, Susan E., *Spirit Epicleses in the Acts of Thomas*, Tübingen: Mohr Siebeck, 2010.

Myrc, John, *Mirk's Festial: A Collection of Homilies, Early English Texts*, London: K. Paul and Trench, Trübner, 1906.

Naaman, Paul. *The Maronites: The Origins of an Antiochene Church*, Collegeville: Liturgical Press, Cistercian Publications, 2011.

Naduthadam, Sébastien, 'L'Anaphore de Mar Nestorius, Edition Critique et Etude', thesis presented to the Institut Catholique de Paris, 1992.

Neale, J. M. and G. H. Forbes, *The Ancient Liturgies of the Gallican Church*, Burntisland: The Pitligo Press, 1855.

Nederlandse Commissie voor Liturgie, 'Daarom stellen wij dit teken van ons geloof', Missaal deel 1, Ordo Missae, Hilversum: N. V. Gooi en Sticht, 1970.

Nelson Burnett, Amy, *Teaching the Reformation: Ministers and Their Message in Basel, 1529–1629*, Oxford: Oxford University Press, 2006.

Nelson Burnett, Amy, *Karlstadt and the Origins of the Eucharistic Controversy*, New York: Oxford University Press, 2011.

Nelson Burnett, Amy, *The Eucharistic Pamphlets of Andreas Bodenstein von Karlstadt*, Kirksville: Truman State University Press, 2011.

Nettl, Paul, *Luther and Music*, Philadelphia: Muhlenberg Press, 1948.

Neusner, Jacob, *A History of the Jews in Babylonia: 1. The Parthian period*, 2nd edn, Leiden: Brill, 1969.

Nevin, John Williamson, *The Mystical Presence and the Doctrine of the Reformed Church on the Lord's Supper*, ed. Linden J. DeBie, Eugene: Wipf and Stock, 2012.

Niederwimmer, Kurt, *The Didache*, Minneapolis: Fortress Press, 1998.

Nischan, Bodo, 'The "Fractio Panis": A Reformed Communion Practice in Late Reformation Germany', *Church History* 53 (1984), pp. 17–29.

Nischan, Bodo, *Prince, People, and Confession: The Second Reformation in Brandenburg*. Philadelphia: University of Pennsylvania Press, 1994.

Nocent, Adrien, 'Les apologies dans la celebration eucharistique', in A. Pistoia and A. M. Triacca (eds), *Liturgie et Rémission des Péchés*, Rome: Edizioni Liturgiche, 1975, pp. 179–96.

Notley, R. Steven, 'The Eschatological Thinking of the Dead Sea Sect and the Order of Blessings in the Christian Eucharist', in R. Steven Notley, Marc Turnage and Brian Becker (eds), *Jesus' Last Week*, Jerusalem Studies in the Synoptic Gospels, vol. 1, Leiden: Brill, 2006, pp. 121–38.

O'Callaghan, Joseph F., 'The Integration of Christian Spain into Europe: The Role of Alfonso VI of León-Castile', in Bernard F. Reilly (ed.), *Santiago, Saint-Denis, and Saint Peter: The Reception of the Roman Liturgy in León-Castile in 1080*, New York: Fordham University Press, 1985, pp. 101–20.

O'Donoghue, Neil Xavier, *The Eucharist in Pre-Norman Ireland*, Notre Dame: University of Notre Dame Press, 2011.

O'Loughlin, Thomas, *The Didache: A Window on the Earliest Christians*, London: SPCK, 2010.

O'Malley, Brendan (ed.), *A Celtic Primer: The Complete Celtic Worship Resource and Collection*, Harrisburg: Morehouse Publishing, 2002.

O'Neill, J. C., 'Bread and Wine', *Scottish Journal of Theology* 48 (1995), pp. 169–84.

Odenthal, Andreas, *Liturgie vom Frühen Mittelalter zum Zeitalter der Konfessionalisierung*, Tübingen: Mohr Siebeck, 2011.

Ohl, Jeremiah F., 'The Liturgical Deterioration of the Seventeenth and Eighteenth Centuries', *Memoirs of the Lutheran Liturgical Association IV* (1901–2), pp. 67–78.

Old, H. O., *The Patristic Roots of Reformed Worship*, Zurich: Theologischer Verlag, 1970.

Olsen, Oliver K., 'Contemporary Trends in Liturgy Viewed from the Perspective of Classical Lutheran Theology', *Lutheran Quarterly* 26 (1974), pp. 101–57.

Olson, Oliver K., 'The "Fractio Panis" in Heidelberg and Antwerp', in Derk Visser (ed.), *Controversy and Conciliation: The Reformation and the Palatinate 1559–1583*, Alison Park: Pickwick Publications, 1986, pp. 147–53.

Olson, Oliver K., *Matthias Flacius and the Survival of Luther's Reform*, Wiesbaden: Harrassowitz Verlag, 2002.

Oosterhuis, Huub, *Open Your Hearts*, New York: Herder and Herder, 1971.

Orme, W. (ed.), *The Practical Works of the Rev. Richard Baxter*, 20 vols, London, 1830.

Orthodox Eastern Church, Monks of New Skete, *The Divine Liturgy of Our Father among the Saints, James of Jerusalem*, New York: Monks of New Skete, 1996.

Osborne, K. B., *Christian Sacraments in a Postmodern World: A Theology for the Third Millennium*, New York: Paulist Press, 2000.

Ossom-Batsa, George, *The Institution of the Eucharist in the Gospel of Mark: A Study of the Function of Mark 14, 22–25 within the Gospel Narrative*, Frankfurt am Main: Peter Lang, 2001.

Ostervald, J. F., *A Compendium of Christian Theology*, trans. John McMains, Hartford: Nathaniel Patten Publishing, 1788.

Packer, J. I. and G. E. Duffield (eds), *The Work of Thomas Cranmer*, Philadelphia: Fortress Press, 1965.

Pahl, Irmgard, *Coena Domini I. Die Abendmahlsliturgie der Reformationskirchen im 16./17. Jahrhundert*, Fribourg: University of Fribourg, 1983.

Palmer Wandel, Lee, *The Eucharist in the Reformation: Incarnation and Liturgy*, Cambridge: Cambridge University Press, 2006.

Palmer, Andrew, 'The Fourth-Century Liturgy of Edessa Reflected in Ephraim's *Madroshe* 4 and 5 on Faith', in István Perczel, Réka Forrai and György Geréby (eds), *The Eucharist in Theology and Philosophy: Issues of Doctrinal History in East and West from the Patristic Age to the Reformation*, Leuven: Leuven University Press, 2005, pp. 320–62.

Paniker, P. T. Givergis, 'The Holy Qurbono in the Syro-Malankara Church', in J. Madey (ed.), *The Eucharistic Liturgy in the Christian East*, Kottayam: Prakasam Publications, and Paderborn: Ostkirchendienst, 1982, pp. 135–71.

Parenti, Stefano, 'La "vittoria" nella chiesa de Constantinopoli della Liturgia di Crisostomo sulla Liturgia de Basilio', in Robert F. Taft and Gabriele Winkler (eds), *Comparative Liturgy Fifty Years after Anton Baumstark (1872–1948)*, Rome: Pontifico Istituto Orientale, 2001, pp. 907–28.

Parenti, Stefano and Elena Velkovska (eds), *L'Eucologio Barberini gr.336*, CLV Edizioni Liturgiche: Rome, 1995.

Patrich, Joseph, 'Archaeological and Literary Evidence for the Evolution of the "Great Entrance"', in Béatrice Caseau, Jean-Claude Cheynet and Vincent

Déroche (eds), *Pèlerinages et Lieux Saints dans l'Antiquité et le Moyen Âge: Mélangues offerts à Pierre Maraval*, Paris: Association des Amis du Centre d'Histoire et Civilisation de Byzance, 2006, pp. 341–93.

Paul, K. P., *The Eucharist Service of the Syrian Jacobite Church of Malabar*, reprint, Piscataway: Gorgias Press, 2003.

Peaston, A. Elliott, *The Prayer Book Revisions of the Victorian Evangelicals*, Dublin: APCK, 1963.

Pecklers, Keith F., *The Unread Vision: The Liturgical Movement in the United States of America 1926–1955*, Collegeville: Liturgical Press, 1998.

Pecklers, Keith F., *Dynamic Equivalence: The Living Language of Christian Worship*, Collegeville: Liturgical Press, 2003.

The Peculiar People, Church Order and Order of Advancing of Members into the Ministry, Southend-on-Sea: The Peculiar People, nd.

Penn, Stephen, 'Wyclif and the Sacraments', in Ian Christopher Levy (ed.), *A Companion to John Wyclif: Late Medieval Theologian*, Leiden: Brill, 2006, pp. 241–91.

'Pentecostal Communion Service – Pastor Andrew Evans', http://www.youtube.com/watch?v=98fOIk8hDYk.

Perkins, Willams, *Works 1*, Cambridge, 1616.

Perrin, Nicholas, *Jesus the Temple*, Grand Rapids: Baker, and London: SPCK, 2010.

Petkūnas, Darius, *Holy Communion Rites in the Polish and Lithuanian Reformed Agendas of the 16th and Early 17th Centuries*, Klaipėda: Klaipėdos Universiteto Leidykla, 2007.

Pettegree, Andrew, *Foreign Protestant Communities in Sixteenth-Century London*, Oxford: Clarendon Press, 1986.

Pfaff, Richard W., 'Prescription and Reality in the Rubrics of Sarum Rite Service Books', in Lesley Smith and Benedicta Ward (eds), *Intellectual Life in the Middle Ages: Essays Presented to Margaret Gibson*, London: The Hambledon Press, 1992, pp. 197–205.

Pfaff, Richard W., *The Liturgy in Medieval England: A History*, Cambridge: Cambridge University Press, 2009.

Phillipson, David, *Ancient Churches of Ethiopia*, New Haven: Yale University Press, 2009.

Pierce, Joanne M., 'The Evolution of the *Ordo Missae* in the Early Middle Ages', in Lizette Larson-Miller, *Medieval Liturgy: A Book of Essays*, New York: Garland Publishing, 1997, pp. 3–24.

Pierce, Joanne M. and John F. Romano, 'The Ordo Missae of the Roman Rite: Historical Background', in Edward Foley (ed.), *A Commentary on the Order of Mass of the Roman Missal*, Collegeville: Liturgical Press, 2011, pp. 3–33.

Pincus, Steve, *1688: The First Modern Revolution*, New Haven: Yale University Press, 2009.

Pinell, Jordi, *Liturgia Hispánica*, Barcelona: Centre de Pastoral Litúrgica, 1998.

Piovanelli, Pierluigi, 'The Adventures of the Apocrypha in Ethiopia', in Alessandro Bausi (ed.), *Languages and Cultures of Eastern Christianity: Ethiopia*, Aldershot: Ashgate, 2012, pp. 87–109.

Pipkin, H. Wayne and John H. Yoder (eds), *Balthasar Hubmaier: Theologian of Anabaptism*, Scotsdale: Herald Press, 1989.

Pitre, Brant, *Jesus and the Jewish Roots of the Eucharist: Unlocking the Secrets of the Last Supper*, New York: Doubleday, 2011.

Pocock, Nicholas (ed.), *Records of the Reformation: The Divorce 1527–1533*, vol. 2, Oxford: Clarendon Press, 1870.

Podmore, Colin, *The Moravian Church in England, 1728–1760*, Oxford: Clarendon Press, 1998.

Poirier, John C., *The Tongues of Angels*, Tübingen: Mohr Siebeck, 2010.

Porter, H. B., 'An American Assembly of Anaphoral Prayers', in Bryan D. Spinks (ed.), *The Sacrifice of Praise: Studies on the Themes of Thanksgiving and Redemption in the Central Prayers of the Eucharistic and Baptismal Liturgies. In Honour of Arthur Hubert Couratin*, Rome: CLV Edizioni Liturgiche, 1981, pp. 181–96.

Pott, Thomas, *Byzantine Liturgical Reform*, Crestwood: St Vladimir's Seminary Press, 2010.

Power, David N., *The Eucharistic Mystery: Revitalizing the Tradition*, New York: Crossroad, 1994.

Powers, Joseph M., *Eucharistic Theology*, New York: Seabury Press, 1967.

Poythress, Diane, *Reformer of Basel: The Life, Thought, and Influence of Johannes Oecolampadius*, Grand Rapids: Reformation Heritage Books, 2011.

Praetorius, Michael, *Mass for Christmas Morning*, Archiv Produktion, 439 250–2.

Prenter, Regin, *Theologie und Gottesdienst*, Århus: Forlaget Aros, 1977.

Pusey, Edward, 'The Holy Eucharist a Comfort to the Penitent', http://anglicanhistory.org/pusey/pusey4.html.

Puthur, Bosco (ed.), *Studies on the Anaphora of Addai and Mari*, LRC Publications 9, Mount St Thomas: Kochi, 2004.

Quere, Ralph Walter, *Melanchthon's Christum Cognoscere: Christ's Efficacious Presence in the Eucharistic Theology of Melanchthon*, Nieuwkoop: B. De Graaf, 1977.

Quere, Ralph Walter, *In the Context of Unity: A History of the Development of Lutheran Book of Worship*, Minneapolis: Lutheran University Press, 2003.

Quitslund, Sonya A., *Beauduin: A Prophet Vindicated*, New York: Newman Press, 1983.

Radding, Charles M. and Francis Newton, *Theology, Rhetoric, and Politics in the Eucharistic Controversy, 1078–1079*, New York: Columbia University Press, 2003.

Raes, Alphonse, 'Les Paroles de la consecration dans les anaphoraes syriennes', *Orientalia Christiana Periodica* 3 (1937), pp. 486–504.

Raes, Alphonse, *Anaphorae Syriacae*, Rome: Ponticial Oriental Institute, 1939.

Raes, Alphonse, 'L'authenticité de la Liturgie Byzantine de S. Jean Chrysostome', *Orientalia Christiana Periodica* 24 (1958), pp. 5–16.

Raes, Alphonse, 'Un nouveau document de la liturgie de S. Basile', *Orientalia Christiana Periodica* 26 (1960), pp. 401–11.

Rahmani, I. E., *I Fasti della Chiesa Patriarchale Antiochena*, reprint, Rome: Pontifical Oriental Institute, 1920, reprint, Piscataway: Gorgias Press, 2010.

Rahner, Karl, *Theological Investigations IV*, Baltimore: Helicon Press, 1966.

Raitt, Jill, *The Eucharistic Theology of Theodore Beza: Development of the Reformed Doctrine*, Chambersburg: AAR Studies in Religion, 1972.

Ratcliff, E. C., 'Christian Worship and Liturgy', in K. E. Kirk (ed.), *The Study of Theology*, London: Hodder and Stoughton, 1939, pp. 407–80.

Ratcliff, E. C., 'The English Usage of Eucharistic Consecration 1548–1662 – II?', *Theology* 60 (1957), pp. 273–80.

Ratcliff, E. C., 'The Institution Narrative of the Roman Canon Missae: Its Beginning and Early Background', *Studia Patristica* 2 (1957), pp. 64–82.

Ratcliff, E. C., 'The Eucharistic Institution Narrative of Justin Martyr's First Apology', *Journal of Ecclesiastical History* 22 (1971), pp. 97–102, reprinted in *E. C. Ratcliff: Liturgical Studies*, ed. A. H. Couratin and D. H. Tripp, London: SPCK, 1976.

Ratcliff, E. C. (ed.), *Expositio Antiquae Liturgiae Gallicanae*, London: Henry Bradshaw Society, 1971.

Rathey, Markus, 'St. Matthew', colloquium presentation, Yale Institute of Sacred Music, 2011.

Raw, Barbara C., *Anglo-Saxon Crucifixion Iconography and the Art of the Monastic Revival*, Cambridge: Cambridge University Press, 1990.

Ray, Walter, 'The Strasbourg Papyrus', in Paul F. Bradshaw (ed.), *Essays on Early Eastern Eucharistic Prayers*, Collegeville: Liturgical Press, 1997, pp. 39–56.

Ray, Walter, 'Rome and Alexandria: Two Cities, One Anaphoral Tradition', in Maxwell Johnson (ed.), *Issues in Eucharistic Praying East and West*, Collegeville: Liturgical Press, 2010, pp. 99–127.

Ray, Walter, 'The Barcelona Papyrus and the Early Egyptian Eucharistic Prayer', *Studia Liturgica* 41 (2011), pp. 211–29.

Re:Quest, 'I Go to a Pentecostal Church: Communion', http://www.request.org.uk/main/churches/pentecostal/pentecostal02.htm.

Reed, Jonathan, 'The Hebrew Epic and the Didache', in Clayton Jefford (ed.), *The Didache in Context: Essays on Its Text, History, and Transmission*, Supplements to Novum Testamentum, Leiden: Brill, 1995, pp. 213–25.

Reed, Luther D., *The Lutheran Liturgy*, Philadelphia: Fortress Press, 1947.

Reeve, Paul W. and Ardis E. Parshall (eds), *Mormonism: A Historical Encyclopedia*, Santa Barbara: ABC-CLIO, 2010.

Reif, Stefan, *Judaism and Hebrew Prayer: New Perspectives on Jewish Liturgical History*, Cambridge: Cambridge University Press, 1993.

Rempel, John D., *The Lord's Supper in Anabaptism: A Study in the Christology of Balthasar Hubmaier, Pilgram Marpeck and Dirk Philips*, Waterloo and Scotsdale: Herald Press, 1992.

Renaudot, E., *Liturgiarum Orientalium Collectio*, vol. 1, Frankfurt am Main, 1847, reprint, Farnborough: Gregg International, 1970.

Renhart, Erich and Jasmine Dum-Tragut, *Armenische Liturgien*, Graz: Schnider, 2001.

Renoux, A., 'L'Anaphore Arménienne de Saint Grégoire l'illumateur', in B. Botte et al. (eds), *Eucharisties d'Orient et l'Occident*, Paris: Cerf, 1970, pp. 83–108.

Renoux, Charles A., 'La Célébration de la Parole dans le rite Arménien avant le Xe siècle', in A. M. Triacca and A. Pistoia (eds), *L'Eucharistie: Célérations, Rites, Piétés*, Rome: CLV Edizioni Liturgiche, 1995, pp. 321–30.

Reuben, Catherine, *La Trudaction des Psaumes de David par Clément Marot: Aspects poétiques et théologiques*, Paris: H. Champion, 2001.

Reumann, John, *The Supper of the Lord: The New Testament, Ecumenical Dialogues, and Faith and Order on Eucharist*, Philadelphia: Fortress Press, 1985.

Rex, Richard, 'Not a Lollard Mass after All?', *Journal of Theological Studies* 62 (2011), pp. 207–17.

Riches, John, *Jesus and the Transformation of Judaism*, London: Darton, Longman and Todd, 1980.

Robeck Jr, Cecil M., *The Azusa Street Mission and Revival: The Birth of the Global Pentecostal Movement*, Memphis: Thomas Nelson, 2006.

Roberts, Alexander and James Donaldson (eds), *The Ante-Nicene Fathers: The Writings of the Fathers down to* A.D. *325.*, vol. 5, Buffalo: The Christian Literature Company, 1886.

Roberts, Alexander and James Donaldson (eds), *The Ante-Nicene Fathers: Hippolytus, Cyprian, Caius, Novatian*, New York: Charles Scribner's Sons, 1903.

Roberts, C. H. and B. Capelle, *An Early Euchologium: The Dêr-Balizeh Papyrus Enlarged and Reedited*, Louvain: Université de Louvain Institut Orientaliste, 1949.

Roca-Puig, R., *Anàfora De Barcelona: I Altres Pregàries 9 Missa del segle IV*, Barcelona: Grafos, 1984.

Rodgers, Dirk W., *John à Laso in England*, New York and Frankfurt: Peter Lang, 1994.

Rogers, Elizabeth Frances, *Peter Lombard and the Sacramental System* (1917), reprint, Merrick: Richwood Publishing Company, 1976.

Roguet, A. M. and Lancelot Sheppard, 'Translation of the Roman Canon', in Lancelot Sheppard (ed.), *The New Liturgy: A Comprehensive Introduction*, London: Darton, Longman and Todd, 1970, pp. 161–73.

Rorem, Paul, 'Luther's Objections to a Eucharistic Prayer', *The Cresset* 38:5 (1975), pp. 12–16.

Rorem, Paul, *Calvin and Bullinger on the Lord's Supper*, Alcuin/GROW Liturgical Study 12, Bramcote: Grove Books, 1989.

Rose, Els, *Missale Gothicum. e codice Vaticano Regienesi latino 317 editum*, Turnhout: Brepols, 2005.

Roseman, Philipp W., *Peter Lombard*, Oxford: Oxford University Press, 2004.

Rosenmüller, Johann Georg, *Pastoralanweisung*, 1788, in Günther Stiller, *Johann Sebastian Bach and Liturgical Life in Leipzig*, St Louis: Concordia Publishing House, 1984.

Rough Edge, *The Beat Eucharist*, Rough Edge, 2010.

Rowe, Kenneth E., 'The Palatinate Liturgy and the Pennsylvania Germans', in Heather Murray Elkins and Edward C. Zaraoza (eds), *Pulpit, Table, and Song: Essays in Celebration of Howard G. Hageman*, Lanham: Scarecrow Press, 1996, pp. 53–76.

Rowell, Geoffrey and Christine Hall (eds), *The Gestures of God: Explorations in Sacramentaility*, London: Continuum, 2004.

Roy, Neil J., 'The Mother of God, the Forerunner, and the Saints of the Roman Canon: A Euchological *Deëis*', in Maxwell Johnson (ed.), *Issues in Eucharistic Praying*, Collegeville: Liturgical Press, 2011, pp. 327–48.

Royel, Awa, 'East Meets East: Byzantine Liturgical Influences on the Rite of the Church of the East', *Journal of the Canadian Society for Syriac Studies* 8 (2008), pp. 44–55.

Royel, Awa, 'From Mosul to Turfan: the *Hūdrā* in the Liturgy of the Assyrian Church of the East. A Survey of Its Historical Development and its Liturgical Anomolies at Turfan', forthcoming in proceedings of the 8th Christianity in Iraq Conference, May 2011.

Royel, Awa, 'The Sacrament of the Holy Leaven (*Malkā*) in the Assyrian Church of the East', *International Congress on the Anaphora of Mar Addai & Mari*, Rome, October 2011.

Royel, Awa, *Mysteries of the Kingdom: The Sacraments of the Assyrian Church of the East*, CIRED, San Jose: Medius Corp., 2011.

Rubin, Miri, *Corpus Christ: The Eucharist in Late Medieval Culture*, Cambridge: Cambridge University Press, 1991.

Rundell, Simon, *Creative Ideas for Alternative Sacramental Worship*, Norwich: Canterbury Press, 2010.

Russo, Nicholas V., 'The Validity of the Anaphora of Addai and Mari: Critique of the Critiques', in Maxwell E. Johnson (ed.), *Issues in Eucharistic Praying in East and West*, Collegeville: Liturgical Press, 2010, pp. 21–62.

Ryan, John Barry, *The Eucharistic Prayer: A Study in Contemporary Liturgy*, New York: Paulist Press, 1974.

Sader, Jean, *Le Lieu de Culte et la Messe Syro-Occidentale selon le 'De Oblatione' de Jean de Dara: Étude d'archéologie et de liturgie*, Rome: Pontifical Oriental Institute, 1983.

Safrai, Shmuel, 'Early Testimonies in the New Testament of Laws and Practices Relating to Pilgrimage and Passover', in R. Steven Notley, Marc Turnage and Brian Becker (eds), *Jesus' Last Week*, Jerusalem Studies in the Synoptic Gospels, vol. 1, Leiden: Brill, 2006, pp. 41–51.

Saka, Ishaq, *Commentary on the Liturgy of the Syrian Orthodox Church of Antioch*, Piscataway: Gorgias Press, 2008.

Samuel, Mar Athanasius Yeshue, *Anaphoras: The Book of the Divine Liturgies According to the Rites of the Syrian Orthodox Church of Antioch*, Lodi, NJ: Mar Athanasius Samuel, 1991.

Sasse, Herman, *This is My Body*, Adelaide: Lutheran Publishing House, 1977.

Saulnier, Stéphane, *Calendrical Variations in Second Temple Judaism: New Perspectives on the 'Date of the Last Supper' Debate*, Leiden: Brill, 2012.

Saxon, Elizabeth, *The Eucharist in Romanesque France: Iconography and Theology*, Woodbridge: Boydell Press, 2006.

Schaefer, Mary M., 'Twelfth Century Latin Commentaries on the Mass: The Relationship of the Priest to Christ and the People', *Studia Liturgica Rotterdam* 15.2 (1982), pp. 176–86.

Schäfer, Peter, *The Origins of Jewish Mysticism*, Princeton: Princeton University Press, 2011.

Schäferdiek, Knut, 'Acts of John', in Wilhelm Schneemelcher (ed.), *New Testament Apocrypha*, vol. 2, *Writings Related to the Apostles; Apocalypses and Related Subjects*, Louisville: Westminster/John Knox, 1989, pp. 152–209.

Schaff, Philip, *The Creeds of Christendom*, vol. 3 (1876), reprint, Grand Rapids: Baker Books, 1998.

Schattauer, Thomas, 'The Reconstruction of Rite: The Liturgical Legacy of Wilhelm Löhe', in Nathan Mitchell and John F. Baldovin (eds), *Rule of Prayer, Rule of Faith: Essays in Honor of Aidan Kavanagh,* OSB, Collegeville: Pueblo Press, 1996, pp. 243–77.

Schatull, Nicole, *Die Liturgie in der Herrnhuter Brüdergemeine Zinzendorfs*, Tübingen: Francke Verlag, 2005.

Schiffman, Lawrence H., *The Eschatological Community of the Dead Sea Scrolls*, Atlanta: Scholars Press, 1989.

Schillebeeckx, Edward, *The Eucharist*, New York: Sheed and Ward, 1967.

Schleiermacher, Friedrich, *The Christian Faith* (1821, 1830), reprint, Edinburgh: T & T Clark, 1989.

Schmidt-Clausing, Fritz, *Zwinglis liturgische Formulare*, Frankfurt am Main: Verlag Otto Lembeck, 1970.

Schmidt-Lauber, Hans-Christoph, 'The Lutheran Tradition in German Lands', in Geoffrey Wainwright and Karen B. Westerfield Tucker (eds), *The Oxford History of Christian Worship*, Oxford: Oxford University Press, 2006, pp. 395–421.

Schmidt, Leigh Eric, *Holy Fairs: Scotland and the Making of American Revivalism*, 2nd edn, Grand Rapids: Eerdmans, 2001.

Schneemelcher, Wilhelm (ed.), *New Testament Apocrypha*, vol. 2, London: Lutterworth Press, 1965.

Schneiders, Marc, 'The Origins of the Early Irish Liturgy', in Próinséas Ní Chatháin and Michael Richter (eds), *Ireland and Europe in the Early Middle Ages*, Stuttgart: Klett-Cotta, 1996, pp. 76–98.

Schoonenberg, Piet, 'Transubstantiation: How Far is this Doctrine Historically Determined?', in Hans Küng (ed.), *The Sacraments: An Ecumenical Dilemma*, New York: Paulist Press, 1967.

Schultz, Hans-Joachim, *The Byzantine Liturgy*, New York: Pueblo Publishing, 1986.

Schwiebert, Jonathan, *Knowledge and the Coming Kingdom: The Didache's Meal Ritual and Its Place in Early Christianity*, London: T & T Clark, 2008.

Scruton, Roger, *I Drink Therefore I am: A Philosopher's Guide to Wine*, London: Continuum Press, 2010.

Searle, Mark, 'Semper Reformanda: The Opening and Closing Rites of the Mass', in Peter C. Finn and James M. Schellman (eds), *Shaping English Liturgy*, Washington: Pastoral Press, 1990, pp. 53–92.

Segelberg, Eric, 'The Coptic–Gnostic Gospel According to Philip and Its Sacramental System', *Numen* 7 (1960), pp. 189–200.

Segger, Glen, 'Petition for Peace: A Theological Analysis of Richard Baxter's Reformed Liturgy in Its Ecclesiological Context', PhD dissertation, Drew University, 2008.

Sehling, E., *Die Evangelischen Kirchenordnungen des XVI. Jahrhunderts*, five vols, Leipzig, 1902–13.

Senn, Frank C., 'Liturgia Svecanae Ecclesiae: An Attempt at Eucharistic Restoration during the Swedish Reformation', *Studia Liturgica* 14 (1980–1), pp. 20–36.

Senn, Frank C., *Christian Liturgy: Catholic and Evangelical*, Minneapolis: Fortress Press, 1997.
Senn, Frank C., 'The Mass in Sweden: From Swedish to Latin?', in Karen Maag and John D. Witvliet (eds), *Worship in Medieval and Early Modern Europe: Change and Continuity in Religious Practice*, Notre Dame: University of Notre Dame Press, 2004, pp. 63–83.
Severus of Antioch, 'Homélies cathedrals – 124 & 125', in *PO* 29, Paris: Firmin-Didot, 1960.
Shaw, P. E., *The Catholic Apostolic Church, Sometimes Called Irvingite: A Historical Study*, Morningside Heights: King's Crown Press, 1946.
Sheerin, Daniel J., 'The Anaphora of the Liturgy of St. John Chrysostom: Stylistic Notes', in David Jasper and R. C. D. Jasper (eds), *Language and the Worship of the Church*, Basingstoke: Macmillan Press, 1990, pp. 44–81.
Shemunkasho, Aho, *Konsekration und Konsekrationsgeschehen in der syrischen eucharistischen Anaphora und in der Liturgie der anderen Mysterien*, Piscataway: Gorgias Press, 2008.
Shenouda III, 'Priesthood', trans. Amir Hanna, revised Maher Malek, COEPA 1997, http://tasbeha.org/content/hh_books/Priesthd/index.html.
Shenouda III, 'Saint Gregory the Theologian: According to the Rites of the Coptic Orthodox Church', http://www.copticchurch.net/topics/liturgy/stgregory.pdf.
Shepherd, M. H., 'The Formation and Influence of the Antiochene Liturgy', *Dumbarton Oaks Papers* 15 (1961), pp. 25–44.
Shepherd, M. H., 'Eusebius and the Liturgy of St. James', *Yearbook of Liturgical Studies* 4 (1963), pp. 109–25.
Shimoff, S. R., 'Banquets: The Limits of Hellenization', *Journal for the Study of Judaism* 27 (1996), pp. 440–52.
Basra, Shlemon of, *Book of the Bee*, ed. and trans. E. A.Wallis Budge, Oxford, 1886, http://www.sacred-texts.com/chr/bb/bb47.htm.
Shmidman, Avi, 'Developments within the Statutory Text of the Birkat ha-Mazon in Light of Its Poetic Counterparts', in Albert Gerhards and Clemens Leonhard (eds), *Jewish and Christian Liturgy and Worship: New Insights into its History and Intersection*, Leiden: Brill, 2007, pp. 109–26.
Shrikian, Gorun, *An Interpretation of the Holy Liturgy or Soorp Badarak of the Armenian Apostolic Church*, New York: Armenian Apostolic Church of America, 1984.
Simpson, Ray, *Celtic Worship through the Year: Prayers, Readings and Creative Activities for Ordinary Days and Saints' Days*, London: Hodder and Stoughton, 1998.
Skaf, Aftimos, 'Analyse Textuelle de L'Anamnèse et de l'épiclèse dans la Liturgie de Saint Jean Chrysostome', in Ayoub Chawan (ed.), *Mélanges offerts à Jean Tabet*, Lebanon: Publications de l'Institut de Liturgie à l'Université Saint-Esprit de Kaslik, 2005, pp. 93–105.
Skoyles Jarkins, Stepanie K., *Aphrahat the Persian Sage and the Temple of God*, Piscataway: Gorgias Press, 2008.
Sleman, Fr Abraam D., *The Divine Liturgy of St. Basil*, www.copticchurch.net.
Smend, Julius, *Die Evangelischen Deutschen Messen Bis Zu Luthers Deutscher Messe*, Göttingen: Vanderhoeck and Ruprecht, 1896.

Smith, Dennis E. and Hal E. Taussig, *Many Tables: The Eucharist in the New Testament and Liturgy Today*, London: SCM Press, 1990.
Smith, Dennis E., *From Symposium to Eucharist: The Banquet in the Early Christian World*, Minnapolis: Fortress Press, 2003.
Smith, James David, *The Eucharistic Doctrine of the Later Nonjurors*, Cambridge: Grove Books, 2000.
Smith, John Arthur, *Music in Ancient Judaism and Early Christianity*, Farnham: Ashgate, 2011.
Smyth, C. H., *Cranmer and the Reformation under Edward VI*, London: SPCK, 1926.
Smyth, Matthieu, *La Liturgie Oubliée: La prière eucharistique en Gaul antique et dans l'Occident non romain*, Paris: Cerf, 2003.
Smyth, Matthieu, 'The Anaphora of the So-called "Apostolic Tradition" and the Roman Eucharistic Prayer', in Maxwell E. Johnson (ed.), *Issues in Eucharistic Praying in East and West*, Collegeville: Liturgical Press, 2010, pp. 71–97.
Sorrell, Mark, *The Peculiar People*, Exeter: Paternoster Press, 1979.
Spener, Philipp, *Pia Desideria* (1675), ET in Theodore G. Tappet, *Introduction to Pia Desideria*, Philadelphia: Fortress Press, 1964.
Sperry-White, Grant, *The Testamentum Domini: A Text for Students, with Introduction, Translation, and Notes*, Alcuin/GROW Liturgical Study 19, Bramcote: Grove Books, 1991.
Spinks, Bryan D. and Kenneth Stevenson (eds), *Patterns for Worship: Essays on Eucharistic Prayers*, GS Misc. 333, London: General Synod, nd.
Spinks, Bryan D., 'The Consecratory Epiklesis in the Anaphora of St. James', *Studia Liturgica* 11 (1976), pp. 19–38.
Spinks, Bryan D., 'Christian Worship or Cultural Incantations?', *Studia Liturgica* 12 (1977), pp. 1–19.
Spinks, Bryan D., *Addai and Mari – The Anaphoras of the Apostles: A Text for Students*, Bramcote: Grove Books, 1982.
Spinks, Bryan D., *Luther's Liturgical Criteria and His Reform of the Canon of the Mass*, Grove Liturgical Study 30, Bramcote: Grove Books, 1982.
Spinks, Bryan D., 'A Complete Anaphora? A Note on Strasbourg Gr. 254', *Heythrop Journal* 35 (1984), pp. 51–9.
Spinks, Bryan D., 'Eucharistic Offering in the East Syrian Anaphoras', *Orientalia Christiana Periodica* 50 (1984), pp. 347–71.
Spinks, Bryan D., *Freedom or Order? The Eucharistic Liturgy in English Congregationalism 1645–1980*, Allison Park: Pickwick Publications, 1984.
Spinks, Bryan D., *From the Lord and 'The Best Reformed Churches': A Study of the Eucharistic Liturgy in the English Puritan and Separatist Traditions, 1550–1633*, Rome: CLV Edizioni Liturgiche, 1984.
Spinks, Bryan D., 'Priesthood and Offering in the *kuššāpē* of the East Syrian Anaphoras', *Studia Liturgica* 15 (1984), pp. 104–17.
Spinks, Bryan D., 'Berakah, Anaphoral Theory and Luther', *Lutheran Quarterly* 3 (1989), pp. 267–80.
Spinks, Bryan D., 'The Jerusalem Liturgy of the Catecheses Mystagogae: Syrian or Egyptian', *Studia Patristica* 17:2 (1989), pp. 391–95.
Spinks, Bryan D., '"And with Thy Holy Spirite and Worde": Further Thoughts on the Source of Cranmer's Petition for Sanctification in the 1549 Communion

Service', in Margot Johnson (ed.), *Thomas Cranmer: Essays in Commemoration of the 500th Anniversary of His Birth*, Durham: Turnstone Ventures, 1990, pp. 94–102.

Spinks, Bryan D., 'The Ascension and the Vicarious Humanity of Christ: The Christology and Soteriology behind the Church of Scotland's Anamnesis and Epiklesis', in J. Neil Alexander (ed.), *Time and Community: In Honor of Thomas Julian Talley*, Washington, DC: Pastoral Press, 1990, pp. 185–201.

Spinks, Bryan D., 'Mis-shapen: Gregory Dix and the Four Action Shape of the Liturgy', *Lutheran Quarterly* 4 (1990), pp. 161–77.

Spinks, Bryan D., *The Sanctus in the Eucharistic Prayer*, Cambridge: Cambridge University Press, 1991.

Spinks, Bryan D., *Worship: Prayer from the East*, Washington, DC: Pastoral Press, 1993.

Spinks, Bryan D., 'The Anaphora of Nestorius: Antiochene Lex Credendi through Constantinopolitan Lex Orandi?', *Orientalia Christiana Periodica* 62 (1996), pp. 273–94.

Spinks, Bryan D., 'Trinitarian Theology and the Eucharistic Prayer', *Studia Liturgica* 26 (1996), pp. 209–24.

Spinks, Bryan D., 'Evaluating Liturgical Continuity and Change at the Reformation: A Case Study of Thomas Müntzer, Martin Luther, and Thomas Cranmer', in R. N. Swanson (ed.), *Continuity and Change in Christian Worship*, Woodbridge: Boydell and Brewer, 1999, pp. 151–71.

Spinks, Bryan D., *Mar Nestorius and Mart Theodore the Interpreter: The Forgotten Eucharistic Prayers of East Syria*, Joint Liturgical Study 45, Alcuin Club/GROW, Cambridge: Grove Books, 1999.

Spinks, Bryan D., *Two Faces of Elizabethan Anglican Theology: Sacraments and Salvation in the Thought of William Perkins and Richard Hooker*, Drew University Studies in Liturgy 9, Lanham: Scarecrow Press, 1999.

Spinks, Bryan D., *Sacraments, Ceremonies and the Stuart Divines*, Aldershot: Ashgate, 2002.

Spinks, Bryan D., 'The Origin of the Antipathy to Set Liturgical Forms in the English-Speaking Reformed Tradition', in Lukas Vischer (ed.), *Christian Worship in Reformed Churches Past and Present*, Grand Rapids: Eerdmans, 2003, pp. 66–82.

Spinks, Bryan D., 'The Anaphora of Severus of Antioch. A Note on Its Character and Theology', in J. Getcha and A. Lossky (eds), *θυσία αἰνέσεω: Mélanges liturgiques offerts à la mémoire de l'archevêque Georges Wagner (1930–1993)*, Paris: Presses Saint Serge, 2005, pp. 345–51.

Spinks, Bryan D., 'The Roman Canon Missae', in Albert Gerhards, Heinzgerd Brakmann and Martin Klöckener (eds), *Prex Eucharistica III/I: Ecclesia Antiqua et Occidentalis*, Fribourg: Academic Press, 2005, pp. 129–43.

Spinks, Bryan D., 'The Westminster Confession: The "Bastard Child" of the Church of England', in David M. Loades (ed.), *Word and Worship*, Oxford: The Davenant Press, 2005, pp. 151–61.

Spinks, Bryan D., 'From Elizabeth I to Charles II', in Charles Heffling and Cythia Shattuck (eds), *The Oxford Guide to The Book of Common Prayer*, New York: Oxford University Press, 2006, pp. 44–55.

Spinks, Bryan D., 'The Prayer Book "Crisis" in England', in Charles Hefling and Cynthia Shattuck (eds), *The Book of Common Prayer: A Worldwide Survey*, New York: Oxford University Press, 2006, pp. 239–43.

Spinks, Bryan D., *Reformation and Modern Rituals and Theologies of Baptism: From Luther to Contemporary Practices*, Aldershot: Ashgate, 2006.

Spinks, Bryan D., 'Theodore of Mopsuestia and the Institution Narrative in the East Syrian Anaphora', *Studia Patristica* 40 (2006), pp. 109–14.

Spinks, Bryan D., *Liturgy in the Age of Reason: Worship and Sacraments in England and Scotland 1662–c.1800*, Farnham: Ashgate Publishing, 2008.

Spinks, Bryan D. (ed.), *The Place of Christ in Liturgical Prayer: Trinity, Christology, and Liturgical Theology*, Collegeville: Liturgical Press, 2008.

Spinks, Bryan D., 'A Sacramental Theology in the East Syrian Tradition', *Moscow Theological Conference* 3 (2009), pp. 537–51; English version online at http://petru440.livejournal.com/258975.html.

Spinks, Bryan D., 'German Influence on Edwardian Liturgies', in Dorothea Wendebourg (ed.), *Sister Reformations: The Reformation in Germany and in England*, Tübingen: Mohr Siebeck, 2010, pp. 175–89.

Spinks, Bryan D., 'The Mystery of the Holy Leaven (Malka) in the East Syrian Tradition', in Maxwell E. Johnson (ed.), *Issues in Eucharistic Praying in East and West*, Collegeville: Liturgical Press, 2010, pp. 63–70.

Spinks, Bryan D., *The Worship Mall: Contemporary Responses to Contemporary Culture*, London: SPCK, 2010 and New York: Church Publishing, 2011.

Spinks, Bryan D., 'Revisiting Egyptian Anaphoral Development', in David A. Pitt, Stefanos Alexopoulos and Christian McConnell (eds), *A Living Tradition: On the Intersection of Liturgical History and Pastoral Practice: Festschrift for Maxwell Johnson*, Collegeville: Liturgical Press, 2012, pp. 195–210.

Spinks, Bryan D., 'The Transition from "Excellent Liturgy" to being "Too Narrow for the Religious Life of the Present Generation"', in Stephen Platten and Christopher Woods (eds), *Comfortable Words: Polity, Piety and the Book of Common Prayer*, London: SCM Press, 2012, pp. 98–120.

Spinks, Bryan D., 'Carefully Chosen Words? The Christological Intentionality in the Institution Narrative and the Epiclesis of the Syriac Anaphora of St. James', in Steven Hawkes-Teeples, Bert Groen and Stefanos Alexopoulos (eds), *Studies on the Liturgies of the Christian East: Selected Papers of the Third International Congress of the Society of Oriental Liturgy Volos, May 26–30, 2010*, Leuven: Peeters, 2013, pp. 239–57.

Spinks, Bryan D., 'The Elizabethan Primers: Symptoms of an Ambiguous Settlement or Devotional Weaning?', in Natalie Mears and Alec Ryrie (eds), *Worship and the Parish Church in Early Modern Britain*, Farnham: Ashgate, 2013, pp. 73–87.

Spinks, Bryan D. and Iain R. Torrance (eds), *To Glorify God: Essays on Modern Reformed Liturgy*, Edinburgh: T & T Clark, 1999.

Sprengler-Ruppenthal, Anneliese, *Mysterium und Riten nach der Londoner Kirchordnung der Niederländer*, Köln–Graz: Böhlau Verlag, 1967.

Springer, Michael S., *Restoring Christ's Church: John a Lasco and the Forma ac Ratio*, Aldershot: Ashgate, 2007.

Spruyt, Bart Jan, *Cornelius Henrici Hoen (Honius) and His Epistle on the Eucharist (1525)*, Leiden: Brill, 2006.

Stamps, Robert J., *The Sacrament of the Word Made Flesh: The Eucharistic Theology of Thomas F. Torrance*, Edinburgh: Rutherford House, 2007.

Starck, Johannes F., *Tägliches Handbuch in guten wie in bösen Tagen 1728*, ET Starck's Prayer Book, St Louis: Concordia Publishing House, 2009.

Steinmetz, David C., *Reformers in the Wings*, Philadelphia: Fortress Press, 1971.

Stephens, Peter, *The Holy Spirit in the Theology of Martin Bucer*, Cambridge: Cambridge University Press, 1970.

Stephens, Peter, 'Zwingli's Sacramental Views', in E. J. Furcha and H. Wayne Pipkin (eds), *Prophet, Pastor, Protestant*, Allison Park: Pickwick Publications, 1984, pp. 155–69.

Stephens, Peter W., *The Theology of Huldrych Zwingli*, Oxford: Clarendon Press, 1986.

Stevenson, Kenneth W., 'The Catholic Apostolic Church – Its History and Its Eucharist', *Studia Liturgica* 13 (1979), pp. 21–45.

Stevenson, Kenneth, *Eucharist and Offering*, New York: Pueblo Press, 1986.

Stevenson, Kenneth, *Liturgy and Interpretation*, London: SCM Press, 2011.

Stevick, Daniel B., *The Altar's Fire: Charles Wesley's Hymns on the Lord's Supper, 1745 Introduction and Exposition*, Peterborough: Epworth Press, 2004.

Stewart, Alistair C., *Two Early Egyptian Liturgical Papyri: The Deir Balyzeh Papyrus and the Barcelona Papyrus with Appendices Containing Comparative Material*, Norwich: Hymns Ancient and Modern, 2010.

Stewart-Sykes, Alistair, *Hippolytus: On the Apostolic Tradition*, New York: St Vladimir's Seminary Press, 2001.

Stewart-Sykes, Alistair, *The Didascalia Apostolorum. An English Version with Introduction and Annotation*, Turnhout: Brepols, 2009.

Stoffer, Dale R. (ed.), *The Lord's Supper: Believers Church Perspectives*, Scottdale: Herald Press, 1997.

Stökl Ben Ezra, Daniel, *The Impact of Yom Kippur on Early Christianity*, Tübingen: Mohr Siebeck, 2003.

Stone, Darwell, *A History of the Doctrine of the Eucharist*, two vols, London: Longmans, 1909.

Storck, John and Walter Dorwin Teague, *Flour for Man's Bread: A History of Milling*, Minneapolis: Minnesota University Press, 1952.

Strelcyn, Stefan, 'L'Action de Grâce de N.-D. Marie et l'anaphore de N.-D. Marie dit *Mä'aza Qeddase* dans le Liturgie Éthiopienne', *Journal of Semitic Studies* 24 (1979), pp. 241–9.

Stringer, Martin D., *A Sociological History of Christian Worship*, Cambridge: Cambridge University Press, 2005.

Stringer, Martin, *Rethinking the Origins of the Eucharist*, London: SCM Press, 2011.

Stuber, A., 'Die Diptychon-Formel für die Nomina offerentium im römischen Messkanon', *Ephemerides Liturgicae* 68 (1954), pp. 127–46.

Stuckwisch, D. Richard, *Johann Konrad Wilhelm Löhe: Portrait of a Confessional Lutheran*, Malone: Repristination Press, 1994.

Stuckwisch, D. Richard, 'The Basilian Anaphoras', in Paul F. Bradshaw (ed.), *Essays on Early Eucharistic Prayers*, Collegeville: Liturgical Press, 1997, pp. 109–30.

Stuckwisch, D. Richard, *Philip Melanchthon and the Lutheran Confession of Eucharistic Sacrifice*, reprint, Bynum: Repristination Press, [1997] 2011.

Studdert Kennedy, G. A., *The Hardest Part*, London: American YMCA, 1918.

Suciu, Alin, 'À propos de la datation du manuscript contenant le Grand Euchologe du Monastère Blanc', *Vigiliae Christianae* 65 (2011), pp. 189–98.

Sunday Resources: A Contemporary Liturgical Resource, 'services of the lord's supper', http://www.sundayservices.anglican.asn.au/lordssupper.html.

Sundman, Boel Hössjer, 'Interpretations of the Presence of God in Liturgy', in Oloph Bexell (ed.), *The Meaning of Christian Liturgy: Recent Developments in the Church of Sweden*, Grand Rapids: Eerdmans, 2012, pp. 53–90.

Svenska Kyrkan, 'Liturgy and Worship', http://www.svenskakyrkan.se/default.aspx?id=657790.

Sveshnikov, Sergei, *Break the Holy Bread, Master: A Theology of Communion Bread*, BookSurge.com: np, 2009.

Swedenborg, Emmanuel, *The True Christian Religion Containing the Universal Theology of the New Church*, Amsterdam, 1771, reprint, Boston and New York: Houghton Mifflin Company, 1907.

Syrian Orthodox Church of Antioch: Archdiocese for the Eastern United States, 'Patriarchal Encyclical Letters', http://syrianorthodoxchurch.org/library/patriarchal-encyclical-letters/the-holy-eucharist.

Tabory, Joseph, 'Towards a History of the Paschal Meal', in Paul Bradshaw and Lawrence Hoffman (eds), *Passover and Easter: Origin and History to Modern Times. Two Liturgical Traditions*, vol. 5, Notre Dame: University of Notre Dame Press, 1999, pp. 62–80.

Taft, Robert F., 'How Liturgies Grow: The Evolution of the Byzantine Divine Liturgy', *Orientalia Christiana Periodica* 43 (1970), pp. 355–78.

Taft, Robert F., *The Great Entrance: A History of the Transfer of Gifts and Other Preanaphoral Rites of the Liturgy of St. John Chrysostom*, Rome: Pontificum Institutum Studiorum Orientalium, 1975.

Taft, Robert F., *History of the Liturgy of St. John Chrysostom: The Great Entrance: A History of the Transfer of Gifts & Other Pre Anaphoral Rites*, vol. 2, Rome: Pontificio Istituto Orientale, 1978.

Taft, Robert F., *Beyond East and West: Problems in Liturgical Understanding*, Washington, DC: Pastoral Press, 1984.

Taft, Robert F., 'How Liturgies Grow: The Evolution of the Byzantine Divine Liturgy', in Robert Taft (ed.), *Beyond East and West: Problems in Liturgical Understanding*, Washington, DC: Pastoral Press, 1984, pp. 167–92.

Taft, Robert F., 'The Dialogue before the Anaphora in the Byzantine Eucharistic Liturgy. III: Let us Give Thanks to the Lord – It is Fitting and Right', *Orientalia Christiana Periodica* 55 (1989), pp. 63–74.

Taft, Robert F., 'The Authenticity of the Chrysostom Anaphora Revisited. Determining the Authorship of Liturgical Texts by Computer', *Orientalia Christiana Periodica* 56 (1990), pp. 5–51.

Taft, Robert F., *The Diptychs*, Rome: Pontificium Institutum Studiorum Orientalium, 1991.

Taft, Robert F., 'Holy Things for the Saints: The Ancient Call to Communion and Its Response', in Gerard Austin (ed.), *Fountain of Life*, Washington, DC: Pastoral Press, 1991, pp. 87–102.

Taft, Robert F., 'The Interpolation of the Sanctus into the Anaphora: When and Where? A Review of the Dossier: Part I', *Orientalia Christiana Periodica* 57 (1991), pp. 281–308.

Taft, Robert F., 'The Interpolation of the Sanctus into the Anaphora: When and Where? A Review of the Dossier: Part II', *Orientalia Christiana Periodica* 58 (1992), pp. 83–121.

Taft, Robert F., *The Byzantine Rite: A Short History*, Collegeville: Liturgical Press, 1992.

Taft, Robert F., 'From Logos to Spirit: On the early History of the Epiclesis', in Andreas Heinz and Heinrich Rennings (eds), *Gratias Agamus: Studien zum eucharistischen Hochgebet. Für Balthasar Fischer*, Freiburg: Herder, 1992, pp. 489–502.

Taft, Robert F., 'The Liturgy of the Great Church: An Initial Synthesis of Structure and Interpretation on the Eve of Iconoclasm', Dumbarton Oaks Symposium paper, expanded in Robert F. Taft (ed.), *Liturgy in Byzantium and Beyond*, Aldershot: Ashgate, 1995.

Taft, Robert F., 'The Armenian "Holy Sacrifice (*Surb Patarg*)" as a Mirror of Armenian Liturgical History', in Robert Taft (ed.), *The Armenian Christian Tradition. Scholarly Symposium in Honor of the Visit to the Pontifical Oriental Institute, Rome, of His Holiness Karekin I, Supreme Patriarch and Catholicos of All Armenians, December 12, 1996*, Rome: Pontificio Istituto Orientale, 1997, pp. 1745–97.

Taft, Robert F., *The Precommunion Rites*, Rome: Pontificio Istituto Orientale, 2000.

Taft, Robert F., 'Mass without Consecration? The Historic Agreement on the Eucharist between the Catholic Church and the Assyrian Church of the East. Promulgated 26 October 2001', *Worship* 77 (2003), pp. 482–509.

Taft, Robert F., 'Was the Eucharistic Anaphora Recited Secretly or Aloud? The Ancient Tradition and What Became of It', in Roberta R. Ervine (ed.), *Worship Traditions in Armenia and the Neighboring Christian East*, Crestwood: St Vladimir's Seminary Press and St Nersess Armenian Seminary, 2006, pp. 15–57.

Taft, Robert F., *The Communion, Thanksgiving, and Concluding Rites*, Rome: Pontificio Istituto Orientale, 2008.

Taft, Robert F., 'Is the Liturgy Described in the Mystagogia of Maximus Confessor Byzantine, Palestinian, or Neither?', in *Bollettino della Badia Greca di Grottaferrata* 8 (2011), pp. 223–270.

Takla, Hany N., *Coptic Liturgy: Past, Present, Future*, www.stshenouda.com/coptman/colgsurv.pdf.

Talley, T. J., 'The Eucharistic Prayer of the Ancient Church According to Recent Research: Results and Reflections', *Studia Liturgica* 11 (1975), pp. 138–58.

Tappert, T. G., *The Book of Concord*, Philadelphia: Fortress Press, 1959.

Tarchnišvili, Michael, 'Eine neue Georgische Jakobosliturgie', *Ephemerides Liturgicae* 62 (1948), pp. 49–82.

Taussig, Hal, *In the Beginning was the Meal: Social Experimentation and Early Christian Identity*, Minneapolis: Fortress Press, 2009.

Teicher, J. L., 'Ancient Jewish Eucharistic Prayers in Hebrew', *Jewish Quarterly Review* 54 (1964), pp. 99–109.

Teigen, Bjarne Wollan, *The Lord's Supper in the Theology of Martin Chemnitz*, Brewster: Trinity Lutheran Press, 1986.

Templeton, Julian, 'What's the Problem with God the Father? Some Implications of Impersonal References to God in Reformed Liturgy', in Julian Templeton and Keith Riglin (eds), *Reforming Worship: English Reformed Principles and Practice*, Eugene: Wipf and Stock, 2012, pp. 43–61.

Terian, Abraham, *Macarius of Jerusalem: Letter to the Armenians*, Crestwood: St Vladimir's Seminary Press and St Nersess Armenian Seminary, 2008.

This Far by Faith: An African American Resource for Worship, Minneapolis: Augsburg Fortress Press, 1999.

Thøfner, Margrit, 'Framing the Sacred: Lutheran Church Furnishings in the Holy Roman Empire', in Andrew Spicer (ed.), *Lutheran Churches in Early Modern Europe*, Farnham: Ashgate, 2012, pp. 97–131.

Thomann, Gunther, *John Ernest Grabe's Liturgies: Two Unknown Anglican Liturgies of the Seventeenth Century*, Nurnberg: privately printed, 1989, expanded as *Studies in English Church History*, Stoke on Trent: privately printed, 1995.

Thomas, Gohar Haroutiounian, 'L'anamnèse et l'histoire du salut dans les anaphors de la famille syrienne occidentale', in J. Getcha and A. Lossky (eds), *Θυσία αἰνέσεως. Mélanges liturgiques offerts à la mémoire de l'archevêque Georges Wagner (1930–1993)*, Paris: Presses Saint Serge, 2005, pp. 113–26.

Thompson, Bard, *Liturgies of the Western Church*, New York: Meridian Books, 1961.

Thompson, Bard, 'The Palatinate Liturgy Heidelberg, 1563', *Theology and Life* 6 (1963), pp. 49–67.

Thompson, Nicholas, *Eucharistic Sacrifice and Patristic Tradition in the Theology of Martin Bucer 1534–1546*, Leiden: Brill, 2005.

The Three Coptic Liturgies (Arabic, Coptic and English), Chicago: Copts in Chicago, 2008.

Thurian, Max, *The Eucharistic Memorial*, two vols, London: Lutterworth, 1960 and 1961.

Thurian, Max (ed.), *Ecumenical Perspectives on Baptism, Eucharist and Ministry*, Geneva: WCC, 1983.

Thurian, Max and Geoffrey Wainwright (eds), *Baptism and Eucharist: Ecumenical Convergence in Celebration*, Geneva: WCC, and Grand Rapids: Eerdmans, 1983.

Tillett, Gregory, 'The Fraction in the Coptic Orthodox Liturgy', *The Glastonbury Review* (1999), http://www.coptic.org/language/tilett.htm.

Timms, George, *Dixit Cranmer*, London: A. R. Mowbray, 1947.

Tirot, Paul, 'Histoire des Prières d'Offertoire dans la Liturgie Romaine du VIIè au XVIè siècle', *Ephemerides Liturgicae* 98 (1984), pp. 323–91.

Tomberlin, Daniel, *Pentecostal Sacraments: Encountering God at the Altar*, Cleveland, TN: Center for Pentecostal Leadership and Care, Pentecostal Theological Seminary, 2010.

Tonneau, R. and Robert Devreesse, *Les Homélies Catéchétiques de Théodore de Mopsueste*, Vatican City, 1949.

Toon, Peter, *Evangelical Theology 1833–1856: A Response to Tractarianism*, Atlanta: John Knox Press, 1979.

Torrance, Iain, *Christology after Chalcedon: Severus of Antioch and Sergius the Monophysite*, Norwich: Canterbury Press, 1988.

Torrance, James B., *Worship, Community, and the Triune God of Grace*, Carlisle: Paternoster Press, 1996.

Torrance, Thomas F., *Theology in Reconciliation*, London: Geoffrey Chapman, 1975.

Torrance, Thomas F., *Scottish Theology from John Knox to John McLeod Campbell*, Edinburgh: T & T Clark, 1996.

Tovey, Phillip, *Essays in West Syrian Liturgy*, Kottayam: OIRSI 199, 1998.

Tovey, Phillip, *Inculturation of Christian Worship: Exploring the Eucharist*, Aldershot: Ashgate, 2004.

Triacca, Achille M., 'Le déroulement de la Messe Ambrosienne', in A. M. Triacca and A. Pistoia (eds), *L'Eucharistie: Celebrations, Rites, Piétés*, Rome: CLV Edizioni Liturgiche, 1995, pp. 339–79.

Triacca, Achille M., 'Le Preghiere Eucharistiche Ambrosiane', in Albert Gerhards, Heinzgerd Brakmann and Martin Klöckener (eds), *Prex Eucharistica III/I. Ecclesia Antiqua et Occidentalis*, Fribourg: Academic Press, 2005.

Tripp, D. H., 'The "Sacramental System" of the Gospel of Philip', *Studia Patristica* 17:1 (1982), pp. 251–60.

Turner, H. E. W., 'The Eucharistic Presence', in Archbishop's Commission on Christian Doctrine, *Thinking about the Eucharist*, London: SCM Press, 1972, pp. 99–114.

Turretin, Francis, *Institutes of Elenctic Theology*, ed. James T. Dennison, trans. George Musgrave Giger, three vols, Phillipsburg: Presbyterian and Reformed Publishing Company, 1997.

Tylenda, Joseph N., 'The Ecumenical Intention of Calvin's Early Eucharistic Teaching', in Brian A. Gerrish (ed.), *Reformatio Perennis: Essays on Calvin and the Reformation in Honor of Ford Lewis Battles*, Pittsburgh: Pickwick Press, 1981, pp. 27–47.

Tzadua, Paulos, 'The Divine Liturgy According to the Rite of the Ethiopian Church', in J. Madey (ed.), *The Eucharistic Liturgy in the Christian East*, Kottayam: Prakasam Publications, and Paderborn: Ostkirchendienst, 1982, pp. 37–68.

Umble, John (ed.), 'An Amish Minister's Manual', *Mennonite Quarterly Review* 15 (1941), pp. 95–117.

Understanding the Syriac Orthodox Divine Liturgy, DVD, directed by Archdiocese of the Western United States, 2009.

Underwood, Grant, *The Millenarian World of Early Mormonism*, Urbana and Chicago: University of Illinois, 1993.

United States Conference of Catholic Bishops, 'The Eucharist: A Lutheran–Roman Catholic Statement. Lutheran–Roman Catholic Dialogue: October 1, 1967', http://old.usccb.org/seia/luthrc_eucharist_1968.shtml.

Urdániz, José L. Bandrés, *A Glance Behind the Curtain: Reflections of the Ethiopian Celebration of the Eucharist*, Adigrat: Master Printing Press, 2008.

Ursinus, Zacharias, *The Commentary of Dr. Zacharias Ursinus on the Heidelberg Catechism*, trans. G. W. Williard, 1852, reprint, Grand Rapids: Eerdmans, 1954.

Ussher, James, *The Whole Works of the Most Rev. James Ussher, DD*, ed. C. R. Erlington, vol. 15, Dublin: Hodge and Smith and Co., 1864.
Vadakkel, Jacob, *The East Syrian Anaphora of Mat Theodore of Mopsuestia: Critical Edition, English Translation and Study*, Oriental Institute of Religious Studies, Kottayam: Vadavathoor, 1989, and Cambridge: Grove Books, 1999.
Vagaggini, Cipriano, *The Canon of the Mass and Liturgical Reform*, London: Geoffrey Chapman, 1967.
Vaillancourt, Mark G., *Lanfranc of Canterbury On the Body and Blood of the Lord and Guitmund of Aversa On the Truth of the Body and Blood of Christ in the Eucharist*, Washington, DC: Catholic University of America Press, 2009.
Van de Pavard, Franz, *Zur Geschichte der Messliturgie in Antiocheia und Konstantinopel gegen Ende des vierten Jahrhunderts*, OCA 187, Rome: Pontificio Istituto Orientale, 1970.
Van De Sandt, Huub, *Matthew and the Didache: Two Documents from the same Jewish–Christian Milieu*, Assen: Royal Van Gorcum, and Minneapolis: Fortress Press, 2005.
Van De Sandt, Huub, 'Why Does the Didache Conceive of the Eucharist as a Holy Meal?', *Vigiliae Christianae* 65 (2011), pp. 1–20.
Van De Sandt, Huub and David Flusser, *The Didache: Its Jewish Sources and Its Place in Early Judaism and Christianity*, Assen: Royal Van Gorcum, and Minneapolis: Fortress Press, 2002.
Van Der Meer, F., Brian Battershaw and G. R. Lamb, *Augustine the Bishop*, London and New York: Sheed and Ward, 1961.
Van Dijk, S. J. P. and J. Hazelden Walker, *The Origins of the Modern Roman Liturgy*, London: Darton, Longmans and Todd, 1960.
Varghese, Baby, 'Early History of the Preparation Rites in the Syrian Orthodox Anaphora', in René Lavenant (ed.), *Symposium Syriacum VII*, Rome: Pontificio Istituto Orientale, 1998, pp. 127–38.
Varghese, Baby, *Dionysius Bar Salibi: Commentary on the Eucharist*, Kottayam: SEERI, 1999.
Varghese, Baby, *John of Dara: Commentary on the Eucharist*, Kottayam: SEERI, 1999.
Varghese, Baby, 'Some Common Elements in the East and West Syrian Liturgies', *The Harp* 13 (2000), pp. 65–76.
Varghese, Baby, *West Syrian Liturgical Theology*, Aldershot: Ashgate, 2004.
Varghese, Baby, 'West Syrian Anaphoras other than St. James and Their Theological Importance', in John Berchmans and James Puthuparampil (eds), *Liturgy of St. James: Its Impact on Theologizing in India*, Pune: BVP Publications, 2009, pp. 32–46.
Vellian, Jacob (ed.), *The Romanization Tendency*, Syrian Churches Series, vol. 8, Kottayam: K. P. Press, 1975.
Verhelst, Stéphane, *Liturgia Ibero-Graeca Sancti Iacobi*, Münster: Aschendorff, 2011.
Vermes, Geza, *The Dead Sea Scrolls in English*, London: Penguin, 1975.

Vickers, Brian J., 'The Lord's Supper: Celebrating the Past and Future in the Present', in Thomas R. Schreiner and Matthew R. Crawford (eds), *The Lord's Supper: Remembering and Proclaiming Christ until He Comes*, Nashville: B&H Academic, 2010, pp. 313–40.

Vondey, Wolfgang, *People of Bread: Rediscovering Ecclesiology*, New York: Paulist Press, 2008.

Vorhes McGowan, Anne, 'The Basilian Anaphoras: Rethinking the Question', in Maxwell E. Johnson (ed.), *Issues in Eucharistic Praying in East and West: Essays in Liturgical and Theological Analysis*, Collegeville: Liturgical Press, 2010, pp. 219–61.

Wagner, Georg, 'Zur Herkunft Der Apostolischen Konstitutionem', in R. P. Bernard Botte (ed.), *Mélanges Liturgiques offert*, Louvain: Abbaye du Mont César, 1972, pp. 525–37.

Wagner, Georg, *Der Ursprung der Chrysostomusliturgie*, Münster: Aschendorff, 1973.

Wagner, Rachel, *Godwired: Religion, Ritual and Virtual Reality*, London: Routledge, 2012.

Wainwright, Geoffrey, *Doxology: The Praise of God in Worship, Doctrine and Life: A Systematic Theology*, New York: Oxford University Press, 1980.

Walker Bynum, Caroline, *Fragmentation and Redemption: Essays on Gender and the Human Body in Medieval Religion*, New York: Zone Books, 1991.

Walker Bynum, Caroline, *Wonderful Blood: Theology and Practice in Late Medieval Germany and Beyond*, Philadelphia: University of Pennsylvania Press, 2007.

Walker, Michael, *Baptists at the Table*, Didcot: Baptist Historical Society, 1992.

Wallace-Hadrill, D. S., 'Eusebius and the Institution Narrative in the Eastern Liturgies', *Journal of Theological Studies* 4 (1953), pp. 41–2.

Walters, J. Edward (ed. and trans.), *Hymns on the Unleavened Bread*, Piscataway: Gorgias Press, 2012.

Webb, B., 'The Anaphora of Theodore the Interpreter', *Ephemerides Liturgicae* 104 (1990), pp. 3–22.

Webb, Douglas, 'Le Sens de L'Anaphore de Nestorius', in A. M. Triacca and A. Pistoia (eds), *La Liturgie: sons sens, son esprit, sa méthode*, Rome: CLV, 1982, pp. 349–72.

Webster, Jane S., *Ingesting Jesus: Eating and Drinking in the Gospel of John*, Leiden: Brill, 2003.

Wegman, H. A. J., *Goed of niet goed? Het eucharistisch gebed in Nederland*, (Deel 1), Hilverum: Gooi en Sticht, 1976.

Wegman, H., 'Généalogie hypothétique de la prière eucharistique', *Questions Liturgiques* 61 (1980), pp. 263–78.

Wegman, H. A. J., 'Une anaphore incomplete? Les Fragments sur Papyrus Strasbourg Gr. 254', in R. van den Broek and M. J. Vermeseren (eds), *Studies in Gnosticism and Hellenistic Religions*, Leiden: Brill, 1981, pp. 432–50.

Weisz, Leo, 'Heinrich Bullinger's Agenda', *Zwingliana* 10 (1954–58), pp. 1–23.

West, Maxine E., 'The Sacramentary of Serapion: Worthless Heresy or Precious Resource', Gregory Dix Essay, 1995.

Wetter, Evelin, '"On Sundays for the laity . . . we allow mass vestments, altars and candles to remain": The Role of Pre-Reformation Ecclesiastical Vestments in the Formation of Confessional, Corporate and "National" Identities', in Andrew Spicer (ed.), *Lutheran Churches in Early Modern Europe*, Farnham: Ashgate, 2012, pp. 165–95.

White, Francis, *The Orthodox Faith and Way to the Church Explained and Justified*, London, 1617.

White, James F., 'United Methodist Eucharistic Prayers', in Frank C. Senn (ed.), *New Eucharistic Prayers: An Ecumenical Study of Their Development and Structure*, Mahwah: Paulist Press, 1987, pp. 80–95.

White, James F., *John Wesley's Prayer Book: The Sunday Service of the Methodists in North America*, Akron: OSL Publications, 1991.

White, Susan J., *Christian Worship and Technological Change*, Nashville: Abingdon Press, 1994.

Williams, Rowan, *Eucharistic Sacrifice: The Roots of a Metaphor*, Grove Liturgical Study 31, Bramcote: Grove Books, 1982.

Williams, Rowan, *Arius: Heresy and Tradition*, London: Darton, Longman and Todd, 1987.

Williams, Rowan, 'Language, Reality and Desire in Augustine's De Doctrina', *Journal of Literature and Theology* 3 (1989), pp. 138–50.

Williams, Rowan, *On Christian Theology*, Oxford: Blackwell, 2000.

Williamson, Lamar, *Preaching the Gospel of John: Proclaiming the Living Word*, Louisville: Westminster John Knox Press, 2004.

Willimon, William, 'Communion as a Culinary Art', *The Christian Century* (21 September 1977), pp. 829–30.

Willis, G. G., *Essays in Early Roman Liturgy*, London: SPCK, 1964.

Winkler, Gabriele, 'Armenia and the Gradual Decline of Its Traditional Liturgical Practices as a Result of the Expanding Influence of the Holy See from the 11th to the 14th Century', in A. M. Triacca (ed.), *Liturgie de l'Élise Particulière et Liturgie de l'Élise universelle*, Rome: Edizioni Liturgiche, 1976, pp. 329–68.

Winkler, Gabriele, 'Further Observations in Connection with the Early Form of the Epiklesis', in Gabriele Winkler (ed.), *Studies in Early Christian Liturgy and Its Context*, Aldershot: Ashgate, 1997, pp. 66–80.

Winkler, Gabriele, *Das Sanctus: Über den Ursprung und die Anfänge des Sanctus und sein Fortwirken*, Rome: Pontificio Istituto Orientale, 2002.

Winkler, Gabriele, 'The Sanctus: Some Observations with Regard to Its Origins and Theological Significance', in Bronwen Neil, Geoffrey D. Dunn and Lawrence Cross (eds), *Prayer and Spirituality in the Early Church*, vol. 3, *Liturgy and Life*, Strathfield NSW, Austrialia: St Paul's Publications, 2003, pp. 111–31.

Winkler, Gabriele, 'A New Witness to the Missing Institution Narrative', in Maxwell E. Johnson and L. Edward Phillips (eds), *Studia Liturgica Diversa: Essays in Honor of Paul F. Bradshaw*, Portland: Pastoral Press, 2004, pp. 117–28.

Winkler, Gabriele, *Die Basilius-Anaphora: Edition der beiden armenischen Redaktionen und der relevanten Fragmente, Übersetzung und Zusammenschau aller Versionen im Lichte der orientalischen Überlieferungen*, Anaphorae Orientales vol. 2, Rome: Pontificio Istituto Orientale, 2005.

Winkler, Gabriele, 'On the Formation of the Armenian Anaphoras: A Completely Revised and Updated Overview', *Studi sull'Oriente Cristiano* 11 (2007), pp. 97–130.

Winkler, Gabriele, 'Armenia's Liturgy at the Crossroads of Neighbouring Traditions', *Orientalia Christiana Periodica* 74 (2008), pp. 363–87.

Winkler, Gabriele, 'The Christology of the Anaphora of St. Basil in Its Various Redactions, with some Remarks Concerning the Authorship of Basil', in Bryan D. Spinks (ed.), *The Place of Christ in Liturgical Prayer: Trinity, Christology, and Liturgical Theology*, Collegeville: Liturgical Press, 2008, pp. 112–26.

Winkler, Gabriele, 'Preliminary Observations about the Relationship between the Liturgies of St. Basil and St. James', *Orientalia Christiana Periodica* 78 (2010), pp. 5–55.

Winkler, Gabriele, *Die Armenische Liturgie des Sahak*, Anaphorae Orientales 3, Rome: Pontificio Istituto Orientale, 2011.

Winkler, Gabriele, 'Unsolved Problems Concerning the Background and Significance of the Vocabulary of Praise in some of the Oldest Eucharistic Prayers', in Bert Groen, Steven Hawkes-Teeples and Stefanos Alexopoulos (eds), *Inquiries into Eastern Christian Worship*, Leuven: Peeters, 2012, pp. 133–72.

Witvliet, John D., 'The Anaphora of St. James', in Paul Bradshaw (ed.), *Essays on Early Eastern Eucharistic Prayers*, Collegeville: Liturgical Press, 1997, pp. 153–72.

Wobbermin, G., *Altchristliche liturgische Stücke aus der Kirche Aegyptens nebst dogmatischen Brief des Bischofs Serapion von Thmuis*, Leipzig and Berlin, 1898.

Woodfin, Warren T., *Embodied Icon: Liturgical Vestments and Sacramental Power in Byzantium*, New York: Oxford University Press, 2012.

Woodruff Tait, Jennifer L., *The Poisoned Chalice: Eucharistic Grape Juice and Common-Sense Realism in Victorian Methodism*, Tuscaloosa: University of Alabama Press, 2011.

Woolfenden, Gregory, 'Praying the Anaphora: Aloud or in Silence', *St Vladimir's Theological Quarterly* 51 (2007), pp. 179–202.

World Council of Churches, *Baptism, Eucharist and Ministry*, Geneva: WCC, 1982.

'Wounded Eucharistic Prayer', http://www.freshworship.org/book/print/545.

Wright, David, 'Infant Baptism and the Christian Community in Bucer', in David Wright (ed.), *Martin Bucer: Reforming Church and Community*, Cambridge: Cambridge University Press, 1994, pp. 95–106.

Wright, N. T., *Jesus and the Victory of God*, Minneapolis: Fortress Press, 1996.

Wright, W., *The Apocryphal Acts*, London: Williams and Norgate, 1871.

Wybrew, Hugh, *The Orthodox Liturgy: The Development of the Eucharistic Liturgy in the Byzantine Rite*, London: SPCK, 1989.

Yakubova, L. (comp.), *Chants from the East: The Liturgical Music of the Assyrian Church of the East*, music scores by A. Sahakyan, Chicago: sponsored by the Assyrian Universal Alliance Foundation, 2009.

Yarnold, Edward, 'The Authorship of the *Mystagogic Catecheses* Attributed to Cyril of Jerusalem', *Heythrop Journal* 19 (1978), pp. 143–61.

Yarnold, Edward, *The Awe-Inspiring Rites of Initiation: The Origins of the RCIA*, Collegeville: Liturgical Press, 1994.

Yarnold, Edward, 'Anaphoras without Institution narratives?', *Studia Patristica* 15 (1997), pp. 395–410.

Yasin, Ann Marie, *Saints and Church Spaces in the Late Antique Mediterranean*, Cambridge: Cambridge University Press, 2009.

Yelverton, Eric E., *The Mass in Sweden: Its Development from the Latin Rite from 1531 to 1917*, London: Henry Bradshaw Society, 1920.

Younan, Andrew, *The Mesopotamian School and Theodore of Mopsuetsia*, 2009, http://www.lulu.com/content/5537694.

Yousif, Pierre, 'Le Déroulement de la Messe Chaldéenne', in F. Casingena-Trévedy and I. Jurasz Geuthner (eds), *Les liturgies syriaques*, Paris: Geuthner, 2006, pp. 59–99.

Yousif, Pierre, 'The Divine Liturgy According to the Rite of the Assyro-Chaldean Church', in J. Madey (ed.), *The Eucharistic Liturgy in the Christian East*, Kottayam: Prakasam Publications, and Paderborn: Ostkirchendienst, 1982, pp. 174–237.

Yousif, Pierre, *L'Euchariste Chez Saint Éphrem de Nisibe*, Rome: Pontificium Institutum Orientale, 1984.

Youssif, Pierre, 'The Anaphora of Mar Theodore: East Syrian; Further Evidence', *Studia Anselmiana* 110, *Analecta Liturgica* 17 (1993), pp. 571–91.

Zanetti, Ugo, 'Fraction Prayers in the Coptic Liturgy', *The Harp* 27 (2011), pp. 291–302.

Zanetti, Ugo, 'Deux prières de la fraction de la liturgie de Grégoire, en grec et en copte', *Orientalia Christiana Periodica* 78 (2012), pp. 291–333.

Zeeden, Ernst Walter, *Faith and Act: The Survival of Medieval Ceremonies in the Lutheran Reformation*, St. Louis: Concordia Publishing House, 2012.

Zheltov, Michael, 'The Anaphora and the Thanksgiving Prayer from the Barcelona Papyrus: An Underestimated Testimony to the Anaphoral History of the Fourth Century', *Vigiliae Christianae* 62 (2008), pp. 467–504.

Zheltov, Michel, 'The Moment of Eucharistic Consecration in Byzantine Thought', in Maxwell E. Johnson (ed.), *Issues in Eucharistic Praying in East and West*, Collegeville: Liturgical Press, 2011, pp. 263–306.

Zimmerman, Joyce Ann, 'EP RII: The Mystagogical Implications', in Edward Foley, John F. Baldovin, Mary Collins and Joanne M. Pierce (eds), *A Commentary on the Order of Mass of The Roman Missal*, Collegeville: Liturgical Press, 2011, pp. 503–8.

Zinzendorf, N. L., *Maxims, Theological Ideas and Sentences, out of the Present Ordinary of the Brethren's Churches. His Dissertations and Discourses from the Year 1738 till 1747*, London, 1751.

Zinzendorf, N. L., *Ergänzungsband* VI, Hildesheim: Georg Olms Verlagsbuchhandlung, 1965.

Zuidema, Jason and Theodore Van Raalte, *Early French Reform: The Theology and Spirituality of Guillaume Farel*, Farnham: Ashgate, 2011.

Zwingli, Huldrych, *Huldrych Zwingli Writings*, trans. E. J. Furcha, Allison Park: Pickwick Publications, 1984.

Zwingli, Huldrych, *Huldrych Zwingli Writings*, trans. H. Wayne Pipkin, vol. 2, Allison Park: Pickwick Publications, 1984.

Index

'Ammar al-Basri 142
Ābā,Mar, Catholicos 145
Aboriginal Prayer 386–7
Abraham Qatraya Bar Lipah 142
Acts of Andrew 198
Acts of John 43–4, 52, 58, 66
Acts of Thomas 39–43, 47, 52, 57–8, 66, 132
Addai and Mari *see under* anaphoras
adiaphora 272
Adisho 154
agape 46
Aitken, Robert 373
Alberic of Monte Cassino 222–3
Albigensian heresy 228
Albrecht, Daniel E. 423–4
Alcuin of York 213
Alexander, Philip 55
Alfonso VI, King 192
Alikin, Valeriy 12, 16, 43
AlphaChurch 434
Alternative Service Book (1980) 63, 390
Amalarius of Metz 214–5
Amar, Joseph 78
Ambrose of Milan 68, 83–6, 204, 205, 212, 217, 275
Ambrosian Missal 207
Ambrosian rite 190, 192, 206–7, 210
Ames, William 301, 329
Amish 352–4
Ammann, Jacob 352
Amon, Karl 381
Anabaptists 348–54
anaklinai, anaklino 4
anamnesis 1, 17, 20, 91, 131, 160, 163, 185, 383, 385–6, 389–90, 394, 405, 414, 419
anaphoras
 Addai and Mari 52–8, 60, 66, 67, 72, 76, 80, 97, 133–4, 147, 149, 151, 152, 166, 168–70, 205
 Apostles, Ethiopian 56, 173, 177
 Athanasius, Armenian 184, 185, 187–9
 Athanasius, Epyptian 101
 Athanasius, Ethiopian 178, 182
 Barcelona 60, 97, 99–105, 113, 382
 Basil, Armenian (1) 112, 113, 184–5
 Basil, Armenian (2) 184
 Basil, Byzantine (Byz.Bas) 121–3, 128, 129, 132–4, 149, 150, 333, 338, 340, 381
 Basil, Coptic (Eg.Bas) 57, 108, 109, 111–5, 133, 135
 Basil, Ethiopian 172
 Cyril of Alexandria, Armenian 184, 185
 Cyril, Coptic 59, 92, 94, 98, 106, 108, 109, 113, 115–116, 117, 177
 Dionysius Bar Salibi, Syriac 163
 Eustathius I, Syriac 163
 Gregory, Coptic 108, 111, 117–8
 Gregory, Egyptian 108, 111, 117–8, 136, 177
 Gregory, Ethiopian 172
 Gregory of Nazianzen, Armenian 184, 185
 Gregory the Illuminator, Armenian (arm.Bas.1) 112, 133, 184
 Ignatius of Antioch, Armenian 184
 Ignatius the Maphrian, Syriac 163
 Jacob of Serug, Ethiopian 179–80, 181, 182
 Jacob of Serug, Syriac 163
 James, Greek and Syriac 116, 122, 129, 134–6, 149, 159, 166, 184, 333, 338, 340, 388
 John Bar Shusan, Syriac 163
 John Bostra, Coptic 102–3
 John Bostra, Syriac 159

John Chrysostom, Byzantine (CHR) 121–3, 129–32, 184, 188, 381
John Maron, Syriac 166
John Son of Thunder, Ethiopian 174, 178–9
John the Evangelist, Syriac 164, 166
Louvain 27 (anaphoral fragment) 100, 101, 382
Mark, Greek 59, 92, 94, 98, 106, 108–9, 113, 115, 118
Mark the Evangelist, Syriac 164, 166
Matthew, Coptic 105, 173
Nestorius, East Syrian 147–50, 151–2, 154, 168, 170
Our Lady Mary ascribed to Cyriacus of Bahnasah, Ethiopian 181, 182
Our Lord Jesus Christ, Ethiopian 173, 177
Peter, Syriac 164, 166
Peter III, Syriac, see Sharar *below*
Sahak, Armenian 184–5
Severus of Antioch, Coptic 102
Severus of Antioch, Syriac 102–3, 159, 163
Sharar (Peter III, Syriac) 52, 57, 166, 167, 168–70
Sixtus, Syriac 164
Strasbourg Papyrus (Gr. 254) 59–61, 66, 72, 94, 99, 101, 102, 104, 106, 113, 115–6, 131
Theodore the Interpreter (Mopsuestia) 80, 147–54, 168–70, 185
Thomas, Coptic 102–5
Thomas of Harkel, Syriac 163
Timothy of Alexandria, Syriac 159, 163
Twelve Apostles, Syrian 130, 149, 158, 159, 160, 166
Xystus, Syriac (*see* Sixtus)
anapipto 4
Andrewes, Lancelot 329
Andrieu and Collomp 59
Anglican Church of South India 388
Anglican-Roman Catholic dialogue 397, 402
Anglican tradition 313–46
Anglican-Orthodox dialogue (2006) 415
Anonymous Exposition 142
Antioch 17, 130, 141
Antoninus Pius 30
Aphrahat 42, 57, 141, 142, 151–2
apophenei 91
Apostolic Constitutions (AC) 61–2, 66, 89–92, 108, 129, 130, 185, 338, 340–1
Apostolic Tradition (AT) 59, 62–6, 90–2, 102, 129–130, 172, 200, 382, 390, 391, 425
Aqqapta 144
Armenian rite 183–9
Arndt, Johann 264, 267
Athanasius 95, 98
Augsburg Confession (1530) 254–5, 259, 290
Augsburg Confession, Apology of 254
Augustana Variata (1540) 255
Augustine of Hippo 68, 86–8, 212, 217, 249, 253, 401
Aulén, Gustav 396–7
Ausbund 354
Australian Prayer Book (1978) 392
Auxentius of Milan 192

Babylonian Captivity of the Church (1520) 248, 249, 254
Bach, Johann Sebastian 267, 271
Baldovin, John 203
Bandrés, José L. 173, 182, 183
Banyard, James 372–3
Baptism, Eucharist and Ministry (BEM) 403–6, 407
Baptists, General 353–8
Baptists, Particular 355–8
Barbarini 336 (manuscript) 108, 125, 130, 131, 133
Barcelona Papyrus, *see* anaphoras, Barcelona
Barker, Margaret 20–1
Barrett-Leonard, R. 95
Barrow, Henry 354–5
Barth, Karl 396
Basil of Caesarea 111, 134
Bates, W. H. 59
Batstone, Louise 199
Bauckham, Richard 12
Baumstark, Anton 117
Baxter, Richard 334–7, 341, 344
Bazaar of Heraclides 148
Beat Mass 432–3

Beauduin, Dom Lambert 377
Bedford, Thomas 330
Benedict of Aniane 213
Benedict VIII, Pope 234
Benedict XVI, Pope 5, 245, 435
berakah, berakot 7, 8, 19, 28, 59, 102
Berengar 220–3, 224, 240
Berger, Teresa 38
Berne Disputation 285
Bersier, Eugène 311
Berwick Liturgy (Knox, 1549) 295, 296
Beukers, C. L. 72–3
Beza, Theodore 301
Bickersteth, Edward 342–3, 344
Biel, Gabriel 242
birkat ha-mazon 2, 23, 25, 54–5, 59, 66, 99
Blomberg, Craig L. 4, 12–13, 14
Blond, George 34
Bobbio Missal 209, 212
Bobrinskoy, Boris 132
Boeve, Lieven 407, 417
Bonaventure 235–6
Böntert, Stefan 433–4
Book of Common Order (1562) 294
Book of Common Order (1940/1979) 409
Book of Common Prayer 293–6, 305, 311, 312, 313, 318–346, 389
Book of Common Worship (Church of South India, 1963) 388
Book of Common Worship (1993) 409
Book of Mormon 370–2
Bornert, René 279–80
Botte, Bernard 63, 80, 95, 382
Bouley, Allan 66, 90, 196
Bouyer, Louis 7, 23, 54, 90, 95, 97, 99, 345, 382
Bowman, Matthew 372
Boynton, Susan 195
Bradshaw, Paul 8, 15, 47, 62, 64, 70, 97, 102, 137, 200
bread and bread making 437
Brenner, Scott F. 308
Brent, Alan 63
Brenz, Johann 253
Brevint, Daniel 361
Briconnet, Bishop Guillaume 285
Bridges, William 373
Brightman, F. E. 174–5, 320
Brilioth, Yngve 251, 315
British Joint Liturgical Group 395
British Methodist rite (1975) 387–8, 395
British United Reformed Church (1980) 387–8
Brock, Sebastian 57, 77, 124–5, 130–1, 141, 163
Brown, David 417
Brown, Leslie 388
Brown, Raymond 21
Browne, Robert 354–5
Bryennios, Archbishop Philotheos 22
Bucer, Martin 255, 259, 278, 279–83, 288, 290, 291, 292, 298, 314, 317, 322
Buchanan, Colin 337, 390
Buchinger, Harald 50–1
Bucke, Daniel 355
Budde, Achim 113
Bugenhagen, Johannas 253, 257, 269–70
Bugnini, Annibale 384
Bulgakov, Sergius 139–40, 442
Bullinger, Heinrich 278, 279, 290, 298, 301, 319, 326
Bullinger's *Agenda* (1532/35) 279
Bultmann, Rudolph 1–2, 11, 21
Burchard, Christopher 8–9
Bürki, Bruno 305, 307, 311
Burnett, Amy 249
Byzantine rite 121–40, 211

Cabasilas, Nicholas 124–7, 138
Caecilius, Bishop 47
Caesarius of Arles 198–9
Callistus, Pope 62
Calvin, John 272, 278, 287–92, 294, 295, 296, 298, 301, 306, 307, 308, 312, 326, 327, 331, 346, 413
Camelot, T. 49
Campbell, Archbishop 339
Campbell, George 309
Campbell, Mary 366
canon missae 115, 166, 184, 200, 203–6, 208, 210, 212, 213, 218, 219–20, 234, 238, 242, 249, 251, 252, 270, 275, 280, 285, 319, 348, 381, 382, 384
Canons of Hippolytus 172
Capelle, Bernard 132
Carbié, Robert 245

Cardale, John 366–70
Cardier, Jean 292
Carolingian kingdom 211
Casey, Damien 35
Catechism of the Catholic Church (1994/97) 416–7
Catholic Apostolic Church 310, 366–70, 394
Celtic rite/tradition 190, 207–10
chaburah 2
Chan, Simon 424–5
Charlemagne 196, 211, 213
Charles IX, King of Sweden 271
Charles the Bald 215, 217
Chauvet, Louis-Marie 417–20, 422, 426, 431, 435
Chemnitz, Martin 259–61, 262, 263
Chilton, Bruce 15, 26
CHR, *see* John Chrysostom *under* anaphoras
chortazein 12–13
Christian Sacrament and Sacrifice (Brevint, 1673) 361
Church of South India 416
Church of Sweden rite (1975) 393
Church of Sweden rite (1986) 408, 413, 415
Church Order and Order of Advancing of Members into the Ministry (Peculiar People, 1926) 373–4
Church Service Society 309
Clarke, Samuel 342
Clement of Alexandria 49–50, 94, 95–6, 101
Clement of Rome 34–5
Clowes, John 363–4, 365
Cole, Thomas 294
Collection of Offices (Jeremy Taylor, 1658) 332–3
collegia 3
Collier, Jeremy 339
Common Order (1994) 409, 415–6
Common Worship (2000) 409, 411, 413
Compendium Theologicae Christianae (1626) 302
Confession Fidei Gallicana (1559) 290
Connolly, R. H. 39, 62, 147
Contestatio, Contestiones 198–9, 212
convivium 3, 17
Coptic Orthodox Divine Liturgy 106–8
Coptic Orthodox rite 94–106
Corinth 17
Corley, Kathleen E. 12
Corpus Christi, feast of 229
Cotton, John 304, 311, 358
Countess of Huntingdon's Connexion 361
Couratin, Arthur xi, 390
Coutsoumpos, Panayotis 17
Covenant Hymns (1849) 375
Cowper, William, Bishop of Galway 303
Cranmer, Archbishop Thomas 246, 258, 313–24, 325, 331, 336, 345–6
Crossan, John D. 11
Croxton Play of the Sacrament 229
Cuming, Geoffrey 32–3, 59, 72, 89, 95, 96, 102, 108, 110, 133, 136, 277, 314, 322
Cutrone, Emmanuel 71–2
Cyprian 46, 47–9, 204, 205
Cyril of Alexandria 73, 93, 110, 114, 116, 118, 141, 150, 155, 161, 162, 170, 260
Cyril of Jerusalem, *see Mystagogical Catecheses* of

Dagobert, King 212
d'Ailly, Pierre 248
Darwin, Charles xi
Das Testament Jesu Christi (Oecolampadius) 283
Dashwood, Sir Francis 342
Datheen, Petrus 300
Davies, Horton xii
Davis, Richard 311, 358
Davis, Stephen 113–4, 115
Day, Juliette 68–9
De canone misse epicheiresis (Zwingli) 275–6
de Clerck, Paul 201–2
De Coena Domini (1569) 259–60
De Ecclesiasticis Officiis 191, 196
Deacon, Thomas 340
Deëis 206
Defence of the True and Catholic Doctrine of the Sacrament (Cranmer, 1550) 314, 316
deipnon 3, 4
Deir Balyzeh 96, 106, 382
Denne, Henry 355

Derrynavlan Hoard 208–9
Deutsche Messe (1526) 250, 252–3, 256, 266, 394
Devotional Services 312
Dialogue with Trypho 30, 33–4
Diatessaron 30, 42
Díaz y Díaz, M. C. 194–5, 198
Didache 16, 22–8, 29, 33, 34, 35, 52, 54–5, 58, 59, 61, 65–6, 96–7, 98, 99, 101, 106, 394
Didascalia 38–9, 52, 61, 93
Didymus the Blind 101
Dimitrievskij, A. 94
Dionysius Bar Salibi 155, 157, 162, 164
Diptychs 194
Directory for the Public Worship of God (Westminster *Directory*, 1644) 303–5, 309, 310, 332, 334, 358
Discourse Eighteen on the Augsburg Confession (Zinzendorf) 359–60
Dix, Gregory xi, 1, 16, 51, 63, 89, 97, 315, 326
Döber, Andreas 270
Dodd, C. H. 21
Douglas, Brian 315, 318, 414, 415
Doval, Alexis 68–9
Draper, Jonathan 22, 26
Drummond, Henry 366
Dura Europos 23, 24
Durandus, William 234–5, 335
Durber, Susan 410
Durham House Group 329–30, 337, 340

East Syrian rite 142–54, 166
Eaton, Samuel 356
Ecumenical Movement 377–8
Edward VI, King 324
Edwards, Jonathan 443
ektene 127
Elior, Rachel 55
Elizabeth I, Queen 324
Elwood, Christopher 289
Elyot, Sir Thomas 257
Engberding, Hieronymus 112, 113, 132
Enriching our Worship 410–11
Ephrem the Syrian 42, 68, 77–81, 141, 142, 152, 170, 405, 417, 423, 441, 442
Ephrem of Amida 111
Episcopal rite (1979) 387–8
Erasmus 348
Erastus, Thomas 262
Essenes 6, 9
Ethio-Eritrean rite 171–83
Etro 168
eucharistia 19, 59
Eucharistic Prayer for Zaire 386
Eucharistic Prayers for Masses with Children 384–5
eucharistic prayers for reconciliation 384, 385–6
Euchologion (1867) 310, 394
Eunomian 89, 104, 134
Eusebius of Caesarea 69
Evangelical Lutheran Church of America 393, 411

Falk, Daniel 55, 67
Farag, Mary 98, 102–5
Farel, Guillaume 285–7, 288, 290–2, 295, 317
Feminist theology 410
Fenner, Dudley 325–6, 327
Fenwick, John 132, 135, 160
fermentum 200, 203
Férotin, Marius 191
Feulner, Hans-Jürgen 158, 184, 187
Fiddes, Paul 434
Findikyan, Daniel 187
Finkelstein, Louis 23–5
First Apology (Justin) 30–4
Flacius Illyricus, Mathias 255–6
Florus of Lyons 215
Flower, J. Roswell 427
Flusser, David 25
Form und Gestalt Wie das herren Nachtmal (Oecomlampadius) 284–5
Forma ac Ratio (Laski) 298–300
Forma albo porządek (1581) 300
Formula Missae (1523) 250–3, 256, 258
Formula of Concord (1577) 259, 261
Fotheringham, J. K. 5
Fourth Lateran Council (1215) 228
Fox, John 294
Franklin, Benjamin 342
Freedman, William 21
French Reformed liturgy (1963) 394
Frendo, John 199–200
Frere, Walter Howard, Bishop 345
Fritsch, Emmanuel 172, 175–6, 182
Fuchs, Hermann 159

Gabriel II Ibn Turaik, Pope (Coptic) 106, 172
Gabriel Qatraya 142, 144, 146, 152–3
Gadderar, James 339
Galley, Captain Howard 391
Gallican rite 190, 191–2, 196–200, 206, 208, 210, 213, 233
Gardiner, Stephen 315–7, 321
Garrow, Alan J. P. 26
Gedicke, Simon 261–2
Gelasian, mixed 213
Gelasian, old 212
Gelston, Anthony 32, 72, 149
Gemayel, P.-E. 167
Genevan Form of Prayers (1556) 294–6, 328
Georg, Margrave Johann 261
George of Arbela 153, 154
George of the Arabs 155, 157
Gerber, Christian 265–6
Gerhard, Johann 262–4
Gerhards, Albert 117
Gerhardsson, Birger 12
Germanus 124–5, 128, 138
Germanus of Paris 196
Geroldseck, Theobald von 276
Gerrish, Brian 272, 275, 279, 280, 289, 312, 315
ghanta 148
Ghighla 148
Gilby, Anthony 294
Giles of Rome 235
Giraudo, Cesare 8, 102
Gómez-Ruiz, Raúl 192
Gordon, Bruce 277–8
Gospel of Philip 45
Gotteschalk 218
Grabar 183
Grabe, Johannes 338–9
Grace Church, Ealing 429, 431–2
Grantham, Thomas 356–7
Gratian's *Decretum* 220
Graves, Raphael 90
Green, Chris E. W. 428–9
Green, Ian 325
Gregory Nazianzus 117
Gregory the Great, Pope 200, 213, 275
Gregory the Illuminator 183
Gregory VII, Pope 222, 230
Gruenwald, Isthamar 55
Grund und Ursach 280, 281
Guibert of Nogent 239
Guitmund of Aversa 221–2

Hadewijch 226–7
Hadrianum 213
haecceitas 417
Haile, Getatchew 174, 178, 181
Halperin, Daniel 55
Hammerschmidt, Ernst 117, 172–4
Hammerstaedt, Jurgen 106
Hampton Court Conference (1604) 328
Handley, David 373–4
Hanssens, J. M. 63
Harnack, Adolf von 31–2
Harrod, Samuel 373–4
Hart, D. Bentley 443
Hawes, Samuel 339
Haymo of Faversham 230, 245
Hebert, A. G. 388
Heddle, William 373
Heidegger, Martin 418
Heidelberg Catechism 296
Heinemann, Joseph 18, 23–4
Heintz, Michael 32
Hen, Yitzak 212, 213
Henry VIII, King 313
Herwegen, Abbot Ildefons 377
Hickes, George 339
Hildegard of Bingen 227
Hilles, Richard 319
Himmelfarb, Martha 55
Hincmar of Reims 218
Hindmarsh, James 363–4
Hindmarsh, Robert 363–4
Hispano-Mozarabic (Visigothic) rite 190–6, 198, 199, 200, 206, 210, 233, 386
Hoadly, Benjamin 305, 341
Hoen, Cornelius 249–50, 273–4
Hoey, Robert F. 384
Holden, J. L. 400–1
Holeton, David 241–2
Hooker, Richard 326–7, 330
Hubmaier, Balthasar 348–52
Hūdrā 142, 148
Hudson, Anne 240
Hugh of St Victor 223–4
Humbert, Cardinal 220–2

Humphreys, Colin J. 5–6, 19
Hunter, John 312
Hus, Jan 241, 253
Hutt, Hans 348
Hymns on the Lord's Supper (Wesley, 1745) 361–2
Hystaspes 31

Ignatius of Antioch 30, 37–8, 423
Ignatius Zakka, Patriarch 165
Ildephonse of Toledo 190, 194
illatio, inlatio 194
inclusive language 410
ingenium romanum 381, 395, 405
Innocent I to Decentius of Gubbio, Letter of 200, 202–3
Institutes of Elenctic Theology 302
International Anglican Liturgical Consultation (IALC) 408–9, 413
International Commission on English in the Liturgy (ICEL) 379, 382, 383
Irenaeus, Bishop of Lyons 35–7, 80, 192, 203, 423
Irving, Edward 366, 367
Isaac of Stella 219, 234
Isaac, Bishop of Seleucia–Ctesiphon 142
Isidore of Seville 190, 191, 194–5, 196
Iskander, Athanasius 119–20
Iso'yabh of Arzōn, Patriarch 145
Iso'yahb III, Catholicos 142

Jacob of Burdana 141, 160
Jacob of Edessa 155, 164
Jacobs, Elfriede 285
Jacobs, H. E. 319
Jacquemont, Patrick 51
Jammo, Sarhad 55, 144
Janeras, Sebastià 101
Jarkins, Stephanie K. Skoyles 57
Jasper, R. C. D. 59, 89, 133, 136, 277
Jaubert, Annie 5
Jeanes, Gordon 203–4, 313, 317, 321
Jeffery, Peter 202, 208
Jeremiah II, Patriarch 138
Jeremias, Joachim 5, 7
Jerome of Prague 241
Jessey, Henry 356
Jewish Synagogal prayers 90
John Chrysostom 68, 81–3, 84, 128, 136, 229
John III, King of Sweden 270, 271
John of Dara 155, 157
John of Tella 141, 160
John Scottus Eriugena 220
John XXIII, Pope 377
John, Abbot of Fécamp 220
John Paul II, Pope 245
Johnson, Francis 355
Johnson, John 338–9
Johnson, Maxwell E. 64, 69, 70, 92–3, 95, 96–7, 102, 137
Johnson, Robert 328
Johnson, Todd 113
Jonas, Justus 253, 315
Jones, John 342
Joseph and Aseneth 8–9
Josephus 9–10
Julian, Cilicia 89
Jungmann, Josef 117
Justin Martyr 30–4, 35, 36, 47, 52, 64, 89, 108, 128, 200, 203, 390, 423, 441

Kantz, Kaspar 249
Karant-Nunn, Susan 257
Karlstadt, Andreas Bodenstein von 249–50, 253, 273, 347
Karris, Robert 14
Kass, Leon 437
katakeimai 4
katapempo 91
Kavanagh, Aidan 145, 382, 383
Keach, Benjamin 358
Kebra Nagast 180
Kéchichian, Isaac 188
Kennedy, Geoffrey Studdert 443–4
Kennedy, Hugh 207–8
Kennedy, V. L. 228
Kidane, Habtemichael 180
Kiffin, William 356
Kilmartin, Edward 59, 84, 86, 87, 215
King, Archdale 165, 196–7, 207
King, Fergus 4, 11, 18, 19
King's Book (1543) 315, 320
Kirchenordnungen 256–9
Klawiter, Frederick C. 37–8
Kliefoth, Theodore 269
kline 4
Knox, John 293–6, 312, 330
Koenig, John 444

Konig, Johann 262
Kraiński, Krzyztof 300
Kramer, Bradley 372
Kretschmar, Georg 97
Krodel, Gottfried G. 393
Kucharek, Casimir 131
Küng, Hans 381
kussapa 148
Kyrie eleison, origin of 201–2

La Maniere et fasson (Farel, 1533) 285
La Piana, George 63
La Verdiere, Eugene 12–15
Lambeth Conference (1958) 389, 390
Lanfranc of Bec 221
Lang, Bernhard 7–8
Lang, Martin 173, 177
Laski, Jan (John à Lasco) 298–300, 301, 318
Last Supper 2–21, 28, 29
Latinization 54, 166, 169
Laud, Archbishop William 331
Laudians/Laudianism 329–30
Leabhar Breac 210
Leaver, Robin 374–5
Leclercq, Jean 227
Lee, Robert 309
Leenhardt, F. J. 396
Lees, J. Cameron 309
Lenti, Vincent 210
Lentz, Harold 254
Leo the Great, Pope 200
Léon-Dufour, Xavier 8, 15
Leonhard, Clemens 74
Levering, Matthew 442, 443
Liber Mozarabicus Sacramentorum 191
Liber Ordinum 191
Ligier, Louis 7, 54
Lima Liturgy 405–6, 407, 441
Lindsey, Theophilus 342
Liturgiam Authenticam 411
Liturgical Movement 377–8, 406
Liturgienbüchlein (Moravian, 1755) 360
Liturgy in Times of Rebellion 332
Liturgy of Comprehension (1689) 337
Lloyd, Bishop 339
Locke, John 305, 341
Löhe, Wilhelm 269
Loughlin, Gerard 440
Louis the Pious 213
Lubac, Henri de 419, 425
Lundhaug, Hugo 45
Luther, Martin 242, 246–56, 259, 260, 271, 272, 274, 276, 277, 280, 286, 288, 295, 307, 318, 319, 346, 347, 348, 360
Lutheran *Book of Worship* (1978) 387–8, 393
Lutheran Church- Missouri Synod 393, 409, 415
Lutheran Service Book (2006) 409
Lutheran Worship (1982) 393
Lutheran–Roman Catholic Dialogue 397, 402

Macarius of Jerusalem 69, 73
MacCulloch, Diarmaid 315
Mack, Burton 11
MacMullen, Ramsey 92
Macomber, W. F. 141
Macy, Gary 223
Maertens, Thierry 384
Magne, Jean 63, 203
Mai fragments 200, 204–5
Malaty, Tadros 119–20
Malka 143, 146
Malmø Mass (1529) 269
Manual of Discipline 10
Mar Esa'ya 148, 150
Marburg, Colloquy of (1529) 250, 274
Marion, Jean-Luc 417, 419–22, 431, 435, 440
Mark-Brandenburg rite (1540) 258
Markus 35
Markus, R. A. 86
Marmitha 144
St. Maron 141
Maronite rite 165–9
Marot, Clément 290
Marpeck, Pilgram 352
Marrow of Sacred Theology (Ames, 1623) 301
Marutha, Bishop of Martyropolis 142
Marxsen, Willi 11
Mary, Queen 324
Mashafa Kidan (*Testamentum Domini*) 172, 173
Masses of Mone 196, 198
Mast, Gregg 309
Maximus the Confessor 124–5, 128, 212

Mazza, Enrico 59, 62, 73, 96–7, 102, 204, 382
McCabe, Herbert 429
McGovern, Patrick E. 437–9
McGowan, Andrew 28, 31, 38, 46
McKitterick, Rosamond 211, 212–3
McKnight, Scott 19–20
Mediator Dei (1947) 377
Méhat, André 49
Melanchthon, Phillip 253–5, 259, 283, 290, 314
Melchizadek 21, 84
Melos 180
Méndez Montoya, Angel 440
Mennonites 352
Mercersburg Movement 307–9, 367
Mercier, B.-Ch. 134
merkavah/hekhalot 55–7, 97, 102, 104
Merovingian kingdom 211, 212
Mesedi 187
Meßner, Reinard 173, 177
Methodism 361–3
Methodist Hymn Book 374
Methodist Worship Book (1999) 410
Metoscita, Michel 166
Metzger, Marcel 61–2, 63
Meyendorff, Paul 125
Micron, Marten 298–300
Milavec, Aaron 24–5
Mingana, A. 73
Mishnah 6, 7, 25
missa 145
Missal of Paul VI (1969) 379–86
Missale Gallicanum Vetus 196
Missale Gothicum 196, 198, 212
Missale Hispano-Mozarabicum 196
Missale mixtum 195
Mitchell, Nathan 23, 421
Mithras 31–2
Móel Cáich 208
Moghila, Peter 139
Montague, Richard 329
Moosa, Matti 111
Moravians 359–60, 363, 376
Moreton, Mary Ann 375
Mormon Church (The Church of Jesus Christ Latter Day Saints) 370–2, 375
Mortensen, Claus 269
Morton, Michael 204
Moses Bar Kepha 155, 157, 162
Mozarabs 190–6
Muller, Richard 301
Mundó, Anscari 193
Müntzer, Thomas 249, 347–8
Myconius 284
Myers, Susan 57–8
Myrc, John (Mirk) 320
Mystagogical Catecheses//Mystagogical Catechetical homilies/MC (Cyril of Jerusalem) 68–73, 74, 76, 111, 123, 135
Mystical Presence (Nevin) 308

Nag Hammadi 45
Narsai 142, 145–6, 152–3
Nasrallah Sfeir, Patriarch 166
Neoplatonism 272
Nerses Lambronac'i 184, 187–9
Nestorius 73, 93, 141, 148
Nettl, Paul 252
Nevin, John Williamson xi, 307–9, 312, 442
New Church 363–6
Newton, Isaac 305, 340
Nischan, Bodo 262
Nocent, Adrian 382
Nonjurors/Nonjuring 337–40, 363
North Africa 192, 204
Notley, R. Steven 21
Nowell, Alexander 325, 327

O'Donoghue, Neil 208–10
O'Malley, Brendan 210
O'Neill, John 8–9
Ockham, William 235, 239, 248
Odes of Solomon 42, 58
Odo of Sully 228
Oecolampadius, Johannes 255, 283–4, 286, 287, 298, 315, 317
Ohl, Jeremiah 268–9
Old Gelasian Sacramentary 200, 203, 204, 205, 212
Old, H. O. 282, 312
Olevianus, Caspar 296–7
Olsen, Oliver 393
Oosterhuis, Huub 384, 395
Order of Worship of the Society of the New Church Meeting in Red Cross Street London (1794) 366
Ordines Romani 218, 228

Ordo Romanus Primus 200, 201–3, 218
Origen 49, 50–1, 94, 97, 98
Ortiz, Alfonso 195
Osiander, Andreas 254, 314
Ossom-Batsa, George 13
Ostervald, Jean-Frederic 305
Overall, John 328–9

Palmer, Andrew 80–1
Parsch, Pius 377
Particular Baptist London Confession (1644) 356
Paschasius Radbertus 215–8
Passover 7, 18
Paterson, John 413
Paul the Deacon 213
Paul VI, Pope 245, 377
Paul, St 1, 4, 15, 16, 17, 20, 30
Peculiar People 372–5
Penn, Stephen 240
Pentecostalism 423–9
Perkins, William 326, 327, 329
Perrin, Nicholas 19–20, 21
Peter Cantor 228
Peter Lombard 223, 224–6, 235
Peter Manducator 228
Peter of Poitiers 228
Peter the Fuller 110
Petkūnas, Darius 299
Petri, Laurentius 270
Petri, Olavus 270
Pettegree, Andrew 299
Pfalz-Neuberg rite (1543) 258, 270
Pfeiffer, August 267
Philadelphia Book of Common Prayer (1786) 342
Philips, Dirk 352
Phillips, Edward 64
Philo 6–7
Pinell, Jodi 192–3, 196
Pippin 196, 211
Pius IV, Pope 245
Pius V, Pope 245
Porządek nabożeństwa (1599) 300
Poullain, Valerand 298
Power, David 35, 236, 239
Poynet, Bishop John 325
Prayer Book for Australia (1995) 414
Prayers for Divine Service (1923) 311
Prenter, Regin 396
Proclus of Constantinople 110, 117
Prone 276
Pseudo-Dionysius the Aeropagite 123–4, 155
Pseudo-Germanus 197
Pusey, Edward 343–4
PVindob. G 41043 100, 101

qanona 148
qedussah 55–6
qibbêl and *mâser* 16
Qolo 168
Quenstedt, Johann 262–3
Quere, Ralph Walter 255
Qumran 8–11, 24, 55, 57
qurbana 2

Raes, Alphonse 113
Rahmani, Ignatius 77
Rahner, Karl 396
Rainholds, John 326
Raitt, Jill 301
Ramsbury, William 240
Ramsey, Archbishop Michael 390, 391
Ratcliff, E. C. 32–3, 54, 205, 320, 390
Rathey, Markus 267
Ratramnus 215–8
Rattray, Bishop Thomas 340
Raw, Barbara 214–5
Ray, Walter 59, 99, 204
raza/rozo 81, 154
Readings upon the Liturgy and Other Divine Offices of the Church (Cardale, 1878) 368
'Red Book' of King Johan III 270–1, 393
Reed, Jonathan 22–3
Reed, Luther D. 256
Reformatio Legum (1552) 318
Reformed Liturgy (Savoy Liturgy) 332, 334–7
Regensburg, Colloquy of 290
Reichenau fragment 208, 210
Reif, Stefan 2, 66–7
Remple, John 351–2
Renaudot, E. 115
Renhart, Erich 184
Renoux, A. 112, 184
Revised Common Lectionary 380

Rex, Richard 240
Richard Cousin 228
Richardson, C. C. 315
Ridgley, Thomas 301
Roca-Puig, R. 99
Rodgers, Dirk 298–9
Roland of Bologna 225
Roman rite 63, 190, 200–6
Romanization *see* Latinization
Romano-Frankish *see* Romano-Western synthesis
Romano-Gallican *see* Romano-Western synthesis
Romano-Western synthesis 208, 210, 211–45, 345
Rorem, Paul 393
Rose, Els 198, 199
Rosenmüller, Johann Georg 267–8
Rough Edge 429, 432–3
Roy, Neil 206
Royel, Awa 145, 154
Rule of the Congregation 10
Rundell, Simon 429–31
Ryan, John Barry 384

Sacrosanctum Concilium (Vatican II, 1963) 377–9
Saint-Denis, Abbey of 212
Saka, Ishaq 164
Samaritans 6
Sánchez-Caro, José Manuel 54, 117
Sancroft, William 336, 339
Sanderson, Robert 332
Sarapion, Bishop of Thmuis 95, 111
Sarapion, euchology of 94–9, 106, 116, 117
Sarum, use of 231–4, 345
Saulnier, Stéphane 5
Scandar, Andrew 166
Schaefer, Mary 214
Schäfer, Peter 55–6
Schaff, Philip 307–9
Schiffman, Lawrence 10–11
Schillebeeckx, Edward 396, 397–8
Schleiermacher, Friedrich 306–7
Schmalkald Articles 247, 253
Schmidt-Lauber, Hans-Christoph 256–7
Scholem, G. 55
Schoonenberg, Piet 396
Schwärmer (fanatics) 250
Schwarz, Diobald 281, 290
Schwarz, E. 62, 63
Schwiebert, Jonathan 24–7
Scot's Confession/Scottish Confession (1560) 294, 368
Scotus, Duns 235, 239, 242, 335
Scruton, Roger 438–9, 440
Seabury, Bishop Samuel 342
Second Helvetic Confession 278
Second London Confession (1677) 356
Second Temple Judaism 4, 5, 6, 21, 55
Second Vatican Council 207, 377–9
Sedro 168
Segelberg, Eric 45
Segger, Glen 335
Selina, Countess of Huntingdon 361
Senn, Frank 256, 393
Senodos 172, 173
Sergius I, Pope 200, 203
Sergius the Grammarian 161
Severus of Antioch 110, 123, 141, 159, 161
Sheerin, Daniel 131
Shenouda III, Pope 118
Shimoff, S. R. 4–5
Shlemon of Basra 146
Shmidman, Avi 24
Sibyl 31
Sigismund, Elector Johann 261–2
Simon, Master, of Flanders 225
Simpson, Ray 411
Sintentus, Christian 268–9
skeuophylakion 127
Smith, Dennis 3, 11
Smith, Joseph 370
Smith, Samuel 364
Smyth, John 355–6
Smyth, Matthieu 64, 130, 196
Smythe, C. H. 315
soft points/secondary and tertiary stratum 89, 108
Sommaire (Farel, 1529) 286
Soueif, Archbishop Youssif 167
Spener, Philipp Jakob 264–5
Spilsbury, John 356
Spinkes, Nathaniel 339
Sprengler-Ruppenthal, Anneliese 299
Sprott, G. W. 309
Stamps, Robert 399
Starck, Johann 265
Stational liturgies 121, 202

Stennett, Joseph 358
Step'anos Siwnec'I 184–7
Stephens, Edward 338
Stephens, Peter 279–80
Sternhold and Hopkins 361
Stevenson, Kenneth 131, 134, 137, 160, 202, 369–70, 381
Stevick, Daniel 361
Stewart -Sykes, Alistair, *aka* Stewart, Alistair C. 64, 106
Stirling (hymn book) 374–5
Stökl Ben Ezra, Daniel 13–4
Story, Robert 309–10
Stowe Missal 190, 208–10
Stringer, Martin 16, 17, 34–5, 38
Sunday Service (Wesley 1784) 362–3
Surgant, John 276
Swedenborg, Emmanuel 363–6
Swiss Synod 386
Sydney, diocese of 392, 414
Symeon of Thessalonike 124–9
symposium, symposia 3–5, 14, 38
Synapte 108, 126
Syrian Orthodox rite 155–65

Taborites / Toborite movement 241
Tabory, Joseph 3–4, 7
Taft, Robert 65, 97, 111, 121, 123, 126–9, 160, 183–4
Taille, Maurice de la 396
Taksa 142
Tallaght 208
Talley, Thomas 7, 54, 102
Talmud, Talmudic 5
Tansley, Daniel 373
Tate and Brady 361
Tatian 30, 42
Taussug, Hal 3, 4, 11
Taylor, Jeremy 332–3, 334, 336–7, 341
Teicher, J. L. 23
Templeton, Julian 410
Terian, Abraham 69
Terracina, Thomas 166
Tertullian 46–7, 203
Testament of Levi, 61
Testamentum Domini 62, 66, 106, 172–3
Theodore of Mopsuestia 68, 73–77, 111, 118, 123–5, 127, 129, 134, 145, 170, 197
Thinking About the Eucharist (Church of England, 1972) 400, 402
Third Nephi 370
This Far by Faith. An African American Resource for Worship (1999) 411
Thomas Aquinas 236–9, 335
Thornborough, Bishop John 329
Thorogood, John 373
Thurian, Max 405–6
Tiburtine Baths 30
Timms, George 315
Timothy II, Patriarch 142
Timothy of Constantinople 111
Timothy the Great 144
Tituli churches 30
Toboroite movement 241
movement 21
todah, see *zebah todah*
Tomberlin, Daniel 427–8, 429
Tombes, John 356
Tomlinson, A. J. 427
Tonneau, R., and Devreesse, R. 73
Torrance, T. F. 397, 398–401, 419
Tosefta 6
Tovey, Phillip 175
Tractarians 342–4
Trent, Council of 243–5, 261, 346, 401
Tripp, David 45
Trisagion 110, 126, 144, 157, 168, 177, 187, 197
True Christian Religion Containing the Universal Theology of the New Church (Swedenborg, 1771) 364
Trypho 33
Turner, H. E. W. 400–1, 441
Turretin, Francis 302
Tylenda, Joseph 289
Tzadua, Paulos 172

Ultraquists 241–2
Urban IV, Pope 229
Ursinus, Zachariah 296–7
Ussher, James, Archbishop of Armagh 330

Vadianus 315
Vagaggini, Cipriano 381, 383
Valentinus 45
Van Baal, J. 423
Van de Pavard, Franz 130
Van de Sandt, Huub 22, 25, 27
Van der Meer, F. 86
Varghese, Baby 155, 157

Vermes, Geza 10
Vermigli, Peter Martyr 320
Verona Sacramentary 200, 204, 205
Victor, Pope 161
Vondey, Wolfgang 426

Waddington, Graeme 6
Wagner, Georg 130–1, 149
Wagstaffe, Thomas 339
Walahfrid Strabo 213–4
Walker, Joan Hazelden 22
Wandel, Lee Palmer 296
Ward, Samuel 329–30
Watson, Natalie xi
Watts, Isaac 311, 374
Way of the Churches of Christ in New England (1645) 304
Ways of Worship (WCC Faith and Order, 1951) 378
We Gather Together (USA Methodist, 1980); 395
Wedderburn, James, Bishop 330
Wegman, Herman 54, 59, 102, 382, 384
Welch, Charles 439
Welch, Thomas 439
Wesley, Charles 361–3, 374
Wesley, John 361–3
West, Maxine 97–8
Westcott and Hort 18
Western rites 93, 190–210
Westminster Confession and Catechisms (1647) 303–4
Westminster *Directory* 304, 332, 334, 358
Whiston,William 341
White Monastery 172
White, Francis 329
White, William 342
Whitefield, George 361
Whitgift, Archbishop 325
Whittingham, William 294
Wied, Hermann von, Archbishop of Cologne 258, 314, 319
Williams, Rowan 87, 417, 421–3, 431, 435
Williamson, Lamar 429
Willimon, William 439
Windsor Statement, *see* Anglican-Roman Catholic Dialogue
Wine making and properties of 437–40
Winkler, Gabriele 56–7, 67, 102, 112, 132–3, 136, 184–5
Wobbermin, Georg 95
Wollebius, Johannes 302
Wolmar, Melchior 301
World Council of Churches (WCC) 378, 388, 403, 409, 425
Worship: from the United Reformed Church (2003) 410, 416
Worship the Lord (2005) 409, 416
Wright, David 280
Wright, Joseph 355
Wright, N. T. 15
Württemberg order (1553/1536) 257, 297
Wyclif, John 239–41

Ximénez de Cisneros, Cardinal Francisco 195
Xosrov Anjewac'i 184, 185, 187, 188, 189

Yarnold, Edward 68, 72
Yelveton, Eric E. 271
Yohannan Bar Zobi 142, 147, 153
Yom Kippur 13–14, 20
York, use of 231–4
Young, Robin Darling 50
Yousif, Pierre 78

Zachariah of Mitylene 111
Zaire Mass (1973) 386–7
Zar'a Ya'Eqob, Emperor 173–4, 181
Zealots 6
zebah todah, todah 8, 15
Zeno of Verona 203
zeon 128, 137
Zephyrinus, Pope 62
Zheltov, Michael 60, 99, 101, 138
zikkaron 20
Zimmerman, Joyce Ann 386
Zinzendorf, Count Nikolaus Ludwig von 359–60
Zirkel, Patricia 217
Zizioulas, John 425
Zwingli, Ulrich 250, 272–9, 283, 285, 286, 288, 294, 306, 307, 315, 346, 348, 352, 401

www.ingramcontent.com/pod-product-compliance
Lightning Source LLC
LaVergne TN
LVHW010459231224
799709LV00002B/10